Mar 2014

Walter Benjamin

Walter Benjamin

A Critical Life

Howard Eiland *and* Michael W. Jennings

The Belknap Press of Harvard University Press
CAMBRIDGE, MASSACHUSETTS · LONDON, ENGLAND
2014

Library of Congress Cataloging-in-Publication Data

Eiland, Howard.
  Walter Benjamin : a critical life / Howard Eiland and Michael W. Jennings.
      pages   cm
  Includes bibliographical references and index.
  ISBN 978-0-674-05186-7 (alk. paper)
  1. Benjamin, Walter, 1892–1940. 2. Authors, German—20th century—
Biography. I. Jennings, Michael William. II. Title.
  PT2603.E455Z6455   2013
  838'.91209—dc23
  [B]   2013012858

Book design by Dean Bornstein

For Elizabeth, Dorothea, Matthew, and Rudolph

And for Sarah and Andrew

Contents

Introduction 1

1. A Berlin Childhood: 1892–1912   12

2. Metaphysics of Youth: Berlin and Freiburg, 1912–1914   32

3. The Concept of Criticism:
   Berlin, Munich, and Bern, 1915–1919   75

4. Elective Affinities: Berlin and Heidelberg, 1920–1922   117

5. Academic Nomad: Frankfurt, Berlin, and Capri, 1923–1925   177

6. Weimar Intellectual: Berlin and Moscow, 1925–1928   235

7. The Destructive Character:
   Berlin, Paris, and Ibiza, 1929–1932   314

8. Exile: Paris and Ibiza, 1933–1934   391

9. The Parisian Arcades:
   Paris, San Remo, and Skovsbostrand, 1935–1937   483

10. Baudelaire and the Streets of Paris:
    Paris, San Remo, and Skovsbostrand, 1938–1939   576

11. The Angel of History:
    Paris, Nevers, Marseilles, and Port Bou, 1939–1940   647

Epilogue   677

Abbreviations   681
Notes   682
Selected Bibliography   719
Acknowledgments   734
Index   735

Walter Benjamin

Introduction

THE German Jewish critic and philosopher Walter Benjamin (1892–1940) is now generally regarded as one of the most important witnesses to European modernity. Despite the relative brevity of his writing career—his life was cut short on the Spanish border in flight before the Nazis—he left behind a body of work astonishing in its depth and diversity. In the years following what he called his "apprenticeship in German literature," during which he produced enduring studies of Romantic criticism, of Goethe, and of the Baroque *Trauerspiel* or play of mourning, Benjamin established himself in the 1920s as a discerning advocate of the radical culture emerging from the Soviet Union and of the high modernism that dominated the Parisian literary scene. In the second half of the 1920s, he was at the center of many of the developments now known as "Weimar culture." Along with friends such as Bertolt Brecht and László Moholy-Nagy, he helped shape a new way of seeing—an avant-garde realism—as it was breaking free of the mandarin modernism that had characterized German arts and letters under the Wilhelmine Empire. In this period, as Benjamin gained recognition for his writing, he harbored the not unreasonable hope of becoming "the foremost critic of German literature." At the same time, he and his friend Siegfried Kracauer were virtually inventing popular culture as an object of serious study: Benjamin produced essays on children's literature, toys, gambling, graphology, pornography, travel, folk art, the art of excluded groups such as the mentally ill, and food, and on a wide variety of media including film, radio, photography, and the illustrated press. In the last decade of his life, most of which was spent in exile, much of his writing originated as offshoots of *The Arcades Project*, his cultural history of the emergence of urban commodity capitalism in mid-nineteenth-century France. Although *The Arcades Project* remained a massive unfinished "torso," the research and reflection that informed it generated a series of groundbreaking studies, such as the celebrated 1936 polemic "The Work of Art in the Age of Its Technological Reproducibility" and the essays on Charles Baudelaire that established the poet as the representative writer of modernity. But Benjamin was not only a surpassing critic and revolutionary theorist: he also left a substantial body of writing on the border between fiction, reportage, cultural analysis, and memoir. His 1928 "montage book" *One-Way Street*, and especially *Berlin Childhood around 1900*, which remained unpublished in his lifetime, are modern masterpieces. In the end, many of Benjamin's works defy simple generic classification. Among the prose works long and short are monographs, essays, reviews, collections of philosophical, historiographical, and autobiographical vignettes, radio scripts, editions of letters and of other literary-historical documents, short stories, dialogues, and diaries. There are also poems, translations of French prose and poetry, and myriad fragmentary reflections of differing length and import.

The concentrated "image worlds" evoked on the pages of these works bring into view some of the most turbulent decades of the twentieth century. Growing up in an assimilated, well-to-do Jewish family in Berlin in the years around 1900, Benjamin was a child of the German Empire: his memoirs are filled with recollections of the monumental architecture beloved of the kaiser. But he was also the child of an explosive urban capitalist modernity; by 1900 Berlin was Europe's most modern city, with new technologies burgeoning everywhere. As a young adult he opposed Germany's involvement in the First World War and in consequence spent most of the war years in Switzerland—yet visions of the war's "nights of annihilation" pervade his work. In the course of the Weimar Republic's fourteen-year existence, Benjamin experienced first the bloody conflict between radical left and radical right that followed the end of the war, then the devastating hyperinflation of the early years of the young democracy, and finally the debilitating political fragmentation of the late 1920s that led to the seizure of power by Hitler and the National Socialists in 1933. Like almost every important German intellectual of the day, Benjamin fled the country in the spring of 1933, never to return. He spent the final seven years of his life in a Parisian exile characterized by isolation, poverty, and relative lack of publishing venues. He was never able to forget that "there are places where I can earn a minimal amount, and places where I can subsist on a minimal amount, but nowhere in the world where these two conditions coincide." The final period of his career saw the shadow of coming war extend across Europe.

Why do Benjamin's works continue to speak so compellingly to the general reader and the scholar alike, more than seventy years after his death? There is the power of his ideas, first of all: his work has re-shaped our understanding of many important writers, of the possibilities of writing itself, of the potentials and hazards of technological media, and of the situation of European modernity as a historical phenomenon. Yet one fails to appreciate his full impact if one ignores its distinctively etched verbal medium—the uncanny Benjaminian style. Purely as a crafter of sentences, Benjamin bears comparison to the most supple and penetrating writers of his day. And he was a pioneering formal innovator: his most characteristic works are based on what he came to call, after the poet Stefan George, the *Denkbild* or "figure of thought," an aphoristic prose form combining philosophical analysis with concrete imagery to yield a signature critical mimesis. Even his ostensibly discursive essays are often secretly composed of sequences of these trenchant "thought images," arranged according to the principles of avant-garde montage. It was Benjamin's genius to find the forms within which a profundity and complexity fully comparable to that of contemporaries such as Heidegger and Wittgenstein could resonate through an immediately engaging and memorable prose. Reading him is therefore a sensory, no less than intellectual, experience. It is like the first taste of a tea-soaked madeleine: dimly remembered worlds blossom in the imagination. And as the phrases linger, constellate, and begin permutation, they subtly attune themselves to an emerging recombinatory logic, slowly releasing their destabilizing potential.

Yet for all the brilliant immediacy of his writing, Benjamin the man remains elusive. Like the many-sided oeuvre itself, his personal convictions make up what he called a "contradictory and mobile whole." This incisive formulation, in which one hears an appeal to the patient reader, is indicative of his protean and polycentric cast of mind. But Benjamin's ungraspability also bespeaks a self-conscious practice aimed at maintaining around him a hermetic space for experiment. Theodor W. Adorno once remarked of his friend that he "hardly ever showed his cards," and this deep reserve, with its recourse to an arsenal of masks and other strategies of indirection, served to guard the well of inwardness. Thus the consummate politeness remarked by all—in the end a complex distancing mechanism. Thus the appearance of weighty maturity at every epoch of his conscious life, a gravity that lent to even casual utterances something of the oracular. And thus his stated "policy" of preventing, whenever possible, extended contact between his friends, the better to preserve each individual or group as a sounding board for his ideas. Within this shifting field of operations, Benjamin conducted himself from an early age in such a way as to realize "the many modes of existence inherent in [him]." If Nietzsche saw the self as a social structure composed of many wills, Benjamin conceived it as "a set of pure improvisations from one minute to the next." It was in keeping with a precipitous internal dialectic that this utter lack of personal dogmatism coexisted with a sovereign and sometimes ruthless power of judging. For the pronounced multiplicity of the phenomenon of Walter Benjamin does not exclude the possibility of an inner systematic, or of a textural consistency such as Adorno posits in referring to his friend's extraordinary "centrifugal" unity of consciousness, a consciousness that constitutes itself by diffusing itself into the manifold.

Mediating this untoward complexity of character, then, is sheer, blinding brilliance of mind. The accounts of Benjamin's person left by friends and acquaintances inevitably start and end with an attestation of such power. They stress, too, his ever present high-mindedness and strangely incorporeal presence to others. Pierre Missac, who came to know him late in life, says Benjamin could not tolerate a friend's so much as putting a hand on his shoulder. And his Latvian love, Asja Lacis, once remarked that he gave the impression of having just arrived from another planet. There is in Benjamin a persistent reference to himself as a monk; in practically every room in which he lived alone—his "cell," he liked to say—he hung pictures of saints. This points to the central importance of contemplation in his lifework. At the same time, this semblance of disembodied brilliance was shot through by a vital and sometimes fierce sensuality, evidenced in Benjamin's erotic adventurism, his interest in intoxicating drugs, and his passion for gambling.

Although he once proposed, in a 1913 essay on moral education, that "all morality and religiosity originates in solitude with God," it is therefore misleading to characterize him, as certain influential English-language treatments have done, as a purely saturnine and involuted figure. This is not to say that he was not plagued by long bouts of immobilizing depression (a trait relatives noted elsewhere in his family tree), nor is it to forget that his diaries—and his conversations with his closest friends—return often enough to the thought of suicide. Yet to treat Walter Benjamin as a hopeless melancholic is to caricature and reduce him. For one thing, he was possessed of a delicate, if sometimes biting, sense of humor, and was capable of an owlish gaiety. While his relationships with his closest partners in intellectual exchange—particularly Gershom Scholem, Ernst Bloch, Kracauer, and Adorno—were often testy and even rebarbative, he repeatedly showed himself to be loyal and generous to those who knew him longest. This inner circle from his school days—Alfred Cohn and his sister Jula, Fritz Radt and his sister Grete, Ernst Schoen, and Egon Wissing—were never far from his thoughts, and he acted immediately and decisively to help them in times of trouble, especially when they all shared the privations of exile. Although these virtues were most visible in such friendships, Benjamin's steadfastness, generous patience, and steely resolve in the face of adversity were evident to all who knew him. Here, too, he remains a contradiction. He both craved solitude and complained of loneliness; he often sought community, sometimes working to create it himself, but was just as often loath to commit himself to any group. After serving as an activist organizer of the German Youth Movement in the years leading up to the Great War, he largely retreated from direct public engagement. The sole exception to this practical withdrawal—apart from his struggle to take a leading role through his writings—was his attempt on three widely separated occasions to found a journal; although none of these planned journals ever appeared, and each foundered on a very different shore, the impulse to symposium—the gathering of like-minded thinkers and writers—was an inextinguishable propensity of his philosophic sensibility.

One feature deserves special emphasis. This physically unprepossessing and frequently awkward figure was seldom remembered for these traits by those who met him; instead they remembered his daring. Yes, his gambling was an addiction, as we say today. But it was also a consummate expression of his willingness to play life against the odds, to work against the grain of convention, and to place himself in intellectual positions whose tensions and paradoxy bordered on the aporetic. Walter Benjamin sought the life of a man of letters at the very moment when this type was vanishing from the European scene. He renounced comfort, security, and honors in order to maintain intellectual freedom and the time and space to read, think, and write. Like his friend Kracauer, he analyzed the conditions threatening the existence of the very cultural type he himself embodied. Not just his methodology, then, but his whole being seemed to obey a dialectical rhythm dictating a perpetual gamble. His appearance and physical bearing, including his expressive hand gestures, tortoise-like intermittent gait, melodious voice, and letter-perfect speech; the pleasure he took in the physical act of writing, in the act of waiting, or in compulsive collecting and flânerie; his self-ritualizing idiosyncrasies of taste; and his eccentrically urbane charm—all these testified to an old-world, antiquarian disposition, as though he had been transplanted from the later nineteenth century. (There are very few photographs of Walter Benjamin in which he does not appear as the bourgeois intellectual with coat and tie.) At the same time, he had a keen interest in emerging technological media such as cinema and radio, and in current avant-garde movements including Dadaism, Constructivism, and Surrealism. His radical cast of mind brought him into dialogue with proponents of an avant-garde bent on starting from a tabula rasa. And so, with his penetrating intensity, his elusive way of thinking, and the endless fund of darkness in his intellectual life, his demeanor necessarily excluded the coziness of the late nineteenth-century haute bourgeoisie and favored the innovative. What he wrote of Baudelaire was also a self-characterization: "Charles Baudelaire was a secret agent—an agent of the secret discontent of his class with its own rule."

Over the course of thirty fateful years, from the dynamic idealism of his student days to the dynamic materialism of his maturity and exile, Benjamin's art of thinking developed dramatically in its form, focus, and tone, if not in its basic tenor, attaining at the end a rare crystallization. At every point this thinking fuses, but never simply intermingles, elements of literary, philosophical, political, and theological discourse. Benjamin's unique synthesis has found a response in a now-enormous secondary literature—a literature notable for its lack of unanimity on any given point. Previous studies of this writer, whether biographical or critical, have tended to proceed in a relatively selective manner, imposing a thematic order that usually eliminates whole regions of his work. The result has all too often been a partial or, worse, mythologized and distorted portrait. This biography aims for a more comprehensive treatment by proceeding in a rigorously chronological manner, focusing on the everyday reality out of which Benjamin's writings emerged, and providing an intellectual-historical context for his major works. Such an approach enables attention to the historicity of each phase of his life, and thus to the historicity of his works—their rootedness both in their particular historical moment and in Benjamin's own intellectual concerns—while lending full credence to a perceived arc in his thought. This constantly renewed intellectual trajectory is sustained by fundamental continuities of concern: an ingrained, theologically conditioned sense of latent crisis in the institutions of bourgeois life, as well as an ever-present awareness of ambiguity in the very processes of thinking. Hence the prevalence of certain subtle stylistic features at every phase of his career, such as a general avoidance of straightforward narrative, a proclivity for metaphor and parable as conceptual devices, and a tendency to think in images. The result is a philosophizing fully attuned to the modernist imperative of experiment, that is, the recognition that truth is not a timeless universal and that philosophy is always, so to speak, on the threshold and at stake. From moment to moment, Benjamin's is a risk-filled mode of thought, rigorous but profoundly "essayistic."

Regardless of theme or subject matter, three concerns are always present in Benjamin's work—and each has its ground in the problematic of traditional philosophy. From first to last, he was concerned with experience, with historical remembrance, and with art as the privileged medium of both. In their origins in the theory of perception, these themes point to Kant's critical idealism, and in their fluid

interpenetration they bear the stamp of Nietzsche's Dionysian philosophy of life; as a student Benjamin was immersed in both systems.
It was Nietzsche's critique of the classical principle of substance—the
critique of identity, continuity, causality—and his radical historical
eventism, privileging the present in all historical interpretation, that
furnished the theoretic ground (the groundless ground) for the generation that came of age in the artistically explosive years before the
First World War. Benjamin never afterward evaded the challenge of
thinking simultaneously within and beyond the antinomies of traditional metaphysics, and he never abandoned the interpretation of reality as a spatiotemporal sea of forces, with its depths and its tides of
transformation. In pursuit of the physiognomy of the modern metropolis, though, he eventually moved into areas equally foreign to Idealist and Romantic philosophies of experience, and the image of the sea
alternated with that of a labyrinthine architecture or of a picture
puzzle to be negotiated if not resolved—in any case, a text to be read,
a manifold language.

What is singular about Benjamin as a reader and thinker is the
highly oblique application of this multilevel philosophical perspective to what Miriam Bratu Hansen has called "everyday modernity."
To be sure, relatively little of his work, and especially of the work
produced after 1924, resembles what we usually think of as philosophy. Adorno offered a bracing corrective to this impression as early as
1955: he showed that every piece of Benjaminian cultural criticism
was at the same time "a philosophy of its object." Beginning in 1924
Benjamin analyzed a wide array of cultural objects without regard to
qualitative distinctions between high and low, and indeed typically
took as his subject the "detritus" of history, that is, neglected and inconspicuous traces of vanished milieux and forgotten events. He
concentrated on the marginal, on anecdote and secret history. On the
other hand, he never relinquished the standard of greatness. He first
made his mark in European letters with an essay on Goethe, regularly
turned to prominent contemporaries such as Proust, Kafka, Brecht, and
Valéry, and focused his multifarious studies of nineteenth-century
Paris in the epoch-making achievements of Baudelaire. Such representative artists were the lodestars of his micrological cultural analysis. For his thinking is oriented by a sense of the whole that emerges

solely through absorption in the force field of a pregnant detail, through perception as individualizing as it is allegorical.

But for all its intensive immersion, this is quite emphatically a politically attuned undertaking, although one that operates at a considerable distance from party politics. Benjamin early on defined political action as the art of choosing the lesser evil, and he later cast doubt on the very concept of political goal. Nevertheless, the question of the political became more pressing for him during the last two decades of his life, at a time when the idea of happiness seemed inseparable from the idea of redemption in a world flirting with its own destruction. He spoke of his "communism" (as evolved from his earlier "anarchism") in letters to certain friends and advocated publicly for the rights of the proletariat at the same time that he celebrated the "true humanity" and salutary moral skepticism of a long line of bourgeois literati stretching from Goethe to Gottfried Keller. His enthusiasm for the gigantic social experiment of Soviet Russia effectively disappeared after Trotsky was banished, though he continued to invoke a revolutionary imperative for his own work, citing in programmatic Brechtian fashion the political-educational responsibilities of the writer. These he tried to fulfill not just through his published writing but through the attempts at founding a journal, including one with Brecht as coeditor. As a theoretical extension of his antebellum student activism, with its loose creed of individualistic socialism, Benjamin's Marxism was informed by wide readings in nineteenth- and twentieth-century social theory, including pre-Marxist thinkers and agitators such as Fourier and Saint-Simon, Proudhon and Blanqui. Early and late, he was more a visionary insurrectionist than a hard-line ideologue. Perhaps we can say that for Benjamin himself, as a nonconforming "left-wing outsider," the question of politics came down to a set of personally and socially embodied contradictions. The conflicting claims of the political and the theological, of nihilism and messianism, were not in themselves to be reconciled. Nor could they be circumvented. His existence—always at the crossroads, as he put it once—was a constant straddling of these incommensurables, an ever-renewed wager.

But if Benjamin's deepest *convictions* remain unfathomable, there can be little doubt that he succeeded, after 1924, in reconciling his philosophical *commitments* with a rethinking of the Marxist tradition as it concerns the status of commodity culture in the West. While writing the book on the *Trauerspiel*, he was engaged in internal debate with the Hungarian theorist Georg Lukács, whose *History and Class Consciousness* he read in 1924. Marx's more localized theory of commodity fetishism becomes, in Lukács's reformulation, a globalizing view of society as "second nature"—revealing a social apparatus constructed by the process of commodity exchange, but through which people move *as if* it were given and natural. Even before his adoption of Marxian rhetoric, Benjamin could thus say that his book was dialectical, if not yet materialist. The final step in the development of the theory was taken when Benjamin—and with him Adorno—extended the notion of second nature by defining it as phantasmagoria, using the name of an eighteenth-century optical device. On this view, the social whole is a machine for projecting images of itself as inherently meaningful and coherent. The philosophical concerns animating Benjamin's earliest writings found their realization in this manner of thinking. For, in the context of modern commodity capitalism, the idea of phantasmagoria entails a recognition of constitutive ambiguity and undecidability, whereby what we mean by "the human" is progressively denatured. If a genuine experience and historical remembrance was still to be possible under these conditions, Benjamin argued, works of art would play a pivotal role. In his own radical terms, the emergence of a new "body space" was correlative with the provision of a new "image space." Only through such transformation in the experience of space and time could a new form of human collectivity emerge.

* * *

At his death, Benjamin's enormous writerly output was so scattered and hidden that much of it seemed irrecoverable. Although a great deal of his work had appeared in print, at least as much was never published during his lifetime and existed as drafts, copies, and fragments in the hands of friends in Germany, France, Palestine, and the United States. In the decades following World War II, much of this work was recovered, some of it as late as the 1980s and in the unlikeliest of places: Soviet archives in Moscow and hidden caches in the Bibliothèque Nationale in Paris. With the publication of comprehensive editions of his collected works and of his letters, most of Benjamin's writings are now in print. It is largely from this published record that we derive our picture of his character and life story.

In addition, various retrospective accounts of the man and his thought have been published by friends and associates—most extensively by those who first oversaw the preparation of his collected works, Gershom Scholem and Theodor W. Adorno, and also notably by Hannah Arendt, Ernst Bloch, Pierre Missac, and Jean Selz, along with a number of others, most of them writing in the wake of the posthumous fame that began only in 1955, after Benjamin's name had passed into virtual oblivion in 1933. Our work stands on the shoulders of the thousands who have studied and drawn inspiration from Benjamin's life and thought over the last sixty years.

CHAPTER ONE

A Berlin Childhood

1892–1912

BERLIN, the city of his birth, was never far from Walter Benjamin's mind—even in the long exile that extended from Hitler's seizure of power in March 1933 to Benjamin's death on the Spanish border in flight from the German armies in September 1940. Walter Benedix Schoenflies Benjamin was born July 15, 1892, in a city that had become the capital of a unified German nation only in 1871; but those twenty years had seen explosive growth in population and industry, as well as the development of a modern infrastructure to support them. Berlin's population numbered 800,000 in 1871; shortly after the turn of the century, more than 2 million people lived in what was Europe's most modern city. Eruptive modernization had in fact obliterated much of the historical character of the dignified old Prussian capital— and, in the years of Benjamin's childhood, the symbols of the German empire arose in their place: the Reichstag opened on December 5, 1894, and Kaiser Wilhelm's Berlin Cathedral on February 27, 1905. The pace at which the city grew and renewed itself meant that the exposed iron tracks of the Berlin City Railway, completed in 1882, ran past a veritable collage of building styles—the massive neo-Gothic and neo-Romanesque structures beloved of the rulers of the new empire stood cheek by jowl with the graceful neoclassical and neo-Renaissance buildings characteristic of Prussia around 1800. Berlin's changes, moreover, were hardly limited to the visual and the tactile: the slower, quieter life of streets filled with horse-drawn conveyances had given way, seemingly overnight, to the clattering of the street-car and, soon enough, to the din of a city full of autos. Because of Germany's belated modernization, Benjamin grew up in the first era of modern urban commercialization; Berlin's center came to be dominated by department stores, mass advertising, and a more general availability of industrially produced commodities a full fifty years after this had occurred in Paris. Berlin's first large department store, Wertheim, had opened on the Leipziger Platz in 1896; it counted eighty-three escalators and centered on a multistory, glass-roofed atrium. The birth of Walter Benjamin and that of German urban modernity were more or less coterminous; it is in some ways not surprising that he produced the twentieth century's most influential theory of modernity.

Benjamin grew up in a thoroughly assimilated Jewish family of the Berlin haute bourgeoisie. The oldest of three children, he passed his earliest years in an orderly household that employed a large domestic staff, including a French governess.[1] In the extensive autobiographical writings begun in 1932, "Berlin Chronicle" and *Berlin Childhood around 1900*, Benjamin has drawn a vivid picture of his youth. Around him was a multifarious *Dingwelt*, a world of things appealing to his well nurtured imagination and his omnivorous imitative abilities: delicate china, crystal, and cutlery emerged on festive days, while antique furniture—large, ornate armoires and dining tables with carved legs—readily served in games of masquerade. We read of the young Benjamin giving himself over to a host of ordinary objects, such as his mother's sewing box with its gleaming upper region and its dark underground, the porcelain basins and bowls on his bedroom washstand, which were transfigured at night by the moonlight, the coal stove with the little oven in another corner of his room, where the nursemaid baked an apple for him on winter mornings, or the adjustable writing desk at the window that became his burrow and shell. In reflecting, during the 1930s, on his early years, Benjamin presents the child that he once was, and which lives for him now in images of a vanished existence, as a genius of dwelling, one initiated into the hidden corners of domestic spaces and the secret life of everyday things. At the same time, he portrays the child's love of travel and his proud and sometimes reckless tendency to expand and break through established bounds—that is, to experiment. This dialectic of intimate absorption and wide-ranging exploration remains fundamental to the grown man and his work.

Benjamin's lifelong love of travel was fed by frequent family outings to the North Sea and the Baltic, the Black Forest and Switzerland,

and by summer residences in nearby Potsdam and Neubabelsberg. His childhood was in fact typical for his class: there was butterfly hunting and ice skating, along with swimming lessons, dancing lessons, and lessons in bicycle riding. There were regular visits to the theater, the Imperial Panorama, and the Victory Column at the center of Königsplatz, and above all to the zoo, where the maid led the children every day. His father, Emil Benjamin, held shares in the Berliner Zoo AG that were tied to free admission for his family. In addition, the children often visited the cavernous apartment of their world-traveling maternal grandmother, where Christmas day was celebrated in crowded splendor, and the apartment of an aunt who would set before the young Walter, on his arrival, a large glass cube containing a miniature working mine, complete with tiny laborers and tools. There were soirées at home, when Benjamin's mother wore a ceremonial sash and her most brilliant jewels to welcome "society" into the domain of the familiar. And of course there was the city itself, still veiled for the most part but alive to the child's senses and beckoning in all directions.

Benjamin's father, Emil (1856–1926), a prosperous businessman born in Cologne to a well-established family of merchants in the Rhineland, had spent several years living in Paris before moving to Berlin in the late 1880s; his children remembered him as a worldly and cultured man who was broadly interested in art.[2] Photographs from Benjamin's childhood years depict a rather imposing, self-confident, and dignified person concerned to emphasize his wealth and standing. Emil belonged to the generation that saw a headlong westward migration of the Berlin upper-middle classes at the end of the nineteenth century. After marrying Pauline Schoenflies, thirteen years his junior, in 1891, he settled first in the stately western district of the city, where both his own and his wife's parents were living. Benjamin was born in a large apartment in a house on Magdeburger Platz, just south of the Tiergarten. This once elegant district was home, as Benjamin says, to the "last true élite of bourgeois Berlin." There, amid the burgeoning aspirations and tensions of Wilhelmine society, "the class that had pronounced him one of its number resided in a posture compounded of self-satisfaction and resentment that turned it into something of a ghetto held on lease. In any case, he was confined to this

1. Emil and Pauline Benjamin with their sons Walter and Georg, ca. 1896. Photographer: J. C. Scharwächter, Berlin *(Collection of Dr. Günther Anders, Vienna)*

affluent quarter without knowing of any other. The poor? For rich children of his generation, they lived at the back of beyond" (SW, 2: 605, 600).

As though to escape the advancing specter of urban misery, Emil Benjamin moved his family several times in the space of a few years, each time a little farther westward. In this the family was typical of the well-to-do bourgeoisie: the city center expanded rapidly westward as the century came to a close. Formerly residential streets such as Kleiststraße and Tauentzienstraße were rapidly commercialized, leading throngs of customers and urban strollers to Berlin's newly developed "grand boulevard," the Kurfürstendamm. Benjamin's father first settled outside the city boundaries in Charlottenburg, part of this new west, where, because of the greatly reduced tax burden, he was able to save money for one final move. Benjamin's school years were thus spent in a house on Carmerstraße, just off Savignyplatz, still one of the liveliest and most elegant districts in Berlin's West End; his school, the imposing brick mass of the Kaiser Friedrich School, lay just across the square. In 1912, when Benjamin was twenty, Emil Benjamin purchased an imposing villa on Delbrückstraße in the newly developed Grunewald district, from which he could take a special omnibus to the city center. Although the villa was destroyed in the Second World War, building plans depict a massive four-story structure in an eclectic, historicizing style. The family lived on the spacious ground floor, complete with a large solarium, while the floors above were rented out. Despite a series of profound disagreements with his parents, Benjamin and his young family would often reside in the Delbrückstraße villa well into the 1920s.

By profession an auctioneer, Emil Benjamin was early on a partner in Lepke's auction house, dealers in art and antiques. After his share in this flourishing business was bought out, he invested his capital in various other enterprises, including a medical supplies firm, a wine distributor, and, around 1910, a consortium to build a skating rink, the Ice Palace, which doubled as a nightclub. The latter figures at one point in Benjamin's reminiscences: on a memorable evening, his father decided to take him along to the nightclub on Lutherstraße (he was around eighteen at the time) and got him a box seat in the circle, from which vantage he mainly eyed a prostitute in a tight-fitting white sailor suit at the bar—an image, he says, that determined his erotic fantasies for years afterward. Benjamin characterizes as "reckless" this attempt by his father to bring even his family's amusements into line with his business affairs, as he had done with all its other needs. But such recklessness, however closely connected to his "entrepreneurial nature," was infrequent enough. Besides his father's power and grandeur, Benjamin mentions his decency, courtesy, and civic uprightness. More telling for us is no doubt the fact of his father's connoisscurship: not only did he know wines but, as his son recalls, he could distinguish the quality of a carpet's pile with the ball of his foot if his shoe soles were thin enough. On the telephone, which in those days had already attained a dominant position in the household, his father sometimes revealed a fierceness that contrasted dramatically with his usual affability. In later years, Benjamin himself would feel the full brunt of his father's anger when, in a pattern that was characteristic for intellectuals of his generation, they quarreled repeatedly and bitterly over the direction of Benjamin's career—and over the persistent unwillingness to support himself and his young family that led to repeated requests for ever larger sums from the parental coffers.[3]

His father's hints and instructions to suppliers conjured up for the young Benjamin an image of an unknown and slightly sinister Berlin, which somewhat belied the image of a traditional and "official" commercial order gained from shopping excursions with his mother. Pauline Schoenflies Benjamin (1869–1930), who came from a wealthy and culturally enlightened family of merchants in the town in Brandenburg then known as Landsberg an der Warthe (now Gorzów Wielkopolski, Poland), had her own aura of power and majesty in the eyes of her elder son. This was epitomized in the title "Näh-Frau" (Madam Needlework), which for a long time was how the child construed the slurred pronunciation of "Gnädige Frau" (Madam) in the mouths of the maids. It seemed fitting, for his mother's place at the sewing table, like all seats of authority, had an air of magic, though sometimes that could be oppressive, as when she made the little boy stand still while she mended a detail of the outfit he was wearing. At such moments he felt the spirit of rebellion rising in him, just as, when he was forced to accompany his mother on an errand in the city, he would generally, to her exasperation, lag a half step behind her, as though "determined never to form a united front with anyone, not even my own mother" (SW, 3:404). At other times her magnificence filled him with pride, as when before an evening party she would appear in her shawl of black lace to kiss him goodnight. He listened with pleasure when she played the piano and sang lieder for him or when her basket of keys jingled through the house. Often sick as a young child, he was inured to the ritual of thermometer and spoon, the latter brought near with "loving care" so that the bitter medicine could be poured "unmercifully" down his throat; on these occasions he craved the stories that, as he puts it, were rippling in his mother's hand as she caressed him.

Pauline Benjamin ran her household with an iron will to order and with a clear eye for practical solutions. His mother had a way, Benjamin felt, of testing his very aptitude for practical life, making him conscious of his clumsiness. He even blames her for his inability, at age forty, to make himself a cup of coffee. When he had broken something or fallen down, he would typically hear her say, like many other mothers in Germany, "Ungeschickt läßt grüßen" (Greetings from Mr. Clumsy). This personification of his bungling made perfect sense in the child's animistic universe; it accorded with his own protoallegorical way of seeing or reading the world, by virtue of which ordinary things such as a rolled-up sock, the sound of carpet-beating in the morning, the rain and the snow and the clouds, the stairwell of the municipal reading room, or the chthonic marketplace all served in their different ways to communicate secret tidings to the young observer, engendering a not yet conscious knowledge of his future. It is a way of seeing peculiarly suited to the multifaceted and multilayered life of the city, with its many threshold experiences and its tendency to incorporate older forms as traces within the framework of the new. Partly because of the influence of writers such as Baudelaire and Friedrich Schlegel, the theory and the practice of allegory—in which the apparent sense of a thing or a text is seen to signal some other, possibly very different sense—becomes determinate for Benjamin, and we can see in the adult's "allegorical perception" an outgrowth of the child's divinatory relation to the world of things, a relation in which discovery and assimilation are predicated on mimetic immersion. At the end of *Berlin Childhood around 1900*, as he looks back elegiacally at the lost world of childhood objects, Benjamin summons the presiding figure of "the little hunchback," of whom Mr. Clumsy is understood to be merely an avatar. With his provenance in German folklore, the little hunchback was familiar to many German boys and girls, who knew him as an elusive mischief-maker: "When I go into my little room / To have my little sweet, / I find a little hunchback there / Has eaten half the treat" (quoted in SW, 3:385). Ultimately at issue in Benjamin's citation of this verse is the consuming power of oblivion, the power of dispersion, for whoever is looked at by the little man stands dazed before a heap of fragments. "When I go up to my kitchen stove / To make a little soup, / I find a little hunchback there / Has cracked my little stoup." In Benjamin's allegorizing remembrance, the little hunchback precedes the child wherever he goes, an unseen assessor extracting "the half part of oblivion" from each thing the child turns to, with the result that, in retrospect, a shadow of melancholy falls over all the former scenes of play, as selectively retrieved, concentrated, and brought to life again in the text.

Yet these protestations of his inadequacies in the encounter with the practical world are perhaps not entirely convincing. This was a highly disciplined Prussian household, and its mores left a lasting stamp on Benjamin and his siblings. Although we have no record of Walter's orderliness as a child (other than the autobiographical accounts of his various childhood collections), we know that his brother, Georg, was an obsessive list keeper: he made lists of his toys, of the sites of his summer holidays, and later lists of newspaper clippings related to his interest in nature conservancy.[4] Such a need to register and inventory can likewise be seen in the writer Benjamin, who, for example, kept lists not just of his own publications but of every book he read—or, rather, those he read in their entirety. It is a tendency no doubt inwardly affiliated with his lifelong drive to collect things of beauty or of special interest and to form archives.[5]

Benjamin's memoirs read very much like the retrospective imaginings of an only child. In fact, the age differences among the siblings— Georg was three years younger, Dora nine—led each of the Benjamin children to experience childhood as an "only child." Walter eventually drew closer to Georg when both were university students, and he established a more intimate bond with his brother after 1924, as

2. Walter and Georg Benjamin in
Schreiberhau, ca. 1902 *(Öster-
reichische Nationalbibliothek,
Vienna, ÖLA 237/04)*

shared leftist sympathies brought them together. Dora's adult relationship with Walter was, especially after their mother's death and
Benjamin's separation from his wife, strained and conflict-ridden until the years of exile, when both were living in Paris; together they
fled the French capital in June 1940.

Hilde Benjamin, the wife of Benjamin's brother, Georg (and later
justice minister of the German Democratic Republic), describes the
family as typical liberal bourgeoisie with an orientation just right of
center.[6] Also typical was the matriarchal bonding of the extended
family: Benjamin's grandmothers served as points of contact to aunts,
uncles, and cousins—many of whom played prominent roles in the
academic and cultural life of modern Germany. A great-uncle on his
mother's side, Gustav Hirschfeld, had been a professor of classical
archaeology at Königsberg, and another great-uncle, Arthur Schoenflies, was a professor of mathematics and rector at Frankfurt. One of
Benjamin's cousins was married to the prominent Hamburg professor
of psychology William Stern. Another cousin, Gertrud Kolmar, was a
highly regarded poet, while yet another, Hilde Stern, was active in the
antifascist resistance.[7]

Benjamin's sheltered childhood was disturbed comparatively late by the exigencies of schooling. He received instruction from private tutors until he was nearly nine, initially in a little circle of children from wealthy homes. His first teacher, Helene Pufahl, is memorialized with affectionate humor at the beginning of the section "Two Enigmas" in *Berlin Childhood around 1900*. Late in life, Benjamin still had in his possession a picture postcard with "the beautiful clear signature: Helene Pufahl . . . The 'p' at the beginning was the 'p' of perseverance, of punctuality, of prizewinning performance; 'f' stood for faithful, fruitful, free of errors; and as for the 'l' at the end, it was the figure of lamblike piety and love of learning" (SW, 3:359). His memories of his next tutor, Herr Knoche, could not have been more different: Herr Knoche—Mr. Bone—emerges as the prototype of the sadistic martinet who enlivened his instruction with "frequent intermezzi for thrashing" (SW, 2:624).

In the spring of 1901, when he was almost ten, Benjamin's parents sent him to the Kaiser Friedrich School in Charlottenburg, one of Berlin's better secondary schools, where, as it happened, more than a third of the pupils were Jewish. The school, an impressive brick pile wedged behind the arches of the Berlin municipal railway, gave a "narrow-chested, high-shouldered impression"; it exuded a "sad, spinsterish primness" for Benjamin (SW, 2:626). Of this institution Benjamin claims to retain not a single cheerful memory. Inside reigned a dreary, highly regimented conventionalism in keeping with this external appearance. The young Benjamin was subjected to such disciplinary practices as caning and detention in the lower grades, and he never quite overcame the fear and humiliation that dogged him in the classrooms and corridors, where he felt himself a prisoner watched over at all times by the relentless school clock. Particularly hateful to him was the obligation to raise his cap to teachers, which he did "incessantly"; when, a decade later, he zealously took up the cause of academic reform, he embraced the idea of nonhierarchical relations between teachers and students as a central tenet—though his egalitarianism always coexisted with an aristocratic spirit.

Indeed, Benjamin's instinctive elitism, his fastidiousness and highmindedness, which in later years would sometimes give a hard edge to his analyses of the political left and of popular culture, is already evident here in the schoolyard: he found the streaming horde of noisy, smelly pupils, especially on the crowded stairways, no less repugnant than the "idiotic harangues" of the teachers. It is hardly surprising that the sickly, nearsighted, and bespectacled child found sporting events and class excursions, with their boisterous and distinctly militaristic flavor, wholly alienating. It should be mentioned, however, that a rather different picture of the school emerges from the comments of Benjamin's friend Gershom Scholem, who was later in touch with some of Benjamin's former schoolmates. The Kaiser Friedrich School was "a decidedly progressive institution," directed by an educational reformer; it provided instruction in French from the first year on, in Latin from the fourth or fifth year, and in Greek from the sixth or seventh year—the last on the basis not of grammars but of the text of the *Iliad*.[8]

Even Benjamin admitted that there were positive aspects to the school—and not least its extensive library. Before his school years, his reading had been encouraged by his parents, and he soon became an omnivorous reader. Some of his reading was typical for a boy of his age: James Fenimore Cooper and his German epigone, Karl May. He also devoured ghost stories, a taste that stayed with him throughout his life. Some of this fantasy reading verged on other mature interests: he returned to books such as *The Phantom of the Opera* and the stories of E. T. A. Hoffmann again and again.

His years at the Kaiser Friedrich School did have one lasting effect: he formed friendships with two of his fellow students, Alfred Cohn and Ernst Schoen, that he never lost. Benjamin of course grew close to others later—to Scholem, to Franz Hessel, to Florens Christian Rang, and to Gustav Glück, as well as to Adorno and Brecht. But none of his later friendships were marked by the trust and intimacy that characterized his adult relationship to Cohn and Schoen.

Benjamin's poor health as a child—he was prone to recurrent fevers of long duration—made for many days of not unwelcome absence from school. Concerned about his ongoing illnesses, his parents withdrew him from the Kaiser Friedrich School shortly after Easter 1904 and, after he had spent several months of idleness at home, sent him to the Landerziehungsheim Haubinda, an expensive country boarding school in Thuringia, central Germany, for students of middle-school

3. Benjamin as a schoolboy *(Akademie der Künste, Berlin. Walter Benjamin Archiv)*

age. There, they hoped, the practical work component of the curriculum (mainly farm work and handicrafts) and the hikes through the surrounding countryside would do him good. The two years that Benjamin would spend at Haubinda in fact proved to be two of the most important in his developmental years: they exerted a liberating effect upon him, though not the one his parents had in mind.

On a gentle rise stands a house; from the look of things, it is spring. It has rained during the night, and the ground is a mire this morning; the sky, reflected in the puddles, is white. The house is Haubinda, where students live. It is called a half-timbered building; its indifferent height, which stands without a view over the forests of the plain, is a throne. The path from the door descends to the garden, then turns left and encounters the black country road, which it accompanies. Flower beds lie along the sides of the path, the brown earth lies open.[9]

Rather than strengthening his constitution and inculcating a more positive relationship to the natural world, Haubinda served decisively in the formation of Walter Benjamin's intellect and character.

Founded in 1901 on English models, though not without a strong chauvinist tendency in its general program, Haubinda promoted the exchange of ideas, especially in regular musical and literary discussion evenings, and, in contrast to the ethos of the Prussian state schools of the day, its faculty encouraged a degree of independent inquiry among the students.[10] New schools based on notions of pedagogical reform had sprung up across Germany in the first decade of the twentieth century; in 1900 the Swedish educational theorist and suffragist Ellen Key had declared the new age "the century of the child." It was at Haubinda that Benjamin first encountered the educational reformer Gustav Wyneken (1875–1964), whose radical pedagogics inspired his own student activism until the outbreak of World War I, and whose idea of awakening youth, in particular, played a key role in his thinking. Wyneken taught at Haubinda from 1903 to 1906, when he was dismissed after an altercation with the school's founder, Hermann Lietz. Soon afterward, together with his colleague Paul Geheeb, he established the Freie Schulgemeinde (Free School Community) at Wickersdorf in the Thuringian Forest, where, for some four years, he was able more fully to put his theories into practice.[11] Benjamin studied German literature with Wyneken at Haubinda in 1905–1906. He later remarked on the way these German lessons provided a direction for his interests: "My partiality for literature, which up until then I had indulged in rather haphazard reading, was deepened and given sure direction through the critical-aesthetic norms which the instruction developed in me; at the same time, this instruction awoke my interest in philosophy" (EW, 49 [1911]). Under Wyneken's comprehensive literary-philosophical influence, Benjamin's hatred of school was transformed into an idealization of student life, the classroom becoming a possible model of true community. When, many years later in his Parisian exile, he refers briefly to the "theory of education as root of utopia" (AP, 915), we can hear in the specific historical construction a distant echo of this early influence.

As can be seen in his most important collection of writings from this period, *Schule und Jugendkultur* (School and Youth Culture [1913]), which is at once a handbook of pedagogy and a theory of culture, Wyneken functioned as a kind of philosophical popularizer, combining the Hegelian concept of "objective spirit" with a darker Nietzschean philosophy of life.[12] The keynote of his teachings is the idea of a "new youth" as heralding a new human being—something called for often enough in the troubled decades to follow. Youth as the hope of the human race—as a creative potential in its own right and not merely a transition to the "practical realities" of adulthood—remains an ideal; at present, comments Wyneken, neither young people nor adults have any inkling of it. It is the function of school (superseding family) to awaken the idea of youth, and it does this by propagating culture. What matters here is not the amassing and organizing of information, necessary as this is, but the cultivation of mind and sensibility, the *renewal* of tradition; one studies foreign cultures in order to make them one's own. True spiritual and physical wakefulness *(Wachsein)* necessitates both historical—ultimately, sociological—and "cosmic" awareness, the highest point of which (as in Plato's theory of education) is the appreciation of beauty. Living culture is grounded in art and philosophy. Thus, the Wynekenian educational program moves toward an integration of academic disciplines in a unified world view *(Weltbild)*, both scientific and poetic. Like Nietzsche, Wyneken criticizes "the old humanistic order," which is said to be no longer viable, and calls for emancipation from "relativistic historicism." Cultural formation depends on the emergence of a new "unhistorical" historical consciousness (the formula deriving from Nietzsche's essay of 1873, "On the Advantage and Disadvantage of History for Life," which will become central for Benjamin as well), a consciousness anchored in recognition of the "great cultural significance of the present," whose immediate task is to process the claims of a "continually self-renewing past" (cited in EW, 40). In place of the "shallow rationalism" of the complacent bourgeois, the intellectual-erotic community of teachers and students—regarding one another, male and female, as "comrades"—must learn a "more paradoxical" thinking, one exposed to the dark stream of life and ready, without falling back on supernatural explanations, to receive what is often only an *Aufblitzen*, a sudden flashing up, of ideas. Such emancipated reflection, characterized by freedom *for* its task, points to the possibility of a new critical-historical religiosity beyond the invidious dogmas of the churches. And only such a spiritual sea change can in turn make possible a *Kulturstaat*, a polity devoted to the flowering of culture, something beyond the egoism of nation-states and the strife of parties. The great problem facing any new political union is the present discrepancy between material (technological) development and ideal (moral and juridical) development.

Integral to this synthesizing doctrine is an explicit elitism: a cult of genius, a concept of the leader, a distinction of the "higher man" from the "rabble"—all expounded with the sort of philosophical pathos one finds in Nietzsche, but without any of Nietzsche's philosophical irony. The higher man is distinguished by a sense for the essential and by absorption in art and philosophy, which, according to Wyneken, breed skepticism toward democratizing trends that bring in their wake the rule of mediocrity; the life of true culture is oriented not toward happiness but toward heroism in the form of self-overcoming, the victory over nature. Although his own thinking is shot through with the nineteenth-century vitalism that would feed so many reactionary ideologies in Germany in the years to come, Wyneken does warn against both "external dangers" emanating from the political right and "inner dangers" from the left. In his conception, the individual is fulfilled in subordinating himself to objective spirit, whose unfolding truth is above persons, though not impersonal. But despite the occasional dialectical turn in the argument, Wyneken clearly opposes the spirit of individualism, and this opposition prepared the way for his final espousal of a German nationalism. It was not exactly an aberration—though to many of his followers it seemed a betrayal of his teachings—when, in November 1914, he affirmed the responsibility of youth to dedicate themselves to the

German war effort. It would be difficult to overestimate the effect of Wyneken's teaching on Walter Benjamin's character and ideas, especially during the next seven years, as he emerged as a leading voice in the German Youth Movement, but finally throughout his life.

Benjamin returned to Berlin in the spring of 1907 to finish his last five years of secondary schooling at the Kaiser Friedrich School. His newfound sense of direction informs the reading he now undertook: he speaks of the development, since his leaving Haubinda, of "specifically aesthetic interests" as a "natural synthesis" of his philosophical and literary interests, and he speaks of his preoccupation with the "theory of drama—above all, reflection on the great dramas of Shakespeare, Hebbel, and Ibsen, with close study of *Hamlet* and [Goethe's *Torquato*] *Tasso*, and intensive reading of Hölderlin. . . . Moreover, the contemporary concern with social questions has naturally had an effect on me, and here a taste for psychology played a part" (EW, 50 [1911]). In a further effort to cultivate his own judgment on literary matters, he met with his friend Herbert Belmore (Blumenthal) and other schoolmates to form a weekly reading and discussion circle, which focused on a range of modern German playwrights (including Gerhart Hauptmann and Frank Wedekind) who could not be studied in school, along with German translations of Greek tragedies, Shakespeare, Molière, and other classics.[13] The participants also wrote reviews for discussion after visits to the theater. These literary evenings, which, according to one participant, continued from 1908 until the outbreak of the war, clearly harked back to the musical and literary "chapel" gatherings at Haubinda, even as they looked forward to the various student-organized discussion forums with which Benjamin would be involved during his university years. Presumably, this reading circle is identical to the "circle of friends" Benjamin later says he founded at Kaiser Friedrich, one or two years after his return from Thuringia, with the purpose of spreading the word about Wyneken, whose articles on the mission of the Free School Community at Wickersdorf continued to be a source of inspiration (GB, 1:70).

Wyneken was forced to leave Wickersdorf in April 1910, after new confrontations with his colleagues there and with state authorities. Carrying on the work of school reform, he subsequently embarked on a busy lecture tour while continuing to publish his writings and oversee the running of various journals. It was during this period that his contact with Benjamin deepened; there are numerous entries in Wyneken's diaries from 1912–1913 relating to his outstanding young protégé, to whom he would read in private from his own works. A prominent organ for the dissemination of Wyneken's ideas at this time was the journal *Der Anfang* (The Beginning), published in Berlin in three series between 1908 and 1914. Initially subtitled *Zeitschrift für kommende Kunst und Literatur* (Magazine for Rising Art and Literature) and circulated among high school students in a print run of 150 hectographed copies, *Der Anfang* was edited by a Berlin student of Benjamin's age calling himself Georges Barbizon (Georg Gretor), a committed Wynekenian whose father was also an art dealer. Benjamin began contributing poetry and prose to the magazine in 1910, while still in high school, making use of the multivalent Latin pseudonym "Ardor" to escape the ire of academic and civic officialdom, which predictably arose in short order. His first publication, a poem entitled "The Poet," sounds a note characteristic of the then-current neo-Romanticism: the solitary figure of the poet is spied from the heights of Olympus as he inscribes eternal lines at the edge of the abyss, his gaze directed now within, now toward the gods above, now on "the crowd." In 1911, when the journal began to appear in a printed format and with a new subtitle, *Vereinigte Zeitschriften der Jugend* (United Magazines of Youth), which became simply *Zeitschrift der Jugend* (Magazine of Youth) in 1913–1914, Benjamin's contributions took on a decidedly political, indeed militant color, as he directly addressed the issues of school reform and youth culture. His opening piece in this sequence of programmatic pronouncements, "Sleeping Beauty," has its point of departure in an allegory of Youth's awakening, Wyneken's stated goal. The need for a new youth to lead the way to revolutionary cultural change is the main theme of all Benjamin's publications as a student, if not of his writings as a whole, over the next three years.

The years of Benjamin's involvement with *Der Anfang* also saw his first contacts with an avant-garde cenacle, the Neue Club (New Club), a circle of proto-Expressionist writers that was in existence between 1909 and 1914 in Berlin, where readings were presented in the so-called Neopathetisches Cabaret evenings organized by the club.

Founded by Kurt Hiller, the New Club counted among its members two figures who would emerge as central contributors to German Expressionism, the poets Georg Heym and Jakob van Hoddis (Hans Davidsohn). Benjamin had a number of acquaintances who were active members: Simon Guttmann (later a photojournalist in Berlin and London) was also active in the group that produced *Der Anfang*, and Benjamin knew both Robert Jentzsch and David Baumgardt, who were important presences. We do not know whether Benjamin was acquainted with Heym, the most gifted poet in the group, although Heym was a friend of Guttmann's; but Scholem tells us that Benjamin recited for him verses from Heym's 1911 collection *Eternal Day* from memory—"a very unusual practice for him" (SF, 65–66).[14] Hiller would go on to publish the first anthology of Expressionist poetry, *Der Kondor*, in 1912.

At the end of 1911, Benjamin applied to take the *Abitur*, the school-leaving examination that would qualify him for admission to a university; there was resistance from his father, who would have liked his son to decide on some useful occupation, like other young men his age. (Emil Benjamin was persuaded to change his mind by his intellectual older sister, Friederike Joseephi, Benjamin's favorite aunt, who had taught her nephew graphology. She committed suicide in 1916.)[15] Benjamin underwent a succession of written and oral exams the following February and March. He did creditably in all academic areas except one: he failed the written exam in Greek (a translation from Plato), though he made up for this in his orals.[16] He scored a "satisfactory" in math, a "good" in Latin, and a "very good" for his German essay on an assigned topic concerning Goethe and the Austrian dramatist Franz Grillparzer, which the senior master praised for its deep understanding and elegant style. Even this little essay shows the influence of Wyneken: it focuses on "the problem of the genius," in the context of which Shakespeare's "great brooder" Hamlet is adduced. The genius, it is argued, "runs aground on life" (GS, 7:532–536). Not long before, he had written in a similar vein on Pindar, in what he describes, in "Berlin Chronicle," as his first philosophical essay, "Reflections on Nobility."

Having graduated from the Kaiser Friedrich School in March, Benjamin was soon back in the good graces of his father, it would seem, for he was able to undertake an extended tour of Italy—including the cities of Como, Milan, Verona, Vicenza, Venice, and Padua—over the Pentecost holiday (May 24–June 15). Before this, he had always taken trips in the company of his family. We have accounts of such trips to Switzerland, taken in the summers of 1910 and 1911, in his first letters to Herbert Belmore; these are high-spirited letters filled with literary parodies and reports and judgments on his reading, which ranged from Fritz Mauthner's theory of language to Tolstoy's *Anna Karenina*. Now, at the age of nineteen, he was being allowed to travel abroad with two school friends. It was his first taste of real freedom from family and teachers. He memorialized this "Italian Journey" of 1912, as he had several other excursions going back to 1902, in the form of a travel diary, his longest to date. What is striking in this particular case is the way he conceives the diary as the realization of the journey: "It is from out of the diary I am about to write that the journey should first come to be. In this diary I would like to see develop . . . the silent, self-evident synthesis which an educational journey requires, and which constitutes its essence" (GS, 6:252). The logic is characteristically Benjaminian: the task of writing is to let what has been emerge for the first time in its actuality. Composing the diary of the journey is in effect the real journey, the educational synthesis. Already implicit here is a complicated understanding of the interrelation of time dimensions with the form and content of a literary work, an understanding that—while anticipating the later materialist conception of the "literarization of the conditions of life"—will begin to bear fruit in the ambitious early essays "Metaphysics of Youth" and "Two Poems by Friedrich Hölderlin," if not in the travel diaries themselves. Meanwhile, "My Journey to Italy, Pentecost 1912" attests in abundant detail to the passion for travel and for travel writing that would only grow keener with the passage of years.

Not long after completing the *Abitur*, Benjamin published his short "Epilogue" to his school years. In this little piece, which appeared anonymously in a *Bierzeitung* or humor magazine that he put together with a few fellow pupils from Kaiser Friedrich, he raises the question "What has school given us?"[17] Putting all joking aside, he answers: plenty of knowledge but no ideals to provide direction, no binding sense of duty. Continually accompanying the schoolwork, he says, was the tormenting feeling of arbitrariness and purposelessness: "We could no more take our work seriously than we could take ourselves seriously" (EW, 54). Again he calls for open exchange, open conversations, between teachers and students, as a necessary first step in taking "youthfulness" itself seriously. The indictment of educational institutions, so boldly inaugurated during Benjamin's high school years, would soon be promulgated in much more public ways.

CHAPTER TWO

Metaphysics of Youth

Berlin and Freiburg, 1912–1914

IF most accounts of the years 1912–1914 suggest that the coming of World War I cast a deepening shadow over all of Europe, Walter Benjamin's first university years in Freiburg and Berlin were dominated by rather different concerns. In these years, he began to focus his studies on what we might call a "philosophy of culture." Far more important than those studies themselves, though, was Benjamin's development during his university years of a broad and stinging critique of academic life. At first, that critique took the form of a series of brilliant but highly esoteric—and largely unpublished—essays. Increasingly, however, Benjamin emerged as a leader and orator in various student groups associated with what is today known as the German Youth Movement. This passionate involvement in the life of students generated his first writings concerned to influence a broad public. And even as he considered entering on a potential public role, Benjamin was impelled for the first time to examine his identity as a Jew.

Benjamin began his university studies in April 1912 at the Albert Ludwig University in Freiburg im Breisgau, one of the oldest and most renowned of German universities. Freiburg itself was a small, quiet city better known for the beauty of its landscapes on the southern slopes of the Black Forest than for its cultural life. It is hard to imagine a greater contrast to the hurly-burly of Berlin, though Freiburg would soon become the center of the new phenomenological movement in philosophy that grew up around the teachings of Edmund Husserl and his revolutionizing student, Martin Heidegger, Benjamin's senior by three years. Benjamin matriculated in the department of philology in order to continue his literary studies, and in the summer semester attended a variety of lecture courses, more than in any semester to follow. These included courses such as Religious Life in

Late Antiquity, Medieval German Literature, General History of the Sixteenth Century (with the well-known historian Friedrich Meinecke), Kant's Weltanschauung, The Philosophy of Contemporary Culture, Style and Technique in the Graphic Arts, and Introduction to Epistemology and Metaphysics.

The last of these was taught to well over a hundred students by the prominent Neo-Kantian philosopher Heinrich Rickert, whose teaching started from a critique of both positivism (the Comtean notion that data derived from sensory experience is the only valid source of knowledge) and vitalism (the philosophical focus on "life itself" that had emerged from the critique of rationalism espoused by Schopenhauer and Nietzsche). Rickert's own contribution consisted in a theoretical appropriation of history and culture. Despite the logical-scientific mode of his argumentation, Rickert's historically oriented analysis—reflecting the turn to *Problemgeschichte* (history of problems) that was a hallmark of the Southwest School of Neo-Kantianism—and his attempt to overcome theoretically the antinomies of spirit and nature, form and content, subject and object, and thus to go *beyond* Kant, would exert a not inconsiderable influence on Benjamin. In fact, Benjamin's own philosophical and aesthetic investigations in the course of the next decade can be seen at telling junctures to weave in and out of orbit with the Neo-Kantianism of Rickert and Hermann Cohen, a professor of philosophy at Marburg. In the last year of his life, he could even write to Theodor Adorno, with whom he always made a point of downplaying the Romantic influences on his thought, that he was himself "a pupil of Rickert (as you are a pupil of Cornelius)" (BA, 333).

Also in attendance at Rickert's 1912 lectures on epistemology and metaphysics was the young Heidegger, who would write his inaugural doctoral dissertation under Rickert's direction before the latter's move to Heidelberg in 1916 (when he was succeeded at Freiburg by Husserl). Heidegger and Benjamin would be together again in Rickert's lecture course on logic (actually a new "philosophy of life") and his accompanying seminar on the philosophy of Henri Bergson the following summer, and it is tempting to imagine that they became aware of each other to some degree in the Bergson seminar. As far as we know, however, there was never any personal contact between the two men whose

4. Benjamin as a student, ca. 1912 *(Museum der Dinge, Werkbundarchiv, Berlin)*

writings would display so many points of contact and whose lives would be so different, though Benjamin became acquainted with Heidegger's early work some four years later—and, to be sure, was unfavorably impressed.[1]

Having overburdened himself with great expectations for higher learning, Benjamin experienced his first semester at university as a "deluge" and "chaos," or so he tells Herbert Belmore, his chief correspondent during the first two university years. Sometimes he was able to escape "the specter of 'overwork'" by surrendering to "the gentle meander of a city stroll on the fringes of the university on a bright morning" (GB, 1:46); southwestern Germany could offer more in the way of scenic

5. Herbert Belmore, ca. 1923 *(Collection of M. P. Belmore, Erlangen)*

beauty and sunny weather than he was used to in his native Berlin. More often, however, he felt himself forced to abide by what he called "Freiburg time," which had its peculiarity in comprising a past and a future but never a present. "It's a fact," he remarks to Belmore in mid-May, "that in Freiburg I'm able to think independently about scholarly matters only about one-tenth as often as in Berlin" (C, 14–15).

His decision to study in provincial Freiburg probably had less to do with the prestige of professors such as Rickert and Meinecke than with the fact that Freiburg had become for the moment a center of radical student action. It was the first of a number of German universities to permit students to put into practice a key strategic proposal by Gustav Wyneken: to set up School Reform Units (Abteilungen für

Schulreform) within the existing Independent Students' Associations
(Freie Studentenschaften). The latter had been organized in many
German universities at the turn of the century, in opposition to established student associations such as fraternities and dueling corps, in
order to further certain liberal educational ideals of the nineteenth
century, such as the inner unity of the academic disciplines and the
unfolding of the individual personality within a community of scholars. The Independent Students' Associations were the primary university arm of the Jugendbewegung, the national youth movement that
had initially grown out of a number of small but tightly organized
groups of boys who enjoyed rambling through the countryside around
Berlin.[2] These groups, the Wandervögel or "walking birds," were officially founded in Berlin-Steglitz in 1901, although such groups had met
informally for years in order to devote themselves to the natural world
and to the cultivation of the simple habits that were the result of time
spent outdoors. As youth groups modeled loosely on the Wandervögel
spread throughout Germany, the mild anti-intellectualism and apoliti-
cism of the early groups—"those long-haired, untidy bacchants . . . who
used to wander through the fields and woods, strumming on their
guitars"—gave way to a broad range of special interests, and what had
been a conglomeration of boys' clubs became a youth movement.[3] By
1912 the Free German Youth (Freideutsche Jugend), the umbrella organization for the movement, contained elements ranging from the
pacifist idealists with whom Benjamin was associated to virulently
nationalist, anti-Semitic conservatives.

The Wynekenians were by no means the largest of these groups—
their number is estimated at 3,000 in 1914—though with their antiau-
thoritarian model of the free school community in Wickersdorf, and
as a self-conscious avant-garde, they were certainly the group with the
highest public profile. They presented themselves as champions of academic and cultural reform, having in view the reform of consciousness
in general and the reform of "bourgeois" consciousness in particular.
In the Communist perspective of Hilde Benjamin, wife and biographer of Benjamin's brother, Georg, the young men and women around
Wyneken appear as an "intellectual elite." She quotes a collectively
authored report on the history of the youth movement among German
working-class youth:

The beginnings of this oppositional bourgeois youth movement reach back to the turn of the century. A number of high school students, mainly young people from the petty bourgeoisie and the bourgeoisie, came into conflict with the authoritarian regime prevailing in the secondary schools, where, for the most part, ossified pedants set the tone, demanding unconditional obedience from the pupils. The suppression of every independent intellectual initiative, the alignment of the educational program with the ideology of military preparedness and the cult of the monarchy, stood in contradiction to the humanistic ideals invoked in the teaching. Together with this, the bourgeois morals of the parental home, the pursuit of profit and the hypocrisy, servility, and ruthlessness bound up with it, were repugnant to many. Of these young people, many went on after graduation to study at universities, where they continued to uphold the Wandervögel spirit. They rejected the practices of the reactionary student corps, the obsession with dueling and drinking, the chauvinism and arrogance and contempt for the people. . . . It was not the existing social order but a generational conflict that basically motivated the nonconformism of these young people. . . . They refused any active intervention in the political struggles of the day. Their goal was the education of people who shape their lives "according to their own principles, on their own responsibility, and in inner truthfulness."[4]

Whoever examines the "ethical program" of Benjamin's prewar student-activist writings, with their detailed indictment of mindless classroom exercises and of a narcotizing philistinism born of the collusion of school and family, will discover a good many correspondences with the intellectual and spiritual "nonconformism" described here.

As it turned out, the Wynekenians remained a minority voice within the more conservative body of independent students as well. The School Reform Units, through which Wyneken for a time exercised an influence over student life in the universities, were designed to supplement official course offerings and thereby broaden the educational horizon beyond the scope of narrowly specialized professional and vocational training. The Freiburg School Reform Unit, which sponsored a lecture series in the university and evening discussion groups, offered Benjamin another arena for carrying out his mission "to restore

6. Gustav Wyneken in Haubinda, 1906 (*Archiv der Deutschen Jugendbewegung, Burg Ludwigstein*)

people to their youth" (C, 24). That summer, an essay of his, "School Reform, a Cultural Movement," appeared in a pamphlet published by the Freiburg School Reform Unit, in an edition of 10,000 copies that were distributed free of charge in universities throughout the country. Operating under a new pseudonym, "Eckhart, phil.," Benjamin argues that school reform means not just reform in the transmission of values but the thoroughgoing revision of those values themselves. Beyond the institutional framework per se, educational reform concerns a whole way of thinking; it presupposes less a narrow educational restructuring than a broad ethical program. But education is not just a matter of thinking *sub specie aeternitatis* (in Spinoza's famous phrase); it's a matter of *living* and *working* "under the aspect of eternity." Only as such an expansion of personal and social horizons can education serve the formation of culture, defined in terms of "the natural advance of humanity" (EW, 58). Some three years later, in the culminating statement of his youth philosophy, "The Life of Students," he more clearly differentiates the relevant "historical task" from nebulous conceptions of human "progress" along a straight line of time.

Benjamin's idea of awakening youth, as immediately grounded in the teachings of Wyneken, but with its roots ultimately in nineteenth-century German thought from Schlegel and Novalis to Nietzsche, is documented not only in his letters but especially in a remarkable series of published and unpublished articles from the period 1911–1915. Much more than juvenilia, this outpouring of writing is suffused with the originality that would mark virtually everything Benjamin would later write. The project of youth culture was for him never limited to the program for school reform but sought a revolution in thinking and feeling. Meaningful institutional change could take place only in the wake of cultural transformation. Youth was conceived as the vanguard in the struggle for a "new humanity" and for a "radical new seeing" (EW, 29, 120). It represented not just a cultural-political movement but a philosophy of life, or living philosophy—more specifically, a philosophy of historical time and a philosophy of religion. For the young Benjamin, these dimensions of thought were closely bound up with one another in the very German concept of spirit, *Geist*. Youth was defined as the "constantly reverberating [*vibrierende*] feeling for the abstractness of pure spirit" (C, 55)—this from one of the most rhapsodic of the letters written in 1913–1914 to his friend and companion-in-arms, Carla Seligson, a medical student in Berlin and later the wife of Herbert Belmore. Virtually every word of his formulation carries an esoteric charge, calculated to explode the logic of the fathers. Carla Seligson had asked: "How is it possible?" Very moved, he answers in frankly mystical tones: the goal is simply the feeling of youth in itself, something not everyone is capable of—the "great joy of its presence." In other words, the goal is not "improvement" but fulfillment (Vollendung—a key term in Rickert), something immanent in each individual who becomes young. He goes on:

> Today I felt the awesome truth of Christ's words: Behold, the Kingdom of God is neither here nor there, but within us. I would like to read with you Plato's dialogue on love, where this is said more beautifully and thought more deeply than probably anywhere else. (C, 54 [September 15, 1913])[5]

Being young, he says, means not so much serving the spirit as *awaiting* it. (We may think here of Hamlet's notion of readiness, which is geared toward "play.")[6] The quasi-theological terminology points to what is at stake in the spirit's "abstractness": rather than allow itself to become fixed in any determinate position, the reverberating, "eternally actualizing" soul of youth keeps its gaze free. As Benjamin writes, "This is the most important thing: we must not fasten on any particular idea, [not even] the idea of youth culture" (C, 54; see 52, on freedom). Which is to say, no dogma and no explicit, closed system, let alone any partisanship, but rather illumination (Erleuchtung), drawing "the most distant spirit" into the light. Despite the proximity of these ideas to a "naive" romanticism which in later years Benjamin was largely to repudiate (see SW, 3:51), they signal the ascendancy of that constitutional ambiguity we encounter in his most characteristic work—an ambiguity expressive of his dynamic, dialectical conception of truth as revelation that keeps faith with the hidden. This is not a truth *about* some matter but a truth *in* the matter.[7]

Carla Seligson's question "How is it possible?" was fundamentally a challenge to political action; Benjamin's answer in 1913 had deflected the call to action into the realm of ideas—and very high-minded ones at that. Politics was not a subject Benjamin addressed directly in writing during his university years, except on rare occasions. In his "Dialogue on the Religiosity of the Present," from the fall of 1912, he briefly envisions an "honest socialism," as opposed to the conventional socialism of the day (EW, 71). And there is a point in the letters where he rather casually mentions to a Zionist friend, Ludwig Strauß, that he has not yet decided between a social-democratic and a left-liberal orientation. In any case, he adds, given the fact that politics is the vehicle of political parties, not ideas, in the end political action can be a matter of only one thing: the art of choosing the lesser evil (GB, 1:82–83 [Jan. 7, 1913]). Nevertheless, the faith in "education"—the belief that politics begins in education and comes to fruition in culture—would, for the remainder of his university years, motivate his increasing prominence in the active organization of the political life of his faction of the Youth Movement. And it would continue to motivate his protest against school and family, and continue to provide the model for his severe, aesthetically colored ethical program.

What was specifically ethical in his thinking was an idea of friendship that, like much else in the reformist discourse of the day, has weighty classical precedents—in this case, Plato's concept of *philia* (the friendship of equals) as the agonistic medium of genuine community. Nietzsche's idea of polity as the congregation of "a hundred deep solitudes" also would have played a part here, as would have Kant's "unsocial sociability." Benjamin's formulation—*eine Freundschaft der fremden Freunde*, the friendship of friends who maintain distance in their relations (C, 57)—invokes the dialectic of solitude and community to which he often recurs in his letters of this period. This formulation would be reflected in his conduct in human relationships for the remainder of his life. Solitude is to be cultivated as the precondition for true community, which is necessarily a community of individual intellects and individual consciences. The elaborate distancing strategies that would mark virtually every relationship in Benjamin's life have their source in this conviction: his strictly codified manners, his maintenance of an impermeable wall between his friends, and his rigorous avoidance of personal matters in conversation and correspondence alike.

At the same time, meaningful or fruitful solitude itself presupposes a living community:

> Where are those who are solitary nowadays? Only an idea and a community in the idea can lead them to that, to solitude. I believe it is true that only a person who has made the idea his own (irrelevant "which" idea) can be solitary; I believe such a person must be

solitary. . . . The deepest solitude is that of the ideal human being in relation to the idea, which destroys what is human about him. And this solitude, the deeper sort, we can expect only from a perfect community. . . . The conditions for solitude among people [*Einsamkeit unter Menschen*], with which so few are familiar nowadays, have yet to be created. (C, 50)

He gives a hint of what he has in mind in referring to the "conditions" for the deep solitude in community, for the ideal shattering of what is "all too human," in another letter from this period (summer 1913), where he speaks of his feeling "that all our humanity is a sacrifice to the spirit," and of tolerating therefore no private interests of any kind, "no private feelings, no private will and intellect" (C, 35). These prescriptions, which betray a high-toned moral rigor in addition to abstract youthful enthusiasm, may sound strange coming from a man who, less than a decade later, was passionately collecting rare books and original artworks for his personal pleasure, and who carefully protected his privacy even from his closest friends—while attacking, it must be noted, the quintessentially bourgeois conception of private property. But such contradictions were typical of his multifaceted character and were in keeping with what he would call the "contradictory and mobile whole" formed by his convictions (BS, 108–109). For the philosophical and the political were never mutually exclusive in Benjamin's perspective, and he was continually seeking membership in groups to which he was almost always temperamentally, if not ideologically, ill-suited. In a letter of June 23, 1913, he could write: "The redemption of the unredeemable . . . is the universal meaning we proclaim" (C, 34).[8] Benjamin's attitude here is at once aristocratic and egalitarian, and it is no different with his later, more urbane pronouncements from the depths of exile and poverty.

If, in the years before the First World War, the classic antagonism of *philosophia* and *politeia* was no more susceptible of ready solutions than it ever was, it could still provide an occasion for clarifying and developing theoretical presuppositions. In this respect, Benjamin's youth writings constitute the workshop of his later philosophy. This is especially evident in regard to the problem of time, which exercised some of the best minds of his generation. Crucial to youth's experience of its own presence—youth as the site of "unceasing spiritual revolution" (EW, 205)—is a broadening of the very notion of the present, of that presence *(Gegenwart)* one can only await *(erwarten)*. Of course, Benjamin's understanding of history is metaphysical from the start. That is to say, it transcends the chronological conception of time by keeping in view, at every point, the totality of time (EW, 78; Benjamin's term is *Gesamtheit*). History is struggle between future and past (EW, 123), and the dynamic locus of this struggle is the present. Nietzsche had already posited the epistemological priority of the present in his essay "On the Advantage and Disadvantage of History for Life," cited by Benjamin in a 1913 *Anfang* article, "Teaching and Valuation." In section 6 of his essay, Nietzsche lays down a law of historical interpretation: "only from out of the highest energy of the present [*Kraft der Gegenwart*] can you interpret the past," for "the past always speaks as an oracle."[9] This is not very different from a saying of Novalis, in a fragment on Goethe, from the period 1797–1800: "One makes a great error if one believes there are 'ancients.' Only now is antiquity starting to arise. It arises in the eyes and soul of the artist."[10] Benjamin echoes Nietzsche's critique of nineteenth-century historicism—the critique of the Rankean doctrine that the historian can attain to objective knowledge of the past "as it really was"—at the opening of the essay "The Life of Students." Instead of viewing history in the context of an infinite extent of time, a homogeneous continuum of events considered as causes and effects, he conceives it here as gathered and concentrated in the present moment, as in a "focal point" *(Brennpunkt)*. The critical-historical task, mentioned above, is neither the pursuit of progress nor the restitution of the past but the excavation of this present, the liberation of its hidden energies. For deeply embedded in every present is an "immanent state of perfection" in the form of the most "endangered" and "excoriated" conceptions, and it is precisely such deep-lying deformations that escape the eye of the conventional historiographer.

The idea of the present as living dialectic of past and future likewise informs the "Metaphysics of Youth," written in 1913–1914, perhaps the most important of Benjamin's early unpublished essays. There Benjamin speaks of the present as eternally having been *(die ewig*

gewesene Gegenwart). What we do and think, he says, is filled with
the being of our ancestors—which, having passed away, becomes
futural. Each day, like sleepers, we use "unmeasured energies" of the
self-renewing past. Sometimes, on awaking, we recall the dream and
carry its spectral energies "into the brightness of the day." In this way,
the waking fortifies itself with dreaming, and "rare shafts of insight"
illuminate the layered depths of the present.[11] In awakening its own
historical resonance, the present gathers to a moment of decision, by
which, rooted in the past, it grounds a future (see "The Religious Position of the New Youth" in EW, 168–170). Here, the motif of "awakening youth" clearly anticipates a central concern of his later thinking,
namely, the dialectical image as a momentary constellation of historical tensions, an emergent force field in which the now of recognition
wakens from and to "that dream we name the past."[12] At stake in this
historical dialectic is "the art of experiencing the present as waking
world [*die Gegenwart als Wachwelt*]," what he will come to call "now
time."[13]

This first wave of independent writing accompanied Walter
Benjamin's emergence as a young adult. The abstract moral conde-
scension to be felt in these writings was inherited to some extent
from Wyneken, but many of the attitudes developed here were unique
to Benjamin and would color much of his writing for years to come.
Looking back on his student days from the perspective of imminent
exile in 1932, Benjamin readily admits that the youth movement was
doomed to failure by its very rootedness in the life of the mind: "It
was a final, heroic attempt to change the attitudes of people without
changing their circumstances. We did not know that it was bound to
fail, but there was hardly any of us whose resolve such knowledge
could have altered" (SW, 2:605). At many points where the brilliance
of the work to come breaks through the self-consciously hortatory
tone of these early texts, we glimpse a key aspect of the author's character. From an early age Benjamin was conscious of the special nature
of his gifts, and there is abundant testimony to the frequent recognition of his extraordinary intelligence. As early as his university years,
he sought to use his gifts to obtain a position of intellectual leadership. Since these were gifts of the intellect and of language, he hoped—
then and throughout his life—that the quality of his writings alone

might win him influence in the world. That hope was often expressed directly to friends such as Gershom Scholem and Hugo von Hofmannsthal. After his intensive involvement with the organizations and print organs of the German youth movement, however, the desire for intellectual leadership *of a group* would come to the fore only in three far-flung attempts to found a journal—and not one of these attempts succeeded.

Of course, at the time, leadership in the youth movement did not always seem so heroic. Benjamin complains about virtually every aspect of his first semester at Freiburg. Not only are classes boring and students uncultivated, but the Independent Students' Association strikes him as "a horde of emancipated phrase-mongers and incompetents," though he does take part in the School Reform Unit, which, unlike the more neutral organization of independent students, has kept faith with the Wynekenian radicalism (GB, 1:52). The only advantage he can see in studying at Freiburg is its proximity to Italy, where, on his Pentecost holiday tour, he came to appreciate Renaissance art. In mid-June, his hopes were somewhat revived on his making the acquaintance of "a young artist," presumably Philipp Keller, who was studying medicine at Freiburg, and whose novel *Mixed Feelings* would be published the following year. Benjamin would maintain rather ambivalent relations with Keller and the Expressionist literary circle of which he was a part.[14] Nevertheless, by the end of the summer semester he had resolved to leave Freiburg for Berlin, where he would live at home on Delbrückstraße while attending classes at the university and participating on a wider front of the youth movement.

Before the start of the new semester, he vacationed with a friend from the Kaiser Friedrich School, Franz Sachs, at Stolpmünde (now Ustka, Poland) on the Baltic, reporting to Belmore in August that his "A.N.G. *(Allgemeine normale Geistigkeit),*" his normally functioning intellect, had resurfaced out of the floodwaters of the four months preceding. At Stolpmünde, Sachs introduced him to a high school senior named Kurt Tuchler, a founder of the Zionist youth group Blue-White, with whom Benjamin carried on lengthy conversations and later a correspondence (now lost). These conversations ignited Benjamin's interest in his identity as a Jew—and confronted him for the first time with "Zionism and Zionist activity as a possibility, and hence perhaps as a duty" (C, 17). As it turned out, the talk of "duty" was premature. Prior to his meeting Tuchler, Benjamin's experience of things Jewish had been minimal. His mother, on grounds of family tradition (as he explains in "Berlin Chronicle"), felt some allegiance to the Jewish Reform community in Berlin, while his father's upbringing inclined him more to the Orthodox rite, but, as we have seen, the Benjamin family also celebrated Christmas in high style, and there were Easter egg hunts for the children. Having been raised in a fully assimilated household of the liberal Jewish bourgeoisie, Benjamin harbored no special feeling for Jewish traditions in general, and religious services bored and repelled him. The profound theological interest that animated his writing from the beginning, moving deeper and deeper underground as he grew older, was at odds with all organized religion. How could it be otherwise? Practically speaking, Benjamin's "Jewishness" was manifest in his choice of friends: with very few (though notable) exceptions, every man and woman who became an intimate friend was from the same sort of assimilated, upper-class Jewish household as his own.

The early confrontation with Zionism was thus a function of his newfound interest in Jewishness as a vital and historically complex problem. In a letter to Martin Buber some three years later, he would write: "The problem of the Jewish spirit is one of the most important and persistent objects of my thinking" (GB, 1:283). He earlier carried on his inquiry into the matter with a fellow Freiburg student, Ludwig Strauß, whom he had met through Phillip Keller. Already an accomplished poet and later, after marrying Buber's daughter, a literary historian at Hebrew University in Jerusalem, Strauß was part of the Expressionist circle around the poet and dramatist Walter Hasenclever. Benjamin revealed to Strauß that it was among the Wynekenians, a large proportion of whom were Jewish, that he first took up the question of Jewish identity. Before that, his sense of being Jewish had merely been an exotic "aroma" in his life (GB, 1:61–62). Benjamin's awakening self-consciousness mirrored that of many other young Jewish intellectuals of the period. The hitherto unknown Moritz Goldstein had published an article, "German-Jewish Parnassus," in the prominent art periodical *Der Kunstwart* in March 1912 that soon occasioned a flurry of responses in that and other journals and was the stuff of heated debate across Germany. Goldstein's article casts a harsh light on the problem of German Jewish identity, arguing for the essential home-lessness of the Jewish intellectual. "We Jews," Goldstein writes, "govern the intellectual possessions of a people that denies us the right to do so. . . . Even if we feel ourselves to be wholly German, the others feel us to be wholly un-German." And if the Jewish intellectual attempts to reject the "German" aspects of his makeup, the results are much the same: "If, with a finally awakened manly pride, we were to turn our backs on the German people that dislikes us, could we ever stop being predominantly German?"[15]

In the wake of these debates with other Jewish students, Benjamin had come to feel his Jewishness "at the core of his being" (GB, 1:69). He carefully distinguishes the question of Jewishness, though, from that of political Zionism. To Strauß, he describes the German Zionists as entirely deficient in any developed Jewish consciousness: *Halbmenschen* (half this, half that), "they make propaganda for Palestine, and then get drunk like Germans" (GB, 1:72). He considers the possibility of a "cultural Zionism," but, in view of the undisguised nationalistic tendencies of the Jewish settler movement, he can have no alternative but to keep his distance from "practical Zionism."[16] And though he signals his readiness to collaborate with Strauß on a journal of Jewish affairs, he makes it clear that "a rigorous engagement with the Jewish sphere is something denied me" (GB, 1:77).

Ultimately at issue in the question of Jewish identity, as broached in the exchanges with Ludwig Strauß between September 1912 and January 1913, was for Benjamin the very idea of culture, the need "to preserve the idea of culture, to salvage it from the chaos of the times" (GB, 1:78). Culture is always essentially *human* culture. Although it may seem to us that in this matter he was echoing Nietzsche's emphatic cosmopolitanism, the insistence on the "good European" by a man acutely sensitive to national character, he actually cites Nietzsche here as representative of the *dangers* facing the idea of culture. In the spirit of his mentor Wyneken, he concedes the necessity of a certain warfare, of struggle with the intimate "enemy," in generating a living, rooted culture; especially here, however, one must beware a vulgarization, if not abandonment, of the ideal. "The social biologists in the style of Nietzsche are fishing in troubled waters," he writes (GB, 1:78).

He goes on boldly to criticize Nietzsche's "intellectualized philistinism," manifest not only in the biologism of the doctrine (will to
power) but also in the reduction of the concept of friendship to the narrowly personal. (Benjamin refers to the section entitled "Of the Friend,"
in Part One of *Thus Spoke Zarathustra,* and specifically to the passage
on the friend asleep, where the speaker finds his own face reflected in
that of the other.) Against this, and presumably still in oblique reference to "the Jewish sphere," Benjamin adverts to Wyneken's ideal of
philosophic friendship, "ethical alliance in thought." His arguments
recall the "Dialogue on the Religiosity of the Present," which he finished by mid-October 1912, and which he mentions to Strauß. In this
midnight colloquy between two friends, which, to be sure, names
Nietzsche (together with Tolstoy and Strindberg) as prophet of the new
religious feeling, it is a question of restoring to "our social activity"
the "metaphysical seriousness" it has lost (EW, 65). Once again, a dialectic of solitary and communal, local and collective, is envisioned:
not the "useless energy of piety" but the physical and spiritual "abundance and weightiness of individuality"—indeed, a "new consciousness of personal immediacy"—are requisite for any genuinely religious
grounding of the common life (EW, 75, 78, 67). The emphasis on a deepened social and ethical consciousness (which includes a "consciousness of the proletariat" [EW, 64; see also GB, 1:64]), the concern with
ennobling the conventions of daily life, distinguishes the Benjaminian
religiosity from the Nietzschean. Which is not to gainsay the continuing importance of Nietzsche's philosophy for Benjamin's thinking
and mode of expression, the paradoxical or dialectical character of
which reflects Nietzsche's deconstruction of the system of oppositions
governing traditional metaphysics and its logic of noncontradiction.
Modern culture was delivered over to the groundlessness of being,
the Dionysian ocean of existence, in which all forms of identity are
dispersed, cast in doubt, beginning with the personal "I" (see EW, 169:
"Our own 'I' [is uncertain]"). It was characteristic of Benjamin in the
face of existential unmooring and immersion to affirm a principle of
sobriety.

Benjamin's metaphysically oriented sense of the social was nourished to some degree by his university studies that fall and winter.
Enrolling in philosophy at the Friedrich Wilhelm University, where,

in October 1912, he began the first of five (nonconsecutive) semesters in Berlin, he attended lectures by the distinguished philosophical sociologist Georg Simmel. Simmel taught as an "extraordinary" professor; because he was a Jew, he remained a professor without permanent ("ordinary") status within the faculty. Yet Simmel was perhaps the most popular and influential teacher then in Berlin, and numbered among his students such important social and political theorists as Ernst Bloch, Georg Lukács, and Ludwig Marcuse. He was by all accounts a riveting lecturer who spoke without notes, following the "motion of thought" as he approached a single subject from many angles: Simmel understood his philosophical work to combine epistemological, art historical, and sociological elements.[17] His eye for detail and his attention to the historically and culturally marginal certainly appealed to and nurtured Benjamin's own nascent proclivities. Simmel's groundbreaking essay "The Metropolis and Mental Life" of 1903 was in many ways the inspiration for Benjamin's later "sociological turn" and for the new analysis of the modern metropolis undertaken by Benjamin and Siegfried Kracauer in the early 1920s. Despite some reservations on philosophical grounds, Benjamin in writings from the 1930s will cite passages from Simmel concerned with the phenomenology of urban life, and will draw on Simmel's understanding of the experience of the big city in formulating his own late theory of experience. Of his other teachers at Berlin—he attended lectures in philosophy (notably by the Neo-Kantian Ernst Cassirer), German literature, and art history—we hear virtually nothing. Only the cultural historian Kurt Breysig, practitioner of a "universal history," seems to have stood out among these others for his independent attitude.

The return to Berlin meant renewed contact with *Der Anfang*, which launched its third and last series in the spring of 1913, after a period of preparatory work in which Benjamin was involved. Between May and October, while publishing in other journals as well, he produced five pseudonymous articles on youth for the new *Anfang*, the last of these being the little essay "Experience," which—in a manner prophetic of his lifelong concern with this theme—attacks the philistine "bourgeois" notion of experience, understood as the outgrowing of youth, in the name of a higher, more immediate experience that knows of the "inexperiencable" (EW, 117). We get a sense of the atmosphere surrounding the reorganization of the journal (whose last issue appeared in July 1914) from Martin Gumpert's account in *Hölle im Paradies: Selbstdarstellung eines Arztes* (Hell in Paradise: Memoirs of a Physician), which was published in 1939 and is worth quoting at length.

> One day I was invited to a meeting to consider setting up a new journal. I found myself in a circle of young men I'd not met before. / They had flowing hair, wore open shirts, . . . and they spoke—or, rather, preached—in solemn, mellifluous phrases about turning away from the bourgeois world and about the right of youth to a culture befitting its worth. . . . The concept of leader and of follower played an important role. We read Stefan George and the stern epics of the Swiss poet Carl Spitteler. . . . In those days, one lived in a world of conceptual possibilities [*in "Begriffen"*]. I wanted to analyze and define all elements of existence, to discover its duality, its multiformity, its mystery. Nothing was unimportant; every leaf, every object—behind its material aspect—had a metaphysical significance, which turned it into a cosmic symbol. . . . The youth movement was exclusively middle class. . . . Conscious of this limitation, I penned a clumsy proclamation, arguing that the youth of the working class belonged with us and that we must get to know them and win their support. Wyneken [who oversaw the running of the magazine in 1913–1914] sent the essay back filled with strongly negative comments: it's too early, we still have to concentrate on ourselves. Hence, . . . the danger of intellectualism that grew up in our circle. . . . Politics was considered unintellectual and unworthy. (Quoted in GS, 2:867–870)

To be sure, the young Benjamin—whom Gumpert thought "the most gifted" of the group—followed Wyneken in consistently dismissing any idea of youth's alignment within existing party politics, and he made an effort to keep *Der Anfang*, too, "at a distance from politics." We can be pretty certain nevertheless that he would not have considered his work for the movement unpolitical.

Benjamin understood politics at this point in both narrow and broad senses; educational reform subserved the latter. For if philosophy is made to stand at the center of the curriculum, from the earliest years of schooling onward, then humanity will be changed—or so he argued in his speeches and articles of 1913–1914 (which are effectively summed up in "The Life of Students"). During his first semester at Friedrich Wilhelm University, he worked on several fronts to promote his ideals, with a level of involvement and a prominence that marked a considerable step forward from his activities in Freiburg. He helped organize the Berlin School Reform Unit, and he was elected to the presidium or steering committee of the larger Independent Students' Association. Outside the university, he was active in the Berlin chapter of the League for Free School Communities, and he met often with Wyneken, who on one occasion was a guest at the Benjamin home on Delbrückstraße.

The years 1913 and 1914 saw Benjamin's first, and in some ways only, direct political engagement in public life. Initially in local groups such as those in Berlin and Freiburg, and then increasingly on a national stage, Benjamin sought positions of leadership in the youth movement, attempting to further a program of reform. As the idealistic tone of the writings indicates, however, this direct bodily engagement in the world of politics ran counter to his deepest tendencies. For he was a circumspect and enormously private young man, uncomfortable in groups, happiest in the solitary engagement with the life of the mind or in dialogue with a single interlocutor. Even seemingly direct interchange with a single conversational partner would often take the form of anecdote, analogy, and innuendo. The inscription on Kierkegaard's tombstone—"That Individual"—suggests the nature of Benjamin's lifelong aversion to groups, even, or perhaps especially, groups of his friends. The fervent political activity of the early university years constitutes, then, an absolute exception in Benjamin's patterns of social behavior. Perhaps not surprisingly, this direct activity was always confrontational and very often polarizing. Yet there is abundant testimony to his personal charisma. Ernst Joël speaks of the "unbelievable power" that Benjamin could exercise over one, while Herbert Belmore has claimed that already in high school Benjamin's "precocious cleverness and intense seriousness" made a deep impression on his friends, who became "almost his disciples."[18]

At the close of what must have been another very busy semester, Benjamin decided to return to Freiburg for the summer of 1913. He had failed to win reelection to the steering committee of the Berlin

Independent Students' Association, and Wyneken wanted him to assume control of the School Reform Unit at Freiburg. In addition, there was his friendship with Philipp Keller, which he considered a main reason for returning. He took a pleasant room near the cathedral in Freiburg, "with respectable saints on the walls." Throughout his life—and regardless of the circumstances—it was important to Benjamin that his living quarters be dominated by images, and images of Christian saints were a constant element in the increasingly complex domestic iconography. From Freiburg he wrote at the end of April to Belmore: "Outside my window, the church square with a tall poplar (the yellow sun in its green foliage), and in front of that an old fountain and the sun-drenched walls of the houses—I can stare at this for fifteen minutes at a time. Then . . . I lie down on the sofa for a while and pick up a volume of Goethe. No sooner do I come upon a phrase like "Breite der Gottheit" [breadth of godhead] than I once again lose control" (C, 18). He found Freiburg changed from the previous summer. The Independent Students' Association was virtually moribund: "There are no announcements to be seen on the bulletin board," he tells Carla Seligson, "no organized groups, no lectures" (C, 21). The Freiburg School Reform Unit, in which he participated the year before, had become a literary circle of seven to nine students, who met on Tuesday evenings for readings and discussion. The group was led by Philipp Keller, who "rules despotically and reads aloud to us incessantly" (C, 19). Benjamin's esteem for Keller's Expressionist writings remained high (he would mention Keller's "unfortunately forgotten" book in a review in *Die literarische Welt* in 1929), but he began working against him, and relations between them cooled: "I . . . liberate people from [Keller], after having liberated myself from him, . . . so that they will have a chance to form themselves, unsentimentally and soberly" (C, 23–24). There is no better expression of the principle that guided Benjamin's political activity at the time. Kurt Tuchler remembers the central point of contention in Stolpmünde: "He sought on his part to pull me into his circle of thoughts and above all to persuade me that I should not join a fraternity, as I then intended to do. He urged me to remain 'independent' and to attach myself to him personally."[19] Rejecting the group meant independence—but independence in a form mediated by Benjamin. It is hardly surprising that Keller withdrew from the discussion evenings by the beginning of June and that subsequently Benjamin held sway, giving talks on the writings of the Swiss poet Carl Spitteler (whom he discusses in his *Anfang* piece, "Sleeping Beauty") and reading essays by Wyneken to the group, some of whom he recruited for the *Anfang.*

By far the most important aspect of this time for Benjamin personally was the intense intellectual friendship he struck up that summer with one member of the reading circle, the moody young poet Christoph Friedrich Heinle (1894–1914), who would accompany him back to Berlin for the winter semester. A native of Aachen, Heinle had studied first in Göttingen before matriculating in philology for the summer semester of 1913 at Freiburg, where he participated in the Unit for Art and Literature among the independent students. Benjamin worked together with Fritz Heinle that summer in Freiburg to establish an educational community "for some people and, not least, for ourselves" (C, 67). Benjamin's relationship with Heinle—which would last for little more than a year—is one of the most enigmatic episodes in Benjamin's enigmatic life. At once epochal and impenetrable, the encounter with Heinle would leave a deep mark on Benjamin's intellectual and emotional physiognomy for years to come.

In April, between bouts of wrestling with Kant's *Foundations of the Metaphysics of Morals* (cited in his rigorously antinomian essay "Moral Education," appearing in July), he read Kierkegaard's *Either / Or,* which was having its first European vogue and which excited him "more than any other book."[20] "You probably know," he wrote to Carla Seligson, "that he demands heroism of us on the grounds of Christian ethics (or Jewish ethics, if you will) as mercilessly as Nietzsche does on other grounds, and that he engages in psychological analyses that are as devastating as Nietzsche's" (C, 20). As he was preparing to spend the Pentecost holiday absorbed in "philosophy and rain," he tells Belmore, "fate" intervened in the form of a decision to visit Paris for the first time. He went with Kurt Tuchler, the Zionist he'd met at Stolpmünde ten months earlier, and Tuchler's friend Siegfried Lehmann. He returned with "an awareness of having lived intensely for fourteen days, as only children do," and with a feeling of being "almost more at home in the Louvre and on the Grand Boulevard than I am in the Kaiser Friedrich Museum or on the streets of

7. C. F. Heinle *(Sammlung Wohlfarth, Frankfurt)*

Berlin. . . . By the time I left Paris, I was familiar with its stores, the advertisements in lights, the people on the Grand Boulevard" (C, 27). Tuchler reports that for the whole time they were in Paris, Benjamin went around in a kind of ecstasy. The two-week visit was more "fateful" than Benjamin could have known, for Paris would later become for him not only an all-consuming object of study but a home in exile.

During this time in Paris, the twenty-year-old writer may have had his first sexual experience with a woman he met on the Paris streets.[21] On the other hand, could Benjamin's sexual initiation really have occurred only when he was twenty? As the contemporaneous paintings by Ernst Ludwig Kirchner and poems by Georg Heym suggest, the streets and cafés of Berlin would have furnished ample opportunity for a young man to follow the customs of his class and seek sex with a prostitute or demimondaine. A section of the *Berlin Childhood* entitled "Beggars and Whores" (it is not included in the revised 1938 version) speaks of the "unparalleled excitement which drove me to accost a whore in the street," an encounter that would have occurred during adolescence. "It could take hours before I made my move. The horror I felt in doing so was no different from that which would have filled me in the presence of an automaton requiring merely a question to be set in motion. And so I cast my voice into the slot. The blood was singing in my ears at that point, and I could not catch the words that fell from the thickly painted lips. I fled the scene" (SW, 3:404–405). It is entirely possible, of course, given Benjamin's inherent caution and fastidiousness, that the final consummation after many approaches took place in a foreign capital, far from the scrutiny of friends and family.

In his second semester at Albert Ludwig University, he continued his studies in philosophy, taking a seminar on Kant's *Critique of Judgment* and Schiller's aesthetics—"chemically purified of ideas," he told Belmore—and a course on the philosophy of nature. He took two courses with Rickert this time around. One was a seminar on Bergson's metaphysics, where he "would just sit and pursue [his] own thoughts."[22] (Bergson's theories, which were much discussed in academic circles in the years before the war, would find a powerful echo in Benjamin's essay "Metaphysics of Youth.") The other was a lecture course attended by "all of literary Freiburg": "as an introduction to his logic, [Rickert] is presenting an outline of his system which lays the foundation for a completely new philosophical discipline: philosophy of the perfected life (woman as its representative). As interesting as it is problematic" (C, 31). He took a more critical line on this course and its *Wertphilosophie* (value philosophy) in a letter to Wyneken in mid-June: "For me, what he says is unacceptable, since he considers woman in principle to be incapable of the highest moral development" (GB, 1:117). He was adopting here a position consistent with Wyneken's own views on the necessity of coeducation and of liberating women from "a domestic ideal that grows more questionable every day" (quoted in EW, 42 [1911]). In a memorable letter of June 23, 1913, to Herbert Belmore, who had written of the symbolic significance of the prostitute, he went further into the question of "woman": "You should understand that I consider the types 'man' and

'woman' as somewhat primitive in the thought of civilized humanity. . . . Europe consists of individuals (in whom there are both masculine and feminine elements), not of men and women. . . . What do we
really know of woman? As little as we do of youth. We've never yet
experienced a female culture, any more than we've known a youth
culture" (C, 34).[23] As for the significance of the prostitute, he re-
proaches Belmore for his "shallow aestheticism": "To you, a prostitute
is some kind of beautiful object. You respect her as you do the Mona
Lisa. . . . But in so doing, you think nothing of depriving thousands of
women of their souls and relegating them to an existence in an art
gallery. As if we consort with them so artistically! Are we being honest when we call prostitution 'poetic'? I protest in the name of poetry"
(C, 35). For Benjamin at this stage, the significance of the prostitute
(who will reemerge as a prominent nineteenth-century type in *The
Arcades Project*) lies in the fact that "she drives nature from its last
sanctuary, sexuality." The prostitute thus signifies "the sexualization
of the spirit. . . . She represents culture in eros: Eros, who is the most
powerful individualist, the most hostile to culture—even he can be
perverted; even he can serve culture" (C, 36).

These reflections on the cultural significance of prostitution are
closely connected to the opening sections of Benjamin's esoteric
"Metaphysics of Youth," which very likely was begun in the summer
of 1913 with the composition of two speculative complexes, "The
Conversation" and "The Diary," to which a shorter third part,
"The Ball," was added the following January.[24] As the metaphysics of
youth (a distinctly post-Nietzschean metaphysics, unfolding beyond
the classical idea of substance), it belongs together with the essays
"Two Poems by Friedrich Hölderlin" and "The Life of Students,"
which might be viewed as constituting, respectively, the aesthetics
and the politics of youth. ("The Life of Students" was directly connected with the campaign for school reform and was published for its
topicality, whereas the other two essays were written without a specific audience in mind, were circulated in manuscript among a few
friends, and remained unpublished during the author's lifetime.) Concerned in large measure with the problem of perception in space and
time, Benjamin's metaphysical speculations are cast in a gnomic,
rhapsodic style that has affinities with the visionary modes of Expres-

sionism.[25] In particular, one may think of the darkly luminous prose poems of Georg Trakl, produced at approximately the same time, though Benjamin's essay is neither morbid nor apocalyptic. A sustained and almost unbearably brilliant tour de force, it maps out a way of doing philosophy in concentrated imagistic form. The essay's vocabulary is one of "tension," "interpenetration," "radiation"—various dynamic or "erotic" relations subtending a vibratory reality. The dynamic extends even to the texture of Benjamin's language, which, in the effort to articulate the convolution of dimensions, employs a philosophical paronomasia that sometimes verges on mannerism: "Die ewig gewesene Gegenwart wird wieder werden" (The present that has been eternally will again come to be [EW, 147]). Such language strikes a consciously archaic note, much as the language of Heidegger after the Second World War will do. In this respect, both Benjamin and Heidegger hark back to poetic practices of Hölderlin (whose beautiful lines on youth as the awakening light appear as an epigraph at the beginning of "The Conversation," this title likewise recalling a Hölderlinian motif).

The metaphysical understanding of "youth" thus entails a certain language as well as a certain temporality—a language bound up with questions of gender. In "The Conversation," after the opening paragraphs on the dream energies of the past, Benjamin distinguishes between two conceptions of language, one dominated by "silence," the other by "words." (In his 1916 essay "On Language as Such and on the Language of Man," he distinguishes in the same terms between nature and humanity.) The language of silence is associated with women and the language of words with men, but here we should keep in mind Benjamin's letter of June 23 to Belmore, which insists on the functional—not substantive—significance of "masculine" and "feminine." (Otherwise, a sentence such as the following—"The language of women has remained inchoate"—would seem as "unacceptable" as Rickert's pronouncements on the subject, notwithstanding the references to Sappho, for Benjamin's concept of "woman," in the first part of the essay, is again consciously archaic). In "The Conversation," man is the speaker, given to blasphemy and imbued with despair, and woman the listener, given to silence and imbued with hope.[26] The speaker, we are told, enters the listener, while the listener grounds the speaker. In fact, the silent listener is the "unappropriated source of meaning" in the

conversation, the one who, moreover, "protects meaning from understanding." In all these functions, the listener embodies the speaker's
"womanly past," the past conceived as a reservoir of energies, a depth
of "night" that the speaker, obsessed with the present, penetrates. In
the silence born of conversation (think of Penelope and Odysseus), the
dream energy is renewed and the night made radiant. As Benjamin
formulates the issue a few years later: "The radiant is true only where
it is refracted in the nocturnal" (SW, 1:52–53 ["Socrates"]). Once again,
we have an idea of truth balancing revelation with secrecy. The fate of
conversation is inseparable from the fate of silence.

The distinction between two modes of language is paralleled, in
"The Diary" (the second—properly metaphysical—part of the essay),
by a distinction between two modes of time: "immortal time," inherently youthful, and "developmental time," the time of calendar, clock,
and stock exchange. The distinction owes much to Bergson, whose
idea of living duration, in which past is prolonged in present, is similarly distinguished from the abstract, linear mechanical time of science and common sense, what he calls the logic of solids. (Compare
"Trauerspiel and Tragedy" of 1916, in which "mechanical time" is
opposed to "historical time" [SW, 1:55–56].) For Benjamin, the "pure"
time flows intermittently within the everyday chronological: "In that
self to which events occur and which encounters human beings . . .
courses immortal time." But flowing within, it transcends what contains it, just as the inner silence transcends the words; developmental time, with its "chain of experiences," is overcome (aufgehoben)
in the radiation of youthful time, which is the time of "the diary"
(Tagebuch). As we've seen, keeping a diary could be a serious literary-
philosophical occupation for Benjamin, and it is not surprising that
such a characteristically youthful medium of expression should come
to figure a whole way of seeing and experiencing. In the "Metaphysics
of Youth," the diary is the site of a simultaneous dissolution and fulfillment of the self—an abdication of the self which "calls me 'I' and
torments me with its intimacies" and a liberation to "that other which
seemed to oppress me but which after all I myself am: ray of time."
The transformed time of the daybook is also a transformed space: the
things we encounter in its interval, under "the spell of the book," are

no longer defined apart from the flow of time, as in classical meta-physics, or apart from the perceiving subject, but are themselves part of that flow and that consciousness. They gravitate toward *(leben . . . dahin)* the self, which in turn befalls *(widerfährt)* all things. In this broad oscillation, deepening the space of time, things enter the field of human perception by posing "questions"—the conception is Bergsonian—appeals to which the recollecting self responds: "in the interchange of such vibrations, the self has its life [*lebt das Ich*]."[27] "Things see us," writes Benjamin, in striking anticipation of his late reflections on the aura (see SW, 4:338–339); "their gaze propels [*schwingt*] us into the future." Thus, on our path through the land-scape of events (in the diary everything that happens surrounds us as landscape), we "befall ourselves"—"we, the time of things." Radiat-ing and gravitating, time's rhythm articulates the interplay of subject and object, simultaneous expansion out of and return into the "womb of time." In the sway of this spatiotemporal dialectic, the diary ren-ders past things futural and lets us encounter ourselves, as our own most intimate enemy, as conscience, in "the time of death." It is the sovereign reality of death, at once distant and near, that for an instant *(Augenblick)* bestows immortality on the living. As the entry to mo-mentary redemption, the diary inscribes a fate in the form of "the resurrections of the self." Some five years later, the idea of an afterlife of works will become fundamental to Benjamin's concept of criti-cism, but the correspondence of philosophy and theology (a nondog-matic and noneschatological theology) marks his thinking at every stage of its development, from the 1910 parable "The Three Who Sought Religion" to the 1940 text "On the Concept of History."

Benjamin's second semester at Freiburg came to a close on August 1, 1913, after what he later described as a stretch of "many bad weeks" (C, 53). Enlivening the period, however, was his friendship with Heinle, "an eternal dreamer and very German" (C, 18). A letter in mid-July to Herbert Belmore, who was studying interior design in Berlin, mentions "some poems by Heinle that may win you over," and Benjamin goes on to remark that "we are probably more aggressive here, more full of pathos, more rash and un-reflective (literally!). . . . [T]hat's the way he *is* and I empathize, sympathize, and am often that

way myself" (C, 45). With Heinle Benjamin took long walks through
the Black Forest environs of Freiburg, talking of Wyneken, the youth
movement, and other large ethical matters. (Heinle published a smoldering prose piece on classroom education in the July issue of *Der
Anfang.*) At the end of the month, they joined forces with another
young poet, Anton Müller, son of the editor of the ultramontane
Catholic newspaper *Freiburger Boten:* "Yesterday [the three of us]
climbed around in the woods . . . and talked about original sin . . . and
about dread. I was of the opinion that a dread of nature is the test of a
genuine feeling for nature" (C, 48). Soon after meeting Heinle, Benjamin had tried unsuccessfully to get his new friend's poetry published
in *Der Anfang.* It was the first in a series of such attempts over the
coming years to disseminate and promote Heinle's work. Several of
Benjamin's friends from this time commented on the peculiar nature
of the friendship. Heinle was, by universal consent, an unusually
beautiful young man—Benjamin could still refer to Heinle and his
brother Wolf ten years later as "the most beautiful youths I have ever
known" (to F. C. Rang, Feb. 4, 1923). Yet Benjamin seems not to have
distinguished between this physical manifestation of beauty and the
purported dark beauty of Heinle's character and poetry. Some readers
of Heinle's work have found it to be juvenile, while others have been
stirred by it.[28]

The time in Freiburg was not without its diversions. There was a
visit to an exhibition of German Renaissance art in nearby Basel,
where Benjamin saw the originals of pictures—such as Dürer's
Melancholia—that would have a bearing on his later monumental
study of the German *Trauerspiel.* And in addition to the readings for
his coursework (Kant, Husserl, Rickert), there was much reading for
his own instruction and pleasure: Kierkegaard, Saint Bonaventure,
Sterne, Stendhal, Maupassant, Hesse, and Heinrich Mann. He even
took time to work on a couple of short stories, including the finely
etched "Death of the Father" (EW, 128–131). When his own father, who
still disapproved of his "aspirations," visited him in July, Benjamin
was able to be "very objective and friendly." When the semester ended,
he found it difficult to leave Freiburg, presumably because of the
depth of his attachment to Heinle: "Finally, life there also suddenly
turned beautiful and summery with the arrival of sunny weather at

the end of the semester. The last four evenings we (Heinle and I) were constantly out together past midnight, mostly in the woods" (C, 49). By the beginning of September, after several weeks of travel with his family in the South Tyrol, he was back in Berlin, preparing to continue both his philosophical studies at the Friedrich Wilhelm University and his work in the youth movement, which, having stagnated over the summer, now entered its most intensive phase.

In September 1913 the so-called Sprechsaal (Discussion Hall) got under way in Berlin. This was an organization set up to represent the interests of high school and university students, specifically of that stratum on which *Der Anfang* drew for its readership. The format and themes of its meetings were familiar: evening gatherings for lecture and discussion—on such topics as youth culture, energy and ethics, the modern lyric poem, the Esperanto movement—with the aim of promoting the free exchange of ideas. Over the course of the winter semester 1913–1914 Benjamin devoted much energy to this new cultural forum, acting as co-signatory for the rental of the "Meeting House," the small apartment in the Tiergarten district, his old stomping ground, where both the Discussion Hall and the Bureau for Social Work of the Berlin Independent Students' Association met. Scholem's first recollection of Benjamin is at one of these Sprechsaal meetings in the autumn of 1913: "Without looking at the audience, he delivered his absolutely letter-perfect speech with great intensity to an upper corner of the ceiling, at which he stared the whole time" (SF, 3–4). Concurrently with this engagement, Benjamin was gradually loosening his ties with *Der Anfang*, which published the final contribution by "Ardor" in October. Within a few months he would find himself caught in the middle of an altercation that, no longer entirely reconstructable, was presumably occasioned by Wyneken's decision to step down as supervisor of the magazine. A group led by Heinle and Simon Guttmann, who favored a literary orientation for the journal, tried to take it over from the editors Georges Barbizon and Siegfried Bernfeld, who favored a political (socialist) orientation. Played out in heated debates in the Discussion Hall, the affair was finally settled when the magazine's publisher, Franz Pfemfert, who also edited *Die Aktion*, the influential journal of a politically radical Expressionism, intervened on the side of Barbizon and Bernfeld. His own attempts at mediation having failed, Benjamin would consider writing a farewell piece denouncing the current tendency of the *Anfang* (the December 1913 issue noted the formation of an "Aryan" Sprechsaal in Vienna; see C, 73), but the journal ceased publication before he could go forward with this.

In October Benjamin appeared for the first time before a large public, playing a role at two well-attended national conferences of the school reform and youth movements. At the First Student Pedagogic Conference, organized by a group at the University of Breslau, Benjamin gave a talk entitled "Ends and Means of Student Pedagogic Groups at German Universities," in which he defended the "Freiburg orientation," explicitly Wynekenian, against a more conservative Breslau faction. Calling for a "new philosophic pedagogy" and a "new outlook among students," he affirmed "an *inwardly* grounded and, at the same time, highly social" student activism that would eschew party loyalty (GS, 2:60–66). The two university factions could agree only to keep each other informed. From Breslau, he traveled to Kassel, in central Germany, to attend the First Free German Youth Congress *(Erste Freideutsche Jugendtag)*, convened by several different youth factions and student groups from across Germany and Austria. Regarded today as the climactic event of the German youth movement, the congress took place on Mount Meißner (renamed "High Meißner" for the occasion—and the name stuck) and neighboring Mount Hanstein on the weekend of October 10–12. Various luminaries, such as the writer Gerhart Hauptmann and the philosophers Ludwig Klages and Paul Natorp, sent their greetings and words of counsel. The three-day event was marked by deep-rooted contention as well as communal festivity. As one participant from Bonn, the writer Alfred Kurella, later put it, the people who made up these groups were "approximately equal parts fascist, antifascist, and indifferent philistine."[29] At the opening session of the congress, which took place outside on a rainy Friday night on the grounds of the ruined castle atop Mount Hanstein, there was a sharp clash between agitators for military preparedness and "racial hygiene" and the leaders of the Free School Community at Wickersdorf, Gustav Wyneken and Martin Luserke. The Wickersdorf position was "autonomy of youth" in the face of all "political or half-political special interests." Not saber-rattling but the call of conscience was to be heeded.

For Wyneken, the struggle to foster "the shared feeling of youthful-ness" was ultimately a struggle to preserve the true soul of Germany. His influence was decisive in the congress's adoption of a statement drafted by the delegates that night, a statement whose opening sentence has come to be known as the "Meißner formula." We have seen it quoted: "Free German Youth seeks to shape its life according to its own principles, on its own responsibility, and in inner truthfulness." The ideological conflicts continued during the next two days, how-ever, as the scene shifted to Mount Meißner and the sun came out. Among the crowds of young people in attendance, there were music, folk dancing, athletic competition, and the display of ceremonial at-tire, along with discussion of race relations, abstinence (from liquor and nicotine), and agrarian reform. Benjamin himself took a rather dim view of the proceedings in the terse critique he published a week later in *Die Aktion*, "Youth Was Silent" (the title a response to a lau-datory article earlier published by the journal's editor Franz Pfemfert, "Youth Speaks!"), but he was not insensitive to the presence of some-thing new in the gathering: "We are by no means going to allow our-selves to be overcome by the *fact* of the Free German Youth Congress. To be sure, we experienced a new reality: two thousand up-to-date young people come together, and on High Meißner the onlooker saw a new physical youth, a new tension in the faces. For us, this is just a pledge of the spirit of youth. Excursions, ceremonial attire, folk dances are nothing new and—in the year 1913—still nothing spiritual" (EW, 135). The recurrent bonhomie he found particularly dismaying, for it robbed the young of "the sacred seriousness with which they came to-gether." Both the ideology and the complacency were warrant that "only few" understood the meaning of the word "youth" and its proper mission, namely, "protest against family and school."

Benjamin's leadership in the movement was boosted in February 1914 when he was elected president of the Berlin Independent Stu-dents' Association for the coming summer semester. Before long, he had lined up some eminent speakers for a summer lecture series: the list included Martin Buber, to speak on his recently published book *Daniel*, and Ludwig Klages, the vitalist philosopher and graphologist, to speak on the duality of spirit and intellect. We get an idea of Benja-min's general intentions for the independent students from a letter of

May 23 to his former schoolmate (and future radio collaborator), the composer, writer, and translator Ernst Schoen: "Basically, what we can do is . . . create a cultured kind of meeting" (C, 67). At issue in this ostensibly modest goal is again the generation of an educational community *(Erziehungsgemeinschaft)*, "which depends entirely on the productive individuals who enter its orbit." This individualistic communitarianism, which had filled the letters to Carla Seligson, was a theme of his inaugural address that May, an extended passage of which (all we have of the text today) is quoted in "The Life of Students." The passage begins: "There is a very simple and reliable criterion by which to test the spiritual value of a community. It is to ask: Does the totality of the productive person find expression in it? Is the whole human being committed to it and indispensable to it? Or is the community as superfluous to each individual as he is to it?" (EW, 200). Benjamin goes on here to invoke the "Tolstoyan spirit," associated with a concept of "service on behalf of the poor," as exemplifying that "truly serious spirit of a social work" at the basis of a "truly serious community."[30] By contrast, the present academic community remains caught up in a mechanical—that is to say, philistine—notion of duty and of self-interest, and the students' empathy with "the workers" or "the people" is wholly abstract. The talk went over well. One of the most vivacious members of the circle, Dora Sophie Pollak— Benjamin's future wife—was overwhelmed: "Benjamin's address . . . was like a form of salvation. One could hardly breathe."[31] At its conclusion, Dora presented the speaker with a bouquet of roses. "It's true," Benjamin commented afterward, "that no flowers have ever made me so happy as these" (C, 60).

In June he attended the 14th Free Student Congress at Weimar, which was marked by fierce debates on the political responsibility of the independent student body. The conference saw a resounding defeat for the Wynekenians, most of whose motions were "brutally voted down on a daily basis" (C, 69). A resolution introduced jointly by the Berlin and Munich delegations proposing to defend the right of high school students to hold their own personal convictions, for example, was defeated by a vote of seventeen to five (GS, 2:877). As president of the Berlin group, Benjamin played a prominent part in this national assembly, presenting a talk on the first day entitled "The

New University," which evidently was close in substance to his inaugural address from the month before. There are indications that he spoke without a manuscript in Weimar. His letters from the time reveal that he based his remarks on the educational lectures of Nietzsche and of Johann Gottlieb Fichte.[32] The latter's *Addresses to the German Nation* of 1807 had called for a university system dedicated to propagating the life of reason as the most important precondition for the establishment of a German nation; the former's *On the Future of Our Educational Institutions* of 1872 had polemicized against a state-run educational machine geared to specialization at the expense of genuine self-formation under the aegis of a great teacher and in contact with philosophy and art. For the independent students, this all comes down to "the necessity of moral decision."[33] In a report on the conference proceedings, a representative of the conservative majority offered a rather condescending view of Benjamin's presentation: "It was wonderful to see how he—who has gone his own way in the spirit of his teacher—channeled all his thoughts toward one magnetic pole: the idea of the highest educational formation. The only thing is that this young Wickersdorfer, with characteristic arrogance, put everything into question—the university, science and scholarship, the culture of the past" (quoted in GB, 1:239n). Benjamin himself refers to the "uniform ill will of this gathering," from which the Wynekenians, acting in the name of "a certain decency, a certain spiritual bearing," nevertheless emerged with dignity intact, having salvaged in the end both their own "elevated but lonely stance," in the face of the outside world, and the "fearful respect of the others" (C, 69). For a while they would continue in their efforts to make possible "a community of young people grounded only inwardly and intensively, and no longer in the least politically" (C, 68), though no more than before did the repudiation of party politics and concrete political goals exclude a vision of social change, of serious "social work," and thus a certain political responsibility.

The essay that in the summer of 1914 grew directly out of the inaugural address and the Weimar talk, "The Life of Students," distinguishes itself at the outset from both a call to arms and a manifesto. We have already discussed the pregnant opening paragraph, with its annunciation of a historical task concentrated on disclosing the messianic energies of the present; the retrieval of the historical object for the benefit of the present accords with a Romantic tradition of thought extending from Novalis and Friedrich Schlegel through Baudelaire to Nietzsche. The task at hand is one of reflection, namely, on the advancing "crisis" concealed in the increasingly secure organization of life. More specifically, the essay seeks to describe the significance of student life and the university from a perspective at once metaphysical and historical, and through such an act of criticism *(Kritik)* to "liberate the future from its deformation in the present" (EW, 198). Like Wyneken, Benjamin takes aim at the instrumentalizing of education, "the perversion of the creative spirit into the vocational spirit." He issues an indictment of the whole professional "apparatus" operating in the universities, and the students' uncritical and spineless acquiescence in this situation, as having stifled any true vocation one might feel for learning and teaching. As a corrective to the external business of training and credentialization, he invokes the idea of "inner unity" (which will have its aesthetic counterpart in the Hölderlin essay, begun later that year). What the mechanism of vocational and professional training does, argues Benjamin, is essentially to shut off the various disciplines from their common origin in the idea of knowledge *(Idee des Wissens)*—which is to say, in philosophy understood as "community of learning." The solution for the present "chaotic conception of academic life" is then to restore the disciplines to their origin in philosophic sensibility and praxis, to make all study in a fundamental sense philosophical.

Of course, Benjamin does not concern himself with how such a transformation of academic life might come about, other than to suggest that it is not a matter of confronting lawyers with literary questions, or doctors with legal ones, so much as subordinating the special fields of knowledge to the idea of the whole represented by the university itself—obviously not the same thing as subordinating them to the philosophy department. It is the collectivity of the university as a working ideal that is the true seat of authority. There is a logical development here: from an affirmation of the immanent unity of knowledge to a call for unifying the academic disciplines, and from there to a demand for nonhierarchical relations between teachers and students and between males and females in the university community and in the community at large. It was the role of students—in their devotion to "unceasing spiritual revolution" as well as to "radical doubt"—to constitute an intellectual vanguard: to keep open a space for questioning and discussion, for "the culture of conversation," so as not only to prevent the degeneration of study into an accumulation of information but also to prepare the way for basic changes in the conduct of everyday life in society.[34]

In retrospect, the defeat at Weimar in June could be seen as writing on the wall, announcing the imminent dissolution of the antebellum student movement that had been at the center of Benjamin's activities for more than four years. To be sure, he was reelected president of the Berlin Independent Students' Association in July for another six months, but with the outbreak of war in August he turned away from the concerns of school reform (if not from the idea of education) and indeed broke off relations with most of his comrades in the youth movement. His letters that summer suggest that, at least in the context of his own daily life, the opposition between solitude and community had not been overcome. He voices his need for "a rigorous life" and declares his intention to seek out over vacation "some remote cabin in the woods, in order to find both peace and work"; as it is, he never has time "to become immersed in anything" (C, 73, 70). When he did go on vacation in July, however, it was not to some lonely outpost but to the Bavarian Alps in company with his friend Grete Radt, with whom he had been close since 1913, and her brother Fritz; on their return to Berlin, he and Grete somewhat hastily announced their engagement.[35] At the same time, he was seeing more and more of Dora Pollak and her first husband, the philosophy student Max Pollak; they spent hours together in conversation, and they would sit around the piano while working through a book by the music authority of the Wyneken circle, August Halm. Dora was not always as calm as Benjamin would have liked, but "she always comes to feel again what is fundamentally right and simple, and therefore I know that we are of one mind" (C, 63).

Several of Benjamin's friends have left unflattering portraits of Dora Pollak. For Franz Sachs, she was an "Alma Mahler *en miniature*. She always wanted to have the man in our circle of friends who appeared to her at that time as the coming leader or as intellectually promising, and she tried this with various people, mostly without success, until she landed on W.B. and made him her husband. I don't believe that this marriage was ever happy."[36] And for Herbert Belmore, she was an "ambitious goose who always wanted to swim in the very newest intellectual currents."[37] The tone of these statements, made by two of his oldest friends, is undoubtedly attributable in part to jealousy: Benjamin *was* the intellectual leader of the group, and much sought after. Moreover, Dora was "a decidedly beautiful, elegant woman . . . [who] participated in most of our conversations with much verve and obvious empathy," as Scholem has written, testifying to the "affection for each other" that she and Benjamin felt, at least in 1916 (SF, 27). Dora was in many ways a perfect complement: if Benjamin in the years to come lived the life of the mind, venturing forth into practical matters only occasionally, and then often tentatively and clumsily, Dora, for all her literary and musical talent (she was the daughter of a Viennese professor of English and authority on Shakespeare), was a capable manager—energetic, perspicacious, and goal-oriented—and it was often just this practicality that made possible Benjamin's thought and writing.

These years in the capital saw Benjamin's gradual formation as a metropolitan intellectual. The allure of Berlin's café life played no small part in that formation. In the old West End Café—headquarters for the city's bohemians and best known by its nickname, Café Größenwahn ("Café Delusions of Grandeur")—he met such distinguished figures as the Expressionist poets Else Lasker-Schüler and Robert Jentsch and the publisher Wieland Herzfelde, though, perhaps out of a consciousness of his "youth" in comparison with this elite outside the university, he generally kept his distance from "the sated, self-assured bohemians" (SW, 2:607). A chief attraction of the cafés was the presence of *cocottes*, who formed the shadowy periphery of his erotic life; it is the "incomprehensible" erotic that evidently occasions the remark to Belmore, made right after his twenty-second birthday: "You may no longer think of me as a single person [*nicht mehr einzeln denken*], and it is as if I had only now been born into a divine age, to come into my own. . . . I know I am nothing, but that I exist in God's world" (C, 73). When, more than a decade later, the demimonde was taken up as a subject in *The Arcades Project*, Benjamin

8. Dora Kellner *(Collection Ah Kew Benjamin, London)*

could write from years of firsthand experience. Meanwhile, his academic studies were coming to seem less relevant than ever; as he puts it in a letter of early July, "The university is simply not the place to study" (C, 72).

It was in the West End Café, "in those very first August days" when Germany declared war on Russia and France, that Benjamin and some of his friends decided to enlist in the military—not from any martial fervor, he explains in the "Berlin Chronicle," but in an attempt to secure "a place among friends in the inevitable conscription" (SW, 2:607). Not surprisingly, given his nearsightedness and more general lack of robustness, he was rejected by the recruiting board—for the time being. Then, on August 8, "came the event that was to banish for long afterward both the city and the war from my mind": Fritz Heinle and Rika Seligson (Carla's sister) committed suicide by turning on the gas in the Discussion Hall.[38] Benjamin was awakened the next morning by an express letter that read: "You will find us lying in the Meeting House" (SW, 2:605). Although the newspapers portrayed the event as the sad outcome of a doomed love, the couple's friends saw it as the most somber of war protests. Benjamin himself took charge of Heinle's manuscripts, which he wanted to edit and publish; after years of unsuccessful efforts, they were left behind and subsequently lost when he went into exile in 1933. To commemorate his dead comrade, he penned a cycle of fifty sonnets, adding others over the years, and he would read aloud from these carefully crafted and often poignant poems to close friends (see GS, 7:27–64). Heinle's death was an experience from which Benjamin never fully recovered. While it is virtually impossible to reconstruct, on the basis of either Heinle's work or Benjamin's various statements on the subject, the full significance of the relationship between the two young men, there is ample evidence of the shattering effect of Heinle's suicide on Benjamin. References to Heinle, often coded, pepper his published writings, and Heinle, or rather his corpse, plays a dramatic role in the opening pages of two of Benjamin's most important works, *One-Way Street* and *Berlin Childhood around 1900*. But suicide is more than a literary topos for Benjamin; the image of his dead friend would have presided over his own suicidal impulses, which became increasingly insistent starting in the mid-1920s.

The immediate effect of the double suicide on Benjamin was a period of prolonged inactivity. At some point in September or October, according to Scholem, he had to report to his draft board: "Benjamin presented himself (having rehearsed beforehand) as a palsy victim. He consequently was granted a year's deferment" (SF, 12). Toward the end of October, he wrote a smoldering letter to Ernst Schoen in which he posits the need for a transformed radicalism: "Of course, we all nourish an awareness of the fact that our radicalism was too much a gesture, and that a harder, purer, more invisible radicalism should become axiomatic for us" (C, 74). Such an initiative cannot be sustained by "the swamp that the university today is," though despite the brutality, egomania, and vulgarity, he was continuing to attend lectures.

"The naked accounting I made of my shyness, fear, ambition, and, more important, of my indifference, coldness, and lack of education, terrified and horrified me. Not one of [the scholars] distinguishes himself by tolerating the community of the others. . . . No one is equal to this situation" (C, 74–75). The disillusionment so evident in this letter was, if anything, more apparent in his personal life. The loss of his two comrades precipitated a brusque withdrawal; in a way that remained inexplicable to those affected, he broke with every one of his close friends from the youth movement. Cohn and Schoen had never been involved and so escaped dismissal. But Belmore, to whom Benjamin had been closest during his first university years, was now effectively shunned, and though there would be a brief renewal of contact before a final break in 1917, their friendship was never the same.

During the winter of 1914–1915 Benjamin drew on his mourning for Fritz Heinle to compose his first great literary-philosophical essay, "Two Poems by Friedrich Hölderlin," which, as he fleetingly indicated years later, was written in memory of Heinle (see GS, 2:921). It was also his first extended venture into literary criticism since his high school days. With its self-contained theory of criticism and its highly original reading of Hölderlin, the essay stands apart, though it took shape under the aegis of aesthetic ideas then current in the circle around the German symbolist poet Stefan George. Benjamin's engagement with the lofty and difficult Romantic poet was made possible by the publication of the first critical-historical edition of Hölderlin's works by the George disciple Norbert von Hellingrath, who was himself killed at the front.[39] In fact, Hellingrath's edition, which began appearing in 1913, initiated a sensational resurgence of interest in this poet, who had been all but forgotten in the early years of the Wilhelmine Empire. In the period immediately before the war, the combination of aestheticism and nationalism in the George school led to a widespread misreading of Hölderlin as a nationalist bard: many German soldiers went to the trenches with a special "knapsack edition" of his poems.

At the time, it was not usual to devote a detailed commentary to individual works by a modern author. Like his older contemporary Benedetto Croce, whose *Aesthetics* (1902) opened the way to criticism of the individual work of art as a concrete and irreducible "aesthetic fact," the more or less successful solution of a specific "artistic problem," Benjamin here rejects the categories and classifications of comparative philology and conventional aesthetics. The essay is ambitious in other respects as well. In the course of exacting—sometimes tortuous—analyses, it develops a theory of truth in poetry, a theory that transcends the customary form-content distinction through advancement of the concept of task.[40] Benjamin's key term here is "the poetized" (das Gedichtete, from the past participle of the verb dichten, "to compose artistically"). What has been poetically formed opens up a sphere in which the truth of the particular poem (Gedicht) is in play. Nothing static, the truth resides in the fulfillment of the particular intellectual-perceptual task that each poem—as a work of art—may be said to constitute. It is not a matter of tracing the process of poetic composition, as Benjamin notes at the outset, for "this task is derived from the poem itself" (EW, 171). At the same time, as "the intellectual-perceptual structure of that world to which the poem bears witness," the task precedes the poem. No less than the writing of the "diary" in "Metaphysics of Youth," no less than the messianically charged historical task in "The Life of Students," the constitution of the poetized—with its revelation of "temporal plasticity and spatial happening"—is fundamentally paradoxical. In all three of these crystallizations of his youth philosophy, Benjamin delineates a privileged sphere of perception in which classical ideas of time and space give way to a "spatiotemporal order," involving the reverberation of past in present, center in extension—the nucleus of the distinctively modern metaphysics, or field theory, underlying the concept of origin (Ursprung) and of dialectical image in his later work.

"In the poetized, life determines itself through the poem, the task [or problem] through the solution." Obviously, this cannot be a matter of art's simply copying nature. The determination of a life context in poetry bespeaks "the power of transformation," something akin to the mythic, whereas it is precisely the weakest creations that are characterized by "all too great proximity to life." Although life ultimately "lies at the basis of the poetized," the work of art presupposes "the structuration of perception and the construction of a spiritual world." As Benjamin puts it in the contemporaneous dialogue on aesthetics and color, "The Rainbow," the artist grasps nature in its ground only by generating and constructing it (EW, 215). The poetized thus emerges, differently with each poem, as a way of conceiving the relation between life and the work of art: that is, as a concept of the poem's task. It emerges in the reading of the poem. For "this sphere is at once product [*Erzeugnis*] and subject of the investigation." The emerging configuration of intellectual and perceptual elements of a poem articulates the specific logic and energy of the poem's "inner form" (a term taken from Goethe but also to be found in Wilhelm von Humboldt, whose writings on language Benjamin studied with the philologist Ernst Lewy that winter in Berlin). Which is to say, the "pure poetized" remains essentially methodological, an ideal goal—"the spatiotemporal interpenetration of all configurations in a spiritual quintessence [*Inbegriff*], the poetized that is identical with life." Projecting the absolute interarticulation toward which the poem gathers in a reading, the concept of the poetized makes possible the evaluation of the poem according to its relative "coherence and greatness" (criteria necessarily modified in the aesthetics of the fragment informing Benjamin's later work, where it is a question no longer of "organism"—as in Croce and Bergson—but of "monad," and where truth is more clearly differentiated from "coherence").

Applying his critical "method," Benjamin focuses on two poems by Hölderlin instancing a process of revision, "The Poet's Courage" ("Dichtermut") and the later "Timidity" ("Blödigkeit"). He argues that the tendency of Hölderlin's revision is everywhere toward greater codetermination of intellectual and perceptual elements, resulting in a more perfect marriage of image and idea, a deepening of feeling, in the bolder second "version." More fully worked out in this version is the idea of poetic destiny—"life in song"—as ground of the sacrificial bond between poet and people (or, in the language of Youth, solitude and community). No doubt Benjamin here takes up the cultic view of the poet to be found not only in Hölderlin but also in a long line of successors, reaching from Nietzsche's Zarathustra through the knightly figures of Jugendstil to Stefan George. But, unwilling to rest content with any exaltation in the sublime, he also takes up the Hölderlinian formula *heilignüchtern* (sacredly sober) and emphasizes that "great works of literature will encounter, as the genuine expression of life, not myth but rather a unity produced by the force of the mythic elements straining against one another."[41] The overcoming of myth—a programmatic feature of Benjamin's writing early and late—entails transformation in the idea of the hero. In Hölderlin's revision of "The Poet's Courage," the quality of courage becomes a unique "timidity," understood by Benjamin as "motionless existence, complete passivity, which is the essence of the courageous man."[42] The authentic stance of the poet, who writes from out of the midst of life, is "to surrender himself wholly to relationship [*Beziehung*]. It emanates from him and returns to him." The poet is thus the radiant center of relations, point of indifference. The new-old dialectic of emanation and return—which we have seen operating in "Metaphysics of Youth" and elsewhere—is perhaps reflected at the very end of the Hölderlin essay, as Benjamin quotes late Hölderlin on the inevitable return of myth: "Legends that take leave of the earth . . . return to humankind [*Menschheit*]." Ultimately at stake in the poetic task is therefore the very idea of humanity, of "the people" and "the few," and bound up with it "a new meaning of death," which Benjamin discovers in the second of the two poems analyzed—and, it may be, in the wake of Heinle's suicide. The second poem dissolves the conventional "rigid" opposition between man and death assumed in the first; it bears witness to the interpenetration of life and death in a world "saturated with danger." It is here that Benjamin locates the origin of song, for "death . . . is the poet's world."[43]

Some fifteen years later, just divorced and approaching forty, determined on a new beginning but acutely conscious of the provisional in everything, Benjamin would look back on his activities during the year before the outbreak of World War I with a mixture of pride and regret: "Since I have been unable after all to construct my entire life on the splendid foundations I laid in my twenty-second year" (C, 365). The spiritual-political ferment of those heady times, as eventually transmuted into the more invisible radicalism, had stamped the character of his life, and, though the romantic strain in his thinking would recede in favor of the materialist and anthropological, he would always remain in a fundamental sense the itinerant student, in quest of new beginnings.

CHAPTER THREE

The Concept of Criticism

Berlin, Munich, and Bern, 1915–1919

FOR Benjamin, the coming of the war precipitated a conclusive break not only with the activities of the youth movement (his Dostoevsky essay of 1917 would still invoke the *spirit* of youth) but with Gustav Wyneken himself, who in November 1914 had given a speech in Munich, "Youth and War," in which he called on young people to join in the defense of the fatherland. Benjamin had been distancing himself from his former mentor at least since the previous spring, when he voiced strong criticisms of the theory of "objective spirit" in *Schule und Jugendkultur* (C, 68).[1] His response to Wyneken's speech on war was unequivocal. Writing to Hans Reichenbach, a philosophy student who in February 1915 denounced Wyneken in an open letter, he called the speech, which he could barely bring himself to read through, an "unparalleled disgrace and outrage" (GB, 1:262). At bottom, he considered it an act of self-betrayal. In March he wrote to Wyneken, formally "dissociating" himself from—as a "final proof of loyalty" to—"the first person to introduce me to the life of the spirit." The letter begins in sadness and goes on to cite Wyneken's words on coeducation and on humanity "in the noble sense," before ending on a note of grim determination:

> *Theōria* within you has been blinded. You have committed awful, horrible treason against the women whom your disciples love. Finally, you have sacrificed young people to the state, which had taken everything from you. The young, however, belong only to those with vision who love them and the *idea* in them above all. The idea has slipped out of your erring hands and will continue to suffer unspeakably. The legacy I now wrest from you is that of living with the idea. (C, 76)[2]

It would be hard to overestimate the effect of the break with Wyneken on the young Walter Benjamin. In the nine years since they had met at Haubinda, Wyneken had exerted an overwhelming influence on Benjamin's thought and conduct. Elements of Wyneken's worldview remained with him for life, above all the dynamic Nietzscheanism that shaped his ideal of the "good European." But in most ways the break was total and Benjamin never looked back. Remarkably enough, the letter to Wyneken is one of the few utterances on the war that we have from Benjamin—Gershom Scholem remembers only a solitary conversation on the subject in 1915, in which Benjamin stood "wholeheartedly on the side of [the radical leftist and war opponent Karl] Liebknecht."[3] In this same period, however, he declined an invitation to contribute to a short-lived pacifist journal, *Der Aufbruch*, edited by another outspoken critic of the Wyneken speech, the medical student Ernst Joël, once a comrade and antagonist in the youth movement and, in later years, before he committed suicide, a supervising physician for Benjamin's experiments with hashish.[4]

The coming of war, the suicide of his friends, and the break with his mentor were all in different ways wrenching experiences for the young Benjamin. Yet, in a pattern that would hold true throughout his life, Benjamin was able, in the face of these calamities, to maintain focus on his literary work. Along with the study of Hölderlin, he was working that winter on a very different sort of writer, Charles Baudelaire, whose poems he began translating.[5] The differences between the two great poets mirror tensions within Benjamin's own sensibility. Where Hölderlin was rhapsodic, Baudelaire was ironic— earnestness contrasting with urbanity; and where Hölderlin's jagged lyric foreshadowed certain strains of Expressionism, Baudelaire's sonorous antilyric fed into Surrealism. As far as Benjamin's future career as a writer is concerned, the early turn to Baudelaire was nothing less than fateful, for Baudelairean *modernité* would prove decisive in the formal and thematic development of his writing, and Baudelaire would become in many ways the focal point of his late work. Benjamin's translation of the "Tableaux parisiens" section of *Les fleurs du mal* eventually was published in 1923, in a bilingual edition for which he wrote an important theoretical introduction, "The Task of the Translator." The translation work was thus the foundation for a lifelong, intimate study. Already by 1915 Benjamin was reading Baudelaire's art criticism in connection with his own investigations into color.[6]

During his final semester at Berlin, in the summer of 1915, Benjamin made the acquaintance of Gershom Scholem, who would become one of his closest friends and most constant correspondents, later serving as an editor of his letters and of other writings. Six years Benjamin's junior, a pacifist, socialist, and dedicated Zionist, Scholem was in his first semester as a university student, concentrating in mathematics and philosophy, when they met.[7] They had first noticed each other in early July at a discussion of a speech given by the pacifist Kurt Hiller.[8] Seeing Scholem a few days later at the university library, Benjamin approached him, "made a perfect bow. . . , and asked whether I was the gentleman who had spoken at the Hiller discussion. I said I was. Well, he wanted to speak with me about the things I had said." Scholem was invited to the Benjamin home on Delbrückstraße, where, in Walter's large, book-lined study decorated with a print of Matthias Grünewald's *Isenheim Altarpiece,* they entered on a conversation about the nature of historical process (SF, 5–6).

Scholem would subsequently pioneer the study of the Kabbalah and teach the history of Jewish mysticism at the University of Jerusalem, where he kept an archive of Benjamin's writings. In his memoir of their friendship, first published in 1975, he offers a portrait of the twenty-three-year-old Benjamin that includes some telling details. When speaking before a large audience, Benjamin would assume "a virtually magical appearance," his "rigid stare" on such occasions contrasting with "his usual lively gestures." "Benjamin had a beautiful voice, melodious and easily remembered," and he was fond of reading aloud from poets such as Baudelaire, Hölderlin, and Pindar. He "dressed with studied unobtrusiveness, and was usually bent slightly forward. I don't think I ever saw him walk erect with his head held high." Scholem dwells on the writer's walk, as Benjamin himself will do in regard to Baudelaire: "There was something unmistakable, deliberate, and groping about his walk. . . . He did not like to walk fast, and it was not easy for me, who was much taller, had long legs, and took big, quick steps, to adapt to his gait when we were walking together. Very often he would stop and go on talking. He was easy to recognize from behind by his peculiar gait, which became even more pronounced over the years."

9. Gerhard (Gershom) Scholem in 1917 *(Akademie der Künste, Berlin. Walter Benjamin Archiv)*

Complementing these traits was his "markedly courteous manner," which "created a natural sense of distance." In conversation, Benjamin "chose his words carefully, but his speech was unpretentious and unostentatious; now and then he would lapse into the Berlin dialect . . . [but] more by way of mimicry" (SF, 8–9).

In October 1915 Benjamin obtained another year's deferment from the military: he succeeded in failing the induction examination after staying up all night in Scholem's company and consuming large amounts of black coffee, a practice not uncommon in those days among young men seeking to avoid the draft. At the end of the month, he left Berlin to continue his studies at the Ludwig Maximilian University in Munich, where Grete Radt was also enrolled. (Another female friend, the sculptor Jula Cohn, was now living in the Bavarian capital as well.) He took a small room in the Königinstraße behind the main university buildings and near the English Garden. "In spite of having little hope that the war will be over in a year," he wrote to Scholem, "I am planning to be able to work in peace, at least for a few months, in Munich" (C, 77). Away from his hometown, that "city of the damned" (GB, 1:318), he did in fact lead a "relatively cloistered life." This did not exclude an occasional night on the town, like the evening he went to an art gallery with Grete to hear Heinrich Mann reading from his new essay on Zola, and afterward drank champagne in an exclusive bar. Aside from this event, he had little good to say about either Munich's cultural life or the student life at the university; then as now, young Germans tend to draw a vivid contrast between the raffish, rough-and-tumble quality of life in Berlin and the quieter, wealthier, more traditional atmosphere of the Bavarian capital.

Deprived of any suitable organization for university reform, Benjamin—for a change—could give his undivided attention to his studies. The results were mixed. The biggest disappointment was Heinrich Wölfflin, the renowned Swiss art historian, whose book *Classical Art* he had read in 1912 and found very useful. In person, Wölfflin struck him as mannered, pedantic, and entirely deficient in any properly oriented perception of the artworks he discussed; his course was "a brutal affront to the listeners" (GB, 1:289). With a course on the history of German literature there was likewise "nothing doing." Somewhat more interesting was a seminar on Kant and Descartes given by the Husserlian Moritz Geiger, whose recently published essay on aesthetic pleasure he was studying together with Husserl's *Ideas: On a Pure Phenomenology*. In his own way Benjamin was returning "to the things themselves," as the phenomenologists liked to say.[9] Among the truly "fruitful"—if recondite—courses taken that semester was one on "The History of Old-Church Atonement," in which he and four monks were the only students in attendance, and one on the pre-Columbian culture and language of Mexico, where he sat around a large table in an elegantly furnished private residence with nine other participants, including the poet Rainer Maria Rilke, who "very sleepily and unassumingly gazes obliquely into space, his moustache drooping sadly" (GB, 1:291). Scholem notes that "he was full of admiration . . . for Rilke's politeness—he whose Mandarin courtesy constituted the utmost that I could imagine" (SF, 33).

This seminar was taught by the ethnologist Walter Lehmann, who was a *Privatdozent* at that time and customarily held classes in his home. Scholem remembers a remark Benjamin made a year later in recommending Lehmann as a teacher: "It is the good fortune of this man that he doesn't know what he knows. Otherwise, he would have gone crazy long ago. His unknowing [*Unwissen*] makes him a scholar."[10] Another participant in this class was a tall, blond, and monocled young man of around thirty whom Benjamin liked to refer to as "the universal genius." This was Felix Noeggerath, a student of philosophy and Indo-European philology, with whom Benjamin would often spend hours conversing in a café after Lehmann's class, wrestling with questions of comparative mythology and with "the concept of historical existence . . . that occupies me, and that forms the center of all the problems which are important to us" (GB, 1:300–301). Through Noeggerath, a friend not only of Rilke but of Stefan George and Ludwig Klages, Benjamin gained entrance into the remains of the "Schwabinger Bohème," one of the principal germ cells of German modernism. The list of writers and painters who lived in Schwabing in the early years of the new century is long and illustrious: the members of the "Blauer Reiter," Wassily Kandinsky, Gabriele Münter, and Franz Marc; the political cabaret "Eleven Executioners," around Frank Wedekind; the "Cosmic Circle," around Stefan George, including the philosopher Ludwig Klages, the graphic designer Melchior Lechter, the right-wing mythagogue Alfred Schuler, and the "Countess of Schwabing," Fanny zu Reventlow; as well as Thomas Mann, Rilke himself, and Alfred Kubin. Noeggerath introduced Benjamin to the philosopher and poet Karl Wolfskehl, who (though Jewish) was a key figure within the George circle. Wolfskehl served as coeditor, with George, of the journal *Blätter für die Kunst* from 1892 until the journal's demise in 1919, and as coeditor of the series of poetry anthologies *Deutsche Dichtung* (1901–1903), with which George sought to revitalize German letters. Although the Cosmic Circle had split apart acrimoniously in 1904 over the issue of anti-Semitism, with George defending Wolfskehl against Schuler and Klages, Benjamin would undoubtedly have become acquainted, through Noeggerath and Wolfskehl, not just with prominent representatives of German aestheticism but also with the writings of the Swiss historian and theorist of matriarchy Johann Jakob Bachofen, whose works were the principal inspiration for Schuler's mystical-demagogic efforts to revive pagan practices. The contact with Wolfskehl would be renewed in the late 1920s through conversations and correspondence; Benjamin published an article, "Karl Wolfskehl: On His Sixtieth Birthday," in the *Frankfurter Zeitung* in 1929. And his engagement with the work of Klages and Bachofen would continue to the end of his life: there would be an essay on Bachofen in 1934–1935 (SW, 3:11–24) and in the later 1930s a plan to write about the role of the archetype in the work of Klages and Carl Gustav Jung. Noeggerath, too, would later resurface significantly in Benjamin's life when, after the two men had reestablished contact in 1930, he introduced Benjamin to the island of Ibiza two years later.

In Munich, Benjamin formed another relationship that would last through the coming decades: he became acquainted with the writer Erich Gutkind, whose mystical utopian work *Siderische Geburt* (Sidereal Birth; 1910) had found a wide reception among the Expressionist circles in Munich. He would stay in touch with Gutkind and his wife, Lucie, who lived in Berlin in the 1920s and immigrated to the United States in 1935, for the rest of his life. He also met the Swiss writer Max Pulver, with whom he shared a passion for graphology. He had read Pulver's esoteric poetry and essays in the new journal *Das Reich*, published by followers of the anthroposophist Rudolf Steiner; in 1931 Pulver would publish *The Symbolics of Handwriting*, which went through many editions. Pulver drew his attention to the philosopher Franz von Baader, a contemporary of the early Romantics who was steeped in the traditions of Christian and Jewish mysticism, and whose "eccentric turn of mind" (GS, 3:307) greatly appealed to Benjamin. Before long, he would acquire the sixteen-volume edition of Baader's collected works—the only collected philosophical works in his library at the time, besides those of Plato—from which he was forced to part in 1934 out of financial need. His reading of Baader helped prepare the way not just for the study of early German Romanticism that culminated in his dissertation of 1919 but for a series of essays on history and language composed in the summer and fall of 1916 that would mark his full emergence as a literary theorist.

In April 1916, before the start of the summer semester at Munich, Benjamin returned to Berlin for a few weeks, during which he saw Scholem several times. Their relationship was deepening, and for Scholem in particular it was a momentous experience: "the greatest experience of my life" (LY, 186). Scholem's diaries for the years 1916–1919 depict a seesaw of emotions where Benjamin is concerned—even as they testify to the latter's remarkable intellectual presence. On getting news of Benjamin's imminent visit in early March 1916, he wrote: "It's a thrilling thought to establish community with someone so productive and awe-inspiring. . . . He has a voice." Scholem sensed quite early that Benjamin had "seen history in a new and fabulous way." But "more than any of his particular opinions," he wrote in August, when they met again, "his spiritual being has an inestimable influence on me. It's just as likely that he's gotten something from me." In fact, a central concern for them both, alongside the historical problematic, was the philosophy of language, and it was here particularly that Scholem's knowledge of the Hebrew tradition would inspire Benjamin's thinking, which in turn had a liberating effect on the younger man. For Scholem at this early juncture, Benjamin was "a man of absolute and magnificent greatness" (LY, 186), a man whose person and work were of prophetic proportions: "Walter once said that the messianic realm is always present, which is an insight of *stupendous* importance—though on a plane which I think no one since the prophets has achieved" (LY, 192).[11]

One of their recurring themes was that of justice in its relation to law. In a diary entry of October 8–9, 1916, Scholem copied out some "Notes for a Work on the Category of Justice" from Benjamin's notebook; the text contains decisive formulations, which anticipate the "Critique of Violence" of 1921:

> To every good, as delimited in the order of time and space, there attaches the character of possession, as an expression of its transience. Possession, however, as encompassed in the same finitude, is always unjust. Hence no system based on possession or property . . . can lead to justice. / Rather, justice resides in the condition of a good that

cannot be a possession. This alone is the good through which other goods are divested of ownership. . . . The immense gulf separating law and justice . . . is something indicated in other languages as well.[12]

Scholem compared Benjamin's idea of justice to that of a liberal Zionist writer particularly important to him, Ahad Ha'am, and in general sought to integrate his friend's thinking into his own iconoclastic religious framework. During his studies in Jena in the winter of 1917, he kept photos of Benjamin and Dora on his desk and carried on imaginary conversations with them. By the beginning of March 1918, he could write in his journal: "He and he alone stands in the center of my life" (LY, 261).

This devotion did not contravene the painful recognition, from at least 1917 on, of an "immense chasm between us," a chasm deepened by Scholem's disillusionment with Benjamin's character. Part of this stemmed from Scholem's disappointment with Benjamin's lack of commitment to Judaism—a difference that would continue to separate the two friends: "One must sadly confess that Walter is not a righteous man. . . . Metaphysics turns him into a lunatic. His sense of perception is no longer human: it's that of a madman delivered into the hands of God" (LY, 244). His disapproval was thus rooted in Benjamin's perceived *moral* failings: "I am forced to witness with my own eyes how *the only life* around me lived metaphysically— and this life is great in every sense of the word—carries with it an element of decadence, and in terrifying proportions" (LY, 261). Scholem is not alone in pointing out this ostensible contradiction in Benjamin's character: other erstwhile friends, while acknowledging the radiance of his intellect, viewed his conduct as sometimes scurrilous. Scholem speaks of lies and despotism and ignobility; on more than one occasion, Walter and Dora treat him "like a butler." Nevertheless, Scholem's dismay and disapprobation did not lessen his appreciation of his friend's unique genius, as indicated by a remarkable entry of June 25, 1918, written some three months after Benjamin, in "boundless trust" (and presumably no little consciousness of his own interests), had handed over his papers to Scholem for safekeeping:

From the outside, he's a man fanatically closed off. . . . Basically, he's
entirely invisible, though he has opened himself up to me more than
to anyone else who knows him. . . . He does not communicate himself; he demands that each person *see* him, although he hides himself.
His method is completely unique, for—I can't put it any other way—it
is really the method of revelation, which, with him, does not merely
appear for small stretches at a time, but *wholly* rules the sphere of
his existence. Surely no one since Lao-tzu has lived this way. . . .
There is something in Walter that is boundless, surpassing all order,
something that, by expending all its force, aims to order his work.
This is in fact the completely anonymous quality [*das völlig Na-
menlose*] legitimizing Walter's work. (LY, 255–256)

Scholem's keen apprehension of his friend's invisibility and
ineffableness—that private and anonymous quality in Benjamin that
refused reduction and even characterization—led him early on to respect the necessity of distance in their mutual "community." But his
diaries for these years also record his persistent longing to see Benjamin
share his Zionist beliefs, something that he pretty much knew from
the start could never happen. Complicating this desire, and no doubt
conditioning the ruptures in their relations over the years, was the
deep conscious love Scholem felt for his difficult friend. He would
sometimes find himself playing the role of the spurned lover and later,
vis-à-vis Benjamin's wife, of the rival held at arm's length.

It was during the spring of 1916 that Benjamin's relationship with
the beautiful and talented Dora Pollak took a decisive turn. With the
outbreak of the war, Dora and her wealthy first husband, the journalist
Max Pollak, had moved to Seeshaupt in Bavaria, where they lived in a
villa just south of Munich near Lake Starnberg. From there, in April
1915, she and Benjamin had traveled to Geneva to see Herbert Belmore.
Soon afterward, Dora initiated a violent break from Benjamin—in order, as she put it in a letter to Carla Seligson, to "save my life. . . . If
you love him, then you have to know that his words are great and
divine, his thoughts and works significant, his feelings small and
cramped, and his deeds fully in accord with all of this." Dora Pollak is
not alone in noting Benjamin's lack of empathy with others. Belmore,
Benjamin's closest confidant from these years, later wrote quite bitterly about him after Benjamin had ended the relationship, finding

him in retrospect morally "cramped" and in possession of "a sterile heart." Both Dora and Belmore suggest in their different ways that this relative lack of fellow feeling colored his entire existence. Belmore claims to recall an incident from around this time: "Once, at a students' meeting, a young girl of my acquaintance spoke to me of 'that stupid Mr. Benjamin.' I was amazed and shocked: 'Stupid? But he's the most brilliant man I've ever known!'—'Of course he is,' she replied quietly, 'but have you ever noticed how stupid he is?' What she meant was that Walter Benjamin, although not deprived of instinct and emotions, chose to see life and action through intellect alone."[13]

It was a portent of the future rhythm of their relationship that, within a few months after Benjamin's move to Munich, the breakup between Dora and Benjamin was healed over and he had once again become a frequent visitor to Villa Pollak. In the course of 1916 his engagement to Grete Radt dissolved (she went on to marry his old friend Alfred Cohn), while Dora separated from her husband. When Scholem visited Seeshaupt in mid-August, as divorce proceedings were under way, he found that Benjamin and Dora "openly displayed their affection for each other and treated me as a kind of co-conspirator, although not a word was said about the circumstances that had arisen in their lives" (SF, 27). This was his first time meeting Dora, and, as he notes in his diary, she made a "very positive" impression on him. He later found out that the invitation to stay with them had come at her initiative.

During Scholem's three-day visit to Seeshaupt, wide-ranging discussions alternated with slow-moving chess games (Benjamin "played blindly" and "took forever to make a move"). The two read together from Socrates's speech in Plato's *Symposium*, and, with Dora present, Benjamin read some excerpts from "Socrates," the provocative essay he wrote that summer, commenting that Socrates was "Plato's argument and bulwark against myth."[14] He also read aloud an ode by Pindar in Hölderlin's translation and in the original Greek. Several conversations focused on Idealist philosophy, and especially Kant, Hegel, and Schelling. At one point Benjamin mentioned that he saw his future in a lectureship in philosophy, and at another point he discoursed on the role of ghosts in his own dreams (he dreamed of ghosts floating and dancing around a large, empty house, particularly at the window, which he took to be a symbol of the soul). The subject of Judaism and Zionism came up repeatedly. Benjamin criticized the "agricultural Zionism" championed by Scholem, and he also had harsh things to say about Martin Buber (a man "in a permanent trance"), to whom he had just written a memorable letter declining an invitation to contribute to Buber's journal of Jewish affairs, Der Jude, the first issue of which contained several articles on the European war with which he intensely disagreed.

In this letter to Buber of July 17, 1916, which he read aloud to Scholem, and which was never answered, he confesses his "inability to say something clear on the question of Judaism," though he does not consider his attitude to be "un-Jewish" (C, 81).[15] In fact, he sidesteps the cultural-political question by focusing on the issue of "politically engaged writing." The latter, he declares, in a barely concealed reproach to Buber and his colleagues, should not be taken to mean writing conceived as the instrument of action. In his view, writing is effective only where it stays true to "its (the word's, language's) mystery," where it intimates the relation between knowledge and action precisely within "linguistic magic":

> My concept of objective and, at the same time, highly political style and writing is this: to approach what was denied to the word. Only where this sphere of the wordless [Sphäre des Wortlosen] in unutterably pure [night][16] reveals itself, can the magic spark leap between the word and the motivating deed, where the unity of these two equally real entities resides. Only the intensive aiming of words into the core of innermost silence is truly effective. (C, 80)

We can feel the vocabulary of Youth—the motifs of purity, silence, ungraspable source, and radiant night—beginning to undergo transformation here, though Benjamin's concept of a writing style at once objective and political seems little different at bottom from the programmatic concept of his writings on academic reform, which represent not so much direct appeals to action as efforts to reorient and liberate their readers' general outlook. But if the letter to Buber echoes the metaphysics of youth, it also points ahead to the theory of language that Benjamin was developing on the basis of his reading of German Romanticism and his dialogue with Scholem.

Reflecting on their conversations at Seeshaupt, Scholem wrote Benjamin a lengthy letter on the subject of language and mathematics, appending a number of questions. Benjamin's response, begun in early November, ran to eighteen pages before he broke off and, in a week's time, recast the letter into essay form—"so that I could formulate the subject more precisely." He wrote to Scholem on November 11, announcing the composition of a "short essay" on the nature of language *(Wesen der Sprache)*, "On Language as Such and on the Language of Man," which he designated a work in progress.[17] He could not deal with the question of mathematics, he tells Scholem, but he refers to the "systematic intent" informing the essay's title, which only heightened his awareness of the "fragmentary nature of its ideas" (C, 82; see also 85). Like many other of his works, this one was to remain a work in progress. But from that point on, the theory of language would always be at stake with Benjamin, coming to the fore in such key texts as "The Task of the Translator," the "Epistemo-Critical Prologue" to the *Trauerspiel* book, "Doctrine of the Similar," and "On the Mimetic Faculty." Today, the 1916 essay on language, first published in 1955, has the status of a classic: as an original synthesis of traditional themes, it provides fundamental perspectives on the problematic of language that dominates twentieth-century thought.

Taking its stand against "the bourgeois conception of language," that is, the philistine instrumental view of language as communication of information and nothing more, the essay aligns itself with Benjamin's earlier critique of the instrumentalization of time, of study, and of historical remembrance. The authentic approach to language—a simultaneously philosophical, theological, and political concern—transcends the dichotomy of subject and object, sign and referent. It is not as means but as medium, in the sense of matrix, that the essential nature of language comes to light, in regard to which Benjamin cites the friend and critic of Kant, J. G. Hamann: *"Language, the mother of* reason and *revelation, its alpha and omega"* (EW, 258). For we can treat of language only *within* language. Benjamin in effect retrieves the earlier philological view of language as an evolving universal spirit, *Sprachgeist*, in contrast to the later, more pragmatic Neogrammarian view, out of which Saussurian linguistics developed. That is, like Heidegger after him, he considers the primary linguistic datum to be neither the individual speech act nor the structure of signification but the existence *(Dasein)* of language, the word, as an incommensurable qualitative totality. All speaking and signifying presuppose the "magical" immediacy of intelligibility: things must in some sense speak to us, must always already have spoken to us in their intelligible immediacy, before we can speak of them.[18] As Benjamin puts it, "If the lamp and the mountain and the fox did not communicate themselves to man, how could he name them? . . . Only through the linguistic being of things [*das sprachliche Wesen der Dinge*] can he rise out of himself to knowledge of them." It follows from these epistemological considerations, already adumbrated in "Metaphysics of Youth," that perception is a modality of language, a kind of reading; experience as such is articulated (see SW, 1:96, 92). To state it somewhat differently, language is the canon of perception (GS, 6:66). We recognize things, once again, *in* language, not first of all by means of it. Thus its incommensurability: inhabiting language as we do, we are unable to take its measure, other than to recognize that "the existence of language . . . is coextensive . . . with absolutely everything." For us, there is no outside of language.[19]

Nevertheless, in the context of the linguistic universal, Benjamin provisionally distinguishes between linguistic and nonlinguistic entities, without precluding their ultimate inner identity. What the lamp communicates to us is not "the lamp itself" but the spiritual or intellectual content of the lamp, "the language-lamp." The thing communicates only that part of its being that is communicable, leaving the rest of the matter unexpressed, for "within all linguistic formation a conflict is waged between what is expressed and expressible and what is inexpressible and unexpressed." Neither here nor in the letter to Buber does Benjamin attempt to justify this postulate of the "inexpressible" and "noncommunicable," which in some ways recalls the Kantian *noumenon*, the unknowable "thing in itself" assumed to lie behind appearances. It also recalls Bergson's point that perception relates to matter as part to whole—though from Benjamin's perspective neither Kant nor Bergson adequately addresses the problem of language. In any case, the idea of a certain communication (*Mitteilung*— not the same as *Kommunikation* in the sense of transmission of information) is clearly central to Benjamin's theory, according to which it is in the nature of each thing or event *(es ist jedem wesentlich)* to communicate itself, to impart its spiritual contents, and thus to partake in "the material community of things in their communication."[20] The unceasing "flow of this communication" runs through the whole of nature, understood from high to low as a manifold of translations, a "continuum of transformations."

The "nameless language of things" passes through translation—at once reception and conception—into the "name-language of man," which is the basis of knowledge. As a specifically human inheritance, naming incorporates both intensive and extensive tendencies of language, the communicable and the communicating, and thus constitutes the "language of language."[21] To illuminate the function of naming and its intrinsic relation to perception, Benjamin turns to the opening chapters of the biblical book of Genesis, not as revealed authority but as an index to "the fundamental linguistic facts," taking language in the biblical sense "as an ultimate reality, approachable only in its unfolding, inexplicable and mystical." His highly intuitive reading of the creation story—comparable in some respects to Kafka's aphorisms on biblical themes—turns on the distinction between word and name. "All human language is only reflection of the word in name." His term here is *Reflex:* the unfolding creative word turns back on itself in the cognizing name, in a movement of completion and delimitation—reflection. The name receives and assimilates the "languages issuing from matter," the "communicating muteness" of nature through which God's word radiates. The task of naming would be impossible were not the nameless language and the naming language related in God, released from the same creative word. Our knowledge of things—generated in the names with which we allow their language to pass into us—is essentially creativity relieved of its divine actuality; the knower is made in the image of the creator. "Man is the knower in the same language in which God is creator."[22]

But there is a "withering" of the name and of the power of receptivity toward things. Humanity turns away from things and enters the realm of abstraction, which is rooted, suggests Benjamin, in the "judging word" that "no longer rests blissfully in itself." For the name is the ground of the concrete elements of language. "Knowledge of good and evil abandons the name." That is, the name steps outside itself in such knowledge, seeing that "good and evil, being unname-able and nameless, stand outside the language of names." The state of abstraction, formerly associated (under Wyneken's influence) with a power of detachment motivating the "pure spirit" of youth, now is associated with "the mediateness of all communication." And the abyss of mediation—in which word is reduced to means, to the status of *mere* sign, the product of convention—entails the abyss of chatter *(Geschwätz).*[23] In other words, the adulteration of the spirit of lan-guage, the fall of the *Sprachgeist* into history, is tantamount to the "bourgeois" instrumentalization, though it is only later (in *The Ar-cades Project*) that Benjamin will cite the Marxian version of this idea: that the bourgeois is preeminently abstract man. In Benjamin's interpretation of the story of the Fall, abstraction as a capacity of the linguistic spirit is already latent in humanity, insofar as the Tree of Knowledge grows in paradise. Knowledge of good and evil, the origi-nary sin of self-consciousness, makes manifest the judgment that hangs suspended over humankind, just as sorrow *(Trauer)* now over-spreads nature in her muteness. But it is "for the sake of her redemp-tion [that] the life and language of *man*—not only, as is supposed, of the poet—are in nature."

Not until the prologue to the *Trauerspiel* book, with its theory of origin, and *The Arcades Project,* with its theory of dialectical image, does Benjamin more fully integrate the principle of language with that of history. The language essay of 1916 views history only from the standpoint of myth. It should be noted, however, that in the period preceding the composition of "On Language as Such . . . ," between June and November 1916, Benjamin produced his first esoteric sketches for the study of the seventeenth-century German "mourning play"—"*Trauerspiel* and Tragedy" and "The Role of Language in *Trauerspiel* and Tragedy"—short pieces that directly anticipate the observations on nature's "lament" at the end of the language essay. In these short pieces, Benjamin distinguishes the closed form of tragedy from the unclosed form of *Trauerspiel* (there is no pure *Trauerspiel*) and brings historical time into relation with the "spectral time" and "endless resonance" of the *Trauerspiel,* whose linguistic principle is the word in transformation. In the play of mourning, where everything ulti-mately comes down to the ear for lament, "the dead become ghosts," and events are therefore "allegorical schemata." The analysis of language here is inseparable from the problematic of time.

In the letter of November 11, 1916, to Scholem announcing the language essay, Benjamin comments on a recently published article by a young Freiburg philosopher whom he does not name but who, like himself, is concerned with the distinction between "historical time" and "mechanical time." The article demonstrates, he says, "precisely how this subject should *not* be treated. An awful piece of work . . . [:] what the author says about historical time . . . is nonsense, . . . [and] his statements on mechanical time are, as I suspect, also askew" (C, 82). It was the first publication of Martin Heidegger's inaugural lecture, "The Problem of Historical Time." There would be other disparaging references to Heidegger's idea of historicity, which Benjamin found too abstract, in later writings. Meanwhile, he missed an opportunity to encounter an author who would soon be orbiting in his intellectual universe: Franz Kafka traveled to Munich to give a reading of his short story "In the Penal Colony," on November 10 (see SF, 33–34). Although there are indications that Benjamin first read Kafka as early as 1915 (C, 279), his active concern with this writer did not begin until 1925.

At the end of December, Benjamin was classified by the Berlin draft board as "fit for light field operations," and he soon after received orders to report for duty, orders he did not obey. He was suffering, he told Scholem in a brief, unfailingly courteous note of January 12, from a severe attack of sciatica and could see no one. Shortly before this communication, Dora had arrived from Seeshaupt, and to Scholem she now confided that she was using hypnosis, "to which Benjamin was very susceptible," to produce sciatica-like symptoms (SF, 35–36). The latter were real enough to convince a committee of military doctors who visited Delbrückstraße, and Benjamin was granted a further deferment. Dora stayed on with the Benjamins and, amid "daily quarrels" with his parents, she and Walter made plans to get married. The wedding took place on April 17, 1917, in Berlin. As the only nonrelative in attendance at the ceremony, Scholem presented his friends with a copy of Paul Scheerbart's utopian "asteroid novel," *Lesabéndio* (1913), which made a profound impression on Benjamin; he immediately composed a little essay, "Paul Scheerbart: *Lesabéndio*" (GS, 2:618–620), and returned to the book in various contexts over the years, producing another essay on Scheerbart in 1939–1940 (SW, 4:386–388). A month after being married, the couple took up residence in a sanatorium in Dachau, north of Munich, where Benjamin's "sciatica" could be treated by a specialist. There, with Dora's aid, he managed to obtain a medical certificate enabling them to leave for neutral Switzerland, his refuge for the duration of the war.

When he arrived in Zurich in early July 1917, Walter Benjamin was a married twenty-five-year-old with vague plans to pursue a university career. As with many children of well-to-do families, his parents continued to support their son and his new wife, and posed, for the time being, relatively few questions about the future. The two years that the Benjamins spent in Switzerland were nonetheless difficult ones. The young couple lived in virtually total isolation: the war all but precluded visits from their friends in Germany, and they made very few new acquaintances in their time there. Once they were thrown back upon themselves, the first signs of tension in the marriage began to appear, and Dora increasingly sought out her own friends and indulged in her own pursuits. Perhaps because of this growing isolation, the years in Switzerland were also productive ones for Benjamin, as he was left free to pursue his intellectual interests. Characteristically, those interests led him in many directions at once, and he only occasionally tried to interlace his richly diverse readings.

In Zurich, Benjamin and Dora met with Benjamin's friends Herbert Belmore and his wife, Carla Seligson. There had been a friendly exchange between Benjamin and Belmore at the end of 1916; Benjamin's letter, with its pronouncements on language, criticism, and humor—he touches on Cervantes, Sterne, and Lichtenberg—has all the dash and dazzle of his earlier correspondence with his old schoolmate (C, 83–84).[24] But in Zurich the friendship came to an end for reasons that remain obscure. In an unsigned note to Belmore written on July 10, Benjamin refers to the "disrespect" shown his wife and to manifold "betrayal" (GB, 1:368).[25] Evidently, there were tensions between Dora and Carla. Scholem's explanation—"Benjamin laid claim to unconditional intellectual leadership, to which [Belmore] henceforth would have to subject himself. [Belmore] refused, and this meant the end of a friendship of long standing" (SF, 41–42)—seems simplistic, though we may well credit his remark, made in this context, about the "despotic trait" in Benjamin's character. Given the unflattering nature of Belmore's later remarks on Dora—he calls her an "ambitious goose"—it is entirely possible that the friendship ran aground on Belmore's failure to take Benjamin's new partner seriously.[26] The encounter with Belmore—"the last relationship obscurely entrapping me with things from the past"—was disturbing enough to drive the Benjamins from Zurich; they settled temporarily in St. Moritz. The wealthy town in the Alps restored a sense of inner peace to Benjamin, and he claimed to have finally found a resting place after "years of struggle." He rejoiced at his sense of being "saved," at his having "absorbed the two years before the war as you would a seed," and at "having escaped from the demonic and ghostly influences which are prevalent wherever we turn, and from raw anarchy, the lawlessness of suffering. . . . After so many years, working once again becomes possible" (C, 91).

To be sure, his illness and flight from Germany had not kept him from reading novels, such as Flaubert's *Bouvard and Pécuchet* and Dostoevsky's *The Idiot*. About the latter, which he thought "tremendous," he wrote a short essay that summer, in which the demise of the novel's Christlike hero, Prince Myshkin, is said to betoken the failure of the youth movement *(Scheitern der Bewegung der Jugend)*. "Its life [youth's life, the movement's life] remains immortal but loses itself in its own light." So this is ultimately a fruitful foundering, a failure with an afterlife, an unforgettable failure, just as, in the "force field" of the novel's narrative, all things and people ultimately gravitate toward the completely unapproachable center that is the life of the prince: "His life radiates an order at whose center we find a solitude ripe to the point of disappearance." The "immortality" of this life is therefore a matter not of longevity but of infinite vibration—"the life that infinitely vibrates its immortality. . . . The pure word for life in its immortality, however, is 'youth.'"[27] Along with this study, Benjamin was working on his translations of Baudelaire, and he was reflecting on contemporary movements in painting (he favored Klee, Kandinsky, and Chagall, found Picasso lacking).

He was also at this time "happily steeping" himself in the study of German Romanticism, reading esoteric writers such as Baader and

Franz Joseph Molitor, author of a work on the Kabbalah, and "a lot of Friedrich Schlegel and Novalis." In a letter to Scholem he broached the idea, reminiscent of his youthful concept of spirit, that the

> core of early Romanticism is religion and history. Its infinite profundity and beauty in comparison to *all* late romanticism derives from this circumstance: that the early Romantics did not appeal to religious and historical facts for the intimate bond between these two spheres, but rather tried to produce in their own *thinking* and life the higher sphere in which both spheres had to coincide. . . . Romanticism . . . aimed at the orgiastic disclosure—"orgiastic" in the Eleusinian sense—of all secret sources of tradition, which was to overflow inviolate into all of humanity. . . . [R]omanticism seeks to accomplish for religion what Kant accomplished for theoretical subjects: to reveal its form. But does religion have a *form*‽ In any case, under history early romanticism imagined something analogous to this. (C, 88–89)[28]

He was arranging fragments of Schlegel and Novalis according to their basic systematic import—"a project I have been thinking about for a long time. It is of course purely interpretive. . . . But Romanticism *must* be interpreted (with circumspection)" (C, 88). In fact, these constellations of fragments formed the immediate groundwork for his dissertation on the early Romantic concept of criticism, but *this* project would not take definitive shape until the following spring, after a somewhat frustrating detour through Kant's late writings on history. He was now seriously weighing the possibility of a career in the academy and trying to decide where in Switzerland he would take his doctorate in philosophy.

From St. Moritz in early September 1917 he wrote Scholem an extraordinary letter on the concept of "teachings" *(Lehre)*, a concept central to his thinking at this period. In a contemporary fragment entitled "On Perception," he refers to "philosophy as a whole," all theory and doctrine, as teachings (SW, 1:96). His letter to Scholem draws on his studies of Romanticism as well as the educational theory that was the armature of his youth philosophy. As always, education is understood in connection with the form one's life takes. It is not a question of the teacher's "setting an example," as Scholem had argued in a recently published article. More to the point is an art of living, such as Friedrich Schlegel calls for: "to live classically and to realize antiquity practically within oneself."[29] In Benjamin's synthesizing conception, education is creative renewal, the rediscovery of tradition. He conceives of tradition here, as he had conceived of language the previous year, and as he will conceive of art in the dissertation, as a dynamic medium—one in which the learner is continually transformed into a teacher (*lernen* and *lehren* both derive from a root meaning "to follow a track").[30] Only as solitary learner can the teacher encompass tradition in his or her *own way* and thus renew it—that is, make what has been transmitted in turn transmissible, communicable *(mitteilbar)*. Appropriation of tradition presupposes immersion in the sea of teachings. For *Lehre*

> is like a surging sea, but the only thing that matters to the wave (understood as an image for the human being) is to surrender itself to the sea's motion: in this way, the wave crests and breaks into foam [*zur Kamm wächst und überstürzt mit Schäumen*]. This enormous freedom of the breaking wave [*Freiheit des Überstürzes*] is education in the authentic sense:... tradition emerging precipitously like a wave from living abundance. (C, 94)[31]

Grounded in such existential immersion, authentic education draws new life from the ebb and flow of teachings, thereby extending the teachings, the language. "To educate is only (in spirit) to enrich the theory [*die Lehre bereichern*]." Tradition manifests the ongoing confrontation of past and future, of old and new generations. For the intercourse of generations is also a wave action: "Our descendants come from the spirit of God (human being); like waves, they rise up out of the movement of spirit. Instruction is the one single point of free association between the old and the new generation" (C, 94). Making original use of the classical literary-philosophical trope of the ocean, thus instancing the rediscovery of which he speaks, Benjamin in effect identifies the tide of teachings with that of spirit, and the order of education is seen to coincide with "the religious order of tradition."

The theological concept of teachings plays a role in the essay "On the Program of the Coming Philosophy" (SW, 1:100–110), the major portion of which the twenty-five-year-old Benjamin, never lacking in boldness, drafted in November, in the midst of his turn to Kant's writings on history. In keeping with the tendency of the Southwest School of Neo-Kantianism in which he was educated, Benjamin felt it necessary to preserve "what is *essential* in Kant's thought," specifically the system's typology, which can be compared only to that of Plato: "Only in the spirit of Kant and Plato and, I believe, by means of the revision and further development of Kant, can philosophy become doctrine [*Lehre*] or, at least, be incorporated in it" (C, 97). This letter to Scholem of October 22—which characteristically ranges from the subject of Kant's prose "as a *limes* of literary prose" to Judaism's questionable attitude toward revelation and to the problem of cubism's relation to color—was the immediate point of departure for his "program" of future philosophy.[32]

According to Benjamin, the revision of Kant must aim to rectify the "decisive mistakes of the Kantian epistemology." These mistakes are traceable, he says, to "the relatively empty Enlightenment concept of experience" and, behind this, to the one-sidedly mathematical-mechanical concept of knowledge whose quintessence was Newtonian physics. Benjamin refers summarily to "the religious and historical blindness of the Enlightenment" as something persisting throughout the modern era. Dissatisfied with the Aristotelian-Kantian distinction of *mathein* and *pathein*, intellectual knowledge and sensuous experience, he invokes a "higher" concept of experience to be developed from the structure of knowledge. The most immediate task is therefore the proper understanding of what is meant by "knowledge." Benjamin isolates two closely connected problem areas in the Kantian concept of knowledge: (1) its essentially unexamined assumption of an "empirical consciousness," that is, of "an individual living ego which receives sensations by means of its senses and forms its ideas on the basis of them," a notion which, for all its long-standing authority, Benjamin ironizes as a specimen of "epistemological mythology"; and (2) its reliance on the schema of subject and object, which Kant was finally unable to overcome, despite his profound analysis of the structure of knowledge.

To be sure, the problem of the "psychological concept of consciousness," in its relation to the "sphere of pure knowledge," remains unresolved. As for the subjectivism and dualism of the Kantian system,

Benjamin proposes several correctives, not unrelated in tenor to the early Romantic revision of Kant. The concept of knowledge must be opened up to "a truly time- and eternity-conscious philosophy," and it must be imbued with an awareness of "the linguistic nature of knowledge." The essentially religious and historical deepening and broadening that will result from these transformations in the idea of knowledge bespeak a transformed logic: truth must be understood as something more than correctness (another point of convergence with Heidegger), and the function of synthesis between thesis and antithesis must be supplemented by the function of "a certain nonsynthesis of two concepts in another." Once the sphere of knowledge has been founded "autonomously beyond the subject-object terminology" (for "all meaning—the true, the good, the beautiful—is grounded in itself" [EW, 117]), experience can be understood as "systematic specification of knowledge," types of cognition grounding types of experience.[33] (In the letter of October 22, he speaks of "our self in knowledge.") Benjamin goes on to suggest, with a nod to phenomenology, that the higher concept of experience, making possible a new idea of freedom, presupposes a "pure transcendental consciousness" different in kind from any empirical consciousness—this assuming that the term "consciousness," divested of everything subjective (alles Subjekthaften), can still be used philosophically. In an addendum completed in March 1918, he formulates the problem of subjectivity in experience more radically, adducing a unity of experience to be understood not as a sum of experiences but as "the concrete totality of experience—that is, existence [Dasein]." Concrete totality is the "object and content" of religious teaching; the concrete totality of experience, Benjamin says, is religion. Thus, the metaphysically deepened concept of experience— through which the philosophy of existence communicates with religious teachings—brings into view "the virtual unity of religion and philosophy." As with Heidegger's Kant interpretation of the late twenties (which, in weaving together concepts of time and space with concepts of imagination and "self-affection," similarly fastens on what is left "unsaid" in Kant's first Critique), the attempt to mark out a subjectivity, or field of consciousness, beyond the static atomic self of subjectivism yields results that seem remote indeed from the actual, rationalistic tendency of Kant's thought. The project of "extending"

Kantian philosophy as such would, in Benjamin's case, prove ill-conceived, though the Kantian ideal of critique would remain on his horizon throughout his career, coexisting with the Nietzschean ideal of immersion.[34]

The "Program" essay was written in the small city of Bern, the de facto capital of Switzerland, where the Benjamins had moved in October so that Walter could enroll at the university; he matriculated on October 23, 1917, for the first of four semesters. Study at Bern, it must be said, left few traces on Benjamin's intellectual physiognomy. Among the courses he took in 1917–1918 was "Outline of Philosophy," presented by Anna Tumarkin (who was soon to publish a book on the Romantic *Weltanschauung*), a seminar on the history of German Romanticism with the Germanist Harry Maync, Paul Häberlin's seminar on Freud (in which he wrote a critique of the libido theory), and a lecture course, "Charles Baudelaire, Poet and Critic," given by the archconservative Swiss historian Frédéric Gonzague de Reynold, to whose interpretation of Baudelaire he would return in *The Arcades Project*. It appears that none of these courses engaged him as much as the multifarious reading he was doing on his own—which, besides the texts of German Romanticism, included works by Anatole France, Adalbert Stifter, and Jacob Burckhardt, the correspondence of Nietzsche and Franz Overbeck, and the three-volume *History of Dogma* by the important liberal Protestant theologian Adolf von Harnack—or as much as the passion for book collecting he was beginning to indulge, especially in the area of old and rare children's books.

The most urgent task, though, was the selection of a dissertation topic. In the letter of October 22 to Scholem, Benjamin had mentioned his intention to begin working on the problem of "Kant and history" in the winter, for "the specific relationship of a philosophy with true doctrine"—in other words, its canonical character—will appear most clearly in confrontation with history (C, 98). But barely two months later, after reading "Idea for a Universal History with a Cosmopolitan Intent" and "To Perpetual Peace: A Philosophical Sketch," he found his expectations disappointed: "Kant is less concerned with history than with certain historical constellations of ethical interest. . . . I find Kant's thoughts entirely inappropriate as the starting point for, or as the actual subject of, an independent treatise" (C, 105). Benjamin was not exactly at a loss, however, after this false start on the dissertation. In fact, he was brimming. From the resort town of Locarno in southern Switzerland, where he and Dora were vacationing for a few weeks, he wrote to Scholem on February 23, 1918, of days filled with "the rich and emancipated melody of the end of a great epoch in my life now behind me. The six years [that] have passed since I left school have constituted a single epoch, lived through at a monstrous tempo, [an epoch] which for me contains an infinite amount of the past [*unendlich viel Vergangenheit*]—in other words, of eternity" (C, 117). To Ernst Schoen he wrote a few days later that "connections of the most far-reaching significance" were being revealed to him that winter, "and I can say that now, for the first time, I am forging ahead toward an integration of my thought" (C, 108).[35] By the end of March, he could announce a focus for his dissertation:

> I am waiting for my professor to suggest a topic; in the meantime, I have come upon one myself. Only since Romanticism has the following view become predominant: that a *work* of art in and of itself, and without reference to theory or morality, can be understood in contemplation alone, and that the person contemplating it can do it justice. The relative autonomy of the *work* of art vis-à-vis art, or, better, its *exclusively* transcendental dependence on art, has become the prerequisite of Romantic art criticism. (C, 119)

He was convinced, in other words, that a dissertation on Romantic art criticism would afford him an opportunity to realize the "integration of [his] thought" he now sought. Such integration, uniting idealist philosophy, the study of literary and visual art considered as a medium of cognition, theology, and the philosophy of history, would characterize each of his major works in the decades to come.

The professor mentioned here was Richard Herbertz, whose courses on logic, epistemology, and the history of philosophy Benjamin attended during his semesters at Bern. Herbertz had agreed to supervise his doctoral dissertation on the philosophical foundations of Romantic criticism, giving his official approval of the topic in May. According to Scholem, who would soon be sharing the Benjamins' Swiss exile, Herbertz was a combination of philistinism and nobility of spirit, the latter manifest in his "utterly unenvious admiration for Benjamin's genius." In his seminar, which focused on Aristotle's *Metaphysics,* Benjamin was "the uncontested favorite. . . . Herbertz, who used to talk in the tone of a philosophical barker . . . , had great respect for [him] and treated him like a younger colleague" (SF, 57–58). Getting his doctorate at Bern, Benjamin surmised, would clear the way to doing "genuine research." "I'm pinning all my hopes on my own work" (C, 108, 115). And, for the first time since the 1914–1915 study of Hölderlin, Benjamin's own work afforded him a larger canvas on which to integrate his interests in epistemology and aesthetics.

He and Dora were living in a small apartment on a quiet street near the university. Lacking social contacts, they lived in "total isolation," now and then attending art exhibitions and concerts. Their sense of isolation was exacerbated, paradoxically, by their discovery that Dora was pregnant. In letters, Dora appealed to Scholem to join them in Switzerland. While Benjamin took classes and pursued his studies for the dissertation, she began to make use of her own gifts in a way that provided some income: she wrote detective novels and, for a couple of months in 1919, worked in an office as a translator of English. (Her father, Leon Kellner, a well-known Anglicist at the University of Vienna, was the author of several books on Shakespeare.) Later, in the 1920s, Dora would write for the influential literary weekly *Die literarische Welt* and edit a magazine for women, *Die Praktische Berlinerin.* In the first years of their marriage, she and Benjamin often read together in the evenings; in the spring and summer of 1918, they read poems by Catullus ("There is nothing more salutary than reading the ancient poets to escape the errors . . . of modern aesthetic concepts" [C, 129–130]) and Goethe's *Metamorphosis of Plants.* But more than any other shared activity, she took pleasure in building up their library of illustrated children's books.

On April 11, 1918, their only child, Stefan Rafael, was born. Benjamin noted soon afterward "how a father immediately perceives such a small human being as a *person,* in such a way that the father's own superiority in all matters having to do with existence seems very insignificant by comparison" (C, 123). Benjamin could never be called an attentive father; he was far too absorbed in his own work. Yet, over the coming years, he took great delight in observing young Stefan's behavior and development, especially the development of his speech.

Soon after his birth he began keeping a notebook devoted to the "*opinions et pensées*' of my son" (C, 288), in which he not only recorded peculiar and amusing verbal constructions and distortions—such as "gratophoph" for "photograph" and "Affika" (*Affe* is "ape" in German) for "Africa"—but also described childish games, rituals, and gestures, as well as short scenes from the family's life.[36] The little archive he assembled—the entries stop in 1932—witnesses in minute detail to his long-standing preoccupation with the perceptual world of childhood and the mimetic genius of the child.[37] It gives virtually no hint, however, of the divisions arising between father and son in consequence of Benjamin's long absences from home when the boy was growing up and his relatively infrequent contact with him after his divorce in 1930.

Early in May their friend Scholem, who had likewise been declared unfit for military service, was able to join them in Bern; he would remain in Switzerland until the fall of 1919.[38] Hardly had he arrived in his new environs than Scholem got a taste of Bernese society: he accompanied Walter and Dora to a recital by the eminent pianist and educator Ferruccio Busoni, who played Debussy in a small hall. Not long afterward, he and the Benjamins moved together to the nearby village of Muri, where for three months, until early August, they lived next door to each other, Scholem sometimes accompanying Benjamin to his classes in Bern. Scholem gives an account of the festive mood that reigned over their initial conversations and outings as well as the tensions that developed. Early on, while the war was raging elsewhere, their high spirits found expression in the creation of a fantasy "University of Muri"—"our own academy," as Benjamin put it, complete with satirical course catalogues (listing, for example, in the medical faculty, a seminar entitled "Studies in Liquidation"), university statutes, and reviews of new acquisitions for the library.[39] Benjamin took the role of university rector, concerning himself with such matters as the absence of a department of demonology or the preparation of a festschrift entitled "Memento Muri," sometimes providing written and oral reports to Scholem, who was heard from as beadle of the School of Religion and Philosophy. This running joke, born of a complex ambivalence toward the real academy, would occupy them intermittently for years afterward.[40] There were other such private entertainments.

At lectures in Bern, the two men "often" played a game involving the compilation of lists of names: "This morning at Häberlin's lecture," Scholem writes in his diary for May 10, "we occupied ourselves by identifying the names of famous people starting with 'M.' Walter came up with 64 to my 51. We would have otherwise died of boredom." That evening, after dinner, the three of them played "the mental guessing game 'Concrete or Abstract.' (Walter had to guess 'priesthood')" (LY, 237).

Their conversations in Muri were once again wide-ranging. They spoke of the distinguished old Neo-Kantian Hermann Cohen, whose lectures they had occasionally attended in Berlin and whose influential early work, *Kant's Theory of Experience,* they dissected in daily reading sessions for a while in July, as a follow-up to Benjamin's recent "Program of the Coming Philosophy," in which he had sought to overcome precisely that theory of experience. "We were full of respect and indeed reverence for this figure; thus we approached our reading with great expectations. . . . But Cohen's deductions and interpretations seemed highly questionable to us. . . . Benjamin complained about the 'transcendental confusion' of his presentation . . . [and] termed the book 'a philosophical vespiary'" (SF, 58–60). Although Cohen's insistent rationalism, rigid dualism, and Victorian optimism were all serious drawbacks in the eyes of the two young men, his antipsychologistic and problem-historical orientation spoke to them both, and Benjamin would soon find many uses for the theory of origin and critique of mythology that inform Cohen's towering final achievement, the philosophic interpretation of biblical messianism in his *Religion of Reason out of the Sources of Judaism* (1919).[41]

Having been deeply moved by his recent reading of the correspondence of Nietzsche and Franz Overbeck, and having followed this up with C. A. Bernoulli's new book on the subject, Benjamin talked a lot about Nietzsche, particularly in his final period, referring to him as "the only person who had seen historical experience in the nineteenth century" (SF, 60).[42] He also spoke at length about Goethe—not surprisingly, given his own practices in this regard, he focused on the central role played by concealment in Goethe's "autobiographical life"—and about Stefan George and his circle, for this poet had been an inspiration to the youth movement and would continue to fascinate him for many years, despite the reactionary cultural politics of his circle. And he read aloud from letters and poems by a variety of writers, including himself. Both he and Scholem were interested in the Austrian satirist Karl Kraus, whose periodical *Die Fackel* they picked up fairly regularly in Switzerland, and whose other prose works they were getting to know. Kraus would become the subject of one of his greatest essays more than a decade later. Early in the summer, they returned to Benjamin's "Program of Coming Philosophy" and the conception of a not yet cognitive experience. When Scholem mentioned "mantic disciplines" as an example of such experience, Benjamin replied: "A philosophy that does not include the possibility of soothsaying from *coffee grounds* . . . cannot be a true philosophy" (SF, 59). This emphasis on the precognitive bespeaks the increasingly decisive "anthropological" thrust of Benjamin's thinking, something signaled as well by his early concern with dreams and waking, as well as with myth. In Muri, he expounded a theory of historical evolution from a premythic age of the spectral and demonic to an age of revelation (compare SW, 1:203, 206). "Even then," comments Scholem, referring to Benjamin's later reflections on the mimetic faculty, "he occupied himself with ideas about perception as a reading in the configurations of the surface, which is the way prehistoric man perceived the world around him, particularly the sky. . . . The origin of the constellations as configurations on the sky surface was, so he asserted, the beginning of reading and writing" (SF, 61). Related to these speculations on a preconceptual realm of associations was Benjamin's "profound interest and absorption in the world of the child."

Scholem prints letters from "Stefan" written that summer to "Uncle Gerhard"; in Dora's handwriting, they were at least in part a collaboration with her husband. Among other things, these letters from baby Stefan attest to the increasingly tempestuous character of the Benjamins' marriage. Moreover, some of the tensions disturbing the household were directly occasioned by Scholem's visits. In his diary, he tells how, shortly after his arrival in Switzerland, Dora "urged me in the most loving manner to relax. She knows how much I love her" (LY, 237). Scholem was clearly torn by his feelings for both partners in the marriage. While his intellectual bond to Benjamin proved a bulwark against what he experienced as an incomprehensible fluctuation between warmth and coldness, his love for Dora had trouble with-standing what he saw as her cynicism, hysteria, and "bourgeois na-ture." She could be icy, would sometimes refuse to shake his hand or speak to him, and once sprang up in the middle of a discussion, called him "loutish," and said she wanted nothing more to do with him (LY, 283).[43] "There lurked a deep-seated bitterness and disillusionment," he writes in his memoir, "over the images of one another that we [three] had fashioned for ourselves. Occasionally such feelings were expressed under the veil of an exchange of letters that the infant Stefan and I would leave out for each other." Thus, some six weeks after Scholem's arrival, "Stefan" writes that, if it were up to him, he "certainly would not be here, where it is so unpleasant and you are creating such a bad atmosphere." And he goes on:

> I believe you really know very little about my Papa. There are very few people who know anything about him. Once, when I was still in heaven, you wrote him a letter that made all of us think that you did know him. [See C, 102 (December 3, 1917), concerning Scholem's interpretation of Benjamin's Dostoevsky essay.] But perhaps you don't after all. I think a man like that is born only once in a great while, and then you just have to be kind to him and he will do everything else by himself. You, dear Uncle Gerhard, still think that one has to do a great deal. . . . But I don't want to be smart-alecky, for you know everything much better. That's the whole trou-ble. (SF, 68–69)

This "letter from Stefan" says as much about the bond between Dora and Benjamin as it does about their attitude toward Scholem. Through the many tensions in their marriage, through its long dissolution in the 1920s, and on into the 1930s, when Dora Benjamin repeatedly pro-vided shelter and support to her exiled, indigent husband, their shared conviction that Walter Benjamin's genius needed to be protected at all costs proved to be the granite-like foundation of their relationship.

The tensions between husband and wife became increasingly evi-dent to Scholem. On one occasion, having been invited to dinner, Scholem sat waiting two hours while Dora and Walter screamed at each other upstairs. When they didn't respond to the maid's repeated knocking, he left without supper, highly dismayed. A few days later, they were all very jovial. Scholem mentions the frequent shows of affection between the two, their use of a humorous private language, and what seemed to be a complementarity in their characters. Dora, who would sometimes play the piano and sing lieder while the two men listened, was "very passionate," and this complemented Benjamin's "basic melancholy," occasionally lightened as it was by some "clowning around."

The Benjamins left Muri in mid-August 1918 for a vacation on Lake Brienz, amid Alpine splendors. Returning to Bern in mid-October for the start of the winter semester, they moved into a four-room apartment and hired a live-in nursemaid. Their get-togethers with Scholem became less frequent. In early November, both Dora and Benjamin came down with relatively mild cases of the Spanish flu, which was then ravaging Europe. Later that month, they received a visit from the writer Werner Kraft, who was studying modern languages in Berlin, where he and Benjamin had met in 1915. Kraft was their only houseguest from Germany, other than the deeply embittered poet Wolf Heinle, younger brother of Benjamin's late friend, who stayed with them for a month in March before departing in acrimony (which, however, did not prevent Benjamin from continuing to do what he could for Heinle until his early death in 1923). In general, they enjoyed a rather secluded existence that fall as Benjamin prepared to draft his dissertation, having summoned the "internal anonymity" he needed for the work (C, 125). Neither the collapse of Germany and Austria-Hungary nor the Russian Revolution seems to have touched them at this point in their lives; Benjamin's letters mention the international situation mainly in connection with the possibility of his placing bids in German book auctions.[44]

Early in 1919 Benjamin made the acquaintance of Hugo Ball and his companion (and later wife) Emmy Hennings, who lived in a neighboring building. Ball had been a central figure in the original group of Zurich Dadaists, while Hennings's poetry had formed part of the second wave of Expressionism after 1910. Although Benjamin seldom saw Ball and Hennings in later years, this extended encounter with living representatives of the historical avant-garde gave impetus to his lifelong advocacy of avant-garde aesthetics and politics. Ball had worked in the theater and as a journalist in Berlin and Munich before immigrating in 1915 to Switzerland, where he earned a bit of money as pianist and librettist for a traveling variety company. He emerged dramatically onto the European scene when, in February 1916, he cofounded the Cabaret Voltaire in Zurich along with Hans Arp, Sophie Täuber, Tristan Tzara, Marcel Janko, Richard Huelsenbeck, and Hennings. His performance of the sound poem "Karawane" on stage at the cabaret—he was dressed in a cardboard construction that looked like a cross between a priest's surplice and an armored bird—was seen by few people, but it has become by now a defining moment of avantgarde art in the twentieth century. After the scattering of the original group of Zurich Dadaists across Europe, Ball remained in Switzerland and found work writing for and later editing the *Freie Zeitung*, a self-described "independent organ of democratic politics." The journal represented the views of German pacifists and had a distinctly anarchistic tint; Ball was much influenced by the thought of Bakunin at this time.[45]

In the spring, Ball introduced Benjamin to his "utopian friend," the philosopher Ernst Bloch (1885–1977), who was living at Interlaken on Lake Brienz.[46] The two men hit it off immediately: they shared many things in their intellectual formation. Bloch was born into an assimilated Jewish family in the Palatinate in southern Germany. After writing his doctoral dissertation in Munich on the epistemology of Benjamin's teacher, Heinrich Rickert, in 1908, he moved to Berlin, where he studied with and became an intimate friend of Georg Simmel. In Simmel's private colloquium for colleagues and advanced students, Bloch met the young Hungarian philosopher Georg Lukács, with whom he formed a lifelong friendship. In later years, Bloch and Lukács would make decisive contributions—along with Antonio Gramsci and Karl Korsch—to the renovation of Marxist philosophy. Both Bloch and Lukács had gravitated in 1913 toward the circle around Max Weber in Heidelberg; Bloch soon emerged as the most flamboyant member of what was otherwise a sober and scholarly group. He and his first wife, the sculptor Else von Stritzky, moved to Switzerland in 1917, working on a commission from Weber's journal, the *Archiv für Sozialwissenschaft und Sozialpolitik*. There Bloch was to undertake a sociological assessment of the German pacifist community in exile. When he met Benjamin, he had already published his first major work, *The Spirit of Utopia* (1918), an idiosyncratic melding of Marxist theory and Judeo-Christian messianism. In the course of several lengthy discussions, an intense, mutually profitable relationship developed between the two men. Bloch describes Benjamin in those days as "rather whimsical and eccentric, but in a very fruitful way. He had not written much as yet, but we spent long nights immersed in conversation."[47] Especially useful to Benjamin was the way Bloch consistently challenged "my rejection of *every* contemporary political trend" (C, 148). By the end of 1919, Benjamin would begin a long review (now lost) of Bloch's *Spirit of Utopia*.[48] Benjamin and Bloch remained friends and intellectual comrades to the end of Benjamin's life. Their intellectual interests and even the assumptions underlying their work were so close, however, that their relationship was colored from first to last by a struggle for primacy.

Benjamin completed a rough draft of his dissertation, "The Concept of Criticism in German Romanticism," at the beginning of April 1919. Though he never would have taken on the project without "external inducement," as he explained six months earlier to the faithful correspondent of his Swiss period, his old friend Ernst Schoen, the undertaking was "not wasted time. What I have been learning from it, that is, insight into the relationship of a truth to history, will . . . hardly be at all explicit in the dissertation, but I hope it will be discerned by astute readers" (C, 135–136). Of course, Benjamin's interest in German Romanticism was of long standing. In the 1912 "Dialogue on the Religiosity of the Present," his speaker remarks at one point "that we are all still living deep within the discoveries of Romanticism," and in an article entitled "Romanticism," published in *Der Anfang* the following year, he associates "the new youth" with an emphatically sober "romanticism of truth" (EW, 70, 105). To Schoen he had likewise emphasized the relevance of Romanticism: "The modern concept of criticism has developed from the Romantic concept." The Romantics evolved "a new concept of art that, in many respects, is *our* concept of art" (C, 136). In announcing the completion of his first draft in April, he says that the dissertation "has become what it was meant to be: a pointer to the true nature of Romanticism, of which the secondary literature is completely ignorant" (C, 139). Nevertheless, he felt that the "complicated and conventional" scholarly attitude he'd adopted on this occasion prevented him from getting to "the heart of Romanticism," that is, its messianism (it is touched on in a footnote at the beginning). But this compromise with academic etiquette in no way signifies a less penetrating exposition: "The structure of the work [which moves from epistemology to theory of art] makes great demands on the reader, as does, in part, its prose" (C, 141). The scholarly presentation was hardly "conventional"; rather, Benjamin's artful interweaving of historical, philosophical, and literary perspectives looks forward to the "interdisciplinary" tendencies of the contemporary academy.

Benjamin's dissertation remains a significant contribution to the modern understanding of German Romantic art criticism; it also represents a decisive step in the development of his own concept of criticism. In the dissertation he introduces three theses central to his later work: the notion that the creative destruction or, in Schlegel's terminology, annihilation of the cultural object is a prerequisite to all critique; the assumption that all meaningful criticism intends the redemption of the work's "truth content"; and the understanding of the critical work as an autonomous creation fully commensurate with the "original" work of art. Benjamin's dissertation does not proceed directly to a consideration of Romantic criticism; instead, it indicates the way that criticism developed in connection with the rethinking of Kant's idealism by later philosophers, particularly Johann Gottlieb Fichte.

Philosophically speaking, the dissertation begins where "Program of the Coming Philosophy" left off—with a theory of knowledge transcending the antithesis of subject and object. Whereas the revision of Kant turned on the concept of experience (which plays an important role in Benjamin's later work), the organizing idea in the dissertation is "reflection," understood as the formative principle in art. The problem of knowledge, the problem of the structure of self-consciousness, is accordingly situated within the context of post-Kantian thought, specifically Fichte's concept of reflection, as it is taken up and transformed by Friedrich Schlegel, Novalis, and their circle at the turn of the eighteenth century. Of course, it had long been recognized that thinking has an intrinsic reflexive relation to itself. After Descartes's instauration of the *cogito* at the dawn of modern philosophy—that is, after the establishment of the thinking subject as the foundation of all knowledge—the problematic of self-consciousness was decisively reoriented by Kant's deduction of the categories of perception, which dictate a necessary connection between the perceiving subject and its objects. German Romanticism builds on this connection in such a way that the difference between subject and object practically disappears.

Benjamin is careful to distinguish this problem-historical context from the literary-historical one.[49] In expounding the epistemological foundations of the Romantic concept of criticism (*Kunstkritik*, literally "criticism of art"), he undertakes a "philosophical criticism," as it is termed in the *Trauerspiel* book. At issue once again is the determination of "the task of criticism." As in the Hölderlin essay, the concept of task entails a historical dialectic (it is not yet called that) between the work of art and the work of criticism; in the dissertation it is said that criticism, in the Romantic sense, functions both as a process and as a product of the classical artwork. In his short essay of 1917, "Dostoevsky's *The Idiot*," Benjamin had put the matter more simply: "Every work of art . . . rests on an idea; it 'has an a priori ideal, a necessity in itself to exist,' as Novalis says, and it is precisely this necessity, and nothing else, that criticism has to demonstrate" (EW, 276).[50] The dissertation (which quotes the same passage from Novalis) puts this thesis to work in conceiving the function of criticism as "knowledge in the medium of reflection that is art" (SW, 1:151). In other words, the task of criticism is to realize the artwork's virtual self-reflection in the present. The reader is the "extended author," in Novalis's phrase, quoted by Benjamin. At the center of this theory of reception is the idea of the "afterlife" of the work—an unfolding of artistic possibilities in which the work of criticism necessarily plays a part.

Benjamin understands reception from the point of view of the object received. For, according to early Romantic philosophy, with its consciously mystical strain, to observe a thing is to arouse its self-recognition through a kind of "experiment," which Novalis calls "a subjective and objective process." All knowledge of an object is simultaneous with the coming-into-being of that object.[51] Benjamin's argumentation is as follows. Reflection—defined by Fichte as activity that "returns into itself," delimiting itself in this curvature of itself—is

the form of thinking. There is no self that at some point in its existence begins to reflect; rather, the self exists only *in* reflecting. This is
the "paradox of consciousness"—immediate, underivable, inexplicable (like the existence of language). Whereas for Fichte the thinking
self necessarily bespeaks an "I" that is countered by a "not-I," by
nature, for the Romantics "everything is a self . . . [,] everything real
thinks." This means, as Schlegel puts it, that "everything is in us,
[and] we are only part of ourselves." Reflection in the early Romantic
sense is thus—in a crucial distinction—an ontological principle, not
just a psychological one. Benjamin mentions a fragment of Novalis in
which the whole of terrestrial existence is interpreted as "the reflection of spirits in themselves," while human existence within this
sphere is "partly the dispelling and 'breaking-through of that primitive
reflection.'" There are levels of reflection, then—from the primitive
reflection of things to the more or less heightened reflection of
humans—infinitely many levels. In the vibratory universe of reflection, any particular being functions as a *Zentrum der Reflexion*, a
"center of reflection." Depending on the degree of its reflective power,
which is a formative and transformative power, it can incorporate
other beings, other centers of reflection *(Reflexionszentren)*, into its
own self-knowledge. This holds for "so-called natural things" as well
as persons, all of whom, through intensification of reflection, can
"radiate" their self-knowledge onto other beings. New centers of reflection are continually forming, like weather systems.

The Romantic concept of reflection is thus, as Schlegel defines it
in his famous 116th Athenaeum fragment, "progressive" and "universal." This has two senses. First, reflection is the progressive incorporation of seemingly anything into itself. And second, it tends to
form ever newer and more complex centers of reflection. The Romantics accordingly interpret the infinity of reflection not as an endless
and empty regress—not as something linear—but as a full infinitude
of interconnection. That is how they conceive the absolute: as the
manifold connectedness of the real, in its degrees of unfolding reflection, its "medial" (not substantive) character. "Reflection constitutes
the absolute, and it constitutes it as a medium. . . . [In] the medium
of reflection, . . . the thing and the knowing being merge into each

other. . . . Every instance of knowing is an immanent connection [*Zusammenhang*] in the absolute."[52]

In Benjamin's radical philosophic reading and transformation of Schlegel and Novalis, art itself emerges as the foremost medium of reflection: "Reflection without the 'I' is a reflection in the absolute of art." For the Romantics, he observes, art is an especially "fruitful" determination of the reflective medium; reflection constitutes "the originary and constructive factor [*das Ursprüngliche und Aufbauende*] in art, as in everything spiritual." Aesthetic form is the imprint of reflection as well as the germ of further reflection, that is, of criticism—critical activity in early Romanticism being the crown of creation.

Criticism is here the consummation, indeed the "absolutizing," of the work of art. This has various meanings in Benjamin's presentation, all of them colored by the characteristically Romantic valence of the "chemical." On the one hand, critical action "destroys." It attacks the presentational form of a work, that in which reflection lies enclosed, and, isolating its elements, "decomposes" it. (The Hölderlin essay speaks of the "loosening up" of the functional coherence of the poem.) On the other hand, through demolition it builds *(durch Abbruch zu bauen)*. Criticism unfolds the embedded reflection, articulates "secret tendencies" of the work, and grasps "universal moments" in the particulars. To absolutize the reflection bound up in art forms means "critically setting free the condensed potential [*Prägnanz*] and many-sidedness of these forms . . . , [revealing] their connectedness as moments within the medium. The idea of art as a medium thus creates for the first time the possibility of an undogmatic or free formalism" (SW, 1:158).

In such reflection of forms, the particular presentational form opens a prospect on the absolute "continuum of art forms," in which all presentational forms interpenetrate, so that, for example, all poems of antiquity could become one poem for the Romantics. According to Schlegel in the 116th *Athenaeum* fragment, quoted by Benjamin, Romantic poetry seeks the unity of genres: "It embraces everything . . . from the greatest systems of art that contain in themselves still other systems, to the sigh, to the kiss that the musing child breathes out in artless song." The individual work as such dissolves in the revelation of "the idea of art," which paradoxically demonstrates the "indestructibility of the work." In its critical-reflective import, aesthetic form sets up a "dialectic of self-delimitation and self-expansion," which in turn establishes "the dialectic of unity and infinity in the idea."

In other words, to the degree that it is "criticizable" (a usage that recalls "communicable" and anticipates "translatable"), the work propagates itself through the criticism nascent in it.[53] As in his Hölderlin essay, Benjamin conceives of criticism here as bringing out the individual work's relation to the whole, whether this be understood as education, religion, history, or art—all names for the oceanic absolute of Romanticism. Assimilated to what Schlegel calls "an immeasurable whole," the work of art, in Benjamin's interpretation, enters onto its afterlife *(Überleben)*. This renewal and transformation of the work's "life" is carried out by a set of readers (poets/translators/critics), "each displacing the others," and together embodying stages of the work's continuing reflection, that is, its historical reception and appraisal—for valuation is immanent in knowledge of the artwork. The idea of the afterlife of works—if not exactly the idea of an aesthetic absolute—assumes decisive importance in Benjamin's subsequent writings, from "The Task of the Translator" and the "Epistemo-Critical Prologue" of the *Trauerspiel* book to *The Arcades Project* and its various textual offshoots.[54] At the same time, the idea of reading as an intimate "chemical action" set going in the tissue of the individual work specifically anticipates the theory of critical "alchemy" outlined in the essay "Goethe's *Elective Affinities*," written in 1921–1922, where it is a question of the philosophical experience of the "truth content" in "material content." Never in Benjamin's literary practice, any more than in that of early Romanticism, is criticism "secondary" to the work criticized.

Benjamin added an "esoteric epilogue" to the dissertation in which he contrasted the Romantic idea of form and of the criticizability of artworks to Goethe's notion of an "ideal of content" and his position on the *uncriticizability* of the work. The delineation of this contrast, in fact, lays the ground for the conception of "truth content" in the work of art. Whereas the Romantic idea of art embraces a continuum of interconnected *forms*, the Goethean ideal is a discontinuous presence of privileged *contents:* it can be grasped only in the "limited plurality of pure contents into which it decomposes." This "limited, harmonic discontinuum of pure contents" emerges as the repository of a "true nature," one not immediately to be identified with the "appearing, visible nature of the world." It is a "true, intuitable, *ur-phenomenal nature*" that is visible—more precisely, "visible after the fashion of a likeness" or in the manner of an image *(abbildhaft sichtbar)*—only in art, while in the nature of the world it remains hidden. The analysis augurs the full corrosive effect of a Benjaminian criticism, a criticism intended to accelerate the decomposition of works of art into "torsos," quarries for the intuition of a truth accessible nowhere but within the work conceived as a privileged cognitive medium. Written for "those with whom I would have to share [the dissertation] as *my* work" (C, 141), the epilogue was not submitted to the faculty at Bern, though it was incorporated into the published text of the dissertation. The latter appeared in 1920, arousing little attention; the remaining copies of the book were destroyed in a fire at the publisher's in Bern in October 1923.

After submitting the dissertation, Benjamin spent the rest of the spring studying for his doctoral exams in philosophy, psychology, and modern German literature. Scholem notes in his diary for June 20, 1919: "Walter's attitude vis-à-vis his exam is simply unbearable: he lives in a dissolute and indecent angst." On June 27, he records the outcome: "This afternoon Walter was awarded a summa cum laude. . . . We were together this evening. Dora, letting her guard down, was happy as a child. . . . Walter passed all three—the dissertation, written exam, and oral exam—glowingly. He said they all behaved extremely affably, and were even enthusiastic. No one can tell what's going to happen now. Walter and Dora haven't yet discussed with me their plans for the winter . . . : they go back and forth between earning a living at all costs and becoming a private scholar" (LY, 304, 306). For several weeks that summer, Benjamin tried to prevent the news of his graduation from reaching his parents. This "mystery-mongering" was evidently undertaken with the aim of prolonging their financial support; he went so far as to ask Scholem to keep the news from his own mother. But despite these efforts his parents learned of the completion of his degree and descended on the young couple unannounced

in August, provoking bitter exchanges between Benjamin and his father. The relationship between father and son improved temporarily
in the fall, when prospects of an academic habilitation in Switzerland seemed to open up for Benjamin, but in the end the crisis in his
relations with his parents was not to be remedied. At issue was not
only his ideological differences with them and with the class in which
he was raised but also his ruthless determination to follow his own
star. Bound up with that determination was evidently the assumption
that it was his parents' obligation to support him and his family for as
long as might be necessary.

On July 1, 1919, Benjamin left with Dora and Stefan, both of whom
were ailing, for a two-month vacation at Iseltwald on Lake Brienz,
where he was able to resume his translation of Baudelaire and to pursue his readings in modern French literature. Among other things, he
read Gide's *Strait Is the Gate* (writing an unpublished review of the
novel in the fall);[55] Baudelaire's genial book on opium and hashish intoxication, *Artificial Paradises* (about which he commented, anticipating his own experiences with these drugs some years later, that it
will be necessary to repeat the experiment independently [C, 148]);
and writings by Charles Péguy ("an unbelievably kindred spirit" in
whom he found "immense melancholy that has been mastered"
[C, 147]). According to Scholem, he was also reading Georges Sorel's
Reflections on Violence and Mallarmé's *A Throw of the Dice* around
this time.[56] In a letter of July 24 to Ernst Schoen, he tells of how he
has immersed himself in the contemporary French intellectual
movement without ever losing his awareness of being an outside observer: "In the things I have been reading, there is a point of contact
for me with some strand of the 'present' that I simply cannot attain
vis-à-vis anything German" (C, 144). It would be several years before
Benjamin could follow this first tentative setting of his compass toward France. Starting in 1925, a considerable part of his literary criticism would be devoted to French literature; today his reputation as a
critic rests in no small part on his pioneering studies of Proust, the
Surrealists, and Baudelaire.

Neither the worries about the health of his wife and son, the difficulties with his parents, nor the uncertainty about his future kept
Benjamin from writing. In Iseltwald he produced a short piece entitled

"Analogy and Relationship," which he showed to Scholem at the end of August, and a few weeks later, in Lugano, he drafted an essay for publication, "Fate and Character," which he considered one of his best efforts to date. The essay (which was published in 1921) seeks to rescue the concepts of fate and character from the subjectivism of conventional religion and ethics and open them to the power of the "anonymous" in human being. Fate and character can be apprehended only through signs, not in themselves; each is a kind of context (*Zusammenhang*). Fate is defined here not in terms of character, as is customary, but as "the guilt-context of the living," something that concerns not man as subject but rather "the life in him" (SW, 1:204). This concept of fate holds equally for Greek tragedy and for the operations of the fortune-teller. Likewise, character is defined not in terms of "moral nature" but as an individualizing light in the "colorless (anonymous) sky of man." Benjamin invokes the example of comedy— Molière, in particular—as a realm in which character is presented not for purposes of moral evaluation but as the "sun of individuality," the brilliance of a single trait allowing no other to remain visible in its proximity. He also mentions the medieval doctrine of temperaments, with its small set of morally indifferent categories, as a hint in grasping the nature of human character. For what is at stake in both fate and character is relation to "a natural sphere."

Benjamin departed Bern at the beginning of November 1919, traveling first to Vienna to see his in-laws and then to nearby Breitenstein for a three-and-a-half-month stay at a sanatorium owned by Dora's aunt. Before leaving Bern, he had visited his dissertation advisor, Richard Herbertz, who, to his surprise, offered him the opportunity of earning his postdoctoral degree in philosophy at Bern, with the possibility of an adjunct lectureship to follow (GB, 2:51). Benjamin communicated *this* news immediately to his parents, who were pleased; his father wrote him letters full of advice but stopped short of making any financial commitment. Benjamin's own letters that winter document his resolve to gain the advanced degree, which would qualify him to teach in a Swiss or German university, though he also makes remarks about following the lead of other penniless Jews in Austria and immigrating to Palestine (see C, 150). It is not clear how Dora, who had broken from the Zionist milieu of her upbringing, would have felt about such a move.[57] In Breitenstein they had a warm room and a nanny for Stefan, and Benjamin was able to finish work on "Fate and Character" and to get going on his review of Bloch's *Spirit of Utopia*, at the same time taking notes for the possible habilitation dissertation on the relation of word and concept (C, 156). In addition, he was reading a new play by Paul Claudel and John Galsworthy's "extraordinarily beautiful" novel *The Patrician*. They would continue in their Austrian retreat until mid-February, when it became clear that, with the current inflation, Dora would be unable to find a suitable position enabling them to return to Switzerland. Germany, ravaged by war and in political turmoil, remained their only possible destination.

CHAPTER FOUR

Elective Affinities

Berlin and Heidelberg, 1920–1922

In the years following his return from Switzerland, Benjamin struggled, internally and externally, to find some way to secure an income that could support his young family and allow him the freedom to continue with his writing, which he increasingly defined as a form of criticism modeled on the critical practices of the early German Romantics. His thoughts were burdened by his situation: at the age of twenty-eight, he had neither immediate prospects nor a viable long-term path toward a career. From his base in Berlin, he worked resolutely, if intermittently, over the following four years to build relationships with professors—first in Heidelberg, then in Frankfurt—that could lead to his habilitation and a teaching position. These were years dominated by professional failure and personal duress—the gradual disintegration of his marriage and constantly renewed tensions with even his closest friends—but it is also in these years that Benjamin produced two of the enduring works of twentieth-century criticism, his essay on Goethe's novel *Elective Affinities* and his monograph on the German Baroque play of mourning, *Origin of the German Trauerspiel*.

During his final days in Bern, Benjamin's dissertation advisor, Richard Herbertz, had floated the possibility of a habilitation and adjunct teaching position at the university. Benjamin was gratified, but he never considered this possibility as anything more than a potential stepping-stone to an academic career in Germany, and Herbertz's proposition marks the onset of a four-year period in which Benjamin sought, now eagerly, now with characteristic trepidation, to find a place for himself within the German university system. The prerequisite to any permanent position at a university was the completion of the *Habilitationsschrift*, the "second dissertation" required of all German professors. The first phase of this pursuit—to which Benjamin referred as the "Swiss business"—spanned the years 1920 and 1921. In January 1920 he wrote to Scholem that "all that exists of [my *Habilitations-schrift*] is my intention to work on a particular topic—that is, a research project that falls within the sphere of the larger question of the relationship between word and concept (language and logos)" (C, 156). A number of unpublished fragments from this period document preliminary conceptual work on problems in the philosophy of language, outlining studies of the sort that might well have earned him a position within a philosophy faculty. In the course of the year, his exploration of linguistic questions came to focus on scholastic philosophy, with particular concentration on the thirteenth-century Scottish philosopher John Duns Scotus.[1] To that end, Benjamin read the *Habilitationsschrift* of his contemporary Martin Heidegger, *The Doctrine of Categories and of Meaning in Duns Scotus*, submitted to the philosophy faculty at Freiburg in 1915. Benjamin's initial reaction was scathing: "It is incredible that anyone could qualify for a university position on the basis of such a study. Its execution requires *nothing* more than great diligence and a command of scholastic Latin, and, in spite of all its philosophic fancy dress, it is basically only a piece of good translation work. The author's contemptible groveling at the feet of Rickert and Husserl does not make reading it more pleasant" (C, 168). But this is as much a throwing down of the gauntlet to a challenger as a genuine evaluation of Heidegger's work. Late in the year, motivated at least in part by Heidegger's preemptive strike (see C, 172), Benjamin would abandon his focus on medieval philosophy.

From the beginning, work on the habilitation was driven by tensions wholly characteristic of Benjamin's habits of mind, tensions constituting what he would later call the "contradictory and mobile whole" of his thought. His concentration on the philosophy of language brought into play reflection on epistemology, theology, history, and aesthetics as well. It had been no different with Benjamin's work in the period culminating in the composition of his Bern dissertation, that is, the period 1916–1919: the dissertation on Romantic criticism, and especially the fragments and unpublished essays that document its genesis, had integrated ideas on language, theology, and epistemology within a major statement on aesthetic forms. In the years 1920–1924, his work would follow a similar pattern, as these interests coalesced decisively in the book *Origin of the German Trauer-spiel*, which he submitted as his habilitation thesis at Frankfurt in 1925. Already in February 1920, at a moment of intensive engagement with linguistics, Benjamin could write to Ernst Schoen of the necessity of going beyond conventional disciplinary boundaries and of radically broadening the principle of literary genre: "I am very interested in the principle underlying the great work of literary criticism: the entire field between art and philosophy proper, by which I mean thinking that is at least virtually systematic. There must indeed be an absolutely fundamental [*ursprünglich*] principle of literary genre that encompasses such great works as Petrarch's dialogue on contempt for the world or Nietzsche's aphorisms or the works of Péguy. . . . I am becoming aware of the fundamental justification for and value of criticism in my own work as well. Criticism of art [*Kunstkritik*], with whose foundations I am currently preoccupied, is simply one segment of this broad field" (C, 157–158). This conception of a philosophically oriented criticism of works of art—or rather a philosophy made to arise from the interpretation of literary works—is based on a very particular understanding of the artwork as repository of essential truth. A fragment entitled "Truth and Truths / Knowledge and Elements of Knowledge," probably written in early 1921, takes up this idea of the work of art as a cognitive medium and thus a privileged site of philosophical investigation: "Truths, however, can be expressed neither systematically nor conceptually—much less with acts of knowledge in judgments—but only in art. Works of art are the proper site of truths. . . . These ultimate truths are not elements but genuine parts, pieces or fragments of the truth. . . . Knowledge and truth are never identical; there is no true knowledge and no known truth. Nevertheless, certain pieces of knowledge are indispensable for a presentation [*Darstellung*] of the truth" (SW, 1:278–279). If Benjamin's dissertation had acknowledged Friedrich Schlegel's establishment of a philosophically based critical practice, his reflections in the early 1920s show him moving toward his own theories in this realm, theories that would find their definitive expression in the essay "Goethe's Elective Affinities" of 1921–1922 and in the *Trauerspiel* book of 1923–1925. As the years to come would prove, no philosophy faculty in Germany was prepared to recognize this kind of work as a disciplinary contribution.

But Benjamin knew very well that the completion and acceptance of a habilitation thesis could not alone gain him a place in the closed world of the German university. He would need to form lasting relationships with established academics if he wanted to secure a permanent position in a system built on patronage.

After one more brief stay with Dora's parents in Vienna to cap their five-month sojourn in Austria, the Benjamins arrived back in Berlin at the end of March 1920, having been away for almost three years. They returned to a city in which the marks of economic and political instability were evident on every street corner. It had been little more than a year since the leftist coalition of Independent Socialists and Spartacists had seized large parts of the city in January 1919, forcing the government to move to the provincial town of Weimar in Saxony; this had been followed by an armed uprising in March, engineered by the newly established German Communist Party. These and similar uprisings in Munich, Dresden, Leipzig, and Braunschweig during the spring had been put down, bloodily, by marauding right-wing mercenaries known collectively as the Freikorps. The signing of the Treaty of Versailles on June 28, 1919, and the announcement of the new constitution establishing the Weimar Republic on August 11 had provided a legal framework, though not yet the substance of stability. The treaty itself imposed crippling levels of reparations on Germany; the reparation payments are often cited as a leading cause of the economic crisis that dominated the republic's first five years. March and April 1920 again saw armed insurrection across Germany: the radical right attempted to overthrow the government in Berlin on March 13. The "Kapp Putsch" was thwarted peacefully by resistance from within the government and, unexpectedly, from some elements of the army, and order was restored by March 17. But on March 14, Communist workers had seized much of the Ruhr area, Germany's industrial heartland; within three weeks, the Ruhr uprising was put down savagely by Freikorps units, resulting in more than 3,000 deaths.

In these chaotic early years of the Weimar Republic, Benjamin's parents, who had enjoyed the financial security of the *Großbürgertum* late into the war, found their fortunes in rapid decline. Benjamin's father, as a result, expressed his willingness to support his son's academic aspirations *only* if the younger Benjamins agreed to live in an apartment in the parental home. The time spent with his parents was marked by constant strife; Benjamin later characterized it as a "long, awful time of depression" (GB, 2:108). His parents pushed for a career with some earning potential and steadfastly refused the kind of support that would enable Benjamin to live independently while continuing to study and write as he wished. Benjamin, with equal tenacity, refused to submit to the parental demands, and the young family was soon forced to cast about for alternatives. Scholem was asked for information about living costs in Bavaria; Dora considered working alone in Switzerland in order to accumulate Swiss francs as a hedge against the ongoing decline in the German mark; even Benjamin himself actively sought a position as an editor at leading publishing houses.

In May 1920 Benjamin and his parents came to a "total falling out." He was "dismissed" from his parents' house, as he explains to Scholem in a letter of May 26; "that is, I left before I was thrown out." And in consequence, "things have almost never been as miserable for me, not in my entire life." He tells Scholem that he could no longer tolerate the "shocking treatment" to which Dora was subjected and the "malicious flippancy" with which the question of his future prospects was held at arm's length, though he was unprepared for the sudden disintegration of his relationship with his parents "after years of relative peace," and after it had seemingly weathered "the most severe tests." On his departure, he was given a one-time payment of 30,000 marks against his inheritance and a further 10,000 marks for the establishment of his own home (40,000 marks would have been about $10,000 before the war; with the rapid decline of the German currency, it was worth less than $700 in May 1920) (GB, 2:87; C, 163).[2] Unable to support themselves on this basis, Benjamin and Dora accepted an offer from their friend Erich Gutkind to move to his home in Berlin-Grünau, on the city's perimeter. Here, in a colorful little house designed by the great modernist architect Bruno Taut, the couple made their first faltering attempts to support themselves financially. Now, and in the years to come, Dora assumed primary responsibility for the family's income, looking on her contribution as the practical basis of her husband's intellectual career, in which she fervently believed. She thus took a job translating from English in a telegraph office, while Benjamin earned a little money by writing an occasional graphological analysis.

In Erich Gutkind (1877–1965) they found not just a friend but a kindred spirit. Benjamin and Gutkind had both been raised in prosperous Berlin Jewish families; both had been tutored from an early age in idealist philosophy; both had sought the life of the independent man of letters; both had been denied full parental support in this endeavor; and both were deeply engaged in esoteric writing. Scholem describes Gutkind as "an altogether mystically attuned soul who had delved into virtually all fields of learning in order to find their secret center."[3] Gutkind's first book, *Siderische Geburt: Seraphische Wanderung vom Tode der Welt zur Taufe der Tat* (Sidereal Birth: Seraphic Journey from the Death of the World to the Baptism of the Deed) had been published in a limited edition in 1910; Gutkind sent copies to dozens of German intellectuals. This short text, which combines utopian and mystical elements in a Nietzsche-inspired ecstatic prose, had an influence on the mood, if not the ideas, of the early Expressionist painters and poets, among them Wassily Kandinsky, Gabriele Münter, Jakob van Hoddis, and Theodor Däubler.[4] His entry into the world of early German Expressionism had opened doors for Gutkind in prominent intellectual circles during the war years. In the summer of 1914 he and a friend, the Dutch psychologist Frederik van Eeden, founded one of the more important intellectual associations of the day, the "Forte circle." This group, which took its name from the Tuscan seaside town of Forte dei Marmi, where future meetings were to be held, was initially conceived as a site of pure intellectual exchange among like-minded Brahmins; it soon took on strains of utopian socialism and a certain esotericism. Scholem, who learned of the circle through Gutkind and Martin Buber, describes the idea behind it as "almost incredible . . . : a small group of people would set up a community devoted to intellectual and spiritual activity for a certain period of time in order to engage without any reservations in a creative exchange of ideas; in doing so they might manage to shake the world off its hinges (to put it esoterically but clearly)."[5] The inner circle of the group was made up of Gutkind, van Eeden, Buber, the anarchist and socialist Gustav Landauer, and the Christian conservative Florens Christian

Rang. The Forte circle conducted an aggressive publishing campaign, and their ideas soon attracted intellectuals as diverse as Kandinsky, Upton Sinclair, Walter Rathenau, Rainer Maria Rilke, and Romain Rolland, all of whom became ideationally affiliated with the Forte program.[6] Benjamin was acquainted with some of the members of the circle besides Gutkind: the sinologist Henri Borel and of course Buber himself.

After the years away from Berlin, the Benjamins slowly regained contact with other old friends and began to establish new relationships. Although he had broken during the war years with most of his friends from school and university circles in Berlin, Freiburg, and Munich, Benjamin continued to see Ernst Schoen and Werner Kraft. And his efforts to have his Bern dissertation published and disseminated brought him into contact with Scholem's brother Reinhold, and his father, a printer. He also attempted to reestablish his connection to the university in Berlin, meeting with the linguist and adjunct professor Ernst Lewy, whose lectures he had admired in 1914–1915. Sometime in late spring he met Gutkind's friend from the Forte circle, the conservative intellectual Florens Christian Rang, at whose home in Braunfels, Hesse, he would later be a frequent guest in his travels between Berlin and Frankfurt. At about the same time he met the writer Shmuel Yosef Agnon at the home of Leo Strauß. Agnon, who would win the Nobel Prize for Literature in 1966, had moved from Palestine to Berlin in 1912; Agnon's works would at times be much in Benjamin's thoughts and would enter repeatedly into his discussions with Scholem in years to come.

Benjamin's reading in the spring focused on novels. Alongside a daunting list of detective fiction, he read Stendhal's *Charterhouse of Parma*, Gottfried Keller's *Martin Salander*, Sterne's *Sentimental Journey*, and Jean Paul's *Levana*, which latter elicited a series of comments on child rearing. And he sought to acquaint himself more thoroughly with Expressionist theory, undoubtedly spurred on by conversations with his host, Erich Gutkind, who could draw on firsthand knowledge of the origins of the Blauer Reiter group around Kandinsky in Munich. Of Benjamin's wider reading in this field, only Kandinsky's *Concerning the Spiritual in Art* had impressed him; he called it "probably the only book on expressionism free of cant" (C, 156). Even amid the family quarrels, financial worries, and resulting depression that dominated the early months of 1920, Benjamin continued to write and to plan writings. During the summer he pushed forward his translations of Baudelaire's poetry and began to cast about for a publisher. And as he continued with his reading of Charles Péguy, a student of Bergson, a committed Dreyfusard, and a patriotic socialist, he began to conceive an introduction to and translation of Péguy's essays; he tried to interest such prominent publishers as S. Fischer and Kurt Wolff in this translation project, but with no success. His own dissertation, though, did appear. In August, Scholem's father produced the copies required by the university, while Verlag Francke, in Bern, published the dissertation as a book.

Despite the increasing financial constraints imposed on the household, Benjamin remained not just a reader but a collector. On several occasions a letter to a friend would contain both bitter complaints regarding the utter hopelessness of his financial situation and, a few paragraphs later, reports of major new acquisitions: in March alone he purchased first editions of Baudelaire's poems and Goethe's correspondence. Werner Kraft remembers a visit to the home of Benjamin's parents during which, after the little boy playing on the carpet had been taken away by his mother, Benjamin lovingly displayed a series of recent rare acquisitions.[7] Alongside his collection of literature and philosophy, both Benjamin and Dora continued to add to their collection of children's books, which would finally comprise more than 200 volumes, mostly from the nineteenth century. Nor did the Benjamins' financial straits prevent them from beginning an art collection. For Walter's birthday in July, Dora gave him his first work by Paul Klee, "Die Vorführung des Wunders" (Presentation of the Miracle; 1916), now in the collection of the Museum of Modern Art in New York.

In June, with some prodding by a letter from Scholem, Benjamin made his first attempts to learn Hebrew, studying with Gutkind, who himself had been Scholem's pupil. Scholem believed that Benjamin's situation in Germany made him particularly susceptible at this time to arguments for an "intensive occupation with Judaism."[8] Although these lessons never progressed beyond the most basic introduction, Benjamin did seize upon them as an occasion for extensive book pur-

10. Paul Klee, *Introducing the Miracle* (© 2013 Artists Rights Society [ARS], New York)

chases: Fürst's Hebrew and Chaldaic dictionary of the Hebrew Bible, several volumes of midrash, a bilingual version of the books of the prophets, and a study of Hassidism by Ahron Marcus. The ambivalence toward Judaism that Benjamin first enunciated in letters to Ludwig Strauß in 1912–1913 remained a source of tension in his friendship with Scholem.

By the fall, the Benjamins were on the move again, determined not to fall back on the resources of the parental home, with its oppressive atmosphere. They settled first at a pension—the Bismarck pension in Hubertusallee, a few blocks away from his parents' villa on Delbrückstraße—and then in October, briefly, in an apartment of their own. The fall saw another attempt to learn Hebrew, this time at the university; here, too, the effort was broken off after a few weeks. Benjamin felt compelled to justify this latest action to Scholem in a letter at the beginning of December, citing the incompatibility of work on the habilitation and serious engagement with Hebrew. Scholem waited some time before replying. In his next letter, dated December 29, Benjamin says he has surmised the reason for his friend's "long" silence, and he quotes sentences he had just written to the Gutkinds in response to their "rebukes" for his decision regarding Hebrew study. In his letter to the Gutkinds (now lost), he had insisted that he was "unable to devote [himself] to things Jewish with full intensity before having derived from [his] European apprenticeship what may result at least in some chance of a more peaceful future, family support, and so on" (C, 169–170)—that is, a university position.

The decisions made by Benjamin's younger brother, Georg, at this epoch of their lives offer a telling contrast to Benjamin's own. After serving in the army for the four war years, Georg returned to the university training he had broken off and plunged unhesitatingly into the rigorous course of study that would make him a physician. In the fall of 1920, despite the limitations of a student's income, he moved out of the villa on Delbrückstraße and into a small furnished room in a worker's district in the city's east side. While Walter remained dependent on and embroiled with his parents, Georg broke away financially but maintained harmonious personal relations, spending Sundays and holidays in Grunewald.[9] Their sister, Dora, also lived at home during this time, while she was at the university, but there were frequent quarrels between Walter and his sister, and her name is never mentioned in Benjamin's letters from the period.

In December, the Benjamins tacitly admitted defeat and moved back to Grunewald and Walter's parents. Curiously enough, the return to the parental home coincided with the end of a long period of depression. Although Benjamin had remarked upon occasional, and briefer, bouts of depression during his university years, long periods of serious depression began to plague him in his late twenties and would continue to the end of his life. Erwin Levy, a cousin, saw Benjamin's affliction as typical for Benjamin's father's side of the family—in which suicides were not uncommon.[10]

As distressing as the return to Delbrückstraße must have been, Benjamin nonetheless entered into an unusually productive period. He had published nothing since the dissertation, but December saw him correcting proofs of the essays "Fate and Character" (which he had written in late 1919) and "Dostoevsky's *The Idiot*" (from 1917) for publication in the journal *Die Argonauten*, which was edited by Ernst Blass and published by a small press in Heidelberg run by Richard Weissbach. At the same time, he was boldly plunging into production of a philosophically based "Politics," something that had been simmering since his conversations with Ernst Bloch in Switzerland. Benjamin asserted repeatedly that his theory of politics would bear no relation to any current political movement or even to the events of the day—he spoke of his "rejection of *every* contemporary political tendency" (C, 148)—but the multipartite composition of a political theory in the years 1919 through 1921, work that combined his interests in philosophy, theology, and aesthetics, was inevitably colored by the tumultuous events that made up daily life in the early years of the Republic.

There is little agreement as to Benjamin's political sympathies in the years leading up to his informal espousal of Marxism in 1924. As with his contemporaries Georg Lukács and Ernst Bloch, who would also become prominent leftist theorists, Benjamin's training in the German philosophical and literary traditions was undertaken in an atmosphere Lukács famously characterized as "romantic anticapitalism," a heady mixture of soft political theory, hard philosophy, and high literature. So while Benjamin could read approvingly Bakunin and Rosa Luxemburg—he was "deeply moved by [the] unbelievable beauty and significance" of Luxemburg's letters from prison (C, 171)—he could also establish a deep intellectual relationship with the conservative Florens Christian Rang and subscribe intermittently to the royalist, reactionary, and anti-Semitic newspaper *Action Française*. Scholem characterized the politics he shared with Benjamin at around this time (1919) in aptly paradoxical terms as "theocratic anarchism," which, as far as Benjamin himself is concerned, should probably be understood in an anticlerical Tolstoyan sense, such as is proclaimed in "The Life of Students": "We . . . talked a lot about politics and socialism, and expressed great reservations about socialism and the position of the individual if it was ever put into practice. To our way of thinking, theocratic anarchism was still the most sensible answer to politics."[11]

By the end of 1920 Benjamin had formulated a very specific plan for a three-part exposition of his theories.[12] The first part was to bear the title "The True Politician"; the second part, provisionally entitled "True Politics," would have included two sections, "Deconstruction [*Abbau*] of Violence" (perhaps identical with the essay Benjamin actually completed in 1921, "Critique of Violence") and "Teleology without Goal" (presumably lost). The "third part" would have taken the form of a critique of Paul Scheerbart's utopian novel *Lesabèndio* (which he had first taken up in an unpublished study of 1919). The specific articulation of this plan and the rapid composition of "Critique of Violence" later in the year were possible because Benjamin had been thinking and writing his way toward this project ever since he began work on his review of Bloch's *Spirit of Utopia*. Already in Breitenstein, he had conceived an essay—which he apparently never completed—with the provisional title "There Are No Intellectual Workers," a pointed reply to the leftist writer Kurt Hiller's conception of activism and, more generally, to the widespread—and ineffectual—attempts on the part of bourgeois writers to identify with and emulate the workers' and soldiers' councils (*Arbeiter-* und *Soldatenräte*) that had sprung up spontaneously in 1918 and forced the abdication of the kaiser (see C, 160). At about the same time, he finished the review of Bloch's book. Far more than simple log rolling for a friend's publication, Benjamin's "enormously intensive" work on the review was driven by a desire to define his own political convictions. Conversations with Bloch in Switzerland had already challenged Benjamin to defend his eschewal of current political trends. Now, in 1920, Bloch's idiosyncratic admixture of Marxism and messianism in *The Spirit of Utopia* evoked a mixed reaction from Benjamin. He found the book "not totally without merit," but "facile and overdone" (C, 159–160). The review consisted "only of a detailed and, when possible, laudatory essay on individual trains of thought," but it also included at the end, in esoteric language, a "confrontation" with Bloch's "impossible [undiscutierbar] Christology" and gnostic epistemology (which, insofar as it posits a "dark chamber of the lived moment" and a "not yet conscious" dimension of experience, left its mark on Benjamin's thinking). Although Benjamin sought several publication venues for his review, including the prominent philosophical journal *Kant Studien*, it remained unpublished, and must now count as lost.

Its attempt at a concise formulation of a theological politics suggests that the "Theological-Political Fragment," one of Benjamin's knottiest little texts, was composed at about this time.[13] It begins with the contention that theocracy has no political meaning, only a religious one, for "nothing historical can relate itself, from its own ground [von sich aus], to the messianic." In other words, the "messianic" cannot be a goal of history. "Seen historically," it appears instead as the end *(Ende)* of history, as a certain existential intensity beyond chronological reckoning. The insistence on an unbridgeable gap between historical life and the truly religious suggests important consonances between the theological elements in Benjamin's thought and central tenets of "dialectical theology," especially Karl Barth's assertion of the absolute otherness of God in the second edition of his *Epistle to the Romans*, which would be published in 1921. In the fragment, Benjamin conceives a figure for the paradoxical relation to the messianic:

> If one arrow points to the goal toward which the secular dynamic [Dynamis des Profanen] acts, and another marks the direction of messianic intensity, then certainly the quest of free humanity for happiness runs counter to the messianic direction. But just as a force, by virtue of the path it is moving along, can augment another force on the opposite path, so the secular order—because of its nature as secular [so auch die profane Ordnung des Profanen]—promotes the coming of the messianic kingdom. The secular, therefore, though not itself a category of this kingdom, is a decisive category of its most unobtrusive approach.

Corresponding to an "eternity of downfall," in the simultaneously sacred and profane "rhythm" of existence, is a worldly restitution, happiness in downfall. "For nature is messianic by reason of its eternal and total passing away [*Vergängnis*]." To strive for eternal transience, Benjamin concludes, for the eternal passing of even "those stages of man that are nature," is the task of world politics, whose method must therefore be called nihilism.[14] The undercurrent of nihilism named explicitly here will surge up at intervals throughout Benjamin's career, dominating some texts, such as "The Destructive Character" of 1931, and lending a particular coloration to others, such as "The Task of the Translator" of 1923.

Benjamin's return to Berlin in the spring had coincided precisely with the worst crisis faced by Germany's still nascent democracy: the Kapp Putsch. On March 13, the highest-ranking German general, Walther von Lüttwitz, supported by a brigade of marines and the paramilitary Freikorps, seized control of the government district in Berlin, declared an end to the Social Democratic government, and named Wolfgang Kapp, a right-wing civil servant, as the new chancellor. The Social Democratic chancellor, Wolfgang Bauer, and the federal president, Friedrich Ebert, fled the city along with the majority of upper-level government officials. Deprived of the support of large parts of the army, the government countered in the only way it could, through the declaration of a general strike. This action, together with the refusal of much of the bureaucracy to follow the directives of Kapp, led to the collapse of the putsch; Kapp and Lüttwitz in turn fled the city on March 17. There is not a single reference in Benjamin's correspondence to the highly charged atmosphere in which he and Dora must have found themselves on their return. But from this point forward, the composition of his "Politics" was accelerated. In April 1920 he drafted a note, now lost, called "Life and Violence" (see C, 162). And at some point in the fall he composed "Fantasy on a Passage in *The Spirit of Utopia*," which has not survived either. He continued to read widely, not just in political theory but in related fields as well. His letters are full of comments on topics as diverse as the epistemology of biology and the idea of eloquence, the latter in reference to the treatise on rhetoric by the Romantic political economist Adam Müller.[15] But the chief result of this prolonged meditation on politics was the essay

"Critique of Violence," which he wrote in December 1920 and January 1921.

Benjamin's essay examines the relationship of violence to law and justice, and in particular the role of violence—the use of force—in the traditions of both natural law and positive law. Although the essay's first pages are given over to a rather abstract and dutiful discussion of a timely issue in jurisprudence—the understanding of violence within means-ends relationships—the writing begins to assume a Benjaminian voice when it turns to the function of violence in the institution and preservation of law and lawmaking bodies: "all violence as a means is either lawmaking or law-preserving" (SW, 1:243). As Benjamin himself acknowledges, these remarks were highly topical in late 1920. "When the consciousness of the latent presence of violence in a legal institution disappears, the institution falls into decay. In our time, parliaments provide an example of this. They offer the familiar, woeful spectacle because they have not remained conscious of the revolutionary forces to which they owe their existence." The Weimar National Assembly, of course, owed its existence precisely to the revolutionary forces unleashed in November 1918; by 1920, Benjamin argues polemically, its decay as an institution was made manifest when it used violent means to suppress the widespread leftist uprisings in the Ruhr in the spring of that year, having lost touch with the creative potential for new lawmaking. Benjamin's opprobrium is not limited to the present government, however; he soon turns to the more general question of the function of the general strike in all societies, basing his remarks not just on a reading of the syndicalist Georges Sorel's *Réflexions sur la violence* of 1908 but on more general research into anarchism and violence. In the fall he had contacted Max Nettlau, the leading authority on anarchism in Europe and an acquaintance of Bakunin's, asking for advice on the most important sources. Drawing on Sorel's distinction between the "political general strike" and the "proletarian general strike," he quotes passages from *Reflections on Violence* in order implicitly to castigate the Social Democrats' use of the general strike to maintain their power in the face of the Kapp Putsch: " 'The political general strike demonstrates how the state will lose none of its strength, how power is transferred from the privileged to the privileged.' " And in one of the earliest and most direct indications of a key tenet of his own political philosophy, he cites Sorel's praise for the proletarian general strike, in which " 'the revolution appears as a clear simple revolt.' " For Benjamin, such a "revolutionary movement" is undertaken together with the rejection of "every kind of program, of utopia. . . . Against this deep, moral, and genuinely revolutionary conception, no objection can stand that seeks . . . to brand such a general strike as violent." This refusal to consider the consequences of purifying revolution bespeaks more than Benjamin's frequently adduced adherence to the *Bilderverbot*, the Jewish injunction against images of redeemed life; it is an oblique expression of his nihilism. Like D. H. Lawrence, Walter Benjamin liked to think of the conventional world order going "pop"—being suddenly suspended.

Much of the essay constitutes, then, an intervention into contemporary legal debates on questions of state power and permissible resistance to that power. The essay's second half, however, returns to issues broached in the essay "Fate and Character," issues that will remain central to the major statement of Benjamin's early thought, "Goethe's Elective Affinities": fate itself, the guilt arising from participation in a "more natural life," myth, and the "annihilating violence" of divine intervention in the world. Echoing the argument of Hermann Cohen's *Ethics of the Pure Will* (1904) and his *Religion of Reason out of the Sources of Judaism* (1919),[16] Benjamin here distinguishes for the first time a myth grounded in polytheism and "mere life" from the more noble spiritual force of monotheism: "God opposes myth . . . If mythic violence is lawmaking, divine violence is law-destroying . . . But in annihilating it also expiates . . . Mythic violence is bloody power over mere life for its own sake; divine violence is pure power over all life for the sake of the living." Some commentators have claimed that in "Critique of Violence" Benjamin associates the notions of divine violence and proletarian revolution. As the essay's closing sentences clearly show, Benjamin was not yet in a position fully to reconcile his political and his theological ideas: "But all mythic, lawmaking violence, which we may call 'executive,' is pernicious. Pernicious, too, is the law-preserving, 'administrative' violence that serves it. Divine violence, which is the sign and seal but never the means of sacred dispatch, may be called 'sovereign' violence."[17] Benjamin's essay apostrophizes the erasure of all current forms of state power and indeed of the state itself; beyond the notion of a non-violent general strike, however, it does not specify a revolutionary practice in connection with that divine erasure of "means." The concept of revolution as agent and expression of the messianic event will emerge more explicitly in the 1930s. Benjamin initially submitted "Critique of Violence" for publication in the prestigious cultural journal *Die weissen Blätter*, edited by René Schickele; Emil Lederer, the member of the journal's editorial board who read it, judged "Critique of Violence" to be "too long and too difficult" for the journal's readership but accepted it for the social science journal *Archiv für Sozialwissenschaft und Sozialpolitik*, the editorship of which he had assumed upon Max Weber's death.

Some of the more esoteric reflections in "Critique of Violence" were fueled by a reading of Erich Unger's *Politik und Metaphysik*, which had appeared in January 1921. Benjamin's enthusiasm for Unger and his work knew no bounds at this juncture; he characterized *Politics and Metaphysics* as the "most significant piece of writing on politics in our time" (C, 172). Unger (1887–1950) had, like Benjamin, been raised in an assimilated Jewish family in Berlin. But unlike Benjamin, whose early maturity was shaped by his contact with Wyneken and the youth movement, Unger had begun from an early age to move in neo-Orthodox circles. He had been tutored in the Talmud by Oskar Goldberg while both were students at the Friedrich Gymnasium, and his work as a philosopher of religion never lost touch with these beginnings. The overt religiosity of Unger's work contrasts markedly with Benjamin's own practice. Like the hunchbacked dwarf who controls the action while hidden beneath the chess table in the famous allegory that opens Benjamin's last known work, "On the Concept of History" of 1940, the theological dimension of Benjamin's work after the First World War is generally positioned on a deep or even hidden level. Yet significant shared assumptions laid the ground for Benjamin's positive reception of Unger. As Margarete Kohlenbach has put it, Benjamin and Unger shared the conviction that "philosophical thought is to seek to identify the conditions in which man could objectively experience, and thus know, that which in modern religiosity is at best believed, or somehow sensed, to be true."[18] And each man was persuaded that such philosophical thought must move beyond a

Kantian model that for them was based on an inadequate understanding of human experience and knowledge. Unger's *Politik und Metaphysik* thus conceives politics as an activity whose primary goal is the provision of an arena for psychophysical experience that *may* "correspond to a disclosure of divine reality."[19]

Benjamin's attraction to Unger's thought was only the most evident sign of his fascination in the early 1920s with the circle of Jewish intellectuals around the figure of Oskar Goldberg (1887–1951). Having played a leading role in the early Expressionist Neopathetisches Cabaret and the Neue Club, Goldberg by the end of the world war had begun to propagate an esoteric "doctrine" of Judaism that did not lack, as Scholem has remarked, a demonic dimension. His conviction that the Jews enjoyed a special relationship to God that was originally based on the practice of magic led to the conclusion that contemporary Judaism had fallen away from this ancient magical Hebraism. For Goldberg and the members of his circle, who were in principle opposed to empirical Zionism, this doctrine of "the reality of the Hebrews"—which Scholem describes as "a sort of biological Kabbalah"—was the sole propaedeutic to what Goldberg's disciple Unger would call, in a lecture attended by Benjamin in February 1922, "the stateless founding of a Jewish people."[20] Through remarkable personal magnetism, Goldberg in fact exercised a dictatorial control over this circle, and he exerted an influence on intellectuals in the Weimar Republic that was out of all proportion to the perspicacity of his ideas. Thomas Mann caught some of that baleful influence in his 1947 novel *Doctor Faustus*, where Goldberg appears as the protofascist metaphysician Dr. Chaim Breisacher. Benjamin and Dora came to know both Goldberg and Unger in the home of Dora's friend Elisabeth Richter-Gabo, first wife of the avant-garde filmmaker Hans Richter. Benjamin's reaction to Goldberg himself was visceral. "To be sure, I know very little about him, but his impure aura repelled me emphatically every time I was forced to see him, to the extent that I was unable to shake hands with him" (C, 173). Despite this repugnance, Benjamin continued to move cautiously at the outer edges of the circle, but for one reason only: in order to maintain contact with Unger, whose person and work continued to draw him.

In January 1921 a lull in the hostilities between Benjamin and his father made life in the parental home more bearable. Obviously foreseeing the necessity of a long residence, Benjamin ordered new bookshelves and installed his library—always a source of deep satisfaction for him. A piano was borrowed, and Dora was able to resume playing; Scholem remembers evenings filled with Mozart, Beethoven, and Schubert.[21] Later in the spring, the couple even attempted amateur theatricals, aspiring to play parts in a skit at a ball at the School for Decorative Arts. Benjamin reported that Dora was convinced she could be "a great actress" if only she would set her mind to it, but this debut was denied her owing to the director's "incompetence" (GB, 2:146). It is more difficult to reconstruct exactly what role their young son, Stefan, played in the Benjamins' family life. One of the very few references to Stefan in the letters from this period describes his first trip to the zoo; his father is charmed by his confusion of the llama and the elephant, the ibex and the ape. In the notebook Benjamin was keeping of his son's "opinions and pensées," there are entries from around this period concerning the issue of "quiet" that suggest the priorities in the Benjamin household and the son's reaction to their enforcement: "When I went into the room to insist that he be quiet, he says loudly, after I left it again: 'The bird there (or: the bear) always comes in the room. The bird should not come in there. It is my room. The room will be spoilt. The whole room spoilt. I also shouldn't be disturbed, I have to work too.' "[22]

The couple took advantage of the comforts of the house by entertaining a number of visitors and inviting friends and relatives to stay with them. One of the first of these invitations went to Ernst Bloch, whose wife, Else von Stritzky, had just died in Munich after a long illness. A much less fortunate visit brought Benjamin's old friend Werner Kraft (1896–1991) to Grunewald. Benjamin had met Kraft in 1915 while both were university students. Although Kraft's more practical nature led him to prepare for a career as a librarian (he worked at prominent libraries in Leipzig and Hannover until his forced retirement and immigration to Palestine in 1934), he thought of himself first and foremost as a literary critic. From their earliest encounters, Benjamin had regarded Kraft as a peer and competitor in the field of philosophically-informed criticism. Something occurred during this last visit, for soon afterward Benjamin wrote to Kraft, breaking off their relationship. A draft of this letter—a less brutal version found its way to Kraft—illuminates not only Benjamin's sense of friendship and his total commitment to intellectual interchange but also his inveterate personal imperiousness: "Contact and conversation with my friends belongs to the most serious and most strenuously observed things in my life. . . . Just as I myself am accustomed to follow through on the consequences of every spoken word in my thought, I expect the same from others. . . . For every person with whom one holds a conversation, one is obliged in the most irrevocable way—and especially wherever views differ—never to express such views without attempting to justify them; above all, one should never expose things to the judgment of others when one never seriously intended to accept criticism of them" (GB, 2:142). On his receipt of this communication, Kraft returned all the letters Benjamin had written him in the course of their friendship—upon which Benjamin further protested that Kraft had not sent them by registered mail! Although they would renew contact after a chance meeting in the Bibliothèque Nationale in Paris at the end of 1933, their relationship finally exploded—spectacularly—in the late 1930s when they entered into one final competition, both claiming to have rediscovered the nineteenth-century German writer Carl Gustav Jochmann.

Benjamin had a genius for a certain kind of friendship; his brilliance and intensity drew a long series of formidable intellects into his orbit. Once established, however, the trajectory of friendship was never smooth: Benjamin kept even his closest friends at arm's length, retaining for himself the right to absolute privacy. And, as Scholem remembers, he was intent on keeping each group of friends sealed off hermetically from every other group; he regarded this practice as a virtual law of social intercourse. Despite these habits, which must have made exchange with Benjamin on any mundane topic a tricky thing indeed, there is overwhelming evidence in the letters of his steadfast faithfulness to a few close friends. Both Theodor Adorno and Werner Kraft have remarked upon his generosity and penchant for gift giving. Invited for dinner in the early 1920s, Kraft found a first edition of the Austrian dramatist Franz Grillparzer's *Life Is a Dream (Der*

Traum ein Leben) wrapped in his napkin. Charlotte Wolff, whom Benjamin came to know through Jula Cohn, remembers Benjamin's extraordinary efforts—including a special trip to Dresden in her company—to convince her parents that she should be allowed to study medicine despite the real financial hardship this would entail.[23]

Much of Benjamin's time in the early months of 1921 was given over to his translation of the section "Tableaux parisiens" (Parisian Scenes) from Charles Baudelaire's *Les fleurs du mal.* Benjamin had begun translating Baudelaire as early as 1914, but he was now spurred on by the possibility of a book publication. Through Jula Cohn he had come into contact with Ernst Blass, a poet who also edited the journal *Die Argonauten* for the publisher Richard Weissbach. (This was the journal in which "Fate and Character" and "Dostoevsky's *The Idiot*" would appear later that year.) Blass had forwarded samples of Benjamin's Baudelaire translations to Weissbach late in 1920. Weissbach now offered 1,000 marks for a luxury edition and 15 percent of the sale of a normal edition, and Benjamin signed and returned the contract in early February. At this point, he had completed the translation of all the poems in the cycle except for "Le cygne II"; he told Weissbach that he intended to include a preface in the form of a general disquisition on the problem of translation. Far from wrapping up the translation project, though, the return of the contract served only to mark the inception of a tortuous and, for Benjamin, enormously frustrating path to the book's publication more than three years later.

Baudelaire was not Benjamin's sole literary concern at this time. The great Austrian writer and journalist Karl Kraus delivered four lectures in Berlin in early 1921, and we can assume that Benjamin was in attendance; Kraus would remain a lifelong interest. And Benjamin continued to read and think about the German Romantics. He returned to Goethe with new enthusiasm—he recounts the pleasure he derived from a rereading of his favorite among Goethe's novellas, "The New Melusine"—and he urged Weissbach to republish Friedrich Schlegel's drama *Alarcos,* which Goethe had included in the repertoire at the theater in Weimar in the early nineteenth century, but which had not been reprinted since 1809.

Benjamin's engagement with contemporary visual art deepened in the years following the completion of his dissertation. In March he visited an exhibition of paintings by August Macke, who had been killed on the Western Front in 1914. The "short essay" he says he wrote on these pictures has not survived. He also mentions a painting by Chagall, *Sabbath,* which he liked but which lacked perfection for him: "I am coming more and more to the realization that I can depend sight unseen, as it were, only on the painting of Klee, Macke, and maybe Kandinsky. Everything else has pitfalls that require you to be on guard. Naturally, there are also weak pictures by those three—but I *see* that they are weak" (C, 178). In April Benjamin visited a Klee exhibition, and on a trip to Munich in late spring he purchased for 1,000 marks ($14) a small Klee aquarelle called *Angelus Novus,* painted in 1920. Although we have no record of his first encounter with the little picture, Charlotte Wolff's recollection of Benjamin's delight at an unexpected discovery gives some sense of the animation that could overcome this otherwise "gauche and inhibited man": he "behaved as if something marvelous had been given to him."[24] *Angelus Novus* would become Benjamin's most prized possession; the picture, which hung for a time in Scholem's Munich apartment after its acquisition, continued to serve as a special link between the friends long after Scholem's immigration to Palestine. Already in 1921 Scholem sent Benjamin a poetic meditation on the image as a birthday gift.

Greetings from the Angelus on July 15

I hang nobly on the wall
looking at no one at all,
I have been sent from heaven
I am an angel-man

The person in my room is good
and does not interest me
I stand in the care of the highest
and do not need a face

That world from which I come
is measured, deep, and clear;
what holds me together in its ground
appears here wonderful

In my heart stands the town
into which God has sent me

the angel who bears this seal
is not moved by it.

My wing is ready to beat
I'd gladly turn back
since if I stayed for living time
I'd still have little luck

My eye is quite black and full
my gaze is never empty
I know what I should proclaim
and know a good deal more

———

I am an unsymbolic thing
and signify what I am
you turn the magic ring in vain
for I have no meaning.[25]

Klee's *Angelus Novus* not only lent its name to the title of Benjamin's first, abortive attempt to found a journal but also figured later in an enigmatic autobiographical piece that Benjamin composed on the island of Ibiza in 1933 ("Agesilaus Santander") and, near the end of his life, inspired one of the best-known passages of his writing: the meditation on the angel of history in "On the Concept of History."

Despite these divergent interests, Benjamin's thoughts remained concentrated on the production of his habilitation thesis. A series of fragments written in late 1920 and early 1921, all related to the ongoing search for a topic, suggest the gradual shifts in his thinking. An initial focus on pure linguistics had come to encompass a set of theological problems; the "Outline for a Habilitation Thesis" (SW, 1:269–271) indicates that the topic of the habilitation might at one point have centered on the problem of the theological symbol. Just as in the course of his work on the dissertation, though, Benjamin's gaze gradually shifted from a linguistic plane to an epistemological and aesthetic one. "Like all historical research," he wrote to Scholem in February, "philology promises the pleasures that the neo-Platonists sought in the asceticism of contemplation, but intensified to the highest degree. Perfection rather than completion, guaranteed extinguishing of morality (without smothering its fire). It represents a side of history,

11. Paul Klee, *Angelus Novus*, 1920. India ink, color chalks and brown wash on paper *(Collection, The Israel Museum, Jerusalem. Gift of Fania and Gershom Scholem, John and Paul Herring, Jo Carole, and Ronald Lauder. B87.0994. Photo © The Israel Museum, Jerusalem by Elie Posner)*

or rather a layer of the historical, for which man may perhaps acquire regulative, methodological, as well as constitutive concepts of elementary logic; but the connection between them must remain closed to him. I define philology not as the science or the history of language, but rather at its deepest level as *history of terminology*" (C, 175–176). Although his use of the terms "philology" and "terminology" might indicate that Benjamin's thought remained within the field of linguistics, this important statement actually signals the final shift away from a philosophical linguistics and toward the literary and aesthetic disciplines. Benjamin was in this period an assiduous student of the golden age of German philology, which we might date from the work of Friedrich Schlegel to that of Nietzsche, and this philological tradition is grounded in the interpretation of literary texts.

Benjamin's calm, even implacable pursuit of a research program for the habilitation took place in an atmosphere of domestic and public turmoil. The headlines in the national dailies from early 1921 tell a story of political and economic unrest, with radical right pitted against radical left while a center-left coalition continued in its attempts to legitimate the fledgling Weimar Republic. Many of the most outrageous actions by the far right—assassinations, attempted coups, seditious publications—were tacitly encouraged by a judiciary that had never been purged of its most conservative imperial elements. And the economic misery of the postwar years was exacerbated as the allies forced a final, crippling reparations package on the German government: 226 billion Goldmarks were to be paid over a period of forty-two years. After the breakdown of talks in London regarding the actual payment of the reparations, French troops occupied the Ruhr region—the heartland of German industry. Benjamin is as silent regarding these events as he is to all but his closest friends regarding a domestic crisis: the near-dissolution of his marriage.

Tensions between Dora and Benjamin had increased in the years following the relative calm of their life in Switzerland. Living under a constant financial shadow, and in a house that was a persistent reminder not just of their dependence on Benjamin's parents but of the enmity that now dominated Benjamin's relations with his father, the couple had come by the spring of 1921 to live lives so separate that they could each fall in love with someone else—virtually simultaneously. Benjamin's old friend from the days of the Youth Movement, the sculptor Jula Cohn, visited the family in April, and in the course of her visit Benjamin found that he was deeply in love with a woman he had not seen in five years. Cohn's friend Charlotte Wolff describes her at this time as a somewhat eccentric creature: "She was petite and . . . moved gently and cautiously in a literal and symbolic sense.

She observed her visitors and everything else through a lorgnette with a long ebony handle. . . . Her head was too large for her slight body, and one's attention became fixed on it." Wolff remembers the awe that Cohn aroused, and a " 'touch' of perceptiveness which attracted intellectuals and artists to her."[26] We don't know exactly how Jula Cohn may have initially responded to any overtures from Benjamin. But it must have become clear to him very early that the woman with whom he imagined a new married life could not return the full depth of his affection. That, at least, is the gist of a quietly anguished letter Dora sent Scholem in May: "Above all, I'm worried about Walter. J[ula Cohn] has not decided for him, he wants to leave her and can't manage it, indeed he doesn't know if he should demand it of himself. I know that she doesn't love him, and that she will never love him. She is too honest to deceive herself and too naive—since she's never been in love—to be clear to herself about this. It's the same with love as it is with faith: you know nothing about it before you have it. . . . He asked me today whether or not he should break with her. . . . If his innermost being consents to his falling hopelessly in love, then so be it, he has no choice—and so much the worse for us. We are good to each other, and I would like it if I could be better, but I'm tormented still by many things."[27] Benjamin's enduring and ultimately unrequited love for Jula Cohn would determine much of the story of his private life in the early 1920s. Cohn would finally marry the chemist Fritz Radt, brother of Benjamin's former fiancée, Grete Radt, in 1925—but not before destroying all of the letters Benjamin had written her up to that point. (Another element in the complicated set of interlocking relationships would be the marriage later in 1921 of Cohn's brother Alfred, a close friend of Benjamin's since their days together at the Kaiser Friedrich School, to Grete Radt.)

In fact, the Benjamin we see reflected in the mirrors of the various women with whom he was involved in the course of his life is in many ways consonant with the Benjamin who speaks from the pages of his letters, essays, and books. One aspect of his manifold self-presentation is consistent across all firsthand accounts: the relative lack, or perhaps introversion, of a bodily erotic element. Scholem recalls a conversation with a mutual acquaintance in which the woman claimed that "for her and her female friends [Benjamin] had not even existed as a man, and that it had never even occurred to them that he had that dimension as well. 'Walter was, so to speak, incorporeal.' " In the early 1920s, Dora also spoke openly to Scholem about the physical difficulties that beset the marriage; she herself conceived of the problem as stemming from a superabundant intellectuality that "impeded his libido" (according to Scholem, she would resort to such psychoanalytic terminology in an attempt to understand her husband, claiming also that he suffered from an "obsessive-compulsive neurosis").[28] Other commentators noted a perhaps related tendency: that same bottomless reserve that dominated all his relationships manifested itself erotically as a certain tolerance and deferral. Charlotte Wolff was struck with Benjamin's ability to "dispense with the capitalism of possessive love," an ability that seemed to leave him free of jealousy even during Dora's extended affair with his friend Ernst Schoen. "The intimacy between his wife and his friend did not disturb his peace of mind: on the contrary, it brought the two men closer together. . . . Walter reminded me . . . of Rainer Maria Rilke, for whom nostalgia for the beloved was more desirable than her presence, which he all too often found an encumbrance rather than a pleasure. I realized that Benjamin could not face physical love for any length of time."[29] But if Benjamin "suffered" from anything in this regard, it was from the Nietzschean imperative to summon and construct himself as an ongoing set of improvisations or masks, what Nietzsche had called "foreground truths and perspective estimates," wagers laid to configure a life.[30] The displacement of energy, intellectual and erotic alike, into his work came at a certain cost. In her perceptive and highly sympathetic portrait, Wolff suggests that the price was a personal life dominated by nostalgia and frustration: "His Self was in his work, fed by inspiration from people he loved unrequitedly."[31]

Benjamin's wooing of Jula Cohn took place against the background of Dora's own affair with one of Benjamin's oldest and closest friends, the musician, composer, and musicologist Ernst Schoen (1894–1960). Originally part of Benjamin's circle at the Kaiser Friedrich School in Berlin, Schoen was, along with Alfred Cohn, the only one of his friends from his youth with whom Benjamin had remained in intimate contact. Schoen was by many accounts a remarkable man. His biographer, Sabine Schiller-Lerg, points to an "elegant restraint and

12. Ernst Schoen and Jula Cohn *(Werkbundarchiv—Museum der Dinge, Berlin)*

modesty, a discreet nobility."[32] Adorno, who came to know him only later, remembered Schoen as "one of those profoundly self-assured individuals who loved to yield the limelight—without a trace of resentment and to the point of self-effacement."[33] They were separated during the war years, when Schoen became Benjamin's most important partner in correspondence from Switzerland. In the years immediately following the war, Schoen seems to have drifted, unsure of a professional direction. In Berlin he had studied piano with Ferruccio Busoni and composition with Edgard Varèse; he also studied at several universities, but it is unclear whether he ever completed a degree.[34] In time he would become artistic director at Southwest German Radio in Frankfurt and would get Benjamin involved with the new medium at the end of the 1920s. The Benjamins had reestablished contact with Schoen on their return from Switzerland, and by the winter months of 1920–1921 Dora had fallen in love with him. She actively imagined the breakup of her marriage to Walter and a new life with Schoen. In late April she revealed to Scholem the extent of the disaster: "Today Walter told me that Jula has told her relatives everything, everything, about E[rnst Schoen] and me—told those bourgeois—he is just as horrified as I am . . . but said nothing about herself and Walter—we'll see what can still be saved. No doubt the catastrophe is coming soon."[35] What Dora does not mention in the letter, but presumably knew, was that Cohn herself was infatuated with Schoen.

If Dora wrote to friends about the crisis, Benjamin typically wrote to himself. His notebooks from the early 1920s are bursting with reflections, some topical—on marriage, on sexuality, on shame—and some already incorporated into a philosophical ethics. While he can claim that "two married people are the elements, but two friends the leaders of a community," he is nonetheless tortured by the special claims of marriage: "God, in the sacrament of marriage, makes love proof against the danger of sexuality as well as against that of death."[36] Perhaps the most moving testimony to Benjamin's awareness of the turmoil in his family, and the effect it was having on young Stefan, speaks from the words of a sonnet, "On January 6, 1922," which Benjamin recorded in the notebook that held the growing archive of Stefan's childish sayings:

> Who is this guest, that—though he disrupt
> The mistress's household and bring her misery—
> Its doorway nonetheless opens to him as swiftly
> As a light gate opens to the wind?
>
> His name is discord that returns
> Even if it has long since emptied table and chambers

To the soul alone its triple retinue remains
True now: sleep, tears, and the child

Yet each day's sword-bright sheaf
Breaks the old scar of those who awaken
And before consolation rocks them anew into slumber

If the source of their tears has long run dry
The child's smile alone, his customary ways
Can invite hope into the home.[37]

Scholem saw a contradiction between the "radiant moral aura" of Benjamin's thought and an unscrupulous, amoral element in his "relationship to things of daily life."[38] But this first deep crisis in the Benjamin marriage calls for a less black-and-white assessment: the ideas set down in the essay drafts and fragments from the period provided, if anything, a reflection on and perhaps a check, but not an antithesis, to his actions.

A stubborn mutual loyalty to the idea of their marriage helped the pair survive this crisis, as they would survive a series of crises throughout the 1920s, until Benjamin himself finally took steps to sever their union at the close of the decade. Scholem recounts that the first stage in the dissolution of the marriage began in the spring of 1921 and lasted for two years. "During that period Walter and Dora resumed their marital relationship from time to time, until from 1923 on they lived together only as friends—primarily for the sake of Stefan, whose development Walter followed with great interest, but presumably out of financial considerations as well" (SF, 94). Perhaps the most remarkable aspect of the new phase in their relationship was Dora's ongoing and total involvement with Benjamin's life as an intellectual. She continued to read everything he wrote and everything by others that concerned him deeply, and he continued to be quite unwilling to move forward in any area unless he and Dora were in intellectual agreement. If Dora could readily imagine a life that did not include physical intimacy with her husband, she found it much harder to withdraw from the magnetic attraction of his mind.

In early June 1921 the Benjamins went their separate ways. Dora traveled with Ernst Schoen, first to Munich to visit Scholem, but then to her aunt's sanatorium at Breitenstein, Austria, where she was diagnosed with a serious pulmonary problem. Benjamin confided guiltily to Scholem that he was pretty sure their marriage problems had brought on the medical crisis. Benjamin visited Dora in Austria during the last two weeks in June, but then, after staying in Munich with Scholem and his fiancée, Elsa Burchhardt, for a few days, he went on to Heidelberg for a visit that lasted until the middle of August. He first took a room in a hotel but soon moved into the rooms at Schloßberg 7a of Leo Löwenthal, who would later become one of Adorno's and Horkheimer's principal collaborators at the Institute of Social Research. Although Benjamin's ostensible reason for the extended stay was a further exploration of the possibilities for obtaining his habilitation at Heidelberg, there was another consideration: Jula Cohn was also there, since she was part of the circle around the literary scholar Friedrich Gundolf. After the stormy spring months in Berlin, Benjamin found a new equanimity during the summer in Heidelberg; even Cohn's continued resistance to his overtures could not dampen his mood. And now, perhaps for the only time in his adult life, Benjamin could imagine himself part of a community of scholars.

The university at Heidelberg was, in the early 1920s, widely regarded as one of the most exciting centers of intellectual production and exchange in Germany. The years after the world war were dominated not just by political and economic turmoil, but by a nationwide search for values and leaders in a time seemingly devoid of principles or direction. This state of affairs lent a particular edge to study at a university. In the early twenties, Gundolf was not only the most influential academic representative of the circle around the nationalist symbolist poet Stefan George but also a nationally recognized authority on culture.[39] Gustav Regler recalls the atmosphere in Gundolf's lectures in the period after the war: "The benches were crowded. It was the sort of audience one sees only in times of crisis." Benjamin had drafted, perhaps as early as 1917, a highly polemical critique of Gundolf's monumental study of Goethe. He now went along to several lectures, but reported that Gundolf "appeared to me to be terribly feeble and harmless in terms of the personal impression he makes, quite different from the impression he makes in his books" (C, 182). Benjamin was not alone in this opinion: behind Gundolf it was George himself, with his vision of a Germany revivified through recourse to a premodern past, who gripped Regler and many other students. "[George] invoked the memory of forgotten monarchs, such as the Hohenstaufens, [and praised] their breadth and power of vision. A new dream arose in Heidelberg, and the great hope of unifying East and West seemed not impossible."[40] Several years later, Benjamin described his own encounter with the poet in a short essay in the *Literarische Welt:* "The hours never grew long as I sat reading on a bench in the Schlosspark in Heidelberg, waiting for the moment when he would come by. One day he came slowly toward me, speaking with a younger companion. Now and then I also found him sitting on a bench in the courtyard of the castle. But all this occurred at a time when the decisive tremor of his work had long since reached me. . . . His teachings, however, no matter where I encountered them, awakened in me nothing but distrust and disagreement."[41] The tension in this passage between the ongoing fascination with the *life and poetic production* of the poet and the long since accomplished break with his teachings is perhaps less a residue of the encounter with George than a portent of an ambitious new literary project. Several unfolding circumstances at this time—the constellation of his and Dora's twinned love affairs, represented very concretely for Benjamin in the person of Jula Cohn; his intensive reading of Goethe throughout the year, and particularly of his novel *Die Wahlverwandtschaften* (Elective Affinities; 1809), which concerns the fateful consequences of twinned love affairs; the personal encounter with Gundolf, for whom Benjamin wished to provide a "legally binding condemnation and execution" (C, 196); and the ever present shadow of George—all this became the catalyst for one of Benjamin's most influential and difficult works, "Goethe's Elective Affinities," which was begun in Heidelberg.

The time in Heidelberg was rich in personal contacts for Benjamin. Besides the classes with Gundolf, he also attended lectures by Karl Jaspers, after Heidegger the most influential German philosopher of the mid-twentieth century, and lectures by his old teacher Heinrich Rickert. Benjamin's formula for Jaspers rather wickedly inverts his impression of Gundolf: "feeble and harmless in his thinking, but as a person obviously very remarkable and almost likable"; on the other hand, he found that Rickert had become "gray and mean" (C, 182–183). Perhaps the most exciting contact was with the participants in a se-

ries of "sociological discussion evenings" held at the home of Marianne Weber, a feminist theorist and politician who was also the widow
of the great sociologist Max Weber. Benjamin distinguished himself
in this circle through his general contributions, but in particular by
his delivery of a prepared speech attacking psychoanalysis, which
he claims was accompanied by constant cries of "bravo" from Alfred
Weber, younger brother of Max Weber. Alfred Weber was a prominent
liberal sociologist who, like his brother, based his ideas on economic
analysis; he was certainly the most influential professor in the social
sciences in Heidelberg at the time. It was during these months of contact with Alfred and Marianne Weber and his engagement with issues
in socioeconomics that Benjamin wrote down one of the most spectacular of his many short texts that remained works in progress, never
to be published in his lifetime.

"Capitalism as Religion" gestures toward Max Weber's fundamental insight into the religious nature of the capitalist work ethic, but it
is significant that, as early as 1921, Benjamin grounds his argument
not in Weber, or indeed in scientific Marxism, but instead in Marx's
analysis of the fetish character of the capitalist commodity in *Capital.* Benjamin argues that capitalism is perhaps the most extreme of
all religious cults, founded as it is upon a purely psychological relationship to fetishized objects. Devoid of doctrine or theology, the cult
maintains itself solely through the *permanent* celebration of its rites—
shopping and consumption. And, for Benjamin, this reinvention of
time as feast day without end ironically triggers the most crippling
effect of capitalism: "the cult makes indebtedness and thus guilt pervasive."[42] This inculcation of a guilt-ridden indebtedness leads not to
the "reform of existence" but to its "complete destruction. It is the
expansion of despair, until despair becomes a religious state of the
world." We cannot yet speak of a Benjaminian Marxism, but this last
expression of the romantic anticapitalism that had marked the first
decades of the century remains one of Benjamin's most intriguing
analyses. Much of the fragment itself and the notes that are incorporated into it are couched in academic language; the little text might
well have been intended as the germ cell of the kind of article that
would draw Weber's attention. Benjamin thus left Heidelberg in August
convinced that he had created a place for himself and his habilitation at

the university; he told Scholem that "people with a doctorate who have already been sitting in Rickert's seminars for a year are asking me how to find their way to a habilitation" (GB, 2:176). Here, as would often be the case in the years just ahead, Benjamin misjudged the institution and its willingness to accept him.

Even given his new hope for an academic career, the most promising encounter in Heidelberg was undoubtedly that with Richard Weissbach, who was preparing Benjamin's Baudelaire translations for publication. Weissbach was impressed enough with Benjamin to offer him the editorship of his journal *Die Argonauten*. On Benjamin's refusal, Weissbach sounded him out on the possibility of creating a new journal of his own, with full editorial control—a proposal to which Benjamin assented enthusiastically. Much of the remainder of the year was given over to work on the proposed journal, and especially to the recruitment of suitable contributors. Ultimately, nothing was to come of the idea beyond the short text "Announcement of the Journal *Angelus Novus*," which itself remained unpublished during Benjamin's lifetime. But some of the importance he ascribed to the project is betrayed in the journal's name: Benjamin hoped that his own new angel, like Klee's vivid herald, would proclaim nothing less than "the spirit of its age." Benjamin envisioned a journal that would bring together original works of literature, conceived of as "crucial statements" on the "fate of the German language," with examples of "annihilating" criticism, conceived of as "the guardian of the house," and translations, conceived of as "the strict and irreplaceable school of language-in-the-making." As in the 1918 essay "The Coming Philosophy" and the 1912 "Dialogue on the Religiosity of the Present," Benjamin imagines here an admixture of philosophy and theology as the key to "contemporary relevance": "The universal validity of spiritual utterances must be bound up with the question of whether they can lay claim to a place within future religious orders" (SW, 1:294). And for Benjamin it was the unconcealed spirit life of human language itself, the philosophical mining of the buried historical-semantic dimension beneath its concept-encrusted surface, that alone could guarantee such universal validity. In a memorable letter of January 13, 1924, to Hugo von Hofmannsthal, he will affirm that "every truth has its house, its ancestral palace in language; and that this palace is constructed out of the oldest logoi; and that, compared to truth grounded in this way, the insights of the individual disciplines remain subordinate so long as they wander as it were nomadically, helping themselves here and there in the realm of language. . . . Philosophy, in contrast, experiences the blessed efficacy of an order, by virtue of which its insights always strive for very specific words whose surface, made crusty by concepts, dissolves when it comes into contact with the magnetic force of this order, betraying the forms of linguistic life locked within" (C, 228–229). *Angelus Novus* was conceived from the beginning as a platform for this "magnetic" release of the ancestral truths embedded in language.

Perhaps the most striking feature of Benjamin's plan was his insistence that the effect of the journal would depend entirely upon the reception of the language of the individual contributors. The early 1920s was a remarkable time for the emergence of new journals, yet most of the "little magazines" that sprang up were the production of a self-defined avant-garde group or community. For example, 1922 saw the birth of *Devětsil* (Nine Forces) in Prague, *Mécano* (1922–1923) in Weimar, and *Zenit* (1922–1926) in Belgrade and Zagreb. That year in Berlin, El Lissitzky and Ilya Ehrenburg produced the only two issues of *Veshch' Objet Gegenstand* (Object) that would appear, with parallel texts in Russian, French, and German. In 1923 two more journals were produced in Prague: *Disk* and *Život* (Life), with Karel Teige involved in both. The *Levy front iskusstv*, known as *LEF* (1923–1925; Journal of the Left Front of the Arts), was published in Moscow, with Vladimir Mayakovsky as editor. And the inaugural issues of both *G: Material zur elementaren Gestaltung* (1923–1926) and *Broom* (1923–1924) were released in Berlin. Whereas the goal of these magazines was generally the cultivation of an informed audience, Benjamin inveighed against precisely this goal. In asserting that "nothing links the contributors with one another beyond their own will and consciousness," he specifically abjures the creation of "an atmosphere of mutual understanding and community. . . . The journal should proclaim through the mutual alienness of its contributors how impossible it is in our age to give voice to any communality" (SW, 1:292–296). This is one of the first statements of what will become a guiding precept for Benjamin. His writings in the period 1919–1922 were concerned above all to reveal the ways in which the present moment was infiltrated by myth: in the essays "Fate and Character," "Critique of Violence," and "Goethe's Elective Affinities," myth emerges as the power that dominates and disorients human relations. Benjamin's "Announcement" thus insists that, in relation to the present age, such categories as context, coherence, and shared meaning are fundamentally false categories, and in his writings of the period he will avoid every strategy of representation that imposes a false continuity and homogeneity on the historical moment.

This denial of the possibility of articulating any present community not only flies in the face of the practices and goals of the various European avant-gardes of the day but runs counter to the thinking of his closest friends and intellectual collaborators from the period. Both Gutkind and Rang sought in every way imaginable to create an intellectual community based on shared beliefs that would continue the goals of the Forte Circle. Gutkind's thoughts turned repeatedly to the ideal of a circle of friends living together in isolation from the world, and he envisioned "a center, a cloister": "If only we could live elsewhere for a while! And finally create the refuge for eminent minds— the new island. Should it not now be time?"[43] Although in 1924 Benjamin would willingly join Gutkind and Rang on a journey to such an isolated place—the island of Capri—he never wholly shared their faith in community. The "Announcement" and the first pages of the essay "The Task of the Translator" are his declaration of faith in language alone, that is, in philosophy and art. It goes without saying that had *Angelus Novus* ever appeared, such thinking would have ruled out all but a tiny audience of readers—a mandarin elite capable of following often abstract and esoteric writing, and presumably sharing Benjamin's convictions regarding language. He envisioned, in fact, "a journal that takes not the least consideration of a public capable of paying" (GB, 2:182), and he thereby sounds a note of hermetic autonomy that he would build on later in the year in his essay "The Task of the Translator."

The prospect of bringing out an independent journal seems to have stirred Benjamin's enthusiasm more than any enterprise since the days of the youth movement and his work on *Der Anfang*. Even after it had become apparent that his plans would lead to nothing concrete, the intellectual exhilaration of the idea lingered. The drive for intellectual mastery that manifested itself in many of Benjamin's personal relationships is evident here on a larger scale as a desire for intellectual leadership. Throughout his life he sought out small groups of like-minded thinkers and artists, and more often than not he emerged as the leading figure, or at least the leading intellect, of the group; only his relationship to Bert Brecht in exile in the 1930s stands as an exception. Editorial control of a journal is of course one of the most concrete manifestations of this urge, and *Angelus Novus* would be only the first of several journal projects. The other main factor connecting them was their shared failure.

If the months in Heidelberg had fostered a certain equanimity in Benjamin, the fall, with its eventual return to Berlin and to his marriage, marked a troubled period in his life. The abortive affair with Jula Cohn clearly took its toll; he complained often of depression in its aftermath. But his work on the journal, and the accompanying attempt to gather and direct a group of disparate intellectuals, had its own costs: Benjamin's self-assertion led, in the fall, to breaks with several friends and collaborators. Despite all this, the final months of 1921 proved to be a productive period for him. Charlotte Wolff has left us a remarkable portrait of Benjamin at this time, a portrait alive to the contradictions that showed up everywhere in this intellectual at thirty: "He had not the male bearing of his generation. And there were disturbing features about him which did not fit with the rest of his personality. The rosy apple-cheeks of a child, the black curly hair and fine brow were appealing, but there was sometimes a cynical glint in his eyes. His thick sensuous lips, badly hidden by a moustache, were also an unexpected feature, not fitting with the rest. His posture and gestures were 'uptight' and lacked spontaneity, except when he spoke of things he was involved in or of people he loved. . . . His spindly legs gave the sorry impression of atrophied muscles. He hardly gestured, but kept his arms close to his chest."[44]

After a brief journey to Karlsruhe to meet Scholem, Benjamin in late August took the train to Austria in order to visit Dora at the sanatorium, where she was making a slow and painful recovery from her pulmonary problems. But Benjamin's mind was clearly elsewhere. He continued to make feverish plans for *Angelus Novus* and traveled to

13. Florens Christian Rang,
1901 *(Collection Adalbert Rang,
Amsterdam)*

Munich on September 4, meeting with Ernst Lewy and Scholem to
determine the line the journal would take, and gathering manuscripts
from potential contributors. These often heated discussions focused
on literature (Heinrich Heine, Karl Kraus, and the now forgotten
Walter Calé) and the philosophy of language (Lazarus Geiger, Haim
Steinthal, and Fritz Mauthner).[45] While still in Munich, Benjamin
began to pick up signals from Lewy and his wife that were confirmed
on his return to Berlin: he received a brusque rejection regarding any
collaboration on *Angelus Novus.* The feud that ensued was soon di-
verted into more civilized channels through the intervention of Dora
and Scholem, but relations between Benjamin and Lewy remained
troubled for years.

Before returning to Berlin, he made one more stop, this one like-
wise devoted to recruiting for the journal. He stayed at the home of
Florens Christian Rang in Braunfels an der Lahn from September 7 to
September 12.[46] Born in 1864, Rang was already nearing the end of an

eventful life when Benjamin first met him at Erich Gutkind's house in Berlin in 1920. Trained in law, he had served as a civil service administrator until 1895, when he returned to the university to study theology. He was active as a pastor from 1898 until 1904 and then reentered the ranks of the state bureaucracy. In 1917 he resigned from state service in order to serve as chief executive officer of the Raiffeisen Society in Berlin (Raiffeisen societies and banks, which exist to this day, grew out of a series of communal self-help organizations aimed at workers and farmers and were founded by Wilhelm Raiffeisen in the late nineteenth century). When Benjamin visited him in Braunfels, Rang had recently retired from public life—and was undergoing a gradual political transformation from the nationalist and conservative positions he had held during the First World War toward a more moderate conservatism. Although Rang is today a little-known figure, his contemporaries held him in high esteem. Martin Buber called him "one of the noblest Germans of our time," and Hugo von Hofmannsthal ranked him alongside the era's leading intellectuals.[47] In the three years to come, Rang emerges as Benjamin's most important intellectual partner; he later commented that Rang's death meant the loss of the "ideal reader" of his *Trauerspiel* book.[48]

By the middle of September, both Benjamin and Dora were back in Berlin—and troubles began almost immediately to rain down on them. Dora was forced to undergo an operation on her lungs, and she again recovered slowly and only with nursing care in the home. And Benjamin's father took to bed with an illness that is never specified. Benjamin describes him in September as terminally ill—though he was soon up and about again. The Benjamin marriage itself continued to be held together, however tenuously, through mutual regard alone. In a note enclosed in Benjamin's letter of October 4, Dora reported to Scholem that Walter was again "very dear and good to me. I am doing well neither physically nor psychologically, but I hope things will improve. Things have been worse" (GB, 2:198). Scholem recalls the fragile consideration for each other that haltingly sustained the marriage. "It was as though each was afraid of hurting the other person, as though the demon that occasionally possessed Walter and manifested itself in despotic behavior and claims had completely left him under these somewhat fantastic conditions" (SF, 94–95).

After Lewy's withdrawal, Benjamin began to think of Erich Unger as a principal collaborator for *Angelus Novus*. Yet these plans were complicated by Benjamin's increasing distance from the circle around Oskar Goldberg, a distance maintained despite the circle's ongoing attempts to recruit him along with Scholem. Benjamin's attitude toward Goldberg and his circle is displayed in his account of a lecture by the Baltic German Hugo Lyck at a private home. "Aside from some of the obligatory bourgeoisie, the preposterous audience consisted above all of Ernst Bloch, Alfred Döblin, Martin Gumpert, and several young ladies from Berlin's wild west. Mr. Lyck, an indisputably schizophrenic talent, is known (among those who, for their part, are not) as a perfectly esoteric personality who is teeming with knowledge, in communication with spirits, world traveled, and in possession of all arcana. . . . His religion, ancestry, and income have not yet been ascertained, and I am no slouch at such matters." Yet Benjamin goes on to portray *what* Lyck says as "wholly noteworthy, now and then unquestionably right, and, even when it was false, altogether essential." And why would Benjamin develop a sudden partisanship for so problematic a voice? Because he claimed to see in Lyck the "original source" of the main doctrines of Oskar Goldberg and his circle (GB, 2:224–225).[49] Given these attitudes, it would have come as no surprise that Unger himself confronted Benjamin in early October, demanding to know where he stood vis-à-vis Goldberg; Benjamin did little to veil his repugnance, and a full break loomed. But Dora's diplomatic skills came to the rescue once again. Recognizing the "prestige-character" of the affair for both men, she took Unger aside and, in a "diabolically clever conversation," explained that her husband's antipathy in this case resulted solely from "private idiosyncrasies" (C, 188).

To the break with Lewy and the near-break with Unger must be added the cooling of Benjamin's relations with Ernst Bloch. Few figures in Benjamin's life evoked so complicated a set of reactions. From the earliest days of their acquaintance, Benjamin was drawn to the spirit of Bloch's thinking, and especially to its insistent political drive. Yet his reaction to the writings themselves usually ranged from ambivalence to outright rejection. On reading a draft of Bloch's book-length study of Thomas Münzer, the Reformation theologian and revolutionary, Benjamin called it "Max Weber transposed into the idiom of [comic playwright Carl] Sternheim" (GB, 2:226). Unalloyed enthusiasm—which Benjamin expressed in September for Bloch's review of Georg Lukács's *History and Class Consciousness*—was a rare thing. Now his personal relation to Bloch, which had remained consistently cordial, was troubled. On failing to visit the Benjamins, Bloch wrote to say that he was unable to abide anyone except the "simplest" of people. He went on to explain, according to Benjamin, why Benjamin himself did not fall into this category. Benjamin responded to this perceived slight by making catty remarks about Bloch to friends; he referred in early 1921 to Bloch's search for a wife "throughout Germany." This was a particularly cruel jab, since rumors had circulated for years that Bloch's first marriage was undertaken with an eye to his wife's then considerable fortune. Here, too, Dora worked hard to prevent the friendship from falling into an abyss; Benjamin describes her as "Machiavelline" in her role as mediator (GB, 2:205). Among the Benjamins' other visitors was Wolf Heinle, never an easy guest. Benjamin continued to feel a special responsibility for the brother of his increasingly mythicized friend. Heinle was eking out a living for himself as a potter in Goslar and working at his short fiction. Benjamin showed that he still had an unwavering faith in the Heinles as authors: he planned to publish a selection of Fritz's sonnets as well as stories by Wolf in the first issue of *Angelus Novus*.

In the final months of 1921 Benjamin at last finished work on a text he had originally envisioned as the foreword to the volume of Baudelaire translations, but which he now looked on as his own contribution to the first issue of *Angelus Novus:* the essay "The Task of the Translator." Benjamin's essay is anything but a how-to for translators; it is conceived from the outset in terms of a global theory of the criticism of works of art. Benjamin well understood the importance of this essay in the development of his thought. He had written to Scholem in March that "what is at issue is a subject so crucial to me that I still do not know whether I can develop it with sufficient freedom, given the current stage of my thinking—assuming that I succeed in elucidating it at all" (C, 177). The essay proceeds from a strong claim that was also deeply rooted in Benjamin's thinking about the journal: the notion of the relative autonomy of the work of art vis-à-vis its audience. "No poem is intended for the reader, no picture for the beholder, no symphony for the audience" (SW, 1:253). With this claim, Benjamin seeks to disavow the customary understanding of translation as a mediation between original work and audience. As he had already asserted in the language essay of 1916, no significant linguistic practice can have as its aim merely the transmission of "meaning"; this is particularly true of literary translation, the function of which is not simply the communication of what the original "says" or "tells." For Benjamin, translation is essentially the revelation of something inherent in the original, indeed something that can be revealed *only* in the original's susceptibility to translation: "a specific significance inherent in the original manifests itself in its translatability." If, in the 1919 dissertation on German Romanticism, Benjamin had already decentered the finite work of art, questioning its privileged status and placing it in a continuum with its subsequent criticism, he here completes and radicalizes that notion: translation not only stands, with criticism, as a crucial element of a work's "afterlife" but actually *supersedes* the life of the original. "In [translations] the life of the originals attains its latest, continually renewed, and most complete unfolding."

What, though, is revealed in translation if not the meaning of the original? For Benjamin, it is the "language of truth, a tensionless and even silent depository of the ultimate secrets for which all thought strives." "And this very language, in whose divination and description lies the only perfection for which a philosopher can hope, is concealed in concentrated form in translations." Benjamin's theory of criticism, which attempts to define a practice that can establish the preconditions for the emergence of truth in a fallen world, had focused from the first on the nature of the truth that lay concealed in every present. Benjamin had conceived of that truth as the "elements of the ultimate condition" in the essay "The Life of Students" of 1914–1915, as the "creative word" in the language essay of 1916, and as "true nature" in the afterword to his dissertation in 1919. Now, in the context of a theory of translation, truth is figured as "the very nucleus of pure language." Moreover, "The Task of the Translator" introduces a new dynamism into Benjamin's theory of language. If, in the essay "On Language as Such and on the Language of Man," the logical priority of the word, the immanence of language to all nature, is expounded without reference to historical development, this radiant "nucleus" of truth, as something "symbolizing" and "symbolized," is now presented as an element accessible only as part of a historical process: through language change. "Yet though this nucleus remains present in life as that which is symbolized itself, albeit hidden and fragmentary, it persists in linguistic creations only in its symbolizing capacity. Whereas in the various tongues that ultimate essence, the pure language, is tied only to linguistic elements and their changes, in linguistic creations it is weighted with a heavy and alien meaning. To relieve it of this, to turn the symbolizing into the symbolized itself, . . . is the tremendous and only capacity of translation." This shift in the understanding of truth from what Benjamin, in the afterword to the dissertation, called a "limited, harmonic discontinuum of pure contents" to an "expressionless" element in an open-ended process—the work's composition, translation, and criticism—stems in part from Benjamin's increasing engagement with concrete historical questions; the shift is related, in other words, to the project of a politics.

Translation's special status in the historical process through which truth may emerge lies in its capacity to reveal the "innermost relationship of languages": "in every one of them as a whole, one and the same thing is meant." This one thing is the "pure language," which is "achievable not by any single language but only by the totality of their intentions supplementing one another." Benjamin hypothesizes that each language, in its "way of meaning," harmonizes with the essential "way of meaning" of every other language, and so points toward "language as such." The translator's task is thus intensification of the tendency toward pure language that is latent in the encounter of two different languages: "Pure language . . . no longer means or expresses anything but is, as expressionless and creative word, that which is meant in all languages." Rather than offer evidence for these claims, Benjamin simply invokes a specific practice of translation: Friedrich Hölderlin's remarkable series of translations from classical Greek. These translations take the notion of literalness in translation beyond any conventional measure; Hölderlin's fidelity to Greek syntax and morphology actively disfigures the German of his translations. With the invocation of Hölderlin's practice, Benjamin's essay leaves conceptual argumentation behind and opens onto a series of resonant but discontinuous figural networks. The first metaphorical register derives from the holy of holies: languages develop toward the "messianic end of their history," inspired by translation that puts "the hallowed growth of languages to the test" and "catches fire from the eternal life of the works." A second portrays the emergence of truth from its entrapment in its material matrix through a series of organic and topographic metaphors. If original works are to be found at the center of the "language forest," the translation is outside the center of the forest, facing the "wooded ridge": "it calls into it without entering, aiming at that single spot where the echo is able to give, in its own language, the reverberation of the work in the alien one." The "seed of pure language" cannot, then, ripen in the forest of language unless it is called to life aurally by a distant echo. Third, Benjamin evokes the language of Tikkun in Jewish mysticism, the belief that sacred vessels, variously interpreted as truth or redemption, were shattered at the inception of historical time but can be repaired. "Fragments of a vessel that are to be glued together must match one another in the smallest details, although they need not be like one another. In the same way a translation, instead of imitating the sense of the original, must lovingly and in detail incorporate the original's way of meaning, thus making both the original and the translation recognizable as fragments of a greater language." Fourth, in a startling anticipation of the central figure of his late masterwork, *The Arcades Project*, Benjamin argues for the ultimate transparency of translation, its capacity to allow the light of pure language to shine upon the original: "For if the sentence is the wall before the language of the original, literalness is the arcade." And finally, as the essay draws to a close, Benjamin invokes the language of social revolution in calling for the emancipation of pure language: it is the task of the translator to break through the "decayed barriers" of his own language. These diverse networks of metaphor are deployed without any attempt at hierarchy or systematization; they are an iterative and constantly varied evocation of what for Benjamin would remain the unquantifiable linguistic nature of all truth.

By the end of the year, Benjamin had returned to work on a number of projects: the essay on Goethe's *Elective Affinities*, an introduction to the collected poems of Fritz Heinle, and of course *Angelus*

Novus. The contents of the first issue was fixed by December: poems by Fritz Heinle; "dramatic poems" by Wolf Heinle; two stories, "The New Synagogue" and "Rise and Fall," by Agnon; Rang's essay "The Historical Psychology of the Carnival"; Scholem's study of the "Klagelied" (Song of Lamentation); and Benjamin's "The Task of the Translator" (GB, 2:218). Like his contributions to *Der Anfang,* Benjamin's contributions to his own journal would have appeared under a pseudonym: J. B. Niemann or Jan Beim. He sent the full manuscript of the issue to Weissbach on January 21, 1922. But production of a manuscript hardly had the intended effect: Weissbach, clearly stalling, attempted to involve Benjamin in a long series of ancillary projects, soliciting his advice on illustrations for children's books, Goethe volumes, and editions of minor authors. Of course, Benjamin himself was a master of subtle deflection; his replies combine an often fawning tone with artful refusals of Weissbach's ideas. In the course of the spring, though, misunderstandings and indignation on both sides gradually came to dominate the relationship.

The difficulties with Weissbach—and thus the uncertainties surrounding the fate of the journal—were exacerbated by the demands of final work on the essay "Goethe's Elective Affinities," which took place between December 1921 and February 1922. Benjamin complained of a return of the "noise psychosis" that often accompanied intense intellectual labor, and he was forced to work by night—often by candlelight, as strikes and local uprisings were still the order of the day in Berlin. "Goethe's Elective Affinities" is in many ways the crown of his early work. It contains not only a penetrating critique of Goethe's dark novel of manners but also Benjamin's most thoroughgoing attempt to systematize his theory of criticism. As he put it to Scholem, his essay is conceived not only as "exemplary criticism" but as prolegomenon to "certain purely philosophical expositions"—and "in between lies what I have to say about Goethe" (C, 194). The essay is thus Benjamin's first attempt to bring the critical method he developed after 1915 to bear on a major work of literature. In elaborating the critical positions adumbrated in his early essays and in the dissertation on Romantic *Kunstkritik,* Benjamin shows that ideas with a lofty metaphysical pedigree could be turned to the account of applied criticism.

Few readings of major works have proven so influential *and* so controversial. Goethe's novel is generically ambiguous. It begins as a comedy of manners and ends as a tragedy. At the country estate of Count Eduard and his wife, Charlotte, the arrival of two visitors, Eduard's friend "the captain" and Charlotte's niece Ottilie, sets off the chain of "chemical" reactions referred to in the novel's title: Eduard falls in love with Charlotte's ward, Ottilie, while Charlotte and the captain discover an "inclination" to each other. A night of love between Charlotte and Eduard produces a baby, but a baby that resembles not the biological parents so much as the partners about whom Eduard and Charlotte were dreaming while in one another's arms. The mood grows dire when Ottilie, while crossing a lake at twilight with the infant, accidentally allows the child to fall from the boat and drown. Despite the—only somewhat ambiguous—reassurances of the other three partners, Ottilie falls immovably silent and finally dies of mysterious causes. The very condensation of this plot summary sheds a concentrated light upon one of Benjamin's principal motivations for writing the essay: the intrusion of two new figures into a seemingly harmonious marriage depicted in Goethe's novel precisely mirrors the quadrangle Walter/Dora/Ernst/Jula that produced such a destructive outcome in his own life. It can thus come as no surprise that Benjamin's reading seizes on the question of morals. Yet that reading departs decisively from the autobiographical when he insists that true morality can be reflected only in language use—or, as with Ottilie, in its renunciation. Ottilie, in fact, emerges as the key to the novel. However much she seems, through her silence and seeming purity, to transcend the moral world of the other main characters, for Benjamin her "internal" decision, because it is never enunciated, that is, never articulated in language, remains alien to truth, or, in the essay's own vocabulary, remains bound to "the mythic" and hence to the natural world.

The structure of the essay is careful and significant. It is divided into three sections, and each section in turn contains three parts: an introductory meditation on the theory of criticism in its relation to philosophy, an interpretation of an aspect of the novel, and a biographical commentary on Goethe himself. Despite this apparently dialectical structure, Benjamin's arguments here are more dualistic than dialectical. He is concerned to show how profoundly the element of myth is woven into the lives of the characters as well as into the setting and atmosphere of the novel, and at the same time how relentlessly myth militates against truth—whether truth is understood as revelation or freedom. Although Benjamin nowhere provides an explicit definition of myth, the term recurs in discussions of the relationship of humans to nature—and in that relationship nature exerts a predominantly malevolent effect upon humans.[50] "Charged, as only mythic nature is, with superhuman powers, it comes menacingly into play" (SW, 1:303). At the heart of Benjamin's essay may be heard a sotto voce reading of Hermann Cohen's magisterial philosophical interpretation of the Hebrew prophets in *Religion of Reason out of the Sources of Judaism*. The central distinction of Cohen's work is that between monotheism, understood as love of God, and a paganism rooted in myth. Cohen starts from the assertion of the absolute otherness of God, whose uniqueness prevents his becoming an object of knowledge (an idea with implications for thinkers as different as Franz Rosenzweig and Karl Barth). Positing the uniqueness of divinity, monotheism transcends the idolatry of nature. Cohen's work, in its ethical rationalism, reveals a measured revulsion, to which Benjamin was at times sympathetic, for the manifestations of nature and for the natural, sensuous aspects of human life. Nature is regarded as "nothing in itself," sensuality as "animal selfishness."[51] Myth thus designates for Cohen, as here for Benjamin, the insidious influence of something fundamentally equivocal upon the human spirit. Already in the writings from the period of the youth movement, Benjamin had given expression to his own deeply felt "dread of nature."[52] Now, in his late twenties, that same horror in the face of "the natural" plays a role in the essay—but it is best expressed in a passage of his montage book *One-Way Street* (1928), which he began not long after completing the Goethe essay. There, in a section with the significant title "Gloves," Benjamin writes:

> In an aversion to animals, the predominant feeling is fear of being recognized by them through contact. The horror that stirs deep in man is an obscure awareness that something living within him is so akin to the animal that it might be recognized. All disgust is originally disgust at touching. . . . He may not deny his bestial relationship

with the creature, the invocation of which revolts him: he must make himself its master. (SW, 1:448)[53]

In "Goethe's Elective Affinities," mythic nature is shown to exert a pernicious effect not just upon the characters—the novel's title maps the notion current in the early nineteenth century that some chemical elements have a natural affinity for one another onto a claimed affinity between each character and a natural feature—but upon Goethe himself, and upon the possible existence of truth in a literary text. Benjamin sees in the affinity of the characters to the behavior of natural elements the most pervasive sign of human moral decay; this affinity entails the progressive incursion of creaturely impulses into ethical decisions. For Benjamin, Goethe himself falls prey to the natural: he subjugates his art to nature as its sole adequate model. Note that the title of the essay is "Goethe's Elective Affinities," not "Goethe's *Elective Affinities.*" Like his characters, Goethe is drawn to a corresponding natural element. Benjamin issues here a sober critique of the dominant trope of all Romanticism—the symbol, with its claim to allow an "intimation of immortality" to glimmer through. Thinking that he perceived manifestations of the numinous in every conceivable natural phenomenon, Goethe became entrapped in what Benjamin calls the "chaos of symbols" (SW, 1:315). For Benjamin, Goethe's fabled self-understanding as an Olympian is at bottom nothing more than unchecked pantheism—a "monstrosity."[54]

If Benjamin's reading of the novel's characters and its author presents challenges to the understanding—"Goethe's Elective Affinities" is one of the most refractory critical texts of the twentieth century— those challenges multiply in view of the theory of criticism that informs the text. In the "esoteric afterword" to his dissertation, he had attributed to Goethe the notion that only art can capture scattered images of a "true nature" once present in a prelapsarian world but subsequently hidden and fragmented—what Benjamin there calls "a limited, harmonic discontinuum" (SW, 1:179). Now, in the essay on *Elective Affinities,* Benjamin defines the "truth content" of literature as a function of certain linguistic elements of a text that carry, in concentrated form, a larger truth. Benjamin spells out the task of criticism itself: our last hope of knowing nature, and thus of knowing ourselves, rests in the isolation of certain fragments of a work of art that bear within themselves some hint of a more integral knowledge. Yet Benjamin's conception of the work of art is contingent upon his notion of truth content only to a limited extent. The truth content *(Wahrheitsgehalt)* of literature represents but a small proportion of all effective elements in the text. The remainder, which Benjamin designates the "material content" *(Sachgehalt)*, has no relation to language in its pure cognizing form, that is, to the language of names he described in the 1916 essay on language. The work of verbal art is instead, like other human artifacts, created on analogy to a natural object. Dependent on linguistic forms marked by history, literary texts as a whole constitute the archive of "natural history"; as such, they mime the nature evident to human cognition, a nature shrouded in semblance and myth.

Myth is the peril into which truth has always already fallen. The text is a field riven by the struggle between its emerging and receding truth and those elements dominated by myth, which in itself is equivocal, neither true nor false: "This relationship [of truth and myth] is one of mutual exclusion. There is no truth—since there is no unequivocalness and thus not even error—in myth." And yet "where the presence of truth should be possible, it can be possible solely under the condition of the recognition of myth—that is, the recognition of its crushing indifference to truth" (SW, 1:325–326). Benjamin's depiction of—and intended intervention in—this antinomy remains in many ways the central theme of his early and late work. Although he will increasingly recognize myth itself as a form of knowledge (as would Adorno and Horkheimer in *Dialectic of Enlightenment*), he will also come to identify myth as the form in which the capitalist world presents itself to perception—as natural, as the only possible world. An often-quoted fragment in *The Arcades Project*, his unfinished study of the variegated cultural expression of urban commodity capitalism in mid-nineteenth-century Paris, reads as follows: "To cultivate fields where, until now, only madness has reigned. Forge ahead with the whetted axe of reason, looking neither right nor left so as not to succumb to the horror that beckons from deep in the primeval forest. Every ground must at some point have been made arable by reason, must have been cleared of the undergrowth of delusion and myth.

This is to be accomplished here for the terrain of the nineteenth century" (AP, N1,4).

The task of criticism, then, is the differentiation of truth from myth, or rather the purging and clarification of the mythic element so as to intimate the true. Benjamin's criticism is never merely interpretive or evaluative but rather expiatory and redemptive: it is an activity that "destroys" its object only to plumb it for the truth it might contain. This destructive urge is a constant: it marks the earliest and the latest comments on criticism. In a letter of 1916 he had offered several metaphors for "criticism of spiritual things," which strives for the "differentiation of the genuine from the nongenuine" precisely through moving "the night," which it fights against, to deliver up *its* light. Criticism is a peculiar sort of light that ignites and consumes the work, a chemical substance "that attacks the other only in the sense that, decomposing it, it reveals its inner nature" (C, 84). And in the *Arcades,* a couple of notes from the later 1930s specify that "'construction' presupposes 'destruction,'" and that "the destructive or critical momentum of materialist historiography is registered in that blasting of historical continuity with which the historical object first constitutes itself" (AP, N7,6 and N10a,1).

Benjamin was thus adamant in arguing that a critical method might be developed capable of discriminating truth from myth. He comes close to formulating a critical credo on the opening page of the essay on Goethe:

> Critique seeks the truth content of a work of art; commentary, its material content. The relation between the two is determined by that basic law of literature [*Schrifttum*] according to which the more significant the work, the more inconspicuously and intimately its truth content is bound up with its material content. If, therefore, the works that prove enduring are precisely those whose truth is most deeply sunken in their material content, then, in the course of this duration, the concrete realities [*die Realien*] rise up before the eyes of the beholder all the more distinctly the more they die out in the world. With this, however, to judge by appearances, the material content and the truth content, united at the beginning of a work's history, set themselves apart from each other in the course of its duration, because the truth content always remains to the same ex-

tent hidden as the material content comes to the fore. More and more, therefore, the interpretation of what is striking and curious—that is, the material content—becomes a prerequisite for any later critic. (SW, 1:297)

The necessary and evolving interrelation of truth content and material content—the former ultimately arising from the volatilization of the latter, as the text's manifest historical content is mined for its philosophical import—points to the radical mutation of traditional metaphysical dualism in Benjamin's thinking. The material content, the vast bulk of the text, forms over time a shield that the critic must work through if he or she is to isolate and free the increasingly recessive truth of the work. Benjamin compares the relationship of hidden truth and manifest content to a palimpsest, "whose faded text is covered over by the lineaments of a more powerful script which refers to that text" (SW, 1:298). The preliminary task of the critic thus becomes the penetration of material content. Benjamin distinguishes two divergent critical activities: commentary, which treats the text's material content, and critique, which seeks truth. At its most basic, commentary is the philological groundwork that sets up provisional boundary markers, defines elements, and applies concepts. Beyond the explication of certain presentational elements in a text, however, commentary must elucidate and render transparent those elements of the presentation that overshadow and conceal its truth. It is a preliminary activity in the sense that it prepares the work of art for the more fundamental activity of critique, the discovery and application of its truth: "If, to use a simile, one views the growing work as the flaming pyre, then the commentator stands before it like the chemist, the critic like the alchemist. Whereas, for the former, wood and ash remain the sole objects of his analysis, for the latter only the flame itself preserves an enigma: that of what is alive. Thus, the critic inquires into the truth, whose living flame burns on over the heavy logs of what is past and the light ashes of what has been experienced" (SW, 1:298). Evoked here is the work after its commentary; it has been reduced to rubble as the critic, in his function of commentator, has, like the chemist, separated out its component parts, reducing to ash what is not of the essence. The critic as practitioner of critique is witness to an ineffable truth freed from, indeed *emanating* from, what had previously veiled it. History, that which has been, and the experience of history, its abysmal influence on the present, are taken up and consumed in the living flame of the artwork, while the essence of a purer experience, reflected in the language of the text, breaks free from its entanglement in that text's material content, as from a chthonic element. Commentary frees the truth content of literature not merely through explication but by annihilating that which traps and disguises it; in this violent liberation of truth from "baser metals," the commentator brings about a redemption of fallen language. Benjamin's book on the *Trauerspiel*, written two years later, further develops this metaphorical construction of the relationship of truth and material content, portraying criticism as "the mortification of works." The reduction of the text to a ruin, to the "torso of a symbol," necessarily precedes the discovery of truth: "The object of philosophical criticism is to show that the function of artistic form is as follows: to make historical content, such as provides the basis of every important work of art, into philosophical truth. This transformation [*Umbildung*] of material content into truth content makes the decrease in effectiveness, whereby the attraction of earlier charms diminishes decade by decade, into the basis for a rebirth, in which all ephemeral beauty is completely stripped off, and the work stands as a ruin" (OGT, 182). Only an "annihilating criticism" (SW, 1:293), one that intimately transforms its object and, through mortification of the obsolete historical, turns it into an origin—only such philosophical deconstruction of the function of form, stripping away the glitter—will find its way to truth.

The idea of purgation—clearing out, blasting apart, burning away—plays a leading role in Benjamin's criticism. He consistently couples the quest for truth with the project of sublating and mastering the banal and creaturely. Scholem was the first to point to the uncanny destructive tendency in Benjamin's work, which he convincingly links to his friend's revolutionary messianism. Benjamin's thought is from the outset nihilistic, in the Nietzschean sense of "divine nihilism" (which has a creative dimension). But the concept of destruction here derives not only from theological sources; there is also Benjamin's animus against bourgeois society, which predates by more than a decade his shift to Marxism. If bourgeois self-understanding develops around a series of culturally specific images (of the bourgeoisie itself and its relation to its environment), then genuine political change, in Benjamin's view, necessitates the displacement and eventual shattering of these icons.

With the Goethe essay complete—Benjamin hoped to publish it in the second issue of *Angelus Novus*—he turned in spring 1922 to other projects. Although no text survives, he asserted repeatedly that his most important work at this juncture remained the introduction to Fritz Heinle's writings. He could even claim that the "engagement with Heinle's poetry and life" would be in the "foreground" of his concerns for some time to come. He worked assiduously, for example, to situate Heinle's poetry within a context that reached from classical lyric to the matriarchal theories of the contemporary vitalist philosopher Ludwig Klages. Only remnants of Heinle's poetry survive today, and opinion as to its quality, as we noted, is mixed. Benjamin himself had the only complete copies, and they were lost, along with a number of Benjamin's own writings, when the contents of his Berlin apartment were seized by the Gestapo. Other friends and contemporaries are of little help here, because Benjamin maintained a cultlike veil around the poems themselves. Werner Kraft recalls an evening in Grunewald in the early 1920s during which Benjamin "ecstatically" recited several of Heinle's sonnets, but the very mode of Benjamin's presentation made it impossible to understand the poem itself. Kraft rightly interpreted this entry into the inner sanctum as a mark of particular respect and confidence, but when he asked Benjamin for copies of the poems to read for himself, he received a flat refusal.[55]

Benjamin also devoted scrupulous attention to details of the Baudelaire volume in production, making endless suggestions for typography, layout, and binding, and repeatedly urging Weissbach to advertise widely. As part of an effort to publicize the forthcoming volume, Benjamin participated in an evening program dedicated to Baudelaire at the Reuss und Pollack bookshop on Berlin's Kurfürstendamm on March 15, 1922, delivering a talk on the poet and reading from his own translations. Although he appears to have spoken from memory or perhaps from notes, two brief texts, "Baudelaire II" and "Baudelaire III," found much later among his papers (see SW, 1:361–362), likely represent preliminary versions of his remarks. Both of these texts focus on binary relations within Baudelaire's works and "view of things." Much of "Baudelaire III" fixes on the chiastic relations between Baudelaire's key terms *spleen* and *ideal*. Benjamin argues that spleen is never merely a generalized melancholy but has its source in a "fatally foundering, doomed flight toward the ideal," while the ideal, in its turn, rises from a ground of spleen: "It is images of melancholy that kindle the spiritual most brightly." This reversal, Benjamin is at pains to point out, takes place not in the realm of morality but in that of perception: "What speaks to us in his poetry is not the reprehensible confusion of [moral] judgment but the permissible reversal of perception." If the central motifs of this reading are still grounded in categories through which Baudelaire had traditionally been received, "Baudelaire II" breaks new ground and anticipates leading motifs of Benjamin's work in the 1930s. In that short text he presents Baudelaire as a privileged reader of a special body of photographic work: time itself is portrayed as a photographer who captures the "essence of things" on a photographic plate. These plates, of course, are negatives, and "no one can deduce from the negative . . . the true essence of things as they really are." In a remarkable attempt to evoke the originality of Baudelaire's achievement, Benjamin attributes to him not the ability to develop such a negative, but rather a "presentiment of its real picture. And from this presentiment speaks the negative of essence in all his poems." Thus Baudelaire's vision deep into the nature of things in a poem such as "Le soleil," his figuration of history as a multiple exposure in "Le cygne," and his fundamental sense for the negative—as the transient and always irreversible—in "Une charogne." And Benjamin finds in Baudelaire a capability analogous to the one he attributes to Kafka in his 1934 essay on the latter: an intimate knowledge of the soul's "mythical prehistory." It is the experience of knowledge as primordial guilt that exposes the nature of the negative to Baudelaire's "infinite mental efforts" and gives him his superior understanding of redemption.

In a period notable for the paucity of surviving correspondence, the letters to Weissbach—some importunate, some aggrieved—are practically the only direct record we have of Benjamin's activities in Berlin during the first half of 1922. The indirect evidence, though, is fascinating. Still basically grounded in the world of the Romantics, Benjamin was beginning to breathe the air of a significantly different world, that of the European avant-garde. In Switzerland, Hugo Ball had introduced him to the filmmaker Hans Richter, and Dora Benjamin and Richter's first wife, Elisabeth Richter-Gabo, had become close friends. Formerly a marginal figure among the Zurich Dadaists, Richter by late 1921 had begun to emerge as a catalyst for new directions in advanced art in Berlin. During the following year, through Richter, Benjamin gradually came to know a remarkable group of artists then active in the city. This loose, international affiliation included the former Dadaists Richter, Hannah Höch, and Raoul Hausmann; the constructivists László Moholy-Nagy and El Lissitzky; the young architects Mies van der Rohe and Ludwig Hilberseimer; and such local artists as Gert Caden, Erich Buchholz, and Werner Graeff. Frequent visitors included Theo van Doesburg, who brought with him the ideas circulating among the de Stijl group in Holland, Tristan Tzara, Hans Arp, and Kurt Schwitters. The group met frequently, primarily in Richter's studio at Eschenstraße 7 in Berlin-Friedenau, but also in the studios of Caden and Moholy-Nagy, and in a series of Berlin cafés; debates raged daily regarding the proper direction for a new European art and for new social forms with this art as their base. Late in 1921 Moholy-Nagy, Hausmann, and Arp had published, together with the Russian artist Ivan Puni, "A Call for Elementarist Art," a declaration of a new art developed from possibilities internal to artistic materials and procedures and not from individual creative genius. Building on this basis, the Berlin group gradually agreed upon a set of common principles. Gert Caden has left an account of the central ideas of the group as they were propounded by Richter, Lissitzky, van Doesburg, and Moholy-Nagy: "Not the personal 'line'—what anyone could interpret subjectively—is our goal, but rather the work with objective elements: circle, cone, sphere, cube, cylinder, etc. These elements cannot be objectified further. . . . Thus a dynamic-constructive system of force is created in space, a system of innermost lawfulness and greatest tension.[56] In July 1922 Moholy-Nagy published the seminal essay "Production-Reproduction" in the journal *De Stijl*; this essay explores the relationship between the new art, a new human sensorium that might arise from contact with it, and a new, liberated society that was the ultimate aim of cultural production. With shared positions in place, Richter, van Doesburg, Hausmann, Moholy-Nagy, Schwitters, Graeff, and Lissitzky attended the founding meeting of the Constructivist International, which met on September 25, 1922, in Weimar. At this meeting, vehement disagreements over political orientation seem to have taken place. Moholy-Nagy, with the support of his Hungarian colleagues Alfréd Kemény and Ernő Kállai, advocated a Communist line, with the requirement of the artist's ultimate fidelity to the proletariat. Faced with intractable opposition, Moholy-Nagy and his allies broke away from the main group; Moholy-Nagy, in fact, soon moved to Weimar and ceased to play a role in the discussions in Berlin. Richter, however, with significant input from Lissitzky, Graeff, and Mies, went on to found the journal *G: Zeitschrift für elementare Gestaltung,* one of a number of little magazines—including Corbusier's *Esprit Nouveau,* van Doesburg's *De Stijl,* and Lissitzky's *Vesch*—attempting to define the new direction, which was a fusion of Dadaism and proto-Surrealism within a rigorous framework supplied by constructivism. With the publication of *G* beginning in 1923, the group of artists meeting in Berlin in the early twenties who had established this new direction took on the retrospective designation "G group."[57]

Walter Benjamin and Ernst Schoen were present at many of these discussions; one can imagine them listening and absorbing rather than contributing to ideas that must have seemed for the most part new and contrary to their instincts. When *G* began to appear, both Schoen and Dora Benjamin were credited as contributing editors, while Benjamin himself appears as translator of Tzara's essay "Photography from the Verso." It would be hard to overestimate the importance of this encounter with the avant-garde for Walter Benjamin's subsequent thought and writings. Reverberations from the G group did not appear immediately in his work, but, beginning with the early notations toward his montage book *One-Way Street* in 1923, Benjamin's reconfiguration of central tenets of the G group emerges with increasing definition. Many of his most famous pronouncements in the 1930s, and the essay "The Work of Art in the Age of Its Technological Reproducibility" in particular, are late manifestations of the interest in technology and the historicity of the human sensorium that began to develop in 1922.[58]

By early summer of that year, Benjamin was anxious to see some sign from Weissbach that *Angelus Novus* would appear. He asked him in late June to "set the projected birthday" of *Angelus Novus* by paying his annual editorial salary of 3,200 marks; receiving no reply, he traveled to Heidelberg on July 21, at least in part to negotiate directly with his publisher. Upon his return to Berlin some weeks later, he wrote to Scholem and to Rang announcing the death throes of *Angelus Novus*, whose "life on earth was sputtering out." Weissbach had again announced a "temporary" cessation of all work on the project, but it was by now obvious to Benjamin that the journal would never appear. He made the best of the situation, however, telling both correspondents that the decision had restored "my old freedom of choice" and provided him with additional clarity regarding his academic prospects (C, 200).

In the fall of 1922 Benjamin's attention—and that of his friends—was increasingly claimed by the rapidly deteriorating economic situation in Germany. Erich Gutkind was forced to become a traveling salesman, hawking margarine throughout the country. Benjamin entered once again into painful negotiations with his father regarding a living allowance. And he stepped up his efforts to generate an income by speculating on the used book market, buying cheaply in one place—often in the northern reaches of the city—and selling at a profit in Berlin's still relatively prosperous west end. He reported to Scholem that he had bought one small book in Heidelberg for 35 marks and resold it for 600 in Berlin. By October, however, the tensions with his parents had become unbearable: "I am determined to put an end to my dependence on my parents, no matter what. Because of their pronounced pettiness and need for domination, it has turned into a torture devouring all the energy I have to work and all my joy in life" (C, 201–202). The situation was dangerous enough that Dora's father traveled to Berlin from Vienna in order to serve as mediator. In the course of heated exchanges, Benjamin's father insisted on a position in a bank for his son. However little sympathy one can muster for a thirty-year-old husband and father who maintains nearly total financial dependence on his elderly parents, the notion of Walter Benjamin's serving as a functionary in a bank surely casts doubt on Emil Benjamin's ability to judge his own son. It is not just that Benjamin's genius would have been wasted, but that Benjamin was certainly incapable of functioning in the highly regimented and insular world of a financial institution. He demonstrated his absolute lack of business sense during negotiations with his parents when he pronounced their financial condition to be "very good"—just as the German economy was spiraling downward toward the hyperinflation of 1923. The exchange rate, which had stood at 14 marks to the dollar immediately after the war, had fallen gradually to 77 marks to the dollar by July 1921, and 1922 saw a series of even more drastic declines: the rate was 191 marks to the dollar in January, 493 in midsummer, and 17,972 in January 1923.[59] A more concrete indication is the price of a loaf of bread: 2.80 marks in December 1919, 163 marks in December 1922, 69,000 marks in August 1923, and 399 billion marks at the height of the hyperinflation in December 1923.

Benjamin was not wholly intransigent in the negotiations; he professed himself willing to begin a career, but only a career that would not put an end to his academic ambitions. Dora's parents were ready to assist the young couple in the establishment of a used book store— Erich Gutkind had recently received an infusion of capital from his parents to do precisely this—but a career as a bookseller was likewise deemed unacceptable by the elder Benjamins. Emil Benjamin's "final" offer of 8,000 marks per month (which amounted to about $1.25 in 1922 dollars) in November was roundly rejected, leading to a violent break with the family. Benjamin's situation can now only be described as desperate. He was an untethered intellectual without concrete prospects of employment—in an economy that teetered on the brink of chaos. To be sure, he aspired to become known as a leading critic, but by late 1922 his published output since the days of the youth movement eight years earlier was precisely three slender articles, not counting the mandatory publication of his dissertation, and his most recent projects, including his journal and his Baudelaire translation, had very uncertain futures.

The stressful situation had taken its toll on Dora's health. She and Stefan left the villa on Delbrückstraße in late November, traveling first to her parents' home in Vienna and then, yet again, to her aunt's sanatorium in Breitenstein. In the meantime, Benjamin traveled westward during the frantic month of December, bracketing a final reconnoitering visit to Heidelberg with stays at the homes of Wolf Heinle in Göttingen and Florens Christian Rang in Braunfels. The two visits are surely symptomatic. In visiting the brother of his lost friend, Benjamin sought out one of the only remaining human contacts with the days of the youth movement—by the early 1920s, Benjamin was in touch only with Heinle, Ernst Joël, and Alfred Kurella. Wolf Heinle, however, was in rapidly failing health. Despite the bitter complaints with which Heinle showered him, Benjamin consulted the young man's physician and explored the possibility of a visit to a sanatorium in Davos; in the months to come, he sought to raise money from Heinle's friends for his medical care. And the visit to Rang was no less fraught with meaning: Rang had become his most important partner in intellectual exchange. It may be that Benjamin's dependence on the older man bespeaks a certain intellectual isolation in Berlin. Scholem remembered Rang as "irrepressible, tempestuous, and eruptive." Yet the conversation and correspondence between Benjamin and Rang, which moved freely between issues in politics, drama, literary criticism, and religion, is fully comparable in its range and depth to Benjamin's long-term exchanges with Scholem and with Adorno. As Scholem was the first to point out, Benjamin in the early 1920s "found himself in profound agreement with Rang on the highest political plane, beyond the differences in their religious and metaphysical outlook" (SF, 116).

As 1922 came to an end, Benjamin traveled once more to Heidelberg—less to make a final attempt at establishing an academic home than to reassure himself that, after years of effort, there was no place for him there. Arriving in early December, he rented rooms and continued to work on the essay on lyric poetry that was to serve as the introduction to Heinle's papers. But even this proved a torture, as he was continually disturbed by the noise of children playing next door. He quickly reestablished contact with the economist Emil Lederer, who had published "Critique of Violence" in the *Archiv für Sozialwissenschaft und Sozialpolitik*, hoping through him to obtain a direct line to Jaspers. After a presentation in Lederer's seminar, however, Benjamin was not invited back. He also returned to the sociological evenings at the home of Marianne Weber. Invited to deliver a talk, he found himself in a difficult position. He had nothing suitable prepared, so he plunged ahead with the "next best thing": an oral version of the essay on lyric poetry. Although the talk was a miserable failure, it would have made no difference. Benjamin learned that Alfred Weber had already taken on a candidate for habilitation: "a Jew," as he wrote to Scholem, "by the name of Mannheim." Benjamin had become acquainted with Karl Mannheim, whom he found a "pleasant young man," through Bloch. Mannheim's career as a towering figure in sociology was still ahead of him: he served as an adjunct faculty member at Heidelberg from 1926 to 1930, when he obtained a position in Frankfurt, and after 1933 he was in exile in England, teaching at the London School of Economics. Benjamin's instincts had been right, and Heidelberg was now, definitively, a closed chapter in his life.

[CHAPTER FIVE]

Academic Nomad

Frankfurt, Berlin, and Capri, 1923–1925

BY the beginning of 1923, Benjamin's sole hope for an academic career rested in Frankfurt, where he began the new year. In the early 1920s, Frankfurt's university was still widely regarded as new and experimental. The universities at which Benjamin had previously studied were without exception established institutions, and in some cases quite venerable. The university in Heidelberg had been founded in 1386; Freiburg in 1457; Munich in 1472 (in Ingolstadt, a small city in Bavaria; the Bavarian monarch moved the university to Munich in 1810). Even the university in Berlin, established by Wilhelm von Humboldt on the basis of the ideas of Friedrich Schleiermacher, had been founded in 1810. Frankfurt, on the other hand, had opened its doors only in 1914. And, unlike the other universities, which had been mandated by the royal families in their respective territories and subsequently financed by the state, the university at Frankfurt was made possible by donations and bequests from individuals and corporations. This intermingling of the financial and intellectual worlds was to be found nowhere else in Germany—but was wholly characteristic of Frankfurt. In his 1928 autobiographical novel *Ginster*, Siegfried Kracauer described his hometown as a "metropolis on a river between high hills. Like other cities, it used its past to encourage tourism. Imperial coronations, international congresses, and a nationwide marksman's competition took place within its walls, which had long since been transformed into public parks. . . . Some Christian and Jewish families traced their origins back to their ancestors. But even families without hereditary pedigree have made of themselves bankers with connections to Paris, London, and New York. Cultural institutions and the stock exchange are separated from one another only spatially."[1] Although its endowment had been decimated by the economic decline

following the end of the world war, the city and the state of Hessia assumed the budgetary burden, and in the 1920s the university was
widely regarded as the most dynamic and innovative institution of
higher learning in Germany. Benjamin had no contacts in any discipline within which his work might be recognized; he did, however,
have connections to several scholars working in other fields. His
great-uncle Arthur Moritz Schoenflies was an emeritus professor of
mathematics there; he had been the university's rector in 1920 and
1921 and, though now retired, remained an influential figure. But a
direct intervention on Benjamin's behalf came from an unexpected
quarter—from Gottfried Salomon-Delatour, a sociologist and adjunct
faculty member in Frankfurt whom he may have met through Erich
and Lucie Gutkind. Salomon-Delatour had been a student of Georg
Simmel, who supervised his dissertation. Through these figures, Benjamin hoped to forge an entry to the aesthetics faculty, where he now
saw his best chance for the placement of a habilitation. This attempt,
too, was plagued by misunderstanding and confusion: Salomon gave
samples of Benjamin's work—the Goethe essay and "Critique of
Violence"—not to the professor of aesthetics, Hans Cornelius, but to
Franz Schultz (1877–1950), who held the chair in German literary
history. Salomon, a sociologist, had neither personal nor professional
ties to Schultz; the professor responsible for the history of German
literature must simply have seemed to him to be the likeliest recipient of Benjamin's work. In the months to come, Benjamin made repeated attempts to follow up on Salomon's initiative through regular
approaches to Schultz—who did everything in his power to keep
Benjamin at bay.

During this brief visit to Frankfurt, Benjamin called on the distinguished philosopher of religion Franz Rosenzweig (1886–1929), who
had founded and served as director of the famous Freies Jüdisches
Lehrhaus (Free Jewish House of Learning), an institution dedicated to
Jewish adult education that drew a constellation of major intellectuals as lecturers and teachers. Earlier in 1922, the first symptoms of
amytrophic lateral sclerosis, the disease of which Rosenzweig eventually died, had manifested themselves. By the time of Benjamin's visit,
Rosenzweig was suffering from advanced paralysis and could make
only "fragments of sound," which his wife was able to translate. Much

of the discussion turned on Rosenzweig's masterwork, *The Star of Redemption*, which had appeared in 1921 and which Benjamin had read while working on the Goethe essay. Rosenzweig's text had plunged Benjamin into the sort of inner struggle that frequently marked his reception of influential ideas. Upon reading it, he had written: "I . . . [recognize] that this book necessarily exposes the impartial reader to the danger of overestimating it in terms of its structure. Or only me?" He later remarked that he was "raptly interested" in Rosenzweig's book for a while (C, 194, 494). Although broad similarities exist between Benjamin's and Rosenzweig's ontological theories of language, it is Rosenzweig's attack on the pretensions to totality in idealist philosophy in general and in Hegel in particular that left the deepest mark on Benjamin. For Rosenzweig, the singularity of the relationship between the one God and the individual person takes precedence over the assertion of any larger unity. Philosophy has not understood this. "Philosophy has to rid the world of that which is singular, and this undoing of the Aught is also the reason why it has to be idealistic. For idealism, with its denial of everything that distinguishes the singular from the all, is the tool of the philosopher's trade."[2] For all his sympathy with this polemic and with the existential urgency of Rosenzweig's thinking, Benjamin evidently harbored some reservations about his work, the "dangers" of which may have been associated in his mind with the almost Wagnerian rhapsody of the argumentation and the philosophic affirmation of liturgy and of "blood community."[3] Nevertheless, he commented to Scholem, whose antimilitarism Rosenzweig had somewhat cryptically attacked at the end of the visit, that he "would really like to see Rosenzweig again in spite of everything" (C, 205).

As Benjamin was about to leave, a friend of Rosenzweig's, the historian of law Eugen Rosenstock-Huessy, arrived; the presence of Rosenzweig and Rosenstock-Huessy in the same room may well have produced a certain consternation in Benjamin, for it would have called to mind the issue of conversion. Rosenstock-Huessy, a convert to Christianity, had exchanged a much-discussed series of letters on Jewish-Christian understanding with Rosenzweig while both were at the front during World War I. Rosenzweig himself stood at the threshold of conversion in 1913, though he was deterred by a systematic study of Judaism undertaken in order to clarify and justify his own position. But both men continued to be associated with the Patmos circle, a group of authors published by Patmos Verlag in Würzburg, of whom several of the most prominent were Jewish converts (GB, 2:301n). Benjamin seems to have had as little sympathy for religious conversion as for any other aspect of organized religion. Dora remembers his pithy reaction to an article by Karl Kraus (in his journal *Die Fackel* from November 1922) in which Kraus discussed his 1911 conversion to and subsequent renunciation of the Catholic Church. Benjamin had exclaimed that "one would have to have been Kraus, and not done this, in order to have something to say about it" (quoted in GB, 2:302n).

Benjamin returned to a Berlin beset with the worst crisis Germany had experienced since the end of the world war. The French and Belgian occupation of the Ruhr region, Germany's industrial heartland, was ongoing, with Germany's delinquency in reparation payments announced as the justification. The government in Berlin called for a general strike, and this, coupled with the already crippling loss of economic production in the region, precipitated a deep economic crisis. Benjamin was moved to some of his most emphatic political pronouncements of the 1920s. He understood the Ruhr crisis not just as a "horrible economic situation" but as a "spiritual infection" (GB, 2:305). Following the example of Rang, who was busy producing and soliciting essays and publicity in support of the German government, Benjamin encouraged friends and acquaintances to take public stands and to organize intellectuals. He was well aware—despite his distrust of parliamentary democracy—that Germany was in need of more citizens like Rang, citizens who, as he wrote to Rang himself, "do not allow their gaze into the interior of political things to become clouded, and who maintain their calm without becoming *Realpolitiker*" (GB, 2:305).

The combination of social unrest and his own professional uncertainty plunged Benjamin into a profound depression in the early months of 1923. In the first week of January, he again joined the family at the sanatorium in Breitenstein, where he, Dora, and four-year-old Stefan all lived in one room for the better part of six weeks. His letters from these weeks are marked by a hopelessness and sense of

isolation that was exacerbated by the snow that seemed to fall incessantly: "I really have nothing good to report about myself. . . . I will
still write my habilitation thesis and, after further vain efforts, will
have to trouble myself with a career neither in journalism nor in academics" (C, 205–206). His estimation of his own position was hardly
helped by reports of Wolf Heinle's rapidly deteriorating condition.
Benjamin continued to raise money in support of a stay for Heinle in
a Swiss sanatorium, despite his knowledge that the situation was
"hopeless" (GB, 2:309). Wolf Heinle's death on February 1 from com-
plications arising from advanced tuberculosis plunged Benjamin even
further into despair, a dark mood akin to what he had felt after Fritz
Heinle's suicide in 1914. Benjamin remembered the two brothers as
"the most beautiful young men [he] ever knew," and he felt their loss
as a loss of the "standards by which one takes the measure of one's
own life." He felt that, if anyone were seeking "a thinking that is not
sophistic, a production that is not reproduction, a practice that is
without calculation," he could find his model in the Heinles (C, 206–
207). This sense of loss was compounded by the increasing certainty
of Scholem's departure for Palestine.

As would so often be the case in the course of his life, there emerged
from the deep trough of Benjamin's depression—"adversities . . . beset
me from all sides like wolves and I do not know how to keep them at
bay"—one of his finest works. His travels in Germany, he wrote to
Rang, had confronted him with the national "destiny that is now,
overwhelmingly and perniciously, making itself felt. Of course, these
last days of traveling through Germany have again brought me to
the brink of despair and let me peer into the abyss" (C, 206–207). The
newfound willingness to comment on contemporary social, political,
and economic issues—an attitudinal shift influenced significantly by
Siegfried Kracauer, whom Benjamin met at the end of 1922 or in the
course of 1923[4]—was accompanied by a new reading program, with a
particular focus on collections of aphorisms. There was a rereading of
Nietzsche's aphorisms, and he made a first acquaintance with Hugo
von Hofmannsthal's *Buch der Freunde* (Book of Friends; 1922). Drawing on his own accounts of the crisis in various of his letters, Benjamin
in the course of the year then set down first drafts of a series of short
prose pieces, pieces that would eventually be incorporated into his

inaugural montage book, *One-Way Street*. The first such cycle of short pieces was an analysis of the human implications of the economic crisis, an analysis that bore the working title "Journey through the German Inflation." Later in the year, Benjamin would solemnly present this cycle, in the form of a scroll, as a parting gift to Scholem upon his emigration to Palestine—which gives us an indication of the importance attributed to these first attempts at the short prose form that he would eventually call, after an earlier usage of the term by Stefan George,[5] the "figure of thought" *(Denkbild)*. The short but remarkably complex "Journey through the German Inflation" was published in *One-Way Street* in 1928 under the title "Imperial Panorama." It is characteristic of Benjamin that his analysis of an economic situation and its political implications focuses neither upon economics nor upon politics but upon the effect of this situation on the human perceptual and cognitive capacities: the condition of "naked misery" itself offers resistance to human attempts to comprehend it. "Mass instincts have become confused and estranged from life . . . [, and] society's attachment to its familiar and long-since forfeited life is so rigid as to nullify the genuinely human application of intellect, forethought, even in dire peril. . . . The people cooped up in this country no longer discern the contours of human personality. Every free man appears to them as an eccentric. . . . All things . . . are losing their intrinsic character, while ambiguity displaces authenticity" (SW, 1:451–454). "Imperial Panorama" of course predates Benjamin's intensive engagement with Marxism, but the outlines of a fundamental position in his later thought are discernible here: the conviction that social change must be predicated on the raising to consciousness of the conditions that actually obtain. He was convinced, moreover, that those conditions are currently accessible only in distorted, veiled form.[6] As the fragmentary "Capitalism as Religion" of 1921 had argued, the debasement of the human sensory and cognitive capacities is an operative feature in the maintenance of the power of capital.

Benjamin returned alone from Breitenstein to Berlin in mid-February, but not without stopping first at Heidelberg in order to retrieve the manuscript of *Angelus Novus* from Richard Weissbach. This marked the end of Benjamin's first attempt to found a journal; he never sought another publisher for *Angelus Novus*, a decision undoubtedly influenced by the desperate economic outlook in 1923. With an editorial career—and its possibility of support—cut off, Benjamin noted wistfully that the Gutkinds were able to subsist on the earnings from their bookstore. He, too, longed for a "view onto terra firma" (GB, 2:320), a solid footing that would allow him to realize his "fondest wish": "to be able to give up the apartment at my parents' house" (C, 206). And for Benjamin in early 1923, the only ground he could now imagine under his feet was that of the university. By early March, he was back in Frankfurt, attending with unusual diligence to the academic politics that necessarily went with an attempt at habilitation. In fact, with the Goethe essay behind him, Benjamin was already embarked on a broad-scale program of research for his next project, a study of the Baroque dramatic form known as the *Trauerspiel*—the "play of mourning." Arising in the sixteenth century, the *Trauerspiel* flourished in seventeenth-century Germany; its principal authors included Andreas Gryphius and Daniel Casper von Lohenstein. Although the form was loosely derived from classical tragedy, the fall of its protagonist occasions not the elevated pathos of the tragic protagonist's struggle against his or her fate, but a kind of spectacle of sorrow; Benjamin himself would later describe the play of mourning as "the play before those who mourn." At this stage of the project, Benjamin could not have been certain whether he was working on his habilitation thesis or on an independent scholarly project: he still maintained the hope that Schultz would accept the Goethe essay as his thesis. But it was evidently Schultz himself who first suggested that Benjamin might productively engage the Baroque drama.[7] Although there were stirrings of a revived interest in the *Trauerspiel* by the early 1920s, Baroque drama was still widely disparaged at the time, and the *Trauerspiel* considered a debased, aesthetically vulgar genre. Given his preference for the marginal and apparently inconsequential, not to mention his own suggestive meditations on this Baroque genre some years back,[8] the *Trauerspiel* was bait to which Benjamin could not but rise. Much of his reading in the early months of the year was thus related to his work on the *Trauerspiel* and was marked by the usual admixture of literature, philosophy, theology, and politics. Aside from comprehensive reading of the dramas themselves, he studied the classical scholar Hermann Usener's widely influential treatise on

the naming of the gods; a new translation of the New Testament by
Leander and Carl von Eß; the conservative political theorist Carl
Schmitt's *Political Theology*; and the nineteenth-century realist Carl
Ferdinand Meyer's historical novel *Jürg Jenatsch*, whose protagonist is
based on a sixteenth-century pastor and politician of that name. By
the middle of April, Benjamin could report that he had "fixed" the
central concepts of his analysis of the Baroque drama.

After a week of visits and conversations with his allies and pro-
spective advisors in Frankfurt, Benjamin traveled, at Rang's invitation, to the small city of Gießen in the northern reaches of the state of
Hessen. There, on March 12, he attended the first meeting of the
"Frankfurt Circle," an interfaith group drawn together by Rang and
Martin Buber that included Jews, Catholics, and a range of Protestants
from Quakers to Lutherans. The discussions in Gießen centered on
the possibility, under current conditions, of a political revival informed by religious principles.[9] It was clearly important to Rang to
bring Benjamin and Buber together at this meeting; as Scholem remembers, these two figures, who treated each other with a reserve
that frequently gave way to suspicion, represented for Rang "incarna-
tions of authentic Jewishness" (SF, 116). Benjamin was deeply impressed by the gathering: "an unsuspected side of Germany sprang
before my eyes" (GB, 2:322). Even if we discount some part of his enthusiasm because he was addressing Rang, an organizer of the meeting, his attendance in Gießen must nonetheless be taken seriously.
Walter Benjamin's theological politics made him, by any account, a
central figure in the religious revival that swept Germany in the years
following World War I. Moreover, his fascination with the attempts by
Rang, Buber, Rosenzweig and others to work toward a new German
society conceived as a tolerant commingling of religious faiths certainly colored his own increasing politicization in the early 1920s.
The Frankfurt Circle was hardly the first such group at whose edges
Benjamin had lingered: he knew of the work of the Forte circle through
Erich Gutkind, and his remarks on Rosenstock-Huessy show that he
was fully conversant with the Patmos circle. The most emphatic state-
ment of his engagement, though, is the "Response" he contributed to
Rang's call for the renewing of dialogue between France, Belgium, and
Germany, issued in his pamphlet *Deutsche Bauhütte: Ein Wort an*

uns Deutsche über mögliche Gerechtigkeit gegen Belgien und Frankreich und zur Philosophie der Politik (German Masons' Guild: a Word to Us Germans on the Possibility of Justice toward Belgium and France, and on the Philosophy of Politics). Besides Benjamin and Buber, both the Baptist journalist, novelist, and dramatist Alfons Paquet, who argued for a pacifist Germany as a mediator between east and west, and the Catholic philosopher of religion and psychotherapist Ernst Michel contributed commentaries. After a few observations on the form of the "response" that are characteristic in their problematicization of the genre of the political pamphlet itself—and thus reminiscent of the early pages of "Goethe's Elective Affinities"— Benjamin's "Response" claims for Rang's tract a revelatory potential. "For this text acknowledges the intellectual borders between peoples to the same extent that it condemns their closure. . . . [These lines] confirm that the truth, even in politics, is unambiguous but not simple [*eindeutig . . . aber nicht einfach*]." As Benjamin continues to meditate on the function of truth in politics, the relays between his philosophical literary criticism and a newly focused political involvement become manifest: he argues—in terms that reflect his *own* principles—that Rang's principles emerge from the "interpenetration of ideas," and he specifies "ideas of justice, of law, of politics, of enmity, of the lie. And no lie is greater than obdurate silence" (GB, 2:374). Around this time, in a series of notes for a work on lying, he expanded on this last thought: "The lie has a constitutive relationship to speech (so that lying through silence is immoral)" (GS, 6:64). Ottilie's silence is construed in the Goethe essay as an immoral avoidance of language itself as the only home of truth; now, in 1923, passing over a political crisis in silence is understood not simply as an ethical breach, but once again as avoidance of the pure mediacy and mediating capacity of the word. For Benjamin, the drama of religious revival plays itself out not on the broad stage of politics but on the only apparently circumscribed stage of language.

Siegfried Kracauer, writing in 1922, had offered a positive evaluation of the sudden resurgence of new forms of association in response to the postwar crisis: "Whoever has lived through these times and paid attention feels in the depths of his being that an hour of reckoning has now come for the German spirit. In sleepless nights of listening and waiting one senses, very close by, the hot breath of this spirit. Now that false dreams of power have been dreamed out, now that need and suffering have burst the hard shells that threatened to suffocate it, this spirit, with a monstrous display of power, struggles toward its realization. . . . Nearly all of the innumerable movements that now tremble throughout Germany and shake it to its foundations testify, despite their apparently contradictory directions, to the desire and nature of this spirit. Youth groups that carry forward generalized human ideals or the ideas of the Germanic fraternities; communards whose values are linked to the communism of primitive Christianity; associations of the like-minded that have as their goal a renewal from within; interfaith religious groups; democratic-pacifist unions; and several efforts at popular education: all these seek the same thing, namely, to emerge from abstract ideas anchored in the ego and arrive at concrete communal forms."[10] Writing a decade later, in the essay "Experience and Poverty" of 1933, Benjamin, unsurprisingly, saw the phenomenon differently: "A generation that had gone to school in horse-drawn streetcars now stood in the open air, amid a landscape in which nothing was the same except the clouds and, at its center, in a force field of destructive torrents and explosions, the tiny, fragile human body. With this tremendous development of technology, a completely new poverty has descended on humankind. And the reverse side of this poverty is the oppressive wealth of ideas that has been spread among people, or rather has swamped them entirely—ideas that have come with the revival of astrology and the wisdom of yoga, Christian Science and chiromancy, vegetarianism and gnosis, scholasticism and spiritualism. For this is not a genuine revival but a galvanization" (SW, 2:732). If Kracauer maintains the idealist notion that "concrete communal forms" might arise as the reflection of ideas emanating from a generalized national spirit, Benjamin suggests that the unceasing profusion of this "wealth of ideas" would actually "swamp" people—and that a new experiential poverty or constructive divestiture is actually the only appropriate response to the times.

Feeling that there was nothing more to be done in Frankfurt, at least for the moment, Benjamin returned to Berlin in early April and received a pleasant surprise: the galleys for his volume of Baudelaire translations. Although he still feared that the book would appear only "according to a transcendental time scheme," he nonetheless immediately composed an announcement intended to aid in publicizing the volume: "The present cycle of poems from *Les fleurs du mal* contains a number of poems that appear for the first time in German translation. Two things will ensure a lasting place for these translations. First, that the demand for fidelity, which the translator establishes beyond dispute in his preface, is met in the most conscientious fashion. And second, that the poetic element in Baudelaire's work is comprehended in a convincing way. That the original text—and, to be sure, the first philologically correct original text to appear in Germany—accompanies every translation will be particularly welcome to all admirers of the great poet" (GB, 2:358). The literary news was not all good, however: the publisher Paul Cassirer, who had expressed admiration for "Goethe's Elective Affinities," nonetheless declined to publish the essay. Benjamin submitted it immediately to the prominent scholarly journal *Deutsche Vierteljahresschrift für Literaturwissenschaft und Geistesgeschichte* (German Quarterly for Literary Scholarship and the History of Ideas), edited by Erich Rothacker and Paul Kluckhohn; he had come to know Rothacker in Heidelberg, and hoped not only for a publishing venue but a good word addressed to Rothacker's colleague in Frankfurt, Professor Schultz. Although Rothacker wrote that the essay had left a "strong and significant impression," he was nonetheless willing to print only its first section, and then in shortened form, for he felt that the writing was inflated by many youthful excesses. In pointing to the fundamental impenetrability of the essay, and to its "rank overgrowth of reflection," Rothacker initiated a consequential line of criticism, one that would be taken up by many first-time readers of "Goethe's Elective Affinities" (quoted in GB, 2:332n). Inured to scholarly incomprehension, Benjamin could certainly have accepted an outright rejection; but he had no interest in bastardizing his work, and he communicated this to Rothacker. Rather than drop the matter, though, Rothacker patronizingly promised to enlist Schultz to "work on" Benjamin and get him to agree to this partial acceptance. This must have been the last straw for Benjamin: he withdrew the essay and enlisted Rang's help in an approach to the great Austrian writer Hugo von Hofmannsthal. In turning to Hofmannsthal, Benjamin came into contact with one of the very few intellectuals in the German-speaking world whose human interactions tended to be even more formal and complex than his own. While not negatively disposed toward Benjamin, Hofmannsthal nonetheless asked Rang to remain as intermediary, writing that "Even in these matters, every gesture has, as in a bodily encounter, its own meaning, and we don't want to 'simplify' anything or reduce it to the 'normal'" (Hofmannsthal to Rang, quoted in GB, 2:341–342n).

In early May, Benjamin returned to Frankfurt, prepared for a lengthy stay and a final, concerted effort to establish himself at the university: he evaluated his chances there as not "completely without hope," but admitted that he had no concrete evidence to support this estimation. He stayed at first with his uncle Schoenflies at Grillparzerstraße 59, but soon rented rooms of his own. His already straitened financial circumstances received a further shock from the prices in Frankfurt: "Leading a student life in an expensive city like Frankfurt is no joke nowadays" (GB, 2:334). Although he never felt comfortable in the city on the Main, the following months were busy and productive ones. He saw a great deal of Scholem, who had come to Frankfurt to use the extensive collection of Hebrew materials at the municipal library. Relations between the two old friends had never been easy in the eight years since their first encounter in Berlin; periods of real intimacy and intense intellectual exchange were punctuated by periods of silence and even recrimination, usually the result of some slight perceived by one or the other of these two prickly personalities. The months in Frankfurt were no different. Indeed, their relations were made even more difficult by yet another tempestuous scene that had taken place between Scholem and Dora in Berlin in April—one of the last eruptions of this very particular triangle.[11] Now, in Frankfurt, there were spats about missed and postponed appointments, and serious disagreements regarding the prospect of emigration to Palestine. Nevertheless, they often made their way together through the new intellectual world they found in Frankfurt. With Scholem, Benjamin renewed his contacts at the Jewish Lehrhaus, and he frequented the colony of Jewish writers and intellectuals around Agnon in Bad Homburg, a short distance away in the foothills of the Taunus Mountains.

But the two most important meetings in Frankfurt were Benjamin's alone. During the summer, he began associating with two young men who would remain among his closest intellectual partners: Siegfried Kracauer (whom he may have met some months earlier) and Theodor Adorno. After several years of architectural practice, Kracauer (1889–1966) had in 1921 joined the staff of the *Frankfurter Zeitung*, one of Germany's most prominent newspapers, as a reporter assigned to such local and regional events as exhibitions, conferences, and trade fairs. By the time Benjamin first met him—perhaps introduced by Ernst Bloch—Kracauer had established himself as the newspaper's principal writer on the role of the German intellectual in a period of cultural crisis. The essays Kracauer published in 1922 and 1923 concentrate on two issues: first, the role of classical German humanism—the German "ideal of humanity" propagated by German Idealist philosophy from Kant to Hegel—under conditions of modernization, and second, the ecumenical religious revival in the years after the war. In essays such as "Those Who Wait," "The Group as Bearer of Ideas," and "The Crisis of Science," Kracauer portrayed a cultural and philosophical tradition falling dizzyingly into crisis as its shared values were challenged. His own adherence to the values of the humanistic tradition was as much at stake here as was the more general situation of the German intellectual, but Kracauer in 1923 had no notion of any possible resolution of the crisis. Theodor Wiesengrund Adorno (1903–1969) was in 1923 a student of philosophy and sociology at the University of Frankfurt. Kracauer had been introduced to him in the last years of the war, while Adorno was still a high school student. Although Kracauer was fourteen years older, a deep friendship with strong homoerotic undertones had developed; the two young men read Kant together and talked about philosophy and music on a regular basis. The initial meeting between Benjamin and Adorno was surely arranged by Kracauer, but Adorno also attended seminars offered by Cornelius and Salomon-Delatour in 1923 and came to know Benjamin better there.

Contact with friends old and new was finally inadequate compensation for Benjamin's increasingly frustrating efforts to solidify his position academically. He attended seminars and attempted to insinuate himself into the circles of students around both Hans Cornelius and Franz Schultz. Cornelius, a professor of philosophy, enjoyed a local, rather than national, reputation for his work in Neo-Kantian

14. Siegfried Kracauer, ca. 1928 *(Deutsches Literaturarchiv Marbach)*

philosophy; but as Adorno, who later wrote his own dissertation under Cornelius's supervision, remembered, Cornelius was hardly a blinkered provincial. He was a painter, sculptor, and pianist, and a thinker known for his lack of orthodoxy.[12] For all that, Cornelius explicitly declined to sponsor Benjamin's habilitation process. Benjamin then turned his hopes briefly to Hermann August Korff. After his own habilitation thesis had been accepted by the Frankfurt faculty, Korff had begun to establish a considerable reputation as a scholar of eighteenth-century German literature with a particular interest in Goethe; the first volume of his multivolume *Spirit of the Age of Goethe* had appeared in 1923, and the entire work would soon establish him as the leading authority on German literary classicism. Korff had been under consideration for a post in Frankfurt, and Benjamin allowed himself to imagine that Korff's natural sympathy for Goethe might lead him to accept "Goethe's Elective Affinities" without revision as a habilitation thesis. But in midsummer Korff accepted a position at the university at Gießen. As Benjamin was all too well aware, this left all remaining hope pinned squarely to Schultz. And Schultz now made it unmistakably clear to Benjamin that the only path to habilitation lay through submission of a work written expressly to that end. This was in and of itself not a bad sign; Benjamin understood that Schultz simply wanted to avoid all appearance of taking extraordinary steps for a student with whom he had no prior relationship. The semester's end in August thus found Benjamin back in Berlin, his candidacy no further along than it had been at the end of 1922. The door to the academy had opened a crack, to be sure, but it seemed that it might take a groundbreaking work of literary scholarship to force it open.

By summer 1923, the chaos of the German currency was having catastrophic effects on everyday life. Benjamin wrote from Berlin at the beginning of August that "everything here conveys a miserable impression. The food shortage can compete with that experienced during the war." Streetcars ran irregularly; stores and small businesses disappeared overnight; tensions between the left and the right threatened constantly to erupt in the streets. The Benjamins' one ray of hope was Dora's being hired as private secretary to Karl von Wigand, reporter in Germany for the Hearst newspapers; her salary not only was issued by a stable source but was paid in dollars, still inflation-proof in 1923. Benjamin's commitment to his family, though, remained as tenuous as ever. After a six-month absence, he found his five-year-old son "much changed but well behaved enough" (GB, 2:346). He lived together with Dora and Stefan in their apartment in the parental home in Delbrückstraße for more than three months, but then moved, alone, into a room in a little garden house at Meierottostraße 6 in an elegant part of the city south of the Kurfürstendamm.

He worked with a certain desperation through the fall on his study of the *Trauerspiel*, impelled by the pressures of the economic crisis and the sense that the door in Frankfurt might slam shut at any moment. "I still do not know if I can do it. At all events, I am determined to complete a manuscript. Better to be chased off in disgrace

15. Theodor W. Adorno in 1924 *(Theodor W. Adorno Archiv, Frankfurt am Main)*

than to retreat." Even for Benjamin, the material on which he was working—not just the dramas themselves, but the theoretical apparatus that he was developing alongside his interpretation—was unusually difficult, and he was aware that he needed to strike the right balance between a "forcing" of the refractory material into an argument and the need to make that argument sufficiently subtle (C, 209). Of the many challenges presented by the study of a form as recondite as the Trauerspiel, he wrote to Rang on December 9,

> what has been preoccupying me is the question of the relationship of works of art to historical life. In this regard, it is a foregone conclusion for me that there is no such thing as art history. The concat-

enation of temporal occurrences, for example, does not imply only things that are causally significant for human life. Rather, without a concatenation such as development, maturity, death, and other similar categories, human life would fundamentally not exist at all. But the situation is completely different as regards the work of art. In terms of its essence, it is ahistorical [geschichtslos]. The attempt to place the work of art in the context of historical life does not open up perspectives that lead us to its innermost core. . . . The essential relationship among works of art remains intensive . . . the specific historicity of works of art is the kind that can be revealed not in "art history" but only in interpretation. For in interpretation, relationships among works of art appear that are timeless [zeitlos] yet not without historical relevance. That is to say, the same forces that become explosively and extensively temporal in the world of revelation (and this is what history is) appear concentrated [intensiv] in the silent world (and this is the world of nature and of works of art). . . . Works of art are thus defined as models of a nature that does not await the day, and thus does not await judgment day either; they are defined as models of a nature that is neither the staging ground of history nor a human domicile. (C, 224)

This is the first concerted attempt to define the methodology upon which the book on the *Trauerspiel* would be based: a criticism concerned to disclose the "innermost core" of works of art, in which what is "explosively and extensively temporal" in history appears concentrated and condensed, and thus not so much to show the embeddedness of the artwork in a certain historical moment as to create that moment in the full "now of its recognizability."

There was little good news regarding his other work, the kind of news that might have made his personal situation and work on the *Trauerspiel* easier. Even though he had the galley proofs of the Baudelaire translations in hand, he understood that a book publication might be one of the last productions of a German publishing industry that was "trickling away." Other essays that had been under consideration by editors now languished. The fate of the essay on Goethe's novel was in limbo as Rang carried out a delicate series of preparatory maneuvers with Hofmannsthal; to that end, Benjamin provided Rang a fat packet with "Goethe's Elective Affinities," "Critique of Violence," the selection of translations from Baudelaire that had been published in *The Argonaut,* and a selection of writings by the Heinle brothers for conveyance to Hofmannsthal. And the essay "The True Politician," which Benjamin had given to Buber for inclusion in an anthology, was again without a home, since Buber's project had failed to find a publisher; Benjamin now hoped to place the essay in a volume commemorating Salomon's retirement. Finally, and against all expectation, Weissbach in October published Benjamin's translations of the "Tableaux parisiens" from *Les fleurs du mal,* together with the essay "The Task of the Translator." Benjamin allowed himself to hope that the volume might establish him as an intellectual presence in Germany. But the book disappeared virtually without a trace: there were two reviews, and one of them, in the *Frankfurter Zeitung,* was very unfavorable. This came as an especially hard blow, since Siegfried Kracauer was an editor at this newspaper. Was the general verdict—the silence as well as the savage critique—justified? Werner Fuld has argued persuasively that Benjamin's translations of Baudelaire never manage to escape the orbit of Stefan George's powerful versions of the poems. Scholem himself, on first hearing Benjamin read four of his translations in 1915, took them to be George's work.[13] The silence that greeted the introduction is perhaps harder to fathom. "The Task of the Translator" remains one of the seminal statements on translation; along with the dissertation of 1919, it was the first formulation of Benjamin's pioneering theory of criticism to reach a (potentially) broad audience.

Whatever promise he may have felt in the continued high-risk achievement of his writings was effectively offset by his pessimism regarding his general situation. He saw clearly that his attempt to initiate an academic career was thwarted not just by his failure to find a sponsor but also by "manifestations of decline" that were everywhere apparent in the university system. The newspapers reported on discussions within the Prussian Ministry of Finance regarding proposals for the outright closing of five universities, including those at Frankfurt and Marbach, in response to the economic crisis. Even though protests in parliament and in the streets led to the withdrawal of the plan, the reports forced Benjamin to ask himself how he could contemplate a career as an intellectual within such "decayed forms and conditions of life?" (C, 212). In the final months of 1923, the Weimar

Republic itself came perilously close to dissolving into chaos. As inflation spiraled out of control and the cost of foodstuffs rose to unimaginable levels, public unrest spilled from the kitchen and into the street. In Berlin on November 5, anti-Semitic gangs roughed up Jewish citizens and plundered homes and businesses. And just three days later, on the evening of November 8, Adolf Hitler led some 600 brownshirts from the Bürgerbräukeller toward Odeonsplatz in Munich, hoping first to overthrow the Bavarian government and then to lead a march on Berlin. That the "beer hall putsch" failed and that Hitler was imprisoned bespoke the growing support for the republic, even in conservative Bavaria, but these events also revealed the ongoing fragility of the new Germany and the vulnerability of its Jewish citizens.

Several of Benjamin's closest friends had already left the country, hopeless as it seemed, and in mid-September Scholem carried through on his plan to emigrate to Palestine. Benjamin and those closest to him were once more moved to thoughts of emigration: "The idea of rescuing the independent and private essence of my existence, which is inalienable to me, by fleeing this demoralizing communication with what is empty, worthless, and brutal is gradually becoming self-evident to me" (C, 212). Dora was considering a life in America, while the Gutkinds again pressed for a move to Palestine. Benjamin thus steeled himself for the possibility of leaving. If his final attempt to establish a bridge to the university were to fail, he was determined to save himself "by swimming, that is, by somehow making a go of it abroad, for neither Dora nor I can endure this slow erosion of all our vitality and worldly goods much longer" (C, 209). Foreignness itself posed no problem to Benjamin, but the prospect of isolation from a European intellectual community was something to be dreaded. Benjamin was fully aware of the dangers currently associated with a role in public intellectual life for German Jews. "Only those who belong to a people are called on to speak in the most terrible moments of that people. . . . Jews should certainly not speak out" (C, 215). Why, then, given his clear insights into the increasingly untenable situation of the German Jewish intellectual, did he remain? Why could he countenance "neither the practical possibility nor the theoretical necessity" of leaving Germany for Palestine? In 1923, and then repeatedly in his correspondence with Scholem through the ensuing decade, Benjamin asserted his essential identification not with the German nation or the German people but with German culture. He confided to Rang not only that Gutkind, who was ready to emigrate, had never experienced "what is positive in the German phenomenon" but also that, as far as he himself was concerned, "circumscribed national characteristics were always central: German or French. I will never forget that I am bound to the former and how deep these ties go" (C, 214). Emigration, and the effective severing of his ties to German culture, remained for now unthinkable. Together with Gutkind and Rang, though, he plotted a temporary escape toward the south; he was neither ready nor willing to abandon Germany altogether, but he was certainly eager for a respite from the economic, political, and professional travails of this year.

At some point that fall Benjamin came to know a young man of exactly his own age who worked at the Prussian State Library—Erich Auerbach, who would become, with Benjamin himself, one of the most influential literary scholars of the twentieth century. Auerbach likewise had been born into a Berlin Jewish family and, after attaining his doctorate in the law, embarked on the study of literature, obtaining a second doctorate in 1921 with a dissertation on the novella of the early Renaissance in France and Italy. He would later build on this study in his most famous work, *Mimesis*, written in Istanbul between 1942 and 1945. Although they never became close friends, they were bound by clear intellectual ties, and Benjamin and Auerbach maintained their correspondence even through the darkest days of the 1930s.

Only at the end of the year did Benjamin's prospects improve. In late November he got to see and copy a portion of a letter from Hofmannsthal to Rang that contained by far the most encouraging reaction to his work he had ever received:

> Please don't expect me to express myself more fully about the absolutely incomparable essay by Benjamin that you had the goodness to entrust to me. I can only say that it has marked an epoch in my inner life, and that I have hardly been able to tear my thoughts, insofar as my own work does not demand all my attention, away from it.

The great beauty of the presentation, allied to such a matchless penetration into what is hidden, seems—to speak of seeming externals—miraculous to me—this beauty arises from a wholly secure and pure thought, of a kind that has few equals. If this man is younger, or indeed much younger than I, then I am struck forcibly by his maturity. (Hofmannsthal to Rang, November 20, 1923, quoted in GB, 2:379–380n)

Benjamin's essay thus found a home in Hofmannsthal's journal, *Neue Deutsche Beiträge,* where it appeared in two parts in the issues of April 1924 and January 1925. The recognition of his talent that Hofmannsthal provided remained vital to Benjamin for many years, both psychologically and materially (he would draw on it for connections to presses and journals and for recommendations to fellow writers). The particular confirmation Benjamin found in Hofmannsthal as a reader of his work corresponds exactly to those qualities that for him distinguished Hofmannsthal as a writer, in particular his consciousness of the secret life of language. In January 1924, as we have mentioned, Benjamin wrote to his "new patron": "It is very important to me that you so clearly underscore the conviction guiding me in my literary endeavors and that, if I understand you correctly, you share this conviction. That is to say, the conviction that every truth has its home, its ancestral palace, in language; and that this palace is constructed out of the oldest logoi" (C, 228).

Support from this influential quarter restored Benjamin's confidence on a wide front, including his hopes for the habilitation; he even managed to extract a small annual subvention from his parents by producing his copy of Hofmannsthal's letter. And the news that his Swiss publisher's warehouse had burned to the ground, taking with it all but a few copies of his dissertation, seems not to have dealt him a setback (he could later joke about it with Scholem, suggesting that his friend corner an emerging market by purchasing the remaining thirty-seven copies). The early months of 1924 were devoted to intensive labors on the study of the *Trauerspiel.* While he admitted to Rang that the textual basis for his work was "remarkably—indeed uncannily—narrow," he nonetheless approached his materials with an "eccentric meticulousness": he had selected and arranged more than 600 quotations from his primary sources alone. And his reading was ranging far beyond the seventeenth century. He consulted Rang regarding the theory of Attic tragedy; he returned to Nietzsche's *Birth of Tragedy*; he delved into the "Fragments from the Estate of a Young Physicist" by the early Romantic natural scientist and philosopher Johann Wilhelm Ritter, where he found confirmation of his conviction that the graphic element of script itself, not just the human word, bore revelatory elements within it; and he continued his reading in Protestant theology and political theory. In the former field, Adolf von Harnack's three-volume history of Christian dogma was his guide, but Karl Barth's commentary, *The Epistle to the Romans*, the second, radicalized edition of which had appeared in 1922, would likely have constituted an intertext for the *Trauerspiel*, indirectly informing his understanding of the unmoored "existential" significance of the Reformation.[14] In political theory, he supplemented his knowledge of anarchism and Judeo-Christian political theology by rereading Carl Schmitt's *Political Theology*. By February he had produced an exposé of the entire study—which is now unfortunately lost. And by March he was planning to begin the volume with an ambitious theoretical introduction and follow it with three chapters: "On History in the Mirror of the *Trauerspiel*," "On the Occult Concept of Melancholy in the Sixteenth and Seventeenth Centuries," and "On the Nature of Allegory and Allegorical Art Forms" (C, 238).

The work slowed as spring arrived and Benjamin's anticipation of a trip south came to dominate his days. He was determined to escape the "pernicious influence of the atmosphere here" and its resultant "constraints" (C, 236); perhaps the most telling indication of this determination was his willingness to sacrifice parts of his library in order to finance the trip. He thus prepared for the journey, and the external and internal changes it could bring, with a kind of "exaltation": with Dora's help, he undertook a regimen of fasting and exercise (C, 257). Already in late fall 1923, he and Erich Gutkind had begun to plan a trip to the island of Capri, and by early 1924 a small group was committed to the enterprise: Benjamin, Emma and Florens Christian Rang, Lucie and Erich Gutkind, and the Gutkinds' Hebrew teacher, Dov Flattau. As the plans took on firmer contours, Benjamin's letters began to be inflected by the discourse of the "south" that had formed a key element of the German cultural heritage since at least the eighteenth century. Italy embodied what Germany seemed to lack: if Germany was gray, rainy, and repressed, Italy was sunny, hedonistic, and liberated. An eighteenth-century handbook on Italy carried by many Germans on their upper-middle-class *Bildungsreise* (educational journey) had described the land in the south in glowing terms: "A traveler sensitive enough to be moved by the beauties in which nature in Italy is so rich—they far exceed those of the arts—will encounter a number of scenes of the most varied sort."[15] Here, as in so many things, Goethe captured the essence of this notion of a free natural beauty that could be made to correspond to a new human interiority.

> Do you know the land where the lemon trees blossom?
> Among dark leaves the golden oranges glow.
> A gentle breeze from blue skies drifts.
> The myrtle is still, and the laurel stands high.
> Do you know it well?
> There, there
> would I go with you, my beloved!

Yet Italy was a more complex idea in the German imagination than this apotheosis of nature might suggest; after the publication of Johann Joachim Winckelmann's *History of the Art of Antiquity* in 1764, a firsthand experience of the remains of classical culture and the art of the Renaissance became all but obligatory for the cultured upper middle classes. It is this combination of idealized nature and re-discovery of an acme of art that forms the background to the most famous account of the experience of Italy, Goethe's *Italian Journey*. Published in 1816–1817, thirty years after the journey itself, this text reconstructs the Italian experience from letters and diary notations, and it reconstructs it as a rebirth, a turning point at which Goethe for the first time finds himself in accord with his inmost self. "At last, I have arrived in the First City of the world!" he writes from Rome on November 1, 1786. "Now I have arrived, I have calmed down and feel as if I had found a peace that will last for my whole life. Because, if I may say so, as soon as one sees with one's own eyes the whole which one had hitherto known only in fragments and chaotically, a new life begins."[16] Even before he departed for Capri, Benjamin had already mapped the place in his imagination. The escape to the island was his "most vital" undertaking; he was longing for "more spacious and freer surroundings" (C, 236). It should thus come as no surprise that he considered the time on Capri to be utterly transformative. Looking back on his trip in December 1924, he remarked that "people in Berlin are agreed that there is a conspicuous change in me" (C, 257).

Benjamin was the first member of the little group to arrive, having made stops in Genoa, Pisa, and Naples. Years later, in 1931, he remembered the panic that had gripped him at the thought of being prevented from escaping Germany. He was walking along Unter den Linden in April 1924 when he saw a headline in the evening paper: "Ban on Foreign Travel." The government had announced that, in order to deal with the ongoing currency crisis, Germans would be allowed to travel abroad only if they could deposit a large sum of money to be reclaimed on their return. The prohibition was scheduled to take effect in three days' time, and Benjamin, quite unable to muster the required deposit, could only throw his things together and depart headlong, without his friends—and without the full amount of money he had hoped to have on hand to cover his expenses.[17] He arrived on Capri on April 9 or 10 and settled into the Pension Gaudeamus, where his friends joined him. The entire group soon moved into the upper floor of a private home at Via Sopramonte 18, not far from La Piazzetta, the small square that was the social center of the village of Capri. The apartment had a "magnificent south-facing balcony with a view of the sea and, above all, a promenade on the roof—which, to a Jewish city-dweller's way of thinking, has something of the large landed estate about it" (GB, 2:456).

Benjamin was immediately struck by the "prodigious beauty" of the island, by the "unprecedented splendor" of its vegetation and its whitewashed villas set against an extraordinary azure sea; he spoke repeatedly—he with his dread of nature—of the "healing power of the countryside" (GB, 2:446, 449, 462). The island had been a favored retreat since Roman times, but its status as a haven for European intellectuals dates from the publication of the book *Discovery of the Blue Grotto on the Isle of Capri* by the German painter and writer August Kopisch, who had rediscovered the grotto in 1826. In the twentieth century, Graham Greene, Maxim Gorky, and Norman Douglas all owned homes on the island. In 1924, though, the island was fairly swarming with German intellectuals—what Benjamin called an "itinerant intellectual proletariat" (GS, 3:133). On the island for part of the time he was there were Bert and Marianne Brecht; two of Brecht's friends, the set designer Caspar Neher and the director Bernhard Reich; the designer and illustrator of Stefan George's books, Melchior Lechter; and Benjamin's nemesis from afar, Friedrich Gundolf.

Some aspects of his life didn't change. He almost immediately found himself short of funds, even in a situation in which his living costs were drastically reduced. He wrote to Weissbach toward the end of April asking for help, and for once his publisher responded quickly and positively. And even in distant Italy he found things to fuel the ambivalence and trepidation he felt about a university career. He attended an international congress of philosophy associated with the celebration of the 500th anniversary of the University of Naples. The streets of the university quarter were a cacophony of partying students, yet the meeting rooms for the congress felt isolated and deserted. "As far as I am concerned," he wrote to Scholem, "the entire affair was not necessary to convince me that philosophers are paid the worst because they are the most superfluous lackeys of the international bourgeoisie. What I had not seen before was that they everywhere display their inferiority with such dignified shabbiness." Italy's leading philosopher, Benedetto Croce, a member of the Naples faculty, remained at a "conspicuous distance" from the event (C, 240). Benjamin himself endured one day and then fled, first to Vesuvius and Pompeii and then for the first of many visits to the National Museum in Naples, with its incomparable collection of antiquities. The city's streets and neighborhoods—the "rhythm of its life"— overpowered Benjamin again and again, as they had so many generations of visitors.

By early May he felt settled enough to begin the actual composition of his study of the *Trauerspiel*. The writing, which he thought would go quickly because of the way he had assembled his quotations, instead proceeded slowly, and sometimes agonizingly so. For one thing, the habilitation thesis was not his only task: he had to earn his bread somehow, and a recent acquaintance in Berlin had begun to provide him with work. Franz Hessel (1880–1941), whom Benjamin had met through their mutual friend Charlotte Wolff, was twelve years older than Benjamin, but from a very similar milieu. In the early 1920s Hessel's life as a well-off literatus had come to an end in much the same way as had Benjamin's: his family lost much of their considerable fortune in the economic disaster, and Hessel was forced to support himself. He began to write cultural commentary for the feuilleton section of the German newspapers and, sometime before 1923, became an editor at Rowohlt Verlag, where he had been working as publisher's reader since 1919. In August 1924 he published four of Benjamin's Baudelaire translations in the Rowohlt journal *Vers und Prosa*, which he edited.[18] One of his first major projects for this publisher was a forty-four-volume translation of Honoré de Balzac's complete works; Hessel assigned one of these volumes, the novel *Ursule Mirouet*, to his acquaintance Benjamin. No little part of Benjamin's time on Capri was given over to this assignment.

Despite the pressures of work, for Benjamin the island was an idyll of *luxe, calme, et volupté*. It had been ages since he had experienced such tranquility—only the early days in Switzerland came close. For the first time in years, he was able to appease his insatiable desire for travel, punctuating his days on the island with systematic exploration of the mainland. His own little group made several excursions, and Benjamin himself took every opportunity to accompany visitors—Alfred Sohn-Rethel, Salomon-Delatour and his wife, and, later in the summer, the Blochs—to the region around Naples, visiting Pompeii, Salerno, Ravello, Pozzuoli, and the entire Amalfi coast. Of the many encounters with classical antiquity during these months, it was the visit to the temples at Paestum that was "unequaled. I was alone when I saw them on an August day in the malaria season, when people avoid the area. The cliché I had associated with the words 'Greek temple' on the basis of pictures I had seen does not even come close to the reality. . . . The narrow, burning blue ribbon of the sea is visible not that far from the temples. . . . All three . . . even now exhibit almost glaring, perceptible differences because of their vitality" (C, 249–250). When he remained on the island, he was able to spend a few hours each day reading, writing, and talking in the local watering hole, Zum Kater Hidigeigei (Tomcat Hidigeigei)—about which Benjamin found nothing unpleasant "except for its name" (C, 242). The size of the German intellectual community ensured that there was always

16. Asja Lacis (*Theodor W. Adorno Archiv, Frankfurt am Main*)

someone with whom to talk. His conversational partners ranged from the leftist Reich to the conservative Lechter.

By mid-June Benjamin had made the acquaintance of someone destined to change his life. Asja Lacis (1891–1979) was a Latvian who, after study in Moscow and St. Petersburg, founded a proletarian children's theater at Orjol in central Russia and later directed plays at a workers' theater in Riga. In Berlin in 1922 she had come into contact with the circle around Brecht and formed a relationship with the director and theater critic Bernhard Reich; Lacis and Reich had followed Brecht to Munich in the fall of 1923, where she worked as assistant director for Brecht's production of his *The Life of Edward II of England* at the Kammerspiele.[19] At Easter 1924, after the play's premiere, she and Reich had taken her small daughter, Daga, to Capri so that she could recover from a lung infection; Reich left the island for work in Paris soon after Benjamin's arrival. In the memoir she wrote many years later, Lacis describes her first encounter with Benjamin.

I often went shopping with Daga around the Piazza. One day I wanted to buy some almonds in a store; I didn't know the word for almonds in Italian, and the salesman didn't understand what I wanted from him. Next to me stood a gentleman, who said, "May I help you, Madam?" "Please," I said. I got the almonds and turned back to the Piazza with my packages. The gentleman followed me and asked, "May I accompany you and carry your packages?" I looked at him and he went on: "Allow me to introduce myself— Doctor Walter Benjamin." . . . My first impression: glasses that threw out light like little headlights, thick dark hair, a slender nose, clumsy hands—he had dropped the packages. On the whole, a solid intellectual—one of the well to do. He accompanied me to the house and asked if he might visit me.[20]

Benjamin returned the next day and admitted that he had been observing them for the past two weeks. If she had begun as an object of fascination, Lacis soon became much more to Benjamin: he fell immediately and hopelessly in love, and pursued her throughout the 1920s. He could allude to their love affair, however cautiously, in a letter to Scholem in early July: "All sorts of things have happened here that could only really be communicated in person. . . . What has happened was not in the best interests of my work, which was dangerously interrupted, and was also perhaps not in the best interests of that bourgeois rhythm of life which is indispensable for every project. . . . I made the acquaintance of a Russian revolutionary from Riga, one of the most splendid women I have ever met" (C, 245). Lacis remembers that he immediately forged a friendship with her daughter—as he would later do with Brecht's two children. Benjamin has left a highly mediated remembrance of Daga in the section "Chinese Curios" in *One-Way Street:* "A child in his nightshirt cannot be prevailed upon to greet an arriving visitor. Those present, invoking a higher moral standpoint, admonish him in vain to overcome his prudery. A few minutes later he reappears, now stark naked, before the visitor. In the meantime he has washed" (SW, 1:447).

The months on Capri mark a seismic shift in Benjamin's political orientation and general outlook. Obviously enough, his new love affair provided the liberation of vital impulses for which he had longed in Berlin. Yet Asja Lacis was influential in other, seemingly less obvious ways. She first and foremost represented for Benjamin a doorway into the Soviet culture that had beckoned briefly during his association with the G Group, and in particular with Lissitzky and Moholy-Nagy. During their conversations Benjamin pumped Lacis for information on contemporary Soviet art and artists. They discussed the theater, the literary scene, the work of Libedinsky, Babel, Leonov, Kataev, Serafimovitsch, Mayakovsky, Gastev, Kirillov, Gerassimov, Kollontai, and Larissa Reisner. At the same time, Benjamin was growing passionate about his new discoveries in French culture—not merely Gide and Proust but Vildrac, Duhamel, Radiguet, and Giraudoux. Before meeting Lacis, he was thus already contemplating for his work a shift in emphasis toward France; Lacis, with her connections in Moscow, provided Benjamin with a complementary focus. His letters were soon full of news of publishing plans in Moscow: a long report on "new extreme bourgeois ideologies in Germany" for a newspaper, and a Russian translation of "Descriptive Analysis of the German Decline"—a text that included all of part 10 and some of part 11 of the section "Imperial Panorama" that would finally appear in *One-Way Street* in 1928. Neither of these plans came to fruition, but they are the first seeds of Benjamin's manifold engagement with Soviet culture—and they mark a turn from what he called his "apprenticeship in German literature," that is, his engagement with the German literature produced in the seventeenth, eighteenth, and early nineteenth centuries, to a frontal assault on contemporary culture.

Before 1924, Walter Benjamin had written all of two pieces on contemporary literature: the unpublished essay on Paul Scheerbart of 1917–1919 and a 1913 *Anfang* essay on Gerhart Hauptmann. Beginning in 1924, he channeled his energies in precipitously new directions: toward contemporary culture—with an emphasis on popular forms and on what has been called everyday modernity—and, especially after the final failure of the attempts to secure his habilitation, toward a career as a journalist and wide-ranging cultural critic. At first haltingly, and then, beginning in 1926, with a vengeance, Walter Benjamin turned his attention to contemporary Europe, to the modernist and avant-garde culture being produced in France and the Soviet Union, and especially to popular culture and the media in which it appeared, something Benjamin and Siegfried Kracauer in some ways invented as a field of serious investigation. His range in the period is astonishing. Between 1924 and 1931, Benjamin produced essays on everything from children's literature and children's theater as pedagogic models to gambling and pornography, and on a wide variety of media including film, radio, and photography. Writing for some of the most prominent weeklies and monthlies in Germany, he established himself in the late 1920s as a visible and influential commentator on cultural matters.

Cultural matters did not, however, form the basis of Benjamin's most intensive discussions with Asja Lacis; those were reserved for the question of politics. Soon after meeting Lacis, he could report to Scholem that his "vital liberation" was shot through with "an intensive insight into the actuality of radical communism"—which set off immediate "alarm signals" in his friend (GB, 2:473, 481). Lacis remembers challenging Benjamin to integrate the question of class interest into his study of the *Trauerspiel*.[21] And Benjamin could soon assert that he had seen "the political practice of communism (not as a theoretical problem but, first and foremost, as a binding attitude) in a different light than ever before"—and he credits Lacis with having engineered the realignment (C, 248).

In the final analysis, though, this fusion of eros and politics is not a sufficient explanation for Benjamin's avowed shift leftward. As it happened, the encounter with Lacis was coterminous with a second weighty event: the encounter with the Hungarian political philosopher Georg Lukács's *History and Class Consciousness*, which had been published in 1923. Born into a wealthy Jewish family in Budapest, Lukács had studied at the universities in Budapest and Berlin, and at the latter had joined the circle around Georg Simmel in 1909–1910. It was there that he first became friends with Ernst Bloch; 1913 found both of them in Heidelberg and part of Max Weber's circle. Lukács's first works—*Soul and Form* (1910) and *Theory of the Novel* (1916)—were equally informed by aesthetic and philosophical interests. As we have seen, he later coined the phrase "romantic anti-capitalism" to characterize these works. In 1918 Lukács abruptly shifted his political allegiances—which had consisted of loose affiliations with socialist and anarcho-syndicalist circles in Budapest—and became a member of the new Hungarian Communist Party; the following year, he became a party official—people's commissar for education and culture—in the short-lived Hungarian Socialist Republic. Following the defeat of the Hungarian Red Army by Czech and Romanian forces, Lukács fled to Vienna, where he began work on a series of essays that were intended to provide a philosophical basis for Leninism. Published as *History and Class Consciousness* in 1923, these essays laid the groundwork for what is now commonly referred to as Western Marxism. Of course, Benjamin had already learned a great deal about the man Lukács from Bloch. But that June on Capri he was introduced to his work by Bloch's review of *History and Class Consciousness*, which had just appeared in *Der neue Merkur*. By September, Benjamin had made a first acquaintance with the book itself. His reaction is worth quoting in full:

> While proceeding from political considerations, Lukács arrives at principles that are, at least in part, epistemological and perhaps not entirely as far-reaching as I first assumed. The book astonished me because these principles resonate for me or validate my own thinking. . . . I want to study Lukács's book as soon as possible, and I would be surprised if the foundations of my nihilism were not to manifest themselves in the antagonistic confrontation with the concepts and assertions of the Hegelian dialectic as directed against communism. (C, 248)

What Benjamin does not say here, but what presumably explains the intensity of his reaction, is that he discovered a remarkable consonance between the central ideas of Lukács's book—and in particular those of its chapter "Reification and the Consciousness of the Proletariat"—and the concepts that had emerged in the writing of the book on the *Trauerspiel*.

There is a third factor at work in Benjamin's surging interest in politics: it did not occur in a vacuum. However isolated Capri might have seemed, the hum and buzz of the "big world" often intruded on the island. For one thing, the island had about it a leftist air. Benjamin was aware that Maxim Gorki had founded a "revolutionary academy" on Capri and that Lenin himself had spent time there. The lingering memory of these Soviet luminaries, however, hardly shielded the island from the fascism sweeping across Italy in the early 1920s. On September 16 Benjamin reported that

> Mussolini set foot on this island at noon today. All kinds of festive decorations failed to deceive anyone about the coldness with which the people received the event. People are surprised that the man came to Sicily—he must have had urgent reasons for doing so—and tell each other that he is surrounded in Naples by six thousand secret agents whose job is to protect him. He does not look like the lady-killer the postcards make him out to be: corrupt, indolent, and as arrogant as if he had been generously anointed with rancid oil. His body is plump and unarticulated like the fist of a fat shopkeeper. (C, 246)

While Benjamin never draws the connection explicitly, it was certainly obvious to him that a political standpoint was necessary in a world where fascism could come to dominate a major European nation. As he put it in "Imperial Panorama": "Anyone who does not simply refuse to perceive decline will hasten to claim a special justification for his own continued presence, his activity and involvement in this chaos. . . . A blind determination to save the prestige of personal existence—rather than, through an impartial disdain for its impotence and entanglement, at least to detach it from the background of universal delusion—is triumphing almost everywhere . . . the air is teeming with phantoms, mirages of a glorious cultural future breaking upon us overnight in spite of all, for everyone is committed to the optical illusions of his isolated standpoint" (SW, 1:453).

In part because of the profundity of these changes in his outlook and in part because of the animated atmosphere of the island, Benjamin lingered much longer than he had originally planned and far longer than his friends in the little exile colony. The Rangs remained only four weeks, and the Gutkinds less than seven—yet Benjamin stayed on, surprising even himself. "Now, in the morning, under a cloudy sky with the wind coming from the sea, I sit on my balcony, one of the highest in all Capri, from which you can look far out over the town and onto the sea. By the way, it is striking how often people who come here for a short time cannot make up their minds to leave. The grandest and oldest incident of this kind involved Tiberius, who on three occasions started back to Rome only to turn back before reaching his destination" (C, 243). In the months to come, Benjamin delighted in repeatedly referring his friends to Marie Curie's explanation for Capri's magic appeal: she attributed its hold on those who live there to a very particular radioactivity in the air! And, looking back on his months on Capri from the vantage of 1931, Benjamin remembered that he would have "put up with anything as long as I did not have to leave the island. I even considered in all seriousness the possibility of living in one of its large caves, and the images I still have of this are so vivid that today I no longer know whether they were mere fantasies or were based on one of the adventure stories that abound on the island" (SW, 2:471).

Not everything about the five and a half months on Capri suited him, however. The writing proceeded with agonizing slowness. And the resultant pressure to produce entailed a familiar set of symptoms in Benjamin: the street noise from the lively little town induced him to escape by writing at night, but he continued to be disturbed by night sounds—including the nocturnal movements of the local livestock. In the second half of his stay he suffered from a series of ailments: stomach maladies in early July and blood poisoning that came on late in the month and continued to give him problems throughout the summer. And although he could watch from a safe distance, the arrival of Flattau's friend Eva Gelblum introduced the first note of discord into the little group living on Via Sopramonte. The Gutkinds were particularly affected, and the flap surrounding the young woman may well have hastened their departure. Most disturbing, though, was the arrival of the long-awaited review in the *Frankfurter Zeitung* of Benjamin's volume of Baudelaire translations. Perhaps as a result of politics at the journal, Kracauer had been unable to prevent the review from being assigned to the Austrian writer Stefan Zweig. Although best known today as a biographer, Zweig in 1924 could look back on a successful career as an exemplary haut bourgeois author of poetry, fiction, and essays. Early in the century he had published a small volume of his own Baudelaire translations (which, as Benjamin archly notes in a letter, is now to be found hardly anywhere outside the "poison cabinet of my own library"), and he was now bent on demolishing the latest competition. Benjamin was keenly aware of the likely effect of a review from so prominent an address—it "might have been worse, but could not have been more damaging"—and of how few people would know that it was written by a competing and "exasperated translator of Baudelaire." Far away from anyplace from which he could marshal a counterstrike, Benjamin was reduced to raging against his ostensible friend, the "editorial muscle man" Kracauer: "God preserve me from my friends; I can take care of my enemies myself" (GB, 2:459, 461).

In early July Benjamin moved to a new room in the Villa Dana—presumably in order to save money. Rather than an entire floor of a house, he now lived in a single room, "the likes of which I have probably never had to work in before: in terms of its proportions, it has every monkish refinement and a view overlooking the most beautiful garden in Capri, which I moreover have at my disposal. A room in which it does not seem natural to go to bed and which seems made for hardworking nights. On top of that, I am the first person to have lived in it—at least for quite some time, but I believe the very first. It was a storeroom or a laundry room. Whitewashed walls, bare of pictures, which will remain so" (C, 246). Asja Lacis remembers that Benjamin was unusually pleased with the new quarters, and she recalls her astonishment at her first visit to lodgings that "resembled a cave in a jungle of grapevines and wild roses."[22]

Lacis and Daga became his most frequent companions on trips into Naples and its surroundings. After one of their visits, Benjamin suggested they write an essay together on that most vibrant of cities; he himself had amassed "a great deal of material,—curious and important observations," on his trips to the city, and he now proposed to put this material to use (GB, 2:486). "Naples," the first of Benjamin's memorable "city portraits," manages to paint a vivid picture of the city while stripping it of the layers of myth and prettification under which it had long suffered. As Benjamin would later put it in a corrosive review of a contemporary study of Naples, "The experiences on the first day show how few people can look directly at the undistorted image of this life—an existence without stillness or shade. The person in whom everything having to do with comfort does not die from contact with this soil can look forward to a hopeless struggle. For the others, though, the ones who encounter the filthiest, but also the most passionate and horrified visage from which poverty ever shone on liberation—for them the memory of the city coalesces in a Camorra."[23] "Naples" is thus uncannily alive to both the city's wretchedness and its glory. Benjamin and Lacis fasten on the fanatical Catholicism that pardons its own excesses while at the same time balancing the corrupt and violent rule of the Camorra; on the delight of the impoverished and deformed at the shock occasioned in a visitor who glimpses them; on the hiddenness and impenetrability of the city's spirit and its dependence on illusion and theatricality; on the street life that is at once indolent and frenetic; and on the extraordinary profligacy in the face of numbing poverty. One aspect of the text, however, has come to define it, and that is the authors' characterization of porosity—and a resultant ambiguity—as the defining feature of the city.

> As porous as this stone is the architecture. Building and action interpenetrate in the courtyards, arcades and stairways. In everything, they preserve the scope to become a theater of new, unforeseen constellations. The stamp of the definitive is avoided. No situation appears intended forever, no figure asserts its "thus and not otherwise." . . . Similarly dispersed, porous, and commingled is private life. What distinguishes Naples from other larger cities is something it has in common with the African *kraal*: each private attitude or act is permeated by streams of communal life. To exist—for the northern European the most private of affairs—is here, as in the *kraal*, a collective matter. . . . Just as the living room appears on the street, with chairs, hearth, and altar, so—only much more loudly—the street migrates into the living room. Even the poorest one is as full of wax candles, biscuit saints, sheaves of photos on the wall, and iron bedsteads as the street is of carts, people and lights. Poverty has brought about a stretching of frontiers that mirrors the most radiant freedom of thought. (SW, 1:416, 419–420)

Just as there is no doubt that the essay is in some sense coauthored, there is little doubt that the German prose is entirely Benjamin's.[24]

"Naples" is an important text not just for the complexity of its view of the fabled city; it is also the text that introduces the prose form that Benjamin would utilize and refine over the next fifteen years, the *Denkbild* or "figure of thought." There is no discursive through-argumentation in "Naples." Instead, the observations and reflections are presented in paragraph-length clusters of thought revolving around a central idea. These central ideas recur at intervals through the essay so that the reader is challenged to repudiate constructs based on linear narrative in favor of *constellations* of literary figures and ideas. Benjamin's practice here draws on two masters of German prose style, Georg Christoph Lichtenberg and Friedrich Nietzsche. Lichtenberg (1742–1799), a mathematician and experimental physicist, had begun to record short texts—random insights, pointed observations, and the results of experiments—in a series of notebooks that he called, with considerable self-irony, his *Sudelbücher* (rough copy books or, in Lichtenberg's own usage, "waste books"). Many of these little texts are marked by an aphoristic compression: "When a book and a head collide and make a hollow sound, is that always due to something in the book?" Benjamin was a great admirer of Lichtenberg and occasionally took him as a subject.[25] On the other hand, his relationship with Nietzsche's work is pervasive and profound. Nietzsche's redeployment of the aphorism for philosophical work in a book of his maturity such as *Beyond Good and Evil* provided Benjamin with an important precedent, as did Nietzsche's structural and strategic use of the aphorism, which sets up a discontinuous network of subtly intercommunicating singularities in place of the grand philosophic system, the very possibility of which it shatters. Benjamin's own use of the form is, in decisive respects, more literary than that of either Lichtenberg or Nietzsche, or even that of Romantic aphorists such as Schlegel and Novalis; the emerging configurations in his *Denkbilder* are as much a function of verbal consonances, echoes, and permutations as of ramifying ideas.

Benjamin and Lacis submitted the essay to journals in Latvia and Germany sometime in October; it finally appeared in the *Frankfurter Zeitung* in August 1925. "Naples" is today the most important of the period's literary works documenting the "intellectual occupation" of the island by the Germans in Benjamin's circle. Ernst Bloch borrowed the central motif from Benjamin's essay and published an essay of his own called "Italy and Porosity" in *Die Weltbühne* in June 1926; the young economist Alfred Sohn-Rethel, an acquaintance from Benjamin's Heidelberg days, published a small piece in the *Frankfurter Zeitung* in March 1926 with the wonderful title "The Ideal of What Is

Kaput," in which he claims that "technical devices are fundamentally kaput. . . . For Neapolitans, functioning starts only where something is kaput."[26]

Benjamin's final weeks on Capri were busy ones. Ernst and Linda Bloch arrived in early September, and Benjamin resumed his role as tour guide on the island and the mainland. He later captured a magical night in which he wandered through the streets of Positano with Bloch and Sohn-Rethel. Leaving his companions, Benjamin was drawn upward into a deserted neighborhood.

> I sensed how I was gliding away from those below me, despite the fact that I remained within seeing and hearing range, easily traversable in imagination. A stillness surrounded me, an eventful abandon [*eine Verlassenheit voller Ereignis*]. I pressed myself forward bodily with every step into an event of which I could form neither image nor concept, an event that had no wish to tolerate me. Suddenly I paused between walls and empty windows in a thicket of moon shadows. . . . And here, under the gaze of the companions who had been carried away into insubstantiality, I came to know what it means to approach an enchanted space [*Bannkreis*]. I turned back.[27]

Although Benjamin retained his harshly critical views on his philosophical friend—he was wont to criticize everything about Bloch, from his sentimental reliance on Jewish humor to his willingness to publish "irresponsible, sanctimonious puffery" alongside important work—he reported to Scholem that Bloch was "showing a friendlier, indeed an absolutely radiant and more virtuous side of himself for the first time in a long while, and his conversation is sometimes truly useful" (GB, 2:481). These final weeks saw new cultural and intellectual contacts, of which one of the most memorable was a tea with the Italian Futurists, Filippo Tommaso Marinetti, Ruggero Vasari, and Enrico Prampolini. Marinetti performed a noise poem "in a highly virtuosic manner," complete with "the whinnying of horses, the thunder of cannons, the rattling of wagons, and machine gun fire" (GB, 2:493). And Benjamin continued to collect books whenever he could, including a few rarities for his collection of children's books. The victim of this welter of activity was his habilitation thesis. Work on the *Trauerspiel* project crawled forward, interrupted not just by travel and social life but by recurrent illness (which he now attributed to malnutrition) and by intermittent bouts of depression that compared to any he had yet experienced. By the middle of September, though, he had completed the preface together with the first, and portions of the second, of what he was still conceiving of as the three main parts of the *Trauerspiel* book.

The long sojourn in Capri left indelible traces in Benjamin; his attempts to work through his experiences there in literary form remained a preoccupation to the end of his life. A number of his most notable *Denkbilder* arise from Capri motifs. He included a dream of the crossing from Capri to Positano in the collection "Short Shadows," which appeared in the *Kölnische Zeitung* in February 1932. And Capri figures significantly in the vignette that opens the 1938 version of *Berlin Childhood around 1900*, namely, "Loggias"—which Benjamin described as "the most exact portrait it is given me to make of myself" (C, 424). In evoking the peculiar promise contained in the air of the Berlin courtyards in which he had grown up, Benjamin writes that "a whiff of this air was still present in the vineyards of Capri where I held my beloved in my arms" (SW, 3:345). Yet probably the best summation of the abiding importance of the island comes in a diary entry from 1931: "For I am convinced that to have lived for a long time on Capri gives you a claim on distant journeys, so strong is the belief of anyone who has long lived there that he has all the threads in his hand and that in the fullness of time everything he needs will come to him" (SW, 2:471).

Benjamin finally tore himself away from Capri on October 10, 1924. On the last day of his sojourn, he learned that Florens Christian Rang had died on October 7. His friend had fallen ill soon after his own return from Capri. The initial diagnosis of rheumatism was altered to "an inflammation of the nerves" as his condition worsened; at the end, Rang suffered from an almost total paralysis. Benjamin stopped writing to Rang in early September, when he learned that Rang was no longer capable of receiving letters. There is a noticeable distance as well as an emotional edge in the way he tells Scholem of receiving the news of Rang's death on his last day on the island—"the news for which I have been preparing myself for the past two weeks, but which is only now slowly getting through to me" (C, 252). The years to come would make it clear that a kind of touchstone, something by which to take the measure of his own existence (as he once said of Fritz Heinle), was no longer immediately present. He had long since acknowledged to himself and his friend that Rang stood "for true Germanness" in his eyes (GB, 2:368). And there were also, he believed, aspects of his own work in the first half of the 1920s that only Rang could fully understand; with Rang's death, he later said, the book on the *Trauerspiel* lost its "proper reader" (GB, 3:16). He tells Scholem he wrote Emma Rang that he owed to her husband "whatever essential elements of German culture I have internalized." To Scholem himself, of course, he sent a more balanced picture: "[The life that dwells in these great subjects for reflection] burst forth from him with all the more volcanic force when it lay paralyzed under the crust of the rest of Germany. There was . . . the opportunity for me, weatherproofed and athletic, to test myself on the impossible, battered massif of his thoughts. Often enough I made my way to a pinnacle that afforded me a broad view onto the region of my own unexplored thoughts. His spirit was shot through with madness, just as a massif is with crevices. But, because of his morality, madness could not gain power over this man. I, of course, was familiar with the wonderfully humane climate of his intellectual landscape: it constantly had the freshness of sunrise" (C, 252). For Benjamin, Rang's greatness—he was as much a moral exemplar as an intellectual—was inextricably bound to his person. He was thus seriously concerned that Rang's significance would be misjudged now that his writings alone would bear witness to the man. Rang's "intellectual landscape," he feared, would now appear "ossified . . . after the sun has set" (C, 252). Rang evidently shared this concern: he named Benjamin his literary executor, a role the younger man never took on. Whether Benjamin was finally unwilling or whether Rang's family stood in the way, we do not know. He left a memorial to his friend near the beginning of *One-Way Street*, in the sections entitled "Flag . . ." and ". . . at Half-Mast." The first deals with Rang's departure from Capri, the second with his death:

Flag . . .

> How much more easily the leave-taker is loved! For the flame burns more purely for those vanishing in the distance, fueled by the fleeting scrap of material waving from the ship or railway window. Separation penetrates the disappearing person like a pigment and steeps him in gentle radiance.

. . . at Half-Mast

> When a person very close to us is dying, there is (we dimly apprehend) something in the months to come that—much as we should have liked to share it with him—could happen only through his absence. We greet him, at the last, in a language that he already no longer understands. (SW, 1:450)

Benjamin was in no hurry to return to Berlin. After several days in Naples and Positano, he spent a week in Rome and shorter stays in Pisa, Florence, Perugia, Orvieto, and Assisi. Many of these days were given over to contemplation of Italian art: he visited the Borghese and Vatican Museums in Rome, the cathedrals in Pisa and Orvieto, and San Francesco in Assisi. He concentrated on the quattrocento, about which he admitted to comparatively little firsthand knowledge; his observation of archaeological remains from antiquity likewise went "according to the regulations" (GB, 2:501). But any dissatisfaction he may have felt with his own lack of knowledge was overshadowed by the "harmonious alliance" of the persistently gray and rainy weather with a deep sense of loneliness—Lacis had rejoined Bernhard Reich, and it was clear to Benjamin that he would not see her for years to come—and with the omnipresence of fascism. He continually found his movements constrained by huge crowds gathered to witness fascist spectacles, and he repeatedly—"whether out of resignation or in an attempt to break out" he could not say—joined the crowd and thrust himself to the front, which afforded him glimpses of the king, the fascist politicians, and the parades by fascist youth and fascist militias. "If I were the Italian correspondent for the *Action française* instead of just a reader, I could not have acted any differently" (C, 255).

He returned in mid-November to Berlin, and to his parents' home in the Delbrückstraße, where he was reunited with Dora and Stefan.

By November 22 he could report to Scholem that he had made a fair copy of what he had so far completed of the *Trauerspiel* book—or at least of the part of it he intended to submit in Frankfurt. He was now confident that he had the title right: "Origin of the German *Trauerspiel*." Furthermore, he had compressed the originally planned three parts into two parts with three sections each. Despite lingering doubts about his success in demonstrating the centrality of allegory for Baroque drama—he hoped this thesis would "burst forth from the whole in its totality"—he was nonetheless rather proud of his writing strategy, the creation of a text composed "almost entirely of quotations . . . the craziest mosaic technique imaginable" (C, 256). As happy as he was with the project and its intellectual significance, though, Benjamin looked toward the submission of the habilitation thesis with profound ambivalence. "But this project marks an end for me—and not for any money in the world a beginning. . . . I dread almost everything that would result from a positive resolution to all of this: I dread Frankfurt above all, then lectures, students, etc. All things that take a murderous toll on time, especially since the economical use of time is not my strong suit" (C, 261). Even with his goal seemingly within reach, he was still incapable of seeing himself as a professor.

In fact, after the time on Capri and the turn to contemporary culture, Benjamin was beginning to envision the contours of a life outside the academy: "For the time being, I'm trying to catch the prevailing wind from all directions in my sails" (GB, 3:15). He reentered the literary marketplace with new resolve. In late 1924 and early 1925, he completed two review essays on collecting children's books, returned to various sections of the text that he would eventually publish as *One-Way Street* but which now bore the working title "Plaquette for Friends," and began work on a number of new essays. This period of intense activity marked the prelude to his breakthrough in 1926 as one of the most visible cultural critics in Germany. In Benjamin's mind, this newly attuned cultural activity was intimately related to the shifts in his political allegiances. Characteristically, he formulates this reorientation as provocatively as possible in writing to Scholem, whose reaction he could well anticipate: "I hope someday the Communist signals will come through to you more clearly than they did from Capri. At first, they were indications of a change that awakened in me the will not to mask the actual and political elements of my ideas in the Old Franconian way I did before, but also to develop them by experimenting and taking extreme measures. This of course means that the literary exegesis of German literature will now take a back seat" (C, 257–258). He notes his own "surprise at the various points of contact I have with radical Bolshevist theory," and he indicates his regret that, at the moment, he can neither produce "a coherent written statement about these matters" nor find occasion to "speak in person," since, "regarding this particular subject, I do not have any other means available of expressing myself" (C, 258).

Of the two review essays on children's books, "Old Forgotten Children's Books" is the more significant; it draws not only on the collection that Benjamin and Dora lovingly assembled over the years but also on Benjamin's long-standing interest in the child's perceptual and imaginative life. Since their time in Switzerland, as we've seen, he kept a notebook of his son Stefan's "opinions and pensées," and he was especially attentive to children's games and toys. The little essay also marks a number of new beginnings for Benjamin: it is not only his first published piece to address issues in popular culture but also his first inquiring sketch of the collector, a figure that will preoccupy him in the 1930s. He acknowledges the potential for "arrogance, loneliness, bitterness—those are the dark sides of many a highly educated and contented collector," but he also contends that every serious collector of children's books must hold "on to a childlike delight in this field." Benjamin knew and admired his fellow collector Karl Hobrecker, whom he calls (in a letter to Scholem) "a master in the field and ungrudging promoter of my own collection." But Hobrecker was also a competitor, and Benjamin recounted that Hobrecker's "publisher was inconsolable at not having given me this assignment, once he became familiar with my collection and the life it has with me." In private, he told friends that the old gentleman's text was written in an "avuncular" style, with a "staid humor that sometimes comes off like an unsuccessful pudding" (C, 250–251). Benjamin was intensely interested in the history of pedagogy in Germany, and the little essay contains a brief account of the role of children's books in that development—the first of many analyses growing out of his early concern with the theory and practice of education. But perhaps the

most important contribution of the essay is the distinction drawn between the child's reactions to color illustrations and his reaction to
woodcuts. As Benjamin had suggested in several writings from 1914
on, color illustrations are related to the developing inner life of the
child.[28] "After all, the role of children's books is not to induct their
readers directly into the world of objects, animals, and people—in
other words, into so-called life. Very gradually, the meaning of these
things is discovered in the outside world, but only in proportion
as they are found to correspond to what children already possess
within themselves. The inward nature of this way of seeing is located
in the color, and this is where the dreamy life that objects lead in the
minds of children is acted out. They learn from the bright coloring.
For nowhere else is sensuous, nostalgia-fee contemplation as much at
home as in color" (SW, 1:410). The woodcut is the "polar complement"
to the color illustration, which "immerses the child's imagination in
a dream state within itself. The black-and-white woodcut, the plain
prosaic illustration, leads him out of himself. The compelling invitation to describe, which is implicit in such pictures, arouses the child's
desire to express himself in words. And describing these pictures in
words, he also describes them by enactment. The child inhabits
them." As much as this distinction might seem to imply a straightforward dichotomy between a dreamlike, fluid interiority and an active
agency in the world, Benjamin is concerned less with the dichotomy
than with hidden potentials that might serve to unite the two poles.
In "enacting" the description, children "inscribe the pictures with
their ideas in a more literal sense: they scribble on them. At the same
time as they learn language, they also learn how to write: they learn
hieroglyphs" (SW, 1:411). The essay on children's books is thus the
first public record of Benjamin's return, during the period of the composition of the *Trauerspiel* book, to his 1916 theories of language, with
their strict dichotomy between an instrumental language that communicates information and a paradisiacal language that communicates nothing but bodies forth its own essence as language. The child's
scribbling is an unconscious demonstration of the theory of script
Benjamin was now elaborating. Drawing on his interest in graphology,
which purports to find a revelation of interiority in the ductus of an
individual's handwriting, the notion of "hieroglyphics" articulated

here will become a central feature of the analysis of the *Trauerspiel* form itself.

Alongside this and other attempts to start a career as a critic of contemporary culture, Benjamin also actively sought salaried positions in the world of German letters. Perhaps most promisingly, he agreed to assume the editorship of a new publishing house being founded by a young man named Litthauer or, according to Scholem, Littauer. Benjamin would have drawn no salary for his editorial work but would have received an income for a steady series of articles and travel reports; on the strength of this, he began to imagine the possibilities of direct access to a publisher, including an idea for a new journal and a plan to publish the book on the *Trauerspiel* there.[29] Although the German economy was beginning to stabilize, fledgling publishing ventures were still very risky: Litthauer Verlag folded in the spring without having published a single title. Benjamin also entered into negotiations to become the editor of the weekly culture supplement to the radio magazine of the Südwestdeutschen Rundfunkdienst in Frankfurt. His friend Ernst Schoen was the director of programming there, and the position at first looked like a real possibility—until Benjamin's expectations for compensation became a stumbling block in the negotiations. This unreasonable demand from someone without any income beyond the now much reduced subvention from his parents highlights a character trait that would plague Benjamin to the end of his life: as his financial situation became increasingly hopeless, the intransigence of his demands for compensation befitting his accomplishments increased in direct proportion.

As if the uncertainty over his professional future were not enough to keep Benjamin unsettled, he continued to complicate his personal life by seeing a great deal of Asja Lacis, who had returned to Berlin with Bernhard Reich and her daughter, Daga, at the end of October. The two families intermingled in ways that must have been fraught with tension. At Benjamin's suggestion, Stefan would frequently accompany Daga to their rhythmic gymnastics classes; Lacis remembers Stefan conducting himself, on these occasions, like a "little cavalier, courtly and elegant."[30] Much as he had in Naples, Benjamin served as Lacis's guide in Berlin, introducing her not just to such violent contrasts as that between the rich neighborhoods where his parents lived in the west and the workers' districts such as Wedding and Moabit in the north, but also to his unmistakably haut bourgeois predilection for fine restaurants and rigorously observed table culture. Even as his political affiliations to the left became deeper, Benjamin's class disposition remained unaltered—and unalterable. Walter Benjamin was hardly alone in his enactment of class contradiction, of course; the late 1920s saw many bitter disputes within leftist writers' groups, as increasing demands for solidarity with the proletariat gradually came to exclude bourgeois intellectuals, who drifted back to the Social Democrats. Benjamin was merely one of the most prominent of these intellectuals to maintain a resolutely radical *intellectual* position while retaining, even amid great poverty, the accouterments of bourgeois life.

Lacis was keen to meet Benjamin's brother, Georg, by this time a committed Communist and social activist, but he kept them apart, in accordance with his long-standing policy of hermetically isolating the people in his life from one another. If he excluded his Latvian friend from many of his own affairs, he was nonetheless eager to gain entry through her to a world about which he knew very little: that of contemporary theater. Sometime in the fall of 1924, Bertolt Brecht—who had actively avoided a meeting with Benjamin on Capri—consented to meet him; Lacis remembers that this first encounter was a failure, and that Brecht kept his exchanges with Benjamin to a minimum.[31] The interest in Brecht shows how much Benjamin's understanding of the possibilities open to him had evolved. Although he preserved his ties to a few close friends from his student days, including Ernst Schoen, Jula Radt-Cohn and her husband, Fritz, and Alfred Cohn, and although he maintained his intense interest in esoteric thought and the people who produced it (he tried to place a review of Erich Unger's latest book, *Gegen die Dichtung* [Against Poetry]), Benjamin was starting, on his return from Capri, to move in rather different circles. As the year came to an end, something like domestic peace reigned in the younger Benjamins' apartment in the parental home. For Hanukkah, Stefan received not just a train set but "a splendid Indian costume, one of the most beautiful toys to have come on the market in a long time: colorful feather headdresses, axes, chains. Since someone else happened to give him an African mask . . . this morning I saw him dancing toward me in a grandiose getup" (C, 258).

By February 1925 the book on the *Trauerspiel* had assumed its definitive shape: two major parts, with a theoretical introduction. Benjamin was still revising the second part (on the basis of a nearly complete manuscript), but both the introduction and the first part were already complete. To Scholem he described the introduction as "unmitigated chutzpah—that is to say, neither more nor less than the prolegomena to an epistemology, a kind of second stage of my early work on language . . . dressed up as a theory of ideas" (C, 261). Neither the long-planned third part of the study nor a brief theoretical conclusion intended to balance the preface was ever written. After more than a year's hard work, Benjamin now mailed the second, "tamer" half of the introduction and part 1 to his advisor, Schultz, who he hoped would initiate the complex procedure that would lead to the *venia legendi* or right to teach as a professor at a university. He reckoned that his chances were "not unfavorable," since Schultz was the dean of the philosophical faculty and could thus smooth the way. And he asked Salomon-Delatour to help him find a "highly educated woman who can give me a week's worth of hard work" (GB, 3:9), so that he could dictate the final version of the second part and the introduction. This method of final composition would mark every major work: Benjamin produced a final handwritten version and then dictated it, making small changes as he read to a stenographer for the production of a final version.

He decamped, ambivalent as ever, for Frankfurt on February 13 and set in motion what he hoped would be the penultimate stage of his journey toward habilitation. As the weeks dragged on he became increasingly despondent. The final, technical details of producing a habilitation thesis—the "mechanical work of dictation, the bibliography"—weighed him down. And Frankfurt itself, whether in comparison to Berlin or to Italy, was marked by its "desolation and inhospitability"; he hated both its "urban life and its cityscape" (C, 261, 263). At bottom, Benjamin was in bad shape emotionally. While he remained unenthusiastic about even the most successful outcome to the process, he came increasingly to see that he was in an impossible situation. Schultz, who held the chair in literary history, had in 1923 given Benjamin every reason to hope that he would sponsor Benjamin's work and his candidacy; it had, after all, been Schultz who had suggested the topic to Benjamin. As Burkhardt Lindner has pointed out, Schultz was an ambitious academic who would not have been dismayed to attach his name to a student whose work would gain wide recognition.[32] But when Benjamin met with Schultz in the spring in order to hand him the remainder of the text, he found him "cool and finicky—and clearly poorly informed as well. He had evidently concerned himself only with the introduction, the most recalcitrant part of the whole thing" (C, 263). Schultz told Benjamin on the spot— and before reading the second part—that he intended to withdraw himself as advisor, and he recommended that Benjamin seek habilitation in aesthetics under the sponsorship of Hans Cornelius. This suggestion had a number of implications. First, it was clear that Schultz was washing his hands of Benjamin. Second, this meant that Benjamin would gain his habilitation, if at all, in an entirely different and, from a purely professional point of view, far less desirable field. Aesthetics, when it existed at all in German universities, was housed in a subsection of philosophy or art history. Finally—and this must have been most galling to Benjamin—he had initially approached Cornelius regarding the possibility of a habilitation in philosophy, that is, long before he had settled on the *Trauerspiel* as a topic, and Cornelius had turned a cold shoulder. "I am moderating my hope very rapidly: the question of who will speak for me is simply too difficult. Two years ago, I would have mustered the most fervent moral indignation in view of this state of affairs. Today, I see through the mechanisms of this institution far too well to be capable of that" (C, 268).

Of course, Benjamin could have pressed forward, but he was savvy enough regarding academic politics to know that he would succeed in his attempts in literary history only if Schultz were to support him "most vigorously" (C, 264). Benjamin understood very well that Schultz's withdrawal placed him squarely in an academic no-man's-land. The German university world, then and now, too often works on the basis of patronage: the best positions, and in fact most positions, fall to candidates with powerful individual backers, and powerful backers support candidates who have proven to be their disciples over long periods of time. Benjamin was an outsider, someone with no real affiliation with the university in Frankfurt or with Schultz—and he never pretended to be anything but that. "I am able to identify a number of benevolently neutral gentlemen on the faculty, but know of no one who would actually take up my cause" (C, 266). He could hardly have been surprised, then, when Salomon-Delatour reported that Schultz had said that "the only thing he has against me is that I am not his student" (C, 264).

If Benjamin had long kept to himself his evaluation of Schultz, he now gave Scholem a fuller picture: "This Professor Schultz, who is insignificant as a scholar, is a shrewd cosmopolitan who probably has a better nose for some literary matters than young coffee house habitués. But I have exhausted all there is to say about him with this blurb on his intellectual tinsel-culture. He is mediocre in every other respect, and what he does have in the way of diplomatic skill is paralyzed by a cowardliness clothed in punctilious formality" (C, 263). Schultz's own writings reveal a scholar with neither analytical nor rhetorical talents; it is hardly surprising that he proved himself incapable of either following or championing Benjamin's work. Although evidence is scanty, other factors such as prejudice and political difference may also have played a role: according to an eyewitness, Schultz took part in the book burning in Frankfurt's main square in 1933, at the very moment that the most prominent Jewish literary critic of the Weimar Republic went into forced exile.[33]

Despite his growing—and well-founded—foreboding, Benjamin officially submitted *Origin of the German Trauerspiel* as his habilitation thesis on March 12, 1925. The focus on a neglected dramatic form was unusual, though interest in the literature of the German Baroque had been growing since the late nineteenth century; early in the new century, the term "Second Silesian School" had become generally accepted as the designation for a group of poets and dramatists working in the Baroque style of Daniel Casper von Lohenstein and Christoph Hoffmann von Hoffmanswaldau. These authors—Andreas Gryphius, Johann Christian Hallmann, and a number of anonymous dramatists— were never part of an organized "school" in the seventeenth century. But a series of influential nineteenth-century literary critics, including Georg Gottfried Gervinus (whom Benjamin considered a model), had identified various formal and thematic similarities across a broad range of their works. Within this literary-historical context, Benjamin had early on (1916) seized upon the dramatic form known as *Trauerspiel*, the play of mourning.

The book on the *Trauerspiel* is in certain ways the fulcrum of Walter Benjamin's career. It represents, above all, his first full, historically oriented analysis of modernity. In its focus on a body of literature from an earlier day, it is of a piece with the literary criticism Benjamin had produced through 1924. Unlike every other work he had written so far, however, the study of the Baroque has an explicit dual focus. The penultimate section of the book's "Epistemo-Critical Prologue" establishes extensive parallels between the language and form of the *Trauerspiel* and that of the contemporary drama of Expressionism. "For like Expressionism, the Baroque is not so much an age of genuine artistic practice as an age possessed of an unremitting will to art [*Kunstwollen*]. This is true of all the so-called periods of decadence. . . . In its brokenness [*Zerrissenheit*], the present age reflects certain aspects of the spiritual constitution of the Baroque, even down to the details of its artistic practice."[34] Certain features of modernity, in other words, can come to light *only through* analysis of a reviled, long-past era. The claim implicit here—one that will become explicit in the late 1920s in *The Arcades Project*—is that certain moments in time stand in a synchronous relation to one another, a relation of correspondence; or, as he puts it later, there is a "historical index" such that the character of a particular epoch can sometimes be understood only by confronting it with a distant predecessor. This deep structure of history is nowhere thematized as such in the two main sections of the study itself: Benjamin depends on his reading of the mourning plays, and the power of his writing, to bring to light salient features of his own day in their "now of recognizability." And just as the study intertwines tendencies of the seventeenth and twentieth centuries, it brings the theory of literary criticism Benjamin developed between 1914 and 1924 into relation with the Marxist literary theory initiated by Lukács. In its focus on the "thing-character" of the plays of mourning, the book prepares the ground for Benjamin's later investigation of the fetishized commodity and its global effect, phantasmagoria. Thus, looking back in a letter of 1931, he can say that the *Trauerspiel* book is "already dialectical, if not yet materialist" (GB, 4:18).

The use of the term "will to art" *(Kunstwollen)* in the prologue bespeaks a reconception of Alois Riegl's model of cultural history. Riegl's approach to works of art presupposes that certain artistic epochs are constitutionally incapable of producing "a well-made individual work." Such eras—the late Roman "art industry," the Baroque, precapitalist modernity—instead produce imperfect or broken works in which a no less significant will to art is manifest. In this emphasis on fragmentation and disruption, Benjamin's own understanding of early modernity takes its cue not only from the tradition of Expressionism but also from Baudelaire's hallmark conception of "modern beauty," the aesthetics of the brutal and ugly that animates so many of his poems. Benjamin's concentration on a series of Baroque dramas marked more by the extremity of their formal and stylistic means than by any conventional aesthetic achievement seeks, then, to disclose an era's will to art and thereby its very spiritual constitution. Moreover, the contemporary historical experience of such eras can unfold *only* in such broken works: "Historical life, as that epoch represented it to itself, is the content and true subject [of the Trauerspiel]" (OGT, 62).

For Benjamin, the history that is the "content" of these plays is an inexorable slide toward disaster. The book's first part, "Trauerspiel and Tragedy," derives a broad intellectual history of the era from readings of extended passages of the plays. At the center of that history is what Benjamin takes to be the Lutheran evisceration of the meaning of daily life: "In that excessive reaction which ultimately drove from the field good works as such, and not merely their meritorious or penitential character, . . . human actions were deprived of all value. Something new arose: an empty world" (OGT, 138–139). Traditional readings of eras such as the Baroque emphasize their longing for transcendence and the resultant eschatological coloration of human activity. Benjamin, on the contrary, proposes that the defining feature of the German Baroque is precisely its *lack* of traditional eschatology. "The religious man of the Baroque clings so tightly to the world because he feels himself being driven with it toward a cataract. There is no Baroque eschatology; and just for that reason, there is a mechanism that heaps up and exalts all earthly things before delivering them to their end." The Baroque wins from this hollow world "a profusion of things" and "brings them to light in a drastic shape." The agent of this drastic illumination is neither the prince, the theologian, nor the peasant in revolt: it is the dramatic form of the *Trauerspiel* itself. Benjamin attributes to the work of art not just a revelatory but a destructive capacity, a nihilistic power: the stage littered with random objects "that customarily escape all figuration" clears "an ultimate heaven," making it "capable—as a vacuum—of one day destroying the earth with catastrophic violence" (OGT, 66). Here, as at many points in the study of the Baroque, the full thrust of Benjamin's reading emerges only when the *Trauerspiel* book is read together with *One-Way Street*, crucial sections of which were written contemporaneously. The cleansing violence attributed to the play of mourning is realized, for example, in the concluding section of *One-Way Street*, "To the Planetarium": "In the nights of annihilation of the last war, the frame of mankind was shaken by a feeling that resembled the bliss of the epileptic. And the revolts that followed it were the first attempt of mankind to bring the new body under its control" (SW, 1:487). The term *Trauerspiel* thus refers both to a specific literary form and to the tendency of modern history itself. It is for this reason that Benjamin considers the mourning play "morally responsible" in a way that more aesthetically realized contemporary drama, such as that of Calderón, is not.

Much of the section "Trauerspiel and Tragedy" is given over to formal analysis of these jagged, recondite dramas, and especially to the relationship established between the characters onstage and the viewer. Far from any naturalistic representation or psychological verism, the figures on the Baroque stage are rigid, awkward constructs. How could it be otherwise, asks Benjamin, when they are made to represent the course of a broken, hopeless history? Their halting, wooden actions are driven not by thought or feeling but by "violent physical impulses," while their stilted, often hieratic speech makes manifest their alienation from both nature and grace. But at the center of Benjamin's analysis is less the characters themselves than the relationship said to obtain between stage and onlooker. The spectator experiences the stage as a morally illuminating projection of his own situation in the world; it makes for "an inner space of feeling with no connection to the cosmos." The dramas are thus "not so much play that causes mourning as play through which mourning finds its satisfaction: play [taking place] before the mournful" (OGT, 119).

In the book's second section, "Allegory and Trauerspiel," Benjamin makes a compelling case for the reinstitution of allegory as the constitutive trope not just of the Baroque but of modernity itself. Understood as a narrative relation between symbolic elements, allegory had fallen into disrepute in the eighteenth century; in Benjamin's rehabilitation, however, the trope has little to do with the narrative and representational aspects of the form. Here, allegory emerges as a strictly codified set of signifiers having no *necessary* relationship to what is represented. In the most-cited passage of the book, we read that "any person, any thing, any relationship can mean any other arbitrary thing." The next sentence, which anchors allegory as a historical practice, is less often quoted: "With this possibility an annihilating but just verdict is pronounced on the profane world: it is characterized as a world in which the detail is of no great importance" (OGT, 175). Benjamin attributes to allegory a unique revelatory capacity, by which it can unmask the abyss lurking within every aspect of worldly life. As the production of meaning breaks down in allegory, it is replaced by a "natural history of meaning" (OGT, 166): the inert, hollowed-out figures on the stage, surrounded by objects deprived of inherent significance, reflect a history no longer distinguishable from nature's own incessant agony and undoing. "That is the heart of the allegorical way of seeing, of the Baroque, worldly exposition of history as the Passion of the world [*Leidensge-schichte der Welt*]—meaningful only in the stations of its decline" (OGT, 166).

In the Baroque *Trauerspiel* this "natural history" "wanders onto the stage" in the form of props, emblems, and the depersonalized, cipherlike human figures. These things and thinglike humans can have no intrinsic relation to a meaningful present or to a history of salvation; they are instead invested by the allegorist with a hidden and wholly fallen significance. "For all the wisdom of the melancholic is subject to the nether world; it is won from immersion in the life of

creaturely things, and nothing of the voice of revelation penetrates to
it" (OGT, 152). The relays between the Trauerspiel book and "Goethe's
Elective Affinities" emerge here in full force: the allegorist, like
Goethe before him, confuses the "wisdom" born of nature idolatry
and the glorification of the creaturely with a higher meaning that is
denied him. The melancholic thus betrays himself and the world for
the sake of a mysterious and apparently profound knowledge. This
is the paradox of the *Trauerspiel:* the allegorist, by investing the dead-
ened things on the stage with a hidden meaning, means to redeem
these profane objects. Concealed within that very action, however,
is the *destruction* of the empty world. On the stage of the *Trauerspiel,*
the allegorical objects appear as ruin and rubble—and so open for the
spectator a prospect onto a history from which the false glimmer of
categories such as totality, coherence, and progress has been stripped
away. "In the field of allegorical intuition, the image is a fragment, a
rune. . . . The false appearance of totality is extinguished. For the
eidos disappears, the simile ceases to exist, and the cosmos it contained shrivels up" (OGT, 176). If this knowledge is *potentially* available to the mournful spectator of the original dramas themselves,
Benjamin hopes for a more direct apprehension of the ideological
construction of history in the case of the modern reader. As he would
later say of film and photography—and of the greatest modern allegorist, Baudelaire—allegorical works make available a certain "productive self-alienation" in the beholder. Humans in the Baroque and
modernity alike are allowed to *see* their own alienation, and so to
glimpse the fragmented, oppressive character of history.

Baroque allegory inspires in the spectator, finally, not just "insight
into the transience of things" but a "concern to redeem them for eternity" (OGT, 223). This is a redemption in downfall. As in the essay on
Goethe's *Elective Affinities*, Benjamin intends here to issue a moral
verdict on the allegorist. Precisely in their pretension and ostentation,
the dramas fall prey not merely to the worship of the profane and creaturely, and not merely to the illusion of a redemptive power, but to the
enticement offered by knowledge of good and evil. "Satanic promises"
motivate the work of the allegorist: "What tempts is the illusion of
freedom—in the exploration of what is forbidden; the illusion of independence—in the secession from the community of the pious; the

illusion of infinity—in the empty abyss of evil" (OGT, 230). For all their brokenness, then, these allegorical works hold within themselves a *potential* purgative force. But they are in need of the annihilating force of the criticism Benjamin had been developing in the decade just past if that potential is to be actualized. Benjamin thus offers near the end of the habilitation thesis a concentrated statement of that very criticism:

> From the very beginning they are set up for that erosion by criticism which befell them in the course of time. . . . [The outer form of the *Trauerspiel*] has died away because of its extreme crudity. What has survived is the extraordinary detail of the allegorical references: an object of knowledge which has nested in the consciously constructed ruins. Criticism means the mortification of works . . . : not then—as the Romantics have it—awakening of the consciousness in living works, but the settlement of knowledge in dead ones. . . . The object of philosophical criticism is to show that the function of artistic form is as follows: to make historical content, such as provides the basis of every important work of art, into a philosophical truth. This transformation of material content into truth content makes the decrease in effect, whereby the attraction of earlier charms diminishes decade by decade, into the basis for a rebirth, in which all ephemeral beauty is completely stripped off, and the work stands as a ruin. In the allegorical construction of the baroque *Trauerspiel* such ruins have always stood out clearly as formal elements of the preserved [*geretteten*] work of art. (OGT, 181–182)

What does this mortified, ruined work reveal? The final sentences of the book suggest that "in the ruins of great buildings the idea of the plan speaks more impressively than in lesser buildings, however well preserved they are" (OGT, 235). That which peers out from the ruin of this bygone form is its "idea." And so Benjamin closes his study—and the decade of his life given over to the production of a highly esoteric theory of criticism—with a reference to a text that his readers could not read: the portion of the "Epistemo-Critical Prologue" that he did not submit in 1924, and which was published only in 1928.

The title of Benjamin's prologue is a play on words. The piece is in part an attempt to formulate a theory of cognition—a doctrine of ideas—but at the same time it is a critique of the very suppositions of any such theory. It thus comments both on an ideal state, what Bernd Witte has called "a utopia of knowledge," in which human understanding might attain truth, and on the actual conditions of knowledge that obtain in the world, conditions that render such understanding impossible.[35] At its heart is an esoteric, religiously conditioned theory of the construction of ideas. Benjamin's ideas are neither regulative concepts of the understanding in the Kantian sense nor unified essences in the Platonic sense. They are instead restructurations of certain elements of the world: "Ideas are related to things as constellations are to stars" (OGT, 34). Benjamin's language theory achieves a provisional resolution here. The ideas are in fact made up of "redeemed" elements of language, elements whose profane meaning has been transfigured and whose contingency has been stripped away, elements to which "the primacy of the symbolic character of the word" has been restored (OGT, 36). It is in this sense that the goal of the *Origin of German Trauerspiel* is the discernment of the "idea" of one word: *Trauerspiel* itself.

With Benjamin's work in hand, the philosophical faculty duly appointed a committee to review the work, and Hans Cornelius, the holder of the chair in aesthetics and art theory, was charged with preparing a preliminary evaluation. A brief initial acquaintance with Benjamin's text led Cornelius to take a highly unusual step. He wrote to Benjamin and asked for a brief summary of the habilitation thesis, which Benjamin promptly provided. In vain, as it turned out: Cornelius's negative evaluation was unqualified. It attested that Benjamin's work was "extremely difficult to read," something no doubt experienced by every subsequent reader. But he went on to assert: "I was unable—despite repeated, concentrated efforts—to derive a comprehensible meaning from these [art historical observations]. . . . Under these circumstances, I am not in a position to recommend to the faculty that the work of Dr. Benjamin be accepted as a habilitation thesis for art history. For I am unable . . . to ignore my misgiving that the author, with his incomprehensible mode of expression—which must be interpreted as signifying a lack of scholarly clarity—cannot serve as a guide for students in this area."[36] Cornelius managed in this evaluation to address no single actual claim in Benjamin's text, while creating the impression that the work was uninformed, confused, and chaotic, and that it was the work of a misguided and possibly unstable mind who should never be let loose in front of students.[37] The evaluation had the intended effect. Although it had been expressly commissioned as a first report, no further reports were produced, and the philosophical faculty voted on July 13, 1925, to reject Benjamin's application—scarcely a week after Cornelius had reported. Or rather it voted to recommend to "Dr. Benjamin" that he withdraw his application, thereby saving himself and the faculty the embarrassment of a formal rejection.

By late July, Benjamin still had heard nothing official, but he began to receive signals of the foundering of his attempt. A friend of Dora's parents with connections in Frankfurt had relayed word of the "total hopelessness" of his application. Schultz, as dean, was in no hurry to inform Benjamin of the outcome of the process. He wrote only in late July: "After the receipt of the first evaluation of your habilitation thesis, I was tasked by the faculty with giving you the advice that you might wish to withdraw your application for admission to the habilitation process. In fulfilling this task, I allow myself to inform you that I remain at your disposal until August 6, should you at any time wish to speak with me."[38] As Lindner points out, Schultz attempted to hide behind the formality of the utterance but could not muster even an "unfortunately." Benjamin was inclined neither to visit Schultz nor, initially, to withdraw his application, preferring to leave "the risk of a negative decision completely up to the college faculty" (C, 276). This is not, however, the course he followed: he withdrew his application, and the materials were duly returned to him in the fall. He expressed his outrage in a letter of August 5 to Salomon-Delatour:

> You will understand why I have been silent for so long. Your last letter, of course, had something to do with this; it was so funereal and oppressive, when a round cursing would have done me good. For, if internal causes had not made the academic enterprise into something inconsequential to me, the way I was treated would have had a long-lasting and destructive impact. If my self-estimation were even in the least dependent on those views, then the irresponsible and reckless manner in which the person in charge handled my af-

fair would have dealt me a shock from which my productivity would not soon have recovered. That none of this is the case—in fact, the opposite is true—must remain a private matter. (GB, 3:73)

The decision to accept the faculty's advice and to withdraw in silence was one that Benjamin rued for the rest of his life; he came increasingly to feel that he had been robbed of the chance to fully expose the pedantry, pettiness, and prejudice that robbed him of his degree. And so he came to compose, probably sometime in the fall, a "ten-line preface to the *Trauerspiel* book, which I wrote to take a dig at the University of Frankfurt and which I consider to be one of my most successful pieces" (C, 293). The mordant "Preface to the *Trauerspiel* Book" was enclosed in a letter to Scholem of May 29, 1926:

I would like to tell the story of Sleeping Beauty a second time.

She sleeps in her hedge of thorns. And then, after a certain number of years, she wakes.

But not at the kiss of a fortunate prince.

The cook woke her up when he gave the scullery boy a box on the ear that, resounding from the pent-up force of so many years, echoed through the palace.

A lovely child sleeps behind the thorny hedge of the following pages.

May no fortune's prince in the shining armor of scholarship come near. In the kiss of betrothal she will bite.

The author has therefore had to reserve to himself the role of master cook in order to awaken her. Already long overdue is the box on the ear that would resound through the halls of academe.

For there will awaken also this poor truth, which has pricked itself on an old-fashioned spindle as, in forbidden fashion, it thought to weave for itself, in the little back room, a professorial robe. (GB, 3:164)

However one reads this modern-day fairy tale, one cannot avoid hearing the resounding slap it delivers to the German university and its scholars. With the rejection of Benjamin's submission, the philosophic faculty of the University of Frankfurt brought down on itself a scandal that continues to cast its shadow today. Yes, *Origin of the German*

Trauerspiel—and especially the "Epistemo-Critical Prologue"—is difficult reading, though its difficulty is finally not of a piece with the dark enigmas of "Goethe's Elective Affinities." Presenting an unsurpassed analysis of the historical significance of an ostensibly antiquated artistic form, it stands today as one of the signal achievements of twentieth-century literary criticism.

CHAPTER SIX

Weimar Intellectual

Berlin and Moscow, 1925–1928

BENJAMIN's failure to find an academic home for the *Trauerspiel* book in spring and summer 1925 closed the long chapter of his life in which he had sought to carve out a place for himself in the German university system. He was now faced with a double dilemma: determining a new career path and finding a way to support himself and his family. The family had been supported, precariously, by Dora's work and the provision of free housing by his parents. Dora now lost the second job that had done much to keep them afloat—and this came on the heels of the collapse of the Litthauer publishing house, on which Benjamin had been pinning his hopes. Benjamin could not conceal his bitterness at the spectacle of a wealthy young publisher who had frittered away more than 55,000 marks on "automobile journeys, dinners, tips, interest, etc. The man himself is now headed, as is right and proper with such people, for a sanatorium" (GB, 3:31). All that remained of this once promising enterprise was the impression of an unattractive mixture of high life and idealism.

Benjamin thus redoubled his efforts to find his niche in the German publishing world. He was fortunate that his turn toward public forums for his work coincided with a veritable explosion of the mass media in the Weimar Republic. With the stabilization of the currency, the middle classes began to rediscover the notion of disposable income, and media organs multiplied rapidly to take advantage of the new situation. Berlin soon attained a reputation as the "most important newspaper city of the world"; more than 2,000 periodicals appeared on the shelves of its bookstores and news agents every month.

Through Kracauer, Benjamin already had access to the feuilleton pages of the *Frankfurter Zeitung*. The oldest and most widely read of the left-liberal dailies in Germany, it was founded in 1856 as the

Frankfurter Geschäftsbericht (Frankfurt Business Report) and changed
its name to the *Frankfurter Zeitung* in 1866. Dedicated from its inception to a left-leaning democratic stance, it was the primary oppositional organ in the early years of the German Empire after 1871; the
editors were frequently incarcerated between 1871 and 1879 for their
refusal to divulge the sources of their writers' articles. In the early
years of the Weimar Republic, its readership consisted mainly of liberal entrepreneurs and professionals; as its feuilleton pages attracted
an increasingly prominent series of authors, they soon rivaled the
political and financial pages as magnets for a wider readership. Brecht,
Alfred Döblin, Hermann Hesse, and Heinrich and Thomas Mann
were just a few of the regular contributors. Benjamin published his
first piece for the paper, "Collection of Frankfurt Children's Rhymes,"
on August 16, 1925, and would publish scores of articles, notes, and
glosses in the years to come.

Meanwhile, in May, he had forged a second important relationship
to a journal: *Die literarische Welt,* edited by Willy Haas and published
by Rowohlt Verlag. Haas (1891–1973) had grown up in the Prague Jewish community; his literary interests developed in the circles around
Franz Werfel and Franz Kafka that met at the Café Arco. Making his
way to Berlin after the war, he supported himself by writing several
well-known screenplays, including the book for *The Joyless Street,*
as well as film criticism for the *Film-Kurier.* He later edited Kafka's
Letters to Milena, and Benjamin cites his interpretation of Kafka in
1934. Haas now entrusted Benjamin with a series of reports on developments in French culture, a task eagerly accepted. While retaining
his older interests in Gide and Giraudoux, Benjamin began immersing
himself in the "questionable books of the Surrealists," with an eye to
an article for the journal; he read André Breton's "Manifesto of Surrealism" and initiated a long engagement with the work of Louis Aragon by reading *Une vague de rêves.* He suggested to Scholem that he
would also be able to publish regular reports concerning the goings-on
at Muri (their fantasy university) in *Die literarische Welt,* but only
one such article, a satirical treatment of recent library acquisitions,
ever appeared.[1] For all his initial enthusiasm, however, Benjamin's attitude toward Haas's magazine rapidly became more cautious—and,

in private, critical. He confided to Hofmannsthal, an early supporter
of the journal, that he found Haas too indecisive and too much the
slave of his circulation numbers. "I had originally greeted the appearance of this journal with joy, entirely in the spirit of your remarks,
until I quickly realized that it was on the whole not intended for serious
criticism. I am not blind to the editorial and journalistic necessities
that demand a place in such a weekly for light and lightest writing.
But just for that reason, the weighty should be considered with twice
the care—and not just in terms of its column space" (GB, 3:116). These
protests reveal the extent to which Benjamin remained obdurately
blind to the financial side of the journalistic equation. Haas himself,
on the other hand, was unstinting in his loyalty to Benjamin: "Among
all those who honored my weekly journal *Die literarische Welt* with
their regular collaboration, I held no one in higher esteem than Walter
Benjamin. He was the opposite of a simple polymath—despite his conspicuous knowledge. When he spoke or wrote about a topic, he never
approached it through analogies, metaphors, or definitions: he constantly seemed to dig his way laboriously out of the very kernel of the
matter, like a gnome who keeps his treasures hidden in a mineshaft
whose exit has been buried."[2]

In addition to the regular appearance of his work in the *Frankfurter Zeitung* and *Die literarische Welt,* there were growing opportunities for Benjamin in other, highly visible publishing venues. A
lightly ironic gloss on the military uses of poison gas appeared in the
Vossische Zeitung.[3] And the pieces that would eventually be assembled in *One-Way Street* began to find their way into print. The *Berliner Tageblatt*—along with the *Frankfurter Zeitung* the most widely
read left-liberal paper—published "Thirteen Theses against Snobs" on
July 10. In the course of the next year, one more important venue
opened for Benjamin: the Dutch avant-garde journal *i10* was founded
in 1926 by Arthur Lehning. Ernst Bloch had met Lehning while vacationing in the south of France, and soon introduced Benjamin as a
potential contributor. Although the journal survived for only a year,
it still stands as one of the most important "little magazines" of the
European avant-garde. Lehning was able to publish work by some of the
most advanced artists and writers; his concentration on photography

and film alone were enough to set the journal apart. The fact that Moholy-Nagy was the editor for all contributions concerning photography and film was surely an added incentive for Benjamin.

A small rivulet of other income sources opened that spring and summer of 1925. Benjamin took on several translation and editing projects. The most difficult and time-consuming of these—and finally the most rewarding—was his immersion in the world of Marcel Proust. He undertook the translation of the three-volume section of *In Search of Lost Time* called "Sodom and Gomorrah" despite his sense that the pay was "by no means good; but it is good enough for me to believe that I had to take on this enormous task" (C, 278). He would ultimately receive 2,300 marks for his work (about $550 in 1925 currency), payable in smaller sums throughout the contract, which ran until March 1926. He also accepted a smaller but no simpler assignment, the translation of the prose poem "Anabase" by the French diplomat and writer Saint-John Perse (pseudonym of Alexis Leger). Benjamin considered the work itself "inconsequential," but he was attracted not just by the relative generosity of the contract but also by its literary provenance: Rilke had originally agreed to translate the poem, but now offered to write a preface and see to its publication with his longtime publisher, Insel Verlag, provided that Benjamin—recommended once again by Hofmannsthal and by the publisher Thankmar von Münchhausen—would assume the actual work of translation. Benjamin completed the translation by late summer and sent it to Rilke and to Hofmannsthal—but it would not be published during his lifetime.[4] He also commenced work on a selection of texts by the nineteenth-century language theorist and educational reformer Wilhelm von Humboldt. Hofmannsthal had referred Willy Wiegand, the publisher of Bremer Presse (the house associated with Hofmannsthal's journal *Neue Deutsche Beiträge*) to Benjamin; after one false start brought on by a momentary fit of optimism regarding his academic chances, Benjamin accepted the commission, more out of loyalty to Hofmannsthal than because of its earning potential. The volume in fact never appeared, but Benjamin systematized the preliminary research for the project in the little text "Reflections on Humboldt." The resolutely negative character of his remarks—he castigates Humboldt for his failure to attend to "the magic side of language . . . its anthropological dimension, especially in the pathological sense," and for his corresponding insistence on a Hegelian understanding of language as "part of objective spirit"—may explain his lack of interest in the project.[5] The most important of these agreements was finalized only in August. On the very day of Benjamin's departure for an extended trip, he signed a general contract with Rowohlt Verlag that would provide him a small fixed income for 1926 and guaranteed the publication of three texts: *Origin of the German Trauerspiel, Plaquette for Friends* (the provisional title of the text that would appear as *One-Way Street*), and "Goethe's Elective Affinities."

The furious energy with which Benjamin cast about for publishing venues was underlain by an equally ambitious reading program. Several books had a profound effect on him, and some were surprises—foremost among them Thomas Mann's 1924 epic, *The Magic Mountain.* "I hardly know how to begin to tell you," he wrote Scholem on April 6, "that this man, whom I have hated like few other literary publicists, has gotten quite close to me because of his last great novel. . . . [It is] a book in which something that is unmistakably essential—something that moves me and has always moved me— . . . spoke to me. . . . I can only imagine that an internal change must have taken place in the author while he was writing. Indeed, I am certain this was the case" (C, 265). It was not only the sweeping and intimate portrayal of the key intellectual currents of the early twentieth century that Benjamin found compelling; it was also, his letter suggests, the perception that Thomas Mann had moved beyond the Nietzschean conservatism of his early years toward a new and more dialectical, if still pessimistic and mythically charged, Dionysian humanism (something epitomized in the protagonist's divagations in the chapter "Snow"). In his letter, Benjamin wonders whether Mann has seen his essay on Goethe's *Elective Affinities;* more than a decade later, he would publish sections of his *Berlin Childhood around 1900* in Mann's Swiss exile journal *Maß und Wert,* and Mann would remember Benjamin as the author of "the amazingly perceptive and profound book on the 'German *Trauerspiel,*' really a philosophy and history of allegory."[6] Mann's novel was also the occasion for one of the very few glimpses we have into life in the Delbrückstraße villa. On returning from a hike one day in the fall of 1925, Hilde Lange, a friend of Walter's sister, Dora, found the entire family—the parents and all three children—engrossed in a discussion of *The Magic Mountain*. Benjamin's letters convey the impression of his isolated existence within the household, but this anecdote suggests that some elements of family life united the extended group even at that late period.[7]

Benjamin's first sustained encounter with the work of Franz Kafka (who had died in 1924) also dates from these months. He read the short prose piece "Before the Law" (excerpted from *The Trial*) and pronounced it to be "one of the best German short stories" (C, 279). He was also continuing his education in leftist politics. Already in May he had conceived of such activity as a kind of career choice: "If I have no luck [in the publishing world]," he wrote to Scholem, "I will probably hasten my involvement in Marxist politics and join the Party—with a view of getting to Moscow in the foreseeable future, at least on a temporary basis" (C, 268). His brother, Georg, already firmly ensconced in the German Communist Party, gave Walter an edition of Lenin's work for his thirty-third birthday. Scholem also sent him an exquisite gift: the first edition of Moses Mendelssohn's *Jerusalem, oder Über religiöse Macht und Judenthum* (Jerusalem, or on Religious Power and Judaism) of 1783, along with a copy of Jacques Rivière's groundbreaking 1924 study of Proust (Rivière is an important source in *The Arcades Project*).

Through the long months of uncertainty, dread, and finally failure in connection with Frankfurt, Benjamin had indulged periodically in his favorite psychological "poison"—the thought of travel. His vague longing to escape from his troubles gradually took concrete form as he laid plans for a trip aboard a freighter that would stop at a series of Mediterranean ports of call. He had hoped to convince Asja Lacis to accompany him, but he succeeded only in enticing her to join him on a barge trip from Berlin to Hamburg, where he would board the freighter.[8] On August 19 the ship sailed from Hamburg, with Benjamin in unusually high spirits. Although he was worried about the possible lack of comfort afforded by this least expensive mode of travel, he was soon not just reassured but delighted: "This journey with the so-called freighter is one long aria of the most comfortable situations in life. In every foreign town you bring along your own room, indeed, your own little . . . vagabond household—; you have nothing to do with hotels, rooms, and fellow guests. Now I'm lying on deck, the evening in Genoa before me, and the sounds of unloading freighters all around me as the modernized 'music of the world'" (GB, 3:81). By the end of the month he was able to spend the first longer period ashore, exploring the region around Seville and Córdoba with its "fascinating exoticism"—and extraordinary heat (he reported a temperature in the sun of 122 degrees), which pushed Benjamin's powers to their limit. In Córdoba he saw not only the great mosque but also the work of the Spanish Baroque painter Juan de Valdés Leal, who had "the power of Goya, the sensibility of Rops, and the subject matter of Wiertz" (C, 283). Barcelona made a vivid impression on Benjamin: he was struck by the resemblance of the Ramblas to the Parisian boulevards, but also by the town's wilder, rougher side. He discovered hidden corners of the city in the company of the ship's captain and mates. "These people were the only ones I could talk to. They are uneducated, but not without independent judgment. And then they have something not easily found on the mainland: a sense for the difference between the well and badly brought up" (C, 283). As hard as it may be to imagine Benjamin in earnest discussion with a freighter's crew, it is obvious that he was accepted into the group and even shown a kind of respect. At the end of the trip he promised the captain a copy of his Balzac translation.

After a longer stop in Genoa, where he visited both the Riviera and the famous walk along the promontory from Rapallo to Portofino, the ship docked for several days at Pisa, and Benjamin was able to visit the walled city of Lucca for the first time. There he encountered a peculiar market day that occasioned one of the most memorable figures of thought in *One-Way Street*, "Not for Sale" (in the section entitled "Toys"). Benjamin describes a "mechanical cabinet" housed in a "long, symmetrically divided tent"; as the visitor walks between the tables, mechanical puppets tick into motion, presenting the viewer with a multifold historical and religious allegory within a space defined by "distorting mirrors." "Not for Sale" is one of Benjamin's earliest attempts to fix in imagery history's distortion of itself as it is mirrored in the constructs of consciousness. And, perhaps especially at this early stage of his affiliation with Marxism, he retains a forthright optimism regarding the final effect of the distortion: "You enter the tent by the right-hand opening and leave it by the left" (SW, 1:474–475). Benjamin departed from the ship and his friends in the crew in Naples, where he immediately found that "the city has once again filled the entire space in my heart that it occupied last year" (C, 284). In Naples Benjamin encountered his acquaintances Adorno and Kracauer, who were traveling together, and he engaged to lead them, along with Alfred Sohn-Rethel (who was still living in Positano), on an excursion to Capri, that place where "a week can pass by in a heartbeat" (GB, 3:80). As it happened, Benjamin was now able to reestablish a kind of intimacy with Jula Radt-Cohn, who was traveling in Italy with her husband, Fritz. He would be haunted by Radt-Cohn's presence in his room on Capri long into the next year.

From Capri, Benjamin traveled to Riga, the Latvian capital on the Baltic, arriving in the first days of November. He had come to visit Asja Lacis, but whether the trip was planned or the spontaneous result of awakening memories of their previous summer together we do not know. Something of Lacis's importance to Benjamin at this time in his life, and of the feverish anticipation of his arrival in her place of residence, is caught in the section "Ordnance" in *One-Way Street:*

> I had arrived in Riga to visit a woman friend. Her house, the town, the language were unfamiliar to me. Nobody was expecting me; no one knew me. For two hours I walked the streets in solitude. Never again have I seen them so. From every gate a flame darted; each cornerstone sprayed sparks, and every streetcar came toward me like a fire engine. For she might have stepped out of the gateway, around the corner, been sitting in the streetcar. But of the two of us, I had to be, at any price, the first to see the other. For had she touched me with the match of her eyes, I would have gone up like a powder keg. (SW, 1:461)

Lacis herself had no idea that Benjamin would appear at her doorstep. She was engaged in a series of Communist theater productions, including the establishment of a proletarian children's theater—and the Latvian government was threatening to arrest her for subversion. The appearance of her "holiday lover" made for an unpleasant shock. "It was the day before a premiere. I went to rehearsal, my head full of pressing concerns, and before me stood—Walter Benjamin. He loved surprises, but this time his surprise didn't please me at all. He came from another planet, and I had no time for him."[9] Benjamin lingered, forlorn, in Riga; the entire city seemed pervaded by Lacis's stern rebuke and his resultant melancholy. In "Stereoscope" (in the "Toys" section of *One-Way Street*), he remembered the city in its entirety as a huge market, "a huddling city of low wooden booths" that stretched along a jetty at which small steamers moored alongside the "blackish dwarftown." "At some corners one can find . . . the colored paper rods that penetrate as far as the West only at Christmastime. Like being scolded by the most-loved voice: such are these rods."[10] The rejection had its usual corporeal manifestation: he reported to Salomon that his general state "leaves much to be desired" (GB, 3:100). Although the visit never took on the joyous tones for which he had hoped, he was allowed to visit the theater and to see Lacis occasionally. He happened to attend a production of a play that confronted the solidly middle-class government head-on, and he was carried along by a huge crowd and pressed against a doorpost before finally freeing himself and climbing onto a window ledge; Lacis found him with a crushed hat and rumpled jacket and shirt collar. She recollected that the only thing that had pleased him about the play was a scene in which a gentleman in a top hat chatted with a worker under an umbrella; in which direction Benjamin's sympathies may have run during the scene is a matter of conjecture.[11]

By early December Benjamin was back in Berlin and in the Delbrückstraße villa, living with Dora, Stefan, and Grete Rehbein, the Benjamins' nanny. Seemingly reconciled to the lack of any future with Lacis, he settled into family life and began spending more time with Stefan, who was now seven and a half. He read to him several hours each week, "wandering aimlessly through a fairytale chaos at the bidding of our books" (C, 287). For Hanukkah, Benjamin retrieved the puppet theater from his own childhood and staged, with the help of two friends, a "spectacular" fairy play by the popular Austrian dramatist Ferdinand Raimund for Stefan and his friends (C, 288). Spurred on by this increased contact, he returned to his record of Stefan's childish sayings, which he had been sporadically assembling since 1918. This archive of a child's linguistic world reveals much about Benjamin's understanding of his son and about his own position in his

family, but it is in the main an inventory of charmingly childish ne-
ologisms: misunderstood and misheard words, original compounds,
and amusing phrases. For a thinker such as Benjamin, a child is a virtual laboratory in which the origins of human language lie ready to
hand, and the young Stefan's utterances continued to play a role in
Benjamin's writings until the end of the latter's life. Yet it is also clear
that Benjamin found what he wanted to find in his child, motifs and
practices that were derived from, or that fed into, the world of his own
intellectual interests: telepathic phenomena, somatic imitation of inanimate objects, and manifestations of the unconscious. For readers
of the notebook, it is also a document of linguistic sociology: we see
how family life shapes language—in this case, a family life made to
revolve around Walter's work. He remembers Stefan's first word:
"quiet," no doubt the word heard most often from his mother as
Daddy was reading or writing. One anecdote, evidently recounted by
Grete Rehbein, the nanny, is telling.

> We were away from the house—this was after several days in which
> I had pressed for quiet in the apartment because of a piece I had to
> write—he is alone in the kitchen with Grete. He says: "Grete to be
> very quiet. He has to work now. Very quiet." With that he climbs the
> dark stairs, opens both doors, and goes into his dark room. When
> Grete follows him after a few moments, she sees him standing still
> in the darkness. He says: "Not to disturb him, Grete! He really has
> to work."[12]

A number of motifs are intertwined here: the child's role-playing
as compensation for the absent father; the subordination of all aspects
of family life to the father's work; and the child's conception of work
as a kind of dwelling in dark, splendid isolation. Some ambivalence
on the part of the father toward his son may also be felt here. On one
hand, Benjamin thought so highly of his son's linguistic gifts (or, at
any rate, of the intrinsic interest of the data he had collected) that he
considered having the notebook typed and distributed to his friends;
he referred to it as Stefan's "opinions et pensées," in playful reference
to the long tradition of writers' notebooks. Ernst Schoen, visiting over
Christmas, had indeed prophesied great things for the young man. At
the same time, Benjamin could note, laconically, that his son was pro-

17. Dora Benjamin (sister), late 1920s (*Akademie der Künste, Berlin. Walter Benjamin Archiv*)

moted to the next grade with "thoroughly average" marks (GB, 3:131). Such coolness did not go unremarked. Stefan's daughter Mona Jean Benjamin later remembered that her father—an erudite bookseller in London—was extremely reluctant to discuss his own father. "He found it very hard to talk about a figure who for him was never really a true father bur more an intellectual figure; someone very distant; someone who he remembers as a man who used to bring him toys from foreign countries."[13]

This was also, for Benjamin, a time of increased contact with his siblings. His sister, Dora, was still living at home, so daily contact was inevitable; his brother, Georg, had his own apartment but was a frequent visitor to the Delbrückstraße villa. Dora had attended a school for girls, the Bismarck-Lyceum, in Grunewald near the parental home. Such schools did not, however, offer the diploma necessary for study at a university; although the Prussian state had passed laws in 1908 extending the same school opportunities to girls as those offered boys, there were, in 1918, only forty-five schools in all of Prussia that offered girls the *Abitur* or degree leading to university study.[14] Dora was thus forced to attend private courses designed for women in order to prepare for university. In 1919 the Prussian government relented and allowed girls to enter a boys' gymnasium; Dora immediately seized this opportunity and was admitted to the Grunewald-Realgymnasium, where her brother Georg had graduated in 1914. After her graduation in 1921, she studied economics at the universities in Berlin, Heidelberg, Jena, and finally Greifswald, where she earned her doctorate in 1924 with a dissertation on the impact on child rearing of women's work at home for the garment industry.[15] In the course of the 1920s she published a revised version of her dissertation in book form, as well as several articles on related topics in the journal *Soziale Praxis*, establishing herself as a recognized authority on the complex issues surrounding work and family in the proletarian milieu. Her work—and her close friendship with her future sister-in-law Hilde Benjamin—brought her close to her brother Georg. Three years younger than Walter, Georg had had his studies interrupted by the war; he earned a doctorate in medicine only in 1923, after first joining the Independent Social Democrats in 1920 and the German Communist Party in 1922. Although Benjamin's relationship to his sister remained difficult long into the 1930s, the brothers saw each other frequently and, especially after Walter began moving toward the radical left, a more intimate relationship grew up between them. In early 1926 Georg married Hilde Lange; Benjamin commented that Georg had "trained" Hilde to be a Communist and that her Christian parents would thus have "a doubly bitter pill to swallow" (C, 288). Neither assertion was based in fact. Although Georg had met Hilde Lange while she was visiting his sister, Dora, Lange had found her own path to the left and discovered a kindred spirit in Georg. In the course of the 1920s both Georg and Hilde would assume increasing prominence in the Communist Party. Georg was appointed municipal school physician for Berlin-Wedding in 1925; he complemented his work with proletarian children by publishing a steady stream of articles, both scholarly and popular, on questions of social hygiene. Hilde, who had earned a law degree, was meanwhile continuing her professional preparation, which culminated in her admission to the bar in

18. Georg Benjamin, late 1920s *(Akademie der Künste, Berlin. Walter Benjamin Archiv)*

1929. She went on to become, in the 1950s, a judge notorious for her severity toward opponents of the Communist regime and then, from 1963 to 1967, the minister of justice in the German Democratic Republic. In 1926, however, their tiny apartment in Wedding functioned as a kind of salon where Communist and left-leaning bourgeois intellectuals came together.

For the first time since 1917, Walter Benjamin was without a major project (aside from the Proust translation, which he had undertaken more for financial reasons than out of intellectual necessity)—if by major project we understand a book-length study. Yet Benjamin was coming to see that he could carve a niche for himself in the German publishing world if he established himself as the main conduit for the serious French literature of his day; his familiarity with contemporary France prompted his resolve to "weave this threadbare fact into a solid context." Although he wrote relatively little in late 1925 and early 1926, he was reading "a sinful amount of things"—and most of this was French (C, 288). But his reading also fed his other interests: he read Trotsky on politics (as well as a debate over Lukács and Bukharin's theory of world history [GB, 3:133]), and Ludwig Klages and Carl Albrecht Bernoulli on the Swiss legal scholar, historian, and matriarchal theorist Johann Jacob Bachofen. In a statement that he would repeat with variations well into the 1930s, he asserted to Scholem that "a confrontation with Bachofen and Klages is unavoidable; many things suggest that this confrontation can be strictly conducted only from the perspective of Jewish theology. This, of course, is where these important scholars scent their archenemy—and not without reason" (C, 288). Although he returned to this "confrontation" several times over the next fifteen years, he was never able to write the definitive work on Bachofen and Klages that he envisioned. As always, Benjamin was also consuming great quantities of detective novels. Only now, in correspondence with Kracauer, did he begin to discern a path down which he could turn his personal obsessions, such as detective novels, into objects of serious consideration. Benjamin may thus be the only commentator in the history of the detective genre to view it from the perspective of the doctrine of humors: he remarks to Kracauer that the figure of the detective fits "remarkably uncomfortably" in the old scheme, yet shares qualities not just with the melancholy humor but with the phlegmatic (GB, 3:147).

Whether he was working on or avoiding it, the Proust translation was never far from his mind. This was partly due to awareness of the proximity of Proust's "philosophical perspective" to his own: "Whenever [in the past] I read anything he wrote, I felt we were kindred souls" (C, 278). The literary publishers Die Schmiede had obtained the rights to Proust's novel from Gallimard in 1925; the first volume had appeared that same year in a translation by the writer Rudolf Schottlaender. This first version of Proust's great work met with scathing reviews. Ernst Robert Curtius, a young scholar of Romance languages who had just begun to publish the work that would make him a leading interpreter of the Latin Middle Ages, had decimated it, finding it not merely plodding but riddled with errors. Curtius's review so alarmed Proust's editors at Gallimard that they convinced the French ambassador to intervene with Die Schmiede. By the fall of 1926, Benjamin and his friend Franz Hessel had discussed with the press the prospect of translating the entire novel, including new translations of the two volumes (volumes 1 and 3) previously published. By August of that year, he and Hessel had completed the first volume of their translation (volume 2 of the novel); ultimately, they would complete three volumes and part of a fourth. *A l'ombre des jeunes filles en fleurs* was published in German by Die Schmiede in 1927, and, after Die Schmiede's bankruptcy, *Le Côté de Guermantes* by Piper Verlag in 1930. Benjamin's completed translation of *Sodome et Gomorrhe*, the result of so much feverish labor on Capri in the summer of 1924, was never published, and the manuscript has never been found. Hessel and Benjamin broke off before completing *La prisonnière*. "You might not get far when you read my Proust translation," he writes to Scholem. "Some unusual things would have to happen for it to become readable. The thing is immensely difficult, and there are many reasons why I can devote very little time to it" (C, 289). Not the least of these reasons was the relatively low remuneration. Stylistically, he was faced with the untranslatability of Proust's lavish, expansive sentences, which, with their constantly deferred terminations, "stand in tension to the spirit of the French language in general and . . . lend to the original a good part of its character": the German can't be as "allusive and surprising" (C, 290). His struggles with the translation, however, were leading him toward some highly original and surprising formulations apropos of the great French novelist: "The most problematical side of his genius is his total elimination of the ethical viewpoint [*des Sittlichen*], something that goes together with the supreme subtlety in his observation of everything physical and spiritual. This is perhaps—in part—to be understood as the 'experimental procedure' in this immense laboratory, where time is made the subject of experiments with thousands of reflectors, concave and convex reflections" (C, 290–291). This observation would be refined and elaborated in the essay "On the Image of Proust," which Benjamin published in 1929, one of the great early assessments of the novelist and his masterwork.

He also received a commission, probably through the intervention of Bernhard Reich, to write three hundred lines on Goethe for the new *Great Soviet Encyclopedia*. Although the essay appeared only in late 1928, and in bowdlerized form, Benjamin approached the task with real enthusiasm, and not a little irony. "The divine impudence inherent in the acceptance of such a commission appealed to me," he wrote, "and I think I will manage to concoct something appropriate" (C, 294). He engaged in a series of lively conversations on the role of Goethe in contemporary leftist culture with Georg and Hilde Benjamin and their friends in Wedding; from those discussions, and from wide reading in nineteenth-century literary history, Benjamin concluded that a Marxist perspective on Goethe provided an opportunity to bring the Olympian to earth by treating him historically, as part of a literary history worthy of its name.

> I was not a little amazed to learn how literary history was being written as late as the middle of the last century, and how powerful Julian Schmidt's three-volume *Geschichte der deutschen Literatur seit Lessings Tod* [History of German Literature since Lessing's Death] is—what clear contours it has, like a beautifully structured frieze. One sees what has been lost when books of this kind are produced as reference works, and one sees that the (unimpeachable) demands of more recent scholarly techniques are incompatible with achieving an *eidos*, a vivid image of a life. It is also amazing how the objectivity of this bullheaded chronicler's mentality increases with historical distance, while the measured and lukewarm manner of expressing judgments, which is typical of more recent literary histories, cannot help appearing an insipid and indifferent expression of contemporary taste, precisely because it lacks the personal element that might act as a corrective. (C, 308)

Laboring to produce a review of Hofmannsthal's late drama *The Tower*, Benjamin was keenly aware of his debt to the older writer and determined to produce something laudatory, but he had misgivings about Hofmannsthal's play and its attempt to wrest a modern *Trauerspiel* from an engagement with Calderón's *Life Is a Dream*. Before even beginning to work on the piece, he told Scholem that, although he had not yet read the play, "my private judgment is already clear from the outset; and my countervailing, public one as well" (GB, 3:27).

As the long Berlin winter came to an end, Benjamin's thoughts turned, as they did so often, to escape. As a general pretext, he had the need to conduct more fieldwork in contemporary French culture; it required only a specific catalyst to get him onto the train and away from Germany. That catalyst took the form of an invitation from Franz and Helen Hessel to come and stay with them at Fontenay-aux-Roses, a suburban town just south of Paris, while they continued to work on the translation of Proust. Benjamin followed the call but, instead of moving in with the Hessels, chose to "sample the pleasures of living in a hotel for once" (C, 293). He established himself at the Hôtel du Midi near the Place de Denfert-Rochereau in Montparnasse on March 16. Besides accelerating the work on the translation, and the payments that were tied to it, he hoped to take real steps toward establishing himself as the leading German commentator on French culture. He was aware that he could do this only by refining his spoken and written French; finding the "tempo and temperature" of the real language would make possible genuine connections to leading French writers and intellectuals (C, 302). But there were other reasons for coming. His financial situation continued to be extremely precarious, and he felt that he could live for half or even a third as much as in Germany. And besides the Hessels, Jula Radt-Cohn was also living in the city, and she continued to magnetize him.

The Parisian spring awakened in Benjamin some of the expansive vitality he had known on Capri. "I am witness to nothing less than a terrorist attack by the spring on this city: true explosions of green have broken out in one or two nights in the most varied parts of town" (GB, 3:141–142). Indulging in aimless strolling, he wandered along the quays with their bookstalls, through the Grands Boulevards, and into the out-of-the-way workers' quarters. As had been the case in Berlin, he became a habitué of the Parisian cafés, preferring the Café du Dôme above all others. Constantly on the lookout for restaurants that could provide him with good, inexpensive food, he reported with enthusiasm on a coachman's inn near his hotel that offered cheap multicourse meals. And he was able to expand his knowledge of modernist art by visiting major exhibitions of the work of Cézanne and Ensor. His delight at his new surroundings translated into an enhanced productivity. "I have discovered a regimen that magically entices the goblins to help out. It consists of my sitting down to work as soon as I get up in the morning, without getting dressed, without moistening my hands or body with a single drop of water, indeed without even drinking any. And I do nothing, much less eat breakfast, before finishing the task I set for the day. This induces the strangest side effects imaginable. I can then do what I want in the afternoon or just stroll along the streets" (C, 297).

Daytime flânerie was not Benjamin's only indulgence. Early in his stay, he reported to Jula Radt-Cohn that he was able to work unusually well because he was spending so many evenings absorbing "Paris right down to [his] fingertips" (C, 292). Some of these evenings fed his interest in popular culture: he visited the Cirque d'Hiver and saw the famous Fratellini clowns, whom he found "much more beautiful than you can imagine; you have to double your estimate of their fame among the public because they have attained it with old routines, or topical ones, but never with 'modern' ones" (GB, 3:172). And he published a report in *Die literarische Welt* on an evening of Surrealist farce in a private studio; he continued to be profoundly ambivalent about Surrealist art and found the whole thing "wretched." The darker underbelly of Parisian popular culture had a wholly different effect: he wrote glowingly in letters about the undiscovered *bals musettes* and bawdy dancehalls he visited. Forays into the world of the sex trade, often taken in the company of Franz Hessel, Thankmar von Münchhausen, or both, were alluded to more coyly. Benjamin never described the exact nature of the exploration of the Parisian demimonde by these three Germans. He recalled "in the last few nights rummaging, under very reliable direction, through wonderful folds in the worn stone coat of the city" (GB, 3:166). Dora has filled out the picture somewhat: in divorce proceedings at the end of the decade, she claimed that Hessel supplied Benjamin throughout the 1920s with a series of young women of loose morals.

These two friends were considerably more experienced in the ways of the world than was Benjamin. The writer and publisher Münchhausen (1893–1979) had come to know the Hessels in Paris in 1912, where he moved in the same artistic circles in Montparnasse. He had had an extended affair with Helen Hessel beginning in 1914, while Hessel was in the army (the character Fortunio in the Truffaut film *Jules and Jim* is based on him), and with Marie Laurencin after the war. Like Hessel and Benjamin, he supported himself at this period through journalism and translation work. Benjamin derived more than intellectual stimulation from Münchhausen's company: his friend seemed always to have an attractive woman at his side, and he often provided

19. Franz Hessel, ca. 1928 (*ullstein bild/The Granger Collection, New York*)

Benjamin with a matching companion. On a day trip to Chantilly and Senlis, Münchhausen's "local flame" was "a not terribly significant but not at all irksome painter whose husband melts into the background in a way beyond description"; although Benjamin gives no hint of the identity of his own companion, he does tell Jula Radt-Cohn: "It appears that chic goyim are currently my cup of tea. It was always most pleasant when we were together as couples" (C, 296).

In the course of the 1920s, Franz Hessel would become one of Benjamin's closest friends. Already in his student years in Munich, Hessel had been at the center of the Schwabinger Bohème, living between 1903 and 1906 in the famous "Eckhaus" at Kaulbachstraße 63 with the impoverished Countess Fanny zu Reventlow and a series of her other lovers, including Ludwig Klages and Karl Wolfskehl. This experiment in the "communism of life" brought Hessel into contact not just with the Cosmic Circle but also with the leading figures in the most advanced modernist cenacle in Germany: Rainer Maria

Rilke, Alexej von Jawlensky, Frank Wedekind, Oskar Panizza, and many others.[16] After breaking off his studies—and his relationship with Countess Reventlow—Hessel moved to Paris, where he frequented the art scene in Montparnasse. At the Café du Dôme he met his future wife, the young art student Helen Grund, and the art collector and agent Henri-Pierre Roché; through Roché, Hessel came to know some of the central figures in Parisian modernism, including Pablo Picasso, Gertrude Stein, Max Jacob, Francis Picabia, and Marcel Duchamp. After serving in the war, Hessel had lived a retired life with Helen in Schäftlarn, a village south of Munich; a series of love triangles were acted out that involved not just the Hessels and Roché but also Helen Hessel's sister Johanna and her husband, Hessel's brother Alfred. Until very recently, Franz Hessel was best known for his role in these affairs: Truffaut's *Jules and Jim* is based on the autobiographical novel of the same name that Roché published in 1953. Franz and Helen Hessel had dissolved their marriage after the intensive experience of the ménage à trois depicted in *Jules and Jim* but had remarried in 1922 and now lived together in Paris in a very open arrangement; Helen could name at least six young women with whom Franz had had extended relationships. Hessel continued to work on major projects for Rowohlt Verlag while translating Proust and working on his third novel, *Heimliches Berlin* (Secret Berlin). Like Benjamin (whose *Arcades Project* he helped inaugurate), Hessel had little sense for the pragmatics of daily life; also like Benjamin, he was an unprepossessing figure. His son Stéphane remembered him as "almost bald, of a small stature and somewhat corpulent. His face and his gestures had a gentle effect; he was for us a somewhat distracted sage who lived within himself and had hardly anything to do with [his children]. Not exactly loquacious, he took great pains with his manner of expression and found a playful delight in the ordering of words."[17]

Benjamin's relationship with Helen Hessel was complex. While he detested what he saw as her efforts to involve him in her "social maneuvering," he took considerable pleasure not just in her attempts to flirt with him but in his own efforts to stiffen his "resolve not to respond in kind" (C, 296). Helen had various reasons for living in Paris. She had begun to forge a considerable reputation for herself as a commentator on the world of fashion and was working in Paris as the fashion correspon-

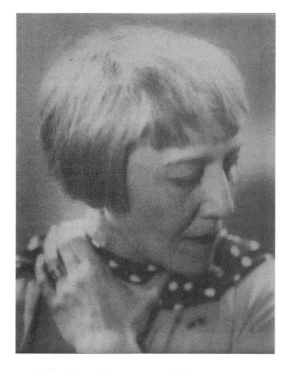

20. Helen Hessel, late 1920s (© *Marianne*
Breslauer / Fotostiftung Schweiz)

dent of the *Frankfurter Zeitung.* (Benjamin would cite her work in his
chapter on fashion in *The Arcades Project.*) The fact that her assignment
took her close to her lover, Roché, was hardly insignificant.

It would be difficult to overestimate the importance of the long
walks Benjamin took with Hessel in Berlin and Paris in the twenties.
For Hessel, the stroll through the urban jungle was undertaken in full
consciousness of its opposition to the instrumentality inherent in
modernization: he called aimless walking a "purely purposeless pleasure." "That strolling absolves you from your more or less wretched
private existence is its most incomparably charming aspect. You keep
company, you communicate, with an array of alien circumstances
and fates. The true stroller is made aware of this by the remarkable
fright experienced when he suddenly encounters an acquaintance in
the dream city of his flânerie and quite simply becomes, with an abrupt
jolt, a determinate individual once again."[18] In the years to come, while

working not just on contemporary French culture but, in the study that bore the working title *The Arcades Project*, on various cultural manifestations of the urban commodity capitalism arising in the nineteenth century, Benjamin came to define the figure of the Parisian flâneur, which has come down to us largely through Baudelaire's poetry and the painting of the Impressionists, as nothing less than an archetype of modern consciousness. And Franz Hessel—with his innate discretion, his sage distraction, and his developed voyeuristic tendencies—embodied the modern flâneur to a superlative degree. In their walks through the streets of the metropolis, Benjamin must have had the first glimmerings of ideas that would come to fruition in what is surely the most gripping analysis of modernity to be produced in the twentieth century.

If Hessel and flânerie provided Benjamin with the peripatetic mode of modern observation, his exchanges with Siegfried Kracauer helped determine what would become his characteristic subject matter. And if Hessel stressed the spontaneously framed optical insight into a particular aspect of urban life, Siegfried Kracauer, in writings from the period such as "Two Planes," "Analysis of a City Map," and "The Hotel Lobby," emphasized the materiality and exteriority of the city, its commonplace objects, textures, and surface structures. During the time in Paris, Benjamin's correspondence with Kracauer took on a new intensity, as they began to share their unpublished studies with each other. With the publication of the essay "Travel and Dance" in the *Frankfurter Zeitung* on March 15, 1925, Kracauer showed the way to a mode of cultural analysis commensurate with the new social forms of capitalist modernity. The essay focuses on popular practices— travel and dance as "spatio-temporal passions"—that have become, on Kracauer's reading, means of coping with the boredom and sameness of life in modern society: travel is reduced to a pure experience of a space that is "less deadeningly familiar" than the everyday, while dancing, as a "representation of rhythm," deflects attention from chronological sequence toward the contemplation of time itself.[19] "Travel and Dance" is a key essay for Kracauer in a number of ways. It shows him turning toward forms and artifacts of everyday modernity as revelatory of the character of the whole historical epoch. In the years to come, in essays with titles such as "Cult of Distraction,"

"Analysis of a City Map," "Calico World," and "The Little Shopgirls Go to the Movies," Kracauer would offer brilliant explorations and critiques of contemporary culture. His gaze was particularly attuned to Berlin's diverse and frenetically active leisure world: spectacles with Tiller girls, movies, shopping, bestsellers. Perhaps the signal accomplishment of these essays is the reorientation of Weimar's critical gaze toward surface phenomena that in traditional culture had been dismissed as ephemeral and, well, superficial.

Benjamin was in frequent touch with Kracauer as he reoriented his work not just toward France and the Soviet Union but toward popular and everyday phenomena. Kracauer's discerning and sometimes minute physiognomic approach to city life brought about fundamental changes in the younger man's work. Benjamin points repeatedly to a new "convergence" between his way of seeing and that of Kracauer. After praising Kracauer's essay "Das Mittelgebirge" (Central German Uplands), he writes, "As you continue to pursue the clichés of the petit bourgeois stagings of dream and longing, I believe that wonderful discoveries lie ahead of you, and we will perhaps encounter each other at the one point at which I've been taking aim with all my energy for the last year . . . : the postcard. Maybe someday you will write that redemption of stamp collecting for which I've been waiting so long without daring to undertake it myself" (GB, 3:177). In writing to his friend about his experiences of Paris, Benjamin emphasizes his attempt to approach the city first in its "exteriority"—its street layout, transportation systems, its cafés and newspapers. It was Kracauer, then, who showed Benjamin how a theory apparently suited only to the refractory objects of a mandarin cultural elite might open up the world around him.

For both writers—and especially for Benjamin—the turn to the popular brought with it a reconsideration of what it meant to write criticism in a politically and historically responsible fashion. A 1926 letter to Kracauer written in Paris confirms Benjamin's awareness of the need for a new directness and transparency: "What is meant [das Gemeinte] has emerged more clearly in my writings in the course of time. There is really nothing that can be more urgently important for a writer" (GB, 3:180). Fortunately, we have been left with a precise record of the gradual change in Benjamin's style and focus: the montage book One-Way Street was composed between 1923 and 1926 and offers not just a snapshot of the new prose form that would dominate Benjamin's Weimar criticism, the *Denkbild* or figure of thought, but a virtual user's guide to the new critical method. First published in 1928, the book consists of sixty short prose pieces; these differ wildly in genre, style, and content. There are aphorisms among the texts, and jokes and dream protocols. There are also descriptive set pieces: cityscapes, landscapes, mindscapes. There are portions of writing manuals; trenchant contemporary political analysis; prescient appreciations of the child's psychology, behavior, and moods; decodings of bourgeois fashion, living arrangements, and courtship patterns that anticipate the Roland Barthes of *Mythologies*; and, time and again, remarkable penetrations into the heart of everyday things, what Benjamin would later call the "exploration of the soul of the commodity."

Many of the pieces in *One-Way Street* first appeared in the feuilleton section of newspapers and magazines, and that medium played a decisive role in the shaping of the prose form on which the book is based. The feuilleton had been introduced in French political journals and newspapers in the nineteenth century. Although it was in some ways the forerunner of the arts and leisure sections of today's newspapers, there were significant differences: (1) rather than a separate section, the feuilleton appeared on the bottom third of most pages of the paper, demarcated by a printed line (in German, feuilleton pieces are commonly said to appear *unter dem Strich*, "below the line"); (2) it consisted mainly of cultural criticism and of serial publications of longer literary texts, but also included significant quantities of other material, including gossip, fashion commentary, and a variety of short forms—aphorisms, epigrams, quick takes on cultural objects and issues—often referred to as "glosses." In the course of the 1920s, a number of prominent writers shaped their writing practice in order to accommodate it to the feuilleton; the *kleine Form* or "little form" that resulted came rapidly to be identified as the primary mode of cultural commentary and criticism in the Weimar Republic. The writer Ernst Penzoldt defined the subject matter of the "little form" in the following way: "poetic observations of the small and big world, daily experience in all its charm, fond strolls, curious encounters, moods, sentimental chatter, glosses and things of that sort."[20] By the late years of the Weimar Republic, the "little form" had become so pervasive as to seem the cognate of metropolitan modernity. In the 1931 novel *Käsebier Conquers the Kurfürstendamm*, by Gabriele Tergit, the publisher of a Berlin daily offers the writer Lambeck the opportunity to write on a regular basis about Berlin. "He was tempted. It would be pleasant to be able to bring his experiences, couched in cultured prose, directly to someone else for once, rather than simply storing them up. . . . Lambeck said, 'Allow me to consider your proposal from the ground up; I just don't know whether the little form suits me or not.' "[21]

The form certainly suited Walter Benjamin. The first section of *One-Way Street*, "Filling Station," is a call to arms for the little form. "Significant literary effectiveness can come into being only in a strict alternation between action and writing; it must nurture the inconspicuous forms that fit its influence in active communities better than does the pretentious, universal gesture of the book—in leaflets, brochures, articles, and placards. Only this prompt language shows itself actively equal to the moment" (SW, 1:444). In a series of rapid claims in the sections to come, Benjamin privileges the fragment over the finished work ("the work is the death mask of its conception"), improvisation over "competence" ("all decisive blows are struck with the left hand"), and waste products and detritus over the carefully crafted (children bring together "materials of widely different kinds in a new, intuitive relationship") (SW, 1:459, 447, 450). Traditional forms of writing were, for Benjamin, simply no longer capable of surviving in capitalist modernity—let alone of providing the framework for meaningful insights into its structure, functioning, and effects. "Script—having found, in the book, a refuge in which it can lead an autonomous existence—is pitilessly dragged out into the street by advertisements and subjected to the brutal heteronomies of economic chaos" (SW, 1:456). As these oppositions imply, Benjamin was convinced that any criticism worth the name was animated by "a moral question": "the critic is the strategist in the literary struggle" (SW, 1:460).

This new understanding of his writing was shaped by Benjamin's evolving political consciousness. He offered a key statement on his position in a letter to Scholem of May 29, 1926, a position he had developed in direct reaction to current conditions in Europe: "Anyone of our generation who feels and understands the historical moment in which he exists in this world, not as mere words, but as a battle, cannot renounce the study and the praxis of the mechanism through which things (and conditions) interact with the masses." Of course, Benjamin knew what to expect from his friend's reaction to the letter: Scholem had already accused him of betraying his earlier work and convictions. The letter is remarkable for its attempt to couch a Communist politics within the framework of religious observance: "I do not concede that there is a difference between [religious and political observance] in terms of their quintessential being. Yet I also do not concede that a mediation between them is possible."[22] Rather than any such mediation, Benjamin acknowledges only a "paradoxical reversal" of one into the other—a reversal that is "ruthless and radical" and which carries with it a task, "not to decide once and for all, but to decide at every moment. . . . If I were to join the Communist Party one day . . . my stance, in regard to the most important things, would be always to proceed radically and never with an eye to consequences." Benjamin's credo ends with a coded endorsement of ideas he had developed while reading Unger's *Metaphysics and Politics*. He considers "Communist 'goals' to be nonsense and nonexistent," yet "this does not diminish the value of Communist action one iota, because it is the corrective for its goal and because there are no meaningfully *political* goals" (C, 300–301). Political action—whether anarchism or communism—remains useful only insofar as it opens a space for meaningful religious experience.

Although the Hessels provided Benjamin with an entry into a number of French and German émigré intellectual circles—he met not only Francis and Gabrielle Picabia but also the writer and translator Pierre Klossowski (younger brother of the painter Balthus) and the photographer Gisèle Freund (with both of whom he would become close friends in the 1930s) at the Hessels' home—he remained acutely aware of his marginal status in Paris and of how difficult it would be for a little-known German intellectual to become part of the fabric of French culture. Benjamin found "as many people as you could possibly want to socialize with pleasantly for a quarter of an hour, but no one who is terribly eager to have anything more to do with you" (C, 301). His solution was a "persistent courtship" of the city. He was aided in this by a powerful ally: time. Benjamin had nowhere to be, and he sensed a newfound patience with his situation. In the course of his stay, he met Jean Cocteau (at the premiere of his "extraordinarily interesting" *Orphée* [GB, 3:182]), heard Paul Valéry lecture, and became acquainted with Jean Paulhan, the editor in chief of the *Nouvelle Revue Française*. And he began living out a kind of Proustian fantasy: introduced by Münchhausen, he made several forays into the part of the cultured Parisian aristocracy that had "remained true to the art-patron manners of old" (GB, 3:130). He attended lectures at the salon of the comte de Pourtalès, "with expensive furniture, adorned by a sprinkling of ladies and gentlemen with the most wicked physiognomies, the likes of which you can only find in Proust." And he was invited to a breakfast given by the Princess di Bassiano at a leading restaurant: "It began with huge portions of caviar and continued in this way. The cooking was done at a stove in the center of the room and everything was displayed before it was served" (C, 296). Although he was often bored, and frequently appalled by the shallowness and cultural pretensions of these events, he was also sometimes reduced to the posture of awestruck impoverished arriviste.

If he met with limited success in his attempts to be accepted by the Parisian intelligentsia, the time in Paris was enlivened—and more than occasionally disturbed—by the steady stream of friends and new acquaintances he encountered. He went out of his way to get to know the Austrian novelist and journalist Joseph Roth, whose 1932 family saga, *Radetzky March*, would chronicle the decline and fall of the Austro-Hungarian Empire. From 1923 until 1932 Roth served as a staff writer at the *Frankfurter Zeitung;* Benjamin approached him at Kracauer's suggestion while Roth was in Paris to write a series of feuilleton articles for the journal. Although the two writers never established any kind of intimate friendship, they would see each other periodically both in Berlin and in Paris until Roth's death in 1939. In the months to come, Benjamin would see as much of Ernst Bloch as he would of the Hessels. Yet Benjamin could not wholly overcome his critical view of his friend—or the suspicion that Bloch was stealing

21. Benjamin portrait bust by Jula Cohn. Photo by
Sasha Stone *(Akademie der Künste, Berlin. Walter
Benjamin Archiv)*

his ideas. "Bloch is an extraordinary individual," he wrote to Jula
Radt-Cohn, "and I revere him as the greatest connoisseur of my writings (he knows what they are about much better even than I, because
he is thoroughly acquainted not only with everything I have ever
written but also with every word I have ever spoken, going back for
years)" (C, 299). On hearing in April that Bloch's work was becoming
fashionable in Jerusalem, he quipped to Scholem that "this is a sign of
a considerable slackening of the instincts" (GB, 3:135).

Although the presence of Jula Radt-Cohn had been part of the appeal of Paris, she left early in his stay, and the remainder of it was
colored by longing for her, set down in an increasingly intimate series
of letters. Benjamin made frequent reference to the now-famous portrait bust she had made of him. "I often think of you," he wrote on
April 30, "and, more than anything, I often wish you were in my
room. It is not at all like the room in Capri, yet it would seem plausi-

ble to you—and you would seem *very plausible to me* in it. . . . I hope
that you notice that I hold you very dear—especially now, as I write—
and keep to the point just as little as a hand when it caresses" (C, 298;
GB, 3:151). Although he could not bring himself to ask her directly to
leave her husband (Jula had married his old friend Fritz Radt in December 1925), he does press her to come to Paris alone: "If you come,
we will have created a situation for ourselves for the first time in
which not everything is coincidence. And we are old enough now for
that: it will do us good" (GB, 3:171). Benjamin's letters to Radt-Cohn
during these years strongly suggest that they shared an intermittent
physical intimacy, one they took pains to hide from Fritz Radt. Also
early in his stay, Salomon-Delatour came through Paris, but Benjamin
noted their increasingly distant relationship by remarking that his
Frankfurt supporter and confidant had "come drably and left sound-
lessly" (GB, 3:157). May was enlivened by a visit from Ernst Schoen
and his wife, who were accompanied by the Russian émigré photographer Sasha Stone, whom Benjamin knew from the G group; Stone
would provide the montage cover of *One-Way Street*.

The stay in Paris was broken by a violent caesura: Benjamin's father
died suddenly on July 18, and Benjamin returned to Berlin for a month.
His relationship with his father had been marked by recurrent strife
ever since his marriage, as Benjamin stubbornly insisted that it was his
father's duty to support his intellectual aspirations and career as a
writer. Yet they had lived together under one roof for much of this time,
and glimmerings of an intimate father-son bond sometimes break
through the vitriol. Certainly the portrait of his father that Benjamin
draws in a series of autobiographical writings from the early 1930s is
that of a man who was caring, if somewhat distant and imposing. The
loss was thus a blow from which Benjamin struggled for a while to recover. He had been plagued for much of the time in Paris by the deep
depression that visited him so often. After a vivid description of joyous
days in Paris, he cautioned Jula to "keep in mind that this kind of hot,
holiday sun does not shine upon me every day" (C, 297). On his return
to Paris following the death of his father, however, he began to experience symptoms of a new sort and severity. Ernst Bloch noted suicidal
tendencies in his old friend, and on Benjamin's arrival back in Berlin, he
reported to friends that he had suffered a "nervous breakdown."

Even while he struggled with depression and nervous ailments, Benjamin was embarking on a new intellectual adventure. During the last weeks of his stay in Paris, he was joined by Bloch and Kracauer, both of whom moved into the Hôtel du Midi; his friends immediately adopted Benjamin's Parisian habits, and the three of them walked and talked until late into the night. Bloch had feuded with Kracauer for years after a devastating review of his 1921 book *Thomas Münzer as the Theologian of Revolution* in the *Frankfurter Zeitung*; but, encountering Kracauer in late August 1926 in a café on the Place de l'Odéon, he strode directly up to him and wished him good day. In Bloch's account, "It took Kracauer's breath away when, after an attack like that on me and after my reaction to it, . . . I went up to him and put out my hand."[23] Living in such close proximity, the three friends experienced a new intellectual solidarity. Bloch tried to win Benjamin's collaboration on the formulation of a "system of materialism," but for Benjamin, intellectual solidarity had its limits. Benjamin was certainly no easy friend, especially on a daily basis, as Scholem had discovered on more than one occasion. Bloch now tried repeatedly to counter Benjamin's melancholy with what he called a "militant optimism." But Benjamin held to the "organization of pessimism." As he was to put it in his great 1929 essay on Surrealism, "Pessimism all along the line. Absolutely. Mistrust in the fate of literature, mistrust in the fate of freedom, mistrust in the fate of European humanity, but three times mistrust in all reconciliation: between classes, between nations, between individuals. And unlimited trust only in IG Farben and the peaceful perfecting of the air force. But what now? What next?" (SW, 2:216–217). Bloch later described life in the hotel as plagued by "trench sickness."[24]

Perhaps in an attempt to leave his depression and nerves behind him, Benjamin traveled south with Bloch, arriving in Marseilles on September 7. Kracauer and his girlfriend (later wife), Elizabeth "Lili" Ehrenreich, had gone ahead, and Benjamin moved into the Hôtel Regina on the Place Sadi Carnot, near the Grand Hôtel de Paris, where Kracauer was staying. His letters from these weeks make it clear that his condition was little better; he told Münchhausen that he had had one nervous breakdown after another, and that "the periods of doing well in between only made it worse in the end" (GB, 3:188). He goes so far as to tell Scholem that his "prospects of recovery are doubtful." Part of his concern was related to the work on Proust: "One could say a lot about the actual work. Let me add . . . that, in a certain sense, it makes me sick. Unproductive involvement with a writer who so splendidly pursues goals that are similar to my own, at least former, goals occasionally induces something like symptoms of intestinal poisoning in me" (C, 305). He seems to have sunk so low that, against his usual practice and inclination, he saw little of the Provençal landscape. An exception was a day trip with Kracauer to Aix-en-Provence, an "unspeakably beautiful city that has been frozen in time." They visited a bullfight outside the city gates, which Benjamin found "inappropriate" and "pathetic," but which inspired Kracauer to produce the little essay called "Lad and Bull."[25] The brief sojourn in Marseilles did have one positive result: he met Jean Ballard, the editor of the *Cahiers du Sud*, and Benjamin persuaded him to take his as yet unwritten essay on Proust; Ballard would often prove a steadfast friend during the years of exile to come.

As he had done during his time in Naples, Benjamin began a portrait of the city. Completed only in 1928 and published in the *Neue schweizer Rundschau* in 1929, "Marseilles" evokes, as any visitor would expect, the image of a rough, bawdy harbor town: the city is figured as "the yellow-studded maw of a seal with salt water running out between the teeth. When this gullet opens to catch the black and brown proletarian bodies thrown to it by ship's companies . . . , it exhales a stink of oil, urine, and printer's ink." Yet Benjamin insists that even the emptiest, most downtrodden districts, such as the prostitutes' quarter, are still marked by the genius loci of the classical age that extended across the Mediterranean. "The high-breasted nymphs, the snake-ringed Medusa's heads over their weather-beaten doorframes have only now become unambiguously the signs of a professional guild." This evocation of the spirit of the city in fact introduces what is a symphonic account: Benjamin's essay, with its ten distinct sections, attempts to evoke Marseilles as it is apprehended by each of the five senses. Just as with the study of nineteenth-century Paris in *The Arcades Project*, he is particularly interested in those threshold areas of the city, and especially the outskirts between Marseilles and the Provençal landscape, which he calls "the state of emergency of a

city, the terrain on which incessantly rages the great decisive battle
between town and country" (SW, 2:232–233, 235). As on Capri, Benjamin's portrait arose from what must have been a fruitful dialogue,
this time with Kracauer, whose pieces "Two Planes" and "Standup
Bars in the South" likewise date from their mutual stay in the area.
"Two Planes" makes an interesting comparison to "Marseilles." If
Benjamin had attempted to capture the spirit of the place, the particular set of sensations that arises in the city, Kracauer's piece focuses
with great intensity on its surface geometry. The visitor to Marseilles
is at the mercy of that surface, caught on a shuttle between the dreamlike tangle of the city's alleyways and the cold rationality of its urban
squares.

Benjamin moved on after only one week, settling for the time being in the village of Agay, near St. Raphaël, where Jula and Fritz Radt
were vacationing. Although he saw them occasionally, Benjamin underwent what amounted to a three-week-long isolation therapy, his
sole companion being Laurence Sterne's *Tristram Shandy*, which he
read in an eighteenth-century German translation and found absorbing. By early October he was back in Berlin, still plagued by the nervous disorders that had driven him from Paris. He intended to stay
until Christmas and then resume his "elliptical" existence, moving
between Berlin and Paris as he continued with the Proust translation.
Although his hometown now held little charm for him, he sought refuge among his books, and even undertook a "general reorganization"
of his library, including an updating of his meticulously maintained
card catalogue. While we don't know the specifics of this reorganization, he had declared before he started that he would dispose of many
books and "limit myself to German literature (recently with a certain
preference for the Baroque, which is made very difficult because of my
finances), French literature, religious studies, fairy tales, and children's books" (C, 306–307).

On returning to Berlin in October, Benjamin was alarmed to find
that Rowohlt was no closer to fulfilling its contract and publishing
his work than it had been when he left. Neither the *Trauerspiel* book
nor *One-Way Street* was yet in galleys, and the house proved unwilling even to give him a new timetable. Although he knew that the gateway to the academy was shut definitively, he still hoped that the study

of the Baroque drama might open other possibilities to him. One of these was entry into the circle around Aby Warburg in Hamburg. This was, at a deep level, a hope with some intellectual foundation. The study of the *Trauerspiel* was profoundly influenced by the work of the first Viennese school of art history, and especially by the work of Alois Riegl; Warburg's own early work had arisen in contact with and parallel to what was happening in Vienna. The *Trauerspiel* study, with its attempt to understand a literary form within a force field of historical and social vectors, should have made Benjamin a natural ally of the Warburg school.

He also worked to maintain his contacts with the Berlin literary scene, which was drifting steadily to the left. He attended a "truly odd" session of the Gruppe 1925 that took the form of a legal trial concerning the leftist writer Johannes R. Becher's latest book, *Levisite oder der einzig gerechte Krieg* (Levisite, or the Solely Just War), which had been banned shortly after its publication in 1925; Alfred Döblin served as prosecutor and the star journalist Egon Erwin Kisch as defense counsel. The group itself was an odd mix of former Expressionists (Alfred Ehrenstein, Walter Hasenclever, Ernst Toller), former Dadaists (George Grosz, Erwin Piscator), and the group of realist writers that we now associate with the Neue Sachlichkeit or New Objectivity (Becher, Döblin, Kurt Tucholsky). Benjamin knew many members of the group socially, including Bloch, Brecht, Döblin, and Roth; others would continue to cross paths with him throughout the 1930s, including the great Austrian novelist Robert Musil.

In November Benjamin learned that Asja Lacis had collapsed in Moscow; it remains unclear whether this was due to a psychological disorder or a neurological one. He rushed to her side and arrived in Moscow on December 6. Although Lacis's breakdown provided the immediate catalyst, Benjamin's visit to Russia was motivated in the end by several complementary factors, personal, political, and professional. The pursuit of the mercurial Lacis—at once discouraging and full of prospects[26]—mirrored the attempt to secure a footing in a rapidly shifting and uncertain cultural terrain, as well as the attempt specifically to capture in writing the technological-primitive life of the city of Moscow, which he compared to a labyrinth, a fortress, and an open-air hospital.

Arriving in Moscow, Benjamin was met by Lacis's companion Bernhard Reich; together, as they would often be in the weeks to come, they went immediately to see Asja herself, who was waiting for them on the street near the Sanatorium Rott, where she was undergoing treatment. Benjamin found her "wild beneath her Russian fur hat, her face somewhat puffy from all the time she had spent bedridden."[27] In the days that followed, Reich was Benjamin's constant companion and guide through the city, introducing him not just to the Kremlin and the other main tourist sites but also to a number of the principal Soviet cultural institutions. Benjamin soon joined Reich as a regular at the Dom Herzena, the headquarters of VAPP, the Organization of Proletarian Writers.

Benjamin's diaries chronicle the enormous difficulties that confronted him in Moscow. The bitter cold of the Moscow winter was exhausting, and the layout of the city itself utterly daunting. He was unable to navigate the sheet ice on the narrow sidewalks, and when he finally felt confident enough to look up, he saw a world capital that was at the same time a small town with two-story houses and as many sleds and carriages as automobiles—an "improvised metropolis that has fallen into place overnight" (MD, 31). He experienced the city as vast and amorphous, but also teeming with people. The sheer exoticism of the inhabitants—Mongols, Cossacks, Buddhist priests, Orthodox monks, and street vendors of every variety—was unimaginable in Berlin. And his almost total lack of Russian ensured that he remained isolated and dependent upon Reich and Lacis—and later upon Nikolaus Basseches, an Austrian journalist who, the son of the Austrian consul general, had been born in Moscow and continued to work at the Austrian legation. He sat for hours and listened to conversations of which he understood only the occasional word; he was forced to rely on hurried translations during films and theatrical performances; and, for all his effort to become an expert on recent trends in Soviet literature, he could finally read not a word.

Benjamin's relationship to Bernhard Reich during these weeks remains hard to fathom. Especially during the first weeks, Reich was enormously generous with his time and with the sharing of his connections to the Russian cultural apparatus. A kind of intimacy grew up between the two men, and when Reich was forced to move from his apartment, he frequently stayed with Benjamin in his hotel room. Yet they were rivals for the same woman, a fact that was apparently never directly acknowledged between the two writers, with their liberated views. The tensions finally bubbled to the surface on January 10, when they had a bitter altercation, ostensibly regarding a piece on Meyerhold that Benjamin had published in *Die literarische Welt* but, as Benjamin well knew, really over Lacis. Asja, on the other hand, was the fully cognizant master of the situation. Benjamin is granted the occasional meaningful glance, and sometimes kisses or hugs; more often, though, he is grateful for just a few moments alone with her. During one of these private interludes he tells her that he wants to have a child by her; she replies that it is his fault alone that they were not living on a "desert isle" with two children of their own, and she enumerates the many times he has spurned or fled from her. Lacis clearly thrived on the attention she received from the two men. When a Soviet general begins to pay court to her over Benjamin's protests, she replies scornfully that Benjamin has been playing the role of the "friend of the family" [*Hausfreund*, the German euphemism for the omnipresent paramour of the lady of the house]: "If he is as dumb as Reich and doesn't throw you out of the house, I have nothing against it. And if he does throw you out, I have nothing against that, either" (MD, 108). So they settled into the brusque oscillation that had characterized their relationship from the first days on Capri: he vacillates between "love and animosity" in the face of her "astonishing hardness, and, despite all her sweetness, her lovelessness" (MD, 34–35). Benjamin thus found himself in a new triangle that clearly recalled the painful days of 1921 during which his marriage foundered on his attraction to Jula Radt-Cohn. It is hardly surprising that at the time of the altercation with Reich he sent yet another intimate note to Jula: "You ought to try now and then to be free of Fritz for an evening. Otherwise when I return there will be 'torment'— something I want just as little as you. Leaving aside the fact that my talent for that is waning (as I grow older). The distance between Berlin and Moscow seems to be just enough to express this with hope of your response. . . . Two kisses. After you have wiped them off, please tear up this letter right away" (GB, 3:227).

The weeks in Moscow were, in still another sense, a reprise of his weeks on Capri in 1924, interlacing the erotic and the political in characteristic fashion. Benjamin's activity as a writer had entered a critical phase: feeling isolated among those of his own generation in Germany, he looked toward Russia—as did, in fact, others of his generation in Germany—for inspiration in dealing with the "sense of crisis" overhanging "the fate of the intelligentsia in bourgeois society" (MD, 47; C, 315; SW, 2:20–21). It was owing to this sense of crisis, which cannot be understood apart from a consideration of class interests and social mandate, that the status of the independent writer was being called into question. Speaking again of his own generation, Benjamin observes that the history of Germany in the period following the First World War was in part the history of the revolutionary education of the left-bourgeois wing of the intelligentsia—a radicalizing occasioned less by the war itself than by the capitulation of the 1918 revolution to the "petty-bourgeois, parvenu spirit of German Social Democracy" (SW, 2:20). What Soviet Russia represented, in this context, was a world-historical experiment in "proletarian government," involving a regimented emancipation from and liquefaction of traditional hierarchical class divisions, such that the life of the worker and the life of the intellectual are interarticulated according to a "new rhythm" of collective existence under the influence of a "new optics."

Experiencing this new rhythm on a daily basis, Benjamin was repeatedly struck by the contrast between Russia's highly developed political consciousness and its relatively primitive social organization. The sheer size of the population "certainly expresses itself as an enormously powerful dynamic factor, but from the point of view of culture, it is a force of nature that is hardly to be overcome" (GB, 3:218). As one might expect, he finds this structural ambivalence expressed symbolically in the private interior. Instead of the cozy bourgeois interior of the West, however, with its "gigantic sideboards distended with carvings, the sunless corners where potted palms sit" and the "soulless luxury of the furnishings" (as evoked in "Manorially Furnished Ten-Room Apartment" in *One-Way Street*), Russian apartments are practically bare. "Of all the Moscow institutions, [the beggars] alone are reliable; they alone refuse to be budged. Everything else here takes place under the banner of the *remont*. Every week the furniture in the bare rooms gets rearranged—this is the sole domestic luxury in which one can indulge and at the same time it provides a radical means of ridding the home of 'coziness' and the attendant melancholia that is its price" (MD, 36). On a visit to a factory, he notes not just the "Lenin niche" but the fact that the same commodity is being produced by hand and by machine, side by side.

Benjamin was witnessing the beginnings of the Stalinization of Soviet cultural policy during his stay. Writing from Moscow to Jula Radt-Cohn on December 26, 1926, he remarked that "the tensions of public life—which in large part have an almost theological character—are so great that, to an unimaginable degree, they seal off everything private" (C, 310—glancing at the near-impossibility of his being alone with Asja). And in his essay "Moscow," worked up from the diary of his journey, he states flatly that "Bolshevism has abolished private life" (SW, 2:30). Russians live estranged in domiciles that are simultaneously office, club, and street. Café life is no more to be found than are artistic schools and *cénacles*. The complacency of bourgeois dwelling, the fetishisms of consumerism, have been expunged at the price of free intellect itself, which has disappeared along with free trade.

The stance of the Russian writer was thus distinguished from that of his European colleagues at this time—nearly three years after the death of Lenin—by the "absolutely public" nature of his activity, which entailed both greater opportunity for work and greater external supervision (according to Benjamin's analysis in "The Political Groupings of Russian Writers" [SW, 2:6]). In theory, all intellectual life in the new Russia subserved the national political debate, which in the winter of 1926–1927, in an atmosphere of postrevolutionary reconstruction, was still characterized by the competing voices of various political groupings, though it was unquestionably dominated by the Communist Party, whose frequently revised directives no intellectual could afford to ignore, any more than the convictions of the aristocratic patron could be ignored in former times.

Although the tone of Benjamin's several pieces on Russian society and culture (see SW, 2:6–49) varies somewhat according to the tenor of the publishing venue—those appearing in *Die literarische Welt* being usually more radical in tone than, say, the essay "Moscow," written for Buber's journal *Die Kreatur*—the concern with "private life," fundamental to his work in other respects (as the figure of the flâneur suggests), remains constant. To be sure, it is private life informed by responsibility to the whole, and by the philosophical critique of atomistic subjectivity—in other words, an ideal at bottom consistent with the concept of collective solitude that was central to Benjamin's youth philosophy. The truly individual human being, as Marx had written in 1844, is necessarily a "species-being" (cited in SW, 2:454). Given this planetary perspective, argues Benjamin, the tensions of public life must come to be encapsulated in private life itself. The cultivation of private life in planetary perspective is integral both to the defense of the poor and traditionally disenfranchised and to the preservation of intellectual freedom, the freedom to dissent and the freedom to engage the works of the past. It is the suppression of such freedom that occasions the tone of satire in some of the most militantly sympathetic of Benjamin's reports, as when he describes the incompatibility between the "old" Russian type of the tortured dreamer and the new man of the revolution, the "intellectual sharpshooter" drilled for political command: in the annihilation of that asocial type, Russia descries "the specter of its own past, a specter that blocks the path to the new industrialized Eden [*Eden der Maschinen*]" (SW, 2:8–9). True objectivity—as attested in such satirical analysis—depends on the dialectic of subject and object, individual and collective; a grasp of the facts presupposes a certain determination:

> At the turning point in historical events that is indicated, if not constituted, by the fact of "Soviet Russia," the question at issue is not which reality is better or which has greater potential. It is only: Which reality is inwardly convergent with the truth? Which truth is inwardly preparing itself to converge with the real? Only he who clearly answers these questions is "objective." Not toward his contemporaries . . . but toward events. . . . Only he who, by decision, has made his dialectical peace with the world can grasp the concrete. But someone who wishes to decide "on the basis of the facts" will find no basis in these facts. (SW, 2:22)

It is in the spirit of such dialectical objectivity that, in describing his essay on Moscow to Buber, Benjamin cites Goethe's famous maxim: "Everything factual is already theory" (C, 313).

He takes no explicit "position," then, on the Russian question—at least not publicly. But the diary of his two months in Moscow is more revealing: "It is becoming clearer and clearer to me that my work needs some sort of solid framework for the immediate future. Obviously, translation cannot provide this. In fact, this construction depends first and foremost on my taking a position. Only purely external considerations hold me back from joining the German Communist Party" (MD, 72). Such considerations lead him to ask himself whether it would not be possible "concretely and economically" to consolidate a position as "left-wing outsider," enabling him to continue working in the sphere to which he has become accustomed. The role of intellectual pacesetter *(Schrittmacher-Position)* he would find seductive, "were it not for the existence of colleagues whose actions demonstrate . . . how dubious this position is" (MD, 73). Does his "illegal incognito among bourgeois authors" make any sense? Could he maintain a "marginal position" without thereby going over to the side of the bourgeoisie or compromising his work? Now might be the moment to join the Party, especially since it is likely to be no more than "an episode" for him; doing so would guarantee a "mandate" and give him the opportunity to rally to the side of the oppressed. He does not fail to consider the personal advantages to be gained from an institutional framework for one's work: it gives Reich the patience, he senses, to put up with behavior from Asja that would make him sick, and "even if this [patience] is only an appearance, that's already a great deal." On the other hand, to be a Communist like Reich in a state ruled by the proletariat means "completely giving up your private independence." At stake here in particular was his "scholarly work with its formal and metaphysical basis," work that in itself, he notes, might have a revolutionary function, especially in regard to its form. He wonders whether, for the sake of this specialized work, he should avoid "certain extremes of 'materialism,'" or instead work out his "disagreements with them" within the Party. What would happen to "all the mental reservations inherent in [his work]" in a society demanding only "banal clarity," as he puts it elsewhere (SW, 2:39)? The stocktaking entry in the diary ends on a relatively conclusive note as he returns to the central issue of private life: "As long as I continue to travel, joining the Party is obviously something fairly inconceivable."

In the years to come, he would remain a freelance writer, "without party or profession" (MD, 60).

For all his conscious ambivalence toward the Communist Party, then, and despite his evident rejection of what would become Stalinism, Benjamin's experience of Moscow was rich and diverse, in keeping with his principle of multidimensional knowledge: "One knows a spot only when one has experienced it in as many dimensions as possible" (MD, 25). He was intent on observing a wide variety of daily affairs, together with the cultural and political affairs of the city. In the stunning cold, he went around "freezing on the outside, on fire within" (MD, 128). He visited shops (toy shops and pastry shops were his delight), restaurants, pubs, museums, offices (where he encountered "Bolshevik bureaucracy"), a factory manufacturing Christmas tree decorations, a children's clinic, and a famous monastery, as well as tourist attractions such as the Kremlin and St. Basil's Cathedral. He took in life on the streets—beggars, homeless children, street vendors, the wild variety of wares, shop signs, and posters, the relative absence of cars and church bells, the distinctive clothing of the inhabitants and their "Asiatic" sense of time, the courteous crush of a streetcar ride and the swift, tender movement of the sleigh brushing against pedestrians, the brilliant colors blossoming in the snow. He went to a play, film, or ballet on a daily basis. Among the recently released films he saw were Eisenstein's *Potemkin*, Pudovkin's *Mother*, Kuleshov's *By the Law*, and Vertov's *One-Sixth of the World*. He saw the ballet *Petrushka*, set to Stravinsky's music; a shortened production (still more than four hours long) of Vsevolod Meyerhold's adaptation of Gogol's *Inspector General*, the extravagant staging of which—involving a series of tableaux—he compared to the architecture of a Muscovite cake; and a production of Mikhail Bulgakov's *Days of the Turbines*, which he found "an absolutely revolting provocation" (MD, 25). He was present at the Meyerhold theater for a crowded public debate involving the writers Vladimir Mayakovsky, Andrei Bely, Anatoly Lunacharsky, and Meyerhold himself. He was interviewed by a Moscow daily newspaper, *Vecherniaia Moskva*, as an expert on literature and the plastic arts.[28] And he took every opportunity to familiarize himself with Moscow's remarkable painting collections. He was overwhelmed at the sight of Matisse's *Dance* and *Music* at the top of the entrance staircase in the Schukin Gallery. Standing before a Cézanne, he hatched an insight that would inform several of his best-known essays: "As I was looking at an extraordinarily beautiful Cézanne, it suddenly occurred to me that it is even linguistically fallacious to speak of 'empathy.' It seemed to me that to the extent that one grasps a painting, one does not in any way enter into its space; rather, this space thrusts itself forward, especially in various very specific spots. It opens up to us in corners and angles in which we believe we can localize crucial experiences of the past; there is something inexplicably familiar about these spots" (MD, 42). This experience of the sedimentation of time in space, making for a strange resonance in the familiar, will drive not just the "Little History of Photography" of 1930 but a set of meditations in *The Arcades Project* from which "The Work of Art in the Age of Its Technological Reproducibility" will emerge in 1935. In the atmosphere of political and cultural agitation found everywhere in Moscow, the present *(Gegenwart)* took on extraordinary importance, as he says in the letter to Jula Radt-Cohn that speaks of the theological tensions of public life in Russia.

One of the most important results of Benjamin's Russian experience, so far as the direction of his future work is concerned, was that it provided an impetus to develop his thoughts about the medium of film. In two pieces for *Die literarische Welt*, "On the Present Situation of Russian Film" and "Reply to Oscar A. H. Schmitz," both published in March 1927, he discusses the current Russian cinema, focusing on Vertov and Eisenstein, respectively, and outlines a film aesthetic that shares salient features with his theory of literary criticism. His position on film, as on so much in vernacular culture, is allied to that of his colleague Siegfried Kracauer, insofar as he views the medium as a preeminent means of investigating social milieux. What he refers to as "the principles of the film medium" are crucial to the task of unfolding the hidden dimensions of a place. The new rhythm and the new optics he found at work in the physiognomy of the Russian workday have their plastic counterpart in this potentially emancipatory medium. Indeed, "with film a new realm of consciousness comes into being":

> To put it in a nutshell, film is the prism in which the spaces of the immediate environment . . . are laid open. . . . In themselves these offices, furnished rooms, saloons, big-city streets, railroad terminals, and factories [were] ugly, incomprehensible, and hopelessly sad. . . . The cinema then exploded this entire prison-world with the dynamite of its fractions of a second, so that now we can take extended journeys of adventure between their widely scattered ruins. The vicinity of a house, of a room, can include dozens of the most unexpected stations. (SW, 2:17)

This incisive passage, which Benjamin incorporated (slightly revised) into his "Work of Art" essay (SW, 3:117), rehearses several characteristic concerns. The "prismatic work" that film performs on a milieu produces new image worlds in the deconstruction of the space, which, on being "exploded," separated out from the customary material nexus, yields "widely scattered ruins." The milieu is thereby critically and creatively "mortified," as Benjamin likes to say. It is excavated like an archaeological site, its underlying sociohistorical strata unearthed. The film's discovery of "unexpected stations" in the midst of the reified everyday opens up an environment that has "resisted every other attempt to unlock its secret." Instrumental to this process of penetration is the sudden change of place or perspective *(sprunghafte Wechsel des Standorts)* effected by the mechanisms of montage, which for Benjamin, as for Brecht, is always a dialectical device, at once isolating and assembling its materials. The filmic "cut" is both a break in the action and a joint in the articulation of a sequence. Benjamin's experiments in what he calls literary montage, and above all the epic montage of *The Arcades Project* (which, making allowances for the difference in scale, one can compare to the "city symphonies" filmed by Vertov and Ruttmann), proceed according to such dialectical logic. The cinematic character of these texts derives not just from their highly localized mise en scène and their rhythm of interruption but from their multiangled disclosure of "collective spaces" and of a "collective in motion."

Having defined the unique promise of the film medium in terms of its topological tendencies, Benjamin raises the crucial, if usually unasked, question of a specifically cinematic plot. The new filmic appropriation of living space, conditioned as it is on the capacities of the recording apparatus, proves that advances in art depend not on new forms or new contents but on technological innovation in media. As it happens, the technological revolution in film has been able to discover "[neither] a form [nor] a content appropriate to it." Where ideology does not dictate subject matter and treatment, the problem of "a meaningful film plot" can be resolved only on a case-by-case basis. Regarding the future of Russian film in particular, which in the postrevolutionary period has been distinguished by its rigorous architectonic depiction of a class movement, Benjamin sees a need for both the cultivation of "a new 'social comedy,'" with "typical situations," and the cultivation of "irony and skepticism in technical matters," an attitude unknown in the Bolshevik technocracy. The Russians, comments Benjamin, are fairly uncritical about the movies they see. Because good foreign films are seldom imported (Chaplin is largely unknown there), they lack European standards of comparison. Indeed, the question of art is in a certain sense passé. As a strictly regulated form of political discourse, that is, as socialist propaganda, the motion picture in Soviet Russia is first of all a sophisticated training device (though it would soon yield its supremacy as informational medium to radio). When, some eight years later, Benjamin returns to the problem of film form in the "Work of Art" essay, he too conceives of film, in its educational, critical-agitational bearing, as a training device *(Übungsinstrument)* for a new shock-informed apperception and for the realization of an "optical unconscious" in the things we encounter. From the beginning, his film aesthetic betokens a new way of seeing.[29] One need only recall the emphasis placed on a transformation of consciousness, a new experience of space and time, in the texts of the youth philosophy more than a decade earlier to appreciate, once again, the continuity of concern in Benjamin's thought through all the discontinuity of form and focus.

Back in Berlin at the beginning of February 1927, he was occupied with the pieces on Russian film and Russian literature for *Die literarische Welt* and was preparing to draft "Moscow" for *Die Kreatur.* The latter piece was cast in the form of "short disparate notes," through which the "creaturely" would be allowed "to speak for itself," and in dealing with which the reader "for the most part . . . will be left to his own devices" (MD, 129, 132).[30] In addition, he had begun

22. Benjamin in 1927. Photo by
Germaine Krull *(Akademie der Künste,
Berlin. Walter Benjamin Archiv)*

working on his article on Goethe for the *Great Soviet Encyclopedia*,
although he now heard from Reich that the editorial board was balk-
ing at his synopsis, which he concluded was too "radical" for them
(C, 312). His conversations with Reich and other literary figures in
Moscow further provided material for his debut at the microphone of
a radio station on March 23, when he broadcast a talk entitled "Young
Russian Writers," presumably a version of the essay "Recent Literature in Russia," published later that spring or summer in Lehning's
Internationale Revue i10. Regular radio work would begin for Benjamin two years later; between 1929 and 1932, he would be heard more
than eighty times on Frankfurt and Berlin stations, usually presenting material he himself had written or was improvising. One of his
main preoccupations in Moscow, however, produced only a truncated
result. He had made repeated visits to the Moscow Toy Museum and
paid for a series of photographs of some of the most important objects,
and he had purchased a vast pile of toys from shops, street markets,
and itinerant vendors. The resulting illustrated essay, "Russian Toys,"
never appeared in the supplement to the *Frankfurter Zeitung* for

which it was intended; it was published, in shortened form, in the *Südwestdeutschen Rundfunkzeitung* in 1930. The original, considerably more extensive manuscript is lost. One further publication in which he took particular delight had reached him in Moscow: *Die literarische Welt* published a wall calendar with caricatures by Rudolf Großman of its frequent contributors, and each caricature was accompanied by a little verse that Benjamin himself composed.

Meanwhile, concurrently with his reports on the new Russia, and amid "a great deal of idleness," he was expanding his coverage of the contemporary French literary scene, coverage that he had begun providing for *Die literarische Welt* the previous August with a piece on Paul Valéry and *symbolisme*. Moreover, the translation of Proust's *A l'ombre des jeunes filles en fleurs*, which he had undertaken in collaboration with Franz Hessel, had appeared in January and was getting generally favorable notice, not least from his allies in Frankfurt and Berlin. A review in the *Frankfurter Zeitung* praised the artfulness and "microscopic" accuracy of the translation, and a letter to the editors of *Die literarische Welt* went even further in lauding the complementary virtues of Benjamin and Hessel as translators.[31] In the years to come, Benjamin would translate several other contemporary French authors, including Louis Aragon, Marcel Jouhandeau, Léon Bloy, and Adrienne Monnier.

Closer to home, the publication of *One-Way Street* and the *Trauerspiel* book—to which Rowohlt was contractually committed—continued to be a source of dismay. Rowohlt kept delaying their long-promised appearance, and Benjamin finally became so frustrated that he refused to return the corrected galleys of the book on the Baroque until he had some assurance that the book of aphorisms and the book version of the study of Goethe's *Elective Affinities* would also appear.

After two unusually quiet months in Berlin, where he lived with Dora and eight-year-old Stefan in the apartment in his parents' Grunewald villa, he was traveling again: the need to keep up with developments in French literature—and his wanderlust—took him to Paris on April 1 for a second extended stay in the French capital. Originally planned for two or three months, the visit stretched to eight months and involved side trips to the Côte d'Azur and the Loire valley. To his delight, he was able to move back into his old room at the Hôtel du Midi, the site of his close intellectual collaboration with Bloch and Kracauer. For the first few weeks he was reading Proust much of the time. At the end of April Scholem stopped off in Paris for a few days while en route to London to study Kabbalistic manuscripts, and he and Benjamin met for the first time in four years. Scholem found his old friend uncommonly relaxed and at the same time in intellectual ferment. Benjamin spoke of his desire to settle permanently in Paris on account of the city's stimulating "atmosphere," while admitting that the difficulties of establishing close contact with Frenchmen made this next to impossible. "It is extraordinarily rare," he wrote to Hofmannsthal, "to achieve the kind of empathy with a Frenchman that would make it possible to converse with him for more than fifteen minutes" (C, 315). The only dependable contact he had so far was with a friend of Hofmannsthal's and Bloch's, the novelist and critic Marcel Brion, editor of the *Cahiers du Sud*, a man he esteemed highly and whom he introduced to Scholem. Benjamin's report on the *Cahiers du Sud* had appeared in *Die literarische Welt* in March. This prominent French journal, in which Brion at the end of 1926 had favorably reviewed Benjamin's Baudelaire translations, would later publish pieces by him in French translation, as the friendship between the two men deepened during Benjamin's exile in Paris in the 1930s.

In mid-May, shortly after Scholem's departure for England, Dora and Stefan arrived for a visit. Benjamin showed Dora around Paris for a few days, and then the little family went off to the Riviera over the Pentecost holiday. Later in June Benjamin won enough money in the casinos at Monte Carlo to finance a week's vacation in Corsica on his own. His taste for gambling (which has something Dostoevskian about it and no doubt ties in with his generally "experimenting" nature), and in particular his fascination with roulette, is reflected in passages of *The Arcades Project*. Among the early drafts of this work, the "brilliant passage on the gambler" (that is, $g^\circ,1$), involving both theological and profane motifs, was singled out by Adorno.[32] "The Gambler" had indeed long been one of Benjamin's preferred incognitos, and not merely in the sense that he was irresistibly drawn to the challenges and dangers of the gaming tables, nor even because he saw gambling—like hashish intoxication—as socially and metaphysically suggestive, particularly in regard to the experience of time it afforded. From his first work to his last, Benjamin took chances on the subject he addressed and on the forms and style of his writing. Much like the gambler who continues to bet as the table seems to be tilted away from him, Benjamin made his own luck. From Corsica he took an airplane back to Antibes, and "this brought me up to date on the latest means of human transportation." It was during this trip to Corsica that he lost "a bundle of irreplaceable manuscripts," including "preliminary sketches, made over a period of years, for the 'Politics.'"[33]

At the beginning of June, Benjamin had written to Hofmannsthal from Pardigon, near Toulon, describing his current projects, which were "mainly devoted to consolidating [his] position in Paris" (C, 315). Feeling "completely isolated" among those of his own generation in Germany, he has turned to France, where, in the Surrealist movement and among individual writers ("especially Aragon"), he finds a kindred spirit: "With the passage of time, I have been tempted to get close to the French spirit in its modern form . . . , completely aside from the fact that it incessantly preoccupies me in its historical guise." The guise he had in mind was nothing less than French classical drama: he was considering a book on Racine, Corneille, and Molière as a kind of counterpart to the book on the *Trauerspiel*. Like so many of his projects, this one, too, fell by the wayside. Perhaps out of solidarity with this renewed historical interest, he rejected Kracauer's suggestion that he purchase a typewriter.

> I see that you have come into possession of such a machine—and I see at the same time that I am still right not to have one. Just recently, this conviction was more than ever confirmed for me on the occasion of the Franco-American tennis tournament. Yes indeed! On that occasion I lost my fountain pen. Or rather: in the tumult, I managed to escape from this fearsome and no longer bearable tyrant to whom I had subjected myself for the last year. I was determined to procure the first cheap replacement that came along and stepped up to a stand in the midst of the crowded Parisian street. Solid citizens stop here at most to fill their pen with fresh ink. There I found the most charming contemporary creature, one that fulfills all my

dreams and that enables a productivity formerly impossible during
the reign of the bygone pen. (GB, 3:262)

This little set piece, written on the same day as the letter to
Hofmannsthal, demonstrates in brief the agility—and slyness—of
Benjamin's intellectual method: even while fetishizing the instruments of his production, he manages to allegorize the instrument and
thereby ironize himself.

At Pardigon he was also working on a long-meditated essay about
the Swiss poet and novelist Gottfried Keller. As he indicates in letters,
his intent in this article, which complements his work on French literature, was to counter the philistine view of Keller as a benevolent
provincial writer by bringing out "distinctly surrealist traits" in his
physiognomy. Work on "Gottfried Keller" continued through mid-
July, and the piece appeared in *Die literarische Welt* in August, inaugurating a series of major essays on important literary figures written
by Benjamin for the German newspapers in the last years of the
Weimar Republic. The Keller essay instances a representative set of
concerns, beginning with the call for a "revaluation of the nineteenth
century" (SW, 2:51–61). Specifically at issue here is an ideological rupture in the history of the German bourgeoisie, as signaled by the
founding of the German Reich in 1871. Keller's work maintains ties
with the "preimperialist" stage of the bourgeoisie, with love of country as opposed to the nationalistic spirit, and with a passionate,
unsentimental liberalism remote from the modern variety. In his
writing, skepticism coexists with an animating vision of happiness,
and this constitutive tension contributes to his distinctive humor,
which is inseparable from his melancholy and choler. No less than
Baudelaire, Keller presides over a space of "nineteenth-century antiquity." It is antiquity eventuating in accordance with a formal law of
"shrinkage" *(Schrumpfung)*—an antiquity contracted into the landscape and the objects of Keller's own unsettled epoch.[34] These things
have for him "the wizened dryness of old fruit, old human faces." In
the mirror world of his description, where the most minuscule cell of
the real has infinite density, "the object returns the gaze of the observer." All these themes would be developed in Benjamin's work over
the course of the coming decade.

In mid-August Benjamin took a five-day trip to Orléans, Blois, and Tours, where, inspired by a passage from Charles Péguy on Victor Hugo, he visited cathedrals and châteaus. The travel diary he kept during this journey to the Loire (now in SW, 2:62–65) records his vivid impressions of the sights, such as the rose window over the main portal of the cathedral at Tours, in which he sees a symbol of "the Church's way of thinking: from the outside, all slaty, scaly, almost leprous; from the inside, blossoming, intoxicating, and golden." The diary also records his feeling of forlornness—"Everything, especially every trivial thing on this journey makes me want to burst into tears"—at being stood up by a Parisian woman with whom, a few weeks earlier, he had fallen in love, "something he did rather easily and frequently in those years" (SF, 133). In this case, consolation was afforded by the comforts of a luxurious hotel room and by the peace and "immediate sense of presence" he found in gazing at great works of architecture. His "Parisian rose," he realized, had been "marvelously planted" between two cathedrals, between his visit to Chartres a month previously and his present experience of St. Gatien in Tours. He had hoped to publish an account of this trip in the *Frankfurter Zeitung*, but this proposal found no support from Kracauer and the other editors.

Benjamin returned to Paris on August 16, and the next day Scholem arrived for a stay of several weeks to do research at the Bibliothèque Nationale. They spent many evenings together, meeting mainly in cafés around the Boulevard Montparnasse. On one occasion Scholem and his wife visited Benjamin's "shabby, tiny, ill-kept room, which contained scarcely more than an iron bedstead and a few other furnishings" (SF, 133). They went to the movies several times (Benjamin especially admired the American actor Adolphe Menjou), and Scholem got to know Benjamin's friend and collaborator Franz Hessel and his wife Helen, who were also in Paris that summer. On the evening of August 23 Scholem accompanied Benjamin (who was wearing a red necktie) to the northern boulevards, where violent mass demonstrations were being held against the execution of Sacco and Venzetti in Boston that night; they barely managed to escape the melee that developed when police on horseback attacked the demonstrators. To Scholem's inquiries about possible commitment to Marxist ideas and methods, Benjamin remarked only that he saw no necessary conflict between radical-revolutionary perspectives and his own mode of production, albeit in dialectical transformation (SF, 135). He was much more forthcoming on the subject of Surrealism and the work of Paul Valéry, and on his (ultimately unrealized) plans for an anthology of Wilhelm von Humboldt's writings on the philosophy of language.

Scholem's visit inaugurated another protracted engagement with the question of a move to Palestine. A new School of Humanities was being established at the Hebrew University in Jerusalem, and Scholem raised the possibility of Benjamin's coming to work there as a university teacher of French and German literature—a position that would require knowledge of Hebrew. When Benjamin responded enthusiastically to this idea and signaled his readiness to learn Hebrew, Scholem arranged a meeting with the chancellor of the Hebrew University, Rabbi Judah L. Magnes, who happened to be in Paris. During a two-hour conversation, Magnes, an American who had studied in Berlin and Heidelberg twenty-five years earlier, listened with emotion as Benjamin, well prepared for the occasion, described his career in the philosophy of language, mentioning his studies of German Romanticism, Hölderlin, Goethe, and the German *Trauerspiel,* as well as his fascination with Baudelaire and Proust. He laid stress on his translation work as a stimulus to philosophical and theological reflection. These things, he said, had made him ever more clearly conscious of his Jewish identity. He stated that he had "done what he could as a critic of significant texts" but that "his position had found virtually no response in Germany." He was therefore looking to Hebrew language and literature as a viable subject (SF, 137–138). The interview led to Magnes's request for letters of recommendation as a first step in considering Benjamin for a teaching position in Jerusalem. Procuring such letters from established academics was no easy matter for Benjamin, who had burned so many bridges behind him. He spent much of the fall sounding out possible referees; among the approaches was a renewed attempt to establish contact with the circle around Warburg. The letters (from Hofmannsthal and from Walter Brecht, the *Ordinarius* for German literature at Munich) reached Magnes in the spring and were pronounced excellent. Benjamin also sent along copies of some of his publications. To Magnes and Scholem he had affirmed his solidarity with the reconstruction work in Palestine, work that he distinguished from political Zionism. Scholem comments drily: "Never before had Benjamin placed himself so decisively in this context, nor did he do so on any subsequent occasion. . . . [The encounter with Magnes] is more fantastic in retrospect than it seemed at the time" (SF, 138–139). It is impossible to determine how serious Benjamin might have been regarding a move to Jerusalem. Letters to people such as Brion and Hofmannsthal over the next couple of years suggest that this was a matter of serious reflection; other utterances suggest that he hoped only to obtain a short-term stipend for the acquisition of Hebrew—or other articles of interest. In the end, he received a one-time payment from Magnes, which eventually spurred him, in late spring 1929, to begin a series of daily lessons with Dr. Max Mayer, an editor at the *Jüdische Rundschau*. The lessons lasted less than a month, derailed first by Mayer's absence from Berlin at a spa and then, permanently, by Benjamin's preoccupation in the fall of 1929 with his divorce proceedings.

Scholem returned to Jerusalem around the end of September. He and Benjamin would see each other only one more time—in 1938, again in Paris. During their weeks together in 1927, Benjamin read aloud passages from a new work on the Paris arcades, what was conceived at this time as an essay of about fifty printed pages, to be completed in the next few months. Little did Benjamin know that the work in question—published posthumously as a thousand-page volume called *The Arcades Project (Das Passagen-Werk)*—would soon outgrow this originally limited conception to become the intended magnum opus and the actual intellectual wellspring of his later years, an ever proliferating philosophical-historical study around which most of his major and minor writings from 1927 through 1940 constellate. In an oft-quoted letter of January 20, 1930, Benjamin characterizes the arcades project as "the theater of all my struggles and all my ideas" (C, 359). Initially, in the summer or fall of 1927, he was planning an article for the Berlin bimonthly *Der Querschnitt*, in which he had published before.[35] The article was to be written in Paris together with Franz Hessel. Hessel's own book on flânerie, *Spazieren in Berlin* (On Foot in Berlin), conceives the modern city—in the wake of Louis Aragon's *Paysan de Paris* (Paris Peasant; 1926)—as a mnemonic; it would appear in 1929 and be reviewed by Benjamin. The short essay "Arcades," a piece of phantasmagorical reportage that grew out of the many discussions with Hessel on the arcades, may in fact have been cowritten with his friend; Benjamin probably thought of it as a draft for this unrealized longer article.[36]

After Benjamin abandoned the collaboration on a newspaper article with Hessel, there was a stage in the gestation of the arcades project—still conceived as an essay—in which, by the end of January 1928, it carried the title "Paris Arcades: A Dialectical Fairyland," the last element, *Féerie*, being the name also of a popular nineteenth-century French theatrical genre that involved allegorical figures and dreamlike décor. Ever since the project's inception in mid-1927, Benjamin had been noting more or less brief reflections on the significance of the arcades and their milieux (these first sketches appearing today as "Paris Arcades I" in *The Arcades Project*). As a nineteenth-century guidebook that Benjamin would later quote describes them, "These arcades, a recent invention of industrial luxury, are glass-roofed, marble-paneled corridors extending through whole blocks of buildings, whose owners have joined together for such enterprises. Lining both sides of these corridors, which get their light from above, are the most elegant shops, so that the *passage* is a city, a world in miniature." Even at this early phase in the project, Benjamin's interest was drawn to the arcades not merely because they served as a telling symbol of the new display and sales strategies associated with urban commodity capitalism but also because of their constitutive ambiguity: as a world in miniature, the arcade is at once street and interior, public and private space.

At this stage, he conceived the work as a kind of Parisian counterpart to *One-Way Street*, a montage text combining aphorisms and anecdotal material on French society and culture of the mid-nineteenth century. Over the course of 1928 and possibly 1929, in connection with his essay plan, he elaborated a set of somewhat longer, more polished drafts ("Paris Arcades II"), the manuscript of which was soon overgrown with quotations, commentaries, and bibliographic references. This conglomerate of reflections and citations forms the core of the central section of *The Arcades Project*, the thirty-six alphabetized folders or "convolutes" (titled by the German editor *Aufzeichnungen und Materialien,* "Notes and Materials") that Benjamin began assembling in the fall or winter of 1928. Eventually the citations—which are drawn from a wide range of nineteenth- and twentieth-century French and German sources—would far outnumber the commentaries and reflections, though, pace Adorno, it is doubtful that Benjamin ever thought of his arcades project purely in terms of *Zitatenkritik* (citation-criticism), of the sort he calls for in notes for an unrealized work on the theory of literary criticism from 1929 or 1930.[37]

Work on the arcades papers—which soon came to include another short essay, "The Ring of Saturn, or Some Remarks on Iron Construction," perhaps intended as a radio broadcast or newspaper article—continued through the end of 1929 or beginning of 1930, when it was broken off for some four years, possibly in consequence of theoretical aporias occasioned by the attempt to reconcile an overtly Surrealist inspiration with the imperatives of a historical materialism. The work was resumed in early 1934 under the purview of "new and incisive sociological perspectives," which gave to the project, now conceived as a book, a "new face" (C, 490; GB, 4:375). This later phase in the work lasted until the spring of 1940, when Benjamin was forced to flee Paris and the Bibliothèque Nationale. During this phase of expansion and new accentuation in the mid- and late 1930s, two highly concentrated synoptic "exposés" were added, one written in German (1935) and the other in French (1939), bringing the total number of texts in the arcades complex to seven. Before leaving Paris, Benjamin entrusted the manuscript of the "Notes and Materials" to fellow writer Georges Bataille, who hid it in a closed archive in the Bibliothèque Nationale, where he worked at the time as a librarian. After the war this manuscript was retrieved and then delivered by personal courier to Adorno in New York at the end of 1947, for in its later phase the work had been carried on under the auspices of the Institute of Social Research.[38] Edited by Adorno's student Rolf Tiedemann, *Das Passagen-Werk* was first published in 1982—an unfinished and fundamentally unfinishable collection of "passages."[39]

Although in letters written during the 1930s Benjamin repeatedly declares his intention to marshal his elaborately organized materials and actually write the book on the arcades, it may be said that in the

course of this fateful decade the research project became an end in itself. The conventional distinction between research and presentation,
Forschung and *Darstellung*, a distinction invoked on occasion by Benjamin himself, gradually ceased to apply in the case of this unique
study.[40] As published today, *The Arcades Project* is de facto a text, like
the notebooks of Joubert, Baudelaire, or Nietzsche. The book can even
be read from beginning to end as an encyclopedic narrative of everyday life in mid-nineteenth-century Paris, though a mode of reading
closer to the divagations of flânerie—the flâneur experiences the city
as historical palimpsest—is no doubt preferable. Whatever may have
been Benjamin's plans for developing the project into a book, it seems
likely that his general aim, as Tiedemann says, was "to bring together theory and materials, citation and interpretation, in a new
constellation, as compared to contemporary methods of presentation" (AP, 931).

Benjamin's own term for the textual format of the arcades project
is "literary montage" (AP, N1a,8), and of course montage as a principle
of artistic construction was in its heyday in the 1920s (one need only
mention in this regard the names of Moholy-Nagy, Heartfield, Eisenstein, and Brecht). Benjamin first made extended use of a montage
method in *One-Way Street*, which, on the model of the multifarious
spectacle afforded by street life in the big city, assembles various sequences of short, aphoristic texts without overt transition between
the sequences. In *The Arcades Project*, where the "profane motifs of
One-Way Street will [be] . . . hellishly intensified" (as Benjamin wrote
in a letter of January 30, 1928, to Scholem), this effect of polyphony
and multiple perspective is greatly magnified by the massive deployment of quotations, commentaries, and reflections, each one of which
may be thought to bear on some thematic concern of the work, and
thus to function, in the context of Benjamin's labyrinthine collection
of arcades phenomena, as a highly condensed "magic encyclopedia" of
the historical epoch under study (AP, H2,7; H2a,1). Each numbered
passage in this giant arcade of a text communicates between the nineteenth and twentieth centuries; each is, at least in theory, a threshold
and corridor leading into the past—into recorded history and into the
primal history *(Urgeschichte)* informing it—and thereby into the present.[41] Reflecting a virtual correspondence between separate mo-

ments in time, and characteristically between the "forehistory" and "afterhistory" of a particular historical phenomenon (Baudelaire, for example, has a forehistory in medieval allegory, an afterhistory in Jugendstil), the *Arcades* passage brings to light for the present—in a flash of legibility—a "dialectical image," something at once documentary and metaphysical.

We have drawn attention to the way this central concept of Benjamin's historical materialism—namely, dialectical image—is anticipated by the ideas of his youth philosophy from the period 1912 to 1919, rooted as that philosophy is in Nietzsche's critique of nineteenth-century historicism, which believed it could scientifically apprehend the past "as it really was." Specifically at issue in Benjamin's concept is the idea of the manifold immanence of the past in the present, the crucial role of the present in interpreting the past, and the idea of the "afterlife of works" as the foundation of what is called tradition. In keeping with this dynamic understanding of historical perception, one sharing salient features with the Surrealist vision of objects and architectures haunted by the ruins of the past, the theory of the dialectical image pivots on the notion of "the now of recognizability."[42] The historical object reveals itself to a present day uniquely capable of recognizing it. As Benjamin conceives the matter, in a schema again deriving from the concerns of his early philosophy, the past moment awakens to a present dreaming of it, at the same time as the present moment, waking to the dream of the past, awakens from that dream and hence to itself. The method of reflection—of reading—depends on an art of experience:

> The new, dialectical method of doing history presents itself as the art of experiencing the present as waking world [*die Kunst, die Gegenwart als Wachwelt zu erfahren*], a world to which that dream we name the past refers in truth. To pass through and carry out *what has been* in remembering the dream!—Therefore: remembering and awakening are most intimately related. Awakening is namely the dialectical, Copernican turn of remembrance [*Eingedenken*]. (AP, K1,3)[43]

In support of his esoteric doctrine of historical dream and historical awakening, Benjamin quotes both Marx ("The reform of consciousness consists *solely* in . . . the awakening of the world from its dream about itself") and Jules Michelet ("Every epoch dreams the one to follow").[44] This esoteric conception was especially important for the first extended phase of work on *The Arcades Project* in the late twenties, the phase directly influenced by the historical phantasmagorias of Surrealism. (Adorno's criticisms in August 1935 [see SW, 3:54–56] eventually led Benjamin to draw back in some measure from this schema, as he accentuated the sociological.) What he terms at one point, in a tacitly theological formulation, "the constellation of awakening" entails a *constructed* awakening "from the existence of our parents" (AP, 907–908; N1,9), an awakening that proceeds—dialectically—through reentry into the dream, that is, into "the historical dreams of the collective" in the preceding century, and through critical penetration of the more or less recessed dream-strata of the past. Hence the micrological thrust of *The Arcades Project:* the inquiry into historical "detritus," as unearthed and collected from the most obsolete and inconspicuous corners of nineteenth-century existence, the repositories of secret histories and collective dreams. These include written advertisements (for beer, for skin lotion, for women's hats), shop signs, business prospectuses, police reports, architectural plans, playbills, political pamphlets, exhibition catalogues, book-length "physiologies" of Parisian social life at midcentury, memoirs, letters, travel diaries, engravings and book illustrations and posters, and a plethora of long-forgotten studies of various aspects of the city on the Seine (such as prostitution, gambling, the streets and quarters, the stock exchange, popular songs, bohemians, the criminal underworld, and so on).

The "dialectics of awakening" thus calls for a theory and practice of citation.[45] Although the word *Zitieren* goes back to Latin *citare*, meaning originally "to set in motion," "to summon," Benjamin's concept transcends the classical distinction between motion and stasis. In *The Arcades Project*, to cite is at once to explode and to salvage: to extract the historical object by blasting it from the reified, homogeneous continuum of pragmatic historiography, and to call to life some part of what has been by integrating it into the newly established context of the collection, transfiguring and actualizing the object in the "force field"—the oscillating standstill *(Stillstand)*—of a dialectical image. The redemption of the past in constellation with the now, adumbrating in language a "nucleus of time lying hidden within the knower and the known alike" (AP, N3,2), takes place in what Benjamin will call, in his 1929 essay "On the Image of Proust," "intertwined time" *(verschränkte Zeit)*.[46] This is the temporality of montage. By means of quotation and commentary—"interpretation in detail"—the principle of montage makes possible a new concreteness, a "heightened graphicness," in the reading and writing of history:

> The first stage in this undertaking [to conjoin a heightened graphicness to the (Marxist) understanding of history] will be to carry over the principle of montage into history. That is, to assemble large-scale constructions out of the smallest and most precisely cut components. Indeed, to discover in the analysis of the small individual moment the crystal of the total event. And, therefore, to break with vulgar historical naturalism. To grasp the construction of history as such. In the structure of commentary. Detritus of history.
>
> (AP, N2,6; see also N2,1)

Elsewhere in the text, Benjamin refers to the small individual moment as a "monad," adapting Leibniz's term to a philosophical eventism beyond the classical idea of substance.[47] The constellation of awakening bespeaks a modernist monadology.

When Benjamin invokes the Marxian understanding of history, as he does in the passage from Convolute N just quoted, he has in mind primarily the twin processes of a technologization and commodification of things, as first manifest on a wide scale in the course of the nineteenth century. At stake in these developments for the arcades project as a whole is "the fate of art in the nineteenth century" (C, 509): this is the general subject of Benjamin's *Passagenwerk*. The question of art's viability or direction becomes the more pressing as these twin processes intensify over time, and indeed as they work in part to bury the question of art. Benjamin focuses on the aesthetic movement known as Jugendstil in order to highlight the increasingly desperate trajectory of an art intent on rising above the marketplace and the technological apparatus, in the process losing its connection with the life of "the people." *The Arcades Project* counters such hopeless idealism by its detailed examination of nineteenth-century vernacular and industrial culture and by its recurrent tracing—within the various dimensions of bourgeois existence—of the protean specter of "abstract man," for whom all things are quantified, made equivalent, as items with a price. In other words, Benjamin counters both aestheticism *and* vulgar materialism. To the leveling and obliterative tendency of capitalism *The Arcades Project* opposes, on one hand, the anamnestic practice of the collector, who undertakes "the Sisyphean task of divesting things of their commodity character" (AP, 9), and, on the other hand, the utopian theory of a Charles Fourier, among others, who looks on the material thing as endowment rather than commodity, and who conceives of a radically different and more humane (if also fantastical) appropriation of technology. According to Benjamin, the "transformation of things [*Wandel der Dinge*] that set in around 1800" brought with it a new tempo of production that opens the way to an ascendancy of fashion in all fields and that alters the traditional relation of art to technology, making it more and more difficult for art to adapt to technological advances (AP, G1,1; see also F3,3). At the same time, this change in the nature of things makes for new possibilities of dwelling (opened up through the principles of transparency and porosity) and new possibilities of communication and expression (the keywords here are simultaneity and interpenetration). In the realm of art, in particular, the nineteenth century—with its "awakening sense for construction" (AP, F6,2)—discloses the prospect of a distinctively "modern beauty," in Baudelaire's famous phrase, a beauty in touch with the velocity, multiplicity, and dissonance of modern experience, especially of modern urban experience, which is nevertheless revealed as resonating antiquity (AP, 22–23).

The kaleidoscopic text of *The Arcades Project* itself exemplifies such constructive dissonance. Reflecting, as we've seen, the interpenetrating and layered transparency of the world of the flâneur, it is everywhere imbued with the "fundamental ambiguity" of the arcades phenomena (AP, Q2,2)—as, for example, in the presentation of fashion, which is seen to be allied to death and to programmed oblivion even as it triumphs over death by recalling the departed (some antiquated device) for its current innovation, and which appears as the indefatigable agent of "false consciousness" even as it represents, through its power to cite the past, a revolutionary potential (AP, 11, 894; SW,

4:395). Likewise in the presentation of the domestic interior, of advertising, of engineering, of museums, of the popular press. Toward all these phenomena, animated as they are by "secret affinities" with one another, and by anticipations and echoes in their objectively constructed historical unfolding, Benjamin manifests his characteristic ambivalence, the expression no doubt of a double vision of the bourgeois world in general. Here, as elsewhere in his later work, the question of art's relation to commodity character is left open.

Benjamin returned to Berlin on October 21. Before leaving Paris, he had attended an international exhibition of photography where, as he saw it, people were gushing over photographs of questionable value. Even a selection of old photos of Paris was disappointing. In a letter of October 16 to Alfred and Grete Cohn, he remarks that old photos of people seem to mean more than old photos of localities, because fashions in clothing provide such a reliable temporal index—an idea borrowed directly from the opening pages of his colleague Siegfried Kracauer's magisterial essay "Photography," which he had read in draft. He mentions that photography has "overnight become a topic of pressing concern" (GB, 3:291).[48] A month later he was singing the praises of Sasha Stone, the Russian-born painter and photographer who was associated with the group around the journal *G*, and whose collage would grace the cover of the upcoming Rowohlt edition of *One-Way Street*—"one of the most effective covers ever," Benjamin crowed (GB, 3:303). And at the end of the year, he would touch on the theme of photomontage in a review of his friend Hessel's novel *Heimliches Berlin* (Unknown Berlin): "This book is technically close to photomontage: housewives, artists, fashionable women, businessmen, scholars are all intercut contrastively with the shadowy outlines of Platonic and comic masks" (SW, 2:70). His thinking about photography finds expression above all in the "Little History of Photography," published in two installments in *Die literarische Welt* in 1931, and in Convolute Y, "Photography," in *The Arcades Project*.

In Paris Benjamin had picked up Flaubert's *Sentimental Education*, which bears on events of 1848 treated in *The Arcades*, and found himself absorbed by this book—to the point that, as he tells the Cohns, he felt unable to focus on contemporary French literature: "Once back in Berlin, I will probably take up another work by Flaubert, if I can bring myself to read anything at all" (GB, 3:291–292). As it happened, he fell ill with jaundice some three weeks after returning to Berlin, and to enliven his sickbed he chose not Flaubert but Kafka, whose posthumously published novel *The Trial* affected him no less profoundly. Indeed, he finished the Kafka novel in a state verging on agony, "so overwhelming is the unpretentious abundance of this book" (GB, 3:312). Under the spell of *The Trial*, he penned a short allegorical piece, "Idea of a Mystery," which he enclosed in a letter of November 18 to Scholem (see SW, 2:68). This little text, which conceives history as a trial *(Prozeß)* in which the nonappearance of the promised messiah is at issue, marked the beginning of an intensive engagement with Kafka's fiction that continued to the end of his life, producing important commentaries in the form of a published essay, a radio talk, and various fragmentary reflections.[49] For Benjamin, Kafka came to represent the distinctively modern storyteller, one whose reappropriation of parable makes uncannily concrete the drastic and comic situation of the decay and oblivion of tradition, of that which parable is supposed to transmit, even as it brings to light the unfathomable prehistoric forces, the creaturely life, informing the existence of the modern city dweller.

Benjamin's bout with jaundice kept him from showing his face around town at a time when, as he tells Scholem, he would have liked to be promoting his two books, *One-Way Street* and *Origin of the German Trauerspiel*, which Rowohlt Verlag was finally publishing early in 1928. He also wanted to attend a lecture by Erich Unger: he reported to Scholem that both Goldberg and Unger, "those antinomian gentlemen," had resumed their publicity efforts for Goldberg's latest theological enterprises. "Of course," he adds, "it is even more of an honor when one is visited oneself" (GB, 3:302). He was referring to a visit he would receive, while he was ailing, from the poet and philosopher Karl Wolfskehl, a friend of Hessel's who had been allied in Munich's Schwabinger Bohème with Stefan George and Ludwig Klages. "It's a good thing I've hardly read a line of his," Benjamin comments to Alfred Cohn; "it enabled me to follow his wonderful conversation without any scruples" (GB, 3:312). He reports that on this occasion Wolfskehl read aloud to him a poem by the nineteenth-century lyric poet Nikolaus Lenau in a manner he would never forget. His account of this visit would appear in *Die literarische Welt* in 1929. That same year Wolfskehl published an article in the *Frankfurter Zeitung*, "Lebensluft" (Air of Life), that would have an influence on Benjamin's conception of aura (from the Greek word meaning "air in motion," "breath"), as Benjamin himself indicates in a letter to Wolfskehl (GB, 3:474–475). The latter in turn was enthusiastic about Benjamin's 1929 essay on Surrealism (GB, 3:460). Wolfskehl was not the only visitor to the Delbrückstraße villa. Hessel came by frequently, and Benjamin had ample time to discuss his experiences in Moscow with his brother, Georg, who was by now deeply involved in the Communist Party and in the provision of adequate medical care to Berlin's poor.

In November and December Benjamin stepped up his efforts to gain entry into the circle surrounding the German art historian Aby Warburg, with whose work he felt a strong affinity. In contrast to a narrowly formalizing or aestheticizing art history, Warburg treated the work of art as a function of social memory. Central to his thinking, as to Benjamin's, is the concept of the afterlife *(Nachleben)* of cultural antiquity—that is, an idea of cultural reception, or more properly confrontation, as simultaneously preservation and transformation. And as with Benjamin, Warburg's global yet highly detailed approach to artworks entails a transcendence of the conventional opposition between form and content, as well as a transcendence of the traditional boundaries separating academic disciplines (such as history, anthropology, psychology, and philology). In a letter of early 1925 to Scholem, Benjamin had called attention to a 1923 publication of the Warburg Institute by Erwin Panofsky and Fritz Saxl, a study of Dürer's engraving "Melancholy" that relied on Warburg's interpretation of Dürer. Benjamin felt certain, as he later tells Hofmannsthal, that his own work would find a favorable hearing with Panofsky (GB, 3:17, 308). At his request, Hofmannsthal sent to Panofsky in Hamburg the August 1927 number of his journal *Neue Deutsche Beiträge*, containing the section on melancholy from Benjamin's forthcoming *Trauerspiel* book,[50] together with a letter of recommendation. Panofsky's response, which Hofmannsthal sent along to Benjamin in December or January, is lost; Benjamin describes it as "cool and resentment-laden." It left him with nothing to do but apologize to Hofmannsthal for his "inopportune request" (GB, 3:325, 332). More encouraging was the news, which reached him the following summer, that Saxl had found the *Trauerspiel* book "very interesting" and wanted to meet the author (GB, 3:407–408n). In the end, however, Benjamin was never able to forge a relationship with the Warburg school—to his detriment and theirs.

At the end of 1927 Benjamin agreed to take part in an experiment involving drug intoxication; it was the first of several such sessions he participated in at various times over the next seven years or so. He experimented for the most part with hashish, which he took orally under the loose supervision of two physician friends, Ernst Joël (a former antagonist in the Berlin youth movement in 1913–1914 [see SW, 2:603–604]) and Fritz Fränkel, who were doing research on narcotics and who recruited Benjamin as a test subject. Later he took hashish on his own, leaving behind an account of an intoxicated evening in Marseilles in 1928. He also on different occasions smoked opium and allowed himself to be injected subcutaneously with mescaline and with the opiate eucodal. He took these drugs, which he looked on as "poison" (Baudelaire's term in his writings on hashish and opium), for the sake of the knowledge to be gained from their use. Or so he claimed. He considered hashish intoxication itself a peculiarly intense form of study, at once dangerous and full of charm, a simultaneous expansion and concentration of the powers of perception. There was a specific connection to the figure of the flâneur in *The Arcades Project*, the nineteenth-century stroller whom Benjamin conceives as uniquely intoxicated by the phantasmagoria of big-city life. Already in a letter of 1919, written after finishing Baudelaire's *Artificial Paradises*, he refers to the poet's attempt to "monitor" the phenomena associated with drug intoxication "for what they have to teach us philosophically," and he speaks of the need to repeat the experiment independently (C, 148). The influence of the Surrealists also played a part in this venture, reflecting as it does the experimental character of Benjamin's intellectual project as a whole. His 1929 essay "Surrealism" underscores the propaedeutic function of intoxicants in achieving a "profane illumination" of the revolutionary energies slumbering in the world of everyday things, and it invokes a dialectics of intoxication *(Dialektik des Rausches)*. Such philosophical justification of drug use appears in the letter of January 30, 1928, in which Benjamin announces to Scholem, with no little secretiveness, his recent entry into "the realm of hashish": "The notes I made [on the first two experiments in December and January] . . . may well turn out to be a very worthwhile supplement to my philosophical observations, with which they are most intimately related, as are, to a certain degree, even my experiences under the influence of the drug" (C, 323).

Records of the experiments were kept by Benjamin and other participants (the first couple of sessions included his friend Ernst Bloch) in the form of written "protocols." Some of these accounts were jotted down in a state of intoxication, while others seem to have been compiled afterward on the basis of notes and personal recollection. Benjamin made use of portions of the drug protocols—both those he produced himself and those produced by his colleagues in which he is described and quoted—in composing two feuilleton pieces published in the early 1930s, "Hashish in Marseilles" and "Myslovice-Braunschweig-Marseilles." The protocols were further mined for sections of *The Arcades Project* dealing with flânerie, with the nineteenth-century domestic interior, and with phenomena of mirroring and superimposition in the arcades. Benjamin spoke in letters of developing his thoughts about hashish into a book, but this project never got off the ground; indeed, it came to number among his "large-scale defeats" (see C, 396). Presumably the book on hashish would have differed from the text published posthumously by Suhrkamp Verlag in 1972 under the title *Über Haschisch*, which contains the surviving protocols of experiments in which Benjamin took part, together with the two feuilleton pieces mentioned.[51] Nevertheless, despite their fragmentary notational character, the drug protocols suggest the tenor of Benjamin's thinking on the subject of intoxication (*Rausch* is a key term in Nietzsche's later philosophy).[52] They also provide revealing glimpses of the man Walter Benjamin—his anxieties and his fearlessness, his sensitivity and his imperiousness, his ardor, his reserve, and his sense of humor—in the waning years of the Weimar Republic, at a time in his life when the promise of regular work as a critic and reviewer blossomed brilliantly only to fade for lack of sustenance, when he became ever more aware of the "disintegration" threatening his thought (C, 396), and when demonic energies were on the rise in private and public spheres alike.

To be sure, Benjamin's interest in drugs by no means represents an unalloyed embrace of the irrational. It was not Symbolist derangement of the senses that he was after but transformation of reason—of the principle of identity and the law of noncontradiction. Among the leading motifs of the drug writings is that of multiple perspective, which is connected to the heightened velocity of thought: the intoxicated person has the sensation of being in more than one place at the same time, or of experiencing a single object from many sides simultaneously. "The opium-smoker or hashish-eater experiences the power of the gaze to suck a hundred sites out of one place" (OH, 85). The principle of identity is thus transformed through the experience of "multivalence."[53] Under the influence of hashish, somewhat as in the animistic world of fairy tales, all objects of perception wear faces, or rather masks—masks within masks; the intoxicated man, like the flâneur or the child at play, becomes a physiognomist for whom everything is a matter of nuance. To characterize this experience of manifold masquerade within the world of things, Benjamin comes up with the formula "colportage phenomenon of space," and in *The Arcades Project* this curious phenomenon is said to be the basic experience of the flâneur, one in which far-off times and places interpenetrate the landscape and the present moment.[54] By such means, intoxication loosens (not displaces) the thread of ratiocination, making for a necessary obliquity of approach, and sensualizing thought by immersing it in a fluid yet punctuated and contoured image space, scene of the "toe dance of reason." At the same time, the "loosening of the self through intoxication" (SW, 2:208), this power of detachment that Benjamin associates, in the second drug protocol, with an ambiguous nirvana (literally, "a blowing out"), enables a quickened empathy with all things, especially the most minuscule. Such "tenderness toward things" (and toward words as things) conditions the apprehension of a changeable, ornamental "aura" emanating from all objects, as reported in the protocol of March 1930.[55] Catalyst to perception more stratified and "richer in spaces," the drug makes possible, suggests Benjamin in "Surrealism," an illuminated intoxication conducing to a deepened sobriety—something, it may be, born of nearness to death. The dialectics of intoxication thus parallels the dialectics of awakening at work in *The Arcades Project*, where awakening means creative reappropriation of the dream, that is, the dream of the past. The talk of the emancipatory possibilities of intoxication in the Surrealism essay should probably be understood in the context of this psychohistorical dialectic.

The early months of 1928 were exciting ones for Benjamin. At the end of January his two books, *One-Way Street* and *Origin of the German Trauerspiel*, were finally published by Rowohlt Verlag. Among the many reviews that appeared in Germany, Switzerland, France, Holland, Hungary, England, and the United States, the most important for Benjamin were those written by his friends and colleagues: Kracauer's review essay "The Writings of Walter Benjamin" in the *Frankfurter Zeitung;* Willy Haas's detailed review of the *Trauerspiel* book on the front page of *Die literarische Welt;* Bloch's memorable article on *One-Way Street,* "Revue Form in Philosophy," in the *Vossische Zeitung;* Hessel's review of *One-Way Street* in *Das Tagebuch;* and Marcel Brion's "Two Books by Walter Benjamin" in *Les nouvelles littéraires.* He also found it noteworthy that Hermann Hesse, who would later try to interest German publishers in Benjamin's *Berlin Childhood around 1900,* wrote an unsolicited letter to Rowohlt praising *One-Way Street* (the letter has not survived). Later in the year he was gratified to see a "very long and approving critique of my things" by Otto Stoessl, a close associate of Karl Kraus, appearing in a Vienna newspaper. He mentions this together with a "very malicious" review in the *Berliner Tageblatt,* the city's leading liberal newspaper (GB, 3:426). The unfavorable notice was by Werner Milch (a professor of Romanticism at Marburg after World War II), who, in the course of rather catty observations on the two books by Benjamin, remarks aptly that, despite the manifest differences in focus and subject matter, both books owe their basic thrust to the early Romantic theory and practice of the fragment.[56] In addition to the largely favorable reception in the newspapers, and despite Benjamin's subsequent claims to the contrary (C, 372), there were a number of sometimes lengthy discussions of the *Trauerspiel* book in various scholarly journals and monographs, representing such fields as philosophy, art history, German literature, sociology, and psychoanalysis.[57]

One incident gives a further indication of Benjamin's growing reputation as a man of letters. When André Gide came to Berlin at the end of January, he took part in a two-hour interview with Benjamin, who was the only German journalist he agreed to see. The encounter, which Benjamin found "enormously interesting" and "delightful," resulted in two articles on Gide, published soon afterward in the *Deutsche allgemeine Zeitung* and *Die literarische Welt*.[58] Writing in February to Hofmannsthal, he said of Gide: "[He] has a thoroughly dialectical nature, characterized by an almost confusing abundance of reservations and barricades. Talking with him in person sometimes intensifies this impression, already conveyed by his writings in their own way, to the point of sublimity, and at other times to the point of being problematical" (C, 326; 324). The point is made without qualification in an article for *Die literarische Welt*, "Conversation with André Gide," where Benjamin emphasizes the "dialectical insight" of the man he calls the subtlest writer alive: "This principled rejection of every golden mean, this commitment to extremes—what else is it but dialectic, not as intellectual method but as life's breath and as passion."[59] Such an attitude entails a resolute cosmopolitanism: Gide is "a man who refuses to accept the claims of a thoroughgoing nationalism, and who recognizes French national identity only if it includes the tension-filled area of European history and the European family of nations" (SW, 2:94, 95, 96).[60]

There were other developments around this time in Benjamin's relations with fellow writers. In mid-February 1928 he met the literary critic Ernst Robert Curtius (1886–1956), who was teaching then at Heidelberg, and whose essays on contemporary French novelists he had first read in 1919; Curtius would publish his influential *European Literature and the Latin Middle Ages* in 1948. In addition, Benjamin had his first meetings in person with Hofmannsthal, to whom he had sent his two books. The *Trauerspiel* book was inscribed with the dedication "For Hugo von Hofmannsthal, / who cleared the way for this book, / with thanks, / February 1, 1928, WB" (GB, 3:333n), a sentence clarified by his remark to Brion that Hofmannsthal had been the first reader of the work (GB, 3:336). His conversation with Hofmannsthal, who visited Benjamin in his apartment in the Grunewald villa, touched on his relation to his own Jewishness as well as on his burgeoning ideas for the arcades project. The encounter was not easy for Benjamin. He was conscious of an "indefeasible reserve on my part, in spite of all my admiration for him," and in spite of "so much genuine understanding and good will on his part." To Scholem he described "an almost senile tendency" in Hofmannsthal, moments "when he sees himself completely misunderstood by everybody" (C, 327–328). The following month Benjamin would publish a review on the theatrical premiere of Hofmannsthal's self-styled *Trauerspiel, Der Turm* (The Tower); although Benjamin's letters reveal a considerable ambivalence toward the play, the review compares its action to the "world of Christian suffering that is portrayed in *Hamlet*" (SW, 2:105).

Also that February, Benjamin became better acquainted with Theodor Wiesengrund Adorno when the latter came to Berlin for some weeks and the two men were able to resume the discussions they had begun in Frankfurt in 1923. Benjamin reported in mid-February to Kracauer (who had first introduced them) that "Wiesengrund and I have been seeing a lot of each other—and to our mutual benefit. He has now met Ernst Bloch as well" (GB, 3:334). Benjamin would see Adorno again at the beginning of June in Königstein, near Frankfurt, where Adorno was a doctoral student, and a month later they would commence the historic twelve-year correspondence that traces the growth of their "philosophical friendship."[61] (Not until the fall of 1936, after Adorno's visit to Paris, were they on a first-name basis, however, and they never used the familiar form of address, as Benjamin did with old friends such as Scholem, Ernst Schoen, and Alfred Cohn; nevertheless, Benjamin's last letter, dictated while he was dying, was a communication to Adorno.) Further cementing the relationship at this point was Benjamin's fondness for Margarete "Gretel" Karplus (1902–1993), later Adorno's wife, whom he had met earlier in the year, and to whom he would write warm and playful letters during the early years of emigration, letters full of penetrating observations on his various projects. Gretel Karplus, in turn, gave generously of her time and her money—she directed a company that manufactured gloves in the mid-thirties—to help Benjamin in various ways after his flight from Berlin in March 1933.

Although Dora had been hard at work translating a detective novel by G. K. Chesterton, giving radio lectures on the education of children, contributing book reviews to *Die literarische Welt* (including one that concerned Joyce's "work in progress"—*Finnegans Wake*), and serving as editor of the magazine *Die praktische Berlinerin*, Benjamin

23. Gretel Karplus, ca. 1932 *(Theodor W. Adorno Archiv, Frankfurt am Main)*

told Scholem in March that their current situation was "gloomy" (GB, 3:348). This was no doubt partly a hint regarding the anticipated stipend from Jerusalem. And however gloomy their financial prospects might have been, Benjamin had nonetheless found time and money for a quick trip to the well-known casino in Sopot, part of the free city of Danzig, in January. His literary prospects were in fact better than they had been for some time. He was producing a steady stream of reviews and feuilleton pieces for *Die literarische Welt,* the *Frankfurter Zeitung,* and other journals on occasion, including the *Neue schweizer Rundschau* and the *Internationale Revue i10.* He had received an invitation from Stefan Großmann, the publisher of the prominent journal *Das Tagebuch,* to become a regular contributor. Moreover, Rowohlt had offered to extend his contract, which would have included a monthly stipend, and he had a competing offer from Hegner

24. Dora Sophie Benjamin, 1927
(Courtesy of the Jewish National
Library)

Verlag, though in the end he turned down both these offers—the former because he was insulted by the conditions offered by Rowohlt,
the latter because he was wary of the "Catholic orientation" of the
press (C, 322).

With so many publishing venues at his disposal, work began to
pour from the villa in Delbrückstraße. In addition to the two accounts of the interview with Gide, there were three pieces published
that spring on children's toys, in which Benjamin discusses the cultural history of toys and adumbrates a "philosophical classification
of toys," treating the world of playthings not in terms of the child's
mind, that is, the psychology of the individual, but in terms of a theory of play.[62] There were also pieces on Karl Kraus's public reading of
Offenbach's *La vie parisienne,* on an exhibition of a unique collection
of nineteenth-century watercolor transparencies, on graphology, on
books by the mentally ill, on the Berlin Food Exhibition, on "Paris as
goddess," and later in the year on the novelist Julien Green, on "the path
to success, in thirteen theses" (which contains the rudiments of a theory of gambling), on Karl Blossfeldt's disclosure of "new image-worlds"

in his volume of botanical photographs, and on Goethe at Weimar. Many of these pieces reflect concerns of *The Arcades Project*. The pieces on Goethe and Weimar, on the other hand, were offshoots of Benjamin's work on the encyclopedia article on Goethe commissioned a year earlier for the *Great Soviet Encyclopedia*; the article itself was written in 1928. During a visit to the Goethe house in Weimar in June to check his documentation, he would unexpectedly find himself alone for twenty minutes in the great author's study, with not even the shadow of a guard to disturb him. "And thus it happens," he observes in recounting this experience to Alfred and Grete Cohn, "that the more cold-bloodedly one accosts things, the more tenderly they sometimes respond" (GB, 3:386).

Among the articles and reviews Benjamin published in early 1928, one short book review, of minor significance in itself, stands out for its uncharacteristically crude invective. Benjamin's review of Eva Fiesel's *Die Sprachphilosophie der deutschen Romantik* (The Philosophy of Language in German Romanticism; 1927) appeared in February in the *Frankfurter Zeitung* and occasioned an angry letter from the author to the newspaper. As editor of the paper's feuilleton pages, Kracauer answered with a letter to Eva Fiesel in support of Benjamin's review. (Neither of these letters has been preserved.) Writing to Kracauer on March 10, Benjamin thanks him for his demonstration of solidarity and praises the "wonderfully exact malice" with which Kracauer came to his defense against the "academic gun moll [*Revolverheldin*]. The Furies are cut from this mold" (GB, 3:341, 343). He goes on in a jocular tone to speak of his requiring a bodyguard in the event of future attacks from readers of reviews. To Scholem he mentions that in her "shameless" letter to the *Frankfurter Zeitung*, the "crazy female" *(törichte Frauenzimmer)* had cited a number of bigwigs as backers of her work, including Heinrich Wölfflin and Ernst Cassirer (GB, 3:346).

In his review, Benjamin characterizes the book as "most likely a dissertation" (which it was not) and places it "high above the average doctoral thesis in German philology." And he adds: "This needs to be stated at the outset in order to forestall misunderstanding of a second statement: It is a typical piece of woman's work [*eine typische Frauenarbeit*]. That is to say, the professional expertise, the level of

learning, are out of all proportion to the low degree of inner sovereignty and genuine engagement with the subject matter" (GS, 3:96).
He goes on to brand the work (in a phrase reminiscent of Nietzsche)
"unmanly historicism," deficient in real understanding of the theory
of language implicit in Romantic thinking.[63] "For the particular contexts can be decisively clarified only on the basis of [intellectual] centers that were inaccessible to [this thinking itself]." He also takes the
author to task for her "unseemly" inattention to the secondary literature and her scanting of bibliographic references.

Benjamin does not seem to have read the book very carefully—he
classes it with the sort of pragmatic scientific linguistics it explicitly
critiques at the end—and he did not trouble to find out anything about
the author. The book was in fact written by someone whose primary
specialization was in another field, namely, classical philology. Eva
Fiesel would become, by the end of the 1920s, an internationally
known authority on the grammar of Etruscan. A victim of the anti-
Semitic laws drafted in 1933, she lost her teaching position in Munich,
despite a formal appeal from colleagues and students, and immigrated
in 1934 to the United States, where she subsequently taught at Yale
and Bryn Mawr.[64] Benjamin's rather odious tone in the review is a
little perplexing. Nothing like it appears in the dozen or so other
reviews he wrote on books by women. If he did harbor antifeminist
sentiments, they never got in the way of his respect for women friends
such as Hannah Arendt, Adrienne Monnier, Gisèle Freund, Elisabeth
Hauptmann, Anna Seghers, and others.[65] Of course, it's possible that
in this case he was reacting defensively to what he took to be an unworthy, if cleverly organized, claim on his own intellectual territory,
one that, moreover, failed to acknowledge his prior contribution to the
field *(The Concept of Criticism in German Romanticism)*. A comparable strain of invective would surface again only in his unpublished
1938 review of Max Brod's book on Kafka (SW, 3:317–321).

For the first time in his career, Benjamin was able to be more selective as to the reviewing work he took on—and he tried to focus on
material related to his studies for *The Arcades Project*. At the beginning of the year, he had confided to Alfred Cohn: "I need to move on
to something new, something altogether different. I am handicapped
by journalistic-diplomatic scribbling" (GB, 3:321). With the arcades

project he was indeed, by his own reckoning, on uncharted ground: "The work on the Paris arcades," he tells Scholem in a letter of May 24, "is taking on an ever more mysterious and insistent mien, and howls into my nights like a small beast if I have failed to water it at the most distant springs during the day. God knows what it will do when . . . I set it free. But this will not happen for a long time, and though I may already be constantly staring into the housing in which it does what comes naturally, I let hardly anyone else have a look inside" (C, 335). Among the far-flung sources he was exploring at this time was the "sparse material" relating to a philosophical description of fashion, "this natural and wholly irrational temporal measure of historical process" (C, 329), which forms the subject of Convolute B of the *Arcades.*

Despite the workload that confined him to his desk, he made occasional forays into Berlin's intellectual life. Scholem's brother Erich invited him to the festive annual dinner for the Berlin circle of bibliophiles. The guests were presented with copies of a remarkable little book called *Amtliches Lehrgedicht der Philosophischen Fakultät der Haupt- und Staats-Universität Muri* (Official Didactic Poem of the Philosophical Faculty of the University of Muri), whose author was Gershom Scholem, the "Beadle of the Department of the Philosophy of Religion" and whose dedicatee was "His Magnificence Walter Benjamin, Rector of the University of Muri." The two friends had composed this compendium of their jokes and academic satires while they were living in the Swiss village of Muri in 1918; Scholem's brother now produced a private edition of 250 copies. And in late March Benjamin was present at the last of a series of four appearances by Karl Kraus at which the great satirist read, with piano accompaniment, from Offenbach's operettas. The performance must have been shattering: Benjamin told Alfred Cohn that his thoughts were in such a state afterward that he was unable to gain perspective on them.

Fleeing the noise and dust of renovations being done to the Delbrückstraße villa, he had moved in April into a new room located "in the deepest, most forgotten section of the Tiergarten," where "nothing but trees peer at me through the two windows" (C, 335). During the two months he lived there, before subletting it to Ernst Bloch, he took advantage of the easy access this room provided to the Prussian

State Library, where he pursued his research on the arcades. An advance he had received from Rowohlt for "a projected book on Kafka, Proust, and so on" (C, 335–336) was helping to maintain the arcades venture. The projected book itself, *Gesammelte Essays zur Literatur*, never materialized, although the contract for the book would be redrawn and expanded two years later.

Alongside his literary efforts, Benjamin spent a great deal of time and effort in the attempt to aid two friends. Arthur Lehning's *i10* was in serious financial trouble, and Benjamin did everything he could to find support for the journal in Germany. He mobilized Kracauer to appeal to the board of the *Frankfurter Zeitung*, and he himself wrote to friends and acquaintances in the publishing world in search of a lifeline. No such support was ever forthcoming, and Lehning's periodical ceased publication at the end of its first year. Alfred Cohn had lost his job, and Benjamin worked assiduously to help him find something appropriate. In the course of the year, he had come to know Gustav Glück, a cultivated Berlin bank official who was part of the circle around Karl Kraus, and the two men discovered a surprising affinity for each other. Although Glück would ultimately serve as the model for Benjamin's famous portrait and provocation, "The Destructive Character," Benjamin turned to him in 1928 for practical advice regarding Alfred Cohn's situation. He also turned to his new acquaintance Gretel Karplus, who was running her family's glove factory in Berlin. Finding no possibilities in a German economy that was, by mid-1929, slipping into recession, Benjamin ultimately encouraged the well-read Cohn to try his hand at journalism, and in fact placed several of his reviews in the *Frankfurter Zeitung* and *Die literarische Welt*.

In his letter of May 24 to Scholem, Benjamin trumpeted his imminent arrival in Jerusalem, at the same time voicing economic considerations: "I have firmly put an autumn visit to Palestine on my agenda for this year. I hope that, before then, Magnes and I will have reached an agreement about the financial terms of my apprenticeship" (C, 335). A few weeks later he met with Magnes in Berlin, and the university chancellor "promised, on his own and without further ado," to provide him with a stipend to study Hebrew (C, 338). Over the next couple of years, Benjamin would postpone the trip to Jerusalem at least seven times, marshaling a variety of excuses (such as his need to finish the arcades project, his need to be near his ailing mother, his need to be with Asja Lacis, or his need to attend to his divorce proceedings), and finally confessing "to a truly pathological inclination to procrastinate in this matter" (C, 350). Though he never set foot in Jerusalem, he did receive a check for 3,642 marks (about $900 in 1928 dollars) from Magnes in October. Thanks for this funding came only eight months later, when Benjamin finally got around to arranging for Hebrew lessons. These were abandoned after a few weeks, as we have seen. Scholem suggests that Benjamin was deceiving himself from the first in his idea of shifting his focus from European to Hebrew literature, and that it took him a while to realize this, because "he did his best to avoid facing his own state of affairs" (SF, 149). Benjamin's letters at this time to Brion, Hofmannsthal, Wolfskehl, and others, letters in which he speaks of his plan to visit Palestine and reconnoiter, lend credence to Scholem's claims. On the other hand, Benjamin never took up Hebrew in earnest, nor did he seem to feel that he should pay back the stipend. When the question of repayment later came up in correspondence with Scholem, and in conversation with Scholem's wife in Berlin, he dodged the issue, leaving the impression that he had acted in bad faith throughout the affair.

The end of spring brought paired calamities. In early May his mother suffered a serious stroke from which she would never fully recover; she stayed on in the villa but required increasing attention. In contrast to his reaction to the sudden death of his father, Benjamin has little to say of this event in his letters, mentioning it only in passing. And at the end of May, he traveled to Frankfurt for the burial of his great-uncle Arthur Schoenflies, who had been a professor of mathematics and a former rector of Frankfurt University, a man in whom, as Benjamin saw it, Jewish and Christian cultural strains were distinctively intermingled (and he could have said the same of himself). During his protracted entanglement with the university in Frankfurt, Benjamin had frequently stayed with his uncle, and the two men had grown close. Back in Berlin, where he was living once more in the family villa, there were deadlines to be met for articles long and short, including "some long articles on French literary currents today" (C, 335). These articles, published in four installments as "Paris Diary," would finally appear in *Die literarische Welt* between April and June 1930. In June and July of 1928 Benjamin and Franz Hessel entered into drawn-out, ultimately fruitless negotiations over the transfer of rights for the Proust translation to Piper Verlag. This development led to his and Hessel's withdrawal from the half-completed project altogether, a project that had had such "an intense effect on [his] writing" (C, 340). In July Benjamin published a short, autobiographically slanted piece on Stefan George, which had been solicited by *Die literarische Welt* for a feature in honor of the poet's sixtieth birthday; among the other contributors were Martin Buber and Bertolt Brecht. Benjamin's close personal relationship with the latter, who came to have a fateful importance in his life, would start the following year.

During the summer of 1928 Benjamin characteristically began meditating a change of scene, though neither he nor Dora had any fixed income: "I sit like a penguin on the barren rocks of my thirty-seven years [he had just turned thirty-six] and brood on the possibility of a lonely Scandinavian cruise. But it is probably too late in the year" (GB, 3:399, to Alfred Cohn). This particular plan would have to wait until the summer of 1930 for its realization, but his financial uncertainties did not stand in the way of shorter trips south. He traveled to Munich in July and found the city a "gruesomely beautiful corpse, so beautiful one doesn't believe in its lifelessness" (GB, 3:402). And he met his friends Jula and Fritz Radt in September in Lugano, Switzerland. From his perch beside the lake he wrote to Scholem of his eagerness to get back to the arcades project and to the kind of work that was free of practical constraints. "It would be splendid," he observes ruefully, "if the ignominious writing I do for profit did not, for its part, need to be maintained at a certain level, so as not to become disgusting to me. I cannot say that I have lacked the opportunity to publish bad stuff. What I have always lacked, despite everything, is only the courage to compose it" (GB, 3:414). At the end of the month he traveled on to Genoa and then Marseilles, where he took hashish in solitude. A further fruit of this return visit to the French port city was the vivid set of vignettes entitled "Marseilles," which he published in the *Neue schweizer Rundschau* the following April (SW, 2:232–236), and of which the nearest analogue in English, perhaps, is James Agee's description of Brooklyn in the late thirties. Benjamin himself compares

"Marseilles" to his piece on Weimar from earlier in the year, though no city so stubbornly resisted his efforts to depict it, he comments, as did Marseilles (C, 352).

The most important of the pieces written "for profit" that fall and winter was the essay "Surrealism," which appeared in three installments in *Die literarische Welt* in February (SW, 2:207–221). Eight months before, this paper had published his translation of excerpts from Louis Aragon's Surrealist travel guide, *Paris Peasant*. Benjamin's engagement with the Surrealists goes back at least to 1925, when he wrote the short piece entitled "Dream Kitsch." As his familiarity with the movement increased, so did his suspicions, though a Surrealist strain of thinking remained determinative in the arcades project, which Benjamin originally conceived as taking possession of "the legacy of Surrealism"—from a distance (C, 342). He saw the Surrealism essay as "an opaque screen placed before the *Arcades*" (C, 347). The essay itself begins and ends with images of technology or, more precisely, of the interpenetration of human bodily and technological forces in a new organized *physis*. Benjamin speaks as an observer removed from the source of the stream and seeking, from the vantage point of his critical power station in the valley, to "gauge the energies of the movement" now that its "heroic phase"—what he also calls "the original movement"—is over. The movement still occupies a highly exposed position situated "between an anarchistic Fronde [violent political opposition] and a revolutionary discipline." It seeks to reach a decision in the face of its competing political and aesthetic imperatives. Surrealism is said to mark a crisis in the arts and in the intelligentsia generally, a crisis in "the humanistic concept of freedom." Just as the classic concept of matter as elementary stuff has dissolved in the wake of the electromagnetic theory of matter, so the idea of human substance and identity is transformed in the new dynamic *physis*.[66] Instead of the atomistic subject and object of classical epistemology, Benjamin has recourse here to categories of image space *(Bildraum)* and body space *(Leibraum)* to characterize the new event-fabric of reality and its wave action or "innervation." This suspension of what Bergson called "the logic of solids" has profound implications for the act of reading. Surrealist texts are emphatically not "literature," though from another angle they represent a "primal upsurge of esoteric poetry." As Benjamin puts it in his "Paris Diary" of 1930:

> At a time when the idea of *poésie pure* was threatening to peter out in sterile academicism, Surrealism gave it a demagogic, almost political emphasis. It rediscovered the great tradition of esoteric poetry that is actually quite removed from *l'art pour l'art* and that is such a secret, salutary practice for poetry. (SW, 2:350)

The Surrealists explode the sphere of poetry from within, pushing the idea of "the poetic life" to the limit. Witness their preoccupation with things outmoded—the first iron constructions, the first factory buildings, the earliest photos, objects that have begun to be extinct, grand pianos, dresses of five years ago—the encounter with which generates images of a pristine intensity. Here of course is one of the main links with *The Arcades Project,* which is no less concerned with bringing the "immense forces of 'atmosphere' concealed in these [obsolete or decrepit] things to the point of explosion." (The formulation also recalls the "prismatic" capacity of film, discussed above.) This soliciting of the energies of the antiquated for present use—a conscious tendency of Benjamin's writings from early on[67]—grounds the possibility of revolutionary experience, revolutionary nihilism, if not yet revolutionary action. It is a matter of revolution, first of all, in the attitude toward what is called ordinary—"we penetrate the mystery only to the degree that we recognize it in the everyday world"—though Benjamin leaves open "the cardinal question" of whether it is in the changing of attitudes or in the changing of external circumstances that we find the conditions for revolution. This question, he says, determines the relation of politics to morality. The "profane illumination" of the world of things, disclosing secret affinities among dispersed phenomena, makes manifest in the space of political action—within what he calls "bodily collective innervation"—an image space to which the powers of contemplation alone are no longer adequate. Here action puts forth its own image *(das Bild aus sich herausstellt)* and is that image. In the remarkable final paragraph of the Surrealism essay, which invokes "The Communist Manifesto," Benjamin adduces "that image space to which profane illumination initiates us [uns heimisch *macht*]," and represents such image space, married to body space, as "the world of universal and integral actuality [*allseitiger und integraler Aktualität*]," a phrase to which he returns at the end of his career, during the composition of "On the Concept of History."[68] The theme of freedom once inspiring the radicalism of youth now reappears in the fullness of "Surrealist experience," with its loosening of the self and measured obliteration of the threshold separating dream and waking world. Such "radical intellectual freedom," as disciplined by the "organization of pessimism," would make possible that integral actuality through which reality surpasses itself, as we read at the end. In expounding this emancipatory potential, Benjamin makes clear that the Surrealists themselves were not always equal to the task of profane illumination entailed in the revolutionary poetic life, drawn as they sometimes were, in their sabotage of liberal-humanistic rationalism and in their "overheated fantasies," to an undialectical conception of myth, dream, and the unconscious.[69]

It would fall to Benjamin himself to explore the implications of the concepts limned so briefly in the essay on Surrealism; his thoughts on politics would henceforth be guided by the notion of the collective as a "body space" that is shaped by and exists within an "image space." Much of his work on media aesthetics in the 1930s can in fact be viewed as the unpacking of these concepts and the specification of the relationship between them. The ultimate goal—the formation and transformation of the collective—occurs through innervation, what Miriam Bratu Hansen has called a "non-destructive, mimetic incorporation of the world."[70] And, as Benjamin claims in the artwork essay of 1936, art is the irreplaceable medium of that incorporation: "Film serves to train human beings in those new apperceptions and reactions demanded by interaction with an apparatus whose role in their lives is expanding almost daily. To make the enormous technological apparatus of our time an object of human innervation—that is the historical task in whose service film finds its true meaning."[71]

If mid-1925 had been the low point in Benjamin's professional career, the three years since had seen his remarkable emergence on the German cultural scene of the late 1920s. It is clear in retrospect that this emergence owed a great deal not just to the brilliance of his writing and the startling originality of his analyses but to his inimitable versatility as well. He could create a journalistic profile in tune with the dominant tendencies of the day, and especially with the Neue Sachlichkeit, which was rapidly displacing the phenomena of the mandarin, imperial culture that had lingered long into the Weimar Republic. But that profile extended well beyond the "new sobriety." His experiences in the Soviet Union and his growing intimacy with Brecht ensured that the leftism frequently shaping his approach was fundamentally different from the left-liberal orientation of most of the Neue Sachlichkeit. And that profile was enlivened at key points by his growing expertise in popular culture and especially by his deep, firsthand knowledge of the European avant-garde movements. The result was a body of work that earned him a rapidly growing reputation and access to a widening spectrum of publishing venues. The "apprenticeship in German literature" was over, and Walter Benjamin was on his way to establishing himself as the most important German cultural critic of his day.

[CHAPTER SEVEN]

The Destructive Character

Berlin, Paris, and Ibiza, 1929–1932

In the course of 1929, Benjamin's erotic entanglements plunged him back into the kind of turmoil he had experienced in 1921, when his marriage first foundered. At some point in the summer of 1928 Benjamin had gotten news of Asja Lacis's upcoming transfer to the Soviet embassy in Berlin, where she was to work as a trade representative for Soviet films. She had arrived in November, in the company of Bernhard Reich—who, however, was there for only a short visit while Bertolt Brecht was finishing *The Threepenny Opera*. (Lacis and Reich had been working with Brecht since 1923, and Brecht would attend some of the screenings she arranged at the embassy in Berlin.) In Reich's absence, Benjamin and Lacis lived together for two months, from December 1928 through January 1929, in an apartment at Düsseldorfer Straße 42, not two miles from his parents' villa, where Dora and ten-year-old Stefan were living with his ailing mother—but by February Benjamin was back in the parental home on Delbrückstraße. Although Lacis evidently had asked him to move out of the apartment they were sharing, she continued to play a major role in his life, and many of his excursions into Berlin's cultural life were undertaken in her company. He also resumed his socializing with Bernhard Reich when his friend and Lacis's life partner returned to Berlin—occasioning a reprise, no doubt, of their awkward dance around Asja in Moscow. It is an indication of the peculiar latitude that all these people allowed themselves in their relations with one another that Benjamin, while still living with Asja in January, attended a festive birthday party for Dora.

In the spring, however, after a series of turbulent scenes, he asked his wife for a divorce so that he could marry his Latvian girlfriend—though it was not at all clear that Asja wanted to marry *him*. It had been seven years since his attraction to Jula Cohn—and Dora's to Ernst Schoen—led to the cessation of conjugal relations between husband and wife. Those seven years were remarkable for the loyalty Dora had shown her husband, supporting him by taking on often demeaning labor, and continuing to serve as a sounding board for his work. Equally remarkable was the perseverance with which the little family unit had managed to live under the same roof in the face of Benjamin's frequent and prolonged absences and his minimal interest in family life. Now, however, Benjamin was determined to make a clean break, and divorce proceedings began on June 29, amid bitter accusations by both parties. They stretched on until March 27, 1930, the date of their divorce. Having initiated the process by accusing his wife of infidelity, Benjamin found himself up against "one of the most cunning and dangerous lawyers in Germany" (GB, 3:489), who had no trouble exposing the weakness of his case. Benjamin ended up losing heavily. The judges rejected his arguments in view of the fact that he had repeatedly conceded to Dora, orally and in writing, the same freedom in sexual matters that for years he had claimed for himself—and this while regularly living off his wife's earnings as a journalist. More recently he had refused all requests to assist in the support of his son. Not surprisingly, he was ordered to pay Dora back the 40,000 marks he owed her, which meant signing over his entire inheritance, including his cherished collection of children's books and his share of the villa in Delbrückstraße.[1]

Shortly before the legal process got started, Benjamin wrote from Delbrückstraße to Hofmannsthal, mentioning his plan to "liquidate [his] Berlin situation" by the beginning of August (GB, 3:473). At approximately the same moment, on June 27, 1929, Dora was writing from Surrey, England, in a more overtly sorrowful vein to Scholem. Her letter provides a revealing glimpse into the marriage and into some of the more profane sides of Benjamin's character, not to mention her own generous nature, and is worth quoting at length:

> Dear Gerhard, things are very bad with Walter. I can't begin to tell you about it, for it breaks my heart. He is altogether under Asja's influence and does things which I can scarcely bring myself to write about—things which make it unlikely that I shall ever again

exchange a word with him in this life. All he is at this point is brains and sex; everything else has ceased to function. And you know or can well imagine that in such cases it's not long before the brains abdicate. That's always been the great danger with him. . . . / Asja's residency permit has expired, and he wanted to marry her as quickly as possible, so as to provide her with German citizenship. Although he has never put aside a penny either for Stefan or for me, he asked me—and I agreed—to lend him half of my future inheritance from my aunt. I gave him all the books, and the next day he asked for the collection of children's books in addition. During the winter he lived with me for months without paying anything, cost me hundreds, and at the same time was spending hundreds on Asja. When I told him my money was running out, he proposed divorce. Right now he owes me over two hundred marks for two months' food, telephone, and other things, although he's received several thousand marks from [Wilhelm] Speyer for collaborating on a play and a novel (I have written proof of this.) / For the past eight years we've given each other our freedom—he's told me all about his smutty affairs and a thousand times has urged me to "find a friend" myself—and for the past six years we've been living apart. And now he makes accusations against me! The contemptible laws of the land are suddenly good enough for him. Of course, standing behind him is the totally unscrupulous Asja, who, as he himself has said to me several times, doesn't love him but merely makes use of him. I know this sounds like a bad novel, but it's true. . . . / He said that if I tore up my marriage contract, he would take on the debt. I promised to have it annulled, but he won't do anything—either for Stefan or about the money he owes me. He doesn't even want to leave me the apartment, which I painted myself and for which I've been paying the rent and the fuel costs for years. . . . I agreed to everything he asked, until I realized that he's the type of man who can't abide by what's settled and always demands something new. He cares no more for Stefan's and my future than for that of a total stranger. / Through it all he suffers terribly. I hear from various eyewitnesses—his friends, mind you—that the two of them fight like cats and dogs. She has an apartment which he pays for and which he used to live in until she made him leave. That's when he came to me again. He said I should have her come live here with me, which I naturally refused to hear of; she was horrible to me some years ago. So now he's taking his revenge.[2]

It is remarkable that, while adducing a pattern of irresponsibility and unscrupulousness on Benjamin's part, and indicating how deeply he's hurt her and their son, Dora nevertheless downplays his responsibility by making him seem a victim of his own sexual intoxication and of Asja's supposed machinations. This interpretation no doubt made it easier for her to forgive him, as she did within a year of the judges' final disposition in the matter.[3] Yet it also sheds a revealing light on the depth of her commitment—not so much to her husband as to his destiny as a writer. The divorce had been a desperate maneuver on his part, a high-stakes erotic and financial gambit. It did not affect her admiration of his intellect, though her compassion never led her to sentimentalize him.

Despite all the upheavals it brought to his daily life, the year 1929 was a high point of productivity for Benjamin, witnessing to his powers of concentration and to what Scholem calls his "store of profound serenity—only poorly described by the word *stoicism*" (SF, 159). In that year he produced more writings—including a great many newspaper reviews, as well as essays, radio scripts, short stories, and a translation—than in any year before or after, at the same time advancing construction of *The Arcades Project* by drafting brilliant short passages of philosophical-historical reflection such as "Paris Arcades" and by gathering citations. In connection with the arcades project, he was studying the late nineteenth-century arts movement known as Jugendstil, developing his ideas about colportage and kitsch (reflected in his published piece "Chambermaids' Romances of the Past Century" [SW, 2:225–231]), and subjecting the architecture of nineteenth-century Paris to intense scrutiny. In that connection he read Sigfried Giedion's *Bauen in Frankreich* (Architecture in France; 1928) in February. He wrote to the author, a Swiss art historian, describing the "electrifying" effect the book had had on him and characterizing its "radical knowing" in a phrase that goes to the heart of his own work: "you are capable of highlighting tradition—or rather, discovering it— within the present day itself" (GB, 3:444). At issue in such researches, as he said to Scholem in March, was his effort "to attain the most extreme concreteness for an era, as it occasionally manifested itself in children's games, in a building, or in a particular situation. A perilous,

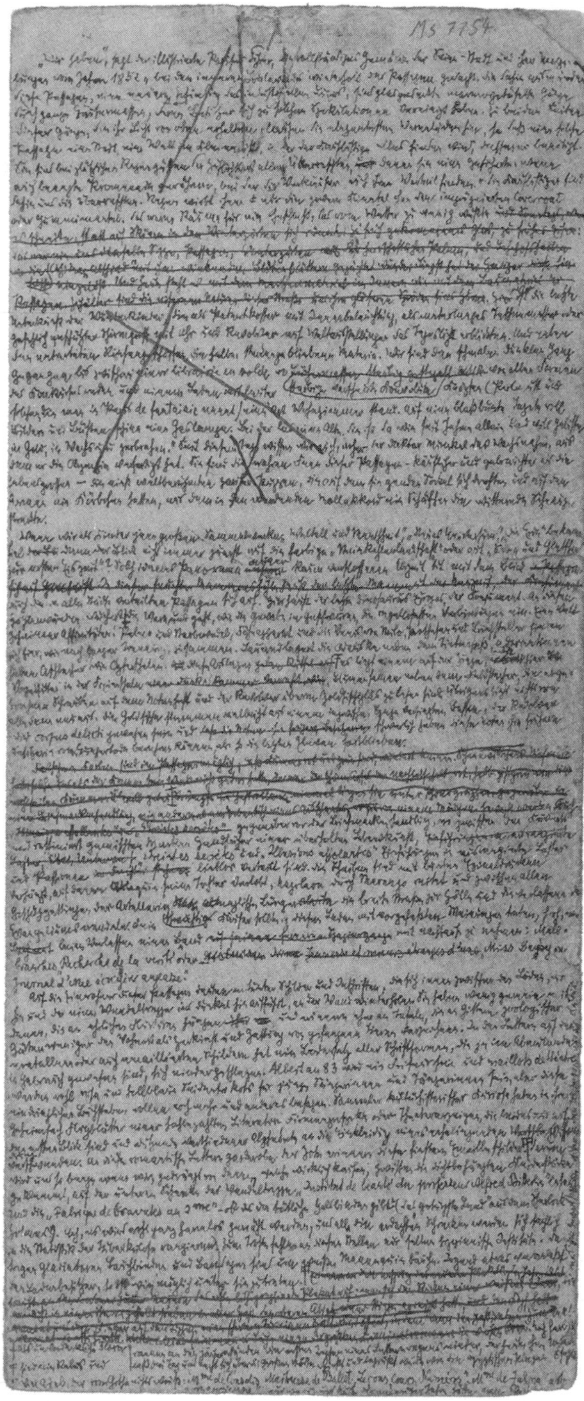

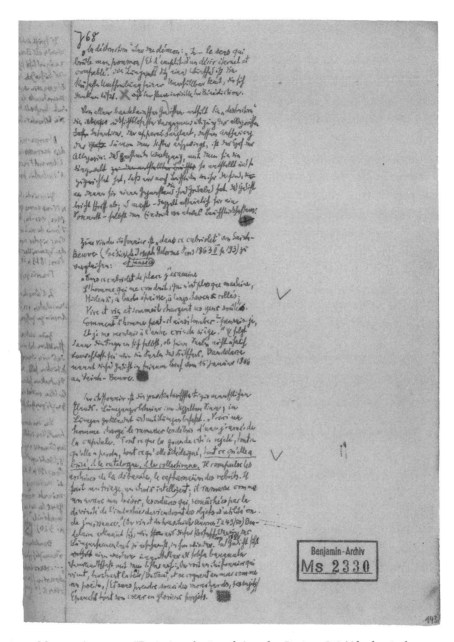

25. Manuscript pages: "Paris Arcades" and *Arcades Project, J68 (Akademie der Künste, Berlin. Walter Benjamin Archiv)*

breathtaking enterprise" (C, 348). This enterprise, already begun in *One-Way Street,* was also carried on in the composition of his signature *Denkbilder,* philosophical vignettes of the sort he was working on in "Short Shadows (I)" (published in November in the *Neue schweizer Rundschau*) and subsequently would employ on an expanded scale in his autobiographical texts, *Berlin Chronicle* and *Berlin Childhood around 1900.*

The year 1929 was also significant in that it saw the emergence of a more overtly Marxist tendency in Benjamin's work. Scholem was the first to note the change, marking the year as "a distinct turning point in [Benjamin's] intellectual life as well as a high point of intensive literary and philosophical activity. It was a visible turning point, which nevertheless did not exclude the continuity of his thought . . .—something that is more clearly discernible now than it was then" (SF, 159). Some part of this turn is clearly attributable to the presence of Asja Lacis in Berlin—just as the earliest stages of his approach to Marxist thought had been mediated by Lacis on Capri. In the course of 1929 Asja took him to meetings of revolutionary proletarian writers in workers' halls and to a series of performances by proletarian theater groups. It was probably already during their two-month cohabitation in the winter of 1928–1929, and it was evidently at Asja's request, that Benjamin drafted a sort of pedagogical manifesto reflecting her decade of experience with children's theater in Soviet Russia.[4] "Program for a Proletarian Children's Theater," which remained unpublished during his lifetime (SW, 2:201–206), attests to his continuing concern with the meaning of childhood in human existence, and hence with the old yet ever new question of education.[5] Every childhood action, writes Benjamin, is "a signal from another world, in which the child lives and commands." It is the responsibility of educators not to dissolve the world of childhood by subjugating children to class interests (as "bourgeois" education—and not least the Wynekenian youth culture itself—attempts to do) but rather to instill seriousness in children by allowing their childhood full scope for play, given that play in one form or another is essential to learning as well as to the fulfillment of childhood. "The education of a child requires that its entire life be engaged," he writes, and the key to this humane pedagogy is the method of improvisation, as cultivated in the theatrical workshops. (Such workshops can be found as well in the utopian schemes of Charles Fourier, the nineteenth-century social theorist who figures prominently in *The Arcades Project*.) As the "dialectical site of education," children's theater inculcates "the power of observation . . . at the heart of un-sentimental love," thereby bringing about the convergence of play with reality. Childhood achievement is geared not toward the "eternity" of the products but toward "the 'moment' of the gesture."[6] Such a moment has its own futurity and resonance: "What is truly revolutionary is the *secret signal* of what is to come that speaks from the gesture of the child." Before she returned to Moscow in 1930, Lacis would try to arrange for Benjamin's immigration to the Soviet Union, in another of her vain attempts to find something for her friend there (according to her own account, she advised Benjamin against moving to Palestine).[7] After this deepening of their intimacy at the end of the twenties, they did not see each other again, though their correspondence would continue until 1936, when Lacis began a ten-year internment in Kazakhstan, while Reich underwent repeated banishment and imprisonment.

While the "heavier Marxist accents" noted by Scholem were in part the result of Lacis's influence, and in part a function of Benjamin's deepening intellectual relationship with Adorno and Horkheimer at this time, the most important catalyst was undoubtedly the friendship that grew up between Benjamin and Bertolt Brecht beginning in May 1929.[8] Although Benjamin is now best known for his work of the mid-1930s, it can be said that with the cementing of the friendship with Brecht, the fundaments of his mature intellectual position were in place by 1929. The admixture of a radical leftist politics, a syncretistic theological concern that drew freely upon theologoumena from Judaism and Christianity, a deep knowledge of the German philosophical tradition, and a cultural theory adequate to the diversity of its objects under the fast-changing conditions of modernity—all of these would characterize his work from now on. It would be his fate, however, that not one of his friends and intellectual partners—to say nothing of his adversaries—would ever comprehend or even tolerate this "contradictory and mobile whole" in its entirety. A letter from his deeply wounded wife to Scholem shows how the shifting, seemingly tenuous filiations in Benjamin's intellectual position could be interpreted, uncharitably, as opportunism:

> Since then he has always made his pacts: with bolshevism, which he was unwilling to disavow, so as not to lose his last excuse (for if he ever did recant, he would have to admit that it's not the sublime principles of this lady that bind him to her but only sexual things); with Zionism, partly for your sake and partly (don't be angry, these are his own words) "because home is wherever someone makes it possible for him to spend money"; with philosophy (for how do his ideas about theocracy and the city of God, or his ideas about violence, accord with this salon bolshevism?); with the literary life (not literature), for he is naturally ashamed to admit to these Zionist whims in front of Hessel and in front of the little ladies Hessel brings him during the pauses in his affair with Asja.[9]

In a way, Benjamin left himself open to such charges because of his refusal to commit himself fully and unreservedly to any of these "pacts." His stance, which is consistent in regard to every established doctrine and belief system, was to approach just close enough to allow the use of certain elements of the system—and no further. This was more than a tendency to bricolage. Like his extreme courtesy and his effort to seal his friends off from one another, it was a strategy designed to maintain his intellectual independence.

At the inception of their friendship, Benjamin was nearly thirty-seven, Brecht thirty-one. Even Benjamin's friends, who tended to be skeptical of Brecht's influence, acknowledged the importance of the relationship. Scholem found that Brecht brought "an entirely new element, an elemental force in the truest sense of the word, into [Benjamin's] life." Hannah Arendt later remarked that the friendship with Brecht was for Benjamin a piece of extraordinary good fortune.[10] Today it can be seen that the foremost German poet of the day was forming an alliance with the foremost literary critic. The two men met frequently for long discussions in Brecht's apartment near the zoo, and Benjamin was soon an accepted member of the tight-knit circle around the dramatist. Their talk ranged widely: from the necessity of winning over the petty bourgeoisie to the side of the left before Hitler enlisted it[11] to the instructive example afforded by Charlie Chaplin, whose recent film *The Circus*, with its brilliant funhouse sequence, had impressed both men,[12] and on whom Benjamin had just published a short piece after reading an article on the Little Tramp by the French poet Philippe Soupault (see SW, 2:199–200, 222–224). Brecht presumably encouraged Benjamin's efforts in radio, having himself just produced a radio play on Lindbergh, and he introduced him to Marxist intellectuals such as Karl Korsch, author of *Marxismus und Philosophie* (1923), editor of *Das Kapital*, and a former Communist member of the Reichstag; Korsch was in fact one of Benjamin's main sources of knowledge regarding Marxism, and he would be cited extensively in *The Arcades Project.*[13] On June 24 Benjamin wrote to Scholem: "You will be interested to know that a very friendly relationship between Brecht and me has recently developed, based less on what he has done (I know only *The Threepenny Opera* and the ballads) than on the well-founded interest one must take in his present plans" (SF, 159). In time Brecht became one of Benjamin's primary subjects: a radio broadcast, "Bert Brecht," in June 1930 would be followed in the course of the decade by some dozen pieces on Brecht's epic theater, poetry, fiction, and conversation. Brecht's theory of montage, with its stress on gesture, quotation, and the dialectic of past and future, his iconoclastic "crude thinking," his cunning use of parable, his satire and undressed humanism, and especially his distinctive voice, which combined an apparent simplicity and even brutality with the utmost subtlety, all were important to Benjamin's own practice as a writer, however much this practice ultimately differed from that of the cigar-chomping Bavarian, who in private considered Benjamin something of a mystic.[14] During the years of exile, Benjamin would find at Brecht's house near Svendborg, on the Danish island of Fyn, one of his few oases, and with Brecht he would renew the sort of personal confrontation with German thinking he had earlier enjoyed with Fritz Heinle and Florens Christian Rang.

The lively engagement with Brecht and his circle was only part of the heady intellectual atmosphere in which Benjamin now moved in the Berlin of the late 1920s—the Berlin that later generations came to think of as the site of "Weimar culture" itself. He continued to see a good deal of his old friends, especially Hessel and his wife, Helen Grund, along with Kracauer, Bloch, Willy Haas, and Wilhelm Speyer. And he still made cautious forays—sometimes accompanied by Erich

26. Bertolt Brecht, ca. 1932 *(Akademie der Künste.
Berlin. Walter Benjamin Archiv)*

Gutkind—into the circle around Oskar Goldberg, if only to report to
Scholem on their machinations: Goldberg and Unger were organizing
weekly discussion evenings under the title "The Philosophical Group."
One of the most important intellectual relationships of these years
was the renewed tie with the artist László Moholy-Nagy, whom he first
met during his involvement with the G Group. As regards the lasting
impact on his thought, the exchanges with Moholy-Nagy were comparable to those with Brecht. Their interchanges had all but ceased between 1923 and 1928, when Moholy-Nagy was a master at the Bauhaus,
first in Weimar and then in Dessau. They had been brought together
again through their work on Arthur Lehning's journal *i10*, for which

Moholy-Nagy served as photography editor. Their discussions in 1929 on photography, film, and other modern media had a crucial bearing on Benjamin's thought in such works as "Little History of Photography," *The Arcades Project,* and "The Work of Art in the Age of Its Technological Reproducibility." Through Moholy-Nagy, who had designed the Kroll Opera's production of Offenbach's *Tales of Hoffmann,* he also made a tentative approach to the Berlin music scene, becoming friendly with the conductor Otto Klemperer. Although some of Benjamin's closest friends were dedicated musicians and composers—Ernst Schoen and Theodor Adorno above all—Benjamin himself repeatedly asserted his near-total incomprehension when it came to musical matters.

There were other new acquaintances as well. Benjamin was seeing the young political philosopher Leo Strauss, who would later become an influential figure in the United States, and who at that time was associated with the Jewish Academy (Akademie für die Wissenschaft des Judentums) in Berlin, where he had just completed a book on Spinoza. Benjamin wrote to Scholem about Strauss: "I won't deny that he awakens my trust and I find him sympathetic" (C, 347). He had also come to know the Viennese writer and theater critic Alfred Polgar through the Hessels, and derived considerable pleasure from his company. In the summer he became personally acquainted with the American-born French novelist Julien Green, whose works he had been recommending to his friends with unusual enthusiasm and whose novel *Adrienne Mesurat* (1927) he had recently reviewed. He would present a radio broadcast on Green in mid-August and, after seeing him again in Paris, publish a luminous essay, "Julien Green," in the *Neue schweizer Rundschau* in April of the following year. This essay contains important statements on the theme of "primal history" *(Urgeschichte)* as it informs the process of dwelling, a process that in Green's novels is still full of archaic magic and dread, for his characters share their lodgings with the ghosts of their ancestors. "The house of the fathers . . . has been transformed into a vista of caverns, chambers, and galleries extending back into the primeval past [*Urzeit*] of mankind" (SW, 2:335). The vision of dwelling spaces haunted by life-forms of both the recent and the remote past—a vision simultaneously historical and ur-historical—is characteristic of Benjamin's own later work.

In view of the success he enjoyed in placing his reviews, interpretations, and commentaries on French authors, it is hardly surprising that the spring found him devoting more and more attention to recent French literature. Even while pursuing his researches into the culture of nineteenth-century France for the arcades project, he found that he was coming "more and more frequently upon passages by young French writers who, while pursuing their own trains of thought, reveal wayward paths that are due to the influence of a magnetic north pole which has disturbed their compass. I am steering straight for it" (C, 340). In the wake of the Surrealism essay—indeed, as its "companion piece" (C, 352)—came the magisterial essay "On the Image of Proust," composed between March and June 1929 and published in *Die literarische Welt* in June and July (SW, 2:237–247). Benjamin had long felt an affinity for Proust's "philosophical way of seeing" (C, 278); while in Moscow he had begun to discern correspondences between Proust's novel and his own *Trauerspiel* book. He found in the "savage nihilism" of the lesbian scene in *Swann's Way* an indication of the way Proust "ventures into the tidy private chamber within the petit bourgeois that bears the inscription *sadism* and then mercilessly smashes everything to pieces, so that nothing remains of the untarnished, clear-cut conception of wickedness, but instead within every fracture evil explicitly shows its true substance—'humanity,' or even 'kindness.' " And that, as he sees It, is the "thrust of my Baroque book" (MD, 94–95). At about that time, that is, in early 1926, he had begun planning an essay about translating Proust. In early 1929 he wrote to Max Rychner, whose journal *Neue schweizer Rundschau* was leading the way in publishing German-language articles on Proust (including one by E. R. Curtius on Proust's perspectivism), that he was still too close to the Proustian text to write about it, but that "German Proust scholarship is sure to have a different look to it, when compared to its French counterpart. There is so much to Proust that is . . . more important than the 'psychologist,' who, so far as I can tell, is almost the exclusive topic of conversation in France" (C, 344). In March he told Scholem that he was "hatching some arabesques on Proust" (C, 349), and in May that he was working on a "very preliminary but cunning essay on Proust," a piece "begun from a thousand-and-one sides but not yet centrally formed" (GB, 3:462). These comments point to his distinctive multiangled approach to Proust's vast novel, this "lifework" in the truest sense, which he judges (without really knowing Joyce's *Ulysses*, it must be said) "the outstanding literary achievement of our time."[15]

He touches on many aspects of the work, including the "vegetative existence of Proust's characters, who are planted so firmly in their social habitat"; the subversive comedy of manners and the deglamorizing of the ego, of love, of morals; the analysis of snobbery and the physiology of chatter; the attentiveness to ordinary objects and the focus on what Benjamin calls the "everyday hour"; the impassioned cult of similarity as extended over wide intervals in time; the consequent transformation of existence into a preserve of memory centered in the vortex of solitude; the historical concreteness of the narration in all its elusiveness, impenetrability, and inconsolable homesickness; and finally the way Proust's sentences, manifesting the "entire muscular activity of the intelligible body," articulate the currents of involuntary remembrance. But the core of Benjamin's essay—voicing as it does a concern that reaches back to his student days, when he was reading Nietzsche and Bergson, and forward to his historical materialism of the 1930s—is the discussion of "intertwined time" *(verschränkte Zeit)*. Benjamin had already suggested in a letter that Proust provides an "entirely new image of life," insofar as he makes the passage of time its measure (C, 290). In the Proust essay he takes issue with the idealist interpretation of the Proustian *thème de l'éternité*: "Proust's eternity is by no means a platonic or a utopian one; it is rapturous [*rauschhaft*]. . . . It is true that in Proust we find rudiments of an enduring idealism, but it is not these elements that determine the greatness of his work. The eternity which Proust opens to view is intertwined time, not boundless time. His true interest is in the passage of time in its most real—that is, intertwined—form." Thus the "counterpoint of aging and remembering" that is fundamental to the novel, in its obsessive quest for happiness. The "universe of intertwining" in Proust opens out in a moment of actualization (closely akin to the "now of recognizability" invoked in the *Arcades* and elsewhere), when *what has been* emerges in a lightning flash of recognition, as Marcel's long-forgotten past first emerges in the taste of a madeleine. The moment of involuntary remembrance is the "shock of rejuvenation" by which some past existence, in its several thicknesses, is awakened and gathered into an image. This concentration and crystallization of the passage of time in a momentary experience of "correspondences" constitutes the rapturous eternity, and it is here above all, in the phenomenon of *Rausch,* of ecstatic presence of mind, that we find the link to Surrealism.

Toward the end of June, shortly before the divorce proceedings began, Benjamin took a two-day auto trip with his old friend from the Haubinda school days, the prolific and cultivated novelist and playwright Wilhelm Speyer (1887–1952), with whom he was collaborating on a detective play. Two of Speyer's most widely read novels, *Charlott etwas verrückt* (Charlotte Somewhat Ruffled; 1927) and *Der Kampf der Tertia* (The Schoolboys Do Battle; 1928) had just been turned into silent films; the film of the latter novel (which concerns the effort of a group of high school students to save a community of cats and dogs from extermination) had been favorably reviewed by Benjamin in *Die literarische Welt* in February. Benjamin no doubt agreed enthusiastically to accompany his old friend: he had begun his daily Hebrew lessons in early May and seemed eager for an excuse to break them off. From Bansin, France, Benjamin wrote to Scholem of his satisfaction with his current literary relations (a feature article on *One-Way Street* had just appeared in a Rotterdam newspaper) and of his dissatisfaction with his friend Ernst Bloch. Back in February, he had complained to Scholem one more time of Bloch's shameless, if subtle, pilfering of his ideas and terminology; now he announced the appearance of "two new books by Bloch, *Traces* and *Essays,* in which a not insubstantial portion of my immortal works, in part somewhat damaged, has been transmitted to posterity" (GB, 3:469).

A longer vacation with Speyer followed in July, with stops at San Gimignano, Volterra, and Siena. Benjamin's letters speak of his delight in the Tuscan landscape, as does a lovely short piece, "San Gimignano," which he published in the *Frankfurter Zeitung* in August. "How hard it can be," this piece begins, "to find words for what lies before our eyes. And when the words do come, they beat with tiny hammers against the real, until they've driven out the image from the midst of the real as though from a copper plate. 'In the evening the women gather at the fountain before the town gate to collect water in great pitchers.' It was only after I'd found these words that the image arose—pitted and deeply shadowed—from the all too dazzling experience." He goes on to describe the way, at dawn, the sun first appears in San Gimignano as a glowing stone on the mountain ridge, and he remarks that "earlier generations must have possessed the art of keeping this stone with them as a talisman, thereby turning the hours into a boon" (GS, 4:364–365). He was equally taken with Volterra, with its great collections of Etruscan art: he found it "magnificent, lying at the center of a kind of snowless, African Engadin—its gigantic desolation and its bald mountaintops are that clear" (GB, 3:477). "San Gimignano" is dedicated to the memory of Hugo von Hofmannsthal, who had died on July 15, Benjamin's birthday. In a letter of July 27 written from Volterra, he tells Scholem how saddened he was by the news, as well as revolted by the insolent tone of the German obituaries.

In this same letter, he mentions coming across a surprisingly beautiful bloom in "George's garden," namely, the 1928 biographical volume on Goethe, Schiller, Hölderlin, and others, *The Poet as Leader in German Classicism*, by Max Kommerell, a literary historian in the circle around Stefan George. Benjamin's review essay, "Against a Masterpiece," which he began in San Gimignano, would appear in *Die literarische Welt* a year later. In it he underlines the "greatness" of the book, the "physiognomic and—in the strictest sense—unpsychological mode of seeing" intrinsic to its "Plutarchan style," the "wealth of authentic anthropological insights" to be found in its pages, but he also levels a decisive critique:

> Whatever form [the present day may take], our task is to seize it by the horns so that we can interrogate the past. It is the bull whose blood must fill the pit if the spirits of the departed are to appear at its edge. It is this deadly thrust of ideas that is absent from the works of the George circle. Instead of offering up sacrifices to the present, they avoid it . . . , [consequently depriving] literature of the interpretation it owes it, and of the right to grow. (SW, 2:383)

This key hermeneutic principle—namely, the operative power ("lifeblood") of the present in all interpretation or interrogation of the past[16]—is reflected in the "philosophy of the flâneur" that informs *The Arcades Project* and which is also the focus of Benjamin's review of Franz Hessel's *On Foot in Berlin*, a book that attests to the two men's intellectual consanguinity. Benjamin's review, "The Return of the Flâneur," published in *Die literarische Welt* in October 1929, is filled with passages from the *Arcades*. It places Hessel's leisurely, elegiac text—characterized as an "Egyptian Dream Book for those who are awake"—in the tradition of Baudelaire, Apollinaire, and Léautaud, the "classics of *flânerie*," and says of the author: "Only a man in whom modernity has already announced its presence, however quietly, can cast such an original and 'early' glance at what has only just become old" (SW, 2:264). Benjamin was busy with a number of other articles in July and August, including a "hostile essay" on the Swiss prose writer Robert Walser (C, 357). In fact, his essay, published in *Das Tagebuch* in September, displays no outward sign of hostility toward this author, who, as Benjamin mentions, was a favorite of Kafka's, though perhaps there is a hint of such an attitude in the discussion of Walser's ostensible neglect of style, construed as a "chaste, artful clumsiness," and in the reference to the childlike nobility of the characters in Walser's delicate, uncanny tales, a quality they share with the heroes of fairy tales, "who likewise emerge from the night and from madness" (SW, 2:258–259).

At the end of August, Benjamin published in *Die literarische Welt* a piece entitled "Conversation with Ernst Schoen," in which he and the composer Schoen—one of his oldest and most intimate friends, who had recently assumed an influential position as artistic director of the radio station Südwestdeutscher Rundfunk in Frankfurt—discussed the educational-political possibilities of radio and television, which, they agreed, should be emancipated from both the promotion of culture with a capital *C* and mere reportage. It had become clear since the introduction of the wireless in Germany in 1923 that politicization of the new mass medium could be effected only through catering to the audience's desire for "entertainment," though such a direction for programming, they argued, need not exclude artistic endeavors of various kinds—broadcast of the Brecht-Weill-Hindemith production of *The Flight of the Lindberghs* and of an Eisler cantata is cited—nor even the airing of experimental works (GS, 4:548–551).[17] Benjamin's discussions with Schoen led to his planning an article on the political aspects of radio the following year; the article was never written, but in a letter to Schoen

Benjamin noted down several areas he meant to cover. These include the trivialization of radio as a consequence, in part, of the failure of a liberal and demagogic press and, in part, of the failure of Wilhelminian ministers; the domination of radio by trade unionism; radio's indifference to things literary; and the corruption in the relations between radio and the press (GB, 3:515–517). The little piece on Schoen fuses two of Benjamin's most pressing interests in the 1920s: it considers questions of didactics and more general educational issues through an optic provided by modern media, including print, radio, photography, and film. Growing out of the consideration of the collection of children's books that he built with Dora—and perhaps more peripherally out of his observation of his son's development—this central tendency of Benjamin's work in the 1920s rarely enters the great essays of the period; rather than forming a cohesive theory, his ideas on education and media are spread across a series of smaller pieces that appeared at widely dispersed times and places in the German feuilleton.

The later 1920s were an occasion not just for meditating on the new communications media. Ernst Schoen also opened the door to regular radio work for Benjamin himself, who, during the latter half of 1929, began doing frequent broadcasts at stations in both Frankfurt and Berlin. Between August 1929 and the spring of 1932 he was heard at the microphone more than eighty times, in a variety of formats. There were talks for young people on diverse topics ("A Berlin Street Urchin," "Witch Trials," "Robber Bands in Old Germany," "The Bastille," "Doctor Faustus," "Bootleggers," "The Lisbon Earthquake"), literary lectures ("Children's Literature," "Books by Thornton Wilder and Ernest Hemingway," "Bert Brecht," "Franz Kafka: *The Great Wall of China*," "On the Trail of Old Letters"), radio dramas (witty and learned conversations under such headings as "What the Germans Read while Their Classic Authors Wrote" or "Lichtenberg," and plays for children such as "A Hullabaloo around Casper"), and finally "radio models" (didactic dramatizations—with example and counterexample—of typical ethical problems of everyday life, focusing on situations in the home, at school, and in the office).[18] For his talks he usually worked from his own script, improvising now and then; on the radio plays he often collaborated with others. Benjamin was adept at recycling material from his newspaper work, tailoring it to more specific audiences and simplifying the language somewhat. In his letters he sometimes deprecates his work for the radio medium as piddling *Brotarbeit*, labor undertaken merely for money, but—true to his claim of the previous year always to maintain "a certain level" in writing for profit—the radio scripts, as we have them, evince both careful construction and a spirited engagement on the part of an author possessed of great urbanity and intellectual charm.

In early August 1929, shortly after his return by bus from Italy, Benjamin moved out of the family villa on Delbrückstraße for the last time—"my residence of ten or twenty years," as he dolefully put it in a brief communication to Scholem (C, 355). He had hoped to soften this blow by arranging for an invitation to the professor and journalist Paul Desjardins's "Décades de Pontigny" at the former Cistercian abbey of Pontigny, an annual gathering of the foremost French artists, writers, and intellectuals; he told Scholem that only foreigners who had "arrived" were invited (GB, 3:428). Although he was unable to attend in 1929 for what he described as "technical" reasons, precisely a decade later, in 1939, he was invited to reside at the abbey and use its famous library. Left homeless in Berlin, Benjamin moved in with the Hessels on Friedrich-Wilhelm-Straße in Schöneberg in the Old West district, his residence in Berlin for the next several months. His review of Hessel's book on Berlin came out in October, and there was some discussion of a possible collaboration on a radio play that Ernst Schoen had apparently commissioned from Hessel, though Hessel ultimately vetoed this idea because, as he complained to Schoen, Benjamin "[tends] to make everything difficult."[19] Schoen, for his part, laid the problem at Hessel's door, referring to his "lunatic obstinacy"; he went so far as to suggest that Benjamin, who seems to have gotten Hessel the commission in the first place, make use of a revolver. Benjamin himself, with a thousand-mark fee at stake, was "very annoyed" at Hessel's refusal to collaborate (GB, 3: 517).

As she was preparing for her return to Moscow, Asja Lacis suffered a breakdown similar to the one that had incapacitated her in Moscow in 1926. Benjamin put her on a train to Frankfurt to be treated by a neurologist who ran a clinic there.[20] On trips to Frankfurt in September and October, during which he not only saw Lacis but gave several radio talks, Benjamin began to intensify his intellectual exchanges with Adorno. At the center of their discussions was the arcades project.

A small group soon formed around Benjamin and Adorno in Königstein, a resort town in the Taunus Mountains. Sitting around a table
at the "Schweizerhäuschen," Benjamin, Lacis, Adorno, Gretel Karplus, and Max Horkheimer engaged in discussions concerning key
concepts of Benjamin's work, such as the "dialectical image."[21] Benjamin read aloud passages from the early drafts of the Arcades and evidently caused a sensation with his theory of the gambler. These
"Königstein conversations" left an imprint on the thinking of all the
participants and helped shape what became known as the Frankfurt
School of cultural theory. In an oft-quoted letter of May 31, 1935, to
Adorno, Benjamin evoked the conversations in Frankfurt and Königstein as marking an epoch in the development of his own thought,
specifically a shift away from the "blithely archaic" Romantic mode
of philosophizing, still "ensnared in nature," and from the "rhapsodic" mode of presentation; such thinking and writing had come to
seem to him, he tells Adorno, naive and obsolete (SW, 3:51). Of course,
the post-Romantic and anti-Romantic reorientation—which is concurrent with the embrace of feuilletonism—can already be recognized in the composition and tonality of One-Way Street, a work inspired in no small measure by Kracauer's urban studies. But by 1935
Kracauer's place as provider of publishing opportunities to Benjamin
had been taken by Adorno and Horkheimer.

That fall, the divorce proceedings began to assume unexpectedly
"cruel" dimensions and, according to Benjamin, began taking their toll.
Toward the end of October, the month of the American stock market
crash, he suffered a ten-day collapse, during which he could neither
speak with nor telephone anyone, let alone write letters (GB, 3:489, 491).
The year 1929—a year that had seen so much success and, in some
ways, was the high-water mark of Benjamin's reputation as a Weimar
literary critic—ended with his sinking into deep depression. For all his
proud protestations that the divorce had been liberating, his exile from
the parental home and from his own family would, in the two years to
come, present him with the greatest emotional challenge of his life.

The new year, 1930, brought a persistent instability to Benjamin's
outward circumstances. Although his work for the newspapers and
the radio continued to keep him more or less afloat for the next few
years, until the National Socialist seizure of power ended his career as

a man of letters in Germany, he was now exposed to the threat of economic crisis—the number of unemployed in the country reached 3 million in March—as he had not been since the days of the hyperinflation of the early 1920s. And his divorce, which he had undertaken quite recklessly, threatened to deprive him of his entire inheritance. Despite all this he now professed to have no regrets. On the contrary, he was determined to derive some intellectual advantage from his presently "makeshift existence" and from the overwhelming sense of "the provisional" that had descended on his daily life. In a letter of April 25 to Scholem, written one day after the issuance of the divorce decree, he spoke of being "completely immersed in this new beginning, starting with where I live [and] how I earn my living" (C, 365).

This attitude of inner resolve in the face of outward uncertainty is evidenced in what Scholem describes as an "extremely personal" letter written several weeks later, a letter that testifies to "the breathtaking, constantly shifting constellations in which I have been caught up for months" (quoted in SF, 162). The letter in question concerns his family and his marriage, both of which he characterizes in terms of dark forces such as one encounters in the novels of Julien Green: "My sister is a match for [his] unloveliest female characters." Relations between Benjamin and his sister, which had never been cordial, had now sunk to a new level. His now ex-wife later told Scholem that Benjamin had been "fearfully exploited" by his sister. Presumably at issue was the disposition of the elder Benjamins' estate.[22] Yet his sister was not the only obstacle confronting him. "And what a struggle I have had to wage against these forces wherever they rise up before me—as they do not only in [the person of my sister] . . . but also in myself" (quoted in SF, 162). The struggle, he tells Scholem, in an oft-cited passage, was taken up belatedly and under disastrous circumstances:

> I doubt whether even you have a fairer and more positive picture of my marriage than I retain to this day and thus presumably forever. Without encroaching on this picture too much, I shall tell you . . . that in the end (and here I speak of years) my marriage had altogether become the exponent of these forces. For a very, very long time I believed that I would never have the strength to find my way out of my marriage; when this strength suddenly came to me in the midst of the deepest suffering and the deepest desolation, I of

course clung to it. Just as the difficulties stemming from this step presently determine my outer existence—after all, it's not easy to be without property and position, home and funds, at the threshold of one's forties—this step itself is now the basis of my inner existence, a foundation that feels solid but has no room for demons. (Quoted in SF, 162)

In his memoir, Scholem underlines the "serious crises and changes" in Benjamin's life at this period and, in this context, quotes a remark of the American historical novelist Joseph Hergesheimer, with whom Benjamin became acquainted in the early 1930s: Benjamin appeared to him like "a man who has just climbed down from one cross and is about to mount another" (quoted in SF, 164). Dora herself would see Benjamin at his mother's cremation in November 1930 and be struck by how "terrible" he looked; she felt sorry for him, she tells Scholem. "Intellectually, he is to me very compelling, exactly as before, although I've grown more independent. He no longer feels anything for me, as I am well aware; is only grateful to me for my decent behavior, and that's all right with me."[23]

In the face of so much misery, Benjamin treated himself with his usual medicine: travel. He spent the days between late December 1929 and late February 1930 in Paris, staying at the Hôtel de l'Aiglon at 232 Boulevard Raspail in Montparnasse. "No sooner do you arrive in the city," he wrote in "Paris Diary," a panoramic account of contemporary French literature that was published in four installments in *Die literarische Welt* from April to June 1930, "than you feel rewarded" (SW, 2:337). Yet the time in Paris was financially precarious. He sought to obtain small amounts of money by calling in loans he had made to equally impecunious friends such as Münchhausen, and by interrupting his sojourn in Paris for his "radio commute" to Frankfurt. Even on so worrying a basis, he worked hard to extend his network of literary contacts in the French capital. In the first days of his stay he met with acquaintances from his earlier visits such as the poets Louis Aragon and Robert Desnos and the critic Léon-Pierre Quint. And he saw Julien Green several times. They came to an agreement that Benjamin would translate his new book—which, however, never happened. During a long evening at the nightclub Le Bateau Ivre, he was regaled with stories about Proust by Léon-Paul Fargue, whom

Benjamin considered "the greatest living poet in France." The highlight was Fargue's account of the famously unsuccessful meeting between Proust and Joyce at a dinner hosted by Fargue.[24] Of the new acquaintances from this time, Marcel Jouhandeau and Emmanuel Berl had the most immediate effect on him. He was struck by the Catholic intellectual Jouhandeau's insight into "the entanglement of piety and vice" in his studies of provincial life, and he was drawn to the Jewish intellectual Berl's "rare critical acumen." He went so far as to affirm the "astonishing" closeness of Berl's point of view to his own (C, 360). More memorable than even these encounters, though, was that with "Monsieur Albert," the man Benjamin took to be the model for Albertine in Proust's *In Search of Lost Time*.[25] He saw Albert for the first time behind the counter in the "small homosexual bathhouse" he managed in the Rue St. Lazare, and recorded their subsequent conversation in a little text called "Evening with Monsieur Albert," which he enclosed in a letter to Scholem. But the most important of these new contacts was that with Adrienne Monnier (1892–1955), the proprietor of the famous bookshop La Maison des Amis des Livres at 7 Rue de l'Odéon, across the street from Sylvia Beach's Shakespeare and Company. In early February, Benjamin entered the shop with a "fleeting, superficial expectation of meeting a pretty, young girl." Instead, he found "a stolid, blond woman with very clear gray-blue eyes, clad in a dress of coarse gray wool of a severe, nun-like cut." He felt instantly that she was "one of those people to whom one can never show enough respect, and who, without seeming to expect that respect in any way, do nothing to reject or deprecate it" (SW, 2:346–347). Monnier's shop served as a meeting place and lecture hall for modernist writers and artists in Paris; in the years to come, Benjamin would meet such figures as Valéry and Gide there. And Monnier herself, who published poems and prose pieces under the pseudonym I.M.S., would prove to be one of Benjamin's most steadfast friends and supporters throughout his exile from Germany in the 1930s.

During one of his trips to Frankfurt from Paris, Benjamin had been asked to contribute a commemorative essay on the death of Franz Rosenzweig, who had succumbed to amyotrophic lateral sclerosis in December 1929. He reported to Scholem that he had turned down the offer because he was now simply too far from Rosenzweig's distinctive world of thought, a world in which he had moved with such passion in the early 1920s. It was in consciousness of the intellectual distance he had traveled since those days that Benjamin was able to offer, from his Parisian vantage, a stocktaking of the last several years. In a letter to Scholem, written in French, he singles out two things from that period. He first acknowledges his growing reputation in Germany and announces his ambition to be acknowledged as "the foremost critic of German literature" (C, 359). Of course, he immediately adds, literary criticism has not been considered a serious genre in Germany for more than fifty years, and anyone wishing to make a name for himself in the area of criticism must first reinvent it as a genre—a further goal that he hoped the volume of his literary essays under contract with Rowohlt would help realize. And he marks the progress made on "Parisian Arcades," now conceived as a book, as the second major accomplishment. In a prescient comment that looks forward to Convolute N of *The Arcades Project,* he notes that the book will require an epistemological introduction much like the one appended to the book on the *Trauerspiel*—and he states his intention of studying Hegel and Marx toward that end.

On his return from Paris in late February 1930, Benjamin resumed lodging with the Hessels while he sought a place of his own. By early April he was on the move again, occupying an apartment in the garden house of the property at Meineckestraße 9, just south of the Kurfürstendamm in Charlottenburg. It was here that he learned of the final dissolution of his marriage on April 24—an event that prompted a retrospective letter to Scholem, still his confessor in the most private things. There, Benjamin lamented the fact that he "was after all unable to construct my entire life on the splendid foundations I laid in my twenty-second year" (C, 365). That twenty-second year, bridging 1913 and 1914, had seen the composition of "Metaphysics of Youth," soon to be followed by "Two Poems by Friedrich Hölderlin." It is not so much that Benjamin now felt he had composed nothing better in the intervening sixteen years, but that those intervening years had seen him increasingly compromise, in the face of financial and other practical necessities, the independent stance he valued so highly.

In the midst of Benjamin's personal crisis, Scholem had in February challenged his friend to render a clear account of his relationship to Judaism. He reminded Benjamin that he had intervened on his be-half with Magnes and the Hebrew University because Benjamin him-self had claimed to want a "productive confrontation with Judaism," but that Benjamin's failure to follow through on his commitments had placed him in an untenable position. Scholem pronounced him-self willing to come to terms with any decision so long as it was ex-pressed in all candor—even if that meant that Benjamin could no longer "in this life consider a true confrontation with Judaism that lies outside the medium of our friendship" (C, 362–363). Benjamin ig-nored the challenge for more than two months, and finally answered Scholem on April 25 by admitting that he had "come to know living Judaism in absolutely no form other than you" (C, 364). Scholem's wife, Escha, visited Benjamin in Berlin in June 1930 and, serving as Scholem's emissary, took up very directly the question of Benjamin's commitment to Judaism, his projected trip to Palestine, and the money he obviously owed to Magnes. To these questions Benjamin avoided giving any answer at all. When asked about the direct expres-sion of his "communist inclinations," he answered "Here's how it is with Gerhard and me: we have convinced each other reciprocally"—a clever evasion if ever there was one.[26] These exchanges effectively mark the end of Scholem's attempts to win Benjamin for the cause of Zionism, or indeed any form of Judaism.

Spring 1930 marked the inception of an ambitious program for the writing—or, in materialist and Brechtian parlance, production—of a series of essays that would position Benjamin in the contemporary cultural-political arena. In fact, so intensive was his commitment to his work at this time that we know relatively little about the events in Benjamin's life outside his study in the year to come. In *One-Way Street*, he had characterized the role of the critic as "strategist in the literary struggle" (SW, 1:460), which was Brechtian *avant la lettre*. Ac-cording to this view, criticism is first of all a moral affair *(moralische Sache)*, and the critic must strive for a "genuine polemics," one that speaks the language of artists. In the course of the next two years, Benjamin sought to realize this idea of literary polemics in a number of review essays, many of them published in the Social Democratic periodical *Die Gesellschaft*. He took aim at both the conservative and fascist right and the moderate, liberal left, mapping for himself a position as left-wing outsider beyond the traditional antinomies, at the same time keeping in view an idea of genuine humanity that would be purged of the sentimentalities at either extreme. In his review of Kommerell's book on German classicism, Benjamin had attempted to find a balanced tone despite the repugnance he felt for the reigning cultural conservatism, with its cult of the Teutonic, the "dangerous anachronism" of its sectarian language, and its obsessive displacement of historical events into a mythological force field, in this case a "salvation history." Much less respectful was his long review of a collection of essays, *War and Warriors,* edited by the novelist and essayist Ernst Jünger, perhaps the leading voice of the intellectual radical right in the Weimar Republic. Benjamin's review, "Theories of German Fascism," seeks to unmask the strategies at work in the war mysticism—abstract, male-oriented, "impious"—of Jünger and his circle. In their vision of the "imperial" warrior he finds a transmutation of the postwar German Freikorps mercenaries, those steel-gray "war engineers of the ruling class" who are essentially the counterparts of the "managerial functionaries in their cutaways"; in their vision of the "nation" he discerns an apology for the ruling class that is supported by this caste of warriors, a ruling class contemptuous of international law and accountable to no one, least of all to itself, and which "bears the sphinx-like countenance of the producer who very soon promises to be the sole consumer of his commodities" (SW, 2:319). The authors in this collection, comments Benjamin, are incapable of calling things by their names, preferring instead to imbue everything martial with the heroic features of German Idealism. Just as Marinetti's glorification of warfare is cited a few years later, in the "Work of Art" essay, as an example of the fascist aestheticizing of politics, so the cult of war is here said to be a translation of the principles of *l'art pour l'art.* The latter is precisely a sophisticated regression to cult value in art, argues Benjamin, a negative theology in flight from social function and objective content, a desperate circumvention of the crisis in the arts that was occasioned by technological advance (photography) and spreading commodification. What is really at issue in the postwar "total mobilization" of which Jünger speaks is the advent of planetary technology, and specifically its misappropriation for destructive ends: "social reality," writes Benjamin at the outset of the review (and it is a thesis he holds to throughout the thirties), "was not sufficiently mature to make technology its own organ, and . . . technology was not strong enough to master the elemental forces of society." It is symptomatic of this sinister apotheosis of the warrior that it lacks any appreciation of peace. Hence the decisive polemical intervention: "We will not tolerate anyone who speaks of war, yet knows nothing but war . . . Did you ever encounter peace in a child, a tree, an animal, the way you encountered a sentry in the field?"

If in his critique of the cultural right Benjamin typically invokes the virtues of sobriety and the perspective of the everyday, in his attack on left-liberal intellectuals he uncompromisingly raises the banner of the revolutionary. His tone on such occasions could be scathing, as in "Left-Wing Melancholy," which was first rejected by the *Frankfurter Zeitung* before being published in *Die Gesellschaft* in 1931. In this piece—nominally a review of a volume of poems by the well-regarded Erich Kästner (best known today as author of the children's book *Emil and the Detectives*)—Benjamin sketches the development of the German left-radical intelligentsia, understood as a phenomenon of "bourgeois dissolution," over the previous fifteen years, from Activism through Expressionism to the New Objectivity (with which Kästner was associated).[27] The political significance of this development is said to lie in "the transposition of revolutionary reflexes (insofar as they arose in the bourgeoisie) into objects of distraction, . . . which can be supplied for consumption" (SW, 2:424; the unequivocally negative take on "distraction" here bespeaks the influence of Brecht). Benjamin contrasts the commodified melancholy and pseudo-nihilism of this cultural tendency—its fundamental complacency masking as despair—with the "truly political poetry" of pre-Expressionist poets such as Georg Heym and Alfred Lichtenstein and contemporary poets such as Brecht. He concludes that the left-liberal idea of humanity, which centers on the attempt to identify the professional life with the private life, is no less than "bestial," for under present-day conditions authentic humanity *(echte Menschlichkeit)* can arise only from the *tension* between these two poles of human existence.

Kästner's poems, which have "forfeited the gift of being disgusted," speak neither to the dispossessed nor to rich industrialists but to a middle stratum of agents, journalists, and department heads whose existence—well-drilled, "morally rosy," rich in repressions and illusions—is the object of Siegfried Kracauer's analysis in his 1930 book *White-Collar Workers*, which Benjamin reviewed that year in both *Die literarische Welt* and *Die Gesellschaft*. We have spoken of Benjamin's intellectual and personal debt to Kracauer, dating back to the early 1920s. In his book on office workers, Kracauer writes from the perspective of the knowing outsider that Benjamin makes his own.[28] As a "revolutionary writer from the bourgeoisie," this outsider and "malcontent" makes his chief responsibility the politicization of his own class; he knows that the proletarianization of the intellectual hardly ever turns him into a proletarian, and that the intellectual's impact can be only indirect. In contrast to the fashionable radicalism, he does not cater to sensation-seeking snobs but, as physiognomist and dream interpreter, takes note of the conspicuous and inconspicuous details of dwelling space, work habits, dress, and furnishings, everywhere treating the faces of social reality like the composite imagery of a picture puzzle, in which the true construction has to be discovered amid the phantasmagoria:

> The products of false consciousness resemble picture puzzles in which the true subject [*Hauptsache*] peeks out from among clouds, foliage, and shadows. And the author has even descended into the advertising sections of white-collar newspapers in order to discover those true subjects that appear embedded like puzzles [*vexierhaft eingebettet erscheinen*] in the phantasmagoria of radiance and youth, education and personality. . . . But the higher reality does not rest content with a fantasy existence, and so makes its presence felt in everyday life in picture-puzzle form, just as poverty does in the bright lights of distraction. (SW, 2:308–309; see also 356)[29]

The true subject of these urban composites—intimating as they do a thoroughly routinized and insulated existence, an existence depoliticized by the pervasiveness of "sports" and inwardly regimented by the framework of ready-made "values"—is the reification and alienation of human relations: "Today, there is no class of people whose thoughts and feelings are more alienated from the concrete reality of their everyday lives than those of white-collar workers." In the face of this collective adaptation to the inhuman side of the contemporary social order, the writer scorns the adventitious observations and crude fact-finding of "reportage," a scion of New Objectivity, and instead "forces a dialectical entry" into the lives he studies, assimilating the language of this class and thereby exposing its ideological substrate to his satirical gaze. He is like a ragpicker (a quintessentially Baudelairean motif) going about at daybreak in moody isolation to gather up "rags of speech," not without letting "one or another of those faded cotton remnants—'humanity,' 'inwardness,' or 'absorption'—flutter derisively in the wind."

The mark of "serious bourgeois writing," then, is serious commitment, as schooled in a mimetic discipline, in close reading and linguistic excavation. This has taken exemplary form in "the principled publicity of private life—a polemical omnipresence . . . practiced by the Surrealists in France and by Karl Kraus in Germany" (SW, 2:407). In such literary-polemical engagement, distinguished both from journalistic "opinion" and from practical party politics, the differences between political and nonpolitical writing effectively disappear, while the differences between radical and opportunistic writing stand out more clearly. That, at least, is the hoped-for effect of the polemics launched in 1930 and 1931. Benjamin sought to supplement these overtly political essays through the publication of his proposed volume of literary criticism, for which he signed a new contract with Rowohlt in April 1930, superseding the original contract of 1928. He worked intensively in the early months of the year on the planned introduction to the volume, tentatively called "The Task of the Critic," which was to consist of three main sections: the task and technique of the critic, the decline of criticism and aesthetics, and the afterlife of works (GS, 6:735; see also SW, 2:416). The volume was to contain his previously published essays on Keller, Hebel, Hessel, Walser, Green, Proust, Gide, Surrealism, and the task of the translator, as well as a major essay on Karl Kraus that was begun in March 1930 and two as yet unwritten essays, "Novelist and Storyteller" and "On Jugendstil" (GB, 3:525n).[30] As it would turn out, however, the collapse of Rowohlt Verlag a year later meant that yet another of Benjamin's planned books would never appear.

The years 1930 and 1931 were not only a time of unusual critical productivity; they also marked a period of sustained reflection on the nature of criticism, such as he had undertaken in the early 1920s. In his notes on the theory of literary criticism from this later period, he refers to the "decay of literary criticism since the Romantic movement" (SW, 2:291), and he pins the blame in part on journalism. The latter is said to have its basis in an "intimate interrelationship between dilettantism and corruption" (SW, 2:350 ["Paris Diary"]). By means of the reviewing business in particular, with its haphazard procedures and general lack of intellectual authority (which is to say, lack of theoretical grounding), "journalism has destroyed criticism" (SW, 2:406).[31] To be sure, the time for aesthetics, in its traditional ahistorical form, has passed; what is required now, in view of the atomization of contemporary criticism, is a "detour through materialist aesthetics, which would situate books in the context of their age. Such criticism would lead to a new, dynamic, dialectical aesthetics," something for which the right sort of *film* criticism can provide a model (SW, 2:292, 294).[32] The divorce of criticism from literary history must be annulled so that the former can become the basis of the latter, its "fundamental discipline [*Grundwissenschaft*]" (SW, 2:415). This transformation of literary history entails the merger of commentary and polemics—that is, the exegetical and the strategic, the events in the work and the judgment concerning them—in a criticism "whose sole medium is the life, the ongoing life, of the works themselves [*das Leben, Fortleben der Werke*]" (SW, 2:372). In this formulation Benjamin has recourse to one of his central literary-historical tenets—the afterlife of works—as first enunciated in his 1919 dissertation on the concept of criticism in German Romanticism (where, to be sure, conventional literary history yields to the history of problems [*Problemgeschichte*]). At the same time, he retrieves the categories of "material content" and "truth content," closely associated with the concepts of "commentary" and "critique," as expounded in his 1921–1922 essay on Goethe's *Elective Affinities*. He brings these ideas together in delineating the responsibility of criticism "to learn to see from inside the work [*im Werke sehen lernen*]," that is, to discover hidden relationships in the work. For to illuminate the work from within means to give an account of "the ways in which the work's truth content and material content interpenetrate" (SW, 2:407–408). It is this access to the interior of the artwork, he adds, that is missing in almost everything that goes by the name of Marxist criticism. At the work's interior, traditional aesthetic aporias, such as the quarrel about form and content, cease to obtain, and the sphere of art itself is left behind.

In this context Benjamin makes use of an idiosyncratic term he shares with Adorno: "shrinkage" *(Schrumpfung)*.[33] Shrinkage is said to be the law governing the transmission of works over time; more precisely, it defines "the entrance of truth content into material content" (SW, 2:408, 415–416). Benjamin specifies a twofold process in this connection: on the one hand, the work is turned to "ruins" by the action of time, while on the other hand, it is "deconstructed" by the work of criticism. As he puts it in the Goethe essay, the material content and the truth content, originally united in the work of art, separate over time, and the critical reading must tease out the truth in the details of a material content grown strange. In the later notes on the theory of criticism, Benjamin's word for this textual deconstruction is *Abmontieren*, which literally means "to dismantle, take to *pieces*."[34] (It is a Brechtian term, related to the terms *Demontierung*, "dismantling," and *Ummontierung*, "reassembling," which are used in reference to the transformative critical function of Brecht's writing; see SW, 2:559, 369–370, and, apropos of Karl Kraus, 436, 439.) The simultaneously destructive and constructive power of criticism, complementing the power of time, shrinks the artwork and packs it into a "microeon—a highly concentrated yet manifold reflection of the historical epoch in which it originated along with the epoch in which it is received and reborn."[35] This is not at all the same as reducing it to historical data, as Marxist criticism tends to do. What Benjamin has in mind is an inner transformation of the work, something effected by its reading. The great problematic of reception—the question of the entire life and effect *(Wirkung)* of works, their fame, their translation, their fate—is given decisive formulation at the end of a relatively little-known essay, "Literary History and the Study of Literature," published in *Die literarische Welt* in April 1931, some three years before work began on the better-known statement of materialist aesthetics, "Eduard Fuchs, Collector and Historian." In his essay on literary history, Benjamin argues that the reception history of a work belongs together with the history of its composition, for

27. Benjamin in 1929. Photo by Charlotte Joël
(Theodor W. Adorno Archiv, Frankfurt am Main)

with its reception the work is "transformed inwardly into a micro-
cosm or, indeed, a microeon." In this way it can become an "organon
of history":

> What is at stake is not to present literary works in the context of
> their age but to present the age that perceives them—our age—in
> the age during which they arose. It is this that makes literature into
> an organon of history [*Organon der Geschichte*]; and to achieve this,
> and not to reduce literature to the materials of history [*Historie*], is
> the task of the literary historian. (SW, 2:464)

In the eyes of Walter Benjamin and other leftist intellectuals, the
crisis in criticism and belles lettres—Benjamin speaks further of
"the crisis in science and art" (C, 370)—was part of a general crisis of
social life.

In the summer of 1930 it seemed that Benjamin might be afforded the opportunity to turn his reflection on criticism into something tangible: he and Brecht agreed to work together to found a journal with the title *Krisis und Kritik*. The idea for the journal—which grew out of an unextinguished faith that literature could play a role, however indirect, in "changing the world"—went back to the conversations between Benjamin and Brecht that began in the spring of 1929. During the summer of 1930, at a time when Benjamin had delivered his radio talk "Bert Brecht" and had published his first Brecht commentary, on passages from *Versuche* (Experiments), in the *Frankfurter Zeitung*, Brecht and Benjamin gathered around them a "very close-knit critical reading circle" with an agenda that included the "annihilation" of Heidegger, whose *Being and Time* had appeared in 1927.[36] In this context, the plan for the journal took on a more definite shape. By September Benjamin had enlisted his publisher, Ernst Rowohlt, who agreed to publish the journal, and formal discussions (with a stenographer present) were undertaken by an editorial board intent on establishing the organizational framework and substantive program for the journal. Rowohlt had stipulated that it be edited by the theater critic and dramatist Herbert Ihering, with Benjamin, Brecht, and Bernard von Brentano, Brecht's friend and the Berlin correspondent for the *Frankfurter Zeitung*, as coeditors.[37]

In a letter to Scholem in early October, Benjamin portrays himself as being at the center of negotiations for the new journal, a project that, he says, characteristically soliciting his friend's discretion, he entered into warily—mindful of the failure of *Angelus Novus*, his earlier journal project, nine years before:

> I cleared the way for the plan's acceptance by the publisher Rowohlt by appointing myself the representative of the journal's organizational and substantive features, which I worked out in long conversations with Brecht. Its formal stance will be scholarly, even academic, rather than journalistic, and it will be called *Krisis und Kritik*. I have thus completely won Rowohlt over to the plan; now the large question arises as to whether it will be possible to unite people who have something to say. . . . Beyond this is the difficulty inherent in working with Brecht. I, of course, assume that I am the one who will be able to deal with that, if anyone can. (C, 368)

Rowohlt had further directed that the political tendency of contributions to the journal should be "sharply to the left" (as if he needed to worry!). As part of his organizational initiative, Benjamin drew up a programmatic "Memorandum Concerning the Journal *Krisis und Kritik*" in October and November 1930, in which he lists some twenty-six potential contributors, including Adorno, Kracauer, Karl Korsch, Georg Lukács, Robert Musil, Alfred Döblin, Sigfried Giedion, Paul Hindemith, Kurt Weill, Erwin Piscator, and Slatan Dudow. He even adds names such as Gottfried Benn and Friedrich Gundolf, hardly exemplars of progressivist thinking.[38] No doubt the project gained impetus from the contemporaneous political successes of the National Socialists, in particular their unexpectedly strong showing in the German Reichstag elections in mid-September. It was necessary to counter the influence of organizations such as the Kampfbund für deutsche Kultur, set up in 1928 by Alfred Rosenberg, Heinrich Himmler, and Georg Straßer to combat "cultural bolshevism" in the artistic avant-garde (Le Corbusier and the Bauhaus were frequent targets). In the fall, Benjamin went so far as to attend a meeting of the Straßer SA group, part of the oppositional National Socialist faction whose leadership was wiped out by Hitler on the Night of the Long Knives in June 1934; at this meeting, as he reported to Brentano in October, he witnessed a "debate that was in part fascinating" (GB, 3:546–547).

In his memorandum on *Krisis und Kritik*, Benjamin takes the position—and it is a position essentially consistent with that of his youth philosophy sixteen years earlier—that the journal will have "political character . . . but not partisan political character." The concept of class struggle was indispensable to intellectual production at this moment, but the intellect and the arts were not to be subordinated to narrow political goals.[39] The journal's critical activity was to be anchored in a clear awareness of "the critical situation at the foundation of today's society." This proviso points to the etymologically informed understanding of the twin terms "crisis" and "criticism": at issue is the idea of a critical or decisive turning point, as one speaks of a crisis in the course of a disease. What is called for at such a moment is a *thinking* intervention, a strategy by which the bourgeois intelligentsia can take account of itself (the journal is emphatically "not an organ of the proletariat"). In the editorial discussions that went on during the fall of 1930, Benjamin speaks of the need for an "enumerating style of writing," one that, in contrast to belletristic and journalistic writing, embraces the spirit of experiment in discerning and reckoning up.[40] Benjamin's own initial contribution to the journal was to be an essay on the self-consciously representative bourgeois novelist Thomas Mann, whose *Magic Mountain* he had found unexpectedly fascinating five years earlier.

With the preliminary discussions for the journal behind him, Benjamin took off in late July for an extended sea cruise through Scandinavia, the fulfillment of a wish made two years earlier. It took him over the Arctic Circle into northern Finland, and on the way back he met up with his old friends Fritz and Jula Radt in the Polish seaside resort of Sopot, site of one of his favorite casinos. On board the ship he wrote the short prose cycle "Nordic Sea," translated Marcel Jouhandeau, and read in the first volume of Ludwig Klages's *The Mind as Adversary of the Soul*, which he considered, despite Klages's "clumsy metaphysical dualism" and his suspect political tendencies, a "great philosophical work" (C, 366).[41] Perhaps the most auspicious thing to happen on the trip was the inception of Benjamin's correspondence with Gretel Karplus (later Adorno's wife). From Trondheim, Norway, he sent her a picture postcard with the kind of courtly inscription that characterized the early years of their friendship: "Once Berlin has been left behind, the world becomes spacious and beautiful, and it even has room on a 2,000-ton steamer, swarming with assorted tourists, for your quietly exhilarated servant. Just now I am offering it the spectacle of a droll, mustachioed old lady sunbathing in an armchair on the ship's terrace—for it simply must be a terrace, whether on the boulevard or in the fjord—with her cup of coffee beside her, scribbling away at her handicraft. So take this simple crochet piece, meant for us as an antimacassar for our friendship, a sign of old affinity from the undeterred traveler" (GB, 3:534–535). He later admitted to Scholem, however, that the experience had been too lonely, and the demands of work too great, for him to have derived any real benefits from the cruise.

On his return to Berlin in early autumn, Benjamin moved into what he thought would be yet another temporary abode, an apartment at Prinzregentenstraße 66 that he sublet from the writer and painter Eva Boy. As it turned out, the new apartment, in the southern reaches of the Bavarian Quarter, home to some of Berlin's most prominent Jewish families, would be Benjamin's last Berlin residence. He was pleasantly surprised by the advantages of his new dwelling—two quiet rooms down the hall from his maternal cousin Egon Wissing and Egon's wife, Gert. In the years remaining before they were all forced to flee the nation of their birth, Benjamin grew very close to the Wissings. They took part in a number of his drug experiments (see OH, 57–70), and Benjamin seems to have been infatuated for a while with Gert Wissing, who would die of pneumonia in Paris in November 1933 (GB, 4:309). The fifth-floor apartment at 66 Prinzregentenstraße had a large study, with a view of ice-skating rinks in the winter and with space for his 2,000-volume library—all presided over by Klee's ink wash drawing *Angelus Novus*. He was even putting together a collection of records for a gramophone someone had given him, and with which he was very happy. As Scholem observes, "It was the last time he had all his possessions together in one place" (SF, 178). With a more permanent living situation, Benjamin was finally able to see more of his twelve-year-old son, Stefan. He tells Scholem of their listening together to a record on which Brecht himself sings, and of the boy's remarking on Brecht's pungent style of thinking and speaking (GB, 3:542).

That fall and winter Benjamin was very busy with reviewing and with radio broadcasts—"so much to do," he told Adorno—in addition to his work on the projected journal and the projected volume of essays. In connection with the two, ultimately unrealized Rowohlt projects in criticism, there was another unrealized project: urged on by Adorno and Max Horkheimer, he was planning to deliver a lecture called "The Philosophy of Literary Criticism" (the title was suggested by Adorno) at the Frankfurt Institut für Sozialforschung, of which Horkheimer became director in October. The lecture was postponed, however, after the death of his mother in early November, and it was never rescheduled. At this time he was also working as a publisher's reader for Rowohlt, consulting at the final stage of manuscript review, and his and Hessel's translation of Proust's *Le Côté de Guermantes*, the third volume of the *Recherche*, was finally coming out from Piper Verlag.

His mother's death on November 2 seems to have had little emotional impact on Benjamin—especially in contrast to the psychological turmoil occasioned by the death of his father four years earlier. Yet it had a major impact on his financial stability. In 1926, on his father's death, Benjamin had received a substantial payment: each of the three siblings received 16,805 Reichsmarks, or about $4,000 in 1930 dollars. In addition, Benjamin had received a one-time payment of 13,000 Reichsmarks in return for signing a contract forgoing his share—up to a fixed amount—in the eventual sale of the Delbrückstraße villa. His divorce further complicated this arrangement: he was forced to take out a mortgage for 40,000 marks on his share of the villa in order to meet his debt to his wife. (In the end, his former wife purchased the house from his siblings using the lion's share of Benjamin's bequest; she retained the villa well into the 1930s.)

Despite his growing reputation as a critic, and despite the forging of alliances with new partners like Brecht, Benjamin continued to cast about for intellectual connections that could further his diverse interests. In December he wrote a brief letter accompanying the delivery of his *Trauerspiel* book to the conservative political philosopher Carl Schmitt, whose treatise *Political Theology: Four Chapters on the Concept of Sovereignty* (1922) had been an important source, saying, "You will quickly notice how much this book, in its exposition of the doctrine of sovereignty in the seventeenth century, owes to you" (GB, 3:558; see also SW, 2:78). He referred to Schmitt's more recent work in political philosophy as a confirmation of his own work in the philosophy of art. Although there is no record of a reply from Schmitt, the copy of Benjamin's book found in Schmitt's library after his death was heavily annotated; Schmitt had made somewhat perfunctory use of Benjamin's book in 1956's *Hamlet or Hecuba*.[42]

Benjamin himself had just received a volume of the selected writings of the Viennese protomodernist architect Adolf Loos, sent to him by the volume's editor, the art historian Franz Glück, who was the brother of his close friend Gustav Glück. Writing in mid-December to thank Franz Glück, Benjamin speaks of the importance of Loos's thinking and creative work to his present studies (GB, 3:559). Loos was a friend and "comrade-in-arms" (as Benjamin describes him) of the Viennese satirist Karl Kraus (1874–1936); he is cited at key moments in the high-powered essay on Kraus that Benjamin had begun the previous March and would work on for nearly a year. Published in four in-

stallments of the *Frankfurter Zeitung* in March 1931, the essay is
dedicated to Gustav Glück (until 1938 director of the foreign section
of the Imperial Credit Bank in Berlin), the model in certain respects
for Benjamin's "The Destructive Character," written later that year,
and a native Viennese who frequented the circle around Karl Kraus
and may have introduced Benjamin to him.[43] Benjamin had been a
reader of Kraus's prose and poetry, as originally published in his journal *Die Fackel* (The Torch), since at least 1918; he had been among the
audience for Kraus's popular performances on the stage and on the
radio, when he would read from his own works, or from Shakespeare,
Goethe, or the libretti of Offenbach; and he had already published four
short pieces on Kraus.[44] His portrait of the man and of his "eccentric
reflection" takes exception to the image of Kraus promulgated by his
acolytes, the image of an "ethical personality," even as it makes him
ultimately the exemplar of a more real humanism.

For Benjamin, Kraus embodies an elemental force—the section
titles of his essay speak for themselves: "Cosmic Man" *(Allmensch)*,
"Demon," "Monster" *(Unmensch)*—and Kraus's critical activity, for
Benjamin, is a form of "cannibalism" that abolishes the distinction
between personal and objective. That is, Kraus puts his "mimetic
genius" to work by imitating the objects of his satirical critique in
order to unmask them, to appropriate them from within and thereby
devour them. He "dismantles" the situation in order to discover the
true question the situation poses. (We have encountered this vocabulary in other of Benjamin's literary-critical projects of the period, in
particular his studies of Kracauer and Brecht.) Benjamin gives us a
vivid picture of Kraus in performance, his wild gestures recalling
those of a fairground showman, his "breathtaking, half-blank, half-
glittering whoremonger's glance" suddenly falling on the spellbound
audience, "inviting them to unholy marriage with the masks in which
they do not recognize themselves." Thus the unmasking of corruption and inauthenticity in Viennese society is simultaneously a mimetic self-(un)masking, a paradoxical process in which the satirist's
whole person is engaged and by which his true face—or rather, "true
mask"—is revealed. The filiation of Kraus's polemical art to prewar
Viennese Expressionism—he is the exact contemporary of Arnold
Schoenberg—is indicated in his self-consciously demonic orchestration

of "idiosyncrasy as the highest critical organ." Before it became a fashion, says Benjamin, Expressionism was the last historical refuge of personality.

The "coincidence of personal and objective elements" can be seen in the way Kraus makes his own private existence—its primordial creaturely and erotic dimension, above all—a public affair; his melancholy hedonism is countered and consummated in cosmopolitan rectitude. This is the secret of his personal polemical authority, which is always grounded in attention to the matter at hand. Historical remembrance redeems private consciousness in a half-mad festive lament. It was no doubt Kraus's lifelong battle against the press that brought these paradoxes to a head, for what was involved here was a denunciation of journalism delivered by a "great journalist": "Only Baudelaire hated, as Kraus did, the satiety of healthy common sense, and the compromise that intellectuals made with it in order to find shelter in journalism. Journalism is betrayal of the literary life, of mind, of the demon" (SW 2:446).

Benjamin's own critique of the press is clearly indebted to Kraus's anatomizing of "the empty phrase," the vehicle by which the journalistic processing of reality proceeds and by which language in the era of mass communication is debased. The despotic topicality of the commercial newspaper world paralyzes the historical imagination, rendering the public incapable of judging, let alone lamenting. Kraus's withering critique of the prevailing "false subjectivity" singles out for special vilification the twin tendencies of "feuilletonism" (deriving from Heine) and "essayism" (deriving from Nietzsche)—tendencies with which he is obviously complicit. But his "deep complicity with his listeners and models" is something he never allows to enter his words, though from time to time, observes Benjamin, it breaks through in his smile and in the creaturely "humming" into which his words depotentiate themselves during performances.

Kraus devours the adversary by quoting him. In his articles, poems, and plays he shows himself a master of the art of citation, an art Benjamin himself practices, with and without quotation marks, in the literary montage of *The Arcades Project*. Kraus makes "even the newspaper quotable." Citation as Kraus's basic polemical procedure and never merely a secondary function—here is one of several points of contact with Brecht. Generation and destruction interpenetrate in citation. That is, the quoted item is wrenched or blasted from its original context, extracted in the manner of a collector's item, to be reborn in the matrix of a new text, becoming in the process material for improvisation, as an old fashion becomes material for a new.[45] The matter quoted is not just summoned—in the sense of "called to life" and salvaged—but judged, and such summary judgment can bring the whole of history to bear on a single news item, a single phrase, a single advertisement. In such ephemera Kraus spies the image of humanity, morally bankrupt as it may be. He is continually citing the classical humanism, with its idea of nature and natural man, as he carries out his mission of destruction in the service of a more ambiguous, deracinated, cosmopolitan humanism, one that will have mastered the demon. In Benjamin's famous formulation: "The monster stands among us as the messenger of a more real humanism." What is called materialist humanism (der reale Humanismus) informs a passage from Marx cited toward the end of the Kraus essay, a passage in which the bourgeois opposition of public and private has been overcome in the vision of a planetary individuality: "Only when the really individual man ... has become in his empirical life, in his individual work, in his individual circumstances a species-being ... , only then is human emancipation complete." Such emancipation—and here the themes of Benjamin's youth philosophy sounded so emphatically at the conclusion of the second part of the essay surface once more—would mean the end of law and the birth of justice in a state of "anarchy," a state without external rule: "anarchy as the only international constitution [Weltverfassung] that is moral and worthy of man."

Karl Kraus's reaction to Benjamin's essay was, unfortunately, in keeping with the character Benjamin had drawn, that of a savage and even despotic satirist. In the mid-May 1931 issue of Die Fackel, there was a passing reference to Benjamin's essay: "All that I really understand of this work—which is certainly well meant and also, it would seem, well thought out—is that it is about me, and that the author appears to know a good many things about me that I myself was previously ignorant of, things that even now I don't clearly recognize; and I can only express the hope that other readers will understand it better than I. (Perhaps it is psychoanalysis.)" This last remark—which may be glossed by Kraus's famous aphorism "Psychoanalysis is a symptom of the disease it pretends to cure"—seems flippant, if not gratuitously malicious, and must have been particularly painful for Benjamin to read. He wrote in June to Scholem, who had been the first to alert him to the passage in *Die Fackel:* "In a word, Kraus's reaction could not reasonably have been expected to be different from what it was; I only hope that my reaction also will be within the realm of what reasonably may be predicted—namely, that I shall never write about him again" (quoted in SF, 175). And he kept to this resolution.

Benjamin had spent the first half of January 1931 just as he had the same period the year before: in Paris, where he continued to solidify his contacts with French writers. On his return to Berlin he found himself immediately embroiled in controversy surrounding *Krise und Kritik*. Internal dissension and external constraints had begun to cloud the project even before Benjamin left for Paris. He and Brecht had foreseen the difficulty of uniting a heterogeneous group of intellectuals and artists but had hoped that their own arguments would carry the day. As it turned out, the attempt to walk a line between a totalizing "bourgeois" conception and a one-sided "proletarian" conception proved unfeasible. Against Benjamin's and Brecht's insistence on developing the technical-constructive dimension of art as the primary *social* responsibility of the artist, others on the board, including the journalist Alfred Kurella (who formerly participated in the youth movement with Benjamin at Freiburg and was now a Communist Party functionary) argued for a strict ideological adherence. Things came to such a pass that in December 1930, in a conversation with Brecht, Benjamin signaled his intention to withdraw from the journal's editorial staff.[46] Finding that the situation had not improved on his return from Paris, he wrote in February 1931 to Brecht, informing him of his resignation as coeditor. None of the three articles being considered for the first issue—the authors were Brentano, Kurella, and the late expatriate, anti-Bolshevik Marxist theorist Georgy Plekhanov— could be called "fundamental works," of the sort he envisioned for the journal; though not without merit, they were attuned more to the "demands of journalistic reality" than to the demands of scholarly description. Were such essays to be published in the journal, "my co-editorship would amount to signing a proclamation. But I never had anything like that in mind." He remained willing to work on the journal, however, and to contribute to the first issue, should Brecht need anything from him (C, 370–371; GB, 4:16). But adding his name to the list of editors, he was convinced, would compromise his intellectual integrity. After Benjamin's departure, the journal project was kept alive for a few more months, until the incipient financial collapse of Rowohlt Verlag ended all talk of *Krisis und Kritik*.

The demise of the journal project did nothing to dampen his political reflections. The question not just of an appropriate political stance but of a way of writing adequate to that stance was in fact much on his mind. When in early March he saw Max Rychner's review of Bernard von Brentano's "Kapitalismus und schöne Literatur," he was prompted to send Rychner the most explicit statement of his new politics that he had yet produced (C, 371–373). This letter, a copy of which was sent off to Scholem on the day it was composed, posits a bridge *(Vermittlung)*—problematical, to be sure—between Benjamin's "very particular position vis-à-vis the philosophy of language" and "the way dialectical materialism looks at things." What motivated his turn to a materialist mode of perception, he says, was not "Communist brochures" but rather his dismay at the complacency of certain " 'representative' works that emanated from the bourgeois side over the last twenty years" (he mentions Heidegger in this context). And it is here that he makes the claim that the *Trauerspiel* book, though it was not yet materialist, was nonetheless already dialectical. Thus it is not any determinate dogma or worldview that Benjamin has in mind when invoking "materialist reflection" but rather a stance *(Haltung)*, a way of seeing—the gravitation of thinking toward "those objects in which each time the truth comes forth at its densest." Such objective insight is legitimized, as Benjamin puts it here, by insight into "the true condition of our contemporary existence," so that every genuine experience of philosophical-historical knowledge becomes self-knowledge on the part of the knower. The argument is characteristic and had just been rehearsed in the essay on Kraus, to which Benjamin refers Rychner. The sense of truth's density, of levels and hierarchies of meaning in the matter, constitutes a link between materialism and theology:

> The *stance* of the materialist seems scientifically and humanly
> more productive in everything that moves us than does that of the
> idealist. If I might express it in summary fashion: I have never been
> able to do research and think in any sense [*Sinn*] other than, if you
> will, a theological one, namely, in accordance with the Talmudic
> teaching about the forty-nine levels of meaning [*Sinnstufen*] in ev-
> ery passage of Torah. And in my experience the tritest Communist
> platitude possesses more *hierarchies of meaning* than does contem-
> porary bourgeois profundity.

In the letter to Rychner, Benjamin was responding to what he clearly
saw as nothing more than a "slight challenge." Sending the letter to
Scholem, though, was a very deliberate instance of throwing oil on
the fire. Scholem had already professed himself displeased by the
"materialist" viewpoint of the Kraus essay; for one thing, he did not
accept the idea that class struggle was a key to understanding history.
Writing from Jericho on March 30, 1931, he outdoes the usual blunt-
ness of his communications to Benjamin (whose replies repeatedly
sought to mollify his irate friend) and goes to the core of his dissatisfaction with Benjamin's personal, political, and religious conduct. He
accuses him of nothing less than self-deception and self-betrayal:
"There is a disconcerting alienation and disjuncture between your
true and your *alleged* way of thinking. . . . Your own solid knowledge
grows out of . . . the metaphysics of language. . . . But your ostensible
attempt to harness [this knowledge] to a framework in which [it suddenly presents itself] as the fruit of materialistic considerations . . .
stamps what you've produced as adventuristic, ambiguous, and in
some cases almost underhanded" (C, 374). Of course, for Benjamin,
ambiguity is never simply a sign of confusion, much less of irresponsibility, but rather is a virtual condition of doing philosophy in the
modern world. Unruffled by Scholem's frontal assault, he refrained
from the "polemical utterance" his friend had hoped to provoke, commenting only that Scholem's ad hominem arguments actually went to
the heart of the problematic with which he and others were concerned
at present. He added—partly for the sake of assurance (he was still
a bourgeois) and partly in defiance (he was not a Zionist)—that he
had no illusions about the location of his productive base in Berlin
Wilmersdorf-West: "The most advanced civilization and the most

'modern' culture not only are aspects of my private comfort but are, in part, simply the means of my production" (C, 377).

Late spring found Benjamin succumbing once again to his wander-lust. He returned to France in the spring of 1931 (May 4–June 21), this time to the Riviera in company with his friends the Speyers and his cousins the Wissings; they stayed in Juan-les-Pins, Saint-Paul de Vence, Sanary, Marseilles, and Le Lavandou. At the last spot, in early June, they met up with Brecht and his retinue of friends and collabora-tors: Carola Neher, Emil Hesse-Burri, Elisabeth Hauptmann, Maria Grossmann, and Bernard and Margot von Brentano. As if Brecht's en-tourage were not already large enough, Kurt Weill and Lotte Lenya soon moved nearby. The holiday trip, with its southern air and open skies, rekindled something of the expansiveness Benjamin had previ-ously experienced on Capri. His diary of the trip, "May-June 1931" (SW, 2:469–485), records his thoughts on various subjects, from Heming-way's writing style and the modern style of interior design to the power of images to still what is always in motion; clearly intended for himself alone, it also mentions such things as a visit to a casino in Nice and his following a pretty girl on the high road at twilight, paus-ing now and then to pick a flower. His expansiveness could even en-compass a confessional moment: he spoke to Gert and Egon Wissing of the "three great loves" of his life (Dora, Jula Cohn, and Asja Lacis), which brought out "three different men" in himself, for genuine love, he has noticed, makes him *resemble* his beloved.

Several of the diary entries from this time indicate that this open-ness was far removed from simple blitheness or lightheartedness. The momentary sense of liberation and even exhilaration with which Benjamin had greeted the divorce decree a year earlier had given way to persistent battle fatigue, and the thought of suicide was often on his mind. It is not always noticed that the period between the spring of 1931 and the summer of 1932, the period during which Benjamin recurrently contemplated suicide, coincided with the period of his most profound estrangement from his former wife. He had been impelled to demand a divorce not just by his hope of marrying Asja Lacis but also by his horror at the "demonic" forces governing his marriage. Yet the rupture in his relationship with Dora deprived Benjamin of his only reliable source of stability and support—both emotional and intellectual.

Without the ballast that Dora had provided from the very start, Benjamin foundered on his own vulnerabilities.

Strangely enough, however, dissatisfaction with his life and his
human relationships—in the context of both "the struggle for money"
and the hopeless cultural-political situation in Germany—coexisted
with a sense of having fulfilled his most cherished wishes. Scholem
remarks that his letters from this period testify to an inner tranquility in the face of outward difficulties. The diary "May-June 1931"
opens on this complex note. He is at once weary of the personal
struggle and secure in the sense of his own personal destiny:

> This dissatisfaction [with my life] involves a growing aversion to, as
> well as a lack of confidence in, the methods I see chosen by people of
> my kind in my situation to assert control over the hopeless situation
> of cultural politics in Germany. . . . And to take the full measure of
> the ideas and impulses that preside over the writing of this diary, I
> need only hint at my growing willingness to take my own life. This
> willingness is not the product of a panic attack; but profound though
> its connection is with my exhaustion from my struggles on the eco-
> nomic front, it would not have been conceivable without my feeling
> of having lived a life whose dearest wishes had been granted, wishes
> that admittedly I have only now come to recognize as the original
> text on a page subsequently covered with the written characters of
> my destiny [*Schriftzügen meines Schicksals*]. (SW, 2:469–470)

The diary continues with a short meditation on wishes (soon to be
adapted in his more formal autobiographical writings), but it does not
return to the question of suicide.

Benjamin's conversations in Le Lavandou with Brecht—who was
now clowning, now fierce—stand out against this dark horizon. As was
usual, their talk ranged over a number of different writers—Shakespeare,
Schiller, Proust, Trotsky—and touched as well on what Benjamin
calls "my favorite topic," that of dwelling *(das Wohnen)*. But a series of
debates about Kafka provided Benjamin with the greatest challenge: he
was reading a recently published posthumous collection of short fiction in preparation for a radio broadcast in Frankfurt on July 3. In fact,
the radio broadcast, "Franz Kafka: *Beim Bau der Chinesischen Mauer*"
(SW, 2:494–500), draws extensively on the conversations held at Le

Lavandou. Although Benjamin does not repeat Brecht's dictum that Kafka is the only authentic Bolshevist writer, he does, it would seem, echo and interpret a number of Brecht's ideas about Kafka, in particular the idea that Kafka's "sole theme" is astonishment at a new order of things in which he is not at home. In Kafka's world, writes Benjamin, modern man dwells in his body the way K., the protagonist of *The Castle,* dwells in the village: "as a stranger, an outcast who is ignorant of the laws that connect this body to higher and vaster orders." Benjamin's remark that Kafka's stories are "pregnant with a moral to which they never give birth," and that this failure of the Law to appear as such is integral to the working of grace in Kafka's fiction, anticipates the argument of the great 1934 essay on Kafka, as well as later pronouncements on this writer.[47]

Benjamin did not hesitate to appropriate what he needed from Brecht, who for his part did not seem to mind; after all, "plagiarism"—of Shakespeare and Marlowe, for example—was an element of Brechtian dramaturgy. But when Adorno, in his inaugural lecture, "The Actuality of Philosophy," delivered at Frankfurt on May 2, made unacknowledged use of an idea from the *Trauerspiel* book, namely, the "intentionless" character of reality as the object of philosophy, Benjamin forthrightly objected. Adorno's early academic career was in fact shaped by his knowing appropriation of Benjamin's work. The direct reference to the *Trauerspiel* book is hardly an isolated instance: the entire lecture is clearly indebted to Benjamin's thinking, as is an important early essay titled "The Idea of Natural History," and Adorno's habilitation thesis, *Kierkegaard: Construction of the Aesthetic,* shows the author in the process of finding his own voice while continuing to rely on the intellectual principles of his friend. It must be said that Adorno made no attempt to hide this indebtedness: his first seminar at Frankfurt took as its subject the book on the *Trauerspiel.* Egon Wissing remembered after Benjamin's death that his cousin had once claimed that "Adorno was my only disciple."[48] Adorno and Benjamin had gotten together in Frankfurt around the beginning of July, presumably during the time Benjamin was there to do his radio show on Kafka, and they discussed the inaugural lecture, copies of which Adorno had sent to Benjamin, Kracauer, and Bloch. At this point Benjamin did not think it necessary for Adorno to refer to the *Trauerspiel* book.

Back in Berlin in mid-July, however, he made a more careful study of the lecture, and after talking the matter over with Bloch—who was, after all, the acknowledged master of recycling Benjaminian ideas—he changed his mind. He wrote Adorno on July 17, quoting a sentence from the lecture in which the task of philosophy is said to be interpretation of the intentionless reality by means of the construction of figures or images out of isolated elements of reality. He comments:

> I subscribe to this sentence. But I could not have written it without at the same time referring to the introduction to the *Trauerspiel* book, where this entirely unique and—in the relative and modest sense in which such a thing can be claimed—new idea was first expressed. For my part, I would have been unable to omit some reference to the *Trauerspiel* book at this point. I need not add that if I were in your position this would be even more the case. (BA, 9)

Adorno's prompt reply is not preserved, but we may deduce its tenor from the close of Benjamin's next letter to him: "I harbor no resentment whatsoever [*von einem Ressentiment . . . nichts in mir bleibt*], or anything remotely like that which you may have feared, and . . . in a personal and substantive sense matters have been most thoroughly cleared up by your last letter." Although this little episode was quickly forgotten, it reveals the tensions that lay beneath the surface of their relationship from early on—even at a moment when the flow of ideas between the two was unambiguously a one-way street.

Summer in Berlin unexpectedly brought a tentative rapprochement with his former wife—much to Stefan's delight. The initial step was a lunch invitation to Delbrückstraße, in the company of a mutual acquaintance, the American writer Joseph Hergesheimer, whose novel *Mountain Blood* Dora would translate in the coming year, and whom she would accompany on a book tour. He was the author of acclaimed short stories and novels, including "Tol'able David" (1917) and *Java Head* (1919)—and a man whom Benjamin esteemed highly. This cautious resumption of contact with his family would have very material consequences for Benjamin in the years ahead. Summer also brought a glimmer of hope for a position at a university: a friend of Adorno's, the musician and writer Hermann Grab, was much taken with Benjamin's work and had asked for and obtained a representative sampling of his writings. He passed them along to Herbert Cysarz, the Baroque specialist cited repeatedly in the *Trauerspiel* book, in the hope that he might find a place for Benjamin at the Karlsuniversität in Prague. We know nothing of Cysarz's reaction, but, like every other attempt to secure Benjamin a place in the academy before and afterward, this led to nothing.

Even positive developments such as these did little to restore his emotional equilibrium. He kept a diary for August, giving it the title "Diary from August 7, 1931, to the Day of My Death." Like the diary from May and June, it begins with the mention of a plan to kill himself (though we hear no more of this after the opening paragraph):

> This diary does not promise to be very long. Today came the negative response from Kippenberg [the head of the Insel publishing house, which Benjamin had hoped would publish a book by him on Goethe's centenary], and this gives my plan the relevance that only futility can guarantee. . . . But if anything can further strengthen the determination—indeed, the peace of mind—with which I think of my intention, it must be the shrewd, dignified use to which I put my last days or weeks. Those just past leave a lot to be desired in this respect. Incapable of action, I just lay on the sofa and read. Frequently, I fell into so deep a reverie at the end of a page that I forgot to turn it. I was mainly preoccupied with my plan—with wondering whether or not it was unavoidable, whether it should best be implemented here in the studio or back in the hotel, and so on. (SW, 2:501)

What he earlier called the "growing willingness" to kill himself is, to all appearances, something new in Benjamin's life, though it might be said that the idea of suicide hangs over his career at least from the moment of the suicide of his friends Fritz Heinle and Rika Seligson in August 1914.[49] Their deaths left an indelible mark on his imagination, finding immediate reflection in the sequence of sonnets he wrote in memory of the young poet. The sight of Heinle's body lying in the mausoleum-like Sprechsaal never left Benjamin. An attempted suicide emerges as the "secret" that organizes his reading of Goethe's *Elective Affinities;* in the section of *One-Way Street* called "Cellar," "the corpse of that boy had been immured as a warning: that whoever one day lives here may in no respect resemble him"; and in the first section of *Berlin Childhood around 1900*, the child "dwells in his loggia . . . as in a mausoleum long intended just for him" (SW, 1:445;

3:346). During the decade to come, the idea of suicide plays a defining role in the theory of modernity developed in *The Arcades Project* and in his Baudelaire studies (where it is said that modernism stands under the sign of suicide). As for the "plan" he hatched in the summer of 1931, and which he almost carried out in a hotel room in Nice the following summer, its realization came only when, with the Gestapo at his back in 1940, his immediate *physical* circumstances seemed desperate, and then it was a matter not so much of carrying out a plan as of meeting an exigency. Perhaps the best indicator of Benjamin's attitude toward the question of suicide in 1931 is provided by the concluding sentence of "The Destructive Character," published in the *Frankfurter Zeitung* in November. As one who uses space without possessing it, and always stands at a crossroads, "the destructive character lives from the feeling not that life is worth living but that suicide is not worth the trouble" (SW, 2:542).

Through it all, Benjamin remained productive on a variety of fronts. Between April 1931 and May 1932 he published in the *Frankfurter Zeitung* a series of twenty-seven letters from the period 1783–1883, the heyday of the bourgeois class in Europe. The letters were selected and provided with short contextualizing introductions by Benjamin, but they appeared in the newspaper without his name. A fruit of his long preoccupation with the bourgeois letter as a literary form, the series became the basis for the volume *Deutsche Menschen* (German Men and Women), which he published pseudonymously in Switzerland in 1936. In connection with the newspaper series, Benjamin wrote a radio talk, "On the Trail of Old Letters," which proposes in characteristic fashion that the distinctions between man and author, person and subject matter, private and objective gradually lose their validity over time, so that to do justice to a single significant letter means going to the heart of the writer's humanity—which is not the same as his psychology: "the more deeply the historian enters into the past, the more the psychology characteristic of . . . slick and cheap biographies becomes devalued, and the more the things, dates, and names come into their own" (SW, 2:557). At issue, once again, is the transmission of "living tradition."

Other notable publications in the summer and fall of 1931 included "Unpacking My Library," which appeared in *Die literarische Welt* in

July, and "Paul Valéry: On His Sixtieth Birthday," appearing in the same paper in October (SW, 2:486–493, 531–535). The former—a good example, like "Food" from a year earlier, of Benjamin's great skill as an essayist—incorporates passages from Convolute H of *The Arcades Project* in its portrait of the collector as a near-extinct type whose intimate relation to his treasures transcends the realm of commodity exchange, and who, as physiognomist of the world of things, navigates the "chaos of memories" awakened by the items in his collection. The latter piece, which sees Valéry as representing, for all his negation of the pathos-filled "human," an advanced stage of the old European humanism, contains memorable reflections on the concept of *poésie pure*, poetry in which the ideas rise out of the music of the voice like islands rising out of the sea. Another piece, the first version of "What Is Epic Theater? A Study of Brecht," was rejected by the *Frankfurter Zeitung* in the fall, after months of editorial delay, as a consequence of the intervention of the newspaper's right-wing theater critic, Bernhard Diebold; it remained unpublished during Benjamin's lifetime. And there was a still more troubling loss: Rowohlt Verlag declared bankruptcy in early summer 1931, taking down with it the planned volume of literary essays on which Benjamin had pinned so many hopes.

The most auspicious of Benjamin's publications that season—harking back to the writings on Russian film, it anticipates central concerns of the "Work of Art" essay of 1935–1936[50]—was "Little History of Photography," which appeared in three installments of *Die literarische Welt* in September and October (SW, 2:507–530). Benjamin's early interest in the medium had been reawakened in the last two years through his renewed contact with László Moholy-Nagy, as well as through his friendship with photographers Sasha Stone in Berlin and Germaine Krull in Paris. With this article Benjamin establishes himself as a leading early theorist of photography, one occupied with the "philosophical questions suggested by the rise and fall of photography." In his view, the flowering of the new medium occurred in its preindustrial phase, indeed in its first decade, and later masters such as Eugène Atget, August Sander, and Moholy-Nagy were to be seen as consciously renewing and transforming the tradition of Nadar, Julia Margaret Cameron, and David Octavius Hill. This assertion of a tradition in photography is not merely a notable contribution: it flies in the face of the widely held notion that "New Vision" photography of the sort promoted at the massive "Film und Foto" exhibition of the Deutscher Werkbund in Stuttgart in 1929 represented a clean break from traditional practices.

Benjamin's analysis has its point of departure in the mysterious charm of early photographs, and particularly of group and individual portraits, those "beautiful and unapproachable" images of the human countenance from a time when it still wore an air of silence. The "aura" of early photographs is a function of this air or "breathy halo"—Benjamin's term *Hauchkreis* brings out the original sense of Greek *aura*, "breath"—emanating from the subjects photographed. "There was an aura about [the people in early photographs], a medium that lent fullness and security to their gaze even as it penetrated that medium." The technical determinant of this auratic appearance was not only the long exposure time, which made for a more painterly synthetic character in the expressions registered, but also the stark chiaroscuro of the images, what Benjamin calls the "absolute continuum from brightest light to darkest shadow," which gave to these incunabula of photography a physiognomic specificity, a delicacy and depth, comparable to what one later finds in the people and milieux of a film by Eisenstein or Pudovkin. But with the rise of commercial photography and the development of faster lenses, there is a "suppression of darkness" in the image, and the aura is "banished from the picture . . . , exactly as it was being banished from reality by the deepening degeneration of the imperialist bourgeoisie." This theory of the "decline of the aura" would play an increasingly prominent role in Benjamin's thinking about art in the years to come.

It is precisely medium-specific properties such as the aura that can activate an apperception of the "new image-worlds" latent in photographs. The "magical value" of old photographs excites "an irresistible compulsion to search such a picture for the tiny spark of contingency, the here and now, with which reality has, so to speak, seared through the image-character of the photograph, disclosing the inconspicuous place where, within the being-such [*Sosein*] of that long-past minute, the future nests still today—and so eloquently that we, looking back, may rediscover it."[51] This notion—that a privileged cognition might be sparked by something inconspicuous and peripheral, whether in a text or in an image—goes back to Benjamin's early writings. It appears in the essay "The Life of Students" of 1914–1915, where we read that "history rests concentrated, as in a focal point," and that "elements of the ultimate condition [*Endzustand*] . . . are deeply embedded in every present in the form of the most endangered, excoriated, and ridiculed creations and ideas" (EW, 197), and it informs the fundamental concept of the "truth content" of art in later writings. In 1931, this basic tendency in Benjamin's thought conditions the idea of the "optical unconscious," that "other nature that speaks to the camera rather than to the eye—'other' above all in the sense that a space informed by human consciousness gives way to one informed by the unconscious." The "image space" first limned in the essay on Surrealism here begins to take on specific contours. That space cannot consist merely in the regime of images produced by the capitalist social apparatus; if the collective is to be transformed, the apperception of new image worlds must take place within the adaptable new possibilities of seeing and doing opened by modern technological media such as photography and film.

It was partly in reaction to the "stifling" atmosphere of conventional commercial photography toward the end of the nineteenth century, with its carefully posed subjects amid pillars and drapes, its penumbral tone and simulated aura, that Atget developed his method of constructive unmasking and disinfecting, by which he "removed the makeup from reality." Turning his back on the landmarks and famous sights of the city, he detailed the inconspicuously ordinary— "he looked for what was unremarked, forgotten, cast adrift"—much as Benjamin himself would do in editing his snapshots of "historical detritus" in *The Arcades Project*. Sander's work in the next generation likewise eschews beautifying effects and shows the typical face of the times (*Antlitz der Zeit* was the title of his sociologically pointed 1929 volume of portraits). Such clean, cool, micrological depiction— precursor to the "salutary estrangement" worked by Surrealist photography—effects "the emancipation of object from aura, which is the most signal achievement of the latest school of photography." The subtle shift in argumentation, resulting in ambivalence toward the phenomenon of "aura," is found again in the more programmatic "Work of Art" essay. Photography both contributes to and dissolves the reification of human relations, obliterating uniqueness and at the same time bringing to light the secret and the fleeting, aiding in the emergence of what Baudelaire called "modern beauty."[52]

At the beginning of October 1931, things were looking bleak—and not just for Benjamin. "The economic order of Germany," he tells Scholem, "has as firm a footing as the high seas and emergency decrees collide with one another like the crests of waves. Unemployment is about to make revolutionary programs just as obsolete as economic and political programs already are. To all appearances, the National Socialists have been delegated to represent the unemployed masses here; the Communists have not as yet established the necessary contact. . . . Anyone who is still employed is, as a consequence of that simple fact, already a member of a workers' aristocracy. A huge class of pensioners . . . is emerging among the unemployed—an inactive class of petit-bourgeois whose element is gambling and idleness" (C, 382). His own profession, he comments drily, has the advantage that one may be fully employed even when not being paid. Without the smallest financial reserves, he has so far succeeded in living from hand to mouth *(au jour le jour durchzukommen)*. And if a couple of larger essays requiring preliminary studies have managed to be born, this is due not only to his grim determination but also to the help of friends, "who now and again do what they can" (GB, 4:53). At the moment he was occupying a small room in the Pension Batavia on Meineckestraße, since Eva Boy was back from Munich and had reclaimed her apartment for a few weeks. Aside from visits with Stefan, he was lacking "all pleasant things": "The constriction of space in which I live and write (not to mention the space I have for thought) is becoming increasingly difficult to bear. Long-range plans are totally impossible . . . , and there are days, and weeks, when I am at a total loss at what to do" (C, 384). Even unexpected, and moderately remunerated, diversions such as the offer to complete a bibliography of the greatest private collection of one of his favorite authors, Georg Christoph Lichtenberg, could not lift his mood.

By the end of the month, however, he was back in the apartment on Prinzregentenstraße—his "Communist cell," where he liked to work lying on the sofa surrounded by all 2,000 of his books and by walls decorated with "only saints' pictures." He was soon writing to Scholem in a more upbeat manner: "Though I don't have the slightest notion of 'what's to come'—I am fine. I could say—and my material difficulties certainly have a share in this—that I feel like an adult for the first time in my life [he was thirty-nine]. Not just no longer young but grown up, in that I have almost realized one of the many modes of existence inherent in me" (C, 385). He had emphasized this Nietzschean theme of the protean self in one of the figures of thought from "Short Shadows (I)": "The so-called inner image of oneself that we all possess is a set of pure improvisations from one minute to the next" (SW, 2:271). A portrait of Benjamin—or at least one of his improvisations—at this period in his life is left us by Max Rychner, editor of the *Neue schweizer Rundschau*, who dined with him in November 1931: "I observed the massive head of the man across from me and couldn't break from this observation: of the eyes—hardly visible, well fortified behind the glasses—which now and then seemed to awaken; of the moustache, obliged to deny the youthful character of the face and functioning like two small flags of some country I couldn't quite identify."[53]

He was as usual working on several projects simultaneously: the scrics of letters for the *Frankfurter Zeitung*; a piece entitled "Various Things of Human Interest about the Great Kant," published in *Die literarische Welt* in December; and, appearing in the same paper in February, "Privileged Thinking," a damning review of Theodor Haecker's book on Virgil, a conventional Christian reading of the poet in which the fundamental question facing all contemporary interpretation of classical texts—is humanism still possible in our age?—is sedulously avoided (SW, 2:574). In addition, Benjamin was acting as judge in an open competition for sound film scripts, reading and evaluating, he tells Scholem, approximately 120 drafts a week. To his way of thinking, the few journals and small newspapers in which his work was appearing represented "the anarchic structure of a private publishing house," and he goes on, in a semiparodic vein, to boast that the main objective of his "promotional strategy"—namely, to publish everything he writes, except for some diary entries—has been successfully carried out now "for about four or five years" (the fate of the first version of "What Is Epic Theater?" was still undecided at that point). But the rueful note quickly returns. Scholem had observed that the "Little History of Photography" derived from prolegomena to the arcades project. Benjamin admits as much with a philosophical shrug: "To be sure, . . . but what more can there ever be than prolegomena and paralipomena?"

At the end of February 1932, Benjamin wrote Scholem of his continuing productiveness—"all this writing, . . . this activity in ten directions"—and of his desire to escape what he calls, in his next letter to his friend, "the ignominy of wheeling and dealing in Berlin" (quoted in SF, 180; C, 390). He had eased the workload somewhat by instituting a division of labor between the composing "hand" and the recording "machine": "I learn more and more to reserve my pen and my hand for the few important subjects and babble the ongoing stuff for the radio and the newspapers into the machine" (quoted in SF, 180). That some of his newspaper work was nevertheless worthy of manual composition is indicated by his remark that the introductions to the series of letters appearing without byline in the *Frankfurter Zeitung* were "written." Between February and May he published numerous pieces besides the review essay "Privileged Thinking," including two articles on the dramaturgical-educational principles of Brecht's Epic Theater, a piece on the Nietzsche Archive created by the philosopher's sister (something reflected in the fantastic and satirical imagery of a mescaline experiment two years later [OH, 94]), a review of Gide's 1931 drama *Oedipe* (Oedipus), and, in collaboration with the editor of *Die literarische Welt*, Willy Haas, "From World Citizen to Haut-Bourgeois," a selection and brief discussion of politically oriented excerpts from writers of the classic bourgeois era, a sort of complement to the series of letters. In addition, during this period Benjamin broadcast several radio talks that display undiminished vitality and wrote and directed several successful radio plays.

In spare or stolen hours during January and February he had been working on a set of "notes . . . concerning the history of [his] relationship to Berlin" (quoted in SF, 180)—this in fulfillment of a contract he had signed the previous October with *Die literarische Welt* for a four-part publication. From these modest beginnings arose not only his most extensive autobiography, "Berlin Chronicle," but the masterwork of his late years, *Berlin Childhood around 1900*. "Berlin Chronicle," even in the advanced draft form in which we have it, obeys the laws of journalistic publication: it was mostly complete by summer

1932. *Berlin Childhood around 1900*, on the other hand, has a composition history almost as long and just as complex as that of *The Arcades Project*; Benjamin worked on the text for the remainder of his life, adding and revising sections and reordering the whole. All this activity in the winter of 1932 did not prevent him from complaining about what appeared to be a missed opportunity: the Goethe centennial was starting up and, "as the only person besides at most two or three others who know something about the subject, I of course have no share in it" (quoted in SF, 181). And he concludes, with a sidelong glance at the possibility of meeting Scholem at some point in the course of his upcoming five-month visit to Europe: "Plans I cannot make. If I had any money, I would bolt before another day goes by." As it happened, he was called on after all to participate in the Goethe centennial by contributing two articles—an annotated bibliography of significant works about Goethe from the poet's day to the present and a review essay on recent studies of *Faust*—to a special Goethe issue of the *Frankfurter Zeitung*.

The windfall provided him with enough income to make his escape from Berlin. From his old friend Felix Noeggerath, the "universal genius" whom he had first met at the University of Munich in 1915, he got word of a unique vacation spot in the Balearic archipelago off the eastern coast of Spain, an unspoiled island retreat offering something like the polar opposite to his present metropolitan existence—and the chance to live on practically nothing. The renewal of contact with Noeggerath is only one of the surprising turns in Benjamin's life at this time. Although both of them had been living in Berlin for years, they had fallen completely out of touch with each other; now, at the mere mention of Ibiza on Noeggerath's part, Benjamin packed up and fled the city for what would be the first of two lengthy stays on the Spanish island.

On April 17 he departed Hamburg for Barcelona on the freighter *Catania*, which ran into "very stormy" weather at the outset of the voyage. During the ten days at sea, Benjamin discovered in himself a "new passion," as he remarks in the posthumously published account "Spain, 1932." It was a passion for collecting "whatever facts and stories I could find," in order to see what they might yield once "purified of all vague impressions" (SW, 2:645–646)—an enterprise comparable to the concern with anecdote and secret history in the arcades project. He got to know the freighter's captain and crew and, over coffee or Van Houten's cocoa, drew them out on a variety of subjects, from the history of the shipping company they worked for to the character of the textbook used in preparing for the helmsman's examination, and he listened to their sailors' yarns, recording some of the material in his notebook. Likewise in Ibiza he heard stories from various characters on the island, and he adapted certain of them into short pieces of his own.[54] Two such pieces deriving from stories told at sea and on the island are "The Handkerchief" and "The Eve of Departure" (SW, 2:658–661, 680–683). The first of these pieces, which would appear in the *Frankfurter Zeitung* in November, and which meditates on the "decline in storytelling" and the relation of the art of storytelling not only to a certain idleness but to wisdom or "counsel" (as distinguished from "explanation"), directly anticipates the now famous essay of 1936, "The Storyteller."

From Barcelona he took the ferry to the island of Ibiza, the smallest and (at that time) least touristed of the Balearic Islands, where, on his arrival in the town of Ibiza, the island's capital and principal port, he learned from Noeggerath that they had both been victims of a con man. Noeggerath had not only suggested Ibiza as the goal of Benjamin's journey but seemingly provided him with the means to prolong his stay there, putting him in touch with a man who promised to rent his Berlin apartment while he was away; this same man had also rented a home on the island to the Noeggeraths, who had generously offered Benjamin a room. Benjamin had quickly settled on these arrangements and was counting on the monthly income for his subsistence in Spain. As it turned out, his sublettor and Noeggerath's landlord was a swindler. He occupied Benjamin's apartment for one week before fleeing from the police, who arrested him later that summer. Not only was Benjamin's rent not forthcoming, but the house that the con man had rented to the Noeggeraths did not even belong to him. After the swindle was discovered, Noeggerath obtained permission to live rent-free for a year in a dilapidated stone farmhouse outside the village of San Antonio, which dwelling he agreed to refurbish at his own expense, while Benjamin found lodgings for 1.80 marks per day, including meals, in a "small peasant's house on the San Antonio bay called Frasquito's house, surrounded by fig trees and situated behind a windmill with broken sails."[55] Although he had to do "without every kind of comfort," and although he was now saddled with paying the rent for his Berlin apartment himself, he was happy to be on Ibiza.

Around the middle of May Benjamin became a guest of the Noeggeraths, who had succeeded in bringing the old farmhouse back to life after years of ruin. The small house, called Ses Casetes, stood on a bluff known as Sa Punta des Molí above the bay of San Antonio. Consisting only of a *porxo* or main room, two bedrooms, and a kitchen, it was full to bursting with Noeggerath and his wife, Marietta, their grown son, Hans Jakob (a student of philology, who was writing a dissertation on the dialect of Ibiza), and Benjamin himself. But Benjamin looked on it all as an idyll: "The most beautiful things are in view from the window giving onto the sea and a rocky island, whose lighthouse shines into my room at night" (C, 392). Although the island offered nothing in the way of modern conveniences—conveniences such as "electric light and butter, liquor and running water, flirting and newspaper reading" (C, 393)—Benjamin soon settled into a rhythm recalling that of his long stay on Capri. The Ibizan landscape was, in subtle ways, both similar and different: its whitewashed houses and its hillsides covered with olive, almond, and fig trees looked much like Capri. As Vicente Valero points out, however, a trip to Ibiza in 1932 was, for the few foreigners who found their way to the island, a journey back in time. Unlike Capri, which had been a magnet for vacationers at least since Roman times and thus had an everyday culture in part shaped by "foreigners," Ibiza remained cut off from most processes of modernization; the primitive goat-based economy of the island made use of no farm machines. As Benjamin recounted in the feuilleton piece "In the Sun," published in the *Kölnische Zeitung* in December, "there were no highways or mail routes leading here, but neither were these just paths made by animals. Instead, here in the open countryside converged the pathways on which farmers and their wives and children and herds, through the centuries, had moved from field to field" (SW, 2:664).

Benjamin found "inner peace" in this relatively untouched rural landscape and in "the beauty and serenity of the people" (C, 390). Indeed, the prose piece "In the Sun" seems to register a new phase in

Benjamin's relationship to the natural world. The old dread still inhabited his senses, more intimately so than ever, but with it now was something distinctly "southern," a relation more soberly personal and bodily than the high-toned metaphysics of youth had ever been, one paying its full debt to the immediate present in a mode of description at once sensual and meditative, an allegorical reportage. The landscape he evokes, in its elemental factual abundance, is rich in signs and historical witness. Like the metropolitan streets he loved to wander, "the ground here sounded hollow . . . [and] responded to every step." Hence, even on pristine Ibiza, Benjamin remained within his own natural-historical image world: "Things change, and trade places; nothing remains and nothing disappears. From all this activity, however, names suddenly emerge; wordlessly they enter the mind of the passer-by, and as his lips shape them, he recognizes them. They come to the surface. And what further need has he of this landscape?" The narrator at the end thus takes the reader back to the remarkable opening of the little text, in which nature appears as an emergent code, a coalescence of names:

> There are, so it is said, seventeen kinds of figs on the island. One ought—the man told himself as he walked in the sun—to know their names. Indeed, not only ought one to have seen the grasses and the animals that give the island its face, its sound, and its scent; not only ought one to have seen the strata of the mountains and the different kinds of soil, which vary from a dusty yellow to a violet brown, with broad splashes of vermilion in between; above all, one ought to know their names. Isn't every region governed by a unique confluence of plants and animals, and isn't every local name a cipher behind which flora and fauna meet for the first and last time? (SW, 2: 662)

Yet this quiet corner of the Mediterranean world (the village of San Antonio, across the bay from the Noeggeraths' house, numbered only 700 inhabitants) was already exposed to the tide of modernization: a hotel was under construction in the port town of Ibiza, fifteen kilometers away (C, 390).

Benjamin's day began at seven with a swim in the sea, where, "far and wide, there is not a single person to be seen along the shore, at most only a sailboat on the horizon at eye level" (C, 392). From his lonely splendor on the beach he would move to a tree trunk in the forest to take a sunbath, or wander shirtless along the coastline and in the interior of the island: he tells Gretel Karplus that he is "leading the kind of life that centenarians confide to reporters as the secret of their longevity" (C, 392). A notable acquaintance from his time on Ibiza, the Frenchman Jean Selz, remembers Benjamin and his peculiar gait as he explored the island: "Benjamin's physical stoutness and the rather Germanic heaviness he presented were in strong contrast to the agility of his mind, which so often made his eyes sparkle behind his glasses. . . . Benjamin had difficulty walking; he couldn't go very fast, but was able to walk for long periods of time. The long walks we took together through the rolling countryside . . . were made even longer by our conversations, which constantly forced him to stop. He admitted that walking kept him from thinking. Whenever something interested him he would say 'Tiens, tiens!' This was the signal that he was about to think, and therefore stop."[56] Among a small enclave of younger German guests on the island at this time, "Tiens-tiens" became a nickname for the ambling Berlin philosopher. In the village, without his being aware of it, he was also known as "el miserable" (the poor wretch), on account of his manifest poverty and sad demeanor.[57]

Aside from the Noeggeraths and Jean Selz and his wife, Benjamin had little contact with other outsiders. There were a few Americans in Santa Eulalia, on the other side of the island, including the writer Eliot Paul, who shared Benjamin's interests in advanced art and had been a coeditor of the important Paris literary journal *transition*, but Benjamin kept well away from them. He had intermittent contact with the few German émigrés, including an odd character from Stuttgart named Jokisch, who had come to Ibiza at the end of the 1920s and had lived in the same little house on Sa Punta des Molí that the Noeggeraths and Benjamin would occupy, and was now residing in the mountain village of San José, in the southeastern part of the island, together with two women. Jokisch supported himself by fishing and, for a while, by the illegal export of a lizard native to those parts; he may also have worked for German intelligence, and was at any rate a vocal supporter of the Nazis.[58] Benjamin captured some of his eccentricities in the figure of the Irishman O'Brien in the story "The Cactus

Hedge" (GS, 4:748–754). From the firsthand compilations of Noegger-ath's son, Hans Jakob (called Jean Jacques), moreover, he would have gained insight into the oral traditions of the island peasantry, their stories, legends, songs, and sayings.

Another fruit of his Ibizan experience was the fragmentary prole-gomenon, as he terms it, to a "rational astrology," prelude to his well-known studies of the mimetic capacity produced the following year. In this little piece he refers to "southern moonlit nights" in which one feels, alive within oneself, mimetic forces long thought to be dead. Such forces were intrinsic, he suggests, to the former authority of astrology, which was a physiognomy of celestial configurations. The perceived constellations of the stars were part of a "cosmos of similar-ity," and events in the heavens could, in principle, be imitated by indi-viduals or groups in antiquity. This ancient science or technology of imitation testified to the presence of "an active mimetic force work-ing expressly inside things," as well as to the presence of "mimetic centers that may be numerous within every being." It was this idea of a primordial mimetic force and "mimetic mode of vision," intimately allied to the concept of experience as "lived similarities," formulated probably around this time (SW, 2:553), that must have come alive for Benjamin amid the landscape and stillness of Ibiza in 1932.

"I have worked hard these last few weeks," he tells Scholem in a letter of June 25, posted from San Antonio (BS, 10). Working without electric light and once again writing everything by hand, he was trying to maintain his high rate of production in order to prolong his stay on the island as much as possible, while continuing to pay the rent for his Berlin apartment. He was also reading widely, as ever: from Stend-hal's *Charterhouse of Parma* to Trotsky's autobiography and his his-tory of the February Revolution (he read Trotsky with "breathless excitement" [C, 393]), from Flaubert's *Bouvard et Pécuchet* and The-odor Fontane's *Der Stechlin* (The Little Thorn) to Julien Green's *Épaves* (Flotsam) and a German translation of Thornton Wilder's novel *Cabala*, from a Marxist study entitled *Lenin and Philosophy* to a his-tory of Protestant sects in the Reformation and a study of the differ-ences between Catholic and Protestant dogma. With several of these texts he was already familiar. And that summer, as he continued to work on the short pieces concerning the history of his relationship to

Berlin, he began rereading Proust as well. In June he received a newly published volume of *Fableaux* (Tales) by Adrienne Monnier, whom he had met, we noted, in her Paris bookshop in 1930, and whom he had interviewed for his "Paris Diary" of that year. He now wrote her back enthusiastically, asking permission to translate one or two of the stories; his translation of her "Vierge sage" (The Wise Virgin) appeared in the *Kölnische Zeitung* in November.

The final weeks of Benjamin's first stay on Ibiza were nevertheless troubled. The news from home was ever more ominous. The National Socialists had seen their first major electoral successes in Bavaria, Prussia, Hamburg, and Württemberg in the spring, and many German cities were becoming the scene of running skirmishes between Nazi paramilitary groups and increasingly defenseless Communists and Socialists. Benjamin had a further, very specific cause for concern: he knew nothing of the fate of his materials for the arcades project, which had been in his apartment and thus accessible to the swindler who lived there for a week. The urge to return to Berlin thus grew pressing, though it was countered by his desire to avoid direct experience of the "opening ceremonies of the Third Reich," as he wrote to Scholem on May 10, 1932 (GB, 4:91). Benjamin's unrest had personal grounds as well. He spent a great deal of time in June with a Russian-German woman named Olga Parem, who had come to Ibiza to visit him. Scholem would subsequently go out of his way to meet this woman, and so confirm the stories he had been told by Dora Kellner and by Ernst Schoen; he recalls that she was "very attractive and vivacious." She and Benjamin had apparently been friends since their introduction by Franz Hessel in 1928. In later years, she told Scholem how much she had enjoyed Benjamin's intellect and charm: "He had an enchanting laugh; when he laughed, a whole world opened up." According to her account, as transmitted by Scholem, "Benjamin was in love with many women in those years and had a 'very beautiful lady friend' in Barcelona, the divorced wife of a Berlin physician." Now, on the island, "Ola" lived with Benjamin and the Noeggeraths in Ses Casetes, and Benjamin arranged with his neighbor Tomás Varó, the son-in-law of his present landlord and a fisherman known throughout the village as "Frasquito," to take them out on the bay every evening before sundown in his little lateen-rigged sailboat. Sometime in the middle of June, Benjamin suddenly proposed marriage to Olga Parem—and was refused.[59]

Despite—or perhaps because of—this turmoil, Benjamin managed to prolong his residence on Ibiza—by a week—and in fact took part in an impromptu celebration of his fortieth birthday on July 15. He spent most of his time in these last weeks in the company of Jean Selz and his wife, Guyet, who invited him to stay with them in their house, La Casita, on the bay in San Antonio. Selz's niece, the artist Dorothée Selz, has described him as "an elegant, very cultivated, reserved, discreet, and extremely modest man"—qualities that won him the trust of other residents of the island. Jean Selz was an expert on European folk art and was familiar with the contemporary art scene in Paris. He and his wife had arrived in Ibiza, on their first visit to the island, in the spring of 1932; they would be instrumental in Benjamin's return to Ibiza the following year.[60] In 1932 they were together right up until the moment of Benjamin's departure from the island at midnight on July 17, when his ship set sail for Majorca. Benjamin describes the scene in a letter to Scholem:

> Their company was so captivating . . . that, when we finally arrived at the quay, the gangplank had been removed and the ship had already begun to move. I had stowed my baggage on board in advance, of course. After calmly shaking hands with my companions, I began to scale the hull of the moving vessel and, aided by anxious Ibizans, managed to clamber over the railing successfully. (BS, 13)

He was headed for the little Italian town of Poveromo (whose name means "poor man"), north of Pisa, to collaborate once again with Wilhelm Speyer, who was working on a new detective play eventually entitled *A Coat, a Hat, a Glove,* and who provided generous, if not immediately forthcoming, remuneration.[61] He arrived in Nice, on his way to Tuscany, less than a week after departing Ibiza and checked into the Hôtel du Petit Parc, an establishment he had chanced upon the previous year when Speyer got his car repaired in the garage opposite, and which had for him "something quite strangely alluring." In his letter of June 25 to Scholem he had raised the possibility that he would spend his birthday in Nice drinking a glass of "festive wine" with "a rather eccentric fellow [*skurrilen Burschen*] whose path has often crossed mine in the course of my various travels"—an unmistakable indication of the recurrence of his suicidal feelings. On July 26, in a mood of "relative equanimity," he wrote to Scholem of his diminishing prospects as a writer and of his mounting sense of failure:

> The literary forms of expression that my thought has forged for itself over the last decade have been wholly conditioned by the preventive measures and antidotes with which I have had to counter the disintegration constantly threatening my thought as a result of such contingencies. And though many—or a sizable number—of my works have been small-scale victories, they are offset by large-scale defeats. I do not want to speak of the projects that had to remain unfinished, or even untouched, but rather to name here the four books that mark off the real site of ruin or catastrophe, whose furthest boundary I am still unable to survey when I let my eyes wander over the next years of my life. (BS, 14–15)

The "four books" in question here are the posthumously published arcades project, the unrealized Rowohlt volume of essays on literature, the collection of German letters that would appear as *Deutsche Menschen* in 1936, and "a truly exceptional book about hashish." The day after writing this unduly pessimistic letter to Scholem, he made preparations to end his life.

The reasons for his taking this step—which, like his "plan" of the previous summer, was revoked at the eleventh hour—remain unclear. Scholem tends to discount the worsening political situation as an explanation. On July 20 the recently appointed reactionary chancellor Franz von Papen had deposed the Social Democratic–led Prussian government, augmenting the spread of political terror and violence across the land and paving the way for Hitler's assumption of power. Now, there is no question that, as a Jew, Benjamin was materially affected by these critical developments. Within a few days of von Papen's coup d'état and his naming himself "imperial commissar for Prussia," the *Frankfurter Zeitung* reported the government's intention to bring the radio medium into line with its program of right-wing propaganda, and in the ensuing weeks the left-leaning directors of the Berlin and Frankfurt radio stations, on whose commissions Benjamin depended for a large part of his income, were dismissed. At the same time, the *Frankfurter Zeitung* began leaving Benjamin's letters and submissions of manuscripts unanswered (though publication of his work in the newspaper would continue—mostly under a pseudonym—for another couple of years). Moreover, in his letter of July 26 Benjamin tells Scholem that the building authorities in Berlin had notified him that he would have to give up his apartment because of alleged code violations.

Whatever his reasons for once again flirting with suicide (Scholem points to the rejection by Olga Parem as a factor), Benjamin on July 27 drafted his will and four farewell letters—to Franz Hessel, to Jula Radt-Cohn, to Ernst Schoen, and to Egon and Gert Wissing.[62] The letters to Hessel and Jula Cohn are particularly vivid expressions of his mental state at this time:

> Dear Hessel,
>
> An impasse with a *vue sur le parc*—what could more magically circumscribe the site of a death-chamber?[63] A well-intentioned gentleman once paid me the compliment of saying I was an artist of life [*ein Lebenskünstler*]. In the selection of this place of departure I hope I have done him an honor. Among those who could make this departure difficult—if my heart did not beat so quickly at the thought of nothingness—there is you. May all the happiness that this beautiful, morning-fresh room promises, as I write, be communicated to your room with the Green Meadow, and may it come to rest there as gently as I myself, let me hope, will be resting soon.
>
> Yours,
> Walter Benjamin

> Dear Jula,
>
> You know that I once loved you very much. And even now that I am about to die, my life has no greater gifts in its possession than those conferred on it by moments of suffering over you. So this greeting shall suffice.
>
> Yours,
> Walter

The letter to Egon and Gert Wissing is similarly impassioned, and indeed is full of tender feeling for his cousins, though it is longer and more circumstantial, being partly taken up with instructions for executing his will. The letter makes it clear that on this day Benjamin was not entirely resolved on killing himself—"not yet absolutely certain that I will put my plan into action." He sounds a lament that echoes that of the previous summer, though he also speaks of having made his peace with death and of how *geborgen,* how hidden and secure, this makes him feel (the term figures significantly in his writings about childhood, pervaded as they are by thoughts of exile and death). He refers to his "profound weariness" and his desire for "healing" rest: "The room I've got now for ten francs a day looks out on a square where children play and the noises of Avenue Gambetta come through muffled by the foliage and palms. This room is the waiting room—modest and inspiring trust—from which, as I think, the great physician will soon summon me into the consulting-room of nothingness [*Parloir des Nichts*]." The opportunities for a writer of his disposition and schooling, he goes on to say, are rapidly disappearing in Germany. "Only life with a woman or with some well defined work" could induce him to put up with the multiplying difficulties, and "both are lacking." To his old friend Schoen, he simply wrote: "Dear Ernst, I know you will think back on me in a friendly spirit and not altogether infrequently. For that I thank you. Yours, Walter." Benjamin never mailed these letters, but he preserved them along with the will.

In the will itself, Benjamin names Scholem as trustee of all the manuscripts in his estate and charges him, in the event of any posthumous publication of his writings, to reserve 40 to 60 percent of the net profits for Stefan.[64] He further bequeaths his entire library to Stefan, with the provision that Egon Wissing, Scholem, and Gustav Glück can each choose from it ten volumes not to exceed 100 marks in value. He also makes individual gifts of paintings and other precious objects to a number of friends, including Ernst Bloch, Asja Lacis, Alfred Cohn, Gretel Karplus, Gert Wissing, Jula Radt-Cohn, Wilhelm Speyer, and Elisabeth Hauptmann. In the letter to the Wissings, he makes an additional bequest to his former wife, Dora.

From Nice Benjamin traveled on to Italy (where he remained for some three months) to join up with Speyer for their collaboration. He wrote to Scholem in a calm spirit from the Villa Irene, a pension in Poveromo, on August 7: "Poveromo lives up to its name: it's a seaside resort for poor people, or at any rate for families with limited funds but lots of children—families from Holland, Switzerland, France, and Italy. I live away from all the bustle, in a simple but quite satisfactory room, and I am rather content, insofar as conditions and prospects allow me to be" (BS, 16). He could expect up to 5,000 marks (10 percent of the box office receipts) for his advice and help in writing Speyer's play, but meanwhile he was almost penniless: "I keep myself going with cigarette money that Speyer has advanced me, and otherwise live on credit"—namely, the "rather long credit line" granted him by the pension where he was living. The collaboration with Speyer, which he found highly diverting, left him plenty of free time, and, his economic woes notwithstanding, he was able to summon his energies and, "for the first time since who knows when," devote himself to a single, well defined project.

This was the composition of *Berlin Childhood around 1900*, begun in Poveromo. The work first arose as a reshaping and expansion of the material on Benjamin's early childhood developed in his "Berlin Chronicle," the lengthy autobiographical piece he had contracted to produce for *Die literarische Welt* nearly a year earlier. He worked on "Berlin Chronicle" mainly on Ibiza, where he began rereading Proust, but in Poveromo he abandoned the commission in order to concentrate on the new project born out of it, which he hoped would be, among other things, more commercially viable. The transformation of the conversationally discursive, autobiographical chronicle format into a more poetic-philosophic mode of presentation, its antecedents in the montage construction of *One-Way Street*, proceeded apace—"I write all day and sometimes well into the night."[65] By September 26 he could announce to Scholem (somewhat prematurely, as it turned out) that the new text, composed of seemingly disparate *Denkbilder*, was "largely finished":

> It is . . . written in small sections: a form I am repeatedly led to adopt, first, by the materially threatened, precarious nature of my work and, second, by considerations as to its commercial prospects. Moreover, the subject matter seems absolutely to demand this form. In short, I am working on a series of sketches [*Folge von Aufzeichnungen*] I will entitle "Berliner Kindheit um 1900." (BS, 19)[66]

Work continued on the *Berlin Childhood* after Benjamin's return to Germany in mid-November; some of the sections went through seven or eight drafts. On his way back to Berlin, he stopped off at Frankfurt and read a large portion of the manuscript to Adorno. The latter recounted his impression to Kracauer on November 21: "I think it is wonderful and entirely original; it even marks a great advance over *One-Way Street,* insofar as all archaic mythology is thoroughly liquidated here and the mythical is sought only in what is most contemporary—in the 'modern' in each case" (quoted in BA, 20n). Adorno could have been thinking of the way metropolitan sites are evoked from the perspective of a child in Benjamin's text, especially chthonic or underground sites such as the indoor public swimming pool, the marketplace, the sidewalks with their gratings looking down into basement apartments, or the otter's pool in the zoo. Benjamin also read portions of the text to Gretel Karplus in Berlin and was gratified by her response.

Although he would continue to add new sections to the work over the next two years, he was able in mid-December 1932 to send Scholem a provisional manuscript of what he was calling his "new book," characterizing it, in spite of fast-darkening horizons, as a reflection of his "sunniest side, relatively speaking," even though "the epithet 'sunny' can't really be applied to [the book's] contents in any strict sense." He adds that, of everything he has written, "this work may be most liable to be misunderstood" (BS, 23–24). Publication of individual sections of the text began on December 24, when "A Christmas Angel" appeared in Berlin's venerable *Vossische Zeitung.* Between December 1932 and September 1935 twenty-six pieces from *Berlin Childhood around 1900* were published in the newspapers, mainly in the *Frankfurter Zeitung* and the *Vossische Zeitung,* and generally under a pseudonym (Detlef Holz or C. Conrad) or anonymously after April 1933. In 1938 Benjamin would publish seven additional pieces in an issue of *Maß und Wert,* the bimonthly émigré journal edited by Thomas Mann. In the spring of that year, a pregnant introductory section was composed, while the rest of the manuscript underwent extensive revision and abridgement (nine complete sections were cut and the remaining text reduced by more than a third), as Benjamin resumed the effort, begun in 1933, to publish the suite of vignettes as a book. It was declined, on account of its difficulty, by at least three publishers in Germany and Switzerland and appeared in book form only posthumously.[67] Today it stands as one of the lesser-known classics of twentieth-century prose writing.

In first describing the work to Scholem, Benjamin had remarked that "these childhood memories . . . are not narratives in the form of a chronicle but rather . . . individual expeditions into the depths of memory" (BS, 19). At issue here is an ontological rather than simply psychological memory—a conception akin to Bergson's idea of memory as the survival of past images, precondition for all human perception and action—memory as an element and not just a faculty. Such a conception is already operative in "Berlin Chronicle," one passage of which was turned into a short piece entitled "Excavation and Memory" (see SW, 2:576, 611). In these laconic reflections, taking a cue from the nature of language, Benjamin argues that memory is not first of all an instrument for surveying the past, not simply a recorder and storehouse. Rather, memory is conceived as the theater (Schauplatz) of the past, the permeable medium of past experience (Medium des Erlebten), "just as the earth is the medium in which ancient cities lie buried. He who seeks to approach his own buried past must conduct himself like a man digging." What is called remembrance is the actualization of a vanished moment in its manifold depth, its meaning. For it may be that "reality takes shape only in memory," speculates Proust in Swann's Way. As Benjamin puts it in his 1929 essay "On the Image of Proust," in a formula bearing on his modern monadology, "A remembered event is infinite, because it is merely a key to everything that happened before it and after it." The excavation of submerged temporal strata, as undertaken in 1932, unearths a trove of images (not a world of characters, as in Proust)—images that, as the precipitate of past experience, constitute "treasures in the sober rooms of our later insights—like torsos in a collector's gallery."

No less important than the patient delving to ever-deeper layers of the past is establishing "the exact location of where in today's ground the ancient treasures have been stored up" (emphasis added), for the living present is also a medium—one in which the images of the past attain form and transparency, and in which the contours of the future are delineated as well: "The present in which the writer lives is this medium. And, dwelling in it, he now cuts another section through the sequence of his experiences [Folge seiner Erfahrung]." In

Berlin Childhood, the palimpsest character of memory and, therefore, of experience—what in the Proust essay is designated "intertwined time"—entails a mode of image overlay, of spatiotemporal superimposition, that turns the text itself into a virtual palimpsest.[68] Just as the flâneur, in his anamnestic intoxication, apperceives traces of the city's past inscribed upon its present-day features, so in Benjamin's sober and lyrical evocation of his early years there is a kind of vertical montage of places and things, as, in obedience to a principle of similitude, remembered sensations give rise to multiple correspondences, including not only other sensations (of forms, colors, smells) but also childhood dreams, fantasies, and reading experiences. Thus the sandstone façade of the Stettiner railroad station bears an image of the sand dunes to which the child and his family are about to journey by train; the damp, cold smell of the stairwell at the entry to the municipal reading room harbors the scent of its iron gallery within; the furnishings of the boy's home—the wallpaper, the console of a tiled stove, his father's leather armchair—are for him stamped with "gorgeous trappings" encountered in adventure novels; and the glass-paneled, oak-framed bookcase, an object of veneration and temptation to the child, wears the image of the fairy-tale chamber that promises heavenly delight, something that in turn contains an image of the old peasant dwelling where stories once accompanied the rhythms of household work. By the same token, the nonchronological, discontinuous narrative as a whole continually superposes, by a variety of references, the author's disenchanted present day on his enchanted past, so everywhere a dead and resurrected world of play is framed in the perspective of exile, and everywhere the man is felt to be prefigured in the child, whose not yet conscious knowledge, embedded in the world of things, is weighed in a philosophic-historical balance, like a dream recalled down to its smallest detail. The stratum of the writer's present day, broken through and made transparent, becomes a window onto remembered experiences that preform it and that also depend on it for the realization of their latent meaning. For it is by virtue of the afterhistory that the forehistory is recognizable.

Together with *The Arcades Project*, which is devoted to the excavation of an earlier historical epoch, Benjamin's portrait of his childhood constitutes his most extended treatment of what he calls, in a

1931 diary entry, his "favorite subject, dwelling."[69] The portrait origi-nates at a time when he was on the verge of homelessness. Earlier in 1932, in his "Ibizan Sequence," he had written of a man who has learned to build his nest in the ruins: "Whatever he did, he made a lit-tle house out of it, as children do when they play" (SW, 2:591). Children ensconce themselves in suddenly available pockets of the thing-world, where for the moment they may be safely hidden away *(geborgen)*. *Berlin Childhood* studies such "subterranean" dwelling (comparable in certain respects to the systematic self-encasement of the étui-man in *The Arcades Project*) in terms of the child's mimetic genius—his capacity for mimicking, and for masking himself with, a host of ordi-nary objects (doors, tables, cabinets, curtains, porcelain), so as to see from out of their midst and from out of their very materiality. For the child, the household is an "arsenal of masks," just as various stations of the surrounding modern city—street corners, parks, courtyards, cabstands—are for him outcroppings of antiquity, thresholds to a precipitous order into which he is readily absorbed, as the old Chinese painter, in the section "The Mummerehlen" (1933), is absorbed into the landscape of his painting. The author's own philosophic immer-sion compares to the rapturous immersion of the child as waking world to dreaming. By means of the text's various framing devices, which bring differing temporal planes into communication, the unre-flective mythic space of childhood dissolves into the space of history, just as the overarching security *(Geborgenheit)* that the child takes for granted dissolves into the adult's sense of crisis. Yet the socially irretrievable childhood world occasions an afterimage, and the demy-thologizing physiognomics yields a higher concreteness and deeper intimacy in historical remembrance.[70]

Take, for example, the evocation of a winter morning in the sec-tion of that name, with its almost imperceptible fusing of space and time in a sequence of thresholds and passages quietly negotiated by the child, as he awaits his cooked breakfast fruit in his bedroom—or rather, as the fruit awaits him:

> It was always so at this hour; only the voice of my nursemaid dis-turbed the solemnity with which the winter morning used to give me up into the keeping of the things in my room. The shutters were

not yet open as I slid aside the bolt of the oven door for the first time, to examine the apple cooking inside. Sometimes, its aroma would scarcely have changed. And then I would wait patiently until I thought I could detect the fine bubbly fragrance that came from a deeper and more secretive cell of the winter's day than even the fragrance of the fir tree on Christmas eve. There lay the apple, the dark, warm fruit that—familiar and yet transformed, like a good friend back from a journey—now awaited me. It was the journey through the dark land of the oven's heat, from which it had extracted the aromas of all the things the day held in store for me. (BC, 62)

The soberly realistic rendering unfolds a world of transformation and convolution, of spatial and temporal plasticity, such as governs events in fairy tales, those earlier emanations of a domestic sphere. The dark and glowing oven chamber that figures here as a source of "aromas" has both a documentary significance, in its reflection of a particular historical epoch and social-technological habitus, and a metaphorical and fabular power of suggestion, functioning within a network of motifs. Such dialectical economy everywhere conditions the distinctive tone of Benjamin's writing in this, his most consummate creation. As Adorno emphasizes in his afterword to the text, the "sunniness" of the presentation is shadowed throughout by melancholy, just as the child's fugitive knowledge is shadowed by the ineffable tidings transmitted from every corner of the mythically animated, enveloping world of things.[71]

Over the summer of 1932, Adorno had sent Benjamin reports of a seminar on recent developments in aesthetics that he, as a twenty-eight-year-old *Privatdozent* (unpaid lecturer), was offering at Frankfurt for a select group of students.[72] The course ran for two semesters and devoted considerable attention to Benjamin's *Trauerspiel* book. Benjamin did not take Adorno up on his invitation to attend a session of the seminar after his return to Germany, although he expressed interest in the idea in a letter. Today, this sophisticated academic appropriation of Benjamin's book within the walls of the very institution where it had been effectively rejected as a habilitation thesis seems not only ironic but prophetic. Benjamin mentioned the course to Scholem, who had been reserved on the subject of Adorno, in a way that could only reinforce his latent prejudice: "When I disclose that he is continuing to use my *Trauerspiel* book in his seminar for the second semester running, without indicating this in the course catalogue, then you have a small cameo that should serve for the moment" (BS, 26).

In November and December, once back in Berlin, Benjamin read the proofs of Adorno's first book, *Kierkegaard: Construction of the Aesthetic,* pausing at one point to commend the author on his "groundbreaking analysis" of the bourgeois interior (part of Kierkegaard's image world) as a socially and historically situated model of metaphysical inwardness: "Not since reading Breton's latest verse (in his *Union libre*) have I felt myself so drawn into my own domain as I have through your exploration of that land of inwardness from whose bourn your hero never returned. Thus it is true that there is still something like a shared work after all" (BA, 20–21). He arranged to review Adorno's book in the *Vossische Zeitung,* where several sections of his *Berlin Childhood* would appear in the coming year. Published in April, the short review calls attention to Adorno's circumventing the already stereotyped existential-theological doctrine of Kierkegaard's thought in favor of "its apparently insignificant relics, . . . its images, similes, and allegories" (SW, 2:704). This point of view is in keeping with Benjamin's own methodological reflections as delineated in another review completed at this time, "The Rigorous Study of Art," which would appear under the pseudonym Detlef Holz in the *Frankfurter Zeitung* in July, after mandatory revision.[73] In this piece, Benjamin invokes the Austrian Alois Riegl as a new type of art scholar, one who is at home in unexplored marginal realms, and one for whom individual works of art, in their manifest materiality first of all, epitomize changes in the realm of perception over time. Such an approach bespeaks the critic's contemplation of his or her own activity as an impetus to rigorous study. The emphasis on marginal cases and inconspicuous data—which goes together with a mode of critical tracing and "scenting out" *(durchspüren)*—clearly recalls the research program of the arcades project (which is likewise concerned with the nineteenth-century bourgeois interior) and its historical-materialist theory of reading, and this in turn points to the connections between the *Arcades* and the *Trauerspiel* book, which makes explicit use of Riegl.

Benjamin traveled by auto from Poveromo back to Germany in mid-November with Wilhelm Speyer at the wheel. He spent the final weeks of 1932 attempting to repair the lines of communication with his two main publishing venues, the *Frankfurter Zeitung* and *Die literarische Welt*. The former had not published anything by him since mid-August, and the editor of the latter, his former collaborator and fellow critic, Willy Haas, had written him in Poveromo to say that his newspaper could not consider further submissions from him for the present. About Haas, with whom he would maintain relations and whose work he would cite and discuss in his 1934 essay on Kafka, he wrote scathingly to Scholem: "The 'intellectuals' among our 'coreligionists' are the first to offer the oppressors hecatombs from their own circles, so as to remain spared themselves" (BS, 23). His efforts on his own behalf met with some success, especially at the *Frankfurter Zeitung*, which began publishing his work again that November: "I have been able to stem the boycott led against me simply by showing up. But whether the energy I invested over these first few weeks will avert the worst cannot yet be judged" (BS, 23). He was also seeking out new contacts. The most important of these, along with the *Vossische Zeitung*, was the *Zeitschrift für Sozialforschung*, the recently inaugurated journal of the Institute of Social Research, which in February would move its offices from Frankfurt to Geneva. Benjamin had met with Max Horkheimer, the director of the institute since 1931, during his stopover in Frankfurt in November, and it was probably then that Horkheimer commissioned the first of the series of critical articles Benjamin would contribute to the journal up through its last German-language number in 1940. His essay, "The Present Social Situation of the French Writer," written mainly in late spring 1933, would appear in the first issue of 1934. Its composition entailed a degree of "fakery" *(Hochstapelei)*, as he himself confessed to Scholem, referring in the first instance, no doubt, to a lack of information (BS, 41). Although Benjamin assured Adorno of the viability of their "shared work," it seemed to Scholem that he sometimes bent over backward to accommodate himself to the institute's sociological line—just as he sometimes contorted himself to appear as someone Scholem could approve. Economic considerations would have been uppermost here: within a few years the institute became in effect Benjamin's primary employer and the sponsor of the refurbished arcades project. Though there were muted complaints about some of the articles proposed for him by Horkheimer, in particular the essay on Eduard Fuchs that was begun in 1934 and finished only two years later, Benjamin's alignment with the institute's program of social research never for long prevented him from pursuing research that did not fit into what he called the "new system of coordinates" (SF, 197).

There were other projects on Benjamin's desk as 1932 came to a close. These included a somewhat fantastical radio play—it was commissioned but not produced by Berlin Broadcasting—on the eighteenth-century German writer and scientist Georg Christoph Lichtenberg, whose aphorisms he had long esteemed; a review essay on Kafka, which, for lack of a commission, remained unwritten; and the composition of new pieces for the *Berlin Childhood*.[74] In connection with work on one of these new *Childhood* pieces, "The Mummerehlen," he drafted in January or February 1933 a succinct exposition of his thoughts on similarity and mimetic behavior, thoughts which had shortly before found expression in the unpublished pieces "On Astrology" and "The Lamp," and which played a crucial, if inconspicuous, role in the conception of "secret affinities" in *The Arcades Project* (see Convolute R2,3).[75] In copying out the new text, "Doctrine of the Similar," for Scholem's archive in late summer 1933, he effectively rewrote it, making a number of changes and additions and producing in the process a still more succinct sister text, "On the Mimetic Faculty," finished in September.[76] He referred to these two texts, which remained unpublished during his lifetime, as "notes" on the philosophy of language. To Scholem, who sent him, at his request, a copy of his 1916 essay, "On Language as Such and on the Language of Man," to aid in the rewrite, he described the new work as merely a gloss or addendum to the essay of 1916, something manifestly "unauthoritative"— a hint. What it dealt with was nothing less than "a new turn in our old tendency to show the ways magic has been vanquished" (BS, 61, 76).

The experience of similarity—both sensuous (as between faces) and nonsensuous (as between man and the stars)—has a history: this was his point of departure. He does not mention the Greek dictum "Like is known by like," but he appropriates the concept of mimesis here as elsewhere for the etiology of perception. In archaic times, it may be supposed, the gift of mimicry played a role in what we today think of as perception, and what we look on as objective processes in nature would have been in principle imitable. Benjamin argues that the once vital powers of "mimetic perception," of "mimetic production and comprehension," powers put to work in primitive magic or clairvoyant practices (such as dances) that preceded the development of religions, passed without residue into language: it is to language in the form of writing and speech that "clairvoyance has, over the course of history, yielded its old powers." These are powers of reading, wakened at first by the "mimetic object-character" of entrails, stars, coincidences, then by more formalized script, such as runes. In any act of reading or writing, similarities are grasped only at critical moments, as they "flash up fleetingly out of the stream of things [aus dem Fluß der Dinge hervorblitzen]." In "profane reading" no less than "magical reading" there is a necessary tempo, a variable swiftness in which the mimetic is fused with the semiotic, for the mimetic in language is manifest only through the material nexus of meaning, as conveyed by combinations of sounds or written characters. Nevertheless, it is evident that language is not just a system of signs. It is more fundamentally a living "medium"—Benjamin had long favored this term—in which objects encounter one another in their significations, that is to say, "in their essences [Essenzen], in their most transient and delicate substances, even in their aromas."[77] As a reservoir of ancient powers of assimilation, language—and writing, in particular—constitutes "the most complete archive of nonsensuous similarity." The concept of nonsensuous similarity is thus central to Benjamin's "new turn" in language theory, for if similarity in general is the organon of experience (AP, 868), then it is nonsensuous similarity in particular that "establishes the ties [die Verspannung stiftet] not only between what is said and what is meant, but also between what is written and what is meant, and equally between the spoken and the written"— each time, he adds, in a completely new way. There is an evident link here with the theory of the dialectical image, which is an image *read* if not literally seen, a historical constellation emerging suddenly— flashing up—in language, through a correspondence of moments.

At one point in *The Arcades Project*, on the subject of the gambler's bodily presence of mind in wagering, Benjamin speaks of a mode of reading that in each case is divinatory (Convolute O13,3), and he further shows how a divinatory relation to things is characteristic of both the nineteenth-century flâneur and the nineteenth-century collector, each in his own way haunted by similarities. Moreover, "The Mummerehlen" and the other *Berlin Childhood* texts likewise portray the child as inhabiting a universe of magical correspondences and as incarnating in his play space an endlessly productive mimetic genius. It was presumably the example of such nonutilitarian and indeed intoxicated activities as gambling, flânerie, collecting, and childhood play—these all reflecting sides of Benjamin's own personality—that made it possible to speak of not only a faculty of becoming similar but also a nonsensuous similarity at work in all reading. For, in general, "our existence no longer includes what once made it possible to speak of this kind of similarity and, above all, to produce it [*hervorzurufen*]."

The final years of the Weimar Republic had seen the publication of a number of Benjamin's now-classic essays: "Surrealism," "Karl Kraus," "On the Image of Proust," and "Little History of Photography." And brilliant insights into an astonishing range of subjects had filled his smaller contributions to German newspapers and journals: insights into cityscapes, French, German, and Russian literature, pedagogy, film, theater, painting and the graphic arts, contemporary political culture, and modern communications media. But no less important were the works that remained unpublished and even uncompleted during these years: they mark, in particular, the inception of the arcades project and of *Berlin Childhood around 1900*, the two projects that would organize virtually all of Benjamin's writing through the long exile lying ahead.

[CHAPTER EIGHT]

Exile

Paris and Ibiza, 1933–1934

IN a resume prepared in June 1940 while applying for an exit visa from France, Benjamin wrote: "For me the inter-war years fall naturally into two periods, before and after 1933."[1] On January 28, 1933, Kurt von Schleicher, who had served as the German chancellor for less than two months, announced his resignation, effectively leaving the appointment of the new Reichskanzler to the president, Paul von Hindenburg, and not to the parliament itself. The semblance of parliamentary democracy had in fact been absent from German politics since at least 1930, when Reichskanzler Heinrich von Brüning, in a desperate attempt to hold together a nation descending into chaos, had begun to rule through emergency decrees. Now, on January 30, Hindenburg named Adolf Hitler the next Reichskanzler; he then dissolved the parliament on February 1. Before the new elections could be held in early March, the Reichstag building burned through the night of February 27–28, an event that may have been orchestrated by the National Socialists themselves. Taking immediate advantage of the situation, Hitler decreed a series of emergency powers for the government, creating conditions that led directly to the establishment of a totalitarian police state over the course of the next year and a half. Opposition parties were banned and opponents of the regime arrested—many to be brutally liquidated. In the immediate aftermath of the fire, a number of Benjamin's friends fled the country, including Brecht, Bloch, Kracauer, Wilhelm Speyer, Bernard von Brentano, and Karl Wolfskehl. Others, such as Ernst Schoen and Fritz Fränkel, were arrested and placed in hastily erected concentration camps. (Schoen, who lost his position as artistic director of the Frankfurt radio station in March, was arrested a second time in April, before he managed to escape to London; Fränkel immigrated that year to Paris, where from

1938 to 1940 he lived in the same building as Benjamin.) Benjamin himself at this time hardly dared step outside into the streets.[2] As Jean-Michel Palmier has put it, "Within just a few months, Germany was drained of its writers, poets, and actors, its painters, architects, directors, and professors. Never before had any country seen a comparable blood-letting of its cultural life."[3] And the intellectuals were only a few thousand among the more than 100,000 Germans—half of whom were Jews—who fled the Reich between 1933 and 1935.[4]

Writing to Scholem on February 28, Benjamin gives memorable expression to the bleakness of the situation: "The little composure that people in my circles were able to muster in the face of the new regime was rapidly spent, and one realizes that the air is hardly fit to breathe anymore—a condition which of course loses significance as one is being strangled. . . . This above all economically" (BS, 27). He goes on to wonder out loud how he will make it through the coming months, whether inside or outside Germany: "There are places where I could earn a minimal income, and places where I could live on a minimal income, but not a single place where these two conditions coincide."

The ill-defined wish to get out of Germany that had recurred throughout the last decade now took on real urgency, as the country was gripped in the spring of 1933 by an unprecedented, if not unforeseen, reign of terror. As he tells Scholem, people were being dragged out of their beds in the middle of the night, tortured, and murdered. The press and the airwaves in Germany were effectively in the hands of the Nazis, and boycotts of Jewish businesses and book burnings were soon to begin. The atmosphere of oppression was palpable everywhere: "Every attitude or manner of expression that does not fully conform to the official one is terrorized. . . . The German atmosphere in which you look first at people's lapels and after that usually do not want to look them in the face anymore, is unbearable" (BS, 34). He emphasizes, though, that it was not fear for his life that determined him to leave the country in all possible haste but, more characteristically, the choking off of the possibilities for publication and intellectual life itself: "Rather, it was the almost mathematical simultaneity with which every conceivable office returned manuscripts, broke off negotiations either in progress or in the final stages, and left inquiries unanswered. . . . Under such conditions, the utmost political reserve, such as I have long and with good reason practiced, may protect the person in question from systematic persecution, but not from starvation." Benjamin's wrenching account of his forced exile from his native land is echoed by many others. The exiles faced pressing material dilemmas—the loss of their profession, reading public, homes, and possessions—but the psychological challenges were in most cases even more overwhelming.

Scholem had arranged for a friend of his, Kitty Marx, a young woman from Königsberg, to visit Benjamin in Berlin at the beginning of March, shortly before her departure for Jerusalem, where that spring she would marry Scholem's friend Karl Steinschneider. Benjamin took an instant liking to Marx, and she was likewise very taken with him. He lent her several books, including Musil's *The Man without Qualities* and the proofs of Brecht's recent didactic play, *The Mother*.[5] Through letters edged with a courtly irony, Benjamin maintained a warm friendship with her over the next five years. According to Scholem, Marx found Benjamin in this period of collective crisis remarkably self-possessed, free of the panic that was gripping so many. She was impressed by the striking composure with which he seemed to face the situation. This composure, comments Scholem, may have had to do with his experience of near-suicide the year before; at any rate, it "found stronger expression in the outward attitude he displayed to other people than in his letters, which often enough bear witness to [his] unrest" (SF, 195).

Benjamin left Berlin on the evening of March 17, well in advance of the first wave of "legal" exclusions of the Jews from German life. April 1 saw the first general boycott of Jewish businesses; as the month went on, measures were taken to exclude Jews from public office and from the professions. Traveling by train to Paris, Benjamin passed out of his native land without incident. During a stopover in Cologne on March 18, he had met with the art historian Carl Linfert, an editor and correspondent of the *Frankfurter Zeitung* who had become an increasingly important partner in intellectual matters—and someone whose work came to play a significant role in Benjamin's own writings. Linfert's essay on eighteenth-century architectural drawing is discussed at the end of Benjamin's review article "The Rigorous Study of Art," and he is cited in *The Arcades Project*. Before his departure from Berlin, Benjamin had written to Felix Noeggerath and Jean Selz, firming up arrangements for another extended stay—it would be five months this time—on Ibiza. This was as far as his plans extended at the moment. Hardly anyone in his position, he remarks to Scholem, could look further into the future. Arriving in Paris on March 19, he checked into the Hôtel Istria, on the Rue Campagne Première in Montparnasse, where he remained until April 5, when he left for Spain. Benjamin may well have chosen the hotel because of its long association with artists. The Surrealists in particular had favored this establishment: Picabia, Duchamp, Man Ray, Tzara, Aragon, and Kiki de Montparnasse all stayed there (as did Rilke, Mayakovsky, and Satie). Louis Aragon even graced the little hotel with a verse:

> Ne s'éteint que ce qui brilla . . .
> Lorsque tu descendais de l'hôtel Istria,
> Tout était différent Rue Campagne Première,
> En mil neuf cent vingt neuf, vers l'heure de midi . . .[6]

During these two weeks in Paris, Benjamin reported to Thankmar von Münchhausen that he sat smoking his pipe *à la terrasse* and shaking his head over the gazettes. But he was also looking toward the future, however bleak it might have appeared—he announced to Scholem that a "new chapter" in their correspondence was being inaugurated. And, unlike some of the refugees who took Nazism to be just one more brief chapter in the turbulent onrush of recent German history, Benjamin was well aware that he was inaugurating a new chapter in his life as well. He thus applied for a French carte d'identité and began, tentatively, to explore possibilities for publishing his work. He met with an old friend from the days of the youth movement and *Der Anfang*, Alfred Kurella, who was now a member of Brecht's circle; Kurella had been included on the editorial board of the aborted journal *Krisis und Kritik* and was soon to be an editor of the French Communist newspaper *Monde*. And while Benjamin knew full well that his flight from Germany would have disastrous consequences for his work, and thus for his ability to earn a living, he was able, despite the crisis, to arrange for a small, ongoing income for the months ahead: he had sublet his Berlin apartment to a "reliable man" by the name of von Schoeller, who in fact would continue there as tenant until the end of 1938. "Through elaborate arrangements" he had also been able to supplement this with a few hundred marks—enough, he hoped, to live for a few months on Ibiza. And there were friends back in Berlin—mainly Gretel Karplus and Thankmar von Münchhausen—who were ready to help out with practical matters such as his apartment and the disposition of the papers, books, and other belongings he had left behind.

A major source of worry was the fact that Dora and Stefan were still in Berlin. "All of this . . . would be bearable, if only Stefan weren't where he still is" (BS, 36). He wrote Dora from Paris at the end of March, proposing that Stefan be sent to Palestine, where Dora's brother Viktor had helped found a village, but his former wife vetoed the suggestion, refusing to be separated from her son. Dora lost her job in April, and she and fifteen-year-old Stefan began learning Italian together in the hope that they might find a safe haven in the south. In the fall of 1934, she would purchase and begin operating a pension in San Remo, a resort town on the Ligurian Sea in northwest Italy, from where she immediately made a heartfelt appeal to Benjamin to come be her guest—which he did.[7] During her year in Nazi Germany, Dora tried in vain to find publishing opportunities for her former husband. Stefan, who considered himself squarely on the left, remained in Germany until the summer of 1935, attending gymnasium and trying to maintain some semblance of a normal teenage life. He joined his mother in San Remo in September of that year, attending the local *liceo* and later continuing his schooling in Vienna (where Dora's parents lived) and London. Dora gave him free rein in all that concerned him because, as she told his father, "he is so reasonable."

In early April Benjamin traveled to Ibiza in the company of the Selzes, stopping off for a few days in Barcelona, where his old friends Alfred and Grete Cohn were living—perhaps, too, to visit the "very beautiful lady friend," the divorced wife of a Berlin physician, about whom Olga Parem spoke to Scholem.[8] After a brief stay at Selz's house in the town of Ibiza, he arrived in the village of San Antonio around the thirteenth of April. He found a place that had changed dramatically in the course of one year. The island itself was no longer the unspoiled asylum it had been but a burgeoning vacation spot, whose

predominantly German summer guests included not a few Nazis. As
Jean Selz puts it, "The magical atmosphere had definitely been tainted."[9]
The noise of new construction filled the air in San Antonio, as the island's residents sought to take advantage of the surge, first of tourists
and now of refugees; even some of the visitors, such as the Noeggeraths, found ways to profit from the situation. They had sublet their
house on Sa Punta des Molí, above the bay of San Antonio, and when
Benjamin arrived they were about to move into a new house, built by
the local doctor on the opposite side of the bay in the village of San
Antonio itself. Benjamin had been guaranteed two months' lodging
with the Noeggeraths and had been looking forward to repossessing
his room of the previous summer and enjoying the lovely stretch of
woods adjacent to it. He found the new arrangements much less con-
genial. Not only was the house architecturally banal and inconve-
niently located, but its paper-thin walls allowed voices to echo
through every room, along with cold gusts of wind, for summer was
late in coming that year. There were some positive features—a larger
room that even included a kind of dressing room, and hot water for his
bath—but Benjamin never regained the feeling of being pleasantly
housed that he had experienced the year before. Noeggerath himself
was altered, seeming more reserved and nothing like the "universal
genius" Benjamin had known as a student. And, most worrisome,
prices were on the rise, so even with the supplements provided by
the sale of part of his coin collection (managed by Thankmar von
Münchhausen in Berlin) Benjamin was hard pressed to survive on his
"European minimum" of sixty or seventy marks a month. He spent
his days in his "forest from the year before" and made frequent trips
to the port town of Ibiza to see the Selzes and to sit in a café (the
town cinema was too dirty for him), escaping for a time the "coloniz-
ing atmosphere . . . , the most hateful of atmospheres," that was enveloping San Antonio. "My long-held mistrust of the whole business of
developers . . . has been all too drastically confirmed here" (C, 415–
416, 419).

His complaints about the island and its changes were of course
exacerbated by the pall cast over all of Europe by the German crisis.
In this regard, Benjamin kept to his long-held practice, avoiding comment on the political situation in his letters and refusing to discuss

such matters in person. He was concerned instead to establish some productive regimen for his now vagabond life, and to rediscover familiar surroundings. As soon as he was out of earshot of the "blastings and hammer blows," the gossip and debating of the "narrow-minded shopkeepers and vacationers," he found that he could recapture some of "the old beauty and solitude of the region" (C, 415–416, 408). Thus, with the aid of a lounge chair, blanket, thermos bottle, and other supplies, he set up his study in a hiding place in the woods, just as he had done the previous summer. At first the cold wind made it all but impossible to work outdoors, and his only "compensation" for the hardships of the day was a warm bath in an enamel tub at the Noeggeraths', a comparative luxury on Ibiza. Later he was able to march out in the early morning to his chosen hillside, where he would retrieve his lounge chair from behind some bushes, secure his books and papers, and write or read undisturbed. He describes his daily routine in San Antonio in a letter to Gretel Karplus (GB, 4:207–208), one of several long letters written to her that summer in which he addresses her for the first time as "Felizitas," his nickname for her,[10] and signs with "Detlef" or "Detlef Holz," one of his current pen names (he also refers to himself as her "adopted child," as distinguished from Adorno, her "problem child"). He usually rises at six or six-thirty, goes down to the ocean for a bath and swim shortly thereafter, and is in his woodland hideout by seven; he would then read Lucretius for an hour. After uncorking his thermos and breakfasting at eight, he works—fortified by stoicism and his meager repast—until one, often pausing around noon for a short walk in the woods. He has lunch in town around two, at a long table where he is careful to observe the prevailing etiquette, and afterward likes to sit under a nearby fig tree to read or "scribble." In the absence of any chess partners, he sometimes passes the later afternoon in card games or dominoes (though his opponents, having for the most part no mental occupation, are "too serious" at it) or in conversation in a café. Back in his room, which he shares with "three hundred flies," he is in bed by nine or nine-thirty, reading a Simenon detective novel by candlelight.

As his stay went on, even this routine failed to provide sufficient relief from the noise and dust of San Antonio, and he began to make frequent excursions into the interior of the island. On one such outing, undertaken in the company of a new acquaintance, he came to know "one of the most beautiful and remote parts of the island." His companion was a twenty-two-year-old Danish engraver named Paul Gauguin, grandson of the famous painter, who was living as the only foreigner in a village buried deep in the Ibizan mountains. After going out with a lobsterman at five in the morning and spending three hours at sea learning about his work, Benjamin and Gauguin—who was "just as uncivilized and just as highly cultivated" as the landscape of the region—were put ashore in a hidden bay. There they were presented with "an image of such immutable perfection that . . . it existed at the very brink of the invisible." What they saw were a few women completely draped in black gathered around some fishing boats, with only their "serious and immobile faces" left uncovered. The sight remained uninterpretable for Benjamin until, over an hour later, as they were hiking up a mountain path toward a village, "a man came walking toward us carrying a tiny white child's coffin under his arm." The women below had been keeners for the dead child but had not wanted to miss the unusual spectacle of a motorboat's arrival on the beach. "In order to find this spectacle striking," comments Benjamin, "you must first understand it." Benjamin suspected that Gauguin had known what he was looking at all along, but "he hardly talks at all" (C, 419–421).

The charms of the Mediterranean could still occasionally work their magic on him. He ends a letter to Gretel Adorno with an idyllic description of the view from his seat on a high terrace: "The town lies below me; the noise from a smithy or from a construction site penetrates up from below like the breathing of the land that begins right at the foot of my bastion—so small is this strip of town. I see to the right of the houses the sea, and behind the houses the island rises up very gently in order to sink, behind a chain of hills that patiently accompany the horizon, into the sea again" (GB, 4:209). And he carried away vivid impressions from his long marches into the island's interior. "In the mountains you find one of the most cultivated and fertile landscapes of the island. The soil is traversed by deep canals that are, however, so narrow that they often flow for a good distance invisibly beneath the high grass—which is of the deepest green. The rushing of these watercourses produces an almost sucking sound. Carob trees, almond trees, olive trees, and conifers grow on the slopes, and the valley floors are covered with corn and beanstalks. Up against the rocks stand blooming oleanders" (GB, 4:231–232).

Although Benjamin worked hard to restrict the circle of those with whom he came in contact—actively avoiding, for example, Raoul Hausmann, the former Dadaist, who was living not far from San Antonio—he nonetheless took advantage of some aspects of the new social situation on the island. He was a regular, for example, at the bar Migjorn (the name means "south wind"), owned by Jean Selz's brother Guy. He remained a frequent visitor in the Selzes' home on Calle de la Conquista in Ibiza, where Jean and his wife, Guyet, regularly played host to a group of writers and artists. And he even made some attempt to learn Spanish, assembling—as he had whenever he returned to his promise to learn Hebrew—a veritable arsenal of methodologies, including a traditional grammar, a word frequency list, and a newfangled "suggestive" approach. The results were also identical to those attained in the study of Hebrew: he remained, by his own admission, without any real competence.

Benjamin spent the last week in May with the Selzes in Ibiza; he needed the relative quiet of their house, with its flower garden and its view of the bay and distant mountains, in order to finish the troublesome study of contemporary French letters that was to mark his debut in Horkheimer's new journal. While he was there, he read to his friends from *Berlin Childhood around 1900,* translating as he went along, and the difficulty he experienced in rendering some of the passages into French prompted Selz to undertake a translation of the work. Although, according to Benjamin, Selz knew no German, the translation got under way as a close collaboration—"we spent hours discussing the slightest words"—and Benjamin pronounced himself well pleased with the initial results.[11] It was also during this stay in the old town of Ibiza in late May that he and Selz smoked opium together, in fulfillment of a wish first expressed by Benjamin the year before. The experience is described at length by Selz in his essay "Une expérience de Walter Benjamin,"[12] and more briefly by Benjamin himself in a letter to Gretel Karplus:

Hardly any clouds [of opium smoke] rise to the ceiling, so deeply do I understand how to draw them out of the long bamboo tube into my insides. . . . At the start of the evening, I was feeling very sad. But I was conscious of that rare state in which the inner and the outer worries balance each other very precisely, giving rise to what is perhaps the only mood in which one really finds solace. We took this as . . . a sign, and after making all the ingenious little arrangements that free one from having to stir during the night, we set to work around two o'clock. . . . The role of assistant, which requires great care, was divided between us, in such a way that each of us was at the same time server and beneficiary of the service, and the conversation was interwoven with the acts of assistance in the same way that the threads which color the sky in a Gobelin tapestry are interwoven with the battle represented in the foreground. . . . Today I've obtained significant results in my study of curtains—for a curtain separated us from the balcony that looked out on the city and the sea. (OH, 14–15)

Selz quotes Benjamin's funny coinage *rideaulogie*—the discipline that studies curtains!—and Benjamin himself, in his written reflections on opium, "Crock Notes" (OH, 81–85), remarks that curtains are "interpreters of the language of the wind." The "Crock Notes"—and, later, *The Arcades Project*—suggest that if the omnipresence and multivalence of ornament in the modern world is to be appreciated, it requires a special approach, a sense of manifold interpretability. Like hashish, opium—they used the code word "crock"—illuminates the "world of surfaces" latent in the everyday: "The opium-smoker or hashish-eater experiences the power of the gaze to suck a hundred sites out of one place."[13]

Of course, "the inner and the outer worries" could not long be dispelled by such means. The "big world" managed to intrude on the little island in unanticipated ways: on May 6 General Francisco Franco visited Ibiza in connection with his duties as the military commander in charge of the Balearic Islands, and Benjamin was forcibly reminded of the rise of the radical right across all of Europe. Early in May he had received news that his brother Georg, who had been active in the German Communist Party since 1922, was in the hands of the SA. First reports had him tortured and blinded in one eye, but these turned out to be exaggerated. Benjamin had spoken by telephone with his younger brother before leaving Berlin, and at that time rumors of his death were already circulating. Georg was arrested in April by uniformed and plainclothes officers and held in "preventive detention" in a police jail in Berlin. During the summer he was transferred to the Sonnenburg concentration camp (which was run by SA and SS units) but was released around Christmas. Afterward, as Benjamin foresaw he would do, he resumed his illegal activities, working for the underground press by translating articles from English, French, and Russian and editing a newsletter. He was arrested again in 1936 and sentenced to six years in prison, at the completion of which he was sent to the Mauthausen concentration camp, where he died in 1942.[14] The news of his brother's arrest—Scholem's brother Werner, meanwhile, was suffering a similar fate—naturally heightened Benjamin's fears for his son. Yet he could not write directly to Dora about these matters without endangering her and Stefan: "There are spies everywhere" (BS, 47). He was able to breathe a little easier when he heard in July that she and their son were on an automobile trip through central Europe. But at the end of May the shock of his dislocation was making itself felt, and Benjamin could tell Scholem that "I am in bad shape. The utter impossibility of having anything at all to draw on threatens your inner equilibrium in the long run—even for someone accustomed, like me, to living under precarious circumstances and without any expectations" (BS, 51).

By late spring Benjamin was already thinking of leaving the island, but he had neither sufficient means nor viable prospects (BG, 23). Writing in May, he told his friends that he already dreaded the "bleakness of winter" awaiting him in Paris, as if the seasons had given way to a permanent state of cold and death. By the middle of July he had, as predicted, exhausted his resources: he was without any dependable source of income beyond the few marks he received from his Berlin tenant. Seeing no possibility of short-term income, he more and more threw himself on the mercy of those few friends in a position to contribute a bit here and there. It was under these circumstances that Benjamin composed his "Sad Poem":

You sit in the chair and write.
You get more and more and more tired.
You go to bed at the right time,
You eat at the right time.
You have money—
Given by the good Lord.
Life is wonderful!
Your heart beats louder and louder and louder,
The sea becomes stiller and stiller and stiller
Right down to its ground. (GS, 6:520)

There is, of course, an element of ironic reveling in the gloom here—at least until the closing tercet, a kind of apocalypse in miniature. It is worth comparing "Sad Poem" to the most famous poem of the German exiles, Brecht's 1938 "To Those Born Later." Where Benjamin renders the sensation of an individual's sinking into historical depths, Brecht looks to a time when that sinking itself will be history:

You who will emerge from the flood
In which we have gone under
Remember
When you speak of our failings
The dark time too
Which you have escaped.[15]

Benjamin could thus take paradoxical comfort in the rainy weather prevailing on the island that summer—his outdoor work habits notwithstanding. As he says to Gretel Karplus, "I love gloomy days, in the south as much as in the north" (GB, 4:249). Yet his misery and sadness were genuine. We have mentioned the report of Vicente Valero, who in the 1990s interviewed many of the oldest inhabitants of the island; he tells us that Benjamin came to be called "el miserable" by the natives there, who recognized his poverty and isolation in his increasingly shabby clothing and shuffling gait.[16] His first three months on the island had already offered a stark contrast to the exuberance with which he greeted his idyll in nature and a primitive society in 1932; the final three months saw a descent into despair. In those months Benjamin gradually withdrew from contact even with his island friends, as he was forced to change his housing repeatedly. His already restricted diet was reduced to a level below subsistence, and the resultant malnutrition, in combination with his state of mind, brought on a series of debilitating illnesses.

But not all literary lines to the outside had been cut just yet. He kept doggedly in touch with certain newspaper correspondents and journal editors, including Carl Linfert, Max Rychner, and Alfred Kurella. The last had immigrated to Paris and was evidently considering a stay on Ibiza; Benjamin wrote him in June, describing the living conditions on the island and its two main towns. He tells Kurella, at that time secretary of a French arm of the Soviet Comintern, that he is very glad to hear from him: "You're standing in the center; I'm at best traveling on a tangent" (GB, 4:224). Yet that tangent, however tenuous, continued to bring him work: "requests for my contributions . . . keep arriving from Germany," he reported from San Antonio in mid-June, "[requests] from offices that showed little interest in me in the past" (BS, 59).[17] He was able to earn, on average, about 100 marks per month, which held him just above the existence minimum of 70–80 marks per month on the island. Nor was his productivity diminished by the precarious circumstances of his day-to-day existence. On the contrary, it was during this period of incipient exile that he composed some of the most magnificent of the *Berlin Childhood* pieces, including "The Moon," "The Little Hunchback," and his "self-portrait" "Loggias." As he tells Gretel Karplus, the "cloak of secrecy" under which he was writing, together with his failure so far to find a publisher for a book version of the *Childhood*—the pseudonymous and anonymous newspaper publication of individual pieces from the series was continuing—made it possible to resist the temptation to finish the work (C, 427–428). These new *Childhood* pieces were written in the interstices of his work schedule, between commissioned labors. On May 30 he was able to finish the most pressing of those, his essay "The Present Social Situation of the French Writer."

Benjamin's wide-ranging survey of the French literary scene was built up from the slimmest of material bases—Noeggerath's library, thirty or forty volumes that Benjamin had left behind on Ibiza the previous year, and several books sent him by Horkheimer from Geneva—and he was keenly aware of the plight this put him in. "The essay, which in any case is sheer fakery," he wrote to Scholem on April 19, "acquires a more or less magical mien by virtue of the fact that I have to write it here, with next to no source material of any kind. It will boldly exhibit that visage in Geneva, but keep it hidden in your presence."[18] Despite the difficulties, he was able—in what was becoming a pattern with him—to take satisfaction at the last in a work over which he had agonized: "It wasn't possible to produce something definitive. Nonetheless, I believe that the reader will gain insight into connections that until now have not been brought out so clearly" (BS, 54).

In the essay itself (SW, 2:744–767), Benjamin traces the contemporary social crisis of the French intellectual back to its initial exposition in the work of Apollinaire. In the pages that follow, he first presents the position of the Catholic right. The work of the "Romantic nihilist" Maurice Barrès, with his demand for an alliance between "Catholic feeling and the spirit of the soil," emerges as the springboard for Julien Benda's better-known indictment of the "treason of the intellectuals." Of the writers on the right, Benjamin treats Charles Péguy in the most balanced fashion—hardly a surprise given his longstanding interest in this poet. He emphasizes the libertarian, anarchistic, and populist elements within Péguy's mystic nationalism, elements he holds to be true remnants of the French Revolution. The analysis of Péguy's populism introduces a series of writers struggling in Zola's wake with the form of the *roman populiste,* and above all Louis-Ferdinand Céline in his explosive first novel, *Voyage au bout de la nuit* (Journey to the End of the Night; 1932). If Benjamin remains predictably skeptical of Céline's achievement, he nonetheless prefers the cold gaze that sees through the prerevolutionary masses—uncovering "their cowardice, their panic-stricken horror, their wishes, their violence"—to the sentimental pablum of liberal writers who sing paeans to the simplicity and moral purity of the common people. Benjamin thus praises Céline for his resistance to the conformism—the willingness to take everything about contemporary France as a given—that condemns most recent literature.

The notion of conformism is the bridge to an analysis of four writers who rise above it: Julien Green, Marcel Proust, Paul Valéry, and André Gide. Green's novels are for Benjamin "nocturnal paintings of the passions," dark works that explode the conventions of the psychological novel. Yet Benjamin finds a contradiction at the heart of Green's writings—that between their formal innovation and their regressive treatment of their subject matter. It is the same contradiction, carried to a higher level, that characterizes for him Proust's great novel.

> For this reason, it makes sense to inquire what the novel of the last decade has achieved for freedom. It is difficult to conceive of any answer, other than to note the defense of homosexuality that Proust has been the first to undertake. However, even though such a comment does justice to the meager revolutionary fruits of literature, it by no means exhausts the meaning of homosexuality in *A la recherche du temps perdu.* On the contrary, homosexuality appears in his work because both the most remote and the most primitive memories of the productive forces of nature are banished from the world he is concerned with. The world Proust depicts excludes everything that is involved in production. (SW, 2:755)

This contradiction between formal innovation and regressive thematics will preoccupy Benjamin in the year to come, spurring him to a meditation on "form-content relations" in progressive literature—the essay "The Author as Producer." The piece on the French writers prepares the ground for that later work in another way as well. In his analysis of Valéry, Benjamin focuses on the writer's conception of and attitude toward his work. Valéry is the great technician among contemporary writers; for him, according to Benjamin, writing is primarily technique. And for Benjamin, as for Valéry, progress is possible not in ideas but in techniques. The artwork is ideally, then, "not a creation, but a construction in which analysis, calculation, and planning play the principal roles" (SW, 2:757). Yet in his conception of the human subject, the intellectual as private person, Valéry is unable to step across "the historical threshold" separating the "harmoniously educated, self-sufficient individual" from the technician and specialist "who is ready to assume a place within a much larger plan." Which brings Benjamin to André Gide.

On Benjamin's reading, the protagonist of Gide's *Lafcadio's Adventures (Les caves du Vatican)* is himself only a technique, a construction—something demonstrated in the famous "gratuitous act" of pushing a fellow railroad passenger out of the train to his death. Benjamin traces a direct line between this action and those of the Surrealists. "For the Surrealists showed themselves increasingly intent on bringing scenes that had originally been initiated in a playful spirit or out of curiosity into harmony with the slogans of the Communist International. And if there could still be any doubt about the meaning of that extreme individualism under whose banner Gide's work was launched, it has lost all validity in the face of his recent statements. For these make clear how, once this extreme individualism had tested itself on the world around it, it inevitably became transformed into Communism" (SW, 2:759). The essay thus passes from the great liberal bourgeois writers to avowed leftists: the Surrealists themselves and André Malraux (the section on Malraux was added in January 1934). Benjamin takes Malraux's *Man's Fate (La condition humaine)*, with its portrayal of the Communist resistance to Chiang Kai-shek's nationalist forces, less as a ringing call to revolution than as an index to the current state of mind of bourgeois leftists in the West: "The climate and problems of civil war are of greater concern to the literary intelligentsia of the West than the weighty facts of social reconstruction in Soviet Russia" (SW, 2:761). It follows that the Surrealists alone can answer the question as to whether there can be a revolutionary literature that is not didactic. In the essay at hand, intended as it was for the *Zeitschrift für Sozialforschung*, Benjamin remains coy in the face of that question—a question he had answered explosively in the great essay on Surrealism of 1929. He suggests here only that Surrealism has "won the forces of intoxication for the revolution"—that is, has linked literature to psychoses, and so made it dangerous. "The Present Social Situation of the French Writer" cannot be counted among Benjamin's most important essays: it is too cautious, too conscious of its publishing venue, and ready to toe the line. Yet, as a carefully angled survey of the state of French letters at a moment of crisis, it far surpasses Benjamin's own estimate of its value. It was received enthusiastically at the institute, and two new commissions followed in short order—an article on the art historian Eduard Fuchs and a review essay on recent publications in the philosophy and sociology of language. But he could not begin working on these until his return to Paris.

From the situation of the contemporary French writer and intellectual Benjamin turned back to the cultural scene in Germany, where Stefan George was celebrating his sixty-fifth birthday. Review copies of two new books on the poet, an icon of cultural conservatism, had put him in the "disagreeable position of having to speak about Stefan George, now, before a German audience" (BS, 58–59). His authoritative and judicious review, "Stefan George in Retrospect," published in the *Frankfurter Zeitung* on July 12 under the pseudonym K. A. Stempflinger, was his last public reckoning with a writer for whose work he had felt the keenest interest as a youth, and for whose voice, as he says at the outset of the review, he has acquired a new ear over time (SW, 2:706–711). At issue here is his mature appreciation of George as an artist of Jugendstil. George remains for him a great and indeed prophetic figure, one who, in his rage against nature and in his gesture of irreconcilability, "stands at the end of an intellectual line that began with Baudelaire" (whose poems George had translated before Benjamin).[19] But with the passage of a quarter century, the "spiritual movement" associated with his name can be seen more clearly as a final, tragic convulsion in the Decadent movement. For all the rigor and nobility of his poetic methods, George's reliance on symbols and "secret signs" in the absence of a living tradition betrays a defensiveness and latent desperation, whose chief symptom is the ascendancy of mere "style" over meaning: "The style is that of Jugendstil—in other words, the style in which the old bourgeoisie disguises the premonition of its own impotence by indulging in poetic flights of fancy on a cosmic scale [*indem es kosmisch in alle Sphären schwärmt*]."

With its "tortured ornamentation," reflecting a determination to translate newly emerging tectonic forms back into the language of arts and crafts, thus cloaking the modernity of its technological means with an effusive figuration of the organic, Jugendstil—the German variant of art nouveau, which took its name from a widely read journal, *Die Jugend* (Youth)—was "a great and quite conscious act of regression." In spite of its Dionysian visions of a future as conjured by the word "youth," it remained a " 'spiritual movement' that aspired to the renewal of human existence without paying heed to politics." The desperate regression of Jugendstil means that even the image of youth "shrinks" to become a "mummy." These words at the end of the review refer sardonically to George's cult of the beautiful dead youth Maximin, but Benjamin is also thinking of the dead—if not exactly deified—comrades of his own youth (Fritz Heinle, Rika Seligson, Wolf Heinle), and of the atrophy of idealism in his generation. For it was the uncompromising melancholy romantics of the antebellum youth movement who, as he puts it, "lived in these poems," finding there refuge and consolation amid the onset of world-night *(weltnacht)*. George was a potent "minstrel" in the experience of that "doomed" generation. The true historical significance of his figure and work, then, is made evident not by those who ascended to university chairs or garnered political power in the name of their master, but rather by "those who—the best of whom, at any rate—can serve as witnesses before the judgment seat of history because they are dead."

Another commission from the *Frankfurter Zeitung* for a commemorative review followed on the heels of the George piece, this time in conjunction with the 200th anniversary of the death of Christoph Martin Wieland, the German Enlightenment poet, novelist, and translator, whose work, Benjamin admitted to Scholem, he hardly knew. With the help of articles in a Festschrift, however, and using the Reclam edition of some of Wieland's works, he labored to complete a biographically oriented article (focusing on Wieland's friendship with Goethe), which appeared in September. During the spring and summer, he was enthusiastically engaged with recently translated novels by Arnold Bennett. He published a review of the German version of *The Old Wives' Tale* (1908) in the *Frankfurter Zeitung* in late May. This review, "Am Kamin" (By the Fireside), develops a metaphor he had first broached in company with Jean Selz the year before, and which reappears in the famous essay of 1936, "The Storyteller": namely, the comparison between the construction of plot in a novel and the building of a fire in a fireplace.[20] Recommending Bennett's *Clayhanger* to Jula Radt-Cohn, as he did to a number of his friends, he comments memorably on the personal affinity he feels for the distinguished Edwardian novelist and critic:

In [Arnold Bennett] I increasingly come to recognize a man whose stance is very much akin currently to my own and who serves to validate it: that is to say, a man for whom a far-reaching lack of illusion[21] and a fundamental mistrust of where the world is going lead neither to moral fanaticism nor to embitterment but to an extremely cunning, clever, and subtle art of living. This leads him to wrest from his own misfortune the chances, and from his own wickedness the few respectable ways to conduct himself, that amount to a human life. (C, 423)

In addition to Bennett's infinitely detailed treatment of English provincial life, and the occasional detective novel, he was reading a German translation of the second volume of Trotsky's *History of the Russian Revolution*, about which he writes to Gretel Karplus in code, so as to foil the Berlin censors: "Of that prodigious novel of peasant life, which I began here last summer, I'm reading now the final volume, 'October,' where Kritrotz's mastery is perhaps even greater than in the first volume" (GB, 4:187). He followed this with Robert Louis Stevenson's *Dr. Jekyll and Mr. Hyde* in German translation. Later in the summer, he was "reading a hodgepodge of things. Even theology, for want of acceptable detective novels." The reference here was to three recent studies: a book on history and dogma, a book on the historical Jesus, and Lucien Febvre's *Un destin: Martin Luther*. After finishing the last, he wrote to Scholem (a sometime student of mathematics) in a modest display of theological humor: "I have now grasped for the fifth or sixth time in my life what is meant by justification through faith. But I have the same trouble here as I have with infinitesimal calculus: as soon as I have mastered it for a few hours, it vanishes again for just as many years" (BS, 76–77).

However restless and itinerant Benjamin had become during his adult years, he was still a Berliner who thrived on a dense network of friends, acquaintances, and intellectual allies and opponents. If the first stay on Ibiza had been a welcome interlude to metropolitan existence, his second stay introduced him to the personal and intellectual isolation he would feel for much of his remaining life. During the months on Ibiza in 1933, his only regular correspondents were Scholem, Gretel Karplus, and Kitty Marx-Steinschneider. Shortly after his arrival on the island in April, he had sent a picture postcard to Siegfried Kracauer, asking for news of the emigration scene. Having fled with his wife to France on February 28, Kracauer was now Paris correspondent for the *Frankfurter Zeitung*, in which Benjamin had just read his piece on the Swiss post-Jugendstil painter Augusto Giacometti (cousin of Alberto Giacometti). He received no word in reply from Kracauer that summer, as can be gathered from a comment he makes to Gretel Karplus some four months later in connection with what he takes to be his own lack of illusions about the chances of finding in Paris any real understanding for his work: "Not surprisingly, I've been informed of Krac's doings only by hearsay; perhaps what makes his case so especially difficult are . . . those deeply rooted illusions peculiar to him" (GB, 4:277). Letters from Scholem were arriving every two to three weeks that spring and during most of the summer, for which Benjamin remained grateful. There was talk once more of Benjamin's considering a move or at least a visit to Palestine. "The problem whether you (a) could, (b) should live here has often been discussed in the circle of your male and female admirers," Scholem tells him in late May, while encouraging him to participate in the discussion himself. Previous to this, Kitty Marx-Steinschneider had invited him to visit her and her husband in their new home in Rehovot, near Jaffa, and offered to pay his way there. Scholem remembers that Benjamin reacted very positively to such invitations but "always had reasons for holding back" (SF, 197). We know now that Scholem's letters painted no very promising picture of employment opportunities for a writer of Benjamin's stripe in Palestine. Already in March of that year he had remarked on the "clear impossibility of your making a living here," and in July he stated flatly: "We see no possibility of your finding work or an occupation here that would be even halfway suitable" (BS, 31, 65). The University of Jerusalem, largely dependent on American donors, had no funds for hiring, and although boatloads of workers from Europe were arriving daily, there was "precious little room for the academics" (BS, 33). Benjamin had written on June 16, by way of participating in the discussion about his coming to Palestine: "I have nothing and am attached to little." He says he would be "glad and fully prepared to come to Palestine" if he could be sure there was more room there than in Europe for "what I know and what I can do. . . . If there is not more [room], then there is less. . . . If I could improve upon my knowledge and my abilities there without abandoning what I have already accomplished, then I would not be the least bit indecisive in taking that step" (BS, 59–60). Scholem's response effectively closed the door on these doubtful speculations. Jerusalem was not a city like others where one could just live and work. "In the long run, only those people are able to live here who, despite all the problems . . . , feel completely at one with this land and with the cause of Judaism, and things are not always so easy for the new arrival, particularly for someone who occupies an intellectually progressive position. . . . My life here is possible only . . . because I feel devoted to this cause, even if in the face of despair and ruination. Otherwise, the suspect nature of a renewal that tends to manifest itself as mostly hubris and linguistic decay would have torn me apart long ago" (BS, 66). Benjamin wrote back, a bit defensively, that he had not for a moment looked on Palestine as "just another—more or less expedient—place for me to reside." But, he added without any evasion, "it is obvious that neither of us is prepared to investigate my 'solidarity with the cause of Zionism.' . . . The result of the investigation could only turn out to be completely negative" (BS, 71).[22] On neither side does the consideration for the other man quite hide the resentment—which, to be sure, never did serious harm to their friendship. In September, Scholem offered to take care of as many of Benjamin's things as he could manage, and his archive of Benjamin's writings was being continually expanded.

As if his immediate worries—lack of money, lack of prospects, lack of a home—were not enough, Benjamin was also faced with the very real problem of the expiration of his German passport. On July 1 he sailed to Mallorca, the largest of the Balearic Islands, in order to apply at the German consulate for a new passport. Since he knew that the provision of new papers to a self-exiled German Jew was anything but certain—he had heard that consular officials were, under some pretext, asking that passports be handed in and then refusing to return them—he undertook a small subterfuge and reported his old passport as lost, so that he would have some document for the worst case. The new passport was issued quickly, allaying his fears. Before returning to Ibiza he spent two days exploring Mallorca on foot and by car, getting to know the landscape, which he found less rich and less mysterious than that of Ibiza. He saw the mountain villages of Deya, "where the lemon and orange gardens are bearing fruit," and Valldemossa, "where the love story between George Sand and Chopin was played out in a Carthusian monastery"; also "palaces on cliffs in which an Austrian archduke lived forty years ago, writing very comprehensive but astonishingly unfounded books about the local chronicles of Mallorca" (GB, 4:257). He also visited with acquaintances, including his former colleague from *Die literarische Welt* Friedrich Burschell and the Austrian novelist and playwright Franz Blei, at a German writers' colony in the village of Cala Ratjada on the island. Although possible access to Blei's legendary library might have tempted Benjamin (he refers to it in a letter), he was resolute in his desire to return to Ibiza.

Benjamin's final months on the island—July, August, and September—saw him torn by conflicting emotions. His poverty, itinerant existence, and persistent illness were pushing him to the brink of desperation. As was so often the case, however, his desperation proved fruitful; out of it now came one of his most significant essays, "Experience and Poverty," written at some point during that summer. In two paragraphs at the beginning that were later adapted in the famous opening section of "The Storyteller," the essay offers a diagnosis of the present state of the culture, as viewed from the perspective of the "generation which from 1914 to 1918 had to experience some of the most monstrous events [*eine der ungeheuersten Erfahrungen*] in the history of the world." The diagnosis is sweeping: we are poorer in communicable experience, in the sort of experience that used to be passed down from generation to generation and that went to form a heritage. Spiritually if not materially, we have become impoverished. "We have given up one portion of the human heritage after another, and have often left it at the pawnbroker's for a hundredth of its true value, in exchange for the small change of 'the contemporary.' The economic crisis is at the door, and behind it is the shadow of the approaching war."[23] The outward signs of this bankruptcy and poverty of experience, ironically enough, bespeak the unprecedented development of technology and of the means of communication over the past hundred years. Benjamin refers to "the horrific mishmash of styles and ideologies produced during the last century," the surfeit of information and ideas that continues to swamp us, and the emergence of a culture divorced from experience or in which "experience is simulated or obtained by underhanded means."

One could read the essay's opening pages as a liberal variant of the critique of modernity issued by representatives of the "conservative revolution" in the teens and twenties. At this point, though, the essay turns the argument on its head and offers the assertion that has made it famous: from the new poverty springs not despair but a new barbarism. In the experience of poverty, the new barbarism starts from scratch and, as a countermeasure to the barren and adulterated, builds on the basis of the minimal. "Among the great creative spirits, there have always been the inexorable ones who begin by clearing a tabula rasa. . . . Such a constructor [*Konstrukteur*] was Descartes . . . Einstein, too." Many of "the best minds" among artists today have likewise turned for inspiration to "the naked man of the contemporary world who lies screaming like a newborn babe in the dirty diapers of the present." He mentions the writers Brecht, Scheerbart, and Gide; the painter Klee; and the architects Loos and Le Corbusier. These very different artists all approach the contemporary world with a "total absence of illusion about the age and at the same time [with] an unlimited commitment to it." Having adopted the cause of the fundamentally new, they are ready, if need be, "to outlive culture"—and they will do so with a laugh. Their laughter will have been a confirmation of their barbarism, but no less of their humanity. It is an inevitably "dehumanized" humanity, one that, with the strangely and delicately engineered figures of a Klee or a Scheerbart, has jettisoned "the traditional, solemn, noble image of man, festooned with all the sacrificial offerings of the past." The new minimalist image of humanity, arising at a point somewhere beyond the traditional distinction between tragedy and comedy, is grounded in "insight and renunciation," along with the spirit of play. Such an ethos is distinguished in principle from that of the powerful few *(wenigen Mächtigen)* who renounce nothing, and who are themselves even "more barbaric, but not in the good way."

The piece is full of echoes and anticipations of other works by Benjamin; his ruminations on the new glass-milieu, the storyteller, the collective dream, can be seen to draw together key motifs from *One-Way Street* and from studies of Brecht, Kraus, Scheerbart, Jugendstil, and the nineteenth-century bourgeois interior. In the space of a few pages, Benjamin draws on these diverse sources—and finally even on an interpretation of Mickey Mouse as a dream in which current conditions are overcome—all in order to imagine the new culture and new forms of experience that might arise from the new barbarism:[24]

> Nature and technology, primitiveness and comfort, have completely merged. And to people who have grown weary of the endless complications of everyday living and to whom the purpose of existence seems to have been reduced to the most distant vanishing point on an endless horizon, it must come as a tremendous relief to find a way of life in which everything is solved in the simplest and most comfortable way, in which a car is no heavier than a straw hat and the fruit on the tree becomes round as quickly as a hot-air balloon.

"Experience and Poverty" is one of Benjamin's most compelling portraits of the uncertain trajectories of modernity. And it was composed in surroundings that he cherished precisely for their archaic qualities. One can imagine him sitting in his lounge chair in the forest on the windy heights of Ibiza, spinning his utopian fable of a society that might one day arise on the ruins of a postfascist Europe.

These months brought him to the edge of poverty, but they also provided, paradoxically enough, the most intense erotic experience he had known since his separation from Asja Lacis. The time in Berlin after Asja's departure had not been spent in isolation, but none of his relationships—either with women of his own class or with the young demimondaines about whom Dora reported in the divorce proceedings—had turned into anything "serious." One of these relationships may have been with Gretel Karplus. Although everyone concerned acted as if the bond between Gretel and Adorno was exclusive, the letters Gretel and Benjamin exchanged in the months after his departure from Berlin sometimes suggest that an intimate relationship had grown up between them during their time together in Germany. The idea that she might break with Adorno is never raised, but the elaborate mechanisms developed to keep certain parts of their correspondence hidden from Teddie attest to a desire on both sides for an ongoing intimacy. This was of course Benjamin's favored form of erotic entanglement: as part of a complicated triangle, preferably with the love object already firmly attached elsewhere. And the time on Ibiza gave him the opportunity to further his experience in this arena.

During his first months away from Berlin, Benjamin was especially lonely. At the end of June, he wrote to Inge Buchholz—whom he seems to have met in Berlin in 1930, and about whom we know next to nothing, not even her maiden name—inviting her to leave for a while, or forever, the man she would later marry and come live with him on Ibiza at his expense (GB, 4:242–245; SF, 196). There is no indication she accepted his offer. But, at about the same time, he met the thirty-one-year-old Dutch painter Anna Maria Blaupot ten Cate, to whom the Noeggeraths' son Jean Jacques had introduced him.[25] Blaupot ten Cate had come to the island in late June or early July, after witnessing the book burning in Berlin on May 10. A love letter drafted in mid-August (but evidently not sent in this form) gives a good idea of Benjamin's feelings for the young woman:

> Dear one, I've just spent a whole hour on the terrace thinking about you. I haven't discovered or learned anything, but thought a great deal, and perceived that you fill up the darkness entirely, and out among the lights of San Antonio you were there again (we won't talk about the stars). In the past, when I've been in love, the woman to whom I felt bound was . . . the only woman on my horizon. . . . Now it's different. You are everything I've ever been able to love in a woman. . . . From your features arises all that makes a woman into guardian, mother, whore. You transform the one into the other, and to each you give a thousand forms. In your arms fate would forever cease to accost me. It could no longer catch me unawares with fear or happiness. The immense stillness that enfolds you hints at how far removed you are from that which claims you by day. It is in this stillness that the transformation of forms takes place. . . ./They play into one another like the waves. (GB, 4:278–279)

Benjamin's pet name for Blaupot ten Cate was "Toet," which meant both "face" and "dessert" or "sweet."[26] And, possibly to Benjamin's surprise, his feelings for her were returned. "I would like to be with you often," she wrote to him in June 1934, "and talk quietly with you, with few words, and also I believe we will now be something different to each other from what we were before. . . . You are more, much more to me than a good friend, you must know that too. Perhaps more than any man could be for me until now."[27] As Valero points out, Benjamin cut himself off from all other contact—both with his shrinking number of friends on the island and with his usual correspondents such as Scholem and Gretel Adorno—and gave himself over for the entire month of August to his new love. Emerging from the depths of hopelessness experienced in July, Benjamin was inspired to a new burst of creativity. He wrote at least two poems to Blaupot ten Cate that summer. And he planned an entire cycle of writings dedicated to her, with the provisional title "Story of a Love in Three Stations" (GS, 6:815). In connection with this plan, he produced two pieces: a story called "The Light," which he ultimately included in his (never published) "Stories from Solitude,"[28] and a text that is one of the most peculiar he ever wrote, the quasi-autobiographical, highly esoteric meditation "Agesilaus Santander"—of which there are two versions completed in Ibiza on two successive days in mid-August (SW, 2:712–716).

The curious title of the latter has associations both with the ancient Spartan king Agesilaos II, mentioned by Xenophon and Plutarch and represented in a tragedy by Corneille, and with the northern Spanish port town of Santander. According to Scholem, who after Benjamin's death discovered, edited, and devoted a detailed commentary to the text (which was probably not intended for publication), the title is above all an anagram of "Der Angelus Satanas" (The Angel Satan)—with a superfluous "i" that, as suggested more recently, can stand for "Ibiza."[29] The angel in "Agesilaus Santander" is a figure based explicitly on Klee's Angelus Novus, the aquarelle Benjamin acquired in 1921. Scholem was the first to notice the affinity between this angel, who, in the text's concluding image, retreats "inexorably" and by sudden starts (stoßweis) into the future from which he has come, and the famous allegory of the "angel of history" in section IX of Benjamin's last signed work, "On the Concept of History." In the two published versions of "Agesilaus Santander," this new angel comes to light by virtue of the author's "secret name," something given him at birth by his parents—this is Benjamin's fiction—so that, in the event he should become a writer, he would not immediately be recognized as a Jew (as he is in Europe with the name "Walter Benjamin"). In its tutelary capacity, the secret name gathers together the forces of life and wards off the uninitiated. (It is one of the horrible ironies of Benjamin's life story that confusion over his name would later permit his burial on Spanish soil and in consecrated ground—not confusion over any "secret" name, but a simple reversal of elements: his death is registered in Port Bou under the name "Benjamin Walter.")

In "Agesilaus Santander," the angel, as it were, steps out of the name, fully armored and on the attack, bereft of human features. At the essay's esoteric midpoint, Benjamin writes that the angel sends "his feminine aspect after the masculine one reproduced in the picture." This conception accords with a statement made in a letter of September 1 to Scholem (who, beyond this veiled allusion, never knew about Blaupot ten Cate): "I have met a woman here who is his [the Angelus's] female counterpart" (BS, 72–73). But this attack that is a gift only brings out the author's strength, namely, his patience— which, like the angel's wings, holds him steady in his song of praise for the woman. Speaking of himself, he says that whenever he was captivated by a woman, "he at once determined to lie in wait for her on her journey through life and to wait until she fell into his hands, ill, aged, and in ragged clothes. In short, nothing could overcome the man's patience." But it is not a matter of conquest. For "the angel resembles everything from which I have had to part: the people, and especially the things." The angel dwells in the lost things like a secret name and "makes them transparent." In doing so, he does not let the author out of his sight—the author himself is "a [gift-giver] who goes away empty-handed"—but draws him along with him on the retrospective passage to the future. In this pursuit that is a retreat, the angel wants only happiness. Such is the conclusion of the second, fuller version:

> He wants happiness—that is to say, the conflict in which the rapture of the unique, the new, the yet unborn is combined with that bliss of experiencing something once more, of possessing once again, of having lived. This is why he has nothing new to hope for on any road other than the road home, when he takes a new person with him. Just like myself; for scarcely had I seen you the first time than I returned with you to where I had come from.

If Benjamin had remarked on the "lack of illusions" that bound him to Arnold Bennett, "Agesilaus Santander" offers a more complex view of his situation in life: despite the recurrent need to retreat and renounce, an engagement with meaningful things, with certain people and experiences, is nonetheless still possible for him, if only by chance or even mishap. With Toet Blaupot ten Cate Benjamin felt the presence of all he had loved in women previously. In the advent of the new and unique, there was an originary return, a journeying back, if not exactly a homecoming. Characteristically for him, the "happiness" was in the waiting, understood as a kind of eddying in time and space.[30]

Blaupot ten Cate was soon to be married to a Frenchman, Louis Sellier, with whom, in 1934, she translated Benjamin's recently published essay "Hashish in Marseilles."[31] She also attempted, without success, to find work for her impecunious admirer with Dutch radio. Benjamin visited with the couple in Paris, where they lived for a while in 1934, and he stayed in touch with Toet through the following year. By November 1935 the relationship had evidently been broken off, though Benjamin could not resist drafting a last, possibly unsent letter in Paris on November 24, which begins by confessing that he cannot quite get it into his head that they're supposed to know nothing of each other (GB, 5:198). The relationships with Inge Buchholz and Toet Blaupot ten Cate, like that with Gretel Karplus, thus fit a pattern of ultimately failed pursuit within a love triangle, such as appears as well in the affairs with Asja Lacis (who was involved with Bernhard Reich) and Jula Cohn (when Benjamin himself was involved with Dora). Moreover, these lost loves all leave their trace in the little noticed sexual thematic of his work. When, in *The Arcades Project* and "Central Park," in a partly bitter-satirical allegorization of Baudelaire's personal habitus, Benjamin speaks of the "Via Dolorosa" of male sexuality, he is indirectly reflecting on the character of his own erotic experiences—and not least on those "stations" mentioned in the cycle for Toet, his own profane "cross" and "passion."[32]

Even during his love affair in the summer of 1933, Benjamin was moving from one improvised dwelling to another in a somewhat futile attempt to find tolerable living and working conditions on Ibiza—

and, above all, to reduce his expenditures to a viable minimum. Toward the end of June, he finally succeeded in quitting the Noeggeraths' noisy, drafty house in favor first of the cheapest and most desolate hotel room imaginable (he was paying one peseta per day; as he wrote, "the price indicates what the room looks like") and then of a room on the other side of the bay in San Antonio, the less developed side, where he had lived the year before and where he could work (in his lounge chair in the adjacent woods) without being disturbed by the hammering and blasting. By arrangement with the owner of a building still under construction, he took up residence—at no cost—in a finished room on the site where some furniture was being stored. The building, of which he was the sole occupant for a few weeks, had no windowpanes or plumbing but was within three minutes of the shore. It stood, in fact, next door to La Casita, the house Jean and Guyet Selz had rented in 1932. "By moving into these quarters," he tells Jula Radt-Cohn, "I have reduced what I need to live and my living expenses to a bare minimum, below which it would seem impossible to go. The fascinating thing about all this is that everything is quite habitable, and if I am lacking anything it is much more noticeable in the area of human relationships than in that of human comfort" (C, 423). The one exception to this lack of companionship was his next-door neighbor, a "very likeable young man who . . . is my secretary" (GB, 4:247).

Valero has unearthed a fascinating subplot to Benjamin's Ibizan story that concerns this evidently clever young man, a German named Maximilian Verspohl. Benjamin and Verspohl had met on the island during Benjamin's first visit in 1932 and had in fact left the island during that time and spent two days in Palma de Mallorca together (GB, 4:132). Verspohl returned to Ibiza with several friends from Hamburg in late spring 1933, moving into La Casita next door to Benjamin's room in the house under construction. Benjamin soon began socializing with the twenty-four-year-old Verspohl and his friends, eating frequently at La Casita, and taking part in a weekly sailing excursion. And Verspohl did in fact serve as Benjamin's "secretary" during these months: he was in possession of a typewriter and typed not only the essays and reviews that Benjamin sent to journals in Germany but a number of other writings as well, all of which were bundled off to Scholem to take their place in his growing archive. This would have seemed an ideal arrangement for Benjamin, until one remembers the numerous rumors that circulated through the islands regarding the presence of Nazi sympathizers and even spies among the recent visitors. Verspohl had presented himself in Ibiza as someone preparing for the study of law at a university; when he returned to Hamburg at the end of 1933, however, he immediately assumed a position in the SS as a staff sergeant. Benjamin had entrusted not just his writings but the series of pseudonyms under which he sought to cloak his identity to a German with Nazi sympathies and, presumably, solid connections to the party apparatus. Benjamin normally entered into new relationships with a high degree of vigilance. The fact that he let his guard down so quickly and on such a broad front, exposing not only himself but his intellectual production, may perhaps be taken as a symptom of the shocks his system had sustained in the months just past.

This cordial if incautious engagement with the young Germans next door was, however, not typical of him. During the summer months Benjamin began to sever his relationships to even his few close friends on the island. As we've seen, the ties that bound him to Felix Noeggerath had begun to fray soon after his arrival that spring. Now, in his final months on Ibiza, he also began to pull away from Jean Selz. Selz later traced the cooling in their relations back to a specific incident. When visiting the port town of Ibiza, Benjamin was in the habit of frequenting the Migjorn, the bar owned by Jean Selz's brother Guy. One night, he very uncharacteristically ordered a complicated "black cocktail" and downed the contents of the tall glass with much aplomb. He then accepted a challenge by a Polish woman to follow her lead and drink two shots of 148-proof gin in rapid succession. He managed to find his way out of the bar, his face impassive, but once outside he collapsed onto the sidewalk, from which he was soon helped up, with considerable difficulty, by Jean Selz. Although Benjamin declared that he wanted to go home immediately, Selz convinced him that he was in no condition to walk the nine miles to San Antonio and his room in the construction site. As it was, it took his friend the rest of the night to get Benjamin into a bed in the Selzes' house, which stood at the top of a steep hill on Conquista Street. When Selz awoke toward midday, Benjamin was gone, having left behind a note of apology and thanks. Although they continued to work intermittently on the French translation of the *Berlin Childhood*, things were not the same as before. "When I did see him again, I felt that something inside him had changed. He couldn't forgive himself for having given such a display, for which he no doubt felt genuine humiliation and, oddly enough, for which he seemed to reproach me."[33] Humiliation no doubt played a role here. But even more than the breach in his carefully maintained protective wall of courtesy, it was presumably the revelation, however momentary, of something like inner desperation that he could not forgive.

A few weeks after his trip to Mallorca, Benjamin's health took a downward turn. His afflictions began with a "very unpleasant" inflammation of sores on his right leg. Luckily for him, this problem announced itself while he was on a visit of a few hours to the town of Ibiza, where there happened to be a German doctor who treated him in his hotel room and who delighted in "painting daily pictures of my chances of dying, should a complication arise" (BS, 69). He was able to drag himself through the town on necessary errands but otherwise was stuck there at the end of July without books or papers, all of which were back in San Antonio. He took advantage of the situation, however, by continuing the translation of *Berlin Childhood* with Selz, who would walk down from Conquista Street every day to meet with him. Sometime during the first week in August he managed to return to San Antonio, but on August 22 he was back in Ibiza, where he had found lodgings for free, and was suffering not only from the inflammation on his leg but from toothache, exhaustion, and fever brought on by the great heat (about which he had earlier joked to Scholem, referring to the "August madness" that commonly strikes foreigners on the island). To the "ensemble of [his] torments" was added the loss of his favored writing instrument—his cherished, compulsively reacquired brand of fountain pen—exposing him to all the "inconveniences that, for me, come with a new, cheap, and unusable writing implement" (GB, 4:280). Also weighing on his mind at this time was the fate of his library back in Berlin. Earlier in the summer, Gretel Karplus had arranged for the transfer to Paris of the "archive" of his manuscripts from his Berlin apartment.[34] But he simply could not afford the cost of packing and shipping his books to Paris.

At the beginning of September, he was again bedridden with the leg inflammation. "I am living totally in the country, thirty minutes . . . from the village of San Antonio. Under such primitive conditions, the fact that you can hardly stand on your feet, hardly speak the native tongue, and in addition even have to work, tends to bring you up against the margins of what is bearable. As soon as I have regained my health, I will return to Paris" (BS, 72). He was without medical aid, his diet was "wretched," water was hard to get, the place was full of flies, and he was lying on "the worst mattress in the world" (BS, 76–77). But work he did. Although, as he mentions to Gretel Karplus, he lost at least two weeks of work time as a result of his poor health, he nonetheless completed several pieces in August and early September, including "On the Mimetic Faculty," "The Moon," the article on Wieland for the *Frankfurter Zeitung,* and "Agesilaus Santander." As this list makes clear, the first months of Benjamin's exile were already representative of what was to come: cut off from his normal milieu and its publishing opportunities, he was forced to accept almost any assignment that came his way. The article on the French writers and the piece on Wieland were in many respects make-work, and Benjamin was keenly aware of the time taken away from his main concerns. What is remarkable, given the constraints of exile, is his ability to produce such deeply personal and even esoteric pieces as "On the Mimetic Faculty," "Agesilaus Santander," and pivotal sections of his *Berlin Childhood*—to say nothing of the weighty pronouncements on modernity in "Experience and Poverty." It was no doubt his awareness of the mixed character of this production that led him to refer later to the "splendor and misery of that last summer on Ibiza" (BS, 140).

Paris was now beckoning, however somberly and ambiguously. At the end of July, Benjamin received a dispatch from the Comité d'aide et d'accueil aux victimes de l'antisémitisme en Allemagne, an organization founded in Paris the previous April under the patronage of Israel Lévi, chief rabbi of France, Baron Edmond de Rothschild, and others.

The letter, Benjamin tells Scholem, was an "official" invitation, "promising [him] free living quarters in a house that Baroness Goldschmidt-Rothschild has reserved in Paris for refugee Jewish intellectuals" (BS, 68). His friend and collaborator Wilhelm Speyer, who—though baptized—came from a Jewish banking family in Frankfurt, had evidently made use of his connections with the world of finance, and Benjamin looked on the invitation as "undoubtedly" implying "a more or less far-reaching introduction," though he did not suppose that on the economic front it represented anything more than "a mere breathing spell." He made formal application to the committee on August 8, mentioning that he had been advised that the house in Paris would be ready in mid-September, and asking that they notify him of their decision by the end of the month (GB, 4:272–273). On September 1 he wrote to Scholem that he was "facing [his] stay in Paris with the utmost reserve. The Parisians are saying: '*Les émigrés sont pires que les boches* [The émigrés are worse than the Krauts]'" (BS, 72). And to Kitty Marx-Steinschneider he later remarked: "You can perhaps best describe what is being done here by Jews and for Jews as negligent benevolence. It combines the prospect of alms—which is seldom realized—with the highest degree of humiliation" (C, 431). As it turned out, the housing reserved by the baroness was by no means free of charge, and a complex series of "oversights and delays" effectively put an end to these modest expectations.

Benjamin arrived in Paris on October 6, seriously ill and without immediate prospects for work. On the day of his departure from Ibiza, September 25 or 26, he had come down with a bad fever, and he made the journey to France under "unimaginable conditions." After checking into a cheap hotel, the Regina de Passy on the Rue de la Tour, in the otherwise expensive Sixteenth Arrondissement, he was diagnosed with malaria and treated with a course of quinine, which cleared his head while still leaving him quite weak. He wrote to Scholem on October 16, having scarcely left his bed for ten days: "I am faced here with as many question marks as there are street corners in Paris. Only one thing is certain, that . . . to try to make a French literary career my means of subsistence . . . would soon rob me of what's left of my no longer unlimited power of initiative. I would prefer any occupation . . . to whiling my time away in the editorial antechambers of the street tabloids" (BS, 82). By the end of the month he had nonetheless begun feeling out local contacts; he visited Léon Pierre-Quint, biographer of Proust and Gide, and came away with some glimmer of hope that the contact might eventually prove useful. "I avoid seeing Germans," he comments to Kitty Marx-Steinschneider; "I still prefer to speak with Frenchmen, who of course are hardly able or willing to do anything, but who have the considerable charm of not talking about their fate" (C, 431).

Concern for his own fate was more than enough. He reckoned his situation, and especially his failure initially to establish any sort of foothold in Paris, to be "desperate." For someone afflicted even at the best of times with profound melancholy, the waves of depression that overcame him now were "deep and well-founded"; they brought on states of indecisiveness that often bordered on paralysis. This sense of loss and isolation came to a preliminary crisis in early November when Gert Wissing, the wife of his cousin Egon, died in Paris. The Wissings had taken part in a number of Benjamin's experiments with hashish in Berlin (see OH, 63, for his description of Gert's dancing), and he counted them among his closest friends. He saw in Gert's death a portent of other fates, including perhaps his own: "She will be the first that we bury here in Paris, but hardly the last" (GB, 4:309).

His financial situation was, if anything, worse than it had been during the summer, if only because the cost of living in Paris was exponentially greater than that on Ibiza. A money order for 300 francs from Gretel Karplus, arriving in early November, momentarily set to rest the "anxieties that in recent days, despite my best efforts to counter them, have left me paralyzed" (GB, 4:309). The money was to be looked on as an advance on the sale of some of Benjamin's books in Berlin, a task that the generous and tactful "Felizitas" was taking in hand for her friend. Earlier in the summer she had wired him the money for a new suit from the tailor, and his thanks were affectionately couched in a wish to see her in Paris: "You know that I am indebted to you for so much that this letter would have been difficult to begin had I started it with an expression of gratitude. . . . Rather, I am hopeful that I will ambush you with my gratitude someplace in an out-of-the-way Parisian bistro when you are least expecting it. I will then see to it that I am not wearing the very suit you gave me and which may more readily provide me with the freedom to do many things other than express this gratitude" (C, 427). The playful irony cannot entirely conceal the suppressed humiliation of an independent spirit forced to live from hand to mouth, and from the crumbs his friends were able to send his way. Jean-Michel Palmier has portrayed the general situation of the exiles, emphasizing the demoralizing circumstances with which they were confronted on a daily basis:

> Without friends, papers or visa, without permission to stay or permit to work, they had to relearn how to live. In a world that often seemed strange and hostile, they felt completely infantilized. Unable to earn a living, abandoned to bureaucratic chicanery, they had to plead their cause to support committees, where these existed, line up at counters to obtain subsidies, papers, information, advice, wait for hours or whole days at consulates, commissariats, prefectures of police, to try to sort out the legal imbroglio that their very existence presented.[35]

With support from his friends, Benjamin moved into another hotel on October 26, the somewhat more reputable Palace on the Rue du Four, a stone's throw from the Boulevard Saint-Germain and steps away from the Flore and the Deux Magots, the literary cafés that he had frequented in more prosperous times. From his window he could see one of the towers of St. Sulpice, "above and behind which the weather habitually speaks its own language" (GB, 4:340). He resided in the hotel until March 24 and was able to return to work, at least sporadically. His emotional state did not prevent him from completing a new (unspecified) section of the *Berlin Childhood*, nor from arranging for a publication with Willy Haas, the former editor of *Die literarische Welt* who was now running a (short-lived) literary weekly in Prague, *Die Welt im Wort*. "Experience and Poverty" appeared on December 7 in this émigré journal, followed the next week by Benjamin's pregnant note—actually, a response to a questionnaire—on a popular work by a great moralist and humorist of the age of Goethe, "J. P. Hebel's *Treasure Chest of the Rhenish Family Friend*" (Benjamin's last published piece on Hebel [GS, 2:628]). For neither publication was Benjamin ever paid, which was as he feared it would be from the moment he accepted the commissions. In mid-November Benjamin published two pieces under a pseudonym in the *Frankfurter Zeitung*, his last remaining German publishing venue. (His final contribution to the newspaper would appear in June 1935.) The first of these was a review of a German-language anthology of German literature for Norwegian high schools, "German in Norway" (GS, 3:404–407), in which—without glancing at the possible political implications of such a volume (whose subtitle was *Die Meister* [The Masters])—he stresses the importance of the unpretentious popular culture of a nation *(das Volkstum)* as the foundation on which its classic art rests. This review was followed three days later by a feuilleton piece, "Thought Figures" *(Denkbilder)*, which employs the format of outwardly discontinuous meditative vignettes that was his forte (SW, 2:723–727).

While Benjamin saw his constant trolling for even the slightest journalistic possibilities as the inevitable consequence of his exile, he knew that the income from these endeavors could only provide him with what amounted to pocket money. It was for this reason that a series of meetings with Max Horkheimer in Paris that autumn could become the key to a continuing existence in exile. His position as a principal contributor to the work of the Institute of Social Research was firmly established in these meetings. The institute had been founded at the Johann Wolfgang Goethe Universität in Frankfurt in 1923 through a donation from the businessmen Hermann and Felix Weil.[36] The first director, Carl Grünberg, was an Austro-Marxist, that is, a Marxist who understood that revolutionary changes in the social structure were contingent upon attaining an absolute majority in a parliamentary democracy.[37] Under Grünberg, the institute and its staff carried out research on orthodox Marxist topics: the history of socialism and the workers' movement. When Grünberg suffered a stroke in 1928, his principal assistant, Friedrich Pollock, became acting director. In 1931 Max Horkheimer was named director of the institute and, at the same time, was named to a chair in social philosophy donated by Felix Weil. Horkheimer (1895–1973) was born into a wealthy Jewish industrial family in Zuffenhausen, near Stuttgart. Unlike most of Benjamin's friends and colleagues from similar backgrounds, he left high school early in order to enter his family's business. He completed an apprenticeship in his father's factory and an internship at a related firm in Brussels before becoming assistant director of the family business in 1914. After brief service at the end of World War I, he withdrew from the firm and rapidly completed the remainder of gymnasium and a university program in Frankfurt in psychology and philosophy, earning his doctorate in philosophy in 1922 with a dissertation entitled "The Antinomy of Teleological Judgment." Horkheimer was by this time the favorite student of Hans Cornelius, the ordinarius for philosophy at Frankfurt, and he became his assistant—a position in a German university somewhere between assistant professor and advanced graduate student. It was in this capacity that Horkheimer, in 1924, had read Benjamin's habilitation thesis on the *Trauerspiel* for Cornelius and contributed to its rejection. Horkheimer successfully submitted his own habilitation thesis (Kant's *Critique of Judgment* as a Connecting Link between Theoretical and Practical Philosophy) in 1925.

When Horkheimer was named director of the Institute of Social Research in 1931, he arrived with a fully articulated research program. In his acceptance address he emphasized that the institute would take a different direction under his leadership. He was determined to use the institute's considerable research and publishing potential to foster interdisciplinary study of the relations between economics, psychology, sociology, history, and culture. The journal *Zeitschrift für Sozialforschung* was established in 1932 as the main publishing organ of this new research effort. Horkheimer assembled a group of young intellectuals around the journal, including Adorno, the literary sociologist Leo Löwenthal, the social psychologist Erich Fromm, and the philosopher and literary historian Herbert Marcuse— names we associate today with the Frankfurt School. Also in 1932, Horkheimer established a branch of the institute in Geneva in order to gain access to the vast statistical archive (focused on the market economics of the industrialized world) at the International Labor Office. As Horkheimer later admitted, he also established the office as a "kind of emergency and evasion headquarters in a neighboring land still under the rule of law."[38] Horkheimer's prescient guidance enabled the institute to resume its work with relatively little disruption when both he and Adorno were dismissed from their teaching positions at Frankfurt in 1933, and when, in May of the following year, he departed for New York.

The years to come, during which Benjamin cemented his position as one of the institute's central contributors on cultural matters, were to see a gradual change from commissioned articles, such as those on the French writers and on the socialist scholar and art collector Eduard Fuchs, to pieces that Benjamin himself suggested. By the time of his meetings with Horkheimer he had not yet started the promised essay on Eduard Fuchs, but he had met with Fuchs himself (who immigrated to Paris in 1933) and been impressed: "He is a remarkable person, who inspires reverence and allows you to imagine what the men who were Social Democrats at the time of the Anti-Socialist Laws [1878–1890] must have been like" (BS, 90). Another article commissioned by Horkheimer was begun in December and finished by the first week in April; this was the review essay on recent developments in the philosophy of language, which appeared in the *Zeitschrift für Sozialforschung* in early 1935 under the title "Problems in the Sociology of Language." The article surveys recent developments in French and German linguistics, concluding, as Benjamin says in letters, just at the point where his own theory begins, that is, with the problem of a "physiognomics of language"—something grounded in the mimetic capability of the living body—effectively transcending the model of language as instrument. Although this essay was long held to be a rather neutral and perfunctory survey of then current directions in the sociology of language, more recent research has uncovered connections between the work of several of the linguists treated here and Benjamin's own thinking on the subject.[39] Several shorter reviews were presumably arranged for Benjamin during these meetings with Horkheimer as well.

A tip from his former wife, Dora, with whom he was regularly corresponding now, led Benjamin to make inquiries of Scholem regarding a newly established publishing house run by a Russian-born woman, Shoshana Persitz, in Tel Aviv. But Scholem dissuaded him from writing her: "A [Hebrew] translation of your essays . . . will not interest the circle of readers in question, since [these essays] occupy a position far too advanced. . . . If you should want at some point to write for such readers, you would have to express yourself in a completely different way, which could be very productive" (BS, 87). However productive a radical simplification and change of focus might or might not have been for Benjamin's work, it was no doubt statements such as this that convinced Benjamin he had no future in Palestine. But he took the counsel good-naturedly and thanked his friend for saving him from unnecessary bother.

His first commission from a French newspaper, the Communist weekly *Monde*, came late in 1933, presumably through the mediation of Alfred Kurella, who was on the editorial staff of the paper. The subject was Baron Haussmann, the prefect of the Seine under Napoleon III and the man largely responsible for the radical renovation and "strategic embellishment" of the city of Paris in the mid-nineteenth century. Kurella left the newspaper in January 1934, after which support for the projected article evidently dried up, for it was never written (see C, 437). But Haussmann, from this point on, was never far from Benjamin's mind: he plays an important role in *The Arcades Project* (Convolute E), and he is also the subject of a short review Benjamin wrote for the *Zeitschrift für Sozialforschung* in 1934. Benjamin's research on Haussmann and on recent sociolinguistics took him once again to the imposing environs of the Bibliothèque Nationale, where he worked in the famous reading room "as on the set of an opera" (GB, 4:365). The library was to become the real center of his activities in Paris in the coming years. "I was amazed," he writes on December 7, "how quickly I found my way back into the complicated catalogue system of the Bibliothèque Nationale" (BS, 90). It was the research on Haussmann that initiated, in early 1934, the second phase of work on *The Arcades Project*, the sociologically accentuated phase that lasted until his flight from Paris in June 1940 (see GB, 4:330). Characteristically, though, Benjamin felt himself unable to carry on with the writing of the "voluminous and meticulous manuscript" until he had first obtained, from Gretel Karplus, blocks of the same notebook paper on which he had started the project; only in this way could he "maintain its external uniformity."

Benjamin studiously avoided contact with all but a small number of Germans in Paris. It is not that he lacked opportunities. A number of informal centers of intellectual exchange for German refugee intellectuals emerged during the years of exile, including the Café Mathieu and the Café Mephisto on the Boulevard Saint-Germain and the Deutscher Klub, whose habitués included Heinrich Mann,

Hermann Kesten, Brecht, Joseph Roth, Klaus Mann, Alfred Döblin, and Lion Feuchtwanger. Yet Benjamin was isolated by his antipathy for the Social Democratic politics of some of these writers, and still more isolated by his preference for one-to-one dialogue with a small group of peers—Brecht, Kracauer, Adorno, and (more rarely now) Ernst Bloch.

With the arrival of Brecht and his collaborator Margarete Steffin in late October or early November, the situation changed for a while. Brecht and Steffin (who were lovers) checked into the Palace Hôtel, where Benjamin was staying, and for the next seven weeks there were lively exchanges between the two men on a regular basis. Benjamin wrote to Gretel Karplus on November 8, employing the shorthand necessary with letters to Germany: "Berthold, whom I see every day, often for long periods, is making an effort to contact publishers on my behalf. Yesterday, Lotte [Lenya] and her husband [Kurt Weill] suddenly showed up at his side" (GB, 4:309). Other émigré Germans, arriving in November and December, were soon incorporated into the extended circle of the intellectually voracious "Berthold," Siegfried Kracauer, Klaus Mann, the playwright and novelist Hermann Kesten, and Brecht's collaborator Elisabeth Hauptmann, the last having just escaped Germany after being held for a week and interrogated by the Gestapo. Brecht and Steffin were working on Threepenny Novel (published 1934), the manuscript of which they gave Benjamin to read.[40] Steffin also found time to help Benjamin assemble the set of letters that was to become Deutsche Menschen (German Men and Women). Brecht voiced strong support for Benjamin's study of Baron Haussmann. In addition, Benjamin and Brecht made preliminary notes and drafts toward a previously floated plan for a detective novel, which, however, never advanced beyond the planning stage.[41]

Shortly before Brecht's arrival in Paris, Benjamin had written that "my accord with Brecht's production represents one of the most important and most defensible points of my entire position" (C, 430). He never wavered in this sentiment, though he was ready enough to acknowledge what Gretel Karplus had called the "great danger" attendant on his susceptibility to the poet's influence; her misgiving was shared even more passionately by Adorno and Scholem. Benjamin's friends were worried—for very different reasons—about the effect of what Brecht himself called his "crude thought" *(plumpes Denken)* on the intricacies of Benjamin's mind and work. Disregarding the enormous subtlety of Brecht's writing—a body of work that has had a greater effect on the German language than that of any writer since Goethe—Benjamin's friends feared that his own subtlety would be sacrificed at the altar of an orthodox, engaged Marxism. These direct assaults on his choice of friends provoked a revealing response from Benjamin. "In the economy of my existence, a very few relationships do indeed occupy a pole that is opposed to the pole of my original being." These relationships were extremely "fruitful." Benjamin goes on, in this letter from June 1934, to assure Karplus: "You in particular are by no means unaware of the fact that my life no less than my thought moves in extreme positions. The amplitude which it maintains by doing so, the freedom to juxtapose things and ideas that are supposed to be incompatible, depends for its specific manifestation on danger [*erhält ihr Gesicht erst durch die Gefahr*]. A danger that in general, and also in the eyes of my friends, appears only in the form of these 'dangerous' relationships" (GB, 4:440–441). Benjamin was as ready as his friends were unready for the juxtaposition of "extreme positions" in his thought. It is in part this very instability, this resistance to the fixed and doctrinaire, that gives his writing the exciting, "living" quality that has engaged several generations of readers.

This concern of others to direct his loyalties was nothing new in Benjamin's life. His former wife and some of his closest friends had seen a similar danger of susceptibility in his relationships to Fritz Heinle and Simon Guttmann and had tried to get Benjamin to open his eyes to these putative dangers. His friends clearly recognized in Benjamin an identificatory impulse, a tendency to merge in some degree his own personality and thought patterns with those of another. Far from a disadvantage, this mimetic capability and open-eyed embrace of "danger" were enabling factors in many of Benjamin's greatest essays: his venturesome identification with Goethe, Kafka, and finally Baudelaire yielded insights that might not have been forthcoming otherwise.

When Brecht and Margarete Steffin left for Denmark on December 19, having invited their friend to join them there, Benjamin was deeply dejected:

The town seems dead to me, now that Brecht is gone. He would like me to follow him to Denmark. Life is supposed to be cheap there. But I am horrified by the winter, the travel costs, and the idea of being dependent on him and him alone. Nevertheless, the next decision I can bring myself to make will take me there. Life among the émigrés is unbearable, life alone is no more bearable, and a life among the French cannot be brought about. So only work remains, but nothing endangers it more than the recognition that it is so obviously the final inner mental resource (it is no longer an external one). (BS, 93–94)

Although Brecht's presence in Paris at this time was relatively brief, it activated a broad network of contacts for Benjamin, many with Communists. Some new acquaintances, such as the Soviet journalist and writer of screenplays Mischa Tschesno-Hell, remained intermittent contacts; others, such as Kurt Kläber, he had already known in Berlin. Kläber had been on the editorial board of the important left journal *Die Linkskurve* (Left-Hand Curve) in the Weimar Republic; in the spring of 1933 he tried to establish, together with Brecht and Bernard von Brentano, a colony for leftist artists in the Swiss canton of Tessin. The renewed contact with Brecht also awakened hopes that some of Benjamin's work might appear in Communist journals. Elisabeth Hauptmann suggested that the essay on French writers would be a valuable addition to the journal *Littérature et Revolution*, which appeared in French, German, English, and Russian; Benjamin urged Brecht to press the matter with his friend Michail Kolzow, a journalist and publisher who occupied prominent positions in party publishing venues. Like so many of Benjamin's approaches to Russian publications, this one had no effect. Mid-December brought other literary losses: on the fourteenth, a new law organizing all journalism in the Third Reich took effect, formalizing the creation in November of the Reichsschriftumskammer, the governmental "chamber" that all German writers were required to join. In the months to come, Benjamin weighed the advantages (a potential gain in publishing outlets) against the disadvantages (a potentially dangerous revelation of his whereabouts) of joining this writers' union and ultimately decided against it. His fear now was that the establishment of this agency would mean still further reductions in his opportunities to publish.

By the turn of the new year, it was increasingly clear to Benjamin that Paris itself presented difficulties to which he had no solution. His life in the city had previously been shaped to a large degree by the presence of friends such as Hessel and Münchhausen—and by sufficient funds to permit him access not just to Parisian cultural life but to its demimonde. His situation in early 1934 could hardly have been more different. Paris itself was dramatically changed. Anxiety was on the rise in France regarding war with a Germany that was increasingly unwilling to honor the limitations placed on it after World War I. And Paris was reeling from the shock of sudden waves of immigrants from Germany, many of them professionals and intellectuals looking for work alongside or even supplanting French citizens. The first wave of refugees had been composed mainly of intellectuals and leftist opponents of the Hitler regime. The aid committees that had been set up estimated that as many as 7,300 refugees had come to France by May 1933; that number would reach 30,000 in 1939. As Manès Sperber put it, "I loved a city whose inhabitants paraded their heart of gold in their songs and street cries, while at the same time they were astonishingly proud of their professed anti-Semitism."[42] Moreover, France itself was by no means immune to Europe's swing toward the radical right. Benjamin was provided with unmistakable evidence of this on the night of February 4. Watching from his window in the Palace Hotel, he saw violent confrontations on the Boulevard Saint-Germain between the police and groups of armed protesters from various right-wing organizations—the Action Française, Croix-de-feu, and Jeunesses Patriotes—who sought to prevent the formation of a left-liberal government under Daladier.

Most of Benjamin's friends and relatives were, of course, dealing with their own exile miseries. Wilhelm Speyer was in Switzerland, but Benjamin was in the process of breaking with him, embittered by Speyer's refusal or inability to deliver Benjamin's share of the proceeds from the detective play they had written together in Poveromo. Siegfried Kracauer and Ernst Schoen were a bit better off, since both had managed to obtain positions providing steady if minimal income: Kracauer as the Paris correspondent of the *Frankfurter Zeitung*, Schoen as a contributor to the BBC, albeit on a temporary basis. Egon Wissing was back in Berlin, grieving the death of his wife and suffering from the addiction to morphine he had shared with her. Others, such as Alfred Cohn, who was living in Barcelona, had managed to bring some small capital with them. Still others, including Ernst Bloch, seemed to have disappeared altogether; Benjamin didn't hear from him for months after Hitler's accession to power, when Bloch and his third wife fled to Switzerland. And still others, including Gretel Karplus; Benjamin's former wife, Dora, and son, Stefan; and his brother, Georg, all seemed trapped in Germany. Gretel Karplus was unable to obtain a passport after a series of decrees issued in July 1933 had classified her and her family as "Eastern Jews," "although Papa," she wrote him, "has lived in the Prinzenallee [in Berlin] for 47 years, and his father was a major industrialist in Vienna!" (GB, 4:331n). His brother, Georg, had been released from the Sonnenburg concentration camp, but he refused to flee Germany—and Benjamin knew very well that he would soon take up his illegal party-organizing work again. "It is horrible," Benjamin wrote to Gretel Adorno in the spring, "how people are strewn about everywhere" (GB, 4:433).

Benjamin was thus left without a single close friend in Paris. "I have hardly ever been as lonely as I am here," he wrote to Scholem in January. "If I were seeking opportunities to sit in a café with émigrés, they would be easy to find. But I avoid them" (C, 434). Intellectual isolation and material hardship remained the keynotes of his existence in Paris. The city was far too expensive for someone forced to live on the money that trickled in from writing and on small amounts received from friends. Adorno, Karplus, and Scholem were tireless in their efforts to seek out patrons and other sources of support, but these efforts usually bore no fruit. There were simply too many penniless exiles and not enough sources of income. He was thus forced to move to ever cheaper hotels and to eat at ever cheaper restaurants, amid fears of a recurrence of the malnutrition and attendant illnesses that had all but incapacitated him on Ibiza. Yet he had no other place to go. And, unlike some of the exiles, he had no illusions about the duration of the Nazi regime: he knew that his expatriation would be of long duration, if not permanent. It was in fact the beginning of a Parisian exile that would, with a few interruptions, extend to the end of Benjamin's life.

Bereft of friends and funds, he struggled against the temptation to give in to depression and confine himself to his room—but he was not always successful. He reports that he lay in bed for days on end "simply in order to need nothing and to see no one," while working as well as he could (GB, 4:355). On better days he wandered into Sylvia Beach's bookshop and lingered over the portraits and autographs of British and American writers; he visited the stalls of the bouquinistes along the Seine and was able, occasionally, to revert to habits so old that they had become "foggy" and buy a choice book; he strolled the boulevards as a latter-day flâneur; and he longed for the warmer weather of the spring, when he might recover the "equanimity and health" that would allow him to walk "with my accustomed thoughts and observations in the Luxembourg Gardens" (GB, 4:340). If he was trapped by day, his imagination was liberated at night in dreams that had a recondite political import. "In these times, when my imagination is preoccupied with the most unworthy problems between sunrise and sunset, I experience at night, more and more often, its emancipation in dreams, which nearly always have a political subject. . . . [These dreams] represent a pictorial atlas of the secret history of National Socialism" (BS, 100).

Remarkably enough, given his paralyzing depressions, he persevered in his attempts to forge a bridgehead in France. In this he was fully mindful, he told Scholem, of the sentiments expressed in one of the passages in Goethe's *Maxims and Reflections:* "Once burned, a child avoids the fire; an oft-scorched old man avoids even warming himself up" (GB, 4:344). For all that, he began to burden even the smallest opportunities in France with his hopes. Although he had yet to place a single essay with a French journal, he made contact with a translator, Jacques Benoist-Méchin, who agreed to translate pieces as they were needed. His letters from the early spring of 1934 were filled with plans for a series of talks on the most advanced German literature, to be delivered in French—subscription lectures that he was to hold at the home of the prominent gynecologist and Communist Jean Dalsace. Aside from the fees they would have brought, Benjamin hoped they might bring him into contact with the French intellectual scene. The talks would have included an introduction on the German reading public and individual lectures on Kafka, Bloch, Brecht, and Kraus. He plunged into the research and writing for the lectures, peppering his letters to his friends with requests for material. The opening lecture would have included not just remarks on antifascist tendencies but a stinging critique of the positions taken by the great Expressionist writer Gottfried Benn. Following the Nazi seizure of power, Benn had assumed the position of acting chair of the Prussian Academy of the Arts, a position left open by Heinrich Mann's precipitate flight from Germany; a declaration of loyalty to the new state was soon demanded of the academy's members. Although there is evidence that Benn's views on Hitler and Nazism were not unambiguous, he nonetheless published a series of essays in support of the regime, beginning with the notorious declaration "The New State and the Intellectuals." As the day of Benjamin's first lecture approached, printed invitations were sent out—but the lectures never took place. Dalsace fell seriously ill and was forced to cancel the entire series.

Benjamin also approached a number of leading intellectuals on his own. He visited Jean Paulhan, the editor of the *Nouvelle Revue Française*, and suggested a piece, in French, on the matriarchal theories of the Swiss anthropologist and jurist Johann Jakob Bachofen (1815–1887). Paulhan's expression of interest in the proposed topic led to much research, a completed essay . . . and a polite but firm rejection. This episode reveals Benjamin's growing confidence in his written French. Earlier in the year he had told Gretel Karplus that his first French-language piece—now lost—contained, according to a native speaker, only a single error. Other approaches—to the professor of German literature Ernest Tonnelat, to the essayist and critic Charles Du Bos, and to the editor of a new French encyclopedia—yielded not even anything so definite as a rejection. Benjamin's difficult transition to the French intellectual scene was typical for intellectual refugees from Germany. They got a generally sympathetic reception from their counterparts in France, and especially from the writers who have been described as the "Rive Gauche": Gide, Malraux, Henri Barbusse, Paul Nizan, Jean Guéhenno, and others.[43] Yet even here the Germans were held at arm's length, invited to cafés and gatherings at bookshops but rarely to dinner in a French home.

Benjamin's attempts to find venues for his work outside France met with disappointment as well. He had yet to be paid for a number of pieces, while others languished in German publishing houses, never to be seen again. Even his friends failed to fulfill their obligations: Willy Haas had never paid him for the pieces published in *Die Welt im Wort,* which had folded and declared bankruptcy in Prague, and Wilhelm Speyer continued to withhold the royalties from the detective play they had written together in 1932. It is a telling sign of the depredations of exile that a relatively small sum—10 percent of the profits from production of a moderately successful play—led Benjamin to consider legal action against an old friend. A noteworthy project intended for the *Zeitschrift für Sozialforschung* fell prey not to rejection but to Benjamin's unwillingness to complete it. He devoted months to the preparation of this "retrospective recapitulation of the cultural politics of *Die neue Zeit,"* the newspaper that was the ideological organ of Germany's Social Democratic Party (BS, 139); he hoped to "demonstrate for once how collective literary products are particularly suited to materialist treatment and analysis and, indeed, can be rationally evaluated only when treated in such a way" (C, 456). Though he mentioned the proposed article in nearly every letter he wrote in the late summer and early fall, the project simply petered out. At Benjamin's instigation, Scholem had asked Moritz Spitzer, editor of the Schocken Library (a series of small, somewhat popular volumes with a largely German Jewish readership), to solicit "one or more small books" from Benjamin (BS, 106). This plan foundered, too, as the German exchange office soon stopped all payments to Schocken authors living abroad.

His ongoing attempts to place *Berlin Childhood around 1900* were a source of particular frustration. Klaus Mann considered publishing some of the pieces in his exile journal *Die Sammlung* early in the year, but this came to nothing. A ray of hope broke through when he received an enthusiastic letter about the manuscript from Hermann Hesse. Hesse was not confident of his ability to help, however: "I have been spared by accident from the book burnings, etc. etc. and am a Swiss citizen; no one has undertaken anything against me aside from private verbal abuse, but my books are receding further and further into the background and are becoming covered with dust, and I'm re-signed to the fact that this will no doubt last for a very long time. Yet I have learned from letters that a thin layer of readers nonetheless still exists for the likes of us" (quoted in GB, 4:364n). Hesse approached two publishers, S. Fischer and Albert Langen, in an effort to find a home for the *Berlin Childhood.* His efforts ultimately bore no fruit, but Benjamin was gratified by the prominent novelist's support. An-other attempt to place the text led to renewed vexation with Scholem. Adorno had recommended the *Berlin Childhood* to Erich Reiss, the publisher of a Jewish press in Berlin. Benjamin thus wrote to Scholem, requesting a kind of letter of reference that could explain the "Jewish aspects" of the book (BS, 102). This of course touched on the sorest point of their friendship—Benjamin's relation to Judaism—and Scholem's reply is characteristically prickly and reproachful:

> I detest Herr Reiss, a fat Berlin-W[est] Jew, half jobber, half snob, and I am not very charmed by the prospect you raise of my intervening with him. On the other hand, it is also unclear to me whether he has read your book or whether the whole thing is just Herr Wiesengr-und's idea. That Reiss is vigorously riding the Zionist wave is well known. . . . It is utterly unclear to me how you imagine that I—acting as the "expert"—could possibly discover Zionist elements in your book, and you will have to lend me a real hand with a list of hints. The only "Jewish" passage in your manuscript was the one I urgently asked you to leave out at the time,[44] and I don't know how you imagine what the procedure will be if you are unable to add sec-tions that are directly relevant in *content,* not just inspired by some metaphysical *posture* which will certainly leave Herr Reiss utterly indifferent. You unfortunately also considerably overestimate my wisdom when you assume I could make your book's "Jewish aspect," which is very obscure to me, clear to a publisher. By the way, I don't know Herr Reiss personally. It goes without saying that, were the publishing house to turn to me *of its own initiative,* I would make every possible effort on your behalf—of that I can assure you—but I must, with a certain skepticism, leave it up to you whether you think it advisable to propose me as a prospective "authority." (BS, 106–107)

Although he proved himself a loyal friend again and again during Benjamin's exile, Scholem consistently refused to do anything that might compromise his own position vis-à-vis other Jewish intellectuals—even in so harmless a situation as this, in which he had no respect for the recipient of any letter he might write. Here, too, the effort to place Benjamin's book came to nothing.

Not all of his literary efforts were frustrated, however. He finished the long review essay he had begun on Ibiza, "Problems in the Sociology of Language," for the *Zeitschrift für Sozialforschung,* and received a small honorarium. He also published several short pieces, some signed with the pseudonym K. A. Stempflinger, in the *Frankfurter Zeitung:* a review of Max Kommerell's book on Jean Paul, a review of two books by Ivan Bunin, and a collective review of new work on Goethe. And in the spring of 1934 he produced two of his most important essays, "The Author as Producer" and "Franz Kafka." "The Author as Producer" was first published twenty-six years after Benjamin's death; the manuscript indicated that it was delivered as a lecture at the Institute for the Study of Fascism in Paris on April 27. This institute, whose members included Arthur Koestler and Manès Sperber, had been founded by Oto Bihalji-Merin and Hans Meins in late 1933. As a research group controlled by the Comintern but financed by French workers and intellectuals, the institute sought to gather and disseminate information and documentation on fascism. Benjamin's talk, one of his most trenchant analyses of the relations between literary form and politics, would have fit well within this program; whether it was ever delivered remains a mystery.

"The Author as Producer" examines the relation between a literary work's political tendency and its aesthetic quality; political tendentiousness has long been held to limit the aesthetic quality of a work. Yet Benjamin starts by proposing that "a work that exhibits the correct [political] tendency must of necessity have every other quality." Far from a doctrinaire call for an overtly politicized literature, Benjamin's essay attempts to rethink the political tendency of a work in terms of its literary quality: "I would like to show you that the tendency of a literary work can be politically correct only if it is also literarily correct. That is to say, the political tendency includes a literary tendency. And I would add straightaway: this literary tendency, which is implicitly or explicitly contained in every correct political tendency of a work, alone constitutes the quality of that work" (SW,

2:769). Benjamin turns the notion of tendentiousness inside out by re-thinking the work's formal qualities—its "literary technique"—in terms of their relationship to the prevailing social relations of production. The question of correct "tendency" is thus seen to turn on the place of the work in the "literary relations of production of its time": does the work's technique represent progress or regression? Benjamin is thinking here not so much of individual techniques within a genre—the modernist manipulation of narrative perspective, say—as of the wholesale recasting of the institution of literature: its genres and forms, its capacity for translation and commentary, and even such apparently marginal aspects as its suitability for plagiarism.

At the center of the essay is a long quotation that is not quite plagiarism: it is Benjamin citing himself as a "left wing author." This quotation offers the daily newspaper as the best example of his claim. The bourgeois press, on this reading, responds to the reader's insatiable, impatient demand for information by opening more and more venues for that reader to give voice to his concerns: letters to the editor, opinion pieces, signed protests. Readers thus become collaborators and, at least in the Soviet press, producers. "For there the reader is at all times ready to become a writer—that is, a describer, or even a prescriber. As an expert—not perhaps in a discipline but perhaps in a post that he holds—he gains access to authorship. Work itself has its turn to speak" (SW, 2:771). Returning to issues he explored as early as *One-Way Street* in the mid-1920s, Benjamin now asserts that "literary competence" emerges more surely from "polytechnical education" than from any literary specialization. The newspaper—"the scene of the limitless debasement of the word"—paradoxically offers itself as a stage for the "literarization of the conditions of living." This is one of Benjamin's most enigmatic formulas. It encapsulates the complex idea that modern life is susceptible to analysis and finally to change only as it is rendered in very specific textual forms. If Benjamin in *One-Way Street* had called for a "prompt language" that alone could be equal to the moment, he here calls for a much vaster reconceptualization of all forms of writing—as production. Only such a revolutionary development, with its roots in the international constructivism he had encountered in the early 1920s, can master "the otherwise insoluble antinomies."

From this theoretical base Benjamin returns to the central problem of the relationship of class affiliation and literary production, a problem that had occasioned raging debates in the Weimar Republic. In "The Author as Producer," he addresses the problem through a critical annihilation of what he calls the "so-called left wing intellectuals." Benjamin savagely rejects the compromises of such writers as Döblin and Heinrich Mann, for whom socialism is "freedom, a spontaneous union of people . . . humanity, tolerance, a peaceful disposition." Their politics, little more than a thinly veiled humanist idealism, had furnished no resistance to fascism; finding a place beside the proletariat was nothing more than tepid moral support. Such "political tendency, however revolutionary it may seem, has a counterrevolutionary function so long as the writer feels his solidarity with the proletariat only in his attitudes, not as a producer." And he returns to a bête noire first trotted out in "Little History of Photography," the photographer Albert Renger-Patzsch, whose photo-book *Die Welt ist schön* (The World Is Beautiful) had remade the genre in 1928. On Benjamin's reading, Renger-Patzsch's photographs fail to reproduce a tenement or garbage dump without "transfiguring" it. Dire poverty is made an object of aesthetic pleasure. And so an apparently progressive photographic practice serves only to "renew from within—that is, fashionably—the world as it is."

In Benjamin's essay, the positive model of an effective artistic practice is provided by Brecht, and in particular by Brecht's notion of "refunctioning" or functional transformation *(Umfunktionierung)*: the idea that cultural materials and practices that had heretofore served the status quo could be "refunctioned" so as not to supply but actually to change the apparatus of production. Brecht's practice, too, is assimilated to Benjamin's call for a general overcoming of specialization. Just as the reader who writes letters to the newspaper becomes an author, writers are called upon to take up photography. "Only by transcending the specialization in the process of intellectual production . . . can one make this production politically useful."[45] Benjamin's talk, with its advocacy of avant-garde practice, its nascent populism, and its Brechtian materialism, flew in the face of the then-current Soviet arts policy. Socialist realism had become state policy in 1932, with the publication of Stalin's "On the Reconstruction of

Literary and Art Organizations"; the Soviet Writers Congress, with its formal acceptance of Socialist Realism and its call for a decided politicization of the arts, would be held in August 1934. If Benjamin's lecture was actually delivered at an institute funded by the Comintern, it must have unleashed a fierce debate.

A conversation with Brecht that summer produced an important addendum to Benjamin's essay:

> Long conversation in Brecht's sickroom . . . centered on my essay "The Author as Producer," in which I develop the theory that a decisive criterion of a revolutionary function of literature lies in the extent to which technical advances lead to a transformation of artistic forms and hence of intellectual means of production. Brecht was willing to concede the validity of this thesis only for a single type— namely, the upper-middle-class writer, a type he thought included himself. "Such a writer," he said, "experiences solidarity with the interests of the proletariat at a single point: the issue of the development of his means of production. But if solidarity exists at this single point, he is, as producer, totally proletarianized. This total proletarianization at a single point leads to a solidarity all along the line." (SW, 2:783)

Five years later, Brecht's claim regarding the possible proletarianization of the bourgeois writer would make its way, almost word for word, into Benjamin's book on Baudelaire.

Benjamin's first letters of the new year evidence his growing preoccupation with the work of Franz Kafka. To Scholem he expressed the hope that he would someday be able to lecture on both Kafka and S. J. Agnon, the Jewish writer whose story "The Great Synagogue" would have figured prominently in the first issue of Benjamin's planned journal *Angelus Novus* in 1921. Discussions on Kafka also played a big part in Benjamin's cautious reestablishment of relations with his old friend Werner Kraft, with whom he had broken in 1921. Until 1933 Kraft had been a librarian in Hannover; he now lived in exile, experiencing the same dilemmas that confronted the other émigré intellectuals. Although they would never rekindle the friendship of earlier times, the two men renewed contact in these days in Paris, and Benjamin read a number of Kraft's essays, including two on Kafka and one on Karl Kraus, with "agreement and respect" (GB, 4:344).

A letter from Scholem on April 19 finally opened the way to writing what was conceived from the beginning as a major statement on Kafka. Scholem had approached Robert Weltsch—editor of the *Jüdische Rundschau*, the largest-circulation Jewish publication still allowed in Germany—regarding the possibility of Benjamin's contributing an essay on Kafka. When Weltsch followed up Scholem's suggestion with an invitation, Benjamin on May 9 accepted enthusiastically, while warning Weltsch that his contribution would not conform to the "straightforward theological explication of Kafka" (C, 442). Benjamin's essay, portions of which were published in the *Jüdische Rundschau* late in the year, rejects not just any straightforwardly religious reading of Kafka's stories but all dogmatically allegorical interpretations that seek to stabilize meaning by assigning fixed values to the various elements of the story: the fathers and the officials in texts such as "The Judgment" and *The Castle* are, in such interpretations, either God, psychic agencies, or the political state. Benjamin explicitly rejects conventional theological, political, and psychoanalytic readings, insisting instead on the final indecipherability of these texts, on their openness and puzzle character: "Kafka had a rare capacity for creating parables for himself. Yet his parables are never exhausted by what is explainable; on the contrary, he took all conceivable precautions against the interpretation of his writings" (SW, 2:804). There is, however, a governing orientation to Benjamin's reading: "the question of the organization of life and labor in human society. This question increasingly occupied Kafka, even as it became impenetrable to him." If Benjamin had addressed these questions—which concern the nature of human experience—in "Experience and Poverty" by examining the consequences of rapidly increasing technologization, he examines them in "Franz Kafka" through the optic of myth. Kafka's protagonists—from Georg Bendemann in "The Judgment" through Josef K. in *The Trial* and K. in *The Castle*, and on to the animal figures of the late short prose—inhabit a world of musty, dark rooms, regardless of the larger institutional structure encompassing them: the family, the court, or the castle. This world is shaped by forces that these figures can neither recognize nor take up a position toward. In a famous evocation of a childhood photograph of Kafka, Benjamin suggests that the boy's "infinitely sad eyes" are looking out over a world in which he can never be at home. What prevents any secure appropriation and makes all existence precipitous? Benjamin suggests that Kafka was wont to think in terms of "ages of the world," and this makes the world he limns a belated one, disturbed by the intrusion of elements from what Benjamin calls a "primordial world" *(Vorwelt)*. Kafka's figures live in a kind of swamp that is alive with the repressed memory of that primordial age; chthonic powers assert their claim on the present age by imposing forgetfulness. The slightest misstep can plunge the protagonist back into that swamp world—into the primitive and prehuman, the creaturely. "The Metamorphosis" is not merely the title of Kafka's best-known story; it designates the specific threat hanging over Kafka's characters, the threat of falling back into an alien life-form. Even if they have not in some way lapsed, Kafka's figures feel the effects of that threat—in the form of shame. They are ashamed before their creatureliness, deformed and humbled by it, bent over beneath its burden like condemned men at the bar. Kafka's figures are all, in one sense or another, awaiting judgment—hopeless even in their hope of acquittal. And there is something beautiful in this "nonsense," Benjamin suggests.

Just as "Goethe's Elective Affinities" was constituted as a repudiation of biographical interpretation by means of biography, "Franz Kafka" is a repudiation of theological interpretation by means of theology. A comparable understanding of myth informs both texts, something akin to Hermann Cohen's wary dread of the animistic prerational realm that lingers on, menacing the traditionally human traits of reasoning and moral action. Benjamin evokes this sense of spiritual crisis in citing a conversation reported by Max Brod, in which Kafka refers to human beings as "nihilistic thoughts, suicidal thoughts, that come into God's head" (SW, 2:798). Brod famously went on to ask Kafka whether there was then any hope in the world. "There is infinite hope," Kafka answered, "just not for us." For whom, then? Benjamin isolates those few, forlorn figures to whom hope seems to cling like the ends of thread clinging to diminutive Odradek (in "The Cares of a Family Man"), figures such as the assistants (in *The Castle*), those creatures who alone, in their imperturbability and elusiveness, seem to escape the quagmire of the family. Yet he also points to moments in Kafka that hint at a productive use for our alienation and deformation; he thus ties the Kafka essay back into his analysis of modernity. As Benjamin worked on the essay that summer in Skovsbostrand, Denmark, where Brecht was living, his conversations with the playwright undoubtedly were a factor in its composition, nowhere more clearly than in the discussion of gesture—a key element of Brechtian dramaturgy. In a magnificent passage, Benjamin unveils the function of the gesture in Kafka, showing first the enormous difficulty of even the simplest gesture in a world so burdened. There, gestures have no inherent meaning, though they might prove to be part of what Benjamin calls a test procedure *(Versuchsanordnung)*. He thus invokes with great subtlety the categories developed in his "Little History of Photography," categories associated with the "optical unconscious." Like the photographic image, the gesture makes of the protagonist a test subject, one alienated from the look of his own stride in the photograph, or from the sound of his own voice in the gramophone.[46] Such gestures can disclose otherwise hidden fragments of our existence, subterranean factors that come to light only in the course of the experiment. Benjamin calls this intimation of the recessive gesture "study." "For it is a storm that blows toward us from forgetting. And study is a sally that rides against it" (SW, 2:814).

Benjamin re-creates this Kafkan world through a brilliant series of evocations and parallels, inviting onto the stage not just some of the writer's most memorable protagonists—Odradek, Sancho Panza, Josephine the mouse singer, the hunter Gracchus—but a range of other types, from Potemkin, Catherine the Great's chancellor, through figures from Grimm's fairy tales. A principal strategy of the essay is thus to displace any reading of the stories by retelling them. This retelling, and our experience of the retelling, is for Benjamin part of the process and trial of reading Kafka. "[Kafka] saw in the mirror that the primordial world held up to him in the form of guilt only the future in the form of the law [*Gericht*]." The process of the trial *(Prozess)* is thus already the verdict. As is the case with Scheherazade, stories delineate a present in the light of what is to come. This is the untoward burden of Benjamin's rejection of dogmatic exegesis. He holds true to Kafka's sense that writing and reading are nothing more nor less than a distillation of the world process—our never-ending trial and only hope. The essay accordingly begins and ends on an autobiographical note. The introductory anecdote describes the visit of the petty undersecretary Schuvalkin to the chancellor Potemkin, who is paralyzed by a deep depression. Immobility brought on by depression was a threat Benjamin had known throughout the last decade—and now, in Paris, it was his constant companion. The essay suggests that our hope for "redemption" lies enclosed within hopelessness itself, and might at some moment awake and enter the world through the tiny, improbable portal of an unconscious, indeed "nonsensical" gesture (BS, 135).[47] At the end of the summer he would comment to Scholem that the study of Kafka was "ideally suited to become the crossroads of the different paths my thought has taken" (BS, 139).

With all this concentrated literary activity, Benjamin was still unable to cover even a fraction of his living costs. His friends had so far made his existence in Paris possible through small gifts of money. In the course of the spring of 1934, Benjamin was gradually able to supplement his irregular income through stipends paid by various organizations and by the ongoing sale of his books. Through the agency of Sylvain Lévy, an Indologist at the Collège de France and a former Dreyfusard, he received that spring a stipend of 700 French francs per month for four months from the Israélite Alliance Universelle. At about the same time, the Institute of Social Research initiated, at Horkheimer's bidding, a stipend of 100 Swiss francs per month that would continue—and be gradually increased—throughout the 1930s. And one of Adorno's efforts on his behalf bore fruit: Adorno's aunt, the pianist Agathe Cavelli-Adorno, convinced a wealthy businesswoman and family friend in Neunkirchen, Elfriede Herzberger, to provide support for Benjamin. The first check, for 450 French francs, came equally from Adorno, his aunt, and Else Herzberger; by the summer, Else Herzberger was providing a more regular though smaller stipend.

It is a telling indication of the desperate situation in which Benjamin now found himself that even these new sources of income could not prevent a further decline in his financial situation; by late March he was forced to move from his cheap hotel in the Sixth Arrondissement, pawning his belongings to settle the bill. Fortunately, his sister, Dora, had recently moved to Paris. Benjamin's relations with his sister had long been troubled, but she now showed herself willing to aid her brother, if only temporarily. Benjamin moved into her small apartment at 16 Rue Jasmin in the Sixteenth Arrondissement. Such proximity after years of cool relations was easy for neither sibling; Benjamin averred that "they didn't sing me this song in the cradle" (BS, 101). He remained for two to three weeks—until Dora's normal renter returned—and then moved again, to an even cheaper hotel, the Floridor, on Place Denfert-Rochereau in the Fourteenth Arrondissement. Meanwhile, his personal relations were reaching a new low. After several times seeing his friend from Ibiza days, Jean Selz (who was continuing to translate sections of the *Berlin Childhood*), Benjamin suddenly dropped all contact, canceling their last appointment in early April by using a patently false pretext. He continued to see—and lend moral support to—his cousin Egon Wissing, but these meetings posed new difficulties. When Wissing was in Berlin earlier in the year, Gretel Karplus had been so taken aback by his condition and behavior that she refused to entrust him with several books intended for Benjamin, and raised serious doubts about Wissing's ability to manage the transport of Benjamin's library to Denmark. Wissing returned to Paris "battered" and a different man, having emerged from his treatment for morphine addiction (GB, 4:361). Yet he remained for Benjamin "someone who once stood very close to me and who perhaps will stand very close again," someone in whose "character and mental formation" he had great faith (GB, 4:378). His family in Germany was still a cause for worry. Dora and Stefan remained in Berlin, while Benjamin's brother, Georg, freed from prison, returned to Berlin from a trip to Switzerland and Italy and immediately resumed, as Benjamin knew he would, his clandestine political work.

Even his correspondence during these months—usually a site for the relief of tensions—was proof against any sense of serenity. In late February he offered Adorno a very pointed critique of his *Singspiel*, "The Treasure of Indian Joe," which was based on scenes from Twain's *The Adventures of Tom Sawyer*. Adorno had written the libretto between November 1932 and August 1933 and had begun to set some parts of the text to music, a task he never completed. Benjamin had been in possession of a copy of the libretto since the early fall, but he delayed his response until late January—a sure sign of trouble brewing between these two fierce intellectuals. When he did reply, it was in very guarded terms, but sufficient to make his objections to the project as a whole palpable to Adorno. Benjamin must have felt justified in attacking Adorno's work where it entered a sphere in which he considered himself expert: culture created for children. Referring to Adorno's libretto as a *Kindermodell*—presumably an allusion both to the genre of radio *Hörmodell* he had worked on himself and to certain of Brecht's plays that were supposed to assume model character for their audiences and other authors—Benjamin objected to the unrelievedly idyllic quality of the setting in rural America and to Adorno's inadequate handling of the specter of death meant to haunt the little opera. One comment in particular must have stung Adorno: a suggestion that his work did not measure up to Jean Cocteau's truly "dangerous" novel of 1929, *Les enfants terribles* (BA, 23–24).

An exchange with Scholem in the spring struck closer to home: it took up again the question of Benjamin's political orientation and its effect on his work. Scholem's important letter also rekindled the old, uncomfortable debate between the friends regarding Benjamin's politics. After reading the relatively mild and straightforward essay "The Present Social Situation of the French Writer," Scholem claimed that he was unable to understand it and asked Benjamin if the piece was a "Communist credo" (BS, 107). Scholem wanted to know where Benjamin stood, and reminded him that he had been unwilling to give clear answers to this question in the past. Scholem's letter elicited a highly revealing response. A draft later found in East Berlin reads: "I have always written according to my convictions—with perhaps a few minor exceptions—but I have never made the attempt to express the contradictory and mobile whole that my convictions represent in their multiplicity, except in very extraordinary cases and then never other than orally" (BS, 108–109). In the letter he finally sent, he defined his Communism as "absolutely nothing other than the expression of certain experiences I have undergone in my thinking and in my life; . . . it is a drastic, not infertile expression of the fact that the present intellectual industry finds it impossible to make room for my thinking, just as the present economic order finds it impossible to accommodate my life; . . . it represents the obvious, reasoned attempt on the part of a man who is completely or almost completely deprived of any means of production to proclaim his right to them, both in his thinking and in his life. . . . Is it really necessary to say all this to you?" (BS, 110). Benjamin continued with a passage on Brecht that showed he was fully aware of the real stakes here: Scholem's objection to his adoption of a Brechtian, engaged politics alongside both his theological inclinations and the carefully modulated leftist social analyses that allied him with the Institute of Social Research. In a letter written that summer, Benjamin again adverted to their controversy while claiming that he could not send Scholem the much more provocative essay, "The Author as Producer," because he had failed to have enough copies made (BS, 113); when Scholem asked for a copy in person in 1938, Benjamin simply replied, "I think I had better not let you read it" (SF, 201).

One bright spot amid so much gloom was the additional help he received in mid-March from the Institute of Social Research (in the person of Friedrich Pollock) for the successful transfer of "about half the library, but the more important half" from his apartment in Berlin to Brecht's house in Denmark (C, 437). He had hoped to transfer the library in its entirety, but his tenant in Berlin, von Schoeller, who had proved so accommodating and reliable, was reluctant to have the apartment wholly denuded of its most prominent furnishings and thus "completely lose its character."[48] The books, in five or six large crates, arrived safely in Denmark. This transfer not only put the library at Benjamin's disposal for his writing but allowed him to make important sales, foremost among them a tortuously negotiated sale of the complete works of Franz von Baader to the library of the Hebrew University in Jerusalem, which he took care of in July. Books, and thoughts of books, thus continued to serve as an escape from the horrors of daily life in exile. He had read André Malraux's new novel, *Man's Fate (La condition humaine),* in January and found it, he tells Gretel Karplus, "interesting, even perhaps fascinating, but not finally productive" (GB, 4:341). It was at this time, however, that he added the section on Malraux to his essay "The Present Social Situation of the French Writer," which appeared in the spring. And detective fiction, never far from his bedside table, continued to be devoured. He read several volumes of Somerset Maugham, including *Ashenden: Or the British Agent,* all in French translation, and recommended them warmly to Gretel Karplus.

Most of his reading, though, was devoted to his work on the Paris arcades—and it took place in the Bibliothèque Nationale. In the course of the 1930s, amid constant changes of abode and even country, the Bibliothèque Nationale was Benjamin's lodestar, the one homestead on which he could count. The other constant was his obsession with his writing materials: his letters are peppered with requests to friends for the paper and notebooks he had used for many years. Binding this all together was the conviction that the arcades project would be his most important work. "The arcades project is the *tertius gaudens* these days between fate and me. I have not only been able to do much more research recently, but also—for the first time in a long while—to imagine ways in which that research might be put to use. That this image diverges greatly from the first, original one is quite understandable" (BS, 100). He thus worked his way through a four-volume history of the French workers' associations by Sigmund Engländer, several excerpts from which appear in *The Arcades Project*. By the end of the spring, he had achieved a preliminary overview and organization of the masses of material that he had collected for the study of Paris. The study now bore the working title "Paris, Capital of the Nineteenth Century"; it would have been divided into five major sections: Fourier, or the Arcades; Daguerre, or the Panorama; Louis Philippe, or the Interior; Grandville, or the World Exhibition; and Haussmann, or the Embellishment of Paris (AP, 914). This reorganization of the project came at a pivotal moment, one at which the earliest stages of the project, with their orientation toward Surrealism and a collective social psychoanalysis, encounter the more historical and sociological orientation that characterized the work after 1934. A letter to Werner Kraft written later that summer from Denmark suggests the connections Benjamin discerned at this time between politics and mass psychology: "You admit that for the time being you do not want to accept communism 'as the solution for humanity.' But of course the issue is precisely to abolish the unproductive pretensions of solutions for humanity by means of the feasible findings of this very system; indeed, to give up entirely the immodest prospect of 'total' systems and at least to make the attempt to construct the days of humanity [*den Lebenstag der Menschheit*] in just as loose a fashion as a rational person who has had a good night's sleep begins his day" (C, 452).

Perhaps with such psychopolitical considerations in mind, he continued to experiment with hallucinogens. Shortly before leaving Paris for Denmark, he took mescaline, allowing himself to be injected subcutaneously by Fritz Fränkel, who had immigrated to France in 1933. Among the welter of notions generated during the nighttime experiment, including speculations on "dawdling," the behavior of children, and the pleasure to be gotten from catatonia, Benjamin's darkly fantastic portrayal of the Nietzsche House in Weimar, which the philosopher's protofascist sister had turned into a shrine, stands out (OH, 94, 96).

In early summer 1934 Benjamin finally, and reluctantly, took Brecht up on his invitation and traveled to Denmark. He could simply no longer afford to support himself in Paris, and Brecht's hospitality seemed the only alternative. It was to be the first of three such extended summer visits, the others coming in 1936 and 1938. Brecht and Helene Weigel were living with their children Stefan and Barbara in an isolated farmhouse in the village of Skovsbostrand, near the town of Svendborg. Svendborg had been industrialized in the nineteenth century but remained a small rural outpost. Situated on the south shore of the island of Fünen, the third largest of the islands that make up a large part of Denmark, Skovsbostrand looks across a channel to the smaller island of Tåsinge to the south. Benjamin experienced this "southern tip" of Fünen as "one of the most remote areas you can imagine" and found its "unexploited" nature and lack of links to the modern world to be a mixed blessing. The town itself offered few distractions: Benjamin soon gave up even on the local cinema, deeming the fare it offered unbearable. He seems to have done relatively little reading that was not directly related to his work: Ilya Ehrenburg's *Vu par un ecrivain d'URSS* (for Benjamin, "the most interesting pages of this author who is in and of himself disagreeable") and Balzac's *Cousine Bette* head a short list. And he was even deprived of the excursions into nature that had become so important for him on Ibiza. He complained repeatedly that there were few paths through the countryside or along the shore, and that the beaches, though abundant, were poor and rocky. Benjamin took a room in a house in the countryside a few minutes from the Brecht enclave; the room served to protect his privacy, but it limited his social relations with Brecht,

Weigel, and the ever-changing cast of characters around the charismatic playwright. That had its good and bad sides. On one hand, he remained wary of the mercurial Brecht, anxious lest he strain their relationship or take excessive advantage of his host's hospitality. Benjamin's relations with Brecht are, in fact, qualitatively different from those with any of his other contemporaries: they are characterized by a certain awe and even subservience that is nowhere else evident. Yet he also deepened his genuine friendship with Brecht, as well as with Weigel and the couple's children, to whom he became close. Even more isolated in Denmark than he had been in France, Benjamin looked forward to his evenings in the big farmhouse with real eagerness: his nightly chess match with Brecht, games of Sixty-Six (a two-handed card game) with Weigel, and gatherings in front of the radio, were for weeks on end his sole source of sociability.

Thus began a period of intensive intellectual exchange and occasional collaboration between two of the twentieth century's most influential intellectuals. Despite the manifest differences in their personalities, Brecht and Benjamin shared a remarkable friendship. As Ruth Berlau, a member of Brecht's circle, remembers: "Whenever Benjamin and Brecht were together in Denmark, an atmosphere of confidence and trust immediately arose between them. Brecht had an enormous liking for Benjamin; in fact, he loved him. I think they understood each other without saying a word. They played chess wordlessly, and when they stood up, they had had a conversation."[49] The discussions seem always to have been held in Brecht's house, never in Benjamin's. They took place, then, under a certain sign and in a certain atmosphere. Benjamin noted two details of Brecht's study. On a beam that supported the ceiling Brecht had painted the words "The truth is concrete." And from the neck of a little wooden donkey that stood on the windowsill hung a small sign on which Brecht had written "Even I must understand it."

Much of their discussion, of course, revolved around Brecht's plays and his conception of theater. Even before leaving Paris for Denmark, Benjamin had written of this to Brecht, stressing the function of the playwright's "extremely light and certain touch" and suggesting that affinities existed between his plays and the ancient Chinese board game of Go, with its initially empty board and its strategy of placing,

rather than moving, pieces. "You place each of your figures and formulations on the right spot, whence they fulfill their proper strategic
function on their own and without having to act" (C, 443). Now, in the
house in Skovsbostrand, they often talked through the evening about
literature, art, society, and politics. We have only Benjamin's record of
these conversations, and it is devoted mainly to Brecht's opinions, so
we must imagine his own part in the dialogue. Their talk often returned to the subject of gesture; this and related exchanges would
help shape the revision of his Kafka essay, which Benjamin undertook
that summer. In order to underscore the importance of gesture, Brecht
pointed to a didactic poem he had composed for the actress Carola
Neher, who had taken leading roles in Brecht's *Happy End* and *Saint
Joan of the Stockyards,* and played Polly in the film version of *The
Threepenny Opera.* "I taught Carola Neher a number of different
things," Brecht said. "She has not only learned to act, but, for example, she has learned how to wash herself. Up to then, she had washed
so as not to be dirty. That was completely beside the point. I taught
her how to wash her face. She acquired such skill in this that I wanted
to make a film of her doing it. But nothing came of it because I was
not making a picture at the time, and she did not want to be filmed by
anyone else. That didactic poem was a model" (SW, 2:783).

In these troubled days, the discussions naturally turned quite often to the role of art in society. Brecht distinguished between "serious" and "unserious" writers in a surprising way: "Let's assume that
you read an excellent political novel and learn later that it was written by Lenin. You'd change your opinion of both Lenin and the novel;
they'd both go down in your estimation" (SW, 2:784). Brecht, of course,
considered himself "unserious." He claimed that he often imagined
himself being examined before a tribunal. When asked if his answers
were serious, he would be forced to admit that they were not entirely
serious. It is as if Brecht somehow anticipated his appearance before
the House Unamerican Activities Committee in October 1947, an
appearance whose brilliant evasiveness has become legendary. He reserved a third category for writers who could not be assigned to either
group, writers such as Kafka, Heinrich von Kleist, and Georg Büchner.
Brecht classified such writers as "failures." These wide-ranging discussions took them across the literature of the West, including the

works of Rimbaud and Johannes R. Becher, Confucius and Euripides, Gerhart Hauptmann and Dostoevsky.

If the evenings were often convivial and stimulating, Benjamin's days were isolated and lonely. He was able to get a lot of work done but, especially considering that he was reunited with his library for the first time in almost eighteen months, it is surprising that he produced no major text during this stay in Denmark. Most of the summer was given over to two projects: the essay on the cultural politics of the German Social Democrats and the revision of the Kafka essay. Brecht was in possession of a full run of the party journal *Die neue Zeit*, and Benjamin assembled a rich archive of excerpts in the course of the summer. As he told Horkheimer, he hoped that the essay would provide a materialist analysis of "collective literary products." And he freely admitted to Horkheimer that he had chosen the topic in order "to serve the goals of the Institute of Social Research," that is to say, its long involvement with the history of the labor movement and social democracy (C, 456). Benjamin's failure to complete the essay, despite the months of work devoted to it, is hardly surprising: the topic was ill suited to his talents and interests, and in the course of time he began to struggle against the orthodoxy that spoke from the materials. By October, he could admit to Alfred Cohn that the essay's theme, "even if it originated with me, is not the expression of my free choice" (GB, 4:508).

The revision of the Kafka essay was another matter altogether: Benjamin based it not just on new ideas but on the discussions with Brecht and on a pregnant exchange of letters with Scholem. An odd, three-part conversation on this topic thus arose, with the essay triangulated between Brecht's historicist and materialist views, Scholem's theological perspective, and Benjamin's own more mediated and idiosyncratic position—all three of which pivoted on the function of parable in Kafka. Brecht's attitude toward Kafka was decidedly ambivalent, and Benjamin's essay did little to change his views. In fact, his reaction to the essay, which he avoided discussing for a while, and which he criticized for its "diary form, in the style of Nietzsche," was in part virulent. Kafka's work was, for Brecht, conditioned by his milieu in Prague, a milieu dominated by bad journalists and pretentious literary types. Given these unfortunate circumstances, literature became Kafka's principal, if not sole, reality. Brecht was savage—and perhaps deliberately a little outrageous—in his judgment: he found real artistic merit in Kafka, but nothing useful. Kafka was a great but failed writer—"a feeble, unattractive figure, a bubble on the iridescent surface of the swamp of Prague's cultural life, and nothing more" (SW, 2:786). A month earlier, he had framed the problem differently, arguing that Kafka's overriding problem was one of "organization." "What gripped his imagination," Brecht remarked, "was his fear of a society of ants: the way in which people become alienated from one another by the forms of their life together" (SW, 2:785). So, because of Kafka's willful ambiguity and even obscurantism—for Brecht, an unconscious abetting of "Jewish fascism" (SW, 2:787)—the task would be to "make a clearing" in Kafka by isolating the "practical suggestions" latent in his stories.[50] Brecht was thus willing to concede that *The Trial* was a prophetic book: "You can see from the Gestapo what could become of the Cheka [Soviet secret police]." Yet Kafka offers too little resistance to the most common sort of contemporary petty bourgeois—that is, to the fascist. Kafka's perspective is "that of a man who has fallen under the wheels," and thus he can answer the supposed "heroism" of fascism only with questions, and especially the question as to his own guaranteed position. "It is a Kafkaesque irony that the man was an insurance agent who appeared to be convinced of nothing more surely than the invalidity of all guarantees" (SW, 2:787).

If Brecht remained suspicious of Benjamin's solidarity with Kafkan undecidability, Scholem was skeptical of Benjamin's appreciation of the theological dimensions of Kafka's project. The central statements of their exchange are worth quoting in full. Scholem had written:

Your portrayal of the preanimistic age as Kafka's seeming present— if I understand you correctly—is really quite piercing and magnificent. The nullity of such a present seems to me to be very problematic, problematic in those final points that are also decisive here. I would like to say that 98% of it makes sense, but the final touch is missing, which you seem to have sensed, since you moved away from that level with your interpretation of shame (you definitely hit the mark there) and of the Law (which is where you get into difficulties!). The existence of secret law foils your interpretation: it should

not exist in a premythical world of chimeric confusion, to say nothing of the very special way in which it even announces its existence.
There you went much too far with your elimination of theology,
throwing the baby out with the bathwater. (BS, 122–123)

Benjamin's reply is free of the defensiveness with which he sometimes responded to the friend who sat in judgment of his inadequate
Judaism. In reflecting on the question of how to conceive, "in Kafka's
sense, the Last Judgment's projection into world history," Benjamin
emphasized Kafka's failure to provide answers, which was a consequence of the nothingness he experienced in the way of redemption.
"I endeavored to show how Kafka sought—on the nether side of that
'nothingness,' in its inside lining, so to speak—to feel his way toward
redemption. This implies that any kind of victory over that nothingness . . . would have been an abomination for him" (BS, 129).

As a kind of answer and intended corrective to Benjamin's reading,
Scholem sent him a long poem—just as he had done during the discussions of the "Angelus Novus." Scholem's recourse to poetry in
both instances may have been a conscious provocation, challenging
the ideas of the premier literary critic of his time through the medium
of manifestly bad verse. Benjamin's reply fastens on key ideas in Scholem's poem, passing its aesthetic merit by in silence:

> 1) I wish tentatively to characterize the relationship of my essay
> to your poem as follows: you take the "nothingness of revelation" as
> your point of departure . . . the salvific-historical perspective of the
> established proceedings of the trial. I take as my starting point the
> small, nonsensical hope, as well as the creatures for whom this hope
> is intended and yet who, on the other hand, are also the creatures in
> which this absurdity is mirrored.
>
> 2) If I characterize shame as Kafka's strongest reaction, this in no
> way contradicts the rest of my interpretation. On the contrary, the
> primal world, Kafka's secret present, is the historical-philosophical
> index that lifts this reaction out of the domain of the private. For
> the work of the Torah—if we abide by Kafka's account—has been
> thwarted.
>
> 3) It is in this context that the problem of the Scripture [Schrift]
> poses itself. Whether the pupils have lost it or whether they are un-
> able to decipher it comes down to the same thing, because, without

the key that belongs to it, the Scripture is not Scripture, but life. Life as it is lived in the village at the foot of the hill on which the castle is built. It is in the attempt to metamorphize life into Scripture that I perceive the meaning of "reversal" [Umkehr], which so many of Kafka's parables endeavor to bring about—I take "The Next Village" and "The Bucket Rider" as examples. Sancho Panza's existence [in "The Truth about Sancho Panza"] is exemplary because it actually consists in rereading one's own existence—however buffoonish and quixotic.

4) I emphasized from the very beginning that the pupils "who have lost the Scripture" do not belong to the hetaeric world, because I rank them as assistants to those creatures for whom, in Kafka's words, there is "an infinite amount of hope."

5) That I do not deny the component of revelation in Kafka's work already follows from my appreciation—by declaring his work to be "distorted"—of its messianic aspect. Kafka's messianic category is the "reversal" or the "studying." You guess correctly that I do not want to shift the path taken by theological interpretation in itself—I practice it myself—but only the arrogant and frivolous form emanating from Prague [that is, Max Brod]. (BS, 134–135)

Just as the great essay on Karl Kraus had done, the essay on Kafka marked a point of crystallization in Benjamin's thought. "The study," he wrote to Werner Kraft in the fall, "brought me to a crossroads in my thoughts and reflections. Devoting additional thought to it promises to do for me precisely what using a compass would do to orient a person on uncharted terrain" (C, 462). But he was also realistic about his chances of supporting himself by writing about German-language literature in the new world of exile. "With the Kafka essay I believe I have closed the series of my literary essays. For the time being, there is no more space for such work. It is perhaps easier to place a book than it is to find a home for writings like that, and so I will turn— insofar as plans are allowed me at all—to larger undertakings. To what extent such things *are* allowed me, though—we won't look too closely into that" (GB, 4:509).

Even as he worked on these larger projects, Benjamin continued to send a steady stream of smaller pieces to Germany. Reviews of books on Schiller and the medieval *Minnesang*, a critique of the work of the Swiss psychoanalyst and existential psychologist Ludwig Binswanger, and two pieces from the *Berlin Childhood* ("Society" and "Blume-shof") appeared in the *Frankfurter Zeitung*. Other venues remained stubbornly closed. He had replied to Moritz Spitzer's invitation to contribute to the next almanac of Schocken Verlag by suggesting that he send part of the Kafka essay, only to learn that Max Brod exercised an "interpretive monopoly" on Kafka's work. This occasioned a dia-tribe against editors that recalls Goethe's famous "God punish the publishers!" It was addressed to Werner Kraft, whose own work on Kafka had met a similar fate: "Since I have never yet come to know an editor who did not attempt to compensate for his total lack of influ-ence with the publisher through self-important dealings with authors, that didn't surprise me at all" (GB, 4:466). And Benjamin himself saw to it that still other venues, such as Klaus Mann's *Die Sammlung*, would never accept his work. Even his abject poverty could not out-weigh his hostility to the easy liberalism that characterized Mann's journal. He thus replied to Mann's offer to be listed as a contributor by stipulating that his name appear only if his contributions were in fact regularly accepted. Which seems reasonable enough until one exam-ines the specifics: he suggested that Mann open the section of the journal reserved for cultural notes *(Glossen)* to commentary on a se-ries of books by Communist authors.

The usually futile attempts to place his work led Benjamin to take a jaundiced view of the successes of some of his friends, and espe-cially of Bloch, so often the butt of sarcastic jokes among Benjamin, Adorno, and Scholem. He told Scholem "that a new volume in the Arsène Lupin series—you know the famous gentleman-*cambrioleur*— is to appear shortly in the form of a new book by Ernst Bloch. *Heritage of Our Times*—I'm quite keen to see it; first, being curious in general, second, because I would like to learn what I, as a child of our time, am likely to inherit here of my own work" (BS, 145). Neither the mockery nor the reiterated charge of sophisticated literary burglary kept Benja-min from adding that he was hoping to see Bloch again soon.

A bit of money trickled in from some of these efforts: Jula Radt-Cohn was holding four marks, the honorarium for "The Little Hunchback" (from *Berlin Childhood*), which had appeared in the *Magdeburgische Zeitung* in July. Although he was furious that Weltsch would pay him only 60 marks for his Kafka essay, he was at this point in no position

28. Ernst Bloch in Milan, 1934 *(Werkbundarchiv— Museum der Dinge, Berlin)*

to withdraw the work. Benjamin had arrived in Denmark almost penniless, having used his last reserves of cash for the transport of his belongings to Skovsbostrand in order to save storage costs in Paris. Thinking that his usual sources of income, however minimal, would continue to be available, he had borrowed enough money from Brecht to see him through the early weeks. And soon after his arrival, he had applied to the Danske Komité til Støtte for landsflygtige Aandsarbejdere (Danish Committee for the Support of Refugee Intellectual Workers) for help. He presented himself in the following terms: "I was forced to leave Germany in March 1933; I was a German citizen in my forty-first year. As an independent scholar and writer, I was not only, at one swoop, deprived of the means of my livelihood by the political upheaval, but I could no longer—although a dissident and belonging to no political party—be sure of my personal freedom. In the same month, my brother was subjected to severe abuse and has been held in a concentration camp since Christmas" (GB, 4:448–449). He goes on to mention his work on writers likely to be known to such a committee (Hofmannsthal, Proust, and Baudelaire), cites his major publications, and points to his ongoing relationship with the *Frankfurter Zeitung.* This appeal seems to have gone unanswered. When his July check from the Herzbergers (Else and her brother Alfons) failed to appear, presumably because of the political turmoil in Germany, he was reduced to utter penury, and he sent out a cry for help to the one source on which he could almost always count: Gretel Karplus. The worst of this latest financial crisis was averted only in mid-September, with the arrival of a check from the Hebrew University for the purchase of his prized sixteen-volume edition of the works of Franz von Baader.

To be sure, world politics were ever present in Skovsbostrand, where Brecht and his circle regularly huddled in front of the radio. "Thus, I was able to listen to Hitler's Reichstag speech, and because it was the very first time I had ever heard him, you can imagine the effect" (BS, 130). More shocking still was the news of Hitler's elimination of Ernst Röhm and his brownshirts, the Sturmabteilung (SA), in what is called today the Night of the Long Knives. The Nazi militia, with its propensity for gratuitous violence, was feared and despised by the regular army. Hitler had long tolerated the SA, which had been instrumental in his rise to power; but he now saw a threat to his rule in the ongoing violence—and in Röhm's ambition. On June 30 and July 1, SS units and Gestapo officers arrested Röhm and key members of the SA's command, killed others on the spot, and, having already moved against Communists and Social Democrats, took advantage of the propaganda umbrella rapidly erected by Goebbels in order to eliminate supporters of Franz von Papen, the vice chancellor, and a number of conservative and centrist politicians on whose loyalty Hitler could not count. At least eighty-five people (including Röhm) died, and the toll may well have been in the hundreds. This massive tremor within the party structure occasioned a spark of hope in even the resigned

Benjamin; Hitler's almost immediate mastery of the situation soon extinguished it.

Events in Austria—the so-called July Putsch, which began on July 25—were an occasion for even greater concern. SS troops, disguised as Austrian soldiers and policemen, broke into the office of the federal chancellor, killing the chancellor, Engelbert Dollfuß, and took control of the Vienna broadcast studio of the main Austrian radio corporation, sending a false news flash that was supposed to serve as the signal for a general Nazi uprising. While much of Austria remained calm, violent clashes in several states between Nazis and the army and police, who remained loyal to the republic, cost more than 200 lives. The putsch failed, as much because of Nazi disorganization as because of the resistance of the security forces. But this first attempt to expand the borders of Nazi Germany sent shock waves across Europe. Benjamin followed the putsch step by step on the radio—"a really memorable experience" (GB, 4:500). The events had a troubling personal side for him, however. He soon learned that Karl Kraus, one of the very few living Europeans he could revere, had expressed his support for Dollfuß in highly questionable terms: "[The Austrian Jews] consider Austrian National Socialism to be not the lesser but the greater evil, 'the perfect horror,' and therefore would have wished that the Social Democrats could look on the protector—however intellectually alien or antipathetic he might be—as the lesser evil. As for ourselves, who have never 'traveled along,' especially not with lies, we can have nothing more to do with this concept. We consider Dollfuß's politics to be the greater good as compared to that of the Social Democrats, and we consider the politics of the latter to be, at best, the lesser evil in comparison with National Socialism."[51] Dollfuß had been the elected chancellor, but had taken advantage of a procedural crisis in the Austrian legislature to impose a state of emergency, sweeping aside parliament in order to rule as a virtual dictator. Although he rejected German Nazism, he had sought to model the Austrian state on the example of Italian fascism. Benjamin was thus dismayed by what he saw as Kraus's "capitulation to Austro-fascism." He was led to ask, "Who is actually left who can still give in?" (C, 458).

By September Benjamin was ready to leave Skovsbostrand. It wasn't that his relationship with Brecht had changed; it remained productive and cordial. But he was lonely. Weigel and the children had fled Fünen because of an outbreak of polio, and the letters from the outside world upon which he was dependent had slowed to a trickle. The weather during the summer had been miserable, so the already sparse opportunities for walks and swims shrank to almost nothing. And for all his gratitude toward Brecht and Weigel, the house and the atmosphere that reigned there were finally not to his liking. The atmosphere was rendered oppressive by the presence of Margarete Steffin. Brecht made an effort to keep his lover away from the others, so she would fail to make an appearance for days on end, but the jealous tension between Weigel and her set the rest of the group on edge. Even the livelier days in the house did not always suit Benjamin; there were often a dozen people in a room at one time, and not all of them made for pleasant company. His days alone in his room in the farmhouse were, as he reported to Horkheimer, conducive to work, but the work he had was not the work he wanted to do—namely, the study of the arcades. For that he needed to be in Paris. Although there are no references, during his first stay in Denmark, to the deep depressions that plagued him, he told his closest friends that his psychological condition was not good; he referred to his currently "exposed inner state" (BS, 138).

He thus longed for some diversion, some break in the pattern of his days, and he could not refrain from comparing the situation in Denmark to his memories of Ibiza. "You see," he wrote on August 19, in a draft of a letter to Toet Blaupot ten Cate,

> even my summer represents a significant contrast to last year's. Back then I couldn't get up early enough—and that is usually the expression of a fulfilled existence. Now it is not just that I sleep longer, but my dreams keep dogging my days, keep recurring. In the last few days, they were about astonishing and beautiful works of architecture: thus I saw B[recht] and Weigel, in the form of two towers or gate-like structures, tottering through a city. The flood of this sleep that breaks so fiercely against the day—like that of the sea agitated by the lunar orb—is moved by the power of your image. I miss your presence more than I can say—and, what is more—more than I could have believed. (GB, 4:482)

The image of Blaupot ten Cate (whom he addresses now with the formal "Sie") has here repressed all memory of the poverty, illness, and desperation of his last days on Ibiza, making them into an idyll compared to which his Danish sojourn must appear drab and lonely indeed.

In fact, Benjamin often found solace for his loneliness in memories of his relationships—even ones that never took place. The draft letter quoted above continues: "For me, too, the time and distance have shown more clearly and more powerfully what determines my tie to you. I am filled by the need for your nearness; my awaiting it governs the rhythm of my days and of my thought. Your nearness could not make itself felt in this way if a piece of you did not live in it. That is now more certain than a year ago." It should be remembered that Anna Maria Blaupot ten Cate was by this time married to the Frenchman Louis Sellier; Benjamin had seen them both that winter in Paris. This was not his only attempt to rekindle an old flame. In August he wrote again to Inge Buchholz, declaring that "a year plays no role for me. On the other hand, I put our four years on the scale, and they weigh little" (GB, 4:477). We know that this letter found its addressee. Inge Buchholz replied that she had burned all of Benjamin's letters and was no longer reachable at any address he had.[52] Only late in September would Benjamin's attempts at amorous correspondence lead anywhere.

On September 18, Benjamin left Skovsbostrand for a time to join the Brechts at Dragør, a small, charming seaside town a few miles from Copenhagen, where Helene Weigel had brought the children. Benjamin was able to indulge in some pleasant hours at the seaside and, in Copenhagen, to drink in the big city life he craved. Hours spent strolling the streets, along with the purchase of a set of transparencies from a "master tattoo artist," lifted his spirits immeasurably. "I've just returned from Copenhagen," he would crow a couple of weeks later to Alfred Cohn, "where I was able to enlarge, by some very lovely pieces, the only collection I can ever, in careless moments, think of continuing with, namely, my collection of colored transparencies. I was able to purchase from a tattoo-artist a number of patterns he'd painted himself—took them off the wall of his little partitioned room, which is located in the rear of a produce shop along a

Copenhagen canal" (GB, 4:508). These transparencies would become some of Benjamin's most cherished possessions in exile, and would grace the walls of many of his hotel rooms and apartments in the years to come. And one day in Dragør he turned the corner and found himself facing a friend from his Berlin days, Wieland Herzfelde (1896–1988), John Heartfield's brother and the publisher of Malik Verlag. Together with Harry Graf Kessler, George Grosz, and Else Lasker-Schüler, Benjamin had been among the early supporters of this publishing house, which was founded in 1917. At that time, Malik Verlag had served as the main organ of the journals produced by the Berlin Dadaists; after 1920, it turned to the publication of books. Its author list included Kurt Tucholsky, Upton Sinclair, John Dos Passos, Maxim Gorki, Vladimir Mayakovsky, and Oskar Maria Graf. With his decidedly leftist politics, Herzfelde had narrowly escaped the grasp of the Gestapo and fled to Prague in spring 1933, leaving behind more than 40,000 volumes to feed the fires of the Nazi book burning. Now, seeing his old friend, Herzfelde exclaimed, "Well, Benjamin. You also probably belong to the generation of '92? We'll surely be seeing each other from time to time. For, you know, the thing about this generation is: that those who were of a more delicate constitution already disappeared before 1914; those who were foolish disappeared between 1914 and 1918; the ones who were left will stick around a while yet" (C, 478). Benjamin no doubt took Herzfelde's cheery prediction for what it was: an indication that he understood Benjamin but ill.

Benjamin found Brecht in an unusually unresolved state of mind in Dragør. Brecht himself traced this unaccustomed indecision to the advantages he enjoyed as compared to most of his fellow emigrants. As Benjamin put it in his "Notes from Svendborg," "Because in general he scarcely acknowledges the emigration as the basis of plans and enterprises, it seems a fortiori to have no relevance for him" (SW, 2:788). This indecision did not prevent Brecht from drawing Benjamin into a literary collaboration. During the first few days of his stay, Benjamin worked together with Brecht and the distinguished Marxist philosopher Karl Korsch (1886–1961) on a Hitler satire "in the style of Renaissance historiography," a prose piece with the working title "The History of Giacomo Ui" (SW, 2:788). Korsch had been active on the left during the German revolution of 1918–1919, while at the same time conducting advanced studies in the law. He was appointed professor of law at the university in Jena in 1923, the same year in which his magnum opus *Marxism and Philosophy* appeared. This book stands alongside the work of Georg Lukács and Antonio Gramsci as the most important theoretical contribution to a critical Marxism in the twentieth century. Korsch also distinguished himself politically during the 1920s by his opposition to Stalinism, a stance that led to his ouster from the Communist Party in 1926. Deprived of his university position in 1933, he at first went underground, then immigrated to Denmark, to Britain, and finally to the United States in 1936—after being called a "Trotskyite Hitler agent" by his former comrades in the Party. Benjamin's acquaintance with Korsch marked a turning point: never a dedicated student of Marx's own writings, Benjamin was introduced to an advanced understanding of Marxism through his reading of Korsch. *Marxism and Philosophy* is one of the more often-cited works in the *Arcades Project*, and it played a significant role in Benjamin's political stance generally, though we should not forget his comment to Adorno on first reading the work in 1930: "Rather faltering steps—so it seems to me—in the right direction" (BA, 7).

Before the collaboration with Brecht and Korsch could make any progress, Benjamin was laid low by an attack of nephritis. His very slow and painful recovery had to be undertaken in a corner of a little house that even he, now hardened to every deprivation, could call "unsatisfactory" and "provisional." His only compensation was his reading of *Crime and Punishment* for the first time, an event that elicited Brecht's remark that it was mainly the reading of this novel that made him ill. "Dostoevsky is of course a great master." Benjamin wrote to Werner Kraft at this time; "but the confusion that lies at the heart of his protagonist is finally shared by the author himself . . . and that confusion is boundless" (GB, 4:506). Benjamin's illness led him to stay a week longer than planned at Dragør. He was sufficiently recovered by September 28 to travel to Gedser, the southernmost town in Denmark, on the island of Falster—a short ferry ride from Rostock. We know nothing about this weekend in Gedser other than the fact that he spent it with Gretel Karplus. And one might conclude from the curtain of silence with which they both shrouded this rendezvous that it was intimate and possibly sexual. At any rate, by October 2 Benjamin was back in Skovsbostrand—and all the more eager to leave Denmark, come what may.

Early October saw him preparing the ground for a return to Paris. He badly wished to resume his arcades work, but there were formidable obstacles in his way. First, he needed to reacquaint himself with the voluminous materials he had assembled for the project; that called for time and relative calm, neither of which he could muster amid the hectic search for support. Moreover, the study could be advanced only in Paris, more specifically at the Bibliothèque Nationale, and the costs of living in Paris were simply beyond his reach at this point (BS, 144). His uncertain financial prospects had been dealt yet another blow by the news that the Institute of Social Research—his only institutional source of support—would be moving to America. "The upshot could easily be a dissolution, or at least a loosening, of my ties to its leaders. What that would mean I won't spell out" (BS, 144). With an eye toward a possibly more stable financial situation, he sent letters to Léon Pierre-Quint and Marcel Brion, announcing his readiness to engage any aspect of the French literary world.

Benjamin left Denmark in late October, his eventual goal being the Italian Riviera, where his former wife had opened her small pension, the Villa Verde, in San Remo. Brecht had already left for London, where he was collaborating with Hanns Eisler on a new musical play, and where he would negotiate the terms for upcoming productions of *Saint Joan of the Stockyards* and *Round Heads and Pointed Heads*. Thus, there was little to keep Benjamin in Denmark, and he was fortified in his resolve to leave by the receipt, a few days before his planned departure, of a collective payment from the *Frankfurter Zeitung* for his summer's work. Ever the traveler, Benjamin stopped for a day in Antwerp, where he had never been, and found a city that could preoccupy the heart of "an old ship's passenger and harbor stroller" (GB, 4:556).

He arrived in Paris on October 24 or 25 and checked into yet another cheap hotel, the Hotel Littré in the Sixth Arrondissement. He remained only a few days but was able to see Kracauer, whose recently completed novel, *Georg*, they discussed, and Jean Paulhan, the director of the *Nouvelle Revue Française*, who gave signs that he might publish Benjamin's essay on Bachofen. As he was about to leave Paris, Benjamin received a letter from Horkheimer that certainly sent tremors through his system. Horkheimer raised the possibility that the institute might be able to bring one additional contributor to America—he stressed that this was unlikely but not impossible—and provide him with a stipend to cover living costs. Would Benjamin be willing to accept such a stipend, which would run for one or two full years?[53] Benjamin's response was unambiguous: "I would most gratefully welcome the chance to work in America, regardless of whether it is to do research at your institute or at an institute associated with yours. Indeed, allow me to say that you have my prior consent to any arrangement that seems appropriate to you" (C, 460). The stipend, unfortunately, never materialized, but from this point on America loomed as a kind of distant horizon for Benjamin.

On the way to San Remo Benjamin stopped briefly in Marseilles in order to meet with Jean Ballard, the editor of the *Cahiers du Sud*, and discuss the possibility of publishing an essay. By early November he was in San Remo, where he had the feeling of having finally arrived at a safe haven in "the most favorable winter station on the Riviera" (GB, 4:531). This large town, on the Mediterranean coast in western Liguria, had been a tourist center since the middle of the eighteenth century, when the first of the grand hotels were built. Tobias Smollett, in his *Travels through France and Italy* of 1766, described it thus: "St. Remo is a pretty considerable town, well-built upon the declivity of a gently rising hill, and has a harbour capable of receiving small vessels, a good number of which are built upon the beach; but ships of any burden are obliged to anchor in the bay, which is far from being secure. . . . There is very little plain ground in this neighbourhood; but the hills are covered with oranges, lemons, pomegranates and olives, which produce a considerable traffic in fine fruit and excellent oil. The women of St. Remo are much more handsome and better tempered than those of Provence."[54] Its setting, with the Maritime Alps plunging directly into the sea, and its unusually stable, springlike microclimate, had drawn prominent visitors since the late nineteenth century, including Russian czarinas, Ottoman sultans, and Persian shahs. Dora Sophie Benjamin was hoping that a tourist trade so well established would survive in a fascist Europe.

In the years since their bitter divorce trial, relations between Dora and Walter had gradually improved. She had actively sought publication possibilities for him while she remained in Berlin, and she now offered him food and shelter in Italy, and not for the last time. Dora had moved to San Remo during the summer, taking a temporary job in the kitchen of the Hotel Miramare in order to cover her expenses and those of Stefan. She reported in July that she was happy to be in Italy, "healthy and cheerful for the first time in years." Although Stefan had accompanied his mother to Italy in the summer, he insisted on returning to his school in Berlin rather than start at the local *liceo* in San Remo, and as we have noted, Dora did not stand in his way. In the fall, she was able to purchase the pension Villa Verde, in part with money that had come to her from the divorce proceedings, and set herself up as a hotelier in San Remo. As one can imagine, Benjamin was acutely aware of the ambiguous position in which his acceptance of Dora's hospitality placed him. In a moment of bemused self-laceration, he asked:

> What should I respond to a person who would tell me that I was lucky to be able to pursue my thoughts while strolling or writing without having to worry about my day-to-day existence and while living in the most splendid of areas—and San Remo is truly exceptionally beautiful? And if someone else were to rise up before me in order to tell me to my face that it was pitiful and a disgrace to nest, as it were, in the ruins of my own past, far from all tasks, friends, and means of production—confronted by that man, I would be all the more likely to fall into an embarrassed silence. (C, 465)

In the relative peace and security of the Italian countryside, he returned to his habit of long walks, with much reading and a good deal of writing. The summerlike weather in early December brought him into the high hills behind San Remo; he visited both Bussana Vecchia and Taggia, mountain towns with magnificent views onto the Mediterranean. At that point he was still so taken with his surroundings that he attempted to entice Kracauer, whom he had found despondent when they met in Paris in October, to come to San Remo. Although he couldn't promise warm weather, he hoped a certain coziness might be appealing: "When it gets cooler, . . . one can take advantage of a fireplace, which I dearly love, and on the basis of which, as you may remember, I once constructed an entire 'Theory of the Novel'" (GB,

4:538).[55] And the prices bore no comparison to those in Paris; he suggested to Kracauer that Dora might take him in as well, for the price of the cheapest pension in town, 20 lire per day.

But as the winter set in, he was plagued by his old feelings of desperation and depression. The pension itself soon proved to be more difficult than he had imagined: no sooner had he arrived than workers poured in. The noise of masons and plumbers brought back memories of the unfinished house on Ibiza. "I sometimes ask myself," he wrote Gretel Adorno on November 25, "whether it was preordained or determined by the stars that I should spend my days amid construction work" (BG, 124). His neurasthenia, however, was the least of his problems. Surrounded every day by foreign tourists and spa visitors whom he found "crass" and "from whom I can scarcely expect anything rewarding" (BS, 149), he had no one with whom he could share ideas. The only intellectually inclined Germans in the vicinity were, as luck would have it, Oskar Goldberg and members of his entourage. "I have fallen into the headquarters of the genuine Magic Jews. For Goldberg has taken up residence here, and he has delegated his disciple [Adolf] Caspary to the cafés, and the *Wirklichkeit der Hebräer* ["Reality of the Hebrews" (1925), Goldberg's major work] to the local newspaper stand, while he himself—who knows?—probably spends his time conducting tests of his numerology in the casino" (BS, 148). Remembering all too well his experiences with Goldberg in the early 1920s, Benjamin avoided any contact with his fellow guests and went out of his way to avoid greeting them. Even the town's cafés, his usual place of refuge in such situations, left him in the lurch, since he found them "even worse than those in the smallest Italian aeries" (BA, 59). In Skovsbostrand he had been deprived of the most basic research facilities; now, in San Remo, the intellectual isolation exerted a still more disastrous effect on his ability to work. "The worst of it," he tells Scholem at the end of the year, "is that I am growing weary. And this is an immediate consequence less of my insecure existence than of the isolation in which its vicissitudes tend to place me" (BS, 149).

The result now, as so often, was a desperate longing to be anywhere but where he was. He still hoped that Horkheimer might call him to America, but he knew that this was unlikely. Thus, when Scholem—having abandoned all hope of bringing Benjamin onto the path of a committed Judaism—suggested in late November that a short, three-to-four-week visit to Palestine might be financed with lectures or other activities, Benjamin responded with the same sort of enthusiasm he had expressed at Horkheimer's inquiry about visiting America. As these plans began to grow more definite in early 1935, Scholem offered Benjamin the choice of a spring or winter visit. Benjamin accepted the winter option, stressing that he couldn't come earlier because he feared that his relationship to the institute was in a critical phase. "As I told you before, the Institute in Geneva—among whose rafters, as you know, my exceedingly battered mortal thread is becoming lost—is moving to America. Since I must endeavor at all costs to maintain personal contact with its leadership, the probable European trip of one or two of its most influential people with whom I am in contact there—they are the directors or at least members of the administration—represents a date I simply cannot ignore" (BS, 153). Scholem read this letter as an unusually direct expression of Benjamin's reservations regarding the institute; the reference to Kafka's *The Trial* (rafters and thread) indicates, at any rate, Benjamin's psychic distance from Horkheimer and his colleagues, and the indecipherability of this group's actions and motives, as far as he was concerned.[56]

As he did so often, Benjamin found refuge from his unhappiness in his dream life. He told Kracauer about a dream in which his "guardian angel" brings him to Balzac. "We had to walk a long time over a pathless area of lush green meadows, through ash or alder trees; all the trees pointed in the direction I had to go, and finally, in a green, leafy arbor, I encountered Balzac, who was sitting at a table smoking a cigar and writing one of his novels. As great as they are, their achievement in an instant appeared more comprehensible to me when I noticed the indescribable stillness surrounding him in this green seclusion" (GB, 5:27). In the early 1920s, at a time when he was actively seeking an academic position, Benjamin had dreamt of encountering Goethe in the poet's study (SW, 1:445–446); now, in his own green seclusion in San Remo, he encounters "Balzac" (the cigar is reminiscent of Brecht) working under conditions much like those he himself had found so productive on Ibiza. This dream of great works emerging in a stillness speaks movingly of Benjamin's ambitions, frustrated as they were by his inability to land in a place "beneficial to my work and my disposition, if not for the eye" (GB, 4:543).

The pension itself proved to be less of a haven than he first imagined. In order to escape the other guests and the evening chill, he was forced to go to bed by 9:00 PM. Dreaming was thus a pleasure for which he had endless amounts of time. Reading was another. He returned to his habit of devouring detective novels, choosing works by Somerset Maugham, the ever-present Simenon, Agatha Christie (whose *Mystery of the Blue Train* he considered overrated), and Pierre Véry. Perhaps the greatest surprise is his enthusiasm for Robert Louis Stevenson's *Master of Ballantrae,* which he recommended to his current correspondents; he ranked it "ahead of almost all great novels, and right behind *The Charterhouse of Parma*" (C, 464). Not all his reading was pure pleasure. He still hoped to place brief reviews of books by Soviet Russian authors, so he read the satirical novel *The Little Golden Calf,* by the writing team of Ilya Ilf and Evgeny Petrov. Horkheimer had been very taken with Benjamin's survey of contemporary French literature, and he now asked for a series of more informal "letters from Paris." Although Benjamin produced the first of these only in 1937, the idea was a sufficient incentive for him to keep up to date on authors treated there (he read Julien Green's latest book, *Visionnaire,* and found it quite disappointing) and to discover new books and authors: Pierre Drieu la Rochelle's *La comédie de Charleroi;* Henry de Montherlant's *Les célibataires* (The Bachelors); and Jean Guéhenno's autobiographic *Journal d'un homme de quarante ans.*

One book made a lasting impression on Benjamin at this time; more precisely, it resurrected the memory of a dead friend. The exiled German historian and theologian Karl Thieme (1902–1963) had sent Benjamin a copy of his 1934 publication *Das alte Wahre: Eine Bildungsgeschichte des Abendlandes* (Old Verities: A History of Personal Formation in the West), and Benjamin fastened upon its critique of *devotio moderna* because it reminded him so powerfully of Florens Christian Rang and the particular "world of theological thinking" to which he had introduced Benjamin. It was ten years since Rang's passing, and Benjamin remained acutely aware of the relevance of Rang's teaching, his sense that "all of Western culture continued to be nourished by the content of Judeo-Christian revelation and its history"

(C, 466–467). He admitted to Carl Linfert that he could not overlook the radical differences between his own perspectives and those of Thieme, differences evident on every page of the latter's book, but he still acknowledged the "indubitable value" of Thieme's work (GB, 4:559).

In December his sense of isolation was relieved by a visit from Stefan, whom he had not seen in almost two years. Benjamin found his sixteen-year-old son composed, confident, and independent. But he lamented his inability to engage the young man in anything other than "serious" discussions—a consequence, perhaps, of Stefan's growing resentment of his all too absent father. Stefan intended to return to Berlin and his schooling, at least until he could be registered in the Italian school system in the spring. Other visits from the outside world remained a rarity; Egon Wissing came in late February, and Fritz Radt and his wife, Jula Cohn, paid a brief visit at the same time, but the departure of these dear friends only increased Benjamin's feeling of isolation. He was coming to the conclusion that life, even life in exile, was happening elsewhere. London was emerging as a center for many of his friends; Ernst Schoen seemed at least tentatively established there, Adorno had a network of contacts there and in Oxford, and Jula and Fritz Radt were considering it as a home. His thoughts turned frequently to Ibiza, "the contours of [which] have engraved themselves so deeply into me," and its little community. He was saddened to learn of the sudden death of young Jean Jacques Noeggerath from typhus; Alfred Cohn reported that the entire island had mourned his passing. As Benjamin told Cohn, this death had a greater effect on him than might have been expected, given the rather casual nature of their acquaintance, for "the thread of his life happened to intersect a knot of my own life" (C, 465). The recurrence of this figure of his "life's thread" suggests an increasing fatalism regarding the course of his existence, though it might be said that he always had a sense of his own destiny. Of course, Benjamin was not the only member of his circle to suffer. Schoen was despondent over his failure to find regular work; Adorno reported that his condition was "dire." And Gretel Karplus's letters, which usually lifted Benjamin's spirits, reflected a troubled stage of her relationship to Adorno. Ailing and unhappy, she had asked Adorno to come to Berlin and have a frank talk about their future together.

Despite the ever-present threat of psychic immobility and even catatonic paralysis—he speaks of the "seething haze of an almost permanent bout of depression" in a letter to Scholem—Benjamin continued to write, and even to receive assignments from both the French and the German émigré press (BS, 154). Many of these undertakings were a necessary evil. His living costs in San Remo were of course negligible, thanks to Dora's generosity, but he knew he could not stay forever, even if he wanted to. He received a generous check for 700 francs from the institute in late January, and a further 500 francs in February, enabling him to build up a modest war chest for the months after his stay at San Remo. Both of these payments he regarded as an honorarium for his essay on the sociology of language. So he continued to write small pieces, rather than the big projects to which he longed to return. As he reported to Alfred Cohn (now a businessman in Barcelona), "I am confining myself to hammering out one piece after another, without much haste and in a semi-craftsmanlike manner" (C, 476). In January he completed his first extended written work in French, the essay on Johann Jakob Bachofen that Jean Paulhan had encouraged him to submit to the *Nouvelle Revue Française* (now in SW, 3:11–24). Still not totally sure of his French, he traveled to Nice in early February in order to go over the penultimate version of the piece with Marcel Brion. The essay aims to inform the French public about a nineteenth-century figure who was little known in France at the time—a scholar whose researches into archaic sepulchral symbolism led to the discovery of a prehistoric "matriarchal era," a Dionysian gynecocracy, in which death was the key to all knowledge and in which the image was "a message from the land of the dead." Benjamin's interest in Bachofen stretched far back into his past; it had arisen during his student days in Munich, the days in which he first came into contact with the circle around Ludwig Klages. As it happened, the essay was ultimately rejected by the *Nouvelle Revue Française* in the spring. Although Jean Paulhan sent it on to the prestigious *Mercure de France* for consideration, it never appeared during Benjamin's lifetime, despite a further proposal in 1940 by Benjamin's friend, the bookseller Adrienne Monnier, to publish it in her *Gazette des amis des livres*. A similar fate befell another commissioned article on which Benjamin was working in early 1935: a review essay about Brecht's *Threepenny Novel*. Benjamin had been unusually taken with the novel, writing to all his friends with exhortations to read it and to send him anything they might hear about its reception. He in fact had placed the review, only to have his vexed relations with Klaus Mann derail the publication. When Benjamin wrote to Mann requesting that his payment for this publication in the Amsterdam-based journal *Die Sammlung* be 250 French francs, instead of the 150 francs proposed by Mann, the twelve-page manuscript was returned without comment, even though the piece was already typeset. "I would obviously have swallowed Mann's impertinence had I foreseen the result," Benjamin wrote to Brecht; adapting a line from the latter's "Song of the Insufficiency of Human Striving" in *The Threepenny Opera*, he added: "I showed myself as not clever enough for this world" (C, 484). On learning of Benjamin's imbroglio, Werner Kraft felt impelled to offer a lesson in the politics of exile: "You might want to take a cue from this: in the future always to be reconciled beforehand to the smaller sum, since even the greater one is so small that the difference hardly matters, where making a bare living is concerned." Kraft was emphatic in his shared sense that such journals keep their authors bound in slavery—and do so "out of a healthy class instinct" (quoted in GB, 5:92n). A third belletristic effort occupying Benjamin at this time, an essay on André Gide called "Letter from Paris," commissioned by the newly founded Moscow organ of the Popular Front, *Das Wort*, did finally appear in November 1936. The second installment of this work, which deals with painting and photography, was likewise commissioned by the journal's editorial board (to which Brecht belonged), but never printed. Ironically, it was this publication in *Das Wort* that later served as grounds for Benjamin's official expatriation, ordered by the Gestapo in February 1939.

In addition to these commissioned articles, Benjamin was engaged in rethinking and expanding the essay on Kafka that had appeared in shortened form in the *Jüdische Rundschau* in December. He had turned to yet another revision of his essay with unusual enthusiasm, spurred on by the possibility of placing a full-length book on Kafka with Schocken. Other factors played a role here. Since his completion of the final version of "Franz Kafka," the first volume of Kafka's collected writings had appeared. And he had received a lengthy, very positive critique of the essay from Adorno, who expressed an "immediate, indeed overwhelming, sense of gratitude" on reading it. "Our agreement in philosophical fundamentals," Adorno went on to say, "has never impressed itself upon my mind more perfectly than it does here" (BA, 66). In fact, Adorno proved to be the ideal early reader of the essay. He understood Benjamin's attempt to elicit what he himself called " 'inverse' theology" in a reading of Kafka's parables; he understood the immanence of myth and the archaic in the construction of modernity; and he understood better than others (Scholem, Kraft, or Brecht) the allegorical function of "script"—writing, the graphic representation of language, scripture—in Benjamin's essay. In early 1935 Benjamin significantly revised and expanded the essay's second section and planned even bigger changes to the fourth and final part. But the contract from Schocken never materialized, and the revision never went beyond a fascinating series of paralipomena.[57] At Werner Kraft's suggestion, he sent the manuscript of the entire essay to the French critic Charles du Bos, hoping he might recommend a French publication venue, but that effort, too, came to naught.

During the months in San Remo, Benjamin continued to work on shorter pieces. Pride of place went to the ongoing *Berlin Childhood around 1900*. He composed a preliminary draft of the section called "Colors," and finished another section called "Halle Gate," which finally became "Winter Evening." He also completed two of his most delightful short works. In early December, the story "To the Minute" appeared in the *Frankfurter Zeitung*. This semiautobiographical piece depicts the anxiety produced by speaking into a studio microphone and reaching a live audience: the speaker loses all sense of time, panics at the thought that he will run over, cuts himself short . . . and finds himself with several minutes of airtime and nothing more to say. And "Conversation above the Corso," which appeared (under a pseudonym, as did "To the Minute") in the *Frankfurter Zeitung* in March, fictionalizes a number of Benjamin's experiences, including aspects of his stay on Ibiza and of his visit to the annual Carnaval de Nice, which he went to see at the end of February 1935 (finding it "much nicer than the snobs make it out to be" [GB, 5:57–58]). The story condenses these experiences and interlaces them with reflections on cultural phenomena tied to "states of exception" such as the carnival. Despite Benjamin's self-deprecating comments in letters (he likened the "Conversation" to one of "those still photographs of a fighter in picturesque positions" [BA, 77]), the story can be appreciated for its mastery in combining casual observation with profound meditation, a combination characteristic of Benjamin's short prose.[58]

Adorno's letter on the Kafka essay reminded Benjamin of what he really wanted to be working on: the study of the Parisian arcades. Following their conversations in the Taunus Mountains in the late 1920s, Adorno had constituted himself the advocate of Benjamin's project to Benjamin himself. He had written a remarkable letter on November 6, 1934, filing a joint claim to the territory Benjamin had staked out as his own, and even going so far as to indicate which approaches were viable and which to be avoided:

> What you say about concluding the period of essay writing and finally resuming work on the Arcades is in fact the brightest piece of news that I have heard from you in many years. You are well aware that I really regard this work as part of our destined contribution to *prima philosophia*, and that there is nothing I desire more than to see you finally capable, after all the long and painful hesitations involved, of bringing this work to a conclusion which does justice to the momentous subject matter. And if I can contribute any aspirations of my own to this work, without your taking this as an immodest suggestion, it would be this: that the work should proceed without qualms to realize every part of the theological content and all the literalness of its most extreme claims, everything that was originally harbored within it (without qualms, that is, concerning any objections stemming from that Brechtian atheism which we should perhaps one day attempt to salvage as a kind of inverse theology, but which we should certainly not duplicate!); further, that for the sake of your own approach you should strongly refrain from associating your thought with social theory in an external manner. For it really seems to me that here, where the most absolutely decisive and fundamental issues are concerned, one has to speak out loudly and clearly, and thereby reveal the undiminished categorial depth of the question, without neglecting theology here; and then, at

this decisive level, I believe that we can all the more easily avail ourselves of the Marxian theory precisely because we have not been forced to appropriate it externally in a subservient fashion: that here the "aesthetic" dimension will be capable of intervening in reality in an incomparably more profound and revolutionary manner than a class theory conceived as some "deus ex machina" is capable of doing. It therefore seems indispensable to me that precisely the most remote themes—that of the "ever-same" and of the infernal—should be expressed with undiminished force, and that the concept of the "dialectical image" should also be expounded with the greatest possible clarity. No one is more aware than I am that every single sentence here is and must be laden with political dynamite; but the further down such dynamite is buried, the greater its explosive force when detonated. I would not dare to offer you "advice" in these matters— what I am attempting to do is simply to stand before you almost like a representative of your own intentions against a certain tyranny, which, as you yourself once did with Kraus, only needs to be named as such in order to be banished. (BA, 53–54)

This intensive engagement—even in its assumption of unsolicited co-proprietorship—struck an immediately encouraging note with Benjamin. In the years to come, however, Adorno's increasingly dictatorial attitude toward what could and could not be said regarding the arcades would have a more baleful effect on the work and its reception—to say nothing of Benjamin's state of mind.

Now, in December 1934, on reading the Kafka essay, Adorno discerned the outlines of the arcades glimmering in the background. He seized on the distinction Benjamin draws in the essay between the concept of "historical age" *(Zeitalter)* and epochal "age of the world" *(Weltalter),* insisting that Benjamin should have reverted to the central organizing conception of history in the arcades project, the relationship between "primal history and modernity." "For us the concept of the historical age is simply non-existent, . . . and we can grasp an epochal age of the world only as an extrapolation from the literally petrified present" (BA, 68). Adorno's reminder here about the centrality of the philosophy of history would have a profound influence on Benjamin's work as he returned to the arcades project in the course of 1935. Whereas the project's first phase, between 1927 and 1930, had been characterized by multifarious notes and sketches displaying the influence of Surrealism and of what we might call "social psycho-analysis," with an emphasis on the notion of a "dreaming collective," Benjamin began to steer the project in a more sociological and histori-cal direction when he took it up again in early 1934, stimulated then by the thought of a major essay on Baron Haussmann's large-scale renovation of Paris, which entailed the demolition of many old neigh-borhoods and many arcades. Adorno's letter reinforced his under-standing that the history of Paris in the nineteenth century was itself an emergent "historical object," one conditioned on continuing ideo-logical construction—or, in Adorno's terms, "extrapolation" from the "literally petrified present." Benjamin's self-appointed task was to re-cover aspects of a "primal history" that had been buried and distorted by conventional historiography; this multiangled excavation would allow a countervailing history to emerge. Now, in San Remo, Benja-min started working through his notes from the first phase of the project with this new perspective in mind. On his return to Paris in the spring, he would launch an extensive elaboration of his research on the arcades. He knew, though, that extended work on the arcades could only be undertaken with major support from the institute. And the institute had a journal to publish. By the end of his stay in Italy, pressure was mounting on Benjamin to commence work on the essay on Eduard Fuchs that Horkheimer had "urgently requested" for the *Zeitschrift.* This was an assignment in every sense of the word, one that Benjamin, by "ingenious stalling," had long evaded. But, as he admitted to Scholem in February, it was an assignment he could no longer duck.

Adorno was not the only friend with whom Benjamin struggled for intellectual mastery. Ernst Bloch had just published his new book, *Heritage of Our Times,* and Benjamin began to hear stories from all sides about how Bloch had invoked him and his work as part of the modernist landscape of the 1920s. Benjamin was in fact determined to mend fences with Bloch, whom he had not seen since leaving Berlin, and who he felt had often over the years "purloined" his ideas. Before he could obtain a copy of the new book, Benjamin drafted a prophylac-tic letter to his old friend (it is one of only two surviving letters of his to Bloch), seeking a meeting and a clearing of the air. "I am convinced

that since our last conversation enough bloody and tear-laden water
has flowed downstream to allow for an exchange of ideas, something
that might furnish new matter for both of us.—And now I come to my
second point: having something new to say does not mean that we
can let old matters rest" (GB, 4:554). The remainder of the letter is
devoted to explaining—presumably to himself as much as to Bloch—
his unusual sensitivity to Bloch's reception of his work. As defensive
as the letter is, it nonetheless shows Benjamin making a concerted
effort to prevent this relationship from falling prey to speculation
and rumor.

When he finally read the book, in mid-January, he shared his ostensibly disparaging but restrained and subtle assessment with Kracauer, soliciting the latter's confidence on the matter, since "Bloch
might already be in Paris" (GB, 5:27). Having compared Bloch's book
to "majestic thunder preceded by brief lightning-like tidings," Benjamin says that this thunder sets up its own "authentic echo"—an echo
resounding out of "hollow spaces." He alludes here to a central concept of Bloch's text, that of the "hollow space [*Hohlraum*] with sparks,"
which is said to be "our condition" at present and presumably for a
long time to come.[59] The literary form proper to such a circumstance
is said to be montage, as realized in the 1920s in all the arts. Montage,
or "philosophical montage," is the method and chief subject of the
book. "There is now," Bloch writes, in a section on the "theater of montage," "no other existence except that of the crack, of dislocation . . . ,
ruins, intersections, and hollow spaces." "Montage in the late bourgeoisie is the hollow space of the latter's world, filled with sparks and
intersections of a 'history of appearance.'" The elaboration of this inconspicuous history, with its "overlapping of historical faces," brings
Bloch before the "hieroglyphs of the nineteenth century," and it is
here in particular that one encounters a whole set of Benjaminian motifs, including colportage, gaslight, world exhibitions, plush, the detective novel, Jugendstil, and so on. Bloch not only makes brilliant
use of what he calls, in his 1928 review of *One-Way Street*, "revue
form in philosophy," but also knowingly appropriates (not without
handsomely crediting Benjamin) the subject matter and constellatory
methods of the arcades project, which he would have learned about in
conversations in Berlin in the late twenties, and which is variously

echoed in Benjamin's feuilleton writing for one who has ears to hear. For his part, Benjamin found Bloch's exposition of this material lacking in "concentration"—precisely the sort of charge that would be leveled at *The Arcades Project* after its publication.

> Instead of allowing the subject at hand to emerge clearly, we find again the old philosophical procedure of "taking a stand" toward each and every issue that has had its day. The subject was obvious enough and, in the chapters on non-contemporaneity, was occasionally treated with great exactitude. . . . The things in question here do not allow themselves to be put right and rectified in empty space [*im leeren Raum*]: they demand a forum. I see the great weakness of the book in its avoidance of this forum and thereby of the forensic evidence as well, the foremost example of which is the *corpus delicti* of the emasculated German intelligentsia. Had it succeeded, it would have become one of the most important books of the last thirty or even one hundred years. (GB, 5:28)

He was less measured—and even more ironic—in his characterization of the book to Alfred Cohn, to whom he wrote on February 6. Along with its self-conscious kaleidoscope style, he disapproved of the book's "exaggerated claims":

> It in no way corresponds to the circumstances in which it has appeared. Instead, it is as out of place as a fine gentleman who, having arrived to inspect an area demolished by an earthquake, has nothing more urgent to do than immediately spread out the Persian carpets his servants had brought along and which were, by the way, already somewhat moth-eaten; set up the gold and silver vessels, which were already somewhat tarnished; have himself wrapped in brocade and damask gowns, which were already somewhat faded. Bloch obviously has excellent intentions and valuable insights. But he does not understand how to put them thoughtfully to work. . . . In such a situation—in a slum—nothing is left for a grand gentleman to do but to give away his Persian carpets as bed covers, cut his brocade into coats, and have his splendid vessels melted down. (C, 478)

Faced with the dreariness of San Remo, Benjamin made a point of traveling to nearby Nice as often as he could. "Not as if there were a lot of people for me [in that city], but still there are one or two. And in addition sensible cafés, bookstores, well-stocked newsstands—in short, everything it is totally impossible for me to get here. While there, I also replenish my supply of detective fiction. I need quite a lot, since my nights here usually begin at about 8:30" (C, 477). One of the people he could meet in Nice was his friend Marcel Brion (1895–1984), a French novelist and critic associated with the literary journal *Cahiers du Sud*. Brion had reviewed Benjamin's book about the German *Trauerspiel* on its appearance in 1928, and he was instrumental in securing the publication of a French translation of Benjamin's "Hashish in Marseilles" in the January 1935 issue of *Cahiers du Sud*—for which he corrected a fair bit of Blaupot ten Cate's uncertain French. A further effort on his part to arrange for a translation of Benjamin's essay "Marseilles" bore no fruit, though Brion continued in various ways to promote Benjamin's work.

Toward the end of February Benjamin suddenly found himself compelled to leave his "place of asylum in San Remo" (C, 480)—where he had planned to stay until May—on account of the unexpected arrival of his former mother-in-law. The months in San Remo had proven to be no easier than those in Svendborg. Not long before he left, he sent Gretel Adorno a pretty bleak final balance:

My dear Felizitas,/as you hear so much from me about my material worries, it would be understandable—and perhaps desirable—for you to assume that I am "otherwise" well. It would be an act of friendship for me to leave you in this assumption./On the other hand, there are moments in which silence acts as a poison—and as it has been forced upon me, at least as far as my voice would reach, you too will now be confronted with it, and will not wish to withdraw from it./I have been experiencing hours and days of the most profound misery, the like of which I do not think I have known in years. Not in the manner of the suffering one finds within periods of contentment, but rather full of a bitterness that flows away into nothingness and is fueled by trifles./It is entirely clear to me that the decisive reason for this is my situation here, my unimaginable isolation. Being cut off not only from people, but also from books, and ultimately—in the worst weather—even from nature. Going to bed before 9 every evening, making the same few journeys every day, on which one knows from the outset that one will not encounter anyone, going through the same stale reflections on the future every day: these are circumstances that, even with a very robust inner constitution—which I had always considered mine to be—must ultimately lead to a severe crisis. / The strange thing is that those conditions which should fortify me most—I mean my work—only heighten the crisis. I have now completed two substantial studies, the "Bachofen" and the review of Bertold's [sic] novel, and my inner burden is not becoming any lighter. / There is nothing to be done; my stay here will have to be terminated one day in any case (my former mother-in-law is coming here), and I cannot even welcome that. There is only one thing that could help: for us to see each other. If only I could absolutely count on it! (BG, 132)

The fear that his work might no longer serve to keep him afloat was no doubt the most insidious of his many ills. On February 22 he wrote to Scholem in his capacity as Benjamin's archivist, lamenting "the present span of history and the course of my life, which have both made the finite collection of my infinitely scattered [verzettelten] production seem less predictable, not to mention less probable, than ever before" (BS, 153). And he saw no end in sight; although he never underestimated Hitler's tenacity, he did underestimate his brutality.[60] Commenting on the remarkable stabilization in Germany after the Röhm upheavals, he predicted to Alfred Cohn that something like a Brüning regime might emerge, that is, government by emergency decree with the parliament left behind (C, 476). Brüning himself, who was chancellor from 1930 to 1932, called his regime "authoritarian democracy." To invoke such a conception in early 1935 is certainly to underestimate the measures in place to ensure Nazi control of Germany, and effectively to disregard the wholesale atrocities already under way there.

CHAPTER NINE

The Parisian Arcades

Paris, San Remo, and Skovsbostrand, 1935–1937

THE first two years of exile had brought unrelieved chaos into Benjamin's life—and into that of virtually every German exile. In 1935, 1936, and 1937, however, a certain tenuous stability would emerge. During these years Benjamin enjoyed gradual increases in his stipend from the Institute of Social Research, and he felt confident of receiving a steady stream of commissions from the *Zeitschrift für Sozialforschung* that could be supplemented by other, more occasional journalistic work; meanwhile, his position in the Parisian intellectual scene had marginally improved. This is not to say that exile became easier, or his long-term outlook any better, but simply that the horrors of the years just past had given way to a somewhat more predictable situation. Under these conditions, Benjamin was able to think in a more sustained manner about his most important work. The arcades project took a major leap forward, as Benjamin was given the opportunity for the first time to present his findings in concentrated form: in the course of 1935, he prepared what he called an exposé of the project, which reflected its current state. In order to compose this prospectus, Benjamin assessed the massive aggregate of material he had assembled during the preceding seven years and, on that basis, reconceived the project's theoretical armature. The result was the terse text known as "Paris, the Capital of the Nineteenth Century." Out of this synoptic involvement with his materials one more essay emerged. "The Work of Art in the Age of Its Technological Reproducibility" was conceived and written as a contemporary pendant to the *Arcades,* its analysis of film culture complementing the examination of the visual arts around 1850 undertaken in the larger project. Between 1935 and 1939 Walter Benjamin engineered one of the most compelling and enduring theories of modernity, and that process had its inception in the nine months between May 1935 and February 1936.

The first days of 1935, though, found Benjamin in flight before his former mother-in-law, who was about to arrive in San Remo. Benjamin hurriedly removed from Dora's modest pension into the considerably grander confines of the Hôtel de Marseille in Monaco, an establishment that had known him in earlier days when, as he put it, "I myself was still a member of the ruling class" (GB, 5:68). What Benjamin does not reveal here—or elsewhere, except in the most oblique literary manner (Convolute O in *The Arcades Project*)—is the cause of his attraction to Monaco: its casino. A letter from his sister of March 1935, in reply to what was clearly a desperate plea for help, contains the first open reference to an affliction that had long plagued Benjamin—and would from now on ensure that his pleas for support to those who knew him best often fell on deaf ears. Dora Benjamin declares herself reluctant to help her brother because she is sure that he has again gambled away what money he does have. And Dora Sophie, his former wife, writes in May to say that she has heard he lost a "large sum" at the roulette tables in Monaco.[1] Scholem, too, in his memoir, notes laconically that he was often unwilling to help for the same reason. We do well, then, to read the urgent entreaties that fill so many of Benjamin's letters in exile against this shadowy background; if one compares his depiction of his living costs with those of other refugees, one comes to the conclusion that they were sometimes exaggerated so as to garner funds for gambling and women. At the time, for example, that he wrote to his sister asking for money, he was receiving 500 francs per month from the Institute of Social Research (then the equivalent of the institute's 100 Swiss francs), plus his rent from Berlin, plus the money that trickled in from his writings. His sister was earning 250 francs per month by providing child care, plus a pittance when she was able to sublet part of her small apartment. Our knowledge of Benjamin's compulsive life in the Parisian demimonde hardly diminishes the true horror of his life in exile. If anything, the very tawdriness of those aspects of his life is perhaps the best indicator of his desperation. In order to understand this behavior from within, one should consider his portrait of the gambler, and the gambler's intoxicated experience of space and time, in *The Arcades Project*.

> Such intoxication depends on the peculiar capacity of the game to provoke presence of mind through the fact that, in rapid succession, it brings to the fore constellations which work—each one wholly independent of the others—to summon up in every instance a thoroughly new, original reaction from the gambler. . . . The superstitious man will be on the lookout for hints; the gambler will react to them even before they can be recognized. (AP, O12a,2; O13,1)

And we should remember that for Benjamin, thinking itself is an existential wager arising from the recognition that truth is groundless and intentionless, and existence a "baseless fabric." The gaming table for him has ontological significance as an image of world play.

Of course, Benjamin was well aware that he could hardly afford to linger long in Monaco—"where the last forty or fifty financial fortunes in the world present themselves to one another in their yachts and Rolls Royces, the whole place shrouded in those dark storm clouds which are the only things I share with them" (BA, 78)—and he began immediately to cast about for ideas as to where to move next. Deprived of the bits of extra income that had formerly allowed him to travel, Benjamin was now limited in his movements to places where he could exist on the support of the institute alone. By far the easiest course would have been an immediate move to Paris, despite its costs, because he was bound in any case to meet with a delegation from the institute there in May. He hesitated, though, first because his best hope for an affordable living situation—his sister's apartment—was not available. Dora Benjamin's "apartment" in the Villa Robert Lindet was actually one large room, and she used it to look after five children from the neighborhood every morning in order to make ends meet; there was simply no place for Benjamin. But he also hesitated because he badly wanted to meet Gretel Karplus and Adorno somewhere in the south of France in the coming weeks. An interim solution would have been a move to Barcelona, where he would have the company of Alfred Cohn. Cohn's reply to Benjamin's inquiry as to whether one could subsist in Barcelona on 100 Swiss francs per month casts an interesting light on the conditions under which the exiles were forced to live:

> One can naturally get by on 100sfr—although in that case one can spend little beyond the cost of food and lodging, if one stays in a pension. Of course there are pensions, Spanish ones, for 150 pesetas (although vacancies are rare), if one takes a room inside the house—so-called airshaft rooms. In spring that is even still bearable. I think it would be more practical for you if you were simply to take a room, which costs 50 pesetas, and is certainly not uncomfortable. You can take your breakfast au zinc, your lunch in an acceptable kosher restaurant for 2 pesetas, which is probably cheapest and sufficient. You might perhaps buy your own evening meal, which yields the following budget (100 sfrs = 238 pesetas):
>
> | | |
> |---|---|
> | Room | 50 with laundry |
> | Breakfast | 18 |
> | Lunch | 60 |
> | Evening meal | 60, as you require! |
> | And fruit during the day, with a café in the afternoon | |
>
> 188, which leaves 50 pesetas for other expenditures (GB, 5:52n).

Racked by indecision, Benjamin in the end remained where he was, staying in Monaco for six weeks, doing little work, carrying on his correspondence, and making frequent excursions into the surrounding high hills. He was soon joined by Egon Wissing, who, in his own plight, had moved to Monaco and thrown himself upon his cousin's mercy. "And," Benjamin wrote to Gretel Karplus, "as unbelievable as it sounds: for more than two weeks I have been supporting us both with my feeble means, which was admittedly possible only by lowering our standard of existence to a level I have never before experienced. Yes, it has been a memorable week for us (and who knows how many similar ones still lie ahead)." Supporting two indigent refugees meant that Benjamin was no longer able to pay his hotel bill. "The weather is fine. If one has ventured far enough into the morning or the afternoon on foot, one reaches a place where, for a moment, one is very glad to be still on hand, in spite of everything. On the way back, however, one often lacks the courage to cross the threshold of the unpaid hotel, where one is greeted by the even more unpaid, in fact utterly unpayable, physiognomy of the patron." He asks Gretel to renew her attempts, hopeless as they may seem at present, to secure him financial support, since "someone who is as rightly intimidated by the face of reality as I am can devote his strength only to the daring of his hopes" (BG, 141–142).

Among the letters preserved from this period is a copy of one to his Latvian lover, Asja Lacis, whom he had not seen since 1929, and who had written at the beginning of the year to report that her prolonged efforts to find him employment in Moscow had turned up nothing. Composed shortly after his forced departure from San Remo, the letter sounds a peculiarly Benjaminian note of gratitude: "Given the miserable state I'm in, it amuses people to waken cheap hopes in me. One thus becomes as morbidly sensitive to hope as somebody with rheumatism is to inflammation. It is *very pleasant* to know a person who, in such circumstances, raises no hopes—even if this is only because she is too lazy to write a letter. This person, then, is you—and you therefore stand on one of the few elevated spots still left in my rather inundated 'soul.' Hence, your not writing meant almost as much to me as your voice would, if I could hear it again after so many years" (GB, 5:54). At the end of the letter, he casually mentions that he is no longer staying with his wife—"that was too difficult in the long run"—and, after giving Asja an address where she can write him in Paris, he adds a sentence harking back to his memoir of his visit to the Soviet Union, the *Moscow Diary:* "I would like to see you, now, in your reindeer coat, and to accompany it through the streets of Moscow" (GB, 5:55). He also tells Asja that Wissing will soon be in Moscow, where he was hoping to be able to practice medicine. Moscow was for Benjamin, too, the third point of a triangle of final escape from Europe that included New York and Jerusalem. He can thus tell Asja, only half in jest, that if Wissing has not found work for him in Moscow within six months, she would hear no more from her Walter. After traveling to Moscow in July 1935 and struggling for several months, Wissing did in fact find work for himself in October at the Central Institute for Cancer Treatment and Research. By the end of the year, however, he had elected to leave the Soviet Union. His letter to Benjamin casts light on the situation of those émigrés who did choose the Soviet Union, as well as on the decision by a figure such as Bertolt Brecht not to go there: "For me—as for all doctors—there would have been no avoiding Soviet citizenship sooner or later—even as early as 1936, according to what I've heard. You know that means the total loss of personal freedom, since one never receives a visa for foreign travel (there is a special directive to the effect that people with relatives outside Russia are under no circumstances to be given a visa)" (GB, 5:56–57n).

Despite the temptations of further flight, Paris ultimately represented the possibility of continuing the arcades project and the necessity of commencing the essay on Eduard Fuchs. The prospect of once again, after so many months, working in a library by now played a role not just in Benjamin's waking life but in his dreams as well. He reported that the years spent working in libraries, "of letting so and so many thousand printed characters run through [his] fingers every week," had created "certain almost physical needs" in him, needs that have long remained unsatisfied (GB, 5:70). He had an unsettling dream of seeing a stranger who, arising from his desk, took a book from *his own* library. Benjamin's agitation led him to reconsider his situation— and propelled him even more powerfully toward Paris. He thus left Monaco in early April, still unsure he could afford life in the French capital.

En route to Paris, Benjamin made a stopover in Nice, spending the night in the Hôtel du Petit Parc, where he had contemplated suicide three years before. From Nice, he traveled on to Paris, moving on April 10 into the Hotel Floridor on the Place Denfert-Rochereau, where he had stayed almost exactly a year before. Benjamin could hardly have known it in April 1935, after a year in which he had been able to produce so little of importance, but the coming year—in which he would finally be able to devote himself to the complex of ideas around the Parisian arcades—would see him compose a number of the works for which he is still best known today. The productiveness of these months was in fact similar to that of the period that saw the composition of the *Trauerspiel* book and the early drafts of *One-Way Street*; this was a similarity of which Benjamin himself was becoming aware.

It is important to note that the remarkable intellectual successes of the year to come were made possible by support from the Institute of Social Research. Benjamin had written from Nice to Max Horkheimer, reaffirming his dedication to the institute: "Nothing is more urgent for me than to link my work to that of the Institute as closely and as productively as possible" (C, 480). Whatever his internal reservations might have been, Benjamin was well aware that the Institute had become his mainstay. Not only had its journal, the *Zeitschrift für Sozialforschung*, become the most important site for the publication of his work, but the stipend provided by the institute since the spring of 1934 was his only regular income during the thirties. In April 1935 a constellation of circumstances bound Benjamin more closely than ever to the institute, and lent crucial impetus to his work on the arcades. Soon after his arrival in Paris, Benjamin finally had the meeting on which he had pinned so many of his hopes during the winter and early spring. This meeting with a director of the institute, Friedrich Pollock, had two important outcomes. First, it relieved the worst of Benjamin's financial concerns, at least in the short run. Pollock doubled his monthly stipend from 500 francs to 1,000 francs for four months (from April through July 1935) and, in addition, paid him 500 francs in cash for resettlement in Paris. And Pollock made a crucial suggestion regarding the study of the arcades: that Benjamin produce a comprehensive exposé of the project. Up to this point, Benjamin had spoken to Horkheimer and his colleagues of the planned book only in the most general terms: a systematic evaluation of those materials— "about which I had hinted here and there, never divulging very much" (BS, 158)—was now imperative for both him and his supporters.

Benjamin straightaway grasped the intellectual lifeline extended to him and plunged into work on the exposé. The composition of the piece was aided, paradoxically, by the annual closing of the Bibliothèque Nationale: deprived of the opportunity to follow the traces of his material into new paths, Benjamin sat in his room and wrote, with only the voluminous notes of his arcades project on which to draw. The result, produced relatively rapidly in the course of the next month, was "Paris, die Hauptstadt des XIX. Jahrhunderts" (Paris, the Capital of the Nineteenth Century), the first of two epitomizing presentations of the arcades complex (the second was written in French in 1939). The completion of the exposé restored, however temporarily, Benjamin's confidence and even will to live: "In this work I see the principal, if not the only, reason not to lose courage in the struggle for existence" (BA, 90). Benjamin commented to Werner Kraft about the surprising speed with which he had been able to bring order—a "crystallization" (BA, 88)—to his heterogeneous compilation of notes and ideas: "The deepest reason for the Saturnian tempo of the thing was the process of total upheaval that a mass of ideas and images had to undergo. They stemmed from the far distant period of my immediately metaphysical, indeed theological thinking, and the upheaval was necessary so that they could nourish with their full force my present disposition. This process went forward in silence; I myself was so little aware of it that I was tremendously surprised when—as a result of an external stimulus—the plan of the work was recently written down in just a few days" (C, 486). He offered a more detailed account of the genesis of the project to Adorno:

> There stands Aragon at the very beginning—*Le paysan de Paris*, of which I could never read more than two or three pages in bed at night before my heart started to beat so strongly that I had to lay the book aside . . . And yet my first sketches for the "Arcades" date from that time.—Then came the Berlin years, during which the best part of my friendship with Hessel was nourished on myriad conversations concerning the arcades project. It was at this time that the subtitle "A Dialectical Fairy Tale [*Feerie*]" first emerged, which is no longer suitable today. This subtitle suggests the rhapsodic character of the presentation as I then conceived it. (BA, 88)

In characterizing that early stage of the project as "rhapsodic," Benjamin concedes its derivation in "an archaic form of philosophizing naïvely caught up in nature." The project as it now stood, he remarked to Adorno, was decisively indebted to the encounter with Brecht, and he asserted that the "aporias" resulting from this encounter—that is, from the confrontation of a historical-materialist perspective with an originally Surrealist one—had been worked through.

Composed in a highly concentrated, almost stenographic style, the 1935 exposé ranges widely over a series of topics (from iron construction and photography to the theory of commodity fetishism and of dialectics at a standstill), defining historical figures (from Charles Fourier and Louis Philippe to Baudelaire and Baron Haussmann) and, finally, nineteenth-century types (from the collector and the flâneur to the conspirator, the prostitute, and the gambler). *The Arcades Project* was founded on a set of complex theoretical positions that Benjamin had gradually refined over the last seven years and which appear as the governing categories of the exposé. And, as its organizing metaphor, the arcades themselves, those metropolitan worlds in miniature, take on new meaning: in their constitutively ambiguous status—half interior, half public sidewalk; half site for the display of commodities, half space for urban leisure—they furnish the primary example of what Benjamin now calls the "dialectical image." In 1935 the dialectical image was conceived as "wish image" and "dream image," a dynamic figuration of the collective consciousness in which the new is permeated with the old and in which the collective "seeks both to overcome and to transfigure the immaturity of the social product and the inadequacies in the social organization of production." The 1935 exposé is in this sense the culmination of the "stage of social psychology" that had characterized the project since the late 1920s. In the exposé, these dream images attest the ability of the collective to see into a better future: "In the dream in which each epoch entertains images of its successor, the latter appears wedded to elements of primal history—that is, to elements of a classless society. And the experiences of such a society—as stored in the unconscious of the collective—engender, through interpenetration with what is new, the utopia that has left its trace in a thousand configurations of life, from enduring edifices to passing fashions." In his 1929 essay on Surrealism, Benjamin had postulated the latent existence of "revolutionary energies" in the outmoded. Indeed, the opening paragraph of the 1915 address "The Life of Students" says as much. In the perhaps more complex model enunciated here, traces of utopia, engendered in the intersection or collision of the new and the antiquated, can be read off of untold aspects of contemporary society. "Paris, the Capital of the Nineteenth Century" was written as a kind of road map for such divinatory reading of social phenomena. Paris's railroad stations, Fourier's phalansteries, Daguerre's panorama, and the barricades themselves—all these emerge in the exposé as wish images that hold within them a potentially revolutionary knowledge. Even those structures and spaces dominated by commodity display and exchange—the world exhibitions, the bourgeois interior, the department stores, and the arcades—are shown to harbor a paradoxical possibility for social change.

The exposé heralded more: an arcades project that would have included an advanced genre and media theory. The democratic potential of the newspapers, the politically neutralizing panoramic literature, and photography's extension, through mass reproduction, of the sphere of commodity exchange are all treated as constituent aspects of the new social modernity that had arisen in Paris by the mid-nineteenth century, together with a new multiperspectival way of seeing. And in its concluding sections Benjamin hinted at the comprehensive theory of modern experience to which his late work is largely devoted. In his consideration of the figure of Baudelaire, Benjamin offers a foretaste of what has become a classic reading of modern literature—his presentation of Baudelaire's poetry as reflecting the transformative "gaze of the alienated man." He portrays Baudelaire here as the quintessential midcentury flâneur, lingering on the threshold of the marketplace—threshold theory *(Schwellenkunde)* is fundamental to *The Arcades Project*—when he is not adrift on the waves of the urban crowd. The crowd is the "veil" through which the familiar city beckons to the flâneur as phantasmagoria; the stroller intermittently encounters the ghosts of far-off times and places restlessly inhabiting phenomena of daily life. Baudelaire's melancholy gaze is thus representative of the flâneur's allegorical mode of perception, in which an ancestral forest of symbols keeps breaking through the evolving cityscape, and in which the historical object, citing past and future simultaneously, like any object of fashion, unfolds as palimpsest and picture puzzle. The exposé lists, without analysis, the motifs that will be central to the later reading of Baudelaire: the poet's shattering impression of a woman in mourning who emerges suddenly from the crowd, his experience of the new and ever-same that stamps the modern face of Paris, and his adumbration of a subterranean Paris, with its chthonic resonance of a mythic past. The final section, on Haussmann's bold and ruthless city planning or "strategic embellishment," stages one of Benjamin's most explicit attempts to come to terms with class conflict. It ends with an emphatic affirmation of dialectical thinking as "the organ of historical awakening," for the realization of "dream elements" in the course of waking up—realization in the sense of both recognition and utilization—is the paradigm of authentic historical thinking.

After its completion, Benjamin wrote to Gershom Scholem on May 20: "With this exposé, which I had promised without giving it much thought, the [arcades] project entered a new phase, in which for the first time it bears more resemblance—a distant resemblance—to a book. . . . This book will unfold the nineteenth century from the perspective of France" (C, 481–482). And in a letter to Adorno that contained a copy of the exposé, Benjamin expressed the hope that he was closer than ever before to the elaboration of a full-length study based on his material. Nothing could have been more welcome to Adorno than this news: he had long held the arcades to be "not only the center of your philosophy but, in light of all that can be spoken philosophically today, the decisive word, a chef d'oeuvre like no other" (BA, 84). Adorno's response was indeed immediate and unequivocal: "After an extremely careful reading of the material," he wrote on June 5, "I believe I can now say that my former reservations about the Institute's attitude have been entirely dispelled. . . . I shall write to Horkheimer at once to urge acceptance of the work en bloc and thereby, of course, appropriate financial support" (BA, 92–93).

For all his enthusiastic support, certain aspects of the exposé obviously troubled Adorno, and he offered a trenchant critique in a letter that August—a letter so searching and precise that it has come to be known by the place where it was posted: the "Hornberg letter," which Benjamin characterized as "great and memorable" (BA, 116). Adorno focuses unrelentingly on the social-psychological theories that had moved to the center of Benjamin's project, and offers a devastating evaluation of the perceived consequences of that development. In characterizing the current state of Benjamin's thinking about the dialectical image as "undialectical," Adorno insisted that "if you locate the dialectical image in consciousness as 'dream,' not only has the concept thereby become disenchanted and commonplace, but it has also forfeited its objective authority, which might legitimate it from a materialist standpoint. The fetish character of the commodity is not a fact of consciousness, but is dialectical in the crucial sense that it produces consciousness" (SW, 3:54). Adorno argues that this ostensible psychologization of the dialectical image ensures that it will succumb to the "magic of bourgeois psychology." Most damning is his claim that Benjamin's understanding of the collective unconscious cannot be clearly differentiated from that of Jung. "The collective unconscious was invented only to distract attention from true objectivity and from the alienated subjectivity that is its correlate. Our task is to polarize and dissolve this 'consciousness' dialectically into society and individual" (SW, 3:55–56). No less biting is Adorno's claim that this psychologization effectively reorients the very notion of the classless society in an undialectical manner, backward toward myth. Throughout his work, Adorno scrupulously avoids any suggestion of a gnostic sublation of modern conditions as a wholesale "phantasmagoria of hell." For him, and soon for Benjamin, any such expressly utopian conception runs the risk of being absorbed, co-opted, and refunctioned by the dominant class—which unfailingly turns the image of utopia against itself into a tool of domination. In the years to come, Adorno would not always prove to be the most generous reader of Benjamin's work (as opposed to later years, when he wrote luminous essays on his departed friend), and Benjamin often bridled at his criticisms. The Hornberg letter is different, though, and Benjamin acknowledged that "all of your reflections—or almost all of them—go to the productive heart of the matter" (BA, 117). He thus gives the appearance of acceding to Adorno's two major points regarding the psychologization of the dialectical image and the careless deployment of the term "classless society." On one "quite decisive" point, however, he stands firm: "how indispensable certain elements I pointed out in this constellation [of the dialectical image] appear to be: namely, the dream figures" (BA, 119). The dialectical image, he insists, cannot be dissociated from the process of "historical awakening"—that is, awakening from and to "that dream we name the past" (AP, K1,3). Such historical dream is to be distinguished from the psychic dream of individual consciousness. In other words, Benjamin's conception is more dialectical and more objective than Adorno thinks. At any rate, Adorno's letter propelled Benjamin into a rearticulation of the theoretical armature of the arcades project. The Hornberg letter and Benjamin's positive response mark the end of the stage of Surrealist-inspired social psychology and the inception of a more resolutely sociological accounting of objects.

The remarkable high that accompanied the composition of "Paris, Capital of the Nineteenth Century" soon gave way, predictably enough, to a crash. Although the usual complaints about noise are absent from Benjamin's letters, his neurasthenia left him exposed to the rapid temperature changes of the Parisian spring, its icy wind and scorching sun, and his "organism oscillated between bouts of fever and bouts of sleeplessness" (GB, 5:102). He confessed to Alfred Cohn that he hadn't felt so poorly in years—and complained that there was almost nothing to cheer him up. He had returned to a Paris that was even less hospitable to German exiles than the one he had left. His daily experience of the French xenophobia that seemed to deepen with every month was exacerbated by more pointed anti-Semitic encounters; even his attempts to obtain aid from various Jewish welfare organizations left a bad taste in his mouth. "If the Jews remain dependent solely on their own kind and the anti-Semites, there probably won't be too many of them left" (GB, 5:103). He realized, nonetheless, that he was in fact among the more fortunate of those members of his circle left on the Continent: "The depredations occasioned by misery, as it gradually enters into alliance with these times, are beginning to be palpable, even in those closest to me" (GB, 5:103).

He was thinking here especially of his cousin Wissing, who, on his return to Paris, had again begun to use morphine. Both Benjamin and Gretel Karplus suspected that their Berlin acquaintance Fritz Fränkel was responsible for Wissing's relapse. Fränkel, a neurologist specializing in addiction, had represented the Königsberg Workers' and Soldiers' Council at the founding of the Spartakusbund, the forerunner of the German Communist Party, during the German Revolution of 1918–1919. His contributions in the 1920s to the party's efforts to improve hygiene and medical care for workers had brought him into contact first with Benjamin's brother, Georg, and later with his sister, Dora, and through them with Benjamin himself. Benjamin's essay "Garlanded Entrance" of 1930 described an exhibition on which both Fränkel and Dora Benjamin had worked. As their acquaintance gradually deepened, both Fränkel and their mutual friend, the neurologist

Ernst Joël, acted as "medical advisors" for the drug experiments Benjamin undertook in Berlin, some of them in the company of Wissing and his first wife, Gert. Fränkel was now living in Paris (in an apartment building in the Rue Dombasle into which Benjamin himself would move in 1938) and seeing Wissing frequently.[2]

More troubling was a new chilliness that had crept into Benjamin's correspondence with Gretel Karplus, a development she addressed in a letter in late June, in which she gently pleads with Benjamin to restore "the one friendship I believed to be unshakable" (BG, 147). The causes were probably complex, not the least of them being a misreading of several letters on both of their parts, but their relationship at this point was certainly clouded by Gretel's resolution of her difficulties with Adorno. This point was brought home to Benjamin when Gretel essentially ventriloquized Adorno's pronouncements on the arcades project. Commenting on the possibility that Benjamin would shape the project in a way that would make it publishable in the *Zeitschrift für Sozialforschung,* she had written on May 28: "I would actually consider that very dangerous, as you would have relatively little space and would never be able to write what your true friends have been awaiting for years, the great philosophical study that exists purely for its own sake and makes no compromises, and whose significance would help to compensate for a great deal of what has happened these last few years. Detlef, it is a matter of rescuing not just you but this work" (BG, 146). Contributing to their vexed relations was the presence of Egon Wissing as intermediary. Gretel had overcome her initial antipathy and grown close to Wissing during his frequent stays in Berlin, and now, as he shuttled back and forth between her and Benjamin, he was evidently doing mischief by playing one off against the other. In his somewhat stern but still friendly response to Gretel's plea for the restoration of their former closeness, Benjamin sought to allay his correspondent's "impatience" by citing "existential conditions," his work, and his "total exhaustion," but he expressed some impatience of his own with regard to Wissing: "I must admit that, at times during this gloomy and disconcerting development, I sometimes feared that my *one* violation of my old maxim in matters of friendship would one day cost me W[issing]'s and yours. And it did not increase my confidence when I saw that—and how—W had already relapsed in his first days here. When one is separated for as long as you and I are, every person who travels between us inevitably becomes a messenger. And W cannot be the right one for me at present. The significance of his failure for me can only be understood if one imagines the way we lived together in the south and all the efforts I made for his sake. To add to all these doubts, I now do not know what level of communication you have found amongst yourselves" (BG, 148). Benjamin's "maxim" was of course his long-observed practice of keeping his friendships in perfect isolation from one another; and his query regarding the "level of communication" between his friends suggests a jealous suspicion that Wissing and Gretel, too, had become intimate. By July some of the old cordiality had crept back into their exchanges, but this vexed interlude certainly marked the end for both of them of any possibility of something more than friendship.

At about the same time—and presumably in Ernst Bloch's company—Benjamin ran into Ernst Kantorowicz (1895–1963), a German Jew whom he detested as an opportunist. Kantorowicz later became famous in English-language intellectual circles in the late 1950s, while working at the Institute for Advanced Study in Princeton, with the publication of his book *The King's Two Bodies*, a study of "medieval political theology" that discriminates within the figure of the king a corporeal person and a symbolic embodiment of the commonwealth. During the period of exile, Kantorowicz was still best known for his very free, heavily theologized biography of the Holy Roman Emperor Friedrich II—a book that cemented his reputation among liberal and leftist intellectuals as an irredeemable partisan of the radical right. In the years after World War I, Kantorowicz had served in the Freikorps, helping to put down with wanton bloodshed the "Greater Poland Uprising" and the Spartacist revolt in Berlin. While studying in Heidelberg, he began to move in the circles around George and Gundolf—and it was this affiliation that shaped the biography that won him a chair at Frankfurt. These associations could not save him from Nazi racial policy, however, and after losing his chair, he had fled abroad and begun a metamorphosis that Benjamin describes in scathing terms: "Only the notorious corks float to the surface, as for example the unspeakably dull and subaltern Kantorowicz, who has promoted himself from theorist of the state party to a position of communist officiousness" (GB, 5:104).

During the summer these difficulties were balanced to a degree by the restoration of amicable relations with two other old friends: Bloch and Helen Hessel. Bloch finally came to Paris in mid-July, and he and Benjamin, long-standing partners and rivals in philosophy, met soon afterward. Benjamin's task was a delicate one: he badly wanted to clear the air and return to cordial relations, but he was also adamant that Bloch understand his strong disapproval of the selective appropriation, however discerning and imaginative, of his arcades motifs in *Heritage of Our Times*. To his surprise and relief, he found Bloch eager to conciliate: Benjamin encountered a "great loyalty" in his old friend. The result, as Benjamin reported to Scholem, was the preservation of a hedged and guarded goodwill: "[Although] the relationship can never evolve to the complete satisfaction of both parties, I will nevertheless most definitely accept responsibility for preserving the association. I, whose weaknesses have surely never included illusions or sentimentality, do so in view of my pure insight into the limitations of this relationship; and, on the other hand, the dispersion of my friends isolates every single one of them, myself included" (BS, 170–171). In the weeks to come, before Bloch's departure for the Côte d'Azur at the end of August, they would see each other often, and Benjamin thus gained a discussion partner such as he had not had since the months in Skovsbostrand. Given his ongoing wariness of Bloch's aptitude for seizing on his ideas, however, he was careful to steer their talk away from the arcades (BS, 165). Benjamin was glad, too, to restore cordial relations with Helen Hessel, with whom he had broken badly in Berlin. They now visited fashion shows together, and Benjamin read her little book on the fashion industry, *Vom Wesen der Mode* (On the Nature of Fashion), whose detailed portrayal of the social and commercial determination of fashion he found excellent—and which he cited at some length in the arcades notes.

On the other hand, Benjamin complained in July that he had not made a single new friend—no "incisive acquaintance"—since his days on Ibiza in 1933; he felt as isolated in Paris as he had been in Skovsbostrand or San Remo. He made every effort to keep up with his French acquaintances—Marcel Brion and Jean Paulhan in the south, and

Adrienne Monnier in Paris—but seemed unable to make new ones. As poet, bookseller, and publisher, Monnier had been a significant figure in Parisian modernism since the early 1920s. Her bookstore, La Maison des Amis des Livres, on the Rue de l'Odéon in the Sixth Arrondissement, was part bookshop, part lending library, and part meeting place and lecture hall. Benjamin had begun to use her lending library as early as 1930, when he was introduced to her by the Germanist Félix Bertaux:

> Madame, a writer and essayist from Berlin, M. Walter Benjamin, said to me yesterday: "Do you know the author of some poems that were published six years ago in the N.R.F. and intensely affected me? Of all the things I have read in French, this made the strongest impression on me." I did not feel entitled to give him your name without your authorization; if, however, you do not absolutely insist on retaining your anonymity vis-à-vis M Benjamin (who has translated Proust), he would be delighted if you would send him word that he could see you. . . . Madame, excuse the indiscretion of my approach, but I was so touched by the devotion of this strange reader that I wanted you, at the least, to be part of it, at the same time that I wanted to renew my personal and lively homage to you.[3]

By 1936 Benjamin's relationship with Monnier had become something very like a "friendship in the German sense" (GB, 5:230), and her shop became an increasingly important point on Benjamin's Paris compass.

Benjamin's isolation was occasionally broken by meetings with Kracauer and with Bloch. The contrast between the fortunes of his friends and their psychological conditions was glaring: Kracauer was usually despondent, still downcast over his failure to find a publisher for his novel *Georg*, and as uncertain about his future as Benjamin; Bloch was his usual ebullient self, fortified by his ongoing publishing successes and by his recent marriage to his third wife, Karola. Benjamin's own antipathy toward Karola was an additional complicating factor: "It is a question of atmosphere: just as there are certain women who understand how to give ample scope to the role of friendship in their husbands' lives—and of no one is this truer than of Else von Stritzky—so there are others in whose presence such things easily

29. Adrienne Monnier. Photo by Gisèle Freund (1912–2000) *(© Gisèle Freund-RMN. Musée National d'Art Moderne, Centre Georges Pompidou, Paris, France © CNAC/MNAM/ Dist. RMN-Grand Palais/Art Resource, NY)*

wither. Linda was already halfway to becoming one of these, and Karola seems to belong among them completely" (BA, 77). Linda Bloch was also in Paris, and miserable, and Benjamin's inherent—if intermittent— generosity showed itself with her: they reconciled their differences and he did what he could to help her.

Fortuitous encounters would occasionally lighten his mood. In late spring he ran into his friend Wieland Herzfelde and Herzfelde's older brother, the former Dadaist John Heartfield (1891–1968). Heartfield, whose singular skill at photomontage had made him a sought-after book, magazine, and poster designer in Berlin, is best remembered today for his covers for the *Arbeiter-Illustrierte Zeitung*, which include some of the most famous of Hitler satires. The brothers were

30. Benjamin at the card catalogue, Bibliothèque Nationale
in Paris. Photo by Gisèle Freund (1912–2000) (© Gisèle
Freund-RMN. © RMN-Grand Palais/Art Resource, NY)

in Paris to attend an exhibition of Heartfield's photomontages in April
and May. Heartfield made an immediate impression on Benjamin,
who saw him more than once during his stay. The discussions inevitably
centered on the rigors of exile; Benjamin extracted from Heartfield the
story of his flight from Germany under harrowing circumstances.
Heartfield's political photomontages had made him an obvious target
for the new regime in 1933, and he had in fact narrowly escaped when
his apartment was stormed by Hitler's brownshirts. And, of course,
there was their shared interest in photography, about which Benjamin
noted "a really good conversation" (C, 494).

The early summer found Benjamin spending his days in various
departments of the Bibliothèque Nationale, pressing forward with his
work on the arcades. He requested, and was granted, access to the
library's notorious "Enfer"—the official designation for the French

state's collection of erotica and pornography that had been started in the 1830s (a selection from this collection was shown to the public for the first time during an exhibition in 2007). It is clear that the composition of the exposé had instilled a new confidence in the importance of the project, and he oversaw the extension of his research into ever more distant corners of the great library. He was now convinced that the project's "conception, so very personal in its origin, addresses the decisive historical interests of our generation" (BS, 165). It is at this time that Benjamin began more fully to formulate the complex interrelationship of a particular past epoch—Paris in the mid-nineteenth century—with the contemporary moment. In order to discern the outlines of those "decisive historical interests" of the present moment, the historian, so he believed, needed to uncover and reconstruct a historical object that had been occluded: he called this "the attempt to retain the image of history in the most inconspicuous arrangements of existence, in its detritus, as it were" (BS, 165). The notes for the project grew rapidly in these months, as Benjamin copied out citations from a growing variety of nineteenth- and twentieth-century sources, and appended his own concise commentaries and reflections. The sheer material volume of the project now made it difficult to be transported, and so at Pollock's suggestion, and with his financial assistance, Benjamin photocopied the entire manuscript of notes and materials assembled thus far.[4] He was also beginning to "explore" the first volume of Marx's *Capital* (BA, 101). Preoccupied as he was with pushing the arcades project forward (and supported by his temporarily increased stipend from the institute), Benjamin wrote very little for publication in 1935. In July the last article he published in Germany during his lifetime appeared under a pseudonym in the *Frankfurter Zeitung.*

As he worked on the arcades project during the remainder of 1935, Benjamin's thoughts were turning increasingly to the visual arts. He visited a major exhibition of images and documents associated with the Paris commune that accompanied the annual commemoration of the event in the suburb of Saint-Denis. And a show with 500 of the greatest works of quattrocento Italian art made a lasting impression. His correspondence with Karl Thieme shows him to be an astute and deeply engaged observer of older artworks, and many of his ideas and observations on the arts are recorded in the arcades manuscript. Although direct discussion of Renaissance painting rarely enters his essays, a footnote on Raphael's Sistine Madonna in the essay "The Work of Art in the Age of Its Technological Reproducibility" of 1936 indicates the lasting impact of this exhibition. That essay, though, shows him probing more deeply into the relationship between photography and film, taking into account other pre-cinematic forms in the nineteenth century as well.

At the end of June he attended an event that could have had epochal significance for him: the International Congress of Writers for the Defense of Culture. This large-scale conference, attended by 230 writers serving as delegates from forty countries, with an audience of three thousand, was held between the twenty-first and twenty-fourth of June at the Palais de la Mutualité in the Rue Saint-Victoire.[5] Billed to the general public as a gathering of writers concerned to preserve Western culture against the threat of fascism, the congress had its initial impetus from within the Comintern in Moscow. Its original organizers were Johannes R. Becher, later minister of culture in the German Democratic Republic, and the novelist Henri Barbusse, editor of the Communist journal *Monde;* working within the framework of the Union of Soviet Writers, the organization that had taken the place of the avant-gardist RAPP in 1934, they hoped to bring a broad range of Western writers into line with Soviet cultural policy. After Barbusse's withdrawal due to illness, André Malraux and Ilya Ehrenburg gradually assumed the role of organizers, broadening the conception of the congress and freeing it from direct Party control. A revised invitation to the congress appeared in *Monde* in March 1935, signed by Malraux, Ehrenburg, Becher, and—giving it an important imprimatur—André Gide; the invitation emphasized the role of the writer as a "defender of the cultural heritage of humanity" and played down all political conclusions.[6] Following on this new orientation, the opening session included speeches by four major authors, E. M. Forster, Julien Benda, Robert Musil, and Jean Cassou, all of whom rejected the unitary notion of "cultural heritage" marketed by the Soviet delegation. Nevertheless, as Anson Rabinbach has pointed out, there was little disagreement with the general characterization of Stalinism as a humanism, and indeed as the only form of humanism capable of successfully resisting the rise of fascism in Europe. This conception of humanism entailed a rejection of the artistic practices of both the revolutionary avant-garde (represented primarily by the Surrealists, who were banned from the congress following an altercation between André Breton and Ehrenburg) and the "bourgeois" writers represented by Benda, Huxley, Forster, and Musil. In their place, there emerged a vaguely defined but explicitly pro-Soviet progressive agenda, striving for a golden mean, so to speak, between the cultural "heritage" (in the jargon of the congress) and the "struggle against capitalist degeneration and fascist barbarism" (in Georgi Dimitrov's words).[7] The novelist and critic Jean Cassou defined the boundaries of that discourse with precision: "Our art does not put itself in the service of the revolution, and the revolution does not dictate to us the responsibilities of our art. But our entire art in its most living dimension, our living conception of culture and tradition, leads us to revolution."[8] Put more baldly, the congress advanced what might be called an antifascist aesthetic—neither revolutionary materialism nor unpolitical liberalism, but rather a cultural synthesis based on the premise that the Russian Revolution represented a moment in what Jean Guéhenno called the "great, long, and patient humanistic revolution which has been taking place since the history of mankind began."[9] Fascism was regression, a return to the Middle Ages. Communism was the future.

Both Benjamin and Brecht, who were able to meet often during the congress, were deeply disappointed. Brecht objected to the "grand words" and "bygone concepts of love of freedom, dignity, and justice" and decried the suppression of such terms as "class" and "property relations."[10] He was at the time working on a satirical novel about European intellectuals, the *Tui-Roman*, and thus, as Benjamin pointed out, "got his money's worth" at the congress. Benjamin, on the other hand, found the opportunity to speak with Brecht "the only gratifying" aspect of the event. The best he could manage was a remark to Horkheimer to the effect that the permanent bureaus created in the course of the congress "might occasionally intervene in a useful manner" (GB, 5:126). He undoubtedly found dispiriting the silent complicity of the writers with the rejection of advanced art that followed from Andrei Zhdanov's speech at the 1934 Moscow Writer's Congress. There, the Communist Party manager Zhdanov had declared the hegemony of "socialist realism" and the proscription of advanced art.

Benjamin's then unpublished talk, "The Author as Producer"—with its claim that only aesthetically progressive art forms can at the same time be politically progressive—now reads as a critique *avant la lettre* of the widespread capitulation to the new Soviet model.

In mid-July, at a time when he was making exciting new discoveries for his arcades project almost on a daily basis, his living conditions improved as well. While his sister was abroad, he was able to move into her apartment in the Villa Robert Lindet, an unprepossessing street in the Fifteenth Arrondissement. His relations with his sister had improved during their mutual exile, no doubt as a result of their common dilemma and their lack of other human contact. Dora worked as a servant in a French home during the first two years of her exile in Paris—a common solution for many women deprived of any opportunity to practice their profession. By early 1935, though, she had made a tentative return to the field of social work in which she had been trained, caring for the children of refugees in her apartment and supplementing this by subletting a portion of her apartment to the mother of her neighbor and friend Fritz Fränkel. But just as she made this new start, there appeared the first signs of the inflammatory disease of the spinal cord—ankylosing spondylitis—that would finally take her life in Switzerland in 1943; the symptoms were accompanied by severe depression. In February 1935 Walter had attempted to help while he was still in San Remo, asking his former wife to send enough money to see his sister through the crisis. As Dora's reply to a request for aid from her brother in March 1935 makes clear, the basis for her existence was at least as precarious as his own: "But I don't think you are admitting to yourself what the struggle for existence means for me, or what it means to work with almost daily severe pain. If I am robbed of the possibility of occasionally taking a couple of weeks off, my situation will be such that I could immediately take my own life. And, at the moment, I still don't want to do that."[11] Remarkably enough, she follows this desperate depiction of her situation with the news that she is enclosing 300 francs of her own money and 300 more that Dora Sophie Benjamin owed her. By the summer, she was earning enough to undertake a trip abroad—and to allow her brother to move into her apartment while she was gone. After two years of being forced to live in hotels, Benjamin now luxuriated in the "feeling of residing in private rooms." Even though he was to remain only until October, he nonetheless tried to make the apartment his own, putting up some prints that Gretel Karplus had given him during their days together in Berlin, and hanging alongside them the cherished transparencies that he had obtained from the Copenhagen tattoo artist.

Despite his more comfortable lodgings, August was a difficult month for Benjamin. His stipend from the institute had reverted to its normal level of 500 francs, and since he had worked on virtually nothing but the arcades since spring, he could count on no revenues from his writing. He thus no longer had the resources to cover even his basic living costs. And Paris in August was a ghost town; the troubled times could not deter the French from departing en masse for their holidays. Benjamin noted that even the émigrés "put their pennies together" and left the city—those who had pennies, that is. He was left alone, his only possibility for travel coming in his dreams. "I think fondly of Barcelona," he wrote to Alfred Cohn. "For your sake; and also because of my unaccustomed summer sedentariness that would there find an end. A steady rain is falling just now, into which one can montage the rhythm of the railway axle, to say nothing of the veil that it weaves around the image of the Sagrada Familia or of the Tibidabo" (GB, 5:146).[12] His "sedentariness" also gave him more time for reading; he supplemented his daily diet of French sources for the arcades with nocturnal wanderings through detective novels and philosophy, including a new book by Leo Strauss, *Philosophy and Law*. A good bit of his reading at this time was driven by a concern very close to home: his brother's incarceration in the Sonnenburg concentration camp. He read Willi Bredel's *Die Prüfung: Der Roman aus einem Konzentrationslager* (The Test: A Concentration Camp Novel), commenting that "this book is certainly worth reading. The question as to why the author could achieve no full success in his representation of a concentration camp leads one to instructive considerations" (GB, 5:130). And, although it is not known whether he was able to obtain it, he asked friends to send him Wolfgang Langhoff's *Die Moorsoldaten*. Langhoff, like Bredel, had been an inmate of a camp, Börgermoor, that lent its name to the "soldiers" of the book's title.

Dora Benjamin returned to her apartment and Benjamin moved out on October 1. Dreading a new series of cheap hotels, he succeeded in finding a more stable situation. He moved into the building at 23 Rue Bénard, where he shared an apartment with another German émigré, Ursel Bud, who was working as a clerical assistant in Paris. Bud, like Benjamin, was a Berlin Jew, but she was twenty years younger and came from a less exalted background, having received commercial training at a vocational school for girls. Like Benjamin, she was later held in an internment camp in France (albeit much longer, from October 1939 through May 1941) and would attempt to flee France through Marseilles in 1942. There all trace of her disappears.[13] Benjamin was able to live in the apartment in the Rue Bénard for two full years, until October 1937, subletting a "very small" but comfortable room (GB, 5:198–199). The neighborhood, in the heart of the Fourteenth Arrondissement, was rather gloomy, but it had good access to the Métro and, best of all, was only a twenty-minute walk to Benjamin's favorite cafés further north along the boulevard du Montparnasse. Benjamin assembled a bit of furniture with the help of his friends Arnold and Milly Levy-Ginsberg, transferred his little collection of prints and transparencies, and found that he had a home. The usual difficulties of moving were compounded, as he tells Brecht's collaborator Margarete Steffin, by "an insurrection of the objects that surround me . . . : since I live on the seventh floor, it began with the elevator's going on strike, followed by a mass migration of the few belongings I care about, culminating in the disappearance of a very beautiful fountain pen that I consider irreplaceable. This was cause for considerable distress" (C, 510–511). By the end of the month, however, this distress had decamped, "swept away, perhaps, by the fantastic fall storms whistling about my aerie day in and day out" (C, 511)— and by the comforts of the new apartment, which he found so pleasant, with hot water in the bathroom and a telephone, and so far above what he had come to expect, that even the "heavy weight" of his work was noticeably lightened (GB, 5:198–199).

Notwithstanding the new apartment and the ongoing stimulation he derived from his work on the arcades, he experienced a return of depression and desperation that autumn. This was of course the general character of Benjamin's exile, but autumn 1935 brought him to a new low point, one he repeatedly characterized as "hopeless." "Things around me have been too bleak and uncertain," he wrote to Scholem, "for me to dare deprive my work of the scarce hours of inner equilibrium. . . . I am provided with the bare necessities for *at most* two weeks a month" (C, 511–512, 514). To Horkheimer he wrote: "My situation is as burdensome as any financial position that does not involve debts can possibly be. . . . I will only mention in passing that I ought to renew my *carte d'identité* [without which he could not visit a doctor or identify himself to authorities] but do not have the 100 francs this requires" (C, 508–509)—a lament that did not go unheeded, since Horkheimer, not uncharacteristically, forwarded an extra 300 francs for the new identity card and a French press pass on October 31. Adorno agreed to exert "moral pressure" on Else Herzberger in the hope that she might renew the allowance that had long since lapsed (GB, 5:113n). Despite these signs of support, Benjamin saw his situation as desperate enough to warrant serious consideration of a move to Moscow, where Wissing had meanwhile succeeded in establishing himself, working at the Central Institute for Cancer Research and Treatment. Wissing, ever the enthusiast, was confident that Benjamin would find work in the Soviet Union and had mobilized a number of contacts to this end—including Lacis and Herwarth Walden. Walden, the gallerist and publisher who had been a central figure in Berlin modernism in the teens and twenties, was now teaching in Moscow. Gretel Karplus raised some very sensible objections to this move, asking Benjamin whether he in fact wanted to live in the same city as Asja Lacis, and whether he could actually adapt to such an enormous change in his living conditions, which would of course be coupled with the loss of his institute stipend. This scheme, too, soon evaporated— and for the last time. The fate of Herwarth Walden provides a cautionary note at this juncture. Although we know relatively little about Walden's years in Moscow, it is clear that he was unable to resist entering into debate with those who equated advanced art with fascism— and this had fatal consequences for him. He died in a Soviet prison in Saratov in 1941. It is difficult to imagine Benjamin acquiescing quietly to an aesthetic regime that would have been as dangerous for him as it was for Walden.

His own misery was compounded by the bad news that continued to pour in from his friends and family. Despite early signs of success, Alfred Cohn's attempts to base an existence in Barcelona were foundering, and he announced that he would have to move once again (a resolution he did not carry through). Benjamin was shattered to think that Cohn might disappear from the "circle of the few people that still exist for me." Noting that the moral crisis of the age was increasingly exacerbated by the material one, he told Cohn that he had begun to keep a "loss list" and that he wasn't sure that he himself would not be found on it one day (GB, 5:183). He was forever worried about Egon Wissing; rumors had reached him that Wissing was endangering his position in Moscow through renewed recourse to morphine. Ever since taking him in on the Riviera, Benjamin had felt an almost paternal responsibility for his wayward cousin. Gretel reassured him that she had heard nothing to suggest that Wissing had succumbed again.

Worst of all was a serious crisis in his relationship with Scholem. Scholem was not so close as the friends from his school days, Cohn and Schoen—but he was his longest-standing partner in intellectual exchange. Although developments in their lives and intellectual orientations—above all, Benjamin's idiosyncratic leftism, which only heightened his opposition to Zionism—had of necessity put distance between them, Benjamin was still remarkably dependent on the give-and-take of his exchanges with Scholem; he knew that he would always get a brutally honest and frequently eye-opening reply to anything he might say or send. In the course of the summer and fall, though, Scholem's end of the correspondence slowed to a trickle, and by December it had effectively ceased. Benjamin took deep offense at this neglect. He asked Kitty Marx-Steinschneider to visit Scholem in order to give him a firsthand account of his Paris friend's desperate situation and to ask why the invitation to Palestine had not been renewed. "These notions provoked a reaction from Scholem," Benjamin wrote to Gretel, "whose pitiful awkwardness (to avoid speaking of falseness) gives me the saddest idea not only of his private nature, but also of the moral climate of the country in which he has been educating himself for the last ten years. None of this had been made explicit in our correspondence, for since I have been faced with the possibility of defeat his approach to it has been as dilatory as it was once insistent.

As you can imagine, however, my own desire to let him know what I think of the awkwardness, cloaked in self-importance and secrecy, with which he evades any active empathy with me is very slight. I do not consider it an exaggeration if I say that he is inclined to see in my situation the avenging hand of the Almighty, whom I have angered through my Danish friendship" (BG, 172–173). Benjamin could let off some steam in writing to Gretel in this vein, which together with everything else must have entertained her, while he grimly resolved to bear with the ideologically conditioned frailties of his friend and archivist. The immediate situation would be resolved only in the coming spring.

He continued to work in the face of adversity throughout the autumn of 1935. Not only his material and personal plight, but the increasingly uncertain fate of his work weighed heavily upon him: "From time to time I dream about the derailed book projects—the *Berlin Childhood around 1900* and the collection of letters—and then I am surprised when I find the strength to embark on a new one. Of course, under such conditions that its fate is even more difficult to predict than the form my own future is likely to take. On the other hand, a book is, as it were, the shelter I step beneath when the weather gets too rough outside" (BS, 171). The new work he refers to here included, first of all, the essay on Eduard Fuchs. He was pushing ahead with the preparatory readings for the essay, which the institute now pressed on him, and which had forced him in August to put his arcades studies on the back burner. He had met with Fuchs, whom he liked personally, on and off throughout the summer, and now hoped that he could finish the article quickly. In fact, the material studies for the project dragged on for another year and a half, during which it was continually set aside for other projects, until the essay was finally drafted, with unexpected and gratifying ease, in January and February of 1937. Although he seems not to have worked on any of the sections of the *Berlin Childhood* during the fall, he did produce memorable works of fiction. The sparkling little tale "Rastelli Erzählt" (Rastelli's Story), a parable of instrumentality, appeared in a Swiss newspaper, the *Neue Zürcher Zeitung*, in November, and was evidently part of "a small stack of short stories" composed that fall "just to double and triple my quota of work" (C, 513). He also put together a lecture on

Goethe's *Elective Affinities* scheduled for February (he tells Scholem and others) at the Institut des Etudes Germaniques at the Sorbonne—an event that may or may not have taken place. And there was the further possibility of a review of Dolf Sternberger's 1934 book on Heidegger, *Der verstandene Tod* (Thinking on Death). Sternberger (1907–1989) had met Benjamin a few years earlier in the home of Ernst Schoen; he was also close to Adorno between 1930 and 1933 and took part in the latter's seminars. In 1934 he joined the editorial board of the *Frankfurter Zeitung*. Benjamin was interested in what Sternberger had to say about "Heidegger and language," but he never undertook to review his book, possibly because of the aversion he felt for the Freiburg philosopher himself, whose worldwide fame filled him with gloom and foreboding (GB, 5:156; GB, 4:332–333).

Above all, there was a new work in the area of aesthetics—a "programmatic" piece, as he characterized it to several of his correspondents—which, taking off from the "Little History of Photography" of 1931, with its examination of the impact of reproduction technology on the composition and reception of artworks, explicitly aligned itself with the epistemological and historiographic principles of the arcades project: that is, with the attempt to recognize the "fate" of art in the nineteenth century from the perspective of the present. The first recorded mention of "The Work of Art in the Age of Its Technological Reproducibility," now Benjamin's best-known essay, is in a letter of October 9 to Gretel Karplus:

> In these last weeks, I have come to recognize that hidden structural character of today's art—of the situation of today's art—which makes it possible to recognize what for us is decisive, but only now taking effect, in the "fate" of art in the nineteenth century. In this regard, I have realized my epistemological theory—which is crystallized around the very esoteric concept of the "now of recognizability" (a concept that, very probably, I haven't shared even with you)—in a decisive example. I have found that aspect of nineteenth-century art which only "now" is recognizable, as it never was before and never will be afterward. (GB, 5:171)

He wrote even more portentously to Horkheimer a week later, describing the work as an advance in the direction of a materialist theory of art. . . . If the subject of the book [on the arcades] is the fate of art in the nineteenth century, this fate has something to say to us only because it is contained in the ticking of a clock whose striking of the hour has just reached *our* ears. What I mean by this is that art's fateful hour has struck, and I have captured its signature in a series of preliminary reflections entitled "The Work of Art in the Age of Its Technological Reproducibility." These reflections attempt to give the questions raised by art theory a truly contemporary form and, to be sure, from the inside, avoiding all *unmediated* reference to politics. (C, 509)

The essay's reflection on film, in particular, as a quintessentially contemporary art, and on its shock-informed reception as symptomatic of profound changes in a human "apperception" everywhere interpenetrated by the "apparatus," served to illuminate the great transformation in the relation of art to technology with which the arcades project was concerned.

Clearly inspired by these fast-erupting ideas, Benjamin suspended his "historical studies" at the Bibliothèque Nationale and followed the "whisperings of his room" (GB, 5:199), spending September and most of October burrowed away, composing what turned out to be the first version of the essay. He returned to this version in December, at which point he began rewriting the whole essay and, after a conversation with Horkheimer (who was in Paris in mid-December), adding footnotes. This second German version, which also incorporated suggestions from Adorno regarding its political-philosophical argument, was completed by the beginning of February 1936. Of the several extant versions of the essay, the second German version is at once the most comprehensive and most specific on a number of key points; Miriam Bratu Hansen dubbed it the "Urtext," and the name has stuck. Benjamin soon afterward initiated a further rewrite, however, which stretched on until March or April of 1939. It was this third and final version—Benjamin himself never ceased regarding it as a work in progress—that formed the basis of the first publication of the essay in German in 1955, the starting point proper for its subsequently widespread dissemination. Published for the first time in May 1936 in the institute's *Zeitschrift* in a French translation, it remains today Benjamin's most oft-cited work.

"The Work of Art in the Age of Its Technological Reproducibility" inquires into the possibilities open to human experience under the conditions of modern capitalism, deeply tied as these are to modern technology.[14] It proceeds from the conviction perhaps best articulated in "Experience and Poverty"—that one of capitalism's principal effects is the destruction of the conditions necessary for an adequate human experience. The essay operates with a seemingly contradictory understanding of *Technik:* technology is at once a main cause of this impoverishment of experience and a potential *remedy.* As Benjamin puts it in "Eduard Fuchs, Collector and Historian," human experience has been denatured by our "bungled reception of technology" (SW, 3:266). In consequence of this misdirected reception, which Benjamin traces in its nineteenth-century provenance in *The Arcades Project,* modern technology functions to anaesthetize human sensory capacities, while at the same time aestheticizing what are at base brutal conditions of production and domination. Yet that very technology has the potential to liberate human experience from its material bondage. The artwork essay analyzes this potential through a bravura reconsideration of new perceptual modes inherent in film. In a multifaceted argument that is constructed thetically, that is, through a montage of individual theses, Benjamin attributes to film two central capacities: first, as a reproducible work of art, it has the capacity to shake the foundations of a cultural tradition on which the hegemonic class has depended for centuries to maintain control; and second, he attributes to film the capacity to effect profound changes in the very structure of the human sensory apparatus. New apperceptions and reactions are necessary if humans are to confront the vast and inimical social apparatus currently in place.

Benjamin's best-known innovation in the essay is his focus on the modern work of art's reproducibility. A work's reproducibility devalues its existence in a particular place and time, thus undermining its uniqueness and authenticity and changing its way of transmitting cultural tradition. "The authenticity of a thing is the quintessence of all that is transmissible in it from its origin on, ranging from its physical duration to the historical testimony relating to it. Since the historical testimony is founded on the physical duration, the former, too, is jeopardized by reproduction, in which the physical duration

plays no part. And what is really jeopardized when the historical testimony is affected is the authority of the object, the weight it derives
from tradition" (SW, 3:103). Benjamin focuses this issue of transmissibility in the concept of aura, "a strange tissue of space and time: the
unique apparition of a distance, however near it may be" (SW, 3:104–
105). A work of art may be said to have an aura if it instances a unique,
authentic status based less on quality, use value, or worth per se than
on its figural distance from the beholder. This distance is not primarily a flat space lying between the monument and its audience but the
bearing of a "strange tissue" of psychological inapproachability, an air
of authority generated by a work on the basis of its position within a
tradition. The aura phenomenon in a work of art reflects sanction—
the privilege of inclusion in a time-tested canon.[15] Benjamin's idea is
of course a scandal and a provocation: he mounts a frontal attack on
the notion of the iconic work of culture, the product of a great genius
that by its very nature modifies our understanding of human experience. The attack is necessary if art is ever to be emancipated from the
spell of cultural tradition—with its rootedness in cult and ritual. For
Benjamin, the "present crisis and renewal of humanity"—one should
keep in mind that this text was written under the advancing shadow
of fascism—eventuates only by means of a "shattering of tradition"
(SW, 3:104)—not the same as its simple abandonment. The sanction of
tradition means integration into cultic practices: "Originally, the embeddedness of an artwork in the context of tradition found expression
in a cult. As we know, the earliest artworks originated in the service
of rituals. . . . In other words: the unique value of the 'authentic' work
of art always has its basis in ritual" (SW, 3:105). At issue here is the
fetishizing of the work of art, something occasioned less through creation than through transmission. If the work of art remains a fetish, a
distanced and distancing object that exerts an irrational and incontro-
vertible power, it may attain to a sacrosanct inviolability within a
culture. It also remains in the hands of a privileged few. The auratic
work exerts claims to power that may parallel and reinforce the claims
to political power made by the class for whom such objects are most
meaningful—the ruling class. The theoretical defense of auratic art was
and is central to the maintenance of their power. It is not just that
such art, with its ritually certified representational or architectonic

strategies, poses no threat to the dominant class, but that the aura of authenticity, authority, and permanence projected by the sanctioned work serves to substantiate the rulers' claims to power.

The work that is reproduced on a mass basis, on the other hand, allows for reception in the situation of the recipient; the viewer is no longer constrained to receive the work in a space consecrated to its cult, such as a museum, concert hall, or church. In the first of the essay's strong claims, Benjamin argues that it is this capacity for reproduction that—especially in film—mobilizes the "liquidation of the value of tradition in the cultural heritage" (SW, 3:104). This presupposes that the cultural heritage itself is instrumental to the maintenance of power by the ruling class. As Benjamin puts it in a fragment from *The Arcades Project,* "the ideologies of the rulers are by their nature more changeable than the ideas of the oppressed. For not only must they, like the ideas of the latter, adapt each time to the situation of social conflict, but they must glorify that situation as fundamentally harmonious" (AP, J77,1). The cultural heritage is precisely that glorification of what is essentially a site of bloody conflict, its aestheticization as something stable and harmonious. "As soon as the criterion of authenticity ceases to be applied to artistic production," however, "the whole social function of art is revolutionized. Instead of being founded on ritual, it is based on a different practice: politics" (SW, 3:106). Reproducibility is thus finally a political capacity of the work of art; its reproducibility shatters its aura and makes for a different kind of reception in a different spectatorial space. Liquidation of the aura enables construction, in the cinema, of a political body through "simultaneous collective reception" of its object.

Having limned the potential social-aesthetic power of film to decompose and fragment the traditional so as to bring hidden areas to light, Benjamin shifts immediately to the other pole of his argument: historical change in the human sensory apparatus. Here he programmatically defines the field in which his work on modern media moves. He concentrates on two related matters: the capacity of the artwork to encode information about its historical period (and, in so doing, potentially to reveal to its audience otherwise inapprehensible aspects of their own milieu), and the capacity of media to effect changes in the structure of perception. Animating all of Benjamin's thought is the conviction that the seemingly most obvious things—who we are, the nature of the physical environment in which we move, the character of our historical moment—are in essence concealed from us. For Benjamin in the thirties, the world in which we live has the character of an optical device: a "phantasmagoria." Originally an eighteenth-century illusionistic device, with which shadows of moving figures were projected onto a wall or screen, phantasmagoria in Benjamin is redefined to fit the world of urban commodity capitalism—an environment so pressingly "real" that we take it to be given and natural, when in fact it is a socioeconomic construct and, in the (Brechtian) language of the artwork essay, an "apparatus." The term "phantasmagoria" thus brings out the power of illusion at work in this environment, a power that imperils not only the general intelligibility of things but also the readiness of humans to form habits and make decisions.

Benjamin argues that if we are to overcome the pervasive reifying power of the social apparatus, new technologized art forms such as film must provide "polytechnic training" in the "organizing and regulating" of responses to the lived environment (SW, 3:114, 117). Benjamin's emphasis on "training" here is anything but casual. Film, on this reading, trains "human beings in the apperceptions and reactions needed to deal with a vast apparatus whose role in their lives is expanding almost daily" (SW, 3:108), and it does so precisely through the most sophisticated recourse to a technical apparatus (camera, editing studio, cinema projection). Film accomplishes this training through a number of devices and capacities inherent in the form. First, films are not merely reproducible: as montage works, they assemble reproductions of processes taking place before the camera. Primary among these is the performance of the film actor, which unfolds before "a group of specialists—executive producer, director, cinematographer, sound recordist, lighting designer, and so on," all of whom can and do intervene in the actor's performance. Although editing usually makes a performance seem continuous and integral, every conventional film performance is a composition of separate takes, each of which has been subjected to the approval of the group of experts. It is a test performance. "Film makes test performances capable of being exhibited, by turning that ability into a test" (SW, 3:111). This disjunctive, testable nature of the performance before the apparatus makes visible something otherwise hidden: the self-alienation of the modern, technologized subject, the susceptibility to measurement and control. The actor thus places the apparatus in the service of a triumph over the apparatus, a triumph of humanity. Reflection on the test performance not only breaks down the "magic" of the cult of the film star. Because the performance is "detachable from the person mirrored," it becomes "transportable" and subject to a different control—that of the viewers, who confront it en masse.

"Man's presentation of himself to the camera" is complemented by another function of film: the "representation of his environment by means of this apparatus" (SW, 3:117). "In the film studio the apparatus has penetrated so deeply into reality that a pure view of that reality, free of the foreign body of equipment, is the result of a special procedure—namely, the shooting by the specially adjusted photographic device and the assembly of that shot with others of the same kind" (SW, 3:115). This paradoxical formulation—a "pure view of reality" produced through the dispositif that is nonetheless "equipment free"—goes to the heart of Benjamin's theories concerning the interpenetration of humanity and apparatus. Through the camera we discover, in his famous phrase, the "optical unconscious." The constitutive tropes of cinema—the close-up and enlargement, slow motion, tracking and panning, superimposition and dissolve—give us new insights into the spatial and temporal "necessities governing our lives" and in this way disclose a "vast and unsuspected field of action [Spielraum]" (SW, 3:117).

Related to this analysis of film production are subtle indications regarding its reception. For Benjamin, the viewing of a film cannot have the same character as the contemplation of an auratic work of art. "A person who concentrates before a work of art is absorbed by it; he enters into the work, just as, according to legend, a Chinese painter entered his completed painting while beholding it. By contrast, the distracted masses absorb the work of art into themselves. Their waves lap around it; they encompass it with their tide" (SW, 3:119).[16] The vast social apparatus, which produces a semblance of harmony and integrity that masks the brutal heteronomies of modern life, can be seen through and dealt with, Benjamin suggests here, only by a more decentered reception, a distracted and diffuse encompassing that eschews contemplative absorption into works complicit with the semblance of harmony. What is required is the cultivation of a cinematographic plasticity of perspective. The unprecedented "tasks" put before the modern viewer—tasks of navigating the shattered and dispersed—must be "mastered gradually . . . through habit." The characteristically modern phenomenon of adept "reception in distraction" finds in film "its true training ground" (SW, 3:120). Benjamin placed his faith in such precognitive training as propaedeutic to the fostering of those "apperceptions and reactions" that alone might master the social apparatus.

Much of the artwork essay is characterized, then, by an unflagging technological utopianism—a utopianism for which the author has often been excoriated. Benjamin clearly recognized that the qualities he detected in the new medium are necessary but not sufficient conditions, for they always require an actualization through specific works and are always threatened by appropriation through the interests of big capital. The insistent political rhetoric of the opening and closing sections of the essay, which seek to discriminate fascism's aestheticization of politics from Communism's politicization of art, needs to be seen in the larger historical context of a Europe on the verge of war.

Benjamin capped his announcement of the work-of-art essay to Horkheimer by raising the question of its publication: "I can well imagine that the *Zeitschrift* would be the proper place for [this piece]" (C, 509). In fact, the essay first appeared in the institute's journal—in a significantly abbreviated French translation by Pierre Klossowski—in 1936. It was Horkheimer who stipulated that the essay appear in French translation—a condition amenable to Benjamin, since he now resided in France. Benjamin had come to know his translator, Klossowski, though Georges Bataille, whose acquaintance he had made at the Bibliothèque Nationale. The multitalented Klossowski (1905–2001) was already active as a philosopher and essayist when Benjamin met him; he went on to paint and write novels. His father was an art historian and his mother a painter who studied with Pierre Bonnard; Klossowski and his brother, the painter Balthus, had grown up in a house frequented not just by artists but by writers such as Gide and Rilke. Benjamin was by no means the only German author Klossowski would translate: he produced well-known translations of Wittgenstein, Heidegger, Hölderlin, Kafka, and Nietzsche. In the mid-1930s Klossowski's growing friendship with Georges Bataille (1897–1962) would prove decisive for his intellectual development. And Bataille, in turn, would figure in Walter Benjamin's approach to the most advanced French intellectual circles of the late 1930s.

Bataille had worked since 1922 at the Bibliothèque Nationale, and since 1930 in the Department of Printed Books, where Benjamin presumably came to know him in the course of his many visits. The two men shared certain tastes: Bataille, too, regularly ran through his salary in casinos and brothels.[17] It was only via the development of an intensive interchange with Klossowski concerning the artwork essay, however, that Benjamin began to make his way at the margins of Bataille's intellectual world. In a sense, Bataille sought to define his intellectual career by countering the example of Surrealism. He had begun to move at the borders of the loosely defined Surrealist groups as early as 1924 but always resisted the fascination exerted by André Breton. In 1929 he founded the journal *Documents* as an explicit alternative to Surrealism, gathering around him a group of dissidents from the Breton camp. In that same year Breton published the *Second Manifesto of Surrealism*, calling for a return to first principles—which in practice meant the exclusion of some of Breton's oldest allies from the group, including Antonin Artaud, André Masson, Philippe Soupault, Roger Vitrac, Francis Picabia, and Marcel Duchamp. Yet Breton devoted more space—a full page and a half—to the denunciation of Bataille and his journal than to any of his better-known foes and former friends. The breach with Breton would have seemed to be complete. In 1935, however, Bataille decided that the price of success—defined in terms of intellectual notice—was an alliance with none other than Breton. At a meeting at the Regency café in September 1935, the two men formulated plans for a new movement and a new journal, to be called *Contre-Attaque;* the first manifesto of the group is dated October 7, and was adorned with thirteen signatures, including those of Breton, Bataille, Paul Eluard, Pierre Klossowski, Dora Maar, and Maurice Heine. The founders intended the movement to be revolutionary, antinationalist, anticapitalist, and free of bourgeois morality. Michel Surya has summed it up nicely: "*Contre-Attaque* inscribed pell-mell in its program nothing less than the liberation of children from parental educational tutelage . . . , the free expression of sexual urges . . . , the free play of passions, the free man as candidate for all the pleasures due to him, and so on."[18] Benjamin probably attended the group's second meeting, on January 21, 1936, at which Bataille and Breton were to have spoken. But Breton failed to appear at this or any subsequent meeting, and by April he and Bataille had broken again. Until early 1936 Benjamin succeeded in establishing only rather distant relations with the French world of letters. Through Bataille and Klossowski, though, he began to find more direct and more engaged paths toward the world of radical thought.

Through Benjamin's meticulous collaboration with Klossowski, the French version of the artwork essay was finished at the end of February 1936. Benjamin's own evaluation of Klossowski's translation is of some interest—and, in view of the protracted and difficult editing process undertaken by the institute in the spring, two of his points stand out: "First, that the translation is extremely precise and largely conveys the meaning of the original. Second, that the French version often has a doctrinaire quality that one finds, in my opinion, only rarely in the German version" (GB, 5:243–244). The sociologist Raymond Aron, a professor at the Ecole Normale Supériere, was at this time the French representative of the institute, and he undertook, in this capacity, a revision of Klossowski's text; Benjamin reported that Aron experienced the text as a translation that bore the marks of the participation of the author—and not always to its advantage. Aron's emendations were only the first—and most amenable—of the many changes made once the essay had been submitted. In early March, Horkheimer received an angry letter from Benjamin accusing Hans Klaus Brill, the general secretary of the Paris office of the institute, of making substantial changes to the artwork essay behind the author's back. The thrust of Brill's revisions was clear: he had tamed much of the essay's directly political language. Brill had begun by striking the whole of the essay's first section, with its claims for a radical politics informed by a radical aesthetics; his further revisions were more surprising, including the striking of the word "socialism." Benjamin protested that the "political *groundplan*" of the essay had to be retained if it was to have any "informational value for the avant-garde of the

French intellectuals" (GB, 5:252). Nothing could be more telling as regards the different audiences intended for the essay by its author and its publisher. Benjamin, eager to enlarge his beachhead on the radical aesthetic left, wanted a polemical and engaged language; his remarks show how far he had moved from the more traditional, largely left-center literary figures, such as Gide and Malraux, to whom he had initially been attracted. The institute, understandably concerned about the French state's tolerance for a radically inclined foreign publication, hoped to address a highly cultured left-liberal audience.

Horkheimer's reply to Benjamin's protests is equally telling. As we know now from his correspondence, he had harbored doubts about some aspects of the essay from his very first reading. Writing to Adorno on January 22, he attributed these problems "to the material distress in which he finds himself. I want to attempt everything to help him out of that. Benjamin is one of the few people whose intellectual power makes it imperative that we not allow them to sink."[19] Although he conceded on a few points, Horkheimer told Benjamin categorically that Brill was acting in a responsible manner—and on the basis of Horkheimer's explicit instructions. "You are familiar, as you yourself emphasize, with our own situation. We must do everything in our power to prevent the *Zeitschrift*, as a scholarly organ, from being drawn into political discussions in the press."[20] Despite the letter's frankness in dismissing Benjamin's claims, it did hold out a carrot for him to grasp: any further discussion of the changes would result in a delay in the essay's publication. Benjamin's acquiescence was immediate: he cabled Horkheimer on March 28, "Changes accepted." Benjamin soon realized that his attempts to get his essay published in a form acceptable to him had, if not jeopardized, at least destabilized his position with the institute—which was not only his major source of support but also the only reliable venue for his publications. He thus wrote to Horkheimer on March 30 in order to reassure the institute's director that he would do "everything in my power to restore the Institute's former confidence in me" (GB, 5:267).

Once the essay appeared, Benjamin was tireless in his efforts to find it a wide audience, for he recognized its potentially broad appeal. Stuart Gilbert, who published the first edition of his popular commentary on Joyce's *Ulysses* in 1930, sought an English translator in

London; Benjamin had presumably come to know him through Adrienne Monnier. Monnier also offered to do what she could to acquaint the Parisian intelligentsia with the piece. She wrote a letter that would have introduced Benjamin and an offprint of his essay to a wide circle of her customers and acquaintances, but this plan foundered on the institute's refusal to provide the 150 offprints Benjamin would have needed. Their reasoning, conveyed by Friedrich Pollock, is revealing:

> I was initially inclined to advocate for the fulfillment of your request for a larger printing run and support for the widest possible distribution of offprints, because I believed that we could use your work at the same time in a small publicity campaign for the journal in France. In the meantime I have become convinced that I was wrong. Your study is much too bold and, in regard to certain questions, far too problematic to be distributed in such a programmatic manner in the service of our journal. (Quoted in GB, 5:292n)

We can imagine Benjamin's dismay at this citing of the boldness of his essay, but the institute's pulling back from its "problematic" conclusions must have been truly galling. He also sent a copy of the essay to Bernhard Reich and Asja Lacis in Moscow, hoping to find a publisher there—but Reich's reply was little short of hostile; the essay had produced feelings of "violent repulsion" in him.[21] And he asked Grete Steffin to put the essay into the hands of the great Soviet avant-gardist and Brecht translator Sergei Tretyakov.

As it turned out, the essay needed little help. It had an immediate and major impact, and was widely discussed in Paris. Benjamin reported that the essay was the subject of a public conversation between the philosopher Jean Wahl and the poet Pierre Jean Jouve (GB, 5:352). In late June André Malraux highlighted the work—in particular the theory of distraction that dominates its final pages—in an address to a congress in London that was intended to initiate a new encyclopedia of the arts; although he suggested to Benjamin at a meeting soon after his return from England that he would discuss the essay's central ideas more fully in his next book, this never came to pass. Benjamin himself gave a talk entitled "The Work of Art in the Age of Its Technological Reproducibility" at a discussion evening at the Café Mephisto that was organized on June 22 by the Paris chapter of the Defense League of German Authors Abroad (Schutzverband deutscher Autoren im Ausland). A week later, at a second meeting, his theses on a materialist theory of art were debated by a large audience of émigré writers, and his friend Hans Sahl, a novelist and critic, made a lengthy presentation on Benjamin's work. Writing to Alfred Cohn at the beginning of July, Benjamin comments that, for him, the most interesting thing about that evening was the silence on the part of the Communist Party members in attendance (C, 528–529).

Among these early responses to the essay, Benjamin showed himself especially pleased with that of Alfred Cohn, who had been impressed by "how organically this work develops out of your earliest writings" (quoted in GB, 5:328). In his reply, Benjamin acknowledged the work's "continuity with my earlier studies, in spite of its new and surely oft-surprising tendency," and, in a key formulation, he locates the basis for this continuity of concern in "the fact that, over the years, I have tried to achieve an increasingly precise and uncompromising idea of what constitutes a work of art" (C, 528). Benjamin composed a little allegory for Kitty Marx-Steinschneider that sums up his sense of his current position—and of the readership of the artwork essay:

> Spring has arrived in the meantime; the little tree of life, however, pays no heed at all to the season, refuses to sprout even the slightest buds, and at most produces small fruits. Some few friends of nature look up at the last of these that had, of course, already been promised to you. It will arrive at your house in approximately one month packaged as a French text. As for the friends of nature, this is a small group that has been thrown together by chance—consisting of some emigrants, one or two French amateurs, a Russian who shakes his head at the situation, and some individuals of varying origin and sex who display curiosity less for the fruit than for the little tree. (C, 524)

Although the third version of the artwork essay would continue to occupy his thoughts, Benjamin now had more time, in the spring of 1936, for seeing old friends and making new acquaintances. He was seeing a good deal of the young Maximilien Rubel. Rubel had studied philosophy and sociology in Vienna, where he developed a special interest in the work of Karl Kraus, and had come to Paris in the early 1930s to study German literature at the Sorbonne. Benjamin had probably met him through Werner Kraft, though Kraft shared none of Rubel's and Benjamin's predilection for esoteric and radical Marxism. Rubel would become a vocal supporter of the Spanish anarchists in 1936, the first year of the Spanish Civil War, and would later become a prominent historian of Marx and Marxism and the chief editor of the Pléiade edition of Marx's works. Also that spring, Benjamin established cordial relations with the wealthy English writer Annie Winifred Ellerman, who went by the name Bryher. During the 1920s, Bryher, often in the company of her lover, the poet H. D. (Hilda Doolittle), had moved in the circle around Joyce and in the community of American émigré intellectuals that included Hemingway, Gertrude Stein, Berenice Abbott, and Sylvia Beach. She had proven herself a generous supporter of the arts and was a major backer for Beach's bookshop, Shakespeare and Company. Bryher and her second husband, the writer and filmmaker Kenneth Macpherson, edited the film journal *Close Up* and had founded an independent film company called POOL Productions. Knowing of her involvement with cinema, Benjamin presented her with a copy of the artwork essay bearing the dedication "à Mme Bryher en signe de s[es] sympathies dévoués hommage de l'auteur." It was hardly surprising that she took a lively interest in the essay and actively sought a translator into English.

The spring also brought friends and intellectual partners through Paris. Benjamin held an important meeting with Friedrich Pollock in April, at which Pollock announced that Horkheimer was raising Benjamin's stipend to 1,300 French francs per month, beginning in May—an unmistakable sign that he was back in the good graces of the institute. At this meeting, he also agreed to compose a series of reports on French letters for the *Zeitschrift;* he wrote several of these in the years to come, sharing them with Horkheimer, but they were never published in the journal. Benjamin and Pollock also discussed Benjamin's ongoing efforts to shepherd the publication of Horkheimer's essays in French. Benjamin would continue to spend an enormous amount of time trying to arrange the translation and publication of a volume of Horkheimer's essays with the *Nouvelle Revue*

Française or Gallimard—although these efforts ultimately came to nothing. In May, Karl Thieme was in town, and Benjamin was able to continue their conversations on art. One topic of discussion may well have been the work of the great French master of etching Charles Meryon (1821–1868), whom Benjamin discovered in the early spring through a reference in Baudelaire while working at the Bibliothèque Nationale. Benjamin had been deeply stirred by Meryon's monumental and moody etchings of Paris; Meryon would soon take his place as a salient figure in the study of the arcades. And in May the Protestant theologian Paul Tillich passed through town, and Benjamin managed to speak with him for a while. A prominent exponent of a religious socialism, Tillich had been relieved of his position as a professor of theology at Frankfurt in 1933, and had accepted an invitation from Reinhold Niebuhr to join the faculty at Union Theological Seminary in New York. While still in Frankfurt he served as the supervisor for Adorno's habilitation thesis on Kierkegaard, and both Adorno and Gretel had kept in close touch with him in the intervening years.

In the course of the spring, Benjamin managed to improve relations with Scholem. Benjamin's anger had simmered through the winter, but Scholem finally wrote on April 19, explaining that his apparent unfriendliness was due to the emotional trauma consequent on his having divorced his wife and assumed responsibility for supporting two households. Scholem's wife, Escha, had left him for the philosopher Hugo Bergmann (1883–1975), who had been a friend of Franz Kafka and Max Brod before his departure from Prague for Palestine. With this explanation, their relationship was back on a viable, if initially stiff, footing. Benjamin's letter of May 2 appeals, not without keen wit, to something noble at stake in their relationship: "Even if our correspondence these last months hasn't fared much better than you have, at least you can't deny me the testimonial that I have stood by it with patience. Not in vain, if it eventually regains something of its original character. That's why we must both hope that the elemental spirits of our existence and our work, who are entitled to our dialogue, will not be kept waiting indefinitely on the threshold" (BS, 178).

Everything he heard from Scholem and from Kitty Marx-Steinschneider about the situation in Palestine was deeply troubling.

The constant armed clashes between Palestinians and Jews—with the British security forces looking on without taking sides—had unsettled even the most optimistic Zionists. As always, Benjamin's stance on Palestine was ambivalent, and his position idiosyncratic: "There are, of course, difficulties in formulating questions. For I am always interested in the same thing: what becomes of the hopes that Palestine raises, beyond allowing ten thousand Jews, even one hundred thousand Jews, to eke out a meager existence. A circumstance that, as absolutely essential as it is, may well not run its course without proving to be a new and catastrophic danger among all the dangers threatening Judaism" (C, 526). Of course, he hardly had to look to Palestine for disturbing news of conflict. Writing on April 14 to Alfred Cohn, who remained in Barcelona, he made a rare exception to his policy of refraining from direct commentary on contemporary politics. The significance of the Popular Front was, in any case, a burning issue in 1936: the Spanish Popular Front had won elections in Spain early in the year, leading to the formation of a republican government, and the elections in France in May 1936 had also seen a victory by the Popular Front, leading to the formation of a government under Léon Blum. Even the dire situation in Europe could not lead Benjamin to moderate his stance on this compromised brand of socialism, however. His acid comments on the election posters of the French Popular Front betray a contempt not only for their politics but also for the aesthetics of their media presence: "The election poster . . . of the French Communist Party presents a woman beaming with motherly happiness, a healthy young lad, and a man—I would almost say a gentleman—looking cheerful and decisive: a magnificent vision of the family, whose happy head has strictly avoided any hint of the worker in his attire" (GB, 5:271). Worst of all, however, was the news that his brother, Georg, had been arrested again, and that Hilde Benjamin had succeeded only with the greatest difficulty in convincing a lawyer to represent him.

With more time on his hands now, he could indulge old predilections in his reading. He rediscovered the "freedom to pursue my simple pleasures as a reader, untroubled by all literary considerations. And since personal taste always plays a role in simple pleasures, and no small role at that, recommending such reading is not a whit more reliable than recommendations of what to eat" (C, 525). Three such "dishes" were the newest Simenon mystery novels, which he recommended to several friends as the best relief from "gloomy hours." He reported that he was also reading both Paul Valéry's *Pièces sur l'art* and Heinrich Heine with great interest. It was not remarkable that Benjamin was reading Heine; what was remarkable was that it had taken him so long to discover this affinity—especially since he knew very well that he was distantly related to the great poet. Heine, one of the most important German writers of the nineteenth century, combined radical sympathies with an old-world refinement and skepticism. He was largely responsible for a shift in German literary language from the esoteric and high-flown diction of Romanticism to a lighter, more urbane, and more ironic mode. Although Heine was in Benjamin's day still best known as a poet, Benjamin characteristically took note of a different side of his production. Heine had raised journalistic commentary, and indeed the form of the report, to the level of art. Already suspect because of his Jewishness, he was banished from Germany after his enthusiastic support for the revolutions of 1830; he moved to Paris in 1831, and returned to Germany only twice during the remainder of his life. Beginning in 1832, Heine served as the Paris correspondent of the *Augsburger Allgemeine Zeitung*, at that time the newspaper with the largest readership in Germany. The series of letters he wrote intermixed commentary on the July Monarchy in France with scathing observations on political repression at home; the letters appeared that same year in book form with the title *Französische Zustände* (Conditions in France), and were immediately banned in Prussia and Austria. And it was this sage political feuilletonism, written almost exactly one hundred years earlier by a German Jewish exile in Paris, that Benjamin now perused.

Although relegated for the most part to the margins of French intellectual life, Benjamin could still address—tactfully, but with real insight and no little bite—the work of his German friends and colleagues. He commented at length on Adorno's memorial essay for Alban Berg, cataloguing echoes of his own work—the phrase "the friendliness of the man-eater" is taken from his essay on Karl Kraus—while praising his friend's thoughtful tribute to the great composer who was his teacher. And in late June he responded enthusiastically on reading the proofs of Adorno's "On Jazz." This essay, one of Adorno's most controversial, undertakes a damning critique of jazz music as an aesthetic form that harmonizes a situation of conflict and perpetuates structures of domination. Benjamin immediately recognized parallels between Adorno's reading of swing-era jazz and critical aspects of the artwork essay, particularly a parallel between the syncopation principle in jazz and shock effects in film: "Would it surprise you if I tell you how enormously delighted I am to discover such a profound and spontaneous inner communication between our thoughts? Nor did you have to assure me that this communication already existed before you had looked at my work on film. The way in which you approach the matter has the kind of power and originality which only arises from the exercise of perfect freedom in the creative process—a freedom whose practice in both our cases only serves to substantiate the profound concordance between our own ways of seeing things" (BA, 144). Significantly, Benjamin passes over in silence the profound difference in tendency between his own essay and Adorno's: where Benjamin ascribes a potentially revolutionary force to film, Adorno rules out the possibility of any redemptive power in jazz.

Benjamin's response to an essay on naturalism by Leo Löwenthal that would appear in the *Zeitschrift* is even more interesting, because it provides us with a view into Benjamin's literary workshop. Löwenthal had prepared the essay for publication in the *Zeitschrift*, but it met with mixed reviews; Benjamin was drawn into the discussion after the essay had undergone significant revision. The exchange of letters with Löwenthal soon became a literary debate, with Benjamin offering a "competing theory" to Löwenthal's ideas on the naturalist movement. As he had done in the exposé of the arcades project, Benjamin emphasizes that every historical epoch harbors within its modes of behavior and production structures and tendencies that remain unconscious. It is the task of the critic not just to interrogate the representations of itself that the past has consciously produced, but to make manifest those "threatening or promising images of the future" which have lived within the past unconsciously, like dreams. As Benjamin sees it, Löwenthal takes naturalism too literally, confining himself to the view of society that is immediately legible in its literary works. Benjamin expounds a naturalism whose works far exceed the theories on which they seem to be based. In the new literary history he sketches, the first wave of naturalism (which for him includes Flaubert) was concerned not so much to render a critique of contemporary society as to reveal " 'eternally' destructive forces in action." At its climax, in Ibsen, Benjamin argues, the movement is inextricably bound up with its coterminous moment in the arts, that is, with Jugendstil. And it is here that Benjamin sees Löwenthal's real achievement. Without naming Jugendstil, Löwenthal identifies a number of its characteristic features, including a concept of life that bears the potential for rejuvenation in itself and a vision of a "transfigured" natural space. Naturalism and Jugendstil together "document" a deep historical conflict within the bourgeoisie. That conflict is represented by those figures in Ibsen's late plays who have "run onto the stage (ragged, proletarianized intellectuals)" and who, near the end of a scene, "point their fingers so eagerly at the fata morgana of freedom in the desert of modern society. Those who are going under [*Untergehende*] are, to be sure, not those who overcome [*Übergehende*] (as which they may appear in Nietzsche). But, on their journey into nothingness, they have a number of experiences which ought not to be lost to humanity. They foresee, however obscurely, the fate of the class from which they come. . . . In many currents of naturalism, the human nature of the bourgeois citizen struggles against necessities before which it has capitulated only in our day" (GB, 5:298–299). Benjamin's characteristically broad-gauged and richly suggestive assessment had little effect on Löwenthal's essay, which appeared in the *Zeitschrift* later in the year under the title "Das Individuum in der individualistischen Gesellschaft. Bemerkungen über Ibsen" (The Individual in the Individualistic Society: Remarks on Ibsen).

Excited by the theoretic initiatives broached in the artwork essay, Benjamin was more eager than ever to return to the arcades project. He nevertheless continued to find himself obligated to produce occasional and commissioned pieces that could be published quickly. But there were limits even to this exigency. He once more pushed the essay on Fuchs to the furthest reaches of the back burner and turned instead to an essay commissioned by Fritz Lieb's journal *Orient und Occident*, an essay on the Russian writer Nikolai Leskov. The Swiss theologian Lieb (1892–1970), who wrote a dissertation on Franz von Baader, had been dismissed from his professorship at Basel in 1933. That year he immigrated to France, and in the course of the 1930s he became Benjamin's principal dialogue partner on issues of Christian theology—"by far one of the best people I've gotten to know here" (C, 525). Lieb and Benjamin had a *jour fixe:* they met Thursdays at the Café de Versailles. The resulting essay, "The Storyteller," remains one of Benjamin's most-cited works, although he himself, to all appearances, attributed no particular importance to it.

"The Storyteller: Observations on the Works of Nikolai Leskov," nominally a reading of a lesser-known contemporary of Tolstoy and Dostoevsky, starts with a general assumption comparable to that of the artwork essay written a few months earlier, the assumption that "experience has fallen in value. . . . For never has experience been more thoroughly belied than strategic experience was belied by tactical warfare, economic experience by inflation, bodily experience by mechanical warfare, moral experience by those in power. A generation that had gone to school on horse-drawn streetcars now stood under the open sky in a landscape where nothing remained unchanged but the clouds and, beneath those clouds, in a force field of destructive torrents and explosions, the tiny, fragile human body" (SW, 3:143–144). While the artwork essay confidently looks forward to an increasingly technologized media landscape, however, "The Storyteller" looks backward, severely elegiac, at the decline of storytelling and all that implies. The experience evoked in this opening section of the essay is, Benjamin asserts, no longer capable of oral transmission. The "communicability of experience is decreasing." If the traditional storyteller's function within the community is to pass on "counsel" to his or her listeners, that function withers, along with the sense of community, when "we have no counsel either for ourselves or for others" (SW, 3:145). The novel, as a literary form dependent on the invention of printing, is born in the dissolution of the oral tradition and of the artisanal community it served; a novel is written by an individual to be read in privacy by other individuals, and, unlike the anonymously transmitted folktale, it typically concerns the inner life of individuals in specific times and places.

After showing that the two most characteristic modern prose forms—the novel and the newspaper—are, in different ways, inhospitable to the atmosphere of storytelling, Benjamin arrives at the pivotal theme of death. As modern society shuttles the phenomena of death and dying to the margins not just of social space but of consciousness, the storyteller loses moral authority. "Characteristically, it is not only a man's knowledge or wisdom, but above all his lived life [*gelebtes Leben*] . . . that first assumes transmissible form at the moment of his death" (SW, 3:151). The profound nihilism of this insight, witnessing to a power of death over time, opens the way to a further parallel with the artwork essay: the ebb of storytelling brings with it the waning of a special mnemonics. Unlike the "colorless light" of traditional historiography, with its burden of *explanation*, the craft of storytelling, with its concentrated "germinative power," displays and *interprets* "the great inscrutable course of the world," which otherwise remains "outside all properly historical categories" (SW, 3:152–153). This inscription of the inscrutable "course of the world" is finally a dimension of what the *Trauerspiel* book first called "natural history." In the final pages of his essay, where he quotes from Bloch's *Heritage of Our Times* on fairy tale and legend, Benjamin returns to one of his great themes from the early 1920s, the problem of creatureliness. Leskov, in the end, stands alongside Kafka as a writer capable of transmitting insight into the mythic, primordial world of the creature into which we constantly threaten to sink back. Even in modern literary guise, but with a focused amplitude that no form of information has ever rivaled, storytelling communicates elemental wisdom, truly useful insight into "the hierarchy of the creaturely world, which has its apex in the righteous man, [and] reaches down into the abyss of the inanimate through many gradations" (SW, 3:159). This ability to relate—that is, condense and distill—"an entire life" is Leskov's gift.

If, in the intervening years, the artwork essay has not infrequently been criticized for an unwarranted optimism, "The Storyteller" has given rise to a widespread impression of Benjamin as nostalgic for the way things used to be. Such views neglect Benjamin's uncanny ability to turn almost any assignment to his own ends. The Leskov essay manages to take on a topic that was seemingly worlds removed from the rise of urban commodity capitalism in Paris and to bring it around to a characteristic Benjaminian concern: media and genre forms in their relation to the problem of human experience. The essay might have had a wider contemporary impact if Jean Cassou, editor of the journal *Europe,* had realized his plan of publishing it in French translation. Benjamin undertook the translation himself, but it never appeared during his lifetime.[22]

Alongside this piece, Benjamin tossed off a series of book reviews for the *Zeitschrift* on topics in which he remained interested: the Baroque, popular literature (Gothic fiction), Romanticism, and the novel (Stendhal, Hofmannsthal, Proust, and Joyce).[23] The late spring and early summer seemed to bring further opportunities. In early May he received an invitation from his friend Wieland Herzfelde to contribute a regular column on French literature to the new journal *Das Wort* that would be published in Moscow. Although not on the editorial board (which consisted of Brecht, the journalist and novelist Willi Bredel, and the novelist Lion Feuchtwanger), Herzfelde was intimately involved with the journal's creation. At a meeting in June with Maria Osten (Maria Greßhöhner), who served as coordinator of the journal in Moscow, Benjamin formalized this arrangement, and immediately asked Willi Bredel for an advance payment. He did produce and submit one such letter on French literature, but it was never published. In June an acquaintance from Berlin, Harald Landry, solicited a contribution from Benjamin for a new journal, *Vox Critica.* Landry had been the literary critic for the *Berliner Zeitung* and the *Vossische Zeitung* in Berlin, and had immigrated to London, where he worked for the BBC. An acquaintance of Benjamin's in Paris, the writer Hans Arno Joachim had recommended the artwork essay to Landry. Benjamin was of course still eager to see his essay appear, either in German or in English, but he responded to Landry's request for a shorter version by saying that the essay could not be cut. Like so many other literary projects in these years, this one came to nothing. Perhaps the most exciting of these new suggestions came from Adorno. In late May Adorno suggested to Horkheimer that an essay on Baudelaire and the social theory of Neoromanticism would be very much in the interest of the *Zeitschrift.* And he proposed that Benjamin be commissioned to produce it—or, perhaps, that he and Benjamin might write it together. In their discussions on the arcades, Adorno had come to recognize the centrality of Baudelaire to Benjamin's whole conception; the proposed essay was intended in part as an accelerant for the larger project. Adorno's letter marks a turning point in the work on the arcades. After Benjamin responded enthusiastically to the suggestion, Horkheimer and Adorno began to envision not just an essay but an entire book on Baudelaire as a partial realization of the years of research on nineteenth-century Paris.

Venues for his major works—and especially for the *Berlin Childhood around 1900*—remained elusive. Franz Glück, the brother of his friend Gustav, was looking for likely presses in Vienna; Benjamin wrote to express his thanks, but also to emphasize just how important the autobiographical text was to him, saying, "However pressing the task of securing my existence through my writing may be, in the case of precisely this manuscript all material considerations are for me in last place" (GB, 5:227).

Benjamin had enjoyed a period of relative health and emotional stability with the composition of the artwork essay. Although he had been plagued with a bout of rheumatism in February, his letters are free of the usual complaints from October 1935 through May 1936. As the summer approached, he found himself confronting his demons once again, and his response was what it had been for fifteen years: he found himself desperate to pick up and travel. The urge was stronger than ever, especially since he had spent virtually the whole of 1935 in Paris. "Once the pressure which had weighed upon me for so long on account of my financial situation was lifted," he wrote to Adorno in early June, "I experienced something that is not unusual in these circumstances: in a state of relaxation, my nerves began to give way. I felt as though all of my reserves were exhausted. I also felt the consequences which over a year's uninterrupted stay in Paris under such conditions had brought with it. I realized that I had to do something to repair the state of my spiritual health" (BA, 139). By the end of June he was resolved to move, but still unsure whether he would join Cohn in Barcelona or Brecht in Skovsbostrand. As always, financial and intellectual considerations were intermingled in the decision. The route to Barcelona would allow for attendance at a conference in Pontigny, where he could make himself useful to Horkheimer and the institute, while Denmark might allow him, through Brecht, to firm up his relationship with *Das Wort*, now a serious publishing prospect for him. The ancient abbey buildings at Pontigny, in northwestern Burgundy, had been purchased in 1909 by the journalist and professor Paul Des-jardins as the site for an annual gathering of intellectuals under the rubric Décades de Pontigny; the conferences took place every year from 1910 through 1914 and again from 1922 through 1939. Each day saw a talk by a writer, professor, or scientist that was followed by dis-cussion; the participants had included Gide, Roger Martin du Gard, Jacques Rivière, Heinrich and Thomas Mann, and T. S. Eliot. Seeing a further opportunity to inform Horkheimer about developments in the French intellectual world, Benjamin had offered to attend the confer-ence as the institute's representative and produce a report.

But he eventually chose to rejoin the Brechts in Denmark, hoping that he might combine a period of recovery in Skovsbostrand with a later trip to Pontigny. He left Paris on July 27. Just as he had done two years before, he met his acquaintance Gustav Regler, a writer and journalist, on board the ship. Regler had been a member of the German Communist Party since 1928 and lived mostly in the Soviet Union, where he was now headed. He gave Benjamin a rather gloomy report on the antifascist writers' congress held in London that spring. Arriv-ing in Skovsbostrand in early August, Benjamin quickly reestablished himself in the complicated milieu around Brecht. He rented a room in a nearby house and requisitioned a corner of Brecht's garden as his workplace, leaving his improvised desk in the late afternoon to re-sume their customary conversations and games of chess. The chess games (which Benjamin now seldom won) had become a symbolic field on which they could play out their intellectual rivalry and their intellectual differences in friendly fashion. "I have had a beautiful chess set made here for ten kroner," Brecht crowed to Margarete Steffin, "finer and just as big as Benjamin's!"[24] As Erdmut Wizisla points out, Brecht's brief epitaph, "To Walter Benjamin, Who Killed Himself Flee-ing from Hitler," one of four poems he wrote in tribute to Benjamin in 1941 on learning belatedly of his friend's death, takes its cue from a reminiscence of their chess games:[25]

> Tactics of attrition were what you liked,
> Sitting at the chessboard in the pear tree's shade.

Benjamin soon found his way back into the rituals that held the little community together: the exchange of books and small gifts, including special stamps intended for their sons. The Brecht Archive holds one such gift, a 1931 edition of Balthasar Gracian's *The Art of Worldly Wisdom* (1647) that Benjamin gave his friend on the occasion of one of his visits. Benjamin had long been tempted to write an essay on the Spanish Jesuit's text, the critical materialism and aphoristic grace of which appealed powerfully to him. He inscribed the gift to Brecht with the refrain from the "Song of the Insufficiency of Human Endeavor" in *The Threepenny Opera:* "For man is not clever enough for this life."

And so Benjamin settled into the Danish countryside once again—although its pastoral graces and the hospitality of his friends unfolded against an ominous background. "It is a very beneficent life here, and so friendly that one has to ask oneself every day how long such a thing will last in this Europe" (GB, 5:362). This reflection was prompted in no small measure by the outbreak of war in Spain. "It was a strange feeling for me," he wrote to Alfred Cohn, "to read in the paper today that Ibiza was being bombed" (GB, 5:349). The report no doubt referred to an attack by the Republican air force on Falangist positions, since the rebels as yet had no aircraft of their own. The situation on Ibiza presaged the fate of many Jewish emigrants in Spain: while the Falangists controlled the island, a number of families were arrested and transported to Germany. To his worries about his own family and his brother was thus added concern for Alfred Cohn and his family in Barcelona. Soon after the outbreak of the Spanish Civil War on July 25, the Cohns had sent their children to live with Alfred's sister Jula and her husband, Fritz Radt, who resided near Paris in Boulogne sur Seine. Cohn and his wife remained behind, hoping to hold on to whatever material possessions were still left to them. And in August the Brecht household was transfixed—and horrified—by the news coming from Moscow of the show trials then taking place.

In Denmark, Benjamin was reunited not only with his friends but with the part of his library he had been able to get out of Berlin—that, too, a reunion he had often longed for and about which he would dream in Paris. Spurred on by sometimes heated debates with Brecht, he continued to elaborate the artwork essay, later estimating that he had added as much as 25 percent by the time he left Denmark. Despite his differences of opinion, Brecht recognized the importance of the essay and promoted it to his fellow editors at *Das Wort* in Moscow. This effort came to nothing, but in early August Benjamin received exciting and heartening news: the Vita Nova publishing house in Lucerne was interested in bringing out his collection of twenty-six letters by distinguished Germans from the years 1783 to 1883, together with his accompanying introductions.

On reading the collection in late spring, Karl Thieme had responded with genuine enthusiasm, saying he found the text "quite extraordinary" (quoted in GB, 5:330n). Thieme suggested a clever strategy: if a publisher in Switzerland could be found and the volume appeared under a pseudonym and a sufficiently anodyne title, the German market might well be open to the book. Thieme's efforts soon bore fruit. The publisher of the Vita Nova house, Rudolf Roessler, was yet another exiled German; a member of various anti-Fascist circles, and later an agent of the Soviet secret services, Roessler had already published Karl Löwith, Paul Landsberg, and Nikolai Berdyaev. Some of the letters and a version of Benjamin's preface to the collection had already appeared, serially and under pseudonym, in the *Frankfurter Zeitung* in 1931–1932. Soon afterward Benjamin had attempted to find a publisher for a book-length anthology that would have included sixty letters. The Vita Nova edition—with the title *Deutsche Menschen* (German Men and Women), suggested by the publisher—would appear in November, making it the fastest of all Benjamin's book publications. The volume was published under the pseudonym Benjamin had used most often since 1933, Detlef Holz. He had to write a hasty note to Willi Bredel asking him to delete his name from the forthcoming issue of *Das Wort*, where a letter by Johann Gottfried Seume together with Benjamin's introduction, both identical to the versions in *Deutsche Menschen*, were about to appear under his own name: the pseudonym would have been revealed, with potentially disastrous consequences.

Although Roessler was more interested in the letters themselves than in the accompanying commentary, Benjamin persuaded him to include a new preface and to retain the full versions of his individual introductions to the letters, which Roessler had wanted to reduce to merely biographical information. After a bit of friendly negotiation, Benjamin was delighted that the "particularly crisp tone" of his introductions, which he saw as a necessary complement to the prevailingly "virile and resolute" language of the letters, would stand alongside the prose from an earlier era (GB, 5:345). The published book employed special measures to camouflage any hint of political resistance in the contents of the anthology; besides the Aryan pseudonym and the patriotic-sounding title, there was the use of Gothic type for the lettering of the cover. The book sold well, as Benjamin had predicted it would. It received generally favorable reviews (one reviewer called it "the work of a literary jeweler") and went into a second edition in 1937 before being spotted by the censor the following year and placed on the index of books banned by the Nazi Ministry of Propaganda.

Neither *Deutsche Menschen* itself nor the series of letters published in the *Frankfurter Zeitung* was Benjamin's first attempt to assemble an anthology of letters. As early as 1925 he had been commissioned by the Bremer Presse to put together an anthology of the writings of Wilhelm von Humboldt, which would have contained a number of letters. In 1932 he and Willy Haas published a series of prose excerpts from German writers under the title "From World Citizen to Haut-Bourgeois" in the *Frankfurter Zeitung*. Although few of the selections are letters, the concatenation of prose pieces by Jakob Grimm, Johann Gottfried Herder, Otto von Bismarck, Ludwig Börne, and Jakob Burkhardt, as well as by Kant, Hegel, Goethe, and Heine, clearly foreshadows the form of *Deutsche Menschen*. Moreover, Benjamin's "letter book" is structurally related to montage books such as *One-Way Street* and *Berlin Childhood around 1900*. In his preface, Benjamin asserts that the letters making up the book span a full century, 1783–1883, and, further, that their sequence is "chronological." Neither of these assertions is borne out by the actual contents. Although the letters and Benjamin's commentaries largely fall within the period in question and are arranged in a rough chronological order, the earliest letter in fact comes from 1767, and the very first letter in the sequence was written in 1832; it is then followed by a letter from 1783. Some of the out-of-sequence letters are disguised by Benjamin's failure to include a date. Disguise, indeed, is all-pervasive here: even the manifest classicism of the text, including as it does letters from most of the central figures of the German cultural canon, is now a diversionary maneuver, masking the implicit attack on corruption and complacency. Some of the camouflage, of course, stems from Roessler, whose political and monetary concerns led him to hope for broad sales. Benjamin's own strategies are at once more subtle and more subversive.

The series of letters displays a persistent autobiographical strain, involving themes of privation, exile, crisis, and what Nietzsche called *amor fati.* Commenting on the book, which he read from first page to last in one night, immediately after receiving it in early November, Adorno was struck by "the expression of grief issuing from [it]" (BA, 159); the tonality is so uniformly mournful that one could think of *Deutsche Menschen* as a sequel to *Origin of the German Trauerspiel.* Both texts give expression to a metaphysical theory of "history in the present" that goes back in its essentials to Nietzsche-inspired early works such as "Metaphysics of Youth" and "The Life of Students." The letter book was compiled at a time when Benjamin was refining the idea that certain historical periods are linked by objective structures—that there is a "historical index" through which temporally distant epochs may nonetheless prove to be synchronous. The theme of "true humanity" is, of course, ever present in Benjamin's texts, as is the corresponding inference that today's Germany was intent on replacing it with the antihuman. In the wake of the Berlin Olympiad of 1936, *Deutsche Menschen* invokes another Germany, one where human relationships could be rooted, if not in peace, then at least in civility, amiability, and the possibility of shared mourning. Yet Benjamin's subversive strategies hardly stop with the counterposing of a better tradition to the current debased one. In the copy of *Deutsche Menschen* he sent to Scholem, Benjamin included this inscription: "May you, Gerhard, find a chamber in this ark—which I built when the Fascist flood was starting to rise—for the memories of your youth."[26] The word for "ark" here is *"Arche":* not just the vessel that rose above the flood, but the beginning (Greek *arkhē*) in the word. The deepest impulse toward rescue—that quintessentially Benjaminian term—lies not so much in the ideas expressed in these letters, no matter how profoundly human, but in the historically resonant language of the text. As always with Benjamin, truth lies hidden within the strata of certain words in certain contexts, and he clearly hoped that the encounter with the language of their long-dead countrymen might release, for some readers in the Third Reich, those sparks of recognition that lead to resistance. Benjamin later told Franz Glück that the *Berlin Childhood* and *Deutsche Menschen* were like the subjective and objective aspects, respectively, of one and the same matter (GB, 5:423).

While he was negotiating the editorial form and financial terms for *Deutsche Menschen*, Benjamin was also working to fulfill the commission from *Das Wort* for a report on contemporary French literature. His chosen topic was the debate that had swirled around the second volume of André Gide's journals in spring 1936. Although the journals contained rich evidence of Gide's literary preoccupations from 1914 to 1927, they became notorious for their description of his path to Communism (a path he was soon to abandon). Benjamin chose one response, *Mythes socialistes*, by the anti-Communist writer Thierry Maulnier, as the object of his analysis. Benjamin described his own essay as a theory of fascist art, and in fact it reads like a postscript to the artwork essay, but a postscript into which all the political fervor expurgated from the earlier work has been channeled. It remains one of Benjamin's most tendentious pieces. Like the letter book, this little essay found its way into print with a rapidity to which Benjamin was no longer accustomed: he sent it off in mid-August, and it was published in November.[27] The payment of his honorarium, however, was not so timely, and Benjamin found himself writing a series of increasingly shrill letters and telegrams to Bredel, dunning him for his money.

The last days of Benjamin's stay in Denmark were clouded by yet another dispute with Scholem, who in an August letter had responded coolly to Benjamin's artwork essay: "I found your essay very interesting. This is the first time I have come upon something thought-provoking in a philosophical context about film and photography. But I am far too lacking in specialized knowledge to be able to pass judgment on your prognoses" (BS, 185). Benjamin was stung by this high-handed dismissal of what he considered a crystallization of his current thinking, not to mention the attitude toward film and photography:

> I . . . have sadly taken to heart the fundamental impermeability with which my latest essay seems to confront your understanding

(and I use the word not in its technical sense alone). If nothing in it
pointed you back to the realm of ideas in which we both used to be
at home, then I am going to assume, for the time being, that the reason was less that I have drawn a very novel map of one of its prov-
inces and more that it was in French. Whether I will ever be able to
make it available to you in German must remain as open a question
as whether it would then find you in a more receptive mood. (BS,
186)

Rather than take this as yet another occasion to distance himself
from his old friend, Benjamin suggested to Scholem in the most fervent terms that if they wanted to save the friendship, both of them
would have to bridge the physical distance between Europe and Palestine by working harder to extract more from each other's work.

Having decided not to take Horkheimer up on his offer to represent the institute at the meetings in Pontigny because it would have
meant leaving Denmark before he was ready, Benjamin left Skovsbostrand and the Brechts on September 10, stopping over in Paris for
just one day before traveling on to San Remo, where he arrived in late
September. He arrived during a heat wave, which kept him close to
Dora's pension. Once cooler temperatures set in, he immediately resumed his daily walks into the low mountains. The visit was brief but
restorative, and by early October he was again ready to face the challenge of surviving in Paris. His return was marked by a welcome occasion: Horkheimer had financed a trip to Paris for Adorno. The pretext
was that the two colleagues would work on the volume of Horkheimer's essays being readied for French translation. Despite their
mutual efforts up to that point, the publication of Horkheimer's essays seemed about to run aground. Groethuysen had put the project
on ice at Gallimard, and René Etiemble, whom Benjamin had chosen
as translator, seemed simply to have disappeared. Horkheimer was
understandably frustrated; Adorno fueled the fire by suggesting that
political intrigue lay behind the problems, while Benjamin, who of
course knew the situation and the principals much better, recognized
that good intentions had simply not been thought through. This failure in no way clouded Benjamin's relationship to the institute; if anything, his efforts placed him deeper in Horkheimer's trust. While he
was still with Brecht, Benjamin had suggested to Horkheimer that the

Moscow trials—the topic of repeated discussion in Skovsbostrand—necessitated a collective rethinking of the intellectual direction of the institute. Horkheimer now took up Benjamin's suggestion and began to plan a conference that would include all of the institute's primary contributors and would set a collective position and line of inquiry. That this never came about must be reckoned more to the times than to any change of mind or miscarriage of plans. Benjamin did, however, turn down one request from the institute: he declined to review Bloch's *Heritage of Our Times,* since such a review would "lie neither in his interests nor in mine" (GB, 5:397).

Not all of the days that Adorno and Benjamin spent together in Paris were given over to the advancement of Horkheimer's project. The visit afforded them ample time to further their common interests; in Benjamin's words, it "brought things long since prepared to mature fulfillment," as they rediscovered "a communality in the most important theoretical intentions," an accord that, in view of their long separation, was "at times almost amazing" (BA, 155; C, 533). They discussed their recent work, and of course the current shape and future prospects of the arcades project. Based on his understanding of the arcades project in its immediate historical context, Adorno suggested that Benjamin write an essay against the theories of C. G. Jung; he felt that the opportunity to differentiate Jung's theory of the archaic image and Benjamin's theory of the dialectical image—the heart of Benjamin's historiographical method—would galvanize the project and clarify its epistemology. These few days in Paris represented a breakthrough in their personal relationship. In the early thirties Benjamin had remained wary of what he saw as Adorno's pilfering of his ideas to advance the promising academic career he himself had been denied. There followed years of mostly cordial intellectual interchange colored by subterranean rivalry for Gretel Adorno's attention. Only now, in 1936, did the similarity of their situations in life come together with their long-standing theoretical and political interests. After these days in Paris, they began to address their letters to "Teddie" and "Walter"—although they never broke the barrier imposed by the formal address in German, the *Sie* form.

The optimism engendered by Adorno's visit did not last long. Later in the month, Benjamin learned that his brother, Georg, had been

31. Stefan Benjamin (*Theodor W. Adorno Archiv, Frankfurt am Main*)

sentenced to six years imprisonment in the Brandenburg-Görden prison on October 14, 1936. Scholem responded to Benjamin's terse announcement—"he is said to have reacted with totally unforgettable courage and composure"—by comparing Georg's position to that of his own brother, who was also a political prisoner in Germany. "Ever since [the pacifist Carl von] Ossietzky was awarded the Nobel Prize [in 1935], they have redoubled the revenge they wreak on those political prisoners in preventive custody who have remained healthy: my mother writes me of the many new ordeals involved. But worst of all is the utter unpredictability of how long the imprisonment will last" (BS, 187, 189). And as troubling as this news was, a personal disaster was looming much closer to home. Dora Sophie had begun to report problems with Stefan as early as spring 1936. Stefan had pressed her to allow him to leave the local *liceo*, complaining that the instructional methods were turning him into a parrot. Dora Sophie confided to Benjamin that she saw the root of the problem in Stefan himself: he had been an exceptional student in Berlin but was now receiving mediocre marks and reacted with thoughts of escape. A boarding school in Switzerland offered an alternative, but Dora wasn't in a position to finance a private education. She was struggling to sell the house on Delbrückstraße in Berlin that had come to her through the divorce agreement, but was very worried that the "Jewish laws" then being imposed would prevent any sale whatsoever.[28]

This news of Stefan's struggles undoubtedly took Benjamin by surprise. His correspondence with his son had been intermittent, but the letters they exchanged were generally lighthearted. His son had even been able to make light of an attempted conscription into the Young Fascists, the last step before membership in the Fascist Party. All members of the local "avant-gardist" group in San Remo had been entered automatically into the lists of the Young Fascists, but Stefan had not even known that he was an "avant-gardist." He told the official at the local Fascist headquarters, who inquired about his knowledge of foreign languages, that he was about to go abroad, which won him a temporary reprieve (GB, 5:320n). Stefan did indeed go abroad over the summer, returning to Vienna in order to prepare for the entrance examinations for the Austrian gymnasium. But here, too, he was blocked, and he wrote to his mother that he would instead enroll in hotel school, an idea that was anathema to both of his highly educated parents. By the end of October 1937 Stefan had dropped out of sight and was refusing to answer either letters or telegrams from his parents or calls from Dora's sister. Dora Sophie implored Benjamin to travel to Vienna to find their son, since she could not go herself for fear of being arrested. She had left Germany without paying the substantial tax imposed on all who left, and a warrant had been issued for her arrest (and even publicized in the Berlin papers).[29] Benjamin thus made arrangements to leave Paris on November 5, first telling Franz Glück that he was having his mail forwarded to Vienna. Given their ongoing uncertainty—they knew neither where Stefan was exactly nor what he was about—he did not finally set out until late November, traveling first to San Remo and then, via Ravenna, to Venice, where Stefan had finally agreed to meet his father—though not his mother. The talks between father and son proved productive, and Stefan agreed to return to San Remo with his father.

Benjamin described his son's problem as a "disturbance of the will" (GB, 5:428); however his parents might like to describe it, Stefan was in a worrisome psychological state. Benjamin immediately tried to arrange for his son to be analyzed by a prominent psychoanalyst, his old comrade in arms from the days of the Youth Movement, Siegfried Bernfeld. But after spending more time with the young man, he arrived at a more sensible evaluation. He told Horkheimer that, "in the case of my son, who is now 18, expatriation occurred while he was entering puberty; he has not been able to find his balance since then" (GB, 5:431). Greater familiarity provided deeper insight into his son's moral condition. Although the evidence remains murky, Stefan seems to have descended into the Viennese demimonde with a vengeance, getting money however he could and gambling it away just as fast. Dora Sophie was at her wits' end. She felt that she had to keep Stefan away from Vienna, where the "proximity of all the casinos" was a danger, but couldn't bring him to San Remo. Her explanation of this decision says everything about her own sense of her son's moral deterioration: bringing Stefan to San Remo would mean "establishing himself here as a freeloader and ne'er-do-well, since he naturally won't undertake anything real. I can't trust him with the pension's books, much less with the cash register; he doesn't understand a thing about administering the place, and he has become too slack for manual labor."[30] At the low point in their attempts to help their son, she worried that he might already have become a criminal. It was at this point that she considered the radical solution of having him adopted by his Berlin nursemaid, Friedy Barth, who was now a Swiss citizen living in Bern. We can only imagine Stefan's father's reaction to his problems with money and gambling. Already somewhat guilt-stricken on account of his distanced relationship to his son, Benjamin now must have been prey to real regret.

As it turned out, Stefan's emotional condition began to improve in the course of 1937. He passed the entrance examinations for the Austrian universities in natural history and geography, and even managed to get his name added to the lists of the Viennese fascist union, hoping to attain Austrian nationality or at least a passport. The results of the initial psychoanalysis had disturbed his mother; she accused herself of failing to give her son enough love in the year after their flight from Berlin. On learning of this, Benjamin paid his acquaintance Anja Mendelsohn fifty francs to provide a graphological analysis of his son (Benjamin's letter containing the results is now lost). Finally,

Stefan was seen by a neurologist, Wilhelm Hoffer, who was able to deliver reassuring news. "The general impression is a good one. Externally, Stefan can be addressed as a well developed young man who makes a quite manly impression. . . . At first, he acted shy and awkward—which can be explained as appropriate to his age and the situation." Hoffer told Stefan's parents that their son's bad company and reckless behavior were probably transitional.[31]

Not surprisingly, Stefan's crisis reawakened distrust in the relationship between Benjamin and Dora; he felt that she had acted unilaterally in regard to crucial issues, and she responded with renewed recriminations about Benjamin's relative lack of involvement in his son's life. As on many previous occasions, however, the two found a way that spring to resolve their differences, and by early summer Benjamin would return to the pension in San Remo.

Benjamin's meeting with Stefan in Venice had one unexpected benefit: he traveled via Ravenna and was able to see its famous Byzantine mosaics. "I've finally fulfilled a desire nursed for twenty years: I have now seen the Ravenna mosaics. The impression the mosaics made on me only barely surpasses that made by the sober, fortress-like churches, which have long been stripped of every intermittent ornament adorning their façades. Some have sunk somewhat into the ground; you have to walk down steps to get to them; this heightens the impression one has of turning back into the past" (BS, 188). Although the mosaics left few traces in his written work, another encounter with pictorial art a few weeks later in Paris would have a much more immediate yield. There he had the "extraordinary pleasure" (GB, 5:481) of attending a large exhibition of the works of Constantin Guys, the nineteenth-century artist who was the subject of one of Baudelaire's most important essays, "Le peintre de la vie moderne" (The Painter of Modern Life), cited extensively in *The Arcades Project*.

During the uproar over Stefan, Benjamin had moved back and forth between Paris and San Remo as he and Dora tried to come to grips with the situation. While this was happening, Ursel Bud took the chance to earn some extra money by subletting Benjamin's room; he thus found temporary quarters in an apartment at 185 Rue de Lavel, in the Fifteenth Arrondissement, in the early weeks of December.

He spent the time between Christmas 1936 and the middle of January 1937 in San Remo. Benjamin returned to Paris and his apartment in the Rue Bénard in early January, and turned immediately to the essay on Eduard Fuchs. During his visit to Denmark the previous August, he had once again taken up the preparatory studies for this piece commissioned by the *Zeitschrift für Sozialforschung* in 1933 or 1934; having worked on the project, intermittently and with little enthusiasm, over the course of 1935 and 1936, he now felt that he had no alternative but to complete the study. He was thus able, as Adorno put it, to "hunt down the fox" (*Fuchs* is German for "fox")—that is, to get down to writing the long-deferred essay. He notified both Adorno and Horkheimer at the end of January that he had made a start in drafting the text of the essay and that its completion would likely require another three weeks. The composition of the essay was as intense and rapid an experience as its preparation was dilatory. On March 1 he wrote to Adorno: "I am sure you will have interpreted the simple reason for these days of silence on my part in the most plausible manner. Once the progress of my work on the Fuchs piece reached a critical stage, it tolerated no other competitors, either day or night" (BA, 168). Benjamin was able to complete the actual writing in so short a time because he drew heavily on materials that he had at hand: the remarkable critical historiography with which the essay opens, as well as lengthy sections on the art and politics of nineteenth-century France, were taken directly from *The Arcades Project*, and the consideration of Fuchs's relationship to Marxism and to the Social Democratic Party was bolstered by research undertaken on the party's journal, *Die neue Zeit*, over the course of two summers in Denmark.

The essay reflects on every page Benjamin's ambivalence toward its subject. Eduard Fuchs (1870–1940) had joined the Social Democratic Party in 1886 and by 1888–1889 was already imprisoned for his political activity. He is now best known for his *Illustrierte Sittengeschichte vom Mittelalter bis zur Gegenwart* (Illustrated History of Manners from the Middle Ages to the Present), the three volumes of which appeared between 1909 and 1912, and for *Die Geschichte der erotischen Kunst* (History of Erotic Art), the three volumes of which appeared between 1922 and 1926. Benjamin recognizes in Fuchs a pioneering collector of caricature, erotic art, and genre painting; he underlines the challenge his writing presents to the verities of bourgeois art criticism, with its glorification of the creativity of the individual artist and its overreliance on an outdated classicist conception of beauty; and he acknowledges Fuchs's early attempts to come to terms with mass art and the technologies of reproduction. Yet Benjamin insists on the limitations imposed on Fuchs and his work by his adherence to the Social Democrats' liberal tenets—the insistence that their educational work was directed toward "the public" and not a class, their entrapment in a Darwinian biologism and determinism, their questionable doctrine of progress and unwarranted optimism, and their deeply German moralism.

The essay is remarkable, then, not so much for its engagement with the work of Eduard Fuchs as for the theory of cultural historiography Benjamin sets out in its opening pages. Drawing on the theoretical groundwork of *The Arcades Project*, the Fuchs essay simultaneously points toward the revolutionary historiography Benjamin would develop in the late 1930s. The essay starts from an understanding of the relation between the work of art and its historical moment, an understanding fundamental to Benjamin's critical writings from the very beginning. Rather than an isolated, autonomous creation, the work of art, on this view, constitutes an evolving historical phenomenon, an oscillating "force field" generated by the convergence and integration—the dynamic constellation—of the work's fore- and after-history: "It is by virtue of [its] after-history that [its] fore-history is recognizable as involved in a continuous process of change" (SW, 3:261). Benjamin anticipates here, as he had first done in the dissertation of 1919 on German Romanticism, the reception theories of the later twentieth century, with their appreciation of the role played by a work's historical reception in the meaning of the work itself. He redeploys one of his favorite quotations in support of this idea: Goethe's dictum "Nothing that has had a great effect can really be judged any longer" (SW, 3:262).

This understanding of the work as a fragment of larger historical processes is basic to Benjamin's concept of the dialectical image, which receives a distinctive new formulation in the Fuchs essay. Already in 1931, in the essay "Literary History and the Study of

Literature," Benjamin had claimed that "what is at stake is not to portray literary works in the context of their age, but to represent the age that perceives them—our age—in the age during which they arose" (SW, 2:464). What in 1931 remained a question of the representation of our own age through the representation of those elements of a prior age that are synchronous with it becomes in 1937 the more pressing question of an adequately historical experience of the present day—in truth, Benjamin's perennial theme. As a "fragment of the past," the work of art forms part of a "critical constellation" with "precisely this present." "For it is an irretrievable image of the past that threatens to disappear in any present that does not recognize itself as intimated in that image" (SW, 3:262). If the present is intimated in the image of the past, this means that the "pulse" of the past is beating in every present. In other words, "historical understanding [is] an afterlife of that which has been understood" (SW, 3:262), a proposition transposed from Convolute N2,3 in *The Arcades Project*. Such dialectical articulation of the relation between past and present entails, in Benjamin's decisive formulation, "a history that is originary for every present" (SW, 3:262). This double-edged apprehension—which points back to Nietzsche's proclamation, in *The Advantage and Disadvantage of History for Life*, that the past can be understood only from out of the highest energy of the present, for the past always speaks as an oracle—this deep paradox of historical understanding is both constructive and destructive in its working. " 'Construction' presupposes 'destruction,' " we read in *The Arcades Project*, for "the dissolution of historical semblance must follow the same trajectory as the construction of the dialectical image."[32] In practice, this means that the ostensibly obsolescent and retrograde elements in any epoch must be revalued by the historian in such a way as to bring about "a displacement of the angle of vision (but not of the criteria!)," until in the end "the entire past is brought into the present in a historical apocatastasis" (AP, N1a,3). Benjamin has recourse here to a central term in ancient Stoic, Gnostic, and Patristic thought, *apokatastasis*, which signified the cosmological alternation between the erasure of an historical era through a purging fire and the *restitutio in integrum* that might follow. The originally mythic-cosmological conception has become in Benjamin something that takes place within history.

It is from this perspective that Benjamin can criticize Fuchs's understanding of history for its failure to incorporate a destructive element. At bottom, this is a failure of conscience, a capitulation to "false consciousness." If the continuum of history is not exploded, cultural history is "sealed off" and "frozen" as an object of contemplation; specifically at issue here is "a renunciation of the contemplativeness which characterizes historicism" (SW, 3:262).[33] And this thought is capped by the now often-cited, indeed classic, admonition: "Whatever the historical materialist surveys in art or science has, without exception, a lineage he cannot observe without horror. The products of art and science owe their existence not merely to the effort of the great geniuses who created them, but also, in one degree or another, to the anonymous toil of their contemporaries. There is no document of culture which is not at the same time a document of barbarism" (SW, 3:267). These words will figure crucially three years later in the thetic essay "On the Concept of History."

It is noteworthy that Benjamin's elation at finishing the work did not exclude "a certain feeling of contempt" that had been growing in him as he became more familiar with Fuchs's writings and which he had tried to keep from being perceptible in the essay itself (BA, 169). It is perhaps most evident in his preliminary notes: "Fuchs lacks not only a sense of the destructive in caricature but also a sense of the destructive in sexuality, especially in orgasm. . . . Fuchs has no understanding of the historical dimension of anticipation in art. For him, the artist is, at best, the expression of the historical status quo, never of what is coming" (GS, 2:1356). This mixed mood is reflected in the letter to Horkheimer that accompanied the submitted manuscript:

> You know best how much world history and private history has come to pass since the plans for the project [on Fuchs] were first made. That there were also difficulties intrinsic to these plans is something we talked about. . . . I have tried to do what I felt was right by Fuchs—in part as felicitously, in part with as little infelicity, as was possible. At the same time, I wanted to give the work a more general interest. It was with this in mind that I made an effort, in dealing critically with Fuchs's methodology, to derive positive formulations on the subject of historical materialism. (GB, 5:463)

In the end, Benjamin was concerned less with Fuchs than with the opportunity afforded him to develop his own ideas. In comparing the Fuchs essay with Adorno's critique of Mannheim, Benjamin showed himself well aware of the "dexterity" both men displayed in "advancing [their] innermost thought, inconspicuously in each case, but without making any concessions" (BA, 168). Horkheimer and his colleagues in New York were very pleased with the result. Horkheimer wrote on March 16 to say that the essay would make an especially valuable contribution to the *Zeitschrift* because it furthered the journal's own theoretical aims; he also suggested a number of minor changes to the text, most of which Benjamin went along with. Additional changes suggested by Fuchs himself, to whom Benjamin sent the article, were incorporated in April. Once again, however, there was friction as the actual editing process got under way. The most upsetting development was the editors' decision to cut the essay's opening paragraph, which situates Fuchs's work in the context of the Marxist theory of art. As Leo Löwenthal, speaking for Horkheimer, explained the matter in May, the editors wished, on "tactical" grounds, to avoid giving the impression that they were publishing "a political article."[34] It seems that Benjamin never consented to the deletion of the first paragraph, which appeared in print only with the publication of his *Gesammelte Schriften*. He had to wait until October for the publication of the essay in the *Zeitschrift*, for Horkheimer did not want to influence unfavorably the "endless" negotiations being carried on with the German authorities for the release of Fuchs's collection (GB, 5:550).

The institute's worries proved unfounded; unlike the artwork essay, "Eduard Fuchs" occasioned only a muted contemporary reaction. Benjamin was thrown back on his own resources as he sought some further response. Scholem remained, despite their difficulties, the most trustworthy reader of Benjamin's work, and he duly received the text of the unexpurgated version of the Fuchs essay. His reaction was predictable: while conceding that "the success of the Marxist approach—whose problematic nature leads the reader of Walter Benjamin again and again to dark broodings, even against the author's will—is less visible to an unfortunate admirer like myself," Scholem nonetheless felt compelled to lament the harm done to Benjamin's work by this casting "of your fine insights before dialectical swine" (BS, 206).

Whatever Benjamin's own reservations regarding his "fine insights" might have been, the essay on Fuchs brought to the fore a concern for methodological issues in cultural historiography, a concern close to the heart of his work on the arcades. He conceded as much to Horkheimer at the end of January in a letter that asks about the forms of writing appropriate to modern philosophy, the problem addressed with such rigor in the preface to the *Trauerspiel* book.

> There can naturally be no question of eliminating philosophical terminology. I am in total agreement with you when you say that historical tendencies "that are preserved in certain categories may also not be allowed to be lost in style." I would like to add one further consideration to what you say. . . . I mean that there is a way of using philosophical terminology to feign a nonexistent richness. This is an uncritical use of technical terms. Concrete dialectical analysis of the particular subject being studied, on the other hand, includes a critique of the categories in which it was apprehended at an earlier level of reality and thought. . . . Surely, general intelligibility cannot be a criterion. But it is likely that a certain transparency in details is inherent in concrete dialectical analysis. The general intelligibility of the whole is of course another story altogether. What is pertinent here is to look squarely at the fact you describe: in the long run small groups will play a prominent role in the preservation and transmission of science and art. This is, in fact, not the time to display in kiosks what we believe we have in our hands, probably not entirely without justification; rather, it seems to be a time to think of storing it where it will be safe from bombs. The dialectics of the thing may consist in this: to give the truth, which is nothing less than smoothly constructed [*glatt gefügt*], a place of safekeeping, smoothly constructed like a strongbox. (C, 537)

This important letter documents the ongoing tensions in Benjamin's work between the concerns of a highly educated, mandarin elite (for whom "general intelligibility" is no criterion) and the responsibility of avoiding technical jargon and creating a "concrete dialectical analysis" that maintains "transparency in details." Writing to Horkheimer,

Benjamin tilts to the former; a letter to Brecht on this subject would have looked rather different.

His daily confrontation with methodological questions, however, brought Benjamin no closer to an answer to the pressing question that arose with the completion of the long-delayed essay on Fuchs: what to write next? He could hardly make the decision on his own, for any major change of direction needed Horkheimer's blessing. His discussions with Adorno in the fall had convinced Benjamin that the epistemological dimension of the arcades project could best be served through a confrontation with the "function of psychoanalytic theories of collective psychology, as they have been applied by fascism, on the one hand, and by historical materialism on the other." This confrontation would occur through an analysis of the concept of "archaic images" in Carl Gustav Jung's "Aryan psychology" (GB, 5:463–464). Further reflection led Benjamin to include the work of Ludwig Klages—less his work in graphology than the ideas propagated in his book *On Cosmogenic Eros*—in which he had long been interested. He saw here an opportunity to go to the roots of the idea of the collective unconscious, and the "image fantasies" that arose from it, an anthropological task in keeping with the scheme of the 1935 exposé of the arcades project (GB, 5:489). As he explained in a second letter addressing Horkheimer's serious reservations about the focus on Jung and Klages, it was necessary to return to the "oldest layer of the book's plan"—that is, its inception in the psychoanalytically inflected writings of the Surrealists—in order to clarify the course of his later researches and thinking. At the same time, Benjamin suggested to Horkheimer that, as an alternative to the study of Jung and Klages, he complete a comparison of "bourgeois" and materialist historiography that could serve as an introduction to the book as a whole. It is interesting to note that such a comparison was indeed written in 1938 and that it was intended as an introduction—not to the arcades themselves, but to the book on Baudelaire to which Benjamin eventually turned. Already in the spring of 1937, Benjamin was proposing an expansion of the section on Baudelaire in the 1935 exposé as a third alternative for his writing focus. By late April Horkheimer was urging him in the strongest terms to concentrate on Baudelaire and to forgo the study of collective psychology. Benjamin's interests, it turned out, were beginning to encroach upon the territory reserved for some of Horkheimer's closest collaborators in the institute, Erich Fromm and Herbert Marcuse, and he thus deflected his distant colleague toward Baudelaire. Benjamin agreed, by return post, to revisit the 1935 exposé with an eye to expanding the Baudelaire section into an independent essay. He thus accepted Horkheimer's godfathering with good grace. Since the completion of the artwork essay, a mutual intellectual respect had begun to make itself felt in their exchanges, although there was always a certain reserve on Horkheimer's part, which must have had something to do with his undivulged auxiliary role in the rejection of Benjamin's habilitation thesis on the *Trauerspiel* back in 1925. From Benjamin's point of view, this growing respect was now, with the final acceptance of the essay on Fuchs, a sign of his more secure position in the institute.

Benjamin notified Adorno of this development in his writing plans on April 23, commenting: "Certainly your own suggestion [apropos of Jung] struck me as the most feasible one . . . so far as the work [on the arcades] is concerned. On the other hand, . . . the essential motifs of the book are so interconnected that the various individual themes do not really present themselves as strict alternatives anyway" (BA, 178). Adorno nonetheless continued to campaign for a Benjaminian treatment of Jung and, as late as mid-September, held out hope that "the Jung piece could prove to be your next essay after all" (BA, 208). Nor did Benjamin immediately abandon the project; in early July he could still apprise Scholem of his immersion in a recent volume of Jung's essays from the 1930s. He was fascinated by Jung's proposal of a therapy peculiar to the "Aryan soul," and wanted to take the measure of the "peculiar figuration of clinical nihilism in literature—Benn, Céline, Jung," showing the kind of "auxiliary services" they provided to National Socialism (BS, 197). He admitted that he had no idea where he might eventually publish such a study, but his persistence shows how important this elucidation of the poisoned roots of collective psychology was to his idea of the arcades project.

Knowing he could not live on the institute's bread alone, Benjamin cast about that spring for other projects and publishing venues. The dissemination of the artwork essay—and preferably its longer, German version—in other languages remained a primary concern. Willi Bredel had rejected the German version, claiming that its length made it unsuitable for *Das Wort*. Benjamin's hopes were temporarily raised by a letter from Horkheimer reporting that the assistant curator of the newly established film department at New York's Museum of Modern Art, Jay Leyda (the friend and later translator of Eisenstein), was interested in publishing an English translation of "The Work of Art in the Age of Its Technological Reproducibility." Horkheimer warned Benjamin, though, against providing Leyda with the German version of the essay for which he had asked: he was concerned that any German original might reintroduce elements that had been cut from the French version published in the *Zeitschrift*. Like all other attempts during Benjamin's lifetime to publish an English version of the essay, in whole or in part, this too this never got off the ground.[35]

On learning of the rejection of the artwork essay from Bredel, Benjamin in turn proposed an extremely ambitious project for the pages of *Das Wort:* a political analysis of the "literary movements of the western nations." He hoped to show, through consideration of representative publishing houses and journals in several countries, the political directions actually taken by literary antifascism. And he proposed to undertake a survey of French literary culture as a kind of model study for the project. On a more modest scale, he proposed a study of the mysteries of Georges Simenon, one of his favorite authors, and a study of the Académie Française. Although Benjamin's suggestions came to nothing, these exchanges with Bredel produced one of Benjamin's most cogent epistolary analyses of the difficulties of publishing in exile:

> When, dear Willi Bredel, you mention the difficult position of your friends "out there," you are speaking—as to what concerns me— more truly than you perhaps know. The interest in *production* here is interlaced, indissolubly, with the author's palpable interest in the *reproduction* of his work. The path from manuscript to printed text is longer than it has ever been, and thus the span of time between the work process itself and its remuneration is stretched to the breaking point. There is an optimal period for all writerly work—to say nothing of the collaboration that takes place between editors and author— and any extensive deviation from this optimal period can seriously hinder the work. This experience is, of course, not new to you.

This was anything but a disinterested disquisition. Benjamin went on to assure Bredel that he could derive more profit from their collaboration if his pieces were to appear more quickly—and if the compensation for them were to arrive more rapidly at the author's door (GB, 5:516). Bredel in fact accepted a second "Letter from Paris" on "Painting and Photography" in late March (the first letter, on André Gide, had been published in 1936). But this incisive critical survey, which reports on a volume of essays concerned with the contemporary crisis of painting and suggests that the crisis stems primarily from photography's usurpation of painting's "usefulness" (SW, 3:236–248), was never published—and Benjamin was never paid.

Benjamin also received offers to publish pieces in two distinguished émigré journals: *Maß und Wert* (Measure and Value), a centrist journal published by Thomas Mann and Konrad Falke and edited by Ferdinand Lion, and *Die neue Weltbühne* (The New World Stage), a magazine of "politics, art, and economics" oriented toward the left. *Die Weltbühne*, edited first by Kurt Tucholsky and then by the heroic Carl von Ossietzky, had been one of the most influential weeklies in the Weimar Republic; it was famous for its humane, tolerant, left-liberal line. Banned by the Nazis in 1933, the journal had struggled to find a home, financial stability and a tenable line in exile. By 1937, that line was largely determined by the economic journalist and part owner Hermann Budzislawski. Bloch, who had published several essays there, had acted as intermediary in this last offer. Despite his reservations about both enterprises, Benjamin would take advantage of these offers, publishing reviews in the two journals in the coming year and vignettes from *Berlin Childhood* in *Maß und Wert*.

Benjamin had returned to Paris early in the new year to find the Parisian literati in an uproar over André Gide's latest book. Although Gide had never joined the Communist Party, he had repeatedly shown himself sympathetic to its cause. The Soviet Writers' Union had invited him to tour the country, and he had accepted, traveling widely in 1936. Instead of the newly liberated humanity he hoped to find, however, he found only totalitarianism. His justification for his political recantation, in the book *Return to the USSR*, was scathing. Benjamin's response to the uproar was clearly conditioned by the state of European politics. "As for me," he wrote to Margarete Steffin, "I disapprove of the book without even having read it. Without even knowing whether what it contains is accurate—or whether it is a decisive contribution. . . . A political position cannot be tested before the general public at just any moment. To claim that is pure dilettantism" (GB, 5:438–439). The heated tone of the controversy surrounding Gide's book points to the dark background against which it occurred: in mid-January, Franco's nationalist troops had mounted a major assault on Madrid, which fell on February 8. Any political attack on the radical left, whatever the motivation, was inevitably seen as detrimental to the Republican cause in Spain. And Spain was not the only explosive situation on the horizon: the Great Uprising in Palestine had reached a new crescendo of violence. Benjamin wrote Scholem on February 11: "Though I'm not a man who gives up easily, there are hours when I feel uncertain whether we shall ever see each other again. A cosmopolitan city like Paris has become a very frail entity, and if what I'm told about Palestine is true, then a wind is blowing there in which even Jerusalem could begin to sway to and fro like a reed" (BS, 190).

By his own admission, Benjamin had isolated himself from his friends and acquaintances while composing the Fuchs essay. In the course of the spring he gradually came back into contact with Kracauer and Bloch, as well as with a few other acquaintances. He was seeing more of the Communist novelist and activist Anna Seghers (born Netty Reiling, 1900–1983), with whom he had probably first come in contact through her husband, the Hungarian sociologist and director of the Freien Deutschen Hochschule, László Radványi. Segher's first book, *Revolt of the Fishermen of Santa Barbara* (1928), had made her famous. In exile in Paris, she was a founding member of the Schutzverband deutscher Schriftsteller im Ausland (Defense League of German Authors Abroad). Segher's life in the late 1930s ran in parallel to Benjamin's: her husband was interned in the same camp as Benjamin at Le Vernet, and, after arranging for his release, Seghers, her husband, and their two children traveled to Marseilles, where they joined the swelling numbers of German émigrés seeking escape from Vichy France. There the parallels end. Seghers and her family succeeded in escaping via Martinique and New York, finally settling in Mexico City. She returned to Germany in 1947 and became one of the most prominent cultural figures in the German Democratic Republic. Another significant acquaintance from this period was the philosopher Jean Wahl, who taught at the Sorbonne. Although he had begun his career as a disciple of Henri Bergson, Wahl had by the mid-1930s established himself as the leading Hegelian in France. His teaching and writing had exerted a profound influence on the Collège de Sociologie, and especially on Alexandre Kojève. In the course of the year, Benjamin also got to know Pierre Dubosc, an expert on Chinese art, whose collection of Chinese paintings was exhibited in Paris that spring. Benjamin's little report on the exposition, "Peintures chinoises à la Bibliothèque Nationale," appeared in the journal *Europe* in January 1938.

Benjamin was especially eager for Stephan Lackner (born Ernest Gustave Morgenroth, 1910–2000) to return to Paris, not merely on account of the intellectual companionship the younger man could offer, but also because he and his father Sigmund had become a noninstitutional source of support. For Benjamin was experiencing another mini-crisis. He had put off purchasing eyeglasses for several years and could now see only poorly; he claimed to Lackner that he hardly dared leave his home. The plea for money for eyeglasses was a symptom of yet another financial crisis. The French economy in 1937 was still reeling from the aftershocks of the Great Depression, which had come to France much later than to the rest of the world. There was massive unemployment, and industrial production had sunk to pre–World War I levels. As a result, the franc had become increasingly unstable, and rapid price increases were crippling Benjamin's budget. A letter to Friedrich Pollack from late March gives us a picture of his finances at this time:

Regular Expenditures:

Rent (including my share of utilities, telephone, and concierge fee)[1]	480.—Frs.
Food	720.—Frs.
Clothing maintenance and Laundry	120.—Frs.
Incidentals (hygiene, café, postage, etc.)	350.—Frs.
Transportation	90.—Frs.
Total	1760.—Frs.

Extraordinary Expenditures[2]

Suits (one per year)	50.—Frs.
Shoes (two pair per year)	25.—Frs.
Undergarments	25.—Frs.
Cinema, Exhibits, Theater	50.—Frs.
Medical Care[3]	

1. I live in the furnished apartment of a German immigrant. Through several purchases—drapes, mat, counterpane—I was able to arrange my room so that I could have an occasional French guest.

2. I have no savings from which to meet extraordinary expenses. On the other hand, I have no debts. My income for the year just past consisted, aside from that known to you, of 1200.—Frs. for my book *Deutsche Menschen*, 250.—Frs. for a contribution to the journal *Wort*, and 150.—Frs. for a contribution to the journal *Orient und Okzident* [*sic*].

3. I can provide no amount for this entry. The acquisition of two pairs of new eyeglasses last month caused me difficulty. At the same time I have been forced to seek dental treatment that, after much deferral, can no longer be delayed. (GB, 5:500–501)

The representation of his income, of course, leaves out the small sums he continued to receive from friends on an irregular basis, and we have no way of knowing whether he was still, in March 1937, receiving rent from his Berlin tenant. On the whole, this accounting seems rather modest and suggests that Benjamin was again struggling to meet the most minimal requirements of existence. The accounting also suggests that Benjamin's daily routine—research at the Bibliothèque Nationale, writing at a café—had changed but little since his move to the capital. He reported to Gretel Karplus that he often "planted [himself] next to the only stove on the terrace of the Select; now and again the sun protrudes from the clouds, thus providing the body with what the eye knows as twilight" (BG, 193).

Neither his problems with his eyesight nor the ongoing financial miseries could stem the flow of Benjamin's reading in early 1937. He had just finished James M. Cain's popular first novel, *The Postman Always Rings Twice*, in French translation, and found it "as thrilling as it is discerning" (GB, 5:479). Cain's hard-boiled melodrama was one of a number of different books he read in these months, including Choderlos de Laclos's *Les liaisons dangereuses,* a collection of nineteenth-century English ghost stories in translation, and—an "extraordinary work"—G. K. Chesterton's *Charles Dickens* (also in French translation), the latter of importance for *The Arcades Project.* His reading of Wladimir Weidlé's *Les abeilles d'Aristé: Essai sur le destin actuel des lettres et des arts* produced a mixed reaction; he remarked to Karl Thieme that he shared nothing of the author's general stance yet found certain of the book's observations on contemporary art conducive to further reflection. And he had the same mixed reaction to Bernard von Brentano's new work, *Prozeß ohne Richter* (Trial without a Judge), that he always had to the works of this author: it was "well written but confused" (GB, 5:513).

Benjamin's quest for a topic that would guarantee near-term publication *and* return him to the methodological problems of the arcades project was interrupted in mid-March by the momentous discovery of a little-known text by a little-known author: Carl Gustav Jochmann's book *Über die Sprache* (On Language) was published anonymously in 1828. Jochmann, a Livonian German, had, like Benjamin, immigrated to Paris; for Benjamin, he was "one of the greatest revolutionary writers of the German language." Jochmann's book contained a seventy-page essay, "Die Rückschritte der Poesie" (The Regression of Poetry), which Benjamin likened to "a meteorite that has fallen into the nineteenth century from out of the twentieth." Benjamin's enthusiasm was sparked by a key conjunction in Jochmann's text: that of language and politics. Like Madame de Staël before him, Jochmann located a basic impediment to the political liberation of the German states in the German insistence on the preeminence of literature. Thus Jochmann's "unimaginably bold thesis": "that the regression of poetry is the progress of culture" (GB, 5:480). Benjamin's own edition of the essay, abridged and supplemented with biographical information on the author and short selections from some of Jochmann's other writings, was sent to Horkheimer on March 28 with a long letter in which Benjamin commented that he himself had read the essay "with a pounding heart" and, further, that it would give him considerable pleasure to see it published in the *Zeitschrift* (GB, 5:492). Horkheimer wrote back two weeks later expressing great enthusiasm for the essay in its shortened form and commissioning Benjamin to write a theoretical introduction for its publication in the institute's journal. This introduction was drafted between April and the beginning of July and then, at Horkheimer's bidding, revised the following year. In it Benjamin locates the peculiar beauty of Jochmann's essay in the "measuring out of its philosophic tensions"—a strategically "vacillating" procedure through which a prose of deep-seated philosophic import is engendered without recourse to philosophical terminology. Together with Benjamin's wide-ranging introduction, the edited essay would eventually appear in a double issue of the *Zeitschrift* in early January 1940.

On the day following the mailing of the letter announcing his "discovery" of Jochmann to Horkheimer, Benjamin received an angry note from Werner Kraft. Their relationship had had its ups and downs: it was broken off in 1921 and then resumed in 1933, after a chance meeting of the two émigré authors in the Bibliothèque Nationale. Kraft moved to Jerusalem the next year, and they had carried on a friendly and fruitful correspondence since then, having in common a passion for such contemporary figures as Kafka, Karl Kraus, and Brecht. They both valued the opportunity to exchange ideas and sometimes work. But Kraft was writing on March 29—at the end of a three-month stay in Paris, during which he met with Benjamin—to demand a second and final break in their relations. Benjamin expressed surprise at Kraft's action, wished him well, and returned some books Kraft had lent him (GB, 5:504–505). The circumstances surrounding this break were tangled. Kraft later remarked that he had no concrete motive for ending things between them, "other than . . . my long-suppressed vexation with Herr Benjamin's manner of carrying on a friendship—this mix of lukewarm cordiality, clear-cut distance, want of loyalty, and plain bluff."[36] The breakup, though, was certainly also occasioned by competing claims for the "discovery" of Jochmann. In 1937 Kraft made no reference to Jochmann; he merely broke off relations. Yet among the books Benjamin returned before Kraft's departure for Jerusalem in April 1937 were the collected works of Jochmann—which suggests that Kraft might have originally pointed Benjamin toward the writer and his work. With the publication of Benjamin's article on Jochmann in 1940, Kraft's claims were sounded—vigorously.

He now maintained, having seen Benjamin's piece, that it was he who, in 1936, first made Benjamin aware of this writer, and specifically of the essay "Die Rückschritte der Poesie," which he himself had discovered in the library at Hannover, where he worked as a librarian until 1933. He further claimed that Benjamin had promised him not to write anything on that essay. Benjamin countered in 1940 that he had learned of Jochmann independently of Kraft through his perusal of a specific volume (which he cites) in the Bibliothèque Nationale in the spring of 1936, even though he first came to know the essay in question after Kraft had lent him the books; he went on to dismiss Kraft's claim of priority in the reading of a published text, however rare it might be, as extravagant. As for a promise not to write on Jochmann's unheralded essay, he said he had merely acknowledged to Kraft the difficulties of such an enterprise. It is worth mentioning, in the context of this unresolved controversy, that when Adorno arranged for the first reprint of Benjamin's Jochmann introduction in 1963, he appended a footnote mentioning Kraft's rediscovery of the forgotten author in the early thirties—a rediscovery that, Adorno says, influenced Benjamin when he later produced his essay on "Die Rückschritte der Poesie."

Adorno was among the first to know of Benjamin's edition of the Jochmann essay in the spring of 1937; visiting Paris for a few days in mid-March, he listened to Benjamin read from the essay and soon thereafter sent an enthusiastic letter to Horkheimer. While in Paris, Adorno also accompanied Benjamin on a visit to Eduard Fuchs, who received them in his apartment. There were naturally other pressing matters Benjamin wanted to discuss with Adorno; as he says in a letter from this period, "The more often we get to see each other, the more crucial our meetings will come to seem to us" (BA, 173). These other matters included a projected volume of essays by various authors to be entitled *Massenkunst im Zeitalter des Monopolkapitalismus* (Mass Art under Monopoly Capitalism), which Adorno was planning and which was to include Benjamin's work-of-art essay, as well as other contributions by him (possibly on the detective novel and on film), but which, because of the institute's financial problems, was never realized. And there was Adorno's new essay on the sociologist

Karl Mannheim. Reading this essay at the beginning of the month, right after completing work on the Fuchs piece, Benjamin had been struck by the profound

> analogy between our respective tasks. . . . In the first place, there were those chemical analyses which had to be performed on . . . all those stale dishes of ideas from which every Tom, Dick, and Harry have long been feeding. Everything from this squalid kitchen had to be subjected to laboratory analysis. And then, secondly, there was that show of urbanity we had to cultivate toward the dubious kitchen chef himself, something you practiced rather less, but which I unfortunately practiced a great deal. . . . And I can see that we have also shared the same dexterity in advancing our innermost thought, inconspicuously in each case, but without making any concessions. (BA, 168)

A good deal of their talk was devoted to their mutual acquaintance Alfred Sohn-Rethel. Both Benjamin and Adorno had seen Sohn-Rethel occasionally in Berlin during the late 1920s, although the intensity of their first encounters near Naples in 1924 was never regained. Despite his leftist leanings, Sohn-Rethel had managed to find a niche for himself in Hitler's Germany, working as a researcher between 1931 and 1936 for the Mitteleuropäischen Wirtschaftstag (Central European Economic Council), an association of the leading German corporations and banks. He immigrated to England only in 1937, passing through Switzerland and Paris on the way. Sohn-Rethel conceived his life's work as the construction of a materialist theory of knowledge uniting Kant's critical epistemology and Marx's critique of political economy. In the hope that Adorno might be able to convince the institute to support his work, Sohn-Rethel had sent him a lengthy exposé of the project—under the title "Sociological Theory of Knowledge"—in autumn 1936. Although Adorno was not wholly convinced by the exposé, he asked Sohn-Rethel to draft a clearer synopsis for submission to Horkheimer. Much later on, Sohn-Rethel suggested that Adorno had recommended to Horkheimer that Benjamin be asked to write an evaluation of the work.[37] Given its relentlessly abstract register, Benjamin was not an ideal referee. During Adorno's visit to Paris in mid-March he and Benjamin spent a long evening listening to Sohn-

Rethel's presentation of his ideas. On the basis of this and further conversations—but before reading Sohn-Rethel's work—Benjamin sent a somewhat tentative endorsement of the project to Horkheimer on March 28; he concluded by suggesting that the most promising of Sohn-Rethel's ideas might best be treated in a kind of working group on epistemology and commodity exchange consisting of himself, Sohn-Rethel, and Adorno. During the month of April, Benjamin worked closely with Sohn-Rethel in Paris on a further revision of his exposé, which was duly submitted to Horkheimer. This so-called Paris exposé was published in 1989 under the title "On the Critical Liquidation of Apriorism: A Materialist Analysis" in a version that included Benjamin's annotations. The collaborative text argues that the increasing abstraction of human thought is the result of commodification: the worker's sensuous human labor is abstracted as the product of that labor is drawn into a system of exchange. On Adorno's final recommendation, Sohn-Rethel received an honorarium of 1,000 francs for the exposé, together with a further 1,000 francs in May. No lasting relationship to the institute was ever established, however; Sohn-Rethel moved to England and found a position as economic advisor in the circle around Winston Churchill. It is ironic that Sohn-Rethel's work would afterward influence the more theoretically inclined cadres of the German student movement of the late sixties, the same cadres who subjected Adorno's work to surpassing scorn.

May saw yet another, even more difficult triangulation with Adorno. Their old friend Kracauer had published the book on which he had long been at work, *Orpheus in Paris: Offenbach and the Paris of His Time*. Kracauer's book uses the biographical form as an optic through which to view the social and cultural history of the Paris of the Second Empire. Given the long-standing affinities between the work of Kracauer and of Benjamin, it could not have been surprising that Kracauer envisioned a physiognomy of a cultural era: the book diagnoses Offenbach's operettas as at once symptomatic of the pomp and superficiality of the reign of Napoleon III *and* suggestive of utopian resistance to that regime. Adorno's comments on the book were unsparing. Calling it an "abomination," he claimed that "the few passages that touch on music are crassly erroneous," that "the social observations are no more than old wives' tales," and that Kracauer offers only a squinting "petty bourgeois look . . . at 'society' and indeed the demimonde." Adorno goes so far as to say that Kracauer may have "erased himself from the list of writers to be taken at all seriously" (BA, 184). Not content with private communications to Benjamin, Bloch, and Sohn-Rethel, Adorno first sent what he termed "a most principled and extremely frank" condemnation of the book to Kracauer himself, and then, at the end of the year, published an excoriating review in the *Zeitschrift für Sozialforschung*. Benjamin, whose relations with Kracauer had already become more distant, had no interest in opening the breach further, reserving his opinion for letters to Adorno. His appraisal of the book, while negative, was more measured, if less specific. He attributes what he sees as the book's failing to Kracauer's need to "establish some positive access to the book market." Kracauer's book is thus for Benjamin a popularization that makes "an example of the thing" without saying anything "essential" about Offenbach's work, particularly where the music is concerned. The result is an ill-judged "redemption" of the operetta (BA, 185–186). The two reactions to Kracauer's book evidently share the sense that their friend had encroached on their territory. Adorno saw a rival in the field of cultural musicology (Ernst Krenek called Kracauer's book "the biography of a musician without music"),[38] and Benjamin saw a book that employed some of his own strategies in analyzing the Second Empire. Given Benjamin's characteristic sensitivity to *any* use of his material and approach, his reaction is surprisingly restrained. Moreover, he would cite the book extensively in *The Arcades Project*. Adorno, on the other hand, launched a virtual vendetta, which must have seemed like a brute betrayal to his old friend and onetime mentor. He blackened Kracauer's reputation with a series of deprecating remarks to Horkheimer, knowing they could only entrench Horkheimer's already skeptical opinion. Looking back at the period of exile from a later vantage, Adorno produced one of his most important works in 1950, *Minima Moralia*, which bears the subtitle *Reflections from Damaged Life*. The German exile community was rife with tension and rivalry. This was occasioned not just by the competition for the very limited resources—and recognition—available in foreign lands but also by the horrible psychological and physiological extremes to which these dislocated and dispossessed human beings were subjected. The controversy over Kracauer's Offenbach book reveals, as do few other instances in the friendship between Benjamin, Adorno, and Kracauer, the extent to which the conditions of exile—intellectual homelessness, financial desperation, and social instability—could deform a life and destroy a friendship.

Late spring brought a few diversions: Benjamin attended a concert by Adorno's friend, the violinist and Schoenberg disciple Rudolf Kolisch, in April, and he heard a speech by Anna Seghers in memory of the great German writer Georg Büchner in May. He noted archly to Margarete Steffin that the speech showed once again how much better Seghers spoke than wrote (GB, 5:521). Friedrich Pollock was in town on institute business in April, and Benjamin spent a pleasant evening with him; the two men were growing friendlier, and Benjamin began to refer to him as "Friedrich" in letters to Adorno. The evening, of course, included pleas for additional support: the French currency continued to fluctuate wildly, and Benjamin was not confident that he could hold on to the modest improvements in his standard of living that he had recently achieved. In early June Adorno came through town again, giving them the chance to deepen their personal and philosophical solidarity. There was one more diversion that seemed tailor-made for the author of *The Arcades Project:* the Paris World Exposition. The Exposition Internationale des Arts et Techniques dans la Vie Moderne opened on May 25; it remains perhaps the most politically charged of all world expositions. The Spanish pavilion, built by the Republican government, housed Picasso's *Guernica*. And the monumental German and Russian pavilions—for all their apparent rivalry—mirrored each other's stolid totalitarian architecture and sculpture. The exposition brought permanent changes to the urban landscape of the Sixteenth Arrondissement: the Avenue des Nations-Unies was built to traverse the grounds, while the Palais de Chaillot and the Palais de Tokio were built along the Seine. Yet Benjamin, whose arcades project examines the role of industrial expositions in the formation of the nineteenth-century capitalist metropolis, mentioned to Scholem in early July that he had not set foot on the exhibition grounds.

Benjamin traveled to San Remo on June 28 and remained in Dora's pension until late August, leaving only to attend a philosophy conference in Paris from July 28 through August 12. Ensconced once again in the Italian resort, he returned to his summer routine, with walks into the surrounding hills, a daily swim, and frequent visits to cafés, where he read and wrote. He remarked to a number of friends that he was "in the midst of intensive and by no means unfruitful study of Jung" (BA, 201). As he described the situation in a letter of July 9 to Fritz Lieb: "I was planning to write a critique of Jungian psychology, whose Fascist armor I had promised myself to expose" (C, 542). Yet the yield from these two months of study was comparatively slight, its only trace in Benjamin's extant work being a few scattered citations and one analytical comment in *The Arcades Project* that takes off from the letter of July 2 to Scholem quoted above:

> In Jung's production there is a belated and particularly emphatic elaboration of one of the elements which, as we can recognize today, were first disclosed in explosive fashion by Expressionism. That element is a specifically clinical nihilism, such as one encounters also in the works of Benn, and which has found a camp follower in Céline. This nihilism is born of the shock imparted by the interior of the body to those who treat it. Jung himself traces the heightened interest in psychic life back to Expressionism. He writes: "Art has a way of anticipating future changes in man's fundamental outlook, and expressionist art has taken this subjective turn well in advance of the more general change." See *Seelenprobleme der Gegenwart* (Zurich, Leipzig, and Stuttgart, 1932), p. 415. (AP, N8a, 1)

In the *Arcades* manuscript, Jung was initially placed in Convolute K, "Dream City and Dream House, Dreams of the Future, Anthropological Nihilism, Jung." The quotation above is taken, though, from Convolute N, "On the Theory of Knowledge, Theory of Progress," where Benjamin assembled most of his explicitly methodological reflections. By the summer of 1937 the shock-mediated phenomenon of "clinical nihilism"—the explosive force of revealed bodilyness—had been reckoned a significant aspect of modern experience and the ideology of progress.

That summer was not a productive one for Benjamin. He wrote to Fritz Lieb, "There is a view onto gloom through whatever window we look." Looking to the southwest, he saw war in Spain and a daily threat to the existence of Alfred Cohn and his family in Barcelona. To the northwest was France and the politics of the Popular Front, which he denounced in an unusually open manner, claiming that the " 'leftist' majority pursues a politics with which the rightists would provoke revolts." And far to the northeast, but ever present in the mind of Benjamin and his friends, were the ongoing show trials in Moscow. "The destructive effect of events in Russia will inevitably continue to spread," he wrote to Lieb. "And the bad thing about this is not the facile indignation of the staunch fighters for 'freedom of thought': what appears to me to be much sadder and much more inevitable at the same time is the silence of thinking individuals who, precisely as thinking individuals, would have difficulty in taking themselves for informed individuals. This is the case with me, and probably also with you" (C, 542).

On August 5, just after a section of his essay "Goethes Wahlverwandtschaften" (Goethe's Elective Affinities) had appeared in French translation in *Cahiers du Sud,* he wrote to Scholem: "I am about to embark on another project, which deals with Baudelaire" (BS, 203). This modest statement marks the starting point for the great project that would occupy Benjamin for the next two and a half years. Once back in Paris in September, with the resources of the Bibliothèque Nationale at hand, he commenced his readings for the Baudelaire piece in earnest. By the time he came to draft the essay "The Paris of the Second Empire in Baudelaire"—during three months of highly concentrated labor the following summer—the essay had been reconceived as the central section of a projected book on Baudelaire. Far from abandoning his work on the arcades, Benjamin came in the course of 1938 to consider that book, *Charles Baudelaire: Ein Lyriker im Zeitalter des Hochkapitalismus* (Charles Baudelaire: A Lyric Poet in the Age of High Capitalism), and the essay at its heart, as a "miniature model" of *The Arcades Project* (C, 556).

In response to a request from Adorno, Benjamin traveled up from San Remo to Paris at the end of July, in order to accompany him to the third Conference of the International Congress for Unified Knowledge, held July 29–31, and the ninth International Congress of Philosophy that followed; at both gatherings, Adorno was the official representative of the institute. With Benjamin's help, he composed a report in which he apprised Horkheimer of the proceedings of the conferences and of discussions which he and Benjamin had had with various participants. For his part, Benjamin was able, as he mentioned to Scholem, to follow "very closely the sessions of the special conference that the Viennese logistical school—Carnap, Neurath, Reichenbach—has been holding. One feels free to say: *Molière n'a rien vu.* The *vis comica* of his debating doctors and philosophers pales in comparison with that of these 'empirical philosophers'" (BS, 202). Other presentations were less comical. At the main conference of philosophers, which was meant to mark the 300th anniversary of the publication of Descartes's *Discours de la méthode,* Benjamin heard not just Nazi sympathizers such as Alfred Bäumler but representatives of the current state of German academic philosophy such as the Idealist Arthur Liebert, editor of the journal *Kant-Studien:* "Hardly had he uttered his first words when I found myself carried back twenty-five years into the past, into an atmosphere, to be sure, in which one could have already sensed all the decay of the present" (BS, 203). He was transported, in other words, back into the world of the German academy and into the lecture halls where he had heard Rickert, Jaspers, Cassirer, and the cream of contemporary German philosophy.

Benjamin returned on August 12 to the Villa Verde in San Remo, where Stefan was vacationing. His son's physical and mental health seemed improved, though it was not clear whether he was ready to take the upcoming school examinations. Benjamin and Dora had a series of very difficult discussions with—and about—the young man, which resolved nothing. From the safe haven of San Remo Benjamin was also thinking about his own near-term future. He knew that he would be anchored to Paris for large parts of the coming year as he worked through the extensive material on Baudelaire held at the Bibliothèque Nationale. The very thought of a lengthy sojourn in one place had the usual effect: he began looking for opportunities to get away. Scholem, with whom he was now back on very friendly terms, again urged him to consider spending part of the winter in Jerusalem. Scholem's invitation was accompanied by a detailed evaluation of the report of the Peel Commission, which had been released on July 8 and recommended the partition of Palestine and the creation of a Jewish state. As Scholem reported, there could hardly be a more interesting time for a visit, and Benjamin responded positively, saying that only an as yet unannounced visit to Paris from one of the institute's directors could deter him.

Without access to a library in San Remo, and thus unable to make a real start on the study of Baudelaire, Benjamin turned to the work of his colleagues. He responded with real enthusiasm to Adorno's essay on Alban Berg: "You have clarified my suspicion that the overwhelming impression which *Wozzeck* made on me that evening in Berlin revealed an inner involvement that I was hardly conscious of, even though it can be specified down to the last detail" (BA, 205). In an unpublished letter of 1925 to Berg, Adorno had conveyed his reaction and that of Benjamin, who had accompanied him, to a performance of the opera on December 22, 1925. Focusing on the pivotal scene at the inn and its "exploitation of out of tune singing as a constructive motif," an effect he found "metaphysically profound," Adorno characterized the scene in terminology derived directly from Benjamin's essay on Goethe's *Elective Affinities:* "It is a caesura in Hölderlin's sense, and one which thereby allows the 'expressionless' to break into the music itself" (BA, 120n). Benjamin's reaction to Horkheimer's wide-ranging programmatic essay "Traditional and Critical Theory," which had recently appeared in the *Zeitschrift,* was more muted, though he expressed his unconditional solidarity with its main points.

Benjamin returned to Paris in early September, eager to begin serious work on the Baudelaire essay. His resumed residence in Paris started with a round of probing conversations with Horkheimer. Their meetings went a long way toward solidifying their friendly relations: Horkheimer could look back on his trip to Paris and affirm that "a few hours with Benjamin are among the loveliest things. Of all our friends, he stands closest to us, and by a good way. I will do everything in my power to help him out of his financial misery."[39] Horkheimer agreed, in the course of his visit, to enable Benjamin to finance an apartment of his own, and he set aside a research fund to aid in the acquisition of research material for the arcades project and the study of Baudelaire. Thus fortified, Benjamin plunged immediately into a particularly intense version of his old routine, with daily research at the Bibliothèque Nationale and the rapid expansion of Convolute J of the arcades manuscript, the convolute dedicated to Baudelaire. We know relatively little about Benjamin's life "beyond Baudelaire" in the months to come, so all-consuming was the work.

The good news he had from Horkheimer came amid frustrating practical developments: on his arrival in Paris at the beginning of September, Benjamin found himself closed out of the apartment in which he had sublet a room for the past two years (GB, 5:575–576). Ursel Bud had sent a letter full of equivocations and evasions to him in San Remo at the end of August. It claimed that an uncle needed the room for a "halfway-official" matter, and that the receipt of her own working papers hung in the balance. The letter closed with an offer to make good the expenses that Benjamin would incur during the time he was barred from the room. In the course of several humiliating conversations, which finally included the offer of 600 francs (never actually paid), Benjamin learned that he had been displaced by a "more acceptable tenant, who . . . , being in receipt of an expulsion order himself, . . . was particularly anxious to find unofficial accommodation." Benjamin concluded that the convenient apartment in the Rue Bénard was now a closed chapter in his life. "This could hardly have come at a worse time than now," he tells Adorno, "when the cost of hotels here in Paris, and even the cost of far less salubrious quarters, has risen by fifty per cent or more on account of the world exhibition" (BA, 215). After a short stay in the Hôtel du Panthéon in the Sixth Arrondissement, he moved into the Villa Niccoló, a hotel at 3 Rue Niccoló in the Sixteenth, where he stayed until late September. While he was there, he received a report from Adorno on his marriage to Gretel Karplus, which had taken place on September 8 in Oxford, with Horkheimer and the economist Redvers Opie as witnesses. This news clearly took Benjamin by surprise, and it was some time before he composed a suitable response—which silence the Adornos both interpreted as reproach. Adorno tried to soften the blow by letting Benjamin know that only the witnesses, along with Horkheimer's wife, Maidon, Adorno's parents, and Gretel's mother, were in attendance. He claimed that "no one else knew anything about it, and we could not let you know the details without producing more personal difficulties than the occasion warranted. . . . I implore you to regard the matter as it really is and without taking offense: for that would be doing us an injustice." Adorno's apology concludes on an odd and oddly ambiguous note: "We both belong to you, and we have left Max in no doubt about the fact either; and indeed, I feel that I can now include him in the sentiment as well" (BA, 208). The conclusion suggests that Adorno believed he himself was the object of a struggle for affection between Benjamin and Horkheimer, and that Benjamin's exclusion from the wedding stemmed from this difficulty. Although Benjamin's eventual reply to this letter is lost, it is more likely that any feeling of hurt on his part would have had to do with Gretel rather than Horkheimer. Benjamin's erotic entanglements were complicated, but not, as far as we can tell, by homoerotic intentions. The same cannot be said for Adorno.

Just when Benjamin was feeling that he could no longer afford even the cheapest hotels, he was saved by an offer from Adorno's wealthy friend Else Herzberger to take up residence, rent-free, in the maid's room of her apartment at 1 Rue de Château in Boulogne sur Seine, while mistress and maid were in America (a period of some three months). By September 25 he was installed in the tiny room, where, "if I really look my gift horse in the mouth . . . , I can see myself sitting . . . , wide awake since six o'clock in the morning, listening away to the oceanic rather than intelligible rhythms of the Paris traffic, which rumbles in through the narrow asphalt aperture in front of my bed . . . , for the bed stands right there where the window is. If I lift the shutters, the street itself is witness to my literary labors, and if I close them, I am immediately exposed to the monstrous climatic extremes which the (uncontrollable) central heating creates" (BA, 222). To escape these conditions, he fled every morning to the Bibliothèque Nationale to pursue his research on Baudelaire.

Even a rent-free lodging could not wholly insulate Benjamin from the massive price increases and the devaluation of the French franc (which had occurred earlier in the summer); his financial position had become much weaker than it was at the start of the year. Furthermore, the "dubious semi-demi-socialism of the Blum government" (BA, 222)—a reference to Léon Blum's presidency of the Popular Front government from 1936 to 1937—had led to persistent stagnation in the building industry and thus to housing shortages. But Horkheimer was true to his word. On November 13 Benjamin heard from Friedrich Pollock that, starting immediately, the institute would pay him an increased stipend of US$80 per month—considerably less than the amount paid to regular contributors in New York, but still proof against the rapid swings in the franc. Pollock also informed him that he could expect a special payment of 1,500 francs to help with his search for lodgings. To Adorno, who for months had been pressuring Horkheimer to revise the institute's financial arrangements with its most important Parisian contributor, Benjamin sent his "heartfelt thanks," along with the comment that the new stipend represented "approximately three-quarters of what you originally had in mind for me" (BA, 222).

There were visits in October from friends—Fritz Lieb, Marcel Brion, and Brecht and his wife, Helene Weigel, the latter two in town to oversee a new French production of *The Threepenny Opera* and to rehearse a new one-act play by Brecht, *Gewehre der Frau Carrar* (Señora Carrar's Rifles), in which Helene Weigel had the lead. Accompanying Brecht to the theater to see such plays as Jean Cocteau's *Chevaliers de la table ronde* (The Knights of the Round Table)—"a sinister mystification, attesting to the rapid decline of his abilities" (GB, 5:606)—and Jean Anouilh's *Voyageur sans bagage* (Traveler without Luggage), he was struck by Brecht's manifest distance from the avant-garde and by the increasing importance of realism in his work. Benjamin saw in these visits to the theater, rather myopically perhaps, evidence for its general decline, and thus proof for his prognosis in the artwork essay. Aside from these reunions, there was his fairly regular intercourse with the prickly Kracauer, which had been interrupted of late (their most recent encounter being a rendezvous in the presence of Horkheimer in September), and he was staying in touch with Paris friends such as Adrienne Monnier, the photographer Germaine Krull, and Anna Seghers. "Everything relegates me, even more than is usually the case," he wrote in October, "to the limited circle of some few friends and the narrower or broader circle of my own work" (C, 547).

Although the preparatory studies for the Baudelaire essay remained his main concern, Benjamin was once again active on several publishing fronts simultaneously. He continued to review books for the *Zeitschrift*. Having produced a review of an anthology of Charles Fourier's writings over the summer, at a time when he was also translating "The Storyteller" into French, he was now working on a review of

La photographie en France au dix-neuvième siècle (Photography in France in the Nineteenth Century), a study written by his friend Gisèle Freund, as well as on a review of *Die Macht des Charlatans* (The Power of the Charlatan), by the Austrian journalist Grete de Francesco. All three reviews had a more or less immediate bearing on the arcades project. Fourier is the subject of an individual folder in *The Arcades Project*, Convolute W, which assembles a fascinating array of material on the imagination, the pedagogy, and the social-industrial context of early socialism, while Freund's study (in published and manuscript versions) is cited in several different contexts having to do with the industrial application of photography and with the relation of photography to developments in nineteenth-century genre painting and cultural bohemianism. He even found a place in the arcades complex for a quote from de Francesco's book on the charlatan, about which he had some reservations despite his personal sympathy with the author (BA, 206). The figure of the charlatan is associated with the phantasmagorias of industry in early nineteenth-century France, and specifically with the tactics of commercial advertising being developed in Fourier's time; Fourier himself may be said to have engaged sometimes in a deliberate charlatanism. The cross-fertilization of the review work and the arcades research is in keeping with one of the distinctly nonclassical methodological principles enunciated at the beginning of Convolute N: "how everything one is thinking at a specific moment in time must at all costs be incorporated into the project then at hand" (AP, N1,3).

In September Horkheimer had introduced Benjamin to Emil Oprecht, the Swiss publisher responsible for issuing not only the *Zeitschrift für Sozialforschung* but also the journal *Maß und Wert,* with whose editors Benjamin was already in contact. Together with Oprecht, Benjamin began to plan out an informational article on the Institute of Social Research for this new journal. After communications with the journal's editor, Ferdinand Lion, who explicitly warned against any hint of "Communism," he managed to get started on "Ein deutsches Institut freier Forschung" (A German Institute for Independent Research) in December; the article appeared the following year. At the beginning of November he sent off to Horkheimer the first of a series of long letters surveying contemporary French literature. This first "letter on literature," not intended for publication, focused on Cocteau's new play *Chevaliers de la table ronde* (which he savages) and books by Henri Calet and Denis de Rougemont; it included a glance at Karl Jaspers's book on Nietzsche, which occasioned Benjamin's remark that "for the most part, philosophical criticism, once it has left behind the framework of the historical treatise, . . . can best fulfill its task today by adopting a polemical form" (GB, 5:600). Alongside these projects, his research on Baudelaire at the Bibliothèque Nationale was proceeding apace, and by mid-November he could report to Adorno that he had "been able to look through more or less all the Baudelaire literature I need" (BA, 227). Soon after this, while engaged with the political writings of the nineteenth-century French revolutionary Louis-Auguste Blanqui, he undertook to have a second batch of arcades materials photocopied and sent off to Horkheimer in New York.

On November 15 Benjamin took what was for him a momentous step. After almost five years of exile, he signed a rental agreement for an apartment of his own at 10 Rue Dombasle in the Fifteenth Arrondissement. Although, as it turned out, he could not move in until January 15, he declared himself pleased with the arrangement. The apartment as a whole was cramped, but it was organized around a rather spacious central room, and it had a large terrace upon which Benjamin could entertain visitors in summer. This would be his last place of residence in Paris before his flight in 1940. In the meantime, Else Herzberger was returning from America toward the end of December, and he had to think of where he would live after vacating her *chambre de bonne* and before moving into his new digs. As had been so often the case, the ever-loyal Dora could still offer refuge, and he made plans to visit San Remo at the end of the year.

Before this short break from Paris, where the political situation was growing steadily darker, he attended a lecture on Hegel by the Russian-born philosopher Alexandre Kojève (born Kojevnikoff) at the "Collège de Sociologie."[40] This group of intellectuals, led by Georges Bataille and Roger Caillois, had been founded in March 1937 in the Café Grand Véfour in Palais Royal; its birth was announced in July 1937 in Bataille's journal *Acéphale*. The "college" was a lecture series held every other Saturday night in the back room of the bookstore Galeries du Livre, and Benjamin was a frequent if silent auditor. The group was oriented toward a "sacred sociology" that sought to interrogate the presence of the sacred in the contemporary world, and to extract from that analysis the elements of a new communal structure. Benjamin was clearly drawn to a group (or, as was his habit, to the fringes of a group) that focused on manifestations of the sacred in an apparently secularized world, on new forms of human community, and on the relations between aesthetics and politics. As he became increasingly familiar with the group, he began to discern more nuanced differences between the positions of the three leading voices—Bataille, Caillois, and Michel Leiris—and to take a more active, though never direct, stand against certain positions espoused by each writer. To Horkheimer in November 1937 he described Kojève's delivery as clear and impressive—the philosopher's influence, Benjamin recognized, was already being felt in Paris, not least among the Surrealists—but he found much to criticize in Kojève's "idealist" conception of dialectics (GB, 5:621).

At the beginning of December Benjamin received news that the Adornos would be leaving soon for America, where Adorno had accepted the job of music director of a research project on radio—a project funded by Princeton University—and where he would be working in close collaboration with Horkheimer at the New York office of the Institute of Social Research. Adorno promised that his advocacy of Benjamin's interests within the institute would continue unabated and that he would do whatever he could to bring Benjamin to America, too—"as quickly as possible," since "war will be unavoidable in the relatively near future" (BA, 228). The news of the Adornos' imminent departure came as a blow to Benjamin. His only consolation was that he would be able to see his friends soon, for they would be spending the Christmas holiday in San Remo. And so, in the midst of a strike by public works employees in Paris, he journeyed down to Italy at the end of December, where Stefan, who had decided not to return to Vienna, was now working at Dora's pension. There he saw Theodor and Gretel Adorno for the last time.

[CHAPTER TEN]

Baudelaire and the Streets of Paris

Paris, San Remo, and Skovsbostrand, 1938–1939

THE first days of January 1938 found Benjamin in San Remo, enjoying the company of his friends Theodor and Gretel Adorno. The days were filled with intensive discussion of their work and its guiding principles. Adorno read to Benjamin from the draft of his book *Versuch über Wagner* (In Search of Wagner), several chapters of which would appear under the title "Fragmente über Wagner" in the *Zeitschrift* in 1939. All three friends noted the importance for the Wagner project of one conversation that took place on a café terrace in the little town of Ospedaletti, a few kilometers to the west of San Remo along the Ligurian riviera. Despite his general lack of familiarity with music theory, Benjamin was impressed by Adorno's ability to make Wagner's music "socially transparent." The talk inevitably turned to questions of biography and criticism. Both friends had deplored what they saw as Kracauer's naive interpretation of specific features of Offenbach's life as somehow indicative of larger social tendencies. Benjamin praised Adorno's physiognomic portrait of Wagner because it was embedded in the composer's social sphere without psychological mediation.

Of particular importance to Benjamin were the discussions of the now far advanced Baudelaire project. By the turn of the year, Benjamin was convinced that his study of Baudelaire, if it was to take full advantage of his research on the arcades, would have to be a book and not an article. Benjamin had been engaged with Baudelaire for more than twenty years when he began to organize his new study. He had read *Les fleurs du mal* during World War I and written his first texts on the poet (the unpublished fragments titled "Baudelaire II & III") in 1921 and 1922; his volume of Baudelaire translations, with "The Task of the Translator" as its preface, appeared in 1923. Benjamin was well

32. Charles Baudelaire, 1855. Photo by Nadar *(Musée d'Orsay, Paris)*

aware of the difficulty of embarking on an extended analysis of Baudelaire in 1938. The studies that preceded his had highlighted the early
Baudelaire—the ties to Romanticism, the Swedenborgian mysticism
of the "correspondences," the flight into reverie and the ideal. As early
as 1902 Gide observed that no writer of the nineteenth century had
been discussed with more stupidity than Baudelaire. Perusing his
mass of material in 1938, Benjamin remarked similarly that most of
the commentary on the poet was conducted "as though the *Fleurs du
mal* had never been written." But if Benjamin was to reinvent Baudelaire, presenting him for the first time as the quintessential modern—
alienated, spatially displaced, saturnine—he knew he would need to
break through the "limits of bourgeois thought" and certain "bourgeois reactions." And he was certainly not blind to the ways his own

thinking was shaped by his haut-bourgeois class formation (GB, 6:10–11).

The conversations with the Adornos about the Baudelaire project ranged widely across questions of focus, emphasis, and critical methodology. Benjamin undoubtedly also discussed with them a discovery that was to have a major impact on the project. While still working in the Bibliothèque Nationale in Paris in late fall 1937, he had come across Louis-Auguste Blanqui's cosmological speculation *L'éternité par les astres* (Eternity via the Stars). The great French revolutionary Blanqui (1805–1881) had the distinction of playing a role in all three of the major uprisings in nineteenth-century Paris: the July Revolution of 1830, the Revolution of 1848, and the Paris Commune in 1870. He was arrested and imprisoned after each of the revolts. *L'éternité par les astres* was composed during his final incarceration in the Fort du Taureau at the time of the Paris Commune. Benjamin later admitted to Horkheimer that the text could seem banal and tasteless on a first reading, but after becoming more familiar with the book he recognized in it not only Blanqui's "unconditional submission" to the social order that had defeated him but at the same time "the most terrible accusation against a society that has reflected this image of the cosmos as a projection of itself onto the heavens" (C, 549). Benjamin discerned correspondences between Blanqui's view of life here, at once mechanistic and infernal, and the role played by astral metaphors in Nietzsche and Baudelaire—correspondences that he hoped to work through in the never-completed third section of his book on Baudelaire.

Upon his return to Paris on January 20, he moved into the small apartment on the Rue Dombasle that he would call home for the remainder of his time in the city. As early as February 7 he could report to Horkheimer that his rooms were set up satisfactorily, and he evinced genuine enthusiasm for his terrace, with its view over the housetops. Anticipating the arrival of those books that had been temporarily quartered with Brecht in Denmark, Benjamin confessed how much he had been missing them: "Only now have I noticed how deeply the need for them has lain buried in me" (GB, 6:38). Toward the end of March his shelves were enriched by an unexpected coup: a friend had saved "some ten or twenty" of the books left behind in his Berlin

apartment and sent them along to him in Paris. The young art collector and author Ernst Morgenroth, who wrote under the name Stephan
Lackner during the exile years, remembers the place of honor that
Paul Klee's watercolor *Angelus Novus* was accorded in the apartment's living room. Despite oft-repeated complaints regarding the
noise from the elevator shaft next to his apartment, Benjamin found—to
the benefit of his budget—that he was loath to leave home for his first
months in the new digs, so glad was he to rediscover the security of a
place of his own.

As he gradually ventured out from the Rue Dombasle, he began to
reintegrate himself into the life of the city. Art was one of the first
things to draw him out. Early in February he visited an exhibit of
Klee's recent work at Kahnweiler's Galerie Simon, commenting that
he continued to prefer Klee's aquarelles to his work in oil. A large exhibit of the work of the Surrealists at the Galerie des Beaux-Arts in
the Rue du Faubourg-Saint-Honoré had a more direct impact on his
work:

> The floor of the main room was covered with wood shavings from
> which ferns rose up here and there. Sacks of coal hung from the ceil-
> ing. Lighting was entirely artificial. One found oneself in a *chapelle
> ardent* of painting; and the pictures on view were something like
> the medals of honor on the breasts of the dear departed. . . . The en-
> trance to the establishment was formed of a gallery of papier-maché
> mannequins. The erogenous (and other) zones of the puppets were
> equipped with a coating of tin foil, light bulbs, balls of thread, and
> other magical utensils. The whole thing was as near to dream as a
> costume shop is to Shakespeare. (GB, 6:41)

Lackner remembers Benjamin's appearance at this epoch of his life:
"He had nothing of the bohemian about him. In those days, he had a
little belly that protruded slightly. He usually wore an old, halfway
sporty tweed jacket with a bourgeois cut, a dark or colored shirt, and
gray flannel trousers. I don't believe I ever saw him without a tie. . . .
Sometimes he had an owlish, profound expression behind his round
spectacles, and it took time to decide if he was mocking what he had
just said aloud."[1] That mocking humor was often to be felt in his personal relations. Encountering the philosopher Jean Wahl on the street

one day, he learned that Wahl had just come from a visit to his first mentor, the aging Henri Bergson. Bergson had expressed his anxiety at the prospect of a Chinese invasion of Paris (and this was while the Japanese were still winning) and blamed all of society's problems on the railroads. As he listened, Benjamin thought: "And what will one be able to get out of the eighty-year-old Jean Wahl?" (BG, 219).

Benjamin's days in Paris during the winter of 1938–1939 were enlivened by frequent visits with French and German émigré friends. He saw Kracauer off and on; the intellectual exchanges of the 1920s that lent decisive impetus to the work of both men had given way to rather awkward relations. They spoke about a book on film that Kracauer was writing on commission—but never finished. And there were frequent meetings with Hannah Arendt and her husband-to-be, Heinrich Blücher. Benjamin had come to know Arendt and her first husband, Günther Stern, while they all lived in Berlin; Stern and Benjamin were distant cousins. Arendt (1906–1975) had been raised in an assimilated middle-class family in Königsberg in East Prussia. She studied with many of the most important intellectuals in Weimar Germany: philosophy with Martin Heidegger, Karl Jaspers, and Edmund Husserl, and theology with Rudolf Bultmann and Paul Tillich. She earned her doctorate with a dissertation directed by Jaspers on Augustine's concept of love. Although no one knew it at the time, Arendt had been Martin Heidegger's lover during the middle years of the 1920s; she had met and married Stern in Berlin only in 1929. She fled Berlin, first to Czechoslovakia and Switzerland and then to Paris, after a police interrogation in spring 1933. During the years of exile in Paris, Benjamin and Arendt had gradually grown closer. Beginning in 1936, a small circle of German émigrés had formed around the two of them. Meeting for regular discussion evenings in Benjamin's living quarters, the group included Fritz Fränkel, painter Karl Heidenreich, lawyer Erich Cohn-Bendit, Heinrich Blücher, and Chanan Klenbort, a colleague of Arendt's at a Jewish aid organization.[2] As a young worker, Blücher had taken part in the Spartacist uprisings in Berlin; he later became a Communist activist. Although he had little formal education, he was a devoted autodidact. Benjamin undoubtedly met Blücher in Berlin, either through his brother, Georg, or at the time when Blücher served as an assistant at Fritz Fränkel's neurological clinic. By 1938, Arendt had become one of Benjamin's principal dialogue partners on issues in philosophy and politics. Both Arendt and Benjamin existed on the fringes of academic philosophy in Paris, attending the occasional lecture and striking up the occasional friendship such as those with Alexandre Kojève, Alexandre Koyré, and Jean Wahl; Arendt, with her sympathy for Hegelian and Heideggerian philosophy, was no doubt closer to this loose network than was Benjamin.

On February 11 he welcomed Scholem to Paris—not without mixed feelings. Scholem was on his way to the United States, where he would combine a lecture tour with the opportunity to study collections of cabalist manuscripts. During Scholem's days in Paris, several conversations turned on the issue of Martin Buber and the translation of the Hebrew Bible he had undertaken with Franz Rosenzweig in the midtwenties (it was published between 1925 and 1937). In a letter to the theologian Karl Thieme, who had objected to the translation of many key phrases, Benjamin expressed his own doubts about the project— not so much the appropriateness of the undertaking itself as the *time* at which it was undertaken. For Benjamin, the "temporal index" forced the translators into a number of German turns of phrase that were symptomatic of the age. Scholem's account of his 1938 meetings with Benjamin in Paris—it was the last time they saw each other—stresses the emotionally charged atmosphere in which their discussions took place.[3] "I had not seen Benjamin in eleven years. His appearance had changed somewhat. He had grown stockier, his bearing was more careless, and his mustache had become much bushier. His hair was streaked heavily with gray. We carried on intensive discussions about his work and his basic outlook. . . . The focus of our discussions, however, was of course Benjamin's Marxist orientation." The portraits in miniature offered by Scholem and Stephan Lackner reveal the long-term effects of exile on Benjamin: although only forty-five years old, he was already becoming an old man.

In response to Scholem's criticisms of the artwork essay—he found the philosophy of film forced and attacked the use made of the concept of aura, "which he had employed in an entirely different sense for many years"—Benjamin asserted that his Marxism was not dogmatic but heuristic and experimental in nature, and that, far from an abandonment of his earlier concerns, it represented a relevant and fruitful transposition of the metaphysical and theological perspectives he had developed in the first years of their friendship. The merger of his theory of language with a Marxist view of the world was a task for which he had the highest hopes. Scholem pressed him on his relationship to "his fellow Marxists." Benjamin defended Brecht's achievement of "a totally unmagical language, a language cleansed of all magic," and compared this achievement to that of one of Scholem's and his favorite authors, Paul Scheerbart. He also spoke to Scholem about Brecht's numerous obscene poems, some of which he reckoned among his very best. And on the subject of the Institute of Social Research (whose inner circle Scholem would soon be meeting), Benjamin emphasized his "profound sympathy" with its general orientation but admitted to reservations, his tone sometimes expressing a "bitterness that was definitely not in keeping with the conciliatory vein of his letters to Horkheimer." Regarding the institute's attitude toward the Communist Party, Benjamin "expressed himself very tortuously and would not commit himself in any way," in marked contrast to the impassioned denunciation of the Moscow trials voiced by some of his friends. On one occasion they discussed Kafka and, on another, Louis-Ferdinand Céline. Apropos of the latter's newest book, *Bagatelles pour un massacre*, Benjamin commented that his own experience had convinced him that latent anti-Semitism was widespread even among the leftist intelligentsia in France, and that only very few non-Jews there—he named Adrienne Monnier and Fritz Lieb—were constitutionally free of it. But Scholem noticed that his friend's great liking for France was unchanged, and that further, in contrast to this, there was in Benjamin "an unmistakable coolness and even antipathy to England and America."

After more than four years of living in Paris, Benjamin had expanded his network of personal contacts in a way that embroiled him—even if at the margins—in French literary politics. The émigré photographer Germaine Krull—whom Benjamin met in 1927—had been a resident of Paris longer than he had, and had lived at various times with French intellectuals, but she nonetheless turned to him for help when she sought a publisher for a story, urging him to use his contacts to help place it. And this was not his only attempt to get a friend published; he spoke to people in Paris and wrote to friends abroad about his acquaintance (and patron) Stephan Lackner's novel *Jan Heimatlos*. It was finally this deep engagement with French literary politics that cemented Benjamin's relationship with the Institute of Social Research and with Horkheimer. Benjamin's published contributions accounted for only a part of the services for which he received a monthly stipend. Lengthy letters to Horkheimer—Benjamin's "letters from Paris"—offered a veritable running commentary on the major trends of French thought, covering the entire political spectrum. In March he engaged in an extended exchange with Horkheimer regarding Céline's *Bagatelles pour un massacre*, which he had just discussed with Scholem. Céline's diatribe, which intertwines virulent anti-Semitism with a seemingly incommensurable pacifism, led Benjamin back to ideas he had begun to formulate in San Remo in the summer of 1937, ideas about a distinctively modern "clinical nihilism." In a letter to Horkheimer he constructed a typically surprising causal nexus between Expressionism, Jung, Céline, and the German novelist and physician Alfred Döblin: "I wonder if there isn't a form of nihilism peculiar to physicians that makes its own desolate verse out of the experiences that the doctor has in his anatomy halls and operating rooms, in front of opened stomachs and skulls. Philosophy has left this nihilism alone with these experiences for more than a hundred and fifty years (as early as the Enlightenment, La Mettrie [author of *L'homme-machine*] stood by it)." Benjamin found the "symptomatic value" of Céline's anti-Semitic invective difficult to overestimate; he pointed to a review in the *Nouvelle Revue Française* that, while gesturing toward the book's confusion and lies, nonetheless concluded by calling it "solid" and praising its "far-reaching vision" (GB, 6:24, 40–41). As a result of the decrees against anti-Semitism published by the French government in April 1939, Céline's book was pulled from the shelves by its publisher. In June Benjamin commented acerbically on an article on Wagner by Claudel published in *Le Figaro*, finding it a "fine demonstration of the magnificent vision and unparalleled ability of this horrible man" (BA, 260).

Always attuned to the role played by journals in the construction of intellectual opinion, Benjamin kept Horkheimer apprised of new players and of significant changes in prominent venues. He made sure, for example, that Horkheimer subscribed to *Mesures*, a journal with subterranean ties to the *Nouvelle Revue Française*. *Mesures* was managed by the American émigré Henry Church, but its content was solicited and edited in secret by Jean Paulhan, the editor of the *Nouvelle Revue Française*. The new journal took on edgier work and had a different, though obviously somewhat overlapping, readership: it appealed to the post-Surrealists in the Collège de Sociologie, to the nascent existential movement, and to those interested in the resurgence of mystical thought.[4] Benjamin was also sure to make frequent reference to the *Cahiers du Sud*, the journal with which he himself had the best relationship; he strongly recommended an article by Jean Paulhan on the rebirth of rhetoric that had appeared there. Benjamin was thus not merely a contributor to the institute's publications but a well-placed reporter for a group of intellectuals who would otherwise have been largely cut off from the European intellectual currents that were its lifeblood.

He was aware that the dangers involved in direct engagement with French institutions were, if anything, greater than those he had encountered in Germany fifteen years previously, when he had begun to establish himself as a freelance critic. To Horkheimer he promised to approach the "annihilating institutions [*Instanzen*] of the age aggressively, whenever possible, in my work; defensively, as far as possible, in the way I live my life" (GB, 6:30). His relationships with leading French intellectuals such as Jean Paulhan, and with younger acquaintances such as Raymond Aron and Pierre Klossowski, were governed by this maxim, as was his often silent attendance at literary and political discussions. Only in his writings—as when he published a review of a talk on the Spanish Civil War by the Catholic nationalist Gaston Fessard in the *Zeitschrift*—did he allow himself a measure of critical distance.

The extent to which Benjamin followed his own maxim in his dealings with the Institute of Social Research remains a matter of sharp debate. In the late 1930s, as Benjamin solidified his relationship to the institute, he was careful to portray himself in what he imagined was the light expected of him: as a leftist thinker who was neither too doctrinaire nor too radical, and as an enlightened critic of a world gone wrong. Scholem's reports on his visit to New York, where he met Horkheimer and the Adornos for the first time, indicate that this consciously constricted self-presentation was neither effective nor, in the end, necessary. One of Scholem's first encounters was with Paul and Hannah Tillich, who were living in New York now that Tillich had begun teaching at Union Theological Seminary.

> Our conversation turned to you. The T.'s were profuse in their praise of you (as was I, most conscientiously), and the result was that a somewhat different picture of Horkheimer's relation to you emerged than the one you had postulated in your various esoterically couched warnings. I put on a bit of an act in order to get T. to talk. He said that H. holds you in the *highest* regard, *but that he is entirely clear that, where you're concerned,* one is dealing with a *mystic*—now this is precisely what you had not intended to suggest to him, if I understood you correctly. It was not I, but Tillich, who used the expression. In a word, he said something like this: People are neither so simple-minded that they can't make you out, nor so obtuse that they are put off by it. They are going to make every possible effort on your behalf and were also thinking of bringing you over here. So it now seems to me, judging from the way T. portrays the Institute's relationship to you, that your diplomacy may well be barging through open doors. . . . They seem to have long been aware of much of what you consider secret and don't wish to have brought up, and *nonetheless* are still placing their hopes on you. (BS, 214–215)

Benjamin's reaction to the report that Scholem was obviously sure would shock him is revealing:

> Your portrayal of the conversation with the two Tillichs aroused my profound interest, but caused me much less surprise than you thought it would. The point here is precisely that things whose place is at present in shadow *de part et d'autre* might be cast in a false light when subjected to artificial lighting. I say 'at present' because the current epoch, which makes so many things impossible, most certainly does not preclude this: that the right light should fall on precisely those things in the course of the historical rotation of the sun. I want to take this even further and say that our works can, for their part, be measuring instruments, which, if they function well, measure the tiniest segments of that unimaginably slow rotation. (BS, 216–217)

Benjamin here attempts to explain his innate caution as a function of the historical index: that self-revelation must have its time, and that premature exposure, even to initiates, might be devastating. In this instance, the veil behind which Benjamin thought and acted seems to have been unnecessary but not harmful; in many other cases, his guardedness and even hiddenness did not serve him well at a time when an occasional view behind the veil might have won him friends and supporters.

When Scholem—never a man for half measures—finally met Horkheimer, he took an instant dislike to him, asserting that Horkheimer was "not a pleasant fellow" and indeed that "I wouldn't be surprised in the least if he turned out to be a scoundrel someday." Colored by his judgment of the man, Scholem's impression was that Horkheimer's admiration for Benjamin was at best brittle. "Wiesengrund maintains that Horkheimer is an incessant admirer of your genius. That did become obvious to me after reading some of his writings, but the personal impression I have of the man reinforces my opinion that, perhaps precisely *because* he feels he has to admire you, such a man can of necessity have only an inscrutable relationship to you, vilely burdened by a sense of embitterment" (C, 235–236). It has to be said that Scholem's reading of the Horkheimer-Benjamin relationship seems largely accurate—indeed, highly perspicacious. Horkheimer's increasingly generous support of Benjamin was accompanied by a consistently reserved attitude toward his work and by an apparent reluctance to bring Benjamin to New York.

Scholem, of course, communicated none of his reservations regarding Horkheimer to the other members of the institute, and least of all to Adorno, with whom he immediately established an open and cordial relationship. Scholem was able to confirm Benjamin's impression that Adorno was doing everything in his power to bring Horkheimer to allow Benjamin a decent living, and that his efforts were supported by the high regard in which Benjamin was held by Leo Löwenthal and Herbert Marcuse. Ultimately, of course, the Adornos—and especially Gretel—hoped that a way could be found to bring Benjamin to join them in America. Gretel described their new home repeatedly and in terms carefully tailored to appeal to Benjamin:

I not only like it better here than in London, but am also quite convinced that you would feel exactly the same. What amazes me most
is the fact that things here are by no means all as new and advanced
as one would really think; on the contrary: one can observe the contrast between the most modern and the most shabby things wherever one goes. There is no need to search for the surreal here, for one
stumbles over it at every step. The skyscrapers are imposing in the
early evening, but later, when the offices have closed and the lights
are sparser, they remind one of insufficiently illuminated European
mews. And just think, there are stars here and a horizontal moon
and splendid sunsets like those in the height of summer. (BG, 211)

The indirect references to Benjamin's essay on Surrealism, with its
linkage of the most advanced and the most outmoded, and to the work
on the arcades, with its exploration of modern modes of architectural
illumination, must have been provocative: Benjamin soon had a map
of New York on his wall so that he could follow the movements of his
friends. Yet Gretel, who knew Benjamin better than anyone else did
(excepting perhaps his former wife), was aware how difficult it would
be, despite all her efforts, to separate him from the European culture
in which he felt at home: "But I fear you are so fond of your arcades
that you cannot part with their splendid architecture, and once you
have closed that door, it is possible that a new subject could interest
you again" (BG, 211).

Benjamin's reading in the early months of the year turned to the
Spanish Civil War. He expressed skepticism regarding the political
instructiveness of his acquaintance Malraux's new novel, *L'espoir*
(published in English as *Man's Hope*), which recounts the feverish debates among the revolutionary factions during the war. He was won
over, however, by Georges Bernanos's attack on Franco, *Les grands
cimetières sous la lune* (translated as *A Diary of My Times*), despite
its insistent Catholicism. His most detailed commentary was reserved for *Spanish Testament* by his neighbor Arthur Koestler. After
working for Willi Münzenberg as an active participant in the effort to
ensure the presence of a Soviet point of view in French intellectual
life, Koestler had made three trips to Spain during the Civil War.
Claiming to be a correspondent for the British daily *News Chronicle*,

he ventured into Falangist territory, where he was recognized by a former journalist colleague from Berlin and denounced as a Communist. He was arrested and summarily sentenced to death. Koestler was reprieved from death row only through a prisoner exchange: he was bartered for the wife of one of Franco's fighter pilots. *Spanish Testament* has two parts: a first book comprising nine reports on the war from a tendentiously ideological point of view, and a second book, "Dialogue with Death," that recounts Koestler's experiences in prison awaiting death. Benjamin was equally fascinated by both parts.

Also on the bookshelf was *Un régulier dans le siècle* (A Soldier in This Century), a second installment of the French nationalist Julien Benda's autobiography; Benda's book (as well as his general theme, the "treason of the intellectuals") provoked a series of reflections on the situation of the nontreasonous intellectual. And his reading of the sociologist Norbert Elias's *Über den Prozess der Zivilisation* (translated as *The Civilizing Process*) prompted a respectful letter to the author. Since one of the areas that Benjamin covered for the *Zeitschrift*—and for the few other journals in which he could still place his work—was European Romanticism, he also kept up with recent publications in German and French. He read Marcel Brion's piece on the early Romantic Wilhelm Heinrich Wackenroder, the author of the seminal *Herzensergießungen eines kunstliebenden Klosterbruders* (*Outpourings of an Art-Loving Friar*, 1797); Brion's text had appeared in the special issue of the *Cahiers du Sud* devoted to German Romanticism alongside the excerpt from Benjamin's "Goethe's Elective Affinities." And, in a reference to his own dissertation on Romantic art criticism, he commented to Egon Wissing that the recent appearance of August Wilhelm Schlegel's unpublished correspondence allowed insight into Friedrich Schlegel's conversion and into his reactionary philosophy of history.

As Benjamin read the work of his colleagues at the Institute of Social Research, his newfound confidence in his position allowed him to offer more open criticisms. In response to Herbert Marcuse's programmatic "Philosophie und kritische Theorie," which had appeared in the *Zeitschrift* in 1937, Benjamin offered Horkheimer a counterposition to the institute's unalloyed rationalism:

Critical theory cannot fail to recognize how deeply certain powers of intoxication [*Rausch*] are bound to reason and to its struggle for liberation. What I mean is, all the explanations that humans have ever obtained surreptitiously through the use of narcotics can also be obtained *through the human:* some through the individual— through man or through woman; others through groups; and some, which we dare not even dream of yet, perhaps only through the community of the living. Aren't these explanations, by virtue of the human solidarity from which they arise, truly political in the end? At any rate, they have lent power to those freedom fighters who were as unconquerable as "inner peace," but at the same time as ready to rise as fire. I don't believe that critical theory will view these powers as "neutral." It is true that they seem today to be at the disposal of fascism. This illusion arises only because fascism has perverted and violated not only those productive forces of nature with which we are familiar but also those that are more remote from us. (GB, 6:23)

The timing of this private critique of the institute's idea of critical theory was surely not accidental.

In the course of 1938, Benjamin intensified what was perhaps the most important—and least understood—of his late intellectual relationships: that with the members of the Collège de Sociologie (at which he had heard Kojève the previous year), and in particular Georges Bataille, Roger Caillois, and Michel Leiris. Bataille's name for this loosely knit association of intellectuals is misleading: the "college" had no didactic intent, and its "sociology of the sacred" is not a science "but something on the order of a sickness, a strange infection of the social body, the senile sickness of an ascedious, exhausted, atomized society."[5] The three founders sought not merely a critique of the sacred but its mythic reanimation in society; the final goal was the formation of a new sort of elective community. We know from several sources that Benjamin was a regular attendee at the biweekly lectures of the Collège; Hans Mayer, another German émigré involved with the group, recalls meeting Benjamin for the last time at one of the events. And we know that he was scheduled to give a lecture in the 1939–1940 series, before the war put an end to the Collège.[6]

33. Benjamin in 1938. Photo by Gisèle Freund (1912–2000)
(© Gisèle Freund-RMN. Repro-photo: Philippe Migeat. © CNAC/
MNAM/Dist. RMN-Grand Palais/Art Resource, NY)

Against this rather scant background, a lengthy discussion in a letter
to Horkheimer dated May 28, 1938, has assumed a perhaps distorted
importance in subsequent assessments of the Collège. That letter suggests a stance of total rejection—Caillois's "pathological cruelty" is
described as "repulsive" in its unconscious approximation of positions
better left to Joseph Goebbels. Yet several factors indicate that we
should treat this with some skepticism. First, the letter is addressed to
Horkheimer, the correspondent least likely to view the Collège and

its study of the sacred, violence, and intoxication sympathetically; second, there are clear correspondences between important aspects of Benjamin's own work and that of Bataille in particular—not least their mutual adherence to a kind of late Surrealism. Benjamin of course knew Bataille well (it was Bataille to whom he would entrust the notes and materials making up the bulk of the arcades project when he left Paris in 1940). Although his relationship to Caillois is less clear, it is surely significant that articles published by Caillois in the *Nouvelle Revue Française* and *Mesures* are cited extensively in *The Arcades Project* in connection with Balzac, Baudelaire, and Haussmann, and in a variety of contexts having to do with "modern myth." On balance, we can imagine Benjamin's interest in the project of the Collège—the enablement of a new form of community through the rediscovery of the sacred—and also his skepticism. Bataille's insistence that the idea of community remains "negative"—heuristic or even unachievable—must surely have resonated with him, while Caillois's advocacy for an engaged sacred community might well have repelled him. Of the intellectual positions of the three leading figures in the group, Benjamin was probably most sympathetic to that of Michel Leiris, whose book *L'age de l'homme* he would review in the year to come.

World politics was, of course, never far from the minds and conversations of Benjamin and his friends, especially now that the policy of German annexation was gearing up. Meeting with Hitler at Berchtesgaden on February 12, the Austrian chancellor Schuschnigg had reached what seemed to be a compromise that might ensure Austria's sovereignty in the face of German pressure: he had agreed to appoint the Austrian Nazi Arthur Seyss-Inquart as minister of public security, with full control of all Austrian police. Realizing that even this concession had done no good, Schuschnigg called on March 9 for a plebiscite on the issue of Austria's unification with Germany. Before the vote could take place, Hitler presented Schuschnigg with an ultimatum: cede control of the government or face a German invasion. Finding no support from France or Britain, Schuschnigg resigned as chancellor on March 11, and German troops crossed the border into Austria on the morning of March 12. The Germans, with their Austrian sympathizers, acted as rapidly to suppress opposition as they had in 1933. Within days of the Anschluß more than 70,000 "opponents" of the new regime—prominent figures in the Austrian government, Social Democrats, Communists, and of course Jews—had been arrested, with many of them murdered and many more taken to concentration camps. Karl Thieme wrote an impassioned letter to Benjamin, fearing for their friends and relations in Austria. "I finally say to myself that God must have something enormous planned for his people (his people according to the flesh and his people of the German tongue), seeing that he allows them to suffer something so enormous" (quoted in GB, 6:51n). "As for me, to put it bluntly," Benjamin replied, "I hardly know anymore where to get an idea of *sensible* suffering and dying. In the case of Austria, no less than in the case of Spain, the horrible thing seems to me that martyrdom is suffered not in the name of the individual's own cause, but rather in the name of a suggested compromise: whether it is the precious ethnic culture of Austria being compromised by a discredited industry and government-owned business, or revolutionary thought in Spain being compromised by the Machiavellianism of the Russian leadership and the indigenous leadership's worship of Mammon" (C, 553). Benjamin's friends on the left continued to look toward Russia with trepidation and a sense of lost hope. Germaine Krull, commenting on some of the published recantations, said, "It makes me quite sick and I can't understand what they must have done to these people to make them produce such absurdities." It was typical of Benjamin that he refused to commit what he really thought to paper; but with all the pressures on the emigrants, he must occasionally have given vent to his feelings on the Russian events.

The rapidly deteriorating political situation posed a direct threat to the status of the German exile communities. Alfred Cohn and his family had fled Barcelona and were living in Paris "in great misery" (GB, 6:86). And the composer Ernst Krenek had escaped from Austria, headed for America. Seeing no tolerable escape route himself, Benjamin attempted to push forward his naturalization. On March 9 he submitted a formal request for French citizenship, accompanied by testimonials from André Gide, Paul Valéry, and Jules Romains. The next months were punctuated with attempts to fulfill various outstanding requirements of the naturalization process, and virtually each of these constituted a seemingly insurmountable hurdle. He needed a *certificat de domicile* that showed how long he had been resident in Paris, but since his former sublettor Ursel Bud had rented the room to him without consulting the landlord, said landlord refused to sign the necessary certificate. "One unlearns being surprised," as he commented to Stefan (GB, 6:90). As a replacement, he requested a *certificat de travail* from the institute. He even considered making a quick trip to America solely to obtain a *titre de voyage*, which might have accelerated the naturalization process. In the end, he felt himself lucky even to hold refugee papers; by late spring 1938, these were no longer being granted. Benjamin's application for French citizenship floated among various bureaucratic offices and had still not been acted upon two years later, when the German occupation rendered it moot. From this time on, however, Benjamin's letters sounded an increasingly anxious note as he attempted to keep his French residence permit current while shielding as much information as possible from the prying eyes of the German authorities.

Although the spring was mainly given over to his ongoing work on the Baudelaire essay, other projects required attention as well. Benjamin had published nothing substantial since the essay on Fuchs. In early March he was finally able to complete the essay on the institute for *Maß und Wert*. He—and occasionally Adorno—had struggled to compose a piece that was true to the research orientation of the institute while remaining acceptable to the liberal bourgeois orientation of the journal. Horkheimer had counseled him to reply to a stern warning from Ferdinand Lion, the editor, by feigning surprise at the imputation of "communist aspects" to the institute, and by assuring him that it was an "academic matter in the truest sense of the word."[7] The eleven-page manuscript cost Benjamin unforeseeable effort: "The difficulty of the work lay in countering Lion's presumed intention to sabotage it" (GB, 6:37). In the end, he was able to produce a text acceptable to the journal *and* to Horkheimer, if less so to himself.

For all his skepticism and thinly veiled hostility toward Lion, he was nonetheless pleased that the journal published a brief discussion of *Deutsche Menschen* in early 1938. Royalties from the book remained among his most important sources of income, and Benjamin kept a careful eye on the flow of money from the Vita Nova press. He went so far as to ask Thieme whether Roessler might not be reporting all the sales of the book, but was reassured on hearing Thieme's endorsement of the publisher's probity. He was particularly delighted by the report of one reader of his book, his sister-in-law, Hilde Benjamin, who, with her son, Michael, had remained in Berlin in order to stay close to her imprisoned husband, Georg. She had singled out a passage in a letter by the German exile Georg Forster that was included in Benjamin's collection: "I no longer have a homeland, a fatherland, or friends; all those who were close to me have left me to form other attachments. And if I think of the past and still feel myself bound, that is merely my choice and my idea, not something imposed by circumstance. Happy turns of fate can give me much; unhappy ones can take nothing from me, except the satisfaction of writing these letters, should I be unable to afford the postage."[8] Hilde Benjamin was deeply moved by this letter; her husband, whose situation was not unlike Forster's, defiantly refused in his letters to sympathize with the eighteenth-century intellectual, of whom Benjamin remarks that his "revolutionary freedom" is dependent on "abstinence." Georg Benjamin wrote to his wife: "The hopelessness [these passages] breathe is too great; since I don't know the stance he takes vis-à-vis contemporary events, Forster's person remains unclear to me."[9]

At Adorno's suggestion, Benjamin also took time to compose an exposé of the three "listening models" he produced for the general public in the last years of the Weimar Republic—scripts that had fallen into the hands of the Gestapo. Working for various radio stations from 1925 on, Benjamin had written—and frequently been at the microphone for—a series of radio talks and radio plays. Beginning in 1925 (and at the instigation of Ernst Schoen, the artistic director of the Frankfurt broadcast station), he had also planned a series of programs conceived as "listening models": didactic presentations aimed at very specific work and living situations—and at the education of the audience in the art of proper listening. The title and conception of the series were indebted to Brecht, who conceived each of his plays not just as a singular work of art but as a model of a certain kind of intervention into the practices of theater; the Brechtian didactic plays intend to reform not just the audience but other dramatists and indeed the entire theatrical tradition. Benjamin's exposé, like so much else produced in his final years, remained unpublished during his lifetime.

These projects were so many interruptions to his main preoccupation: Charles Baudelaire. In the late spring Benjamin worked through his mass of notes on the arcades, organizing them into a scheme for a book on Paris in the age of Baudelaire. "After I have spent so long piling up books on books, excerpts on excerpts," he wrote in mid-April, "I am now ready to compose a series of reflections which will furnish the foundation for an entirely transparent structure. For dialectical rigor, I should like this piece to be the equal of my work on the Elective Affinities" (BA, 247). He shared with Scholem a definitive metaphorical formulation of his intentions for the Baudelaire book (a formulation he would revise in AP, Convolute J51a,5). "I want to show Baudelaire as he is embedded in the nineteenth century; the appearance thus created must seem new, and exert a scarcely definable attraction, like that of a stone which has rested for decades in the forest floor and whose impression, after we have rolled it from its place with more or less difficulty, lies before us extraordinarily clear and intact." Some of the social and historical sweep that Benjamin intended for his project is indicated by the authorities he consulted regarding details: the economist and lawyer Otto Leichter (recommended to him by Pollock) and the eminent art historian Meyer Shapiro, who had become an intellectual partner for Adorno in New York.

The contemporary relevance that Benjamin attributes to his work on Baudelaire is given memorable expression in the remarks to Scholem that follow this characterization of his method (and which we have quoted above in a different context): "Our works can, for their part, be measuring instruments which, if they function well, measure the tiniest segments of this unimaginably [slow historical rotation of the sun]" (C, 217). The increasingly frequent comparison of his work to a photographic emulsion uniquely suited to the recording of subtle changes in the social-historical landscape is clearly related to this metaphor of the measuring instrument. As a letter to Horkheimer from mid-April shows, Benjamin's intentions regarding his Baudelaire book had taken solid form. Describing the projected book as a "miniature model" of the arcades, he mapped out its structure in terms of central thematic aspects of the larger project reorganized now around the figure of Baudelaire. His preliminary schematization is revealing:

The work will be in three parts. Their projected titles are: "Idea and Image"; "Antiquity and Modernity"; "The New and Eversame." The first part will show the crucial importance of allegory in the *Fleurs du mal*. It presents the construction of allegorical perception in Baudelaire, while making transparent the fundamental paradox of his doctrine of art—the contradiction between the theory of the natural correspondences and the rejection of nature. . . .

The second part develops, as a formal element of allegorical perception, the "dissolve" through which antiquity comes to light in modernity and modernity in antiquity. . . . The crowd affects this transposition of Paris in decisive fashion. The crowd settles as a veil before the flâneur: it is the newest intoxicant of the lonely individual.—Second, the crowd erases all traces of the individual: it is the newest asylum of the outcast.—The crowd is, finally, the newest and most unfathomable labyrinth in the labyrinth of the city. Through it, previously unknown chthonic features engrave themselves on the cityscape.—To disclose these aspects of Paris was the manifest task of the poet. . . . In Baudelaire's terms, nothing in his own century comes closer to the task of the hero of antiquity than the task of giving form to modernity.

The third part treats the commodity as the fulfillment of allegorical perception in Baudelaire. It turns out that the new, which explodes the appearance of the eversame under whose spell the poet was placed by spleen, is nothing other than the aureole of the commodity. . . . The dissipation of allegorical semblance is rooted in this fulfillment. The unique importance of Baudelaire resides in his being the first and the most unswerving to have apprehended [*dingfest gemacht*] the productive energy of the self-estranged human being—in the double sense of acknowledging this being and intensifying it through the making-fast.[10] The individual formal analyses presented by the work in its various sections thereby converge in a unified context. (C, 556–557)

While working on this schematization of the Baudelaire book in April and May, Benjamin suffered chronic migraine headaches. He finally consulted a specialist, who recommended treatment for malaria; after visiting an ophthalmologist to be examined for the new glasses he needed so badly, however, he found the headaches had disappeared. During these weeks, work on the Baudelaire project slowed nearly to a standstill, and he sought relief in thoughts of his upcoming visit to Denmark and Brecht, which was to begin in late June and last some three months. Life in exile remained extremely precarious—and not merely on account of politics and economics. Benjamin was dependent on his friends in ways other than financial; his letters written in the spring of 1938 are filled with requests and thanks related to the transcription of his work. Throughout this period, Gretel Adorno remained a steadfast source of support, but other, less likely figures spent hours preserving and disseminating the work of this impoverished intellectual who lacked a real publishing base. Although he was frequently asked to contribute to new exile publications, the difficulties involved often led to the abridgment or even bowdlerization of his work. In April Benjamin was asked by an old acquaintance, Johannes Schmidt, to contribute to a new journal, *Freie deutsche Forschung* (Independent German Research); his initial enthusiasm led ultimately only to the publication of one book review. More vexatious still was his experience upon receiving a copy of Dolf Sternberger's second book, *Panorama: Ansichten des 19. Jahrhunderts* (Panoramas of the Nineteenth Century). As he read through the book, Benjamin became convinced that Sternberger had pirated key motifs from his arcades project, as well as from the work of Adorno and Bloch. He was incensed not merely by the apparent plagiarism but by Sternberger's cynical deployment of their ideas under Nazi imprimatur. In a draft of a letter to Sternberger that he may never have sent (it was written ca. April 1938), Benjamin delivered an indictment: "~~You have succeeded in constructing a synthesis between the new world of ideas that you share with Adolf Hitler and an older one, which you shared with me.~~ You have rendered unto Caesar what is Caesar's and taken from the ~~Jew~~ exiled what you needed" (GB, 6:70; Benjamin's strikethroughs). In 1939 Benjamin composed a somewhat tempered but still thoroughly negative review of Sternberger's book. Many years later—on the appearance of a new edition of his book in 1974—Sternberger responded to the review (which remained unpublished during Benjamin's lifetime):

> The judgment W.B. made in Parisian exile at the time, in a manu-
> script which has only recently come to light, was a painful one for

me. I owe him much, not least the sharpening of my eye for the foreign and dead aspects of historical details, as well as a feeling for
proceeding configuratively, but I of course did not yet know any of
his own relevant works. His essay begins sympathetically, ending in
a harsh and angry tone. He too recognized the original critical motivation and characterized it with precision, but he failed to see the
"concept" that would succeed in bringing the remote together,
namely, social analysis. He wanted to achieve such an analysis in
his own great work on the Paris arcades; my book, related in subject
matter, could not possibly satisfy him. I could not then and cannot
now confer on class concepts and economic categories the capacity
to intercept or illuminate historical conceptions. Benjamin himself believed in it at the time, but could not act accordingly: even
in his work, definitions are surpassed by images. (Quoted in BS,
241–242n)

Leaving aside the issue as to whether Sternberger knew the outlines
of Benjamin's work in the 1930s, one notes an inescapable fact about
this rebuttal: its silence on Sternberger's complicity with National
Socialism.

The bitterness of this discovery was alleviated in some measure by
pleasant thoughts of the apparently immanent marriage of Liselotte
Karplus, the sister of his close friend Gretel Karplus Adorno, to his
cousin Egon Wissing. The wedding, which was to have taken place on
May 30, was in fact repeatedly postponed and took place only in 1940.
The visit of his aunt and uncle, Wissing's parents, in Paris, on their
way to the wedding and ultimately to a new life in Brazil, occasioned
thoughts in Benjamin that were marked equally by melancholy and
by acerbic wit. In a letter to his son, Stefan, Benjamin noted that the
Wissings' immigration to Brazil required their conversion to Catholicism. "The saying 'It's enough to make you Catholic' comes from the
Middle Ages; and, happily, we seem to be right back there again" (GB,
6:88).

Before departing for Denmark and a period of concentrated work
on the Baudelaire project, Benjamin devoted a great deal of time and
energy in May and June to the possible publication of two books. As
the years of exile lengthened, he was wishing ever more strongly to
see his *Berlin Childhood around 1900* in print. The text had been re-

jected by at least three publishers, who had apparently complained of its difficulty. During May and June he subjected the text to a thoroughgoing revision, adding a new introductory section while rearranging and abridging the complex of short, meditative texts that had initially appeared in the *Frankfurter Zeitung* and other newspapers at the end of the Weimar Republic. He not only made the prose crisper and less discursive, more concentrated on the imagery, but ruthlessly excised nine complete sections having a more autobiographical accent and more than a third of the remaining text, including passages of rare beauty.[11] Soon after asking Karl Thieme to help find a Swiss publisher for the text, he took the chance of exacerbating his already strained relations with Ferdinand Lion and *Maß und Wert* by proposing publication there. His letter to Lion quotes from the newly composed introductory section of *Berlin Childhood:*

> The text has ripened during my exile; of the past five years, none has gone by without my devoting a month or two to it. . . . The plan for the work dates from 1932. At that time, in Italy, it began to be clear to me that I would soon have to bid a long, perhaps lasting farewell to the city of my birth. Several times in my inner life, I had already experienced the process of inoculation as something salutary. In this situation, too, I resolved to follow suit, and I deliberately called to mind those images which, in exile, are most apt to waken homesickness: images of childhood. My assumption was that the feeling of longing would no more gain mastery over my spirit than a vaccine does over a healthy body. I sought to limit its effect through insight into the irretrievability—not the contingent biographical but the necessary social irretrievability—of the past. (GB, 6:79–80)

As it turned out, *Maß und Wert* published seven sections of *Berlin Childhood* in its July-August issue. It was to be the last portion of the text—for many, Benjamin's masterpiece—to appear in the author's lifetime. His final documented effort at publication very nearly succeeded, however: he had an agreement with the émigré publisher Heidi Hey to produce the book in a private edition. Yet in May this, too, foundered after a series of unpleasant meetings and telephone conversations with Hey, who professed herself hurt and bewildered. Benjamin insisted that he retain total control of every aspect of the publication, including typeface, design, and paper quality. The one document we have, a letter from Hey to Benjamin, suggests that she was a sympathetic reader and a practical-minded publisher who had formulated a plan that was "matter of fact" rather than "fantastic": she promised Benjamin to print a limited number of copies of a bibliophile, numbered edition, and to be responsible for distributing half of the print run, with the other half falling to Benjamin himself. Benjamin chose to forgo this opportunity rather than surrender control of the production of the book—a choice that had everything to do with the importance of the work to him and nothing at all to do with the actual circumstances under which publishers were forced to work in exile.

For all his absorption in Baudelaire during these months, Benjamin often found himself returning to Franz Kafka; his ideas on the French poet and the Czech-Jewish fiction writer became intertwined in fascinating ways. "My reading [of Kafka] is intermittent," he wrote to Scholem on April 14, "because my attention and time are turned almost undividedly to the Baudelaire project." Using Scholem as intermediary, Benjamin hoped to interest Salomon Schocken in a book on Kafka. He wrote a magnificent letter to Scholem in mid-June, articulating his new thinking on Kafka. The letter, composed as a prospectus that could be shared with Schocken and others, has all the polish and epigrammatic force of a finished essay. Adorno had already, in December 1934, echoed Benjamin's own comment about the "unfinished" quality of his just published essay, "Franz Kafka." Adorno was thinking in particular of the essay's relation to the basic categories of the arcades project: "The relationship between primal history and modernity has yet to be conceptualized, and the success of an interpretation of Kafka must, in the last analysis, depend on that conceptualization" (BA, 68).

The 1938 letter on Kafka begins with an attack on Max Brod's recent biography of the writer, before making an apodictic assertion: that Kafka's work "is an ellipsis; its widely spaced focal points are defined, on the one hand, by mystical experience (which is, above all, the experience of tradition) and, on the other hand, by the experience of the modern city-dweller" (SW, 3:325). Benjamin then cites an extended passage from the physicist Arthur Eddington's *The Nature of the Physical World* (1928), which presents the act of walking through an open doorway as an undertaking complicated by atmospheric pressure, gravity, the movement of the earth, and the dynamic and ultimately "loose" nature of the physical world, a world without "solidity of substance." There are clear analogies here: the modern world has a spatial consistency like that depicted in Kafka's short prose text "The Trees," a temporality like that in "A Common Confusion," and a causality akin to that found in "The Cares of a Family Man." In the 1934 essay Benjamin highlighted Kafka's particular gift for "study," that is, for an oblique attentiveness to aspects of a forgotten "preworld," a sphere of inchoate myth whose laws determine the course of daily existence. Now Benjamin presents a Kafka attuned to the social and economic determinants of the modern world. "What is actually and in the precise sense *crazy* [*toll*] about Kafka is that this newest world of experience comes to him by way of the mystical tradition. . . . I would say that this reality is now almost beyond the *individual's* capacity to experience, and that Kafka's world, often so serene and pervaded by angels, is the exact complement of his age" (SW, 3:325–326). Kafka's mystical capability attunes him, in other words, to something like that relation between modernity and primal history whose conceptualization Adorno missed in the 1934 essay, to that underlying field for play (*Spielraum*) concealed beneath the phantasmagorical regimes of commodity capitalism and further obscured by the fragmentary character of modern experience.

In a wonderful aside in another letter, Benjamin shows how deeply his thinking on Kafka's modernity had permeated his reflections on the arcades and on Baudelaire. He claims for that special class of Kafkan figures, among whom the "assistants" are most prominent, a function analogous to that of the flâneur. Just as the flâneur wanders the Parisian Grands Boulevards, allowing disparate, shocklike experiences to be inscribed on his body even as they resonate in his memory, so the "assistant" type, in a state of intoxication akin to a mystical trance, wanders through the Kafkan universe. In their blithe and groundless transparency, such figures alone seem capable of bringing to consciousness the alienating character of historical conditions (BA, 310–311).

The primary thrust of the parallel between Kafka and Baudelaire established in the 1938 Kafka letter is, however, not in any conventional sense thematic; the analysis of experience is in both instances the precondition for a discrimination of *form*. For Benjamin, Kafka's parable form is the truly emancipatory element of his work. "He gave up truth so that he could hold on to its transmissibility, the haggadic element. . . . But [Kafka's works] don't simply lie down at the feet of doctrine, the way Haggadah [story] lies down at the feet of Halakhah [law]. Having crouched down, they unexpectedly cuff doctrine with a weighty paw" (SW, 3:326). Kafka's works bear witness to a "sickening of tradition"; they mark the point at which the transmission of wisdom is hollowed out, becoming transmission tout court. In this they are like the allegorical elements in Baudelaire's poetry. In their pretense to wholeness, organicism, and finally wisdom, the parables share key features with allegory, which, as a critical mimesis, breaks down the fetishized appearance of the commodity, breaking through the mythic powers that distort our comprehension of historical conditions. "Baudelaire's allegory bears traces of the violence that was necessary to demolish the harmonious façade of the world that surrounded him" (AP, J55a,3). Kafka and Baudelaire together exemplify a unique capacity: their works reveal the aura *in the process of its decay*. In the 1938 letter to Scholem, the revelatory and even transformative potential in Kafka is shown to emerge only when his texts are brushed, as Benjamin says, against the grain: "In every true work of art there is a place where, for one who removes there, it blows cool like the wind of a coming dawn. From this it follows that art, which has often been considered refractory to every relation with progress, can provide its true definition. Progress has its seat not in the continuity of elapsing time but in its interferences—where the truly new makes itself felt for the first time, with the sobriety of dawn" (AP, N9a,7).

Benjamin had hoped to ingratiate himself further with Schocken through favorable mention of Max Brod's Kafka biography, but even a casual reading removed that possibility. "I speak of Kafka at this point, however," he wrote to Scholem, "because the biography, in its interweaving of Kafkaesque ignorance and Brodesque sagacity, seems to reveal a district of the spiritual world where white magic and spurious witchcraft interplay in the most edifying manner. I haven't yet been able to read it much, but I at once appropriated for myself the Kafkaesque formulation of the categorical imperative: "'Act in such a way that the angels have something to do'" (BS, 216). The proposed book on Kafka remained a topic for discussion between Scholem and Benjamin well into 1939, before it finally foundered on Schocken's indifference. This failure was perhaps in keeping with what Benjamin wrote, at the end of his letter to Scholem, about the figure of Kafka in its "purity" and its "peculiar beauty": "It is the figure of a failure. The circumstances of this failure are manifold. Perhaps one might say that once he was sure of ultimate failure, then everything on the way to it succeeded for him as in a dream" (SW, 3:327). It follows that Kafka's "failure" is inseparable from his hope and his serenity.

Just before leaving for Denmark, Benjamin sent a long letter to Adorno that was clearly intended as a provocation. He had read carefully a number of chapters from Adorno's Wagner study and was full of enthusiasm for individual points. He took issue, however, with the philosophy of history that informed the work as a whole, and especially with Adorno's deployment of the key Benjaminian category of "redemption" (Rettung).

> It seems to me that any such redemption, undertaken from the perspective of the philosophy of history, is incompatible with one undertaken from a critical perspective that is focused upon progress and regress. Or more precisely—is compatible only in those philosophical connections in which we have ourselves occasionally discussed the question of "progress" sub vocem. The unconditional use of concepts like those of the progressive and the regressive, concepts whose justification I would be the last to deny in the central sections of your work, makes the idea of an attempted "redemption" of Wagner utterly problematic. . . . Redemption is a cyclical form, polemic a progressive one. . . . For the decisive element in such redemption— am I not right?—is never simply something progressive; it can resemble the regressive as much as it resembles the ultimate goal, which is what Kraus calls the origin. (BA, 258–259)

In Benjamin's late thinking on the philosophy of history, the progressive and the regressive hardly contribute to a forward-driven dialectic, let alone to the positive "redemption" of isolated features of the social context. As he puts it in *The Arcades Project:*

Modest methodological proposal for the cultural-historic dialectic. It is very easy to establish oppositions, according to determinate points of view, within the various "fields" of any epoch, such that on one side lies the "productive," "forward-looking," "lively," "positive" part of the epoch, and on the other side the abortive, retrograde, and obsolescent. The very contours of the positive element will appear distinctly only insofar as this element is set off against the negative. On the other hand, every negation has its value solely as background for the delineation of the lively, the positive. It is therefore of decisive importance that a new partition be applied to this initially excluded, negative component so that, by a displacement of the angle of vision (but not of the criteria!), a positive element emerges anew in it too—something different from that previously signified. And so on, ad infinitum, until the entire past is brought into the present in a historical apocatastasis. (AP, N1a,3)

Apocatastasis—the Stoic and patristic notion that conflagration precedes any possible restoration—is at the heart of Benjamin's ever-darkening thoughts on history. This never-completed debate with Adorno on the role of progress must be read in a very particular context: in the same letter in which he challenges Adorno, he notes in passing his friend's plan to write, with Horkheimer "a study of the dialectic," a study that would eventually become *Dialectic of Enlightenment*, with its dedication in memory of Benjamin.

Benjamin departed Paris on June 21, bound for an extended visit with Brecht and his family in Skovsbostrand. He not only looked forward to the change of scene and the opportunity to work without interruption on the Baudelaire project; he felt positively driven from the city. Germany was becoming increasingly aggressive, tensions in France were growing, and he knew that his status as an exile there made his hard-won foothold increasingly tenuous. Upon his arrival in Denmark, he moved into the house next door to Brecht, where his landlord was a police official, a circumstance that he hoped might work to his advantage should he be forced to extend his visa because of war. The first days in Skovsbostrand promised a nearly ideal working environment; he looked forward, he wrote (quoting Baudelaire), to living in the *"contemplation opiniâtre de l'oeuvre de demain."*[12] The house had a large garden, and the window in his attic room looked out from his "spacious, weighty" desk onto the sound on one side and the forest on the other. "The little ships that pass by represent my only distraction—apart from the daily chess interlude with Brecht" (BS, 230). Next door were the Brechts and their two children, Stefan and Barbara, of whom Benjamin was very fond; also the radio, their main source of information about the rapidly shifting world events ("the newspapers arrive here so late that you have to pluck up your courage just to open them"), and his evening meal (C, 568–569). He soon became aware, though, of the drawbacks that had always bothered him: "The weather is gloomy, and does not exactly tempt me to go for any walks; all the better, for there are none to take. My desk does have a climatic advantage: it is situated underneath a slanted roof, where the warmth occasionally emitted by the sparse rays of sunlight lasts a little longer than elsewhere." A bright spot was his recent acquaintance with the work of Katharine Hepburn: "She is magnificent" (BG, 229–230).

His days were fairly uniform: eight or nine hours of work on Baudelaire, followed by a meal, a bit of companionship, and a game or two of chess with Brecht—which, he told Gretel, he tended to lose, even though he sometimes took up to a half hour to make a move.[13] Although remarks in several letters express an intention to return to Paris by mid-July in order to meet Scholem (who at that time would be on his way from New York to Palestine), other evidence, and Scholem's own feelings on the matter, suggest that this was an encounter Benjamin hoped to avoid. The letter of June 12 on Kafka—the distillation of more than a decade's reflection on this writer so close to his heart—can thus be read as a form of anticipatory compensation for the direct exchange that would never take place again.

As he plunged into his Baudelaire materials, he soon realized that the schematization prepared in Paris in the wake of his migraines would have to be redone. As he worked his way back through his material on the arcades and on Baudelaire and began to reorganize, he came to see the Baudelaire project as a direct continuation of his work in the 1920s. The first such indication is a note to Scholem that describes the work on Baudelaire as "a long chain of reflections (which takes the *Elective Affinities* essay as their model)" (BS, 231). He tells his sister that he is "again involved—after a hiatus of ten years—in

writing a book." In 1928 Ernst Rowohlt had published Benjamin's
book on the German *Trauerspiel,* together with his city-book *One-Way
Street.* And it is to *One-Way Street* that Benjamin refers, however unconsciously, when he tells Friedrich Pollock that his Baudelaire book
will afford "a view—arranged perspectivally—into the depths of the
nineteenth century" (GB, 6:133)—a phrase virtually identical to his
description of *One-Way Street* in a 1926 letter to Scholem. By the end
of July it was clear that he would not have the work completed by September 15, the deadline given him by the Institute of Social Research.
He had agreed to this date while still in Paris, thinking that the outline composed there would accelerate the writing process.

Throughout late July, August, and September 1938, Benjamin
worked full throttle on his study of Baudelaire. The new schematization had three parts: an introductory, highly theoretical section entitled "Baudelaire als Allegoriker" (Baudelaire as Allegorist), which would
link Baudelaire to Benjamin's reading of Baroque allegory; a central
section, "Das Paris des Second Empire bei Baudelaire" (The Paris of
the Second Empire in Baudelaire), which would provide the social
"data" or "antithesis" to that theory; and a concluding section, "Die
Ware als poetischer Gegenstand" (The Commodity as Poetic Object),
which would examine the posthistory of Baudelaire's age through
analyses not just of commodity fetishism but also of art nouveau and
the notion of eternal return in Baudelaire, Blanqui, and Nietzsche. In
early August Benjamin suggested to Horkheimer that section two
might be most suitable for publication in the *Zeitschrift für Sozialforschung.* As he conceived this section—which would become the
essay "The Paris of the Second Empire in Baudelaire"—Benjamin began to articulate a series of analogies linking Baudelaire, Louis Napoleon, and the Parisian *bohème,* at the same time that he was articulating "the relation of the metropolitan crowd to modern literature" and
the complex intertwining of antiquity and modernity in Baudelaire's
poems (GB, 6:150). As he would later say of the overall conception of
the Baudelaire book, the "philosophical bow [was] being bent to the
greatest extent possible" (BS, 252).

Work on the Baudelaire essay was accompanied by the wide-ranging
discussions with Brecht that were characteristic of their relationship.
Much of their talk was of literature: Virgil, Dante, Goethe, Anna

Seghers, Brecht's own epic theater and recent poetry.[14] In his journal for August 13, 1938, Brecht mentions a conversation about the crisis of bourgeois sexuality: "Benjamin maintains Freud thinks that sexuality will one day die out completely."[15] But, increasingly, their time together was given over to discussions of recent developments in the Soviet Union. In a letter to Horkheimer, Benjamin attempted to explain the views he held in common with Brecht:

> We have up to now been able to view the Soviet Union as a power that does not determine its foreign policy according to imperialist interests—hence as an anti-imperialist power. We continue to do so, at least for now, because—despite the gravest possible reservations—we still view the Soviet Union as the agent of our interests in a coming war, as well as in the delaying of this war; I assume that this corresponds to your sense of the situation. That this agent is the costliest imaginable, in that we have to pay for it with sacrifices diminishing the interests that matter most to us as producers, Brecht would never think of disputing. (BG, 229)

Even Brecht had come to regard the newest developments—the show trials, the purges, the cowering before Hitler—as "catastrophic for everything we've been working for over the past twenty years" (BG, 229). For example, they feared that Brecht's friend and translator, the great Soviet writer Sergei Tretjakov, had been executed following his arrest—a fear that proved true. Their reservations regarding Soviet policies were hardly limited to the trials and executions: both Brecht and Benjamin were torn between their hope that the Soviet Union might yet prevent a war and their disgust at the excesses of Soviet literary politics. The great debates among German Marxists that took place in journals such as *Das Wort* and concerned the proper direction for a genuinely socialist art are now known collectively as the "Expressionism debate," initiated as they were by Georg Lukács's 1934 article on the alleged decline of Expressionism into obscurantism; Brecht's exploitation of certain Expressionist techniques in his decidedly antiobscurantist plays helped establish a credible counterargument to Lukács.

Benjamin's solidarity with Brecht *and* with Adorno and Horkheimer led him to find ways to mediate between the two camps. He urged Brecht to read every issue of the *Zeitschrift*, and took care to emphasize points of agreement between New York and Skovsbostrand—such as an antipathy to the doctrinaire realism espoused by Lukács. "He knows as well as we that the theoretical position of the *Zeitschrift* gains more weight with every passing day" (GB, 6:134). Benjamin's proximity to Brecht and his vigorous, engaged Marxism continued, however, to worry Benjamin's colleagues at the institute, where a more mediated—some would say infinitely deferred—understanding of engagement reigned. Benjamin's commitment to Brecht exacted more personal costs. He reported to Gretel Adorno, for example, that he was reading much more "party line" literature in Denmark than he did ordinarily. And to Kitty Marx-Steinschneider he commented that his room was coming to resemble a monk's cell—not because of its furnishings but because of its intellectual isolation. "In spite of all my friendship with Brecht, I need to pursue my work in strict seclusion. It contains very distinct moments that he is unable to assimilate. He has been a friend for a long enough time for me to know this and is perceptive enough to respect it" (C, 569).

Even the idyll in the policeman's house, under the pressure of pushing forward the Baudelaire, began to sour. Benjamin confided to the Adornos in late August that the noise of the children in the house might force him to leave. He was considering renting rooms from a mentally ill man, despite his antipathy to such illnesses. Strung between Brecht, the institute, and his own as yet unrealized hopes for the Baudelaire, he sometimes felt trapped. Philosophical discussions with his old friend Gershom Scholem, he wrote, had evidently left Scholem with an image of him not unlike that of "a man who has made his home in a crocodile's jaws, which he keeps pried open with iron braces" (C, 569). In fact, his relations with Scholem had reached a new low. Having departed Paris a few weeks before Scholem could meet him there on his way back from New York, Benjamin now informed his friend that their hopes for a meeting in Paris that fall would not be realized either, since he had to remain in Denmark to complete the Baudelaire. They would be unable to discuss their recent work, and Benjamin would miss the opportunity to meet Scholem's new wife. Any embarrassment over his repeated dodging soon faded, however. On September 30 he sent an aggrieved letter to Scholem: "I find it astonishing that you have let me hear no word from you. Your silence has been an object of my concern for some time now" (BS, 231). Scholem pleaded, rather lamely, that the trip to America had produced a kind of lethargy that kept him from writing for close to three months—but his perturbation at Benjamin's ongoing avoidance of a meeting must have been the real cause.

One sign of Benjamin's concentration in this period—he described his three months of work on the Baudelaire essay as "extremely intense"—is the relative paucity of references to his reading habits. He mentions with some consternation that he had come across a recent issue of the Moscow periodical *Internationale Literatur* in which the writer Alfred Kurella, whom he had known since the days of the youth movement, and with whom he had clashed in the editorial debates surrounding the proposed journal *Krise und Kritik* in 1930–1931, had characterized him as a follower of Heidegger (Kurella had reviewed the excerpt from Benjamin's essay "Goethe's Elective Affinities" published in translation in the French journal *Les Cahiers du Sud*). But otherwise his comments refer to his reading *plans*. Benjamin did consent with pleasure to the publication of excerpts from an earlier letter to Horkheimer—a "letter from Paris" on recent developments in French writing. He asked only that the letter's highly critical account of Georges Bataille, with whom he enjoyed cordial relations, and through whom he had come into contact with the circle of intellectuals around the Collège de Sociologie, be excised before publication.

In September, as Benjamin worked toward concluding "The Paris of the Second Empire in Baudelaire," his letters reveal a profound anxiety that was fully justified by developments in Europe. Germany's insistence on the annexation of the Sudetenland made war in Europe seem inevitable. Benjamin told several of his correspondents that he would rather await the war in Scandinavia than in France, and he asked Horkheimer for names of Scandinavian friends in case his visa expired. It was against this horizon that Benjamin concluded three months of "the most intensive labor" (BS, 231) on his Baudelaire essay and, near the end of the month, left Skovsbostrand for Copenhagen in order to dictate and mail the final version of "The Paris of the Second Empire in Baudelaire."[16] This last stage of composition coincided with what he called "the provisional dénouement" of the European situation: the signing of the Munich accords between Hitler, Mussolini, Neville Chamberlain, and Édouard Daladier on September 29 and Germany's immediate invasion of the Sudetenland. Benjamin consequently saw only the part of his "beloved" Copenhagen that lay between his hotel room and the radio set in the hotel's common room (BA, 277).

On October 4, shortly after his return to Skovsbostrand, Benjamin reported to Adorno that the completion of the essay had been "a race against the war; and despite choking anxiety, I experienced a feeling of triumph on the day I brought the 'flâneur'—planned for almost fifteen years—safely under a roof (if only the fragile one of a manuscript!) just before the end of the world" (BA, 278). In a letter to Horkheimer confirming the mailing of the manuscript, Benjamin characterized the essay as a signature effort: it sets forth "decisive philosophical elements of the *Arcades* project in what I hope are their definitive form." And to the Adornos he restated a conviction betraying a certain anxiety about the essay's reception in New York: his belief that the as yet unwritten—though schematized—first and third parts "provide the armature for the whole: the first presents the character of allegory in Baudelaire as a problem, while the third presents the social resolution of the problem" (BA, 273). He wanted it understood that "the philosophical bases of the *entire* book" would be intelligible only from the standpoint of the third section, "The Commodity as Poetic Object" (C, 573).

In *Charles Baudelaire: A Lyric Poet in the Age of High Capitalism*—his projected book title—Benjamin attempts nothing less than a wholesale reinvention of the great French poet as the representative writer of urban capitalist modernity. For Benjamin, Baudelaire's greatness consists precisely in his *representativeness:* in the manner in which his poetry—often against its express intent—lays open the structure and mechanisms of his age. Of course, Benjamin was hardly alone among his contemporaries in taking Baudelaire as the first exemplary modern writer. In England, Baudelaire was a touchstone for T. S. Eliot, who translated his work into English and in 1930 produced a magisterial essay on Baudelaire's relation to modernity (his view of life "an evangel to his time and to ours"), not to mention the decisive influence of *Les fleurs du mal* on that other great city poem, "The Waste Land." In Germany, Stefan George was a foremost link between Baudelaire and modern German writing; George's translation of *Les fleurs du mal* (1889) is still in many ways unsurpassed. Yet Eliot and George saw in Baudelaire a writer significantly different from the one discovered by Benjamin. For Eliot, as for Swinburne before him, Baudelaire was a key to adequate spiritual comprehension of modernity, an indispensable predecessor in Eliot's own quest to find a religiously informed path through the modern wasteland; for George, as for Nietzsche before him, Baudelaire's poetry opened onto a vast, wholly aestheticized landscape that was proof against the indignities of a utilitarian and philistine society. At stake in this comparison of Benjamin and his contemporaries is more than the leftism of the one versus the conservative—or, in the case of George, protofascist—politics of the others. If Eliot's Baudelaire was a prophetic voice in the spiritual constitution of modernity, and George's Baudelaire the beacon of all genuinely modern aesthetic production, Benjamin made Baudelaire a uniquely problematic object: a largely apolitical writer whose work prepares the ground for a responsible cultural politics in the present. Benjamin resolutely refuses to attribute a single productive social or political insight to Baudelaire himself; the achievement of Benjamin's work on Baudelaire is its exposure of *Les fleurs du mal* as uniquely, scathingly, terrifyingly *symptomatic* of Baudelaire's era—and ours. "The Paris of the Second Empire in Baudelaire" begins, disconcertingly (and that is its keynote), not with a consideration of Baudelaire's poetry, or even of Baudelaire himself, but with a quasi-historiographic evocation of a particular "intellectual physiognomy": the conspiratorial face of the *bohème*. For Benjamin, the bohemians were not primarily *artistes* starving in garrets—think of Rodolfo and Mimi in Puccini's *La Bohème*—but a motley collection of amateur and professional conspirators who imagined the overthrow of the regime of Napoleon III, France's self-appointed emperor. In the opening pages of the essay Benjamin quietly establishes relays between the tactics employed by this social stratum and the *aesthetic* strategies governing Baudelaire's poetry and criticism. If "surprising proclamations and mystery-mongering, sudden sallies, and impenetrable irony were part of the *raison d'état* of the Second Empire," Benjamin writes,

Baudelaire's poetry is likewise distinguished by "the enigmatic stuff of allegory" and "the mystery-mongering of the conspirator." This sociophysiognomic approach to the poet has reference not to a poem where such a sinister physiognomy flashes up at the reader—one might think of "Satan's Litanies," with its apostrophe of Satan as the "Prince of exiles, exiled Prince who, wronged/yet rises ever stronger from defeat"—but rather to the poem "Ragpicker's Wine," with its evocation of the labyrinthine milieu in which the conspirators operated, a series of cheap taverns outside the city gates. This composite of gestural aspects of a particular intellectual physiognomy within the spaces in which it arises is basic to Benjamin's method in his work on Baudelaire. In the figure of the ragpicker we find a highly charged concatenation: "From the littérateur to the professional conspirator, everyone who belonged to the *bohème* could recognize a bit of himself in the ragpicker. Each person was in a more or less blunted state of revolt against society and faced a more or less precarious future." As this quotation from "The Paris of the Second Empire" suggests, the ragpicker was a recognizable social type. Yet with Baudelaire the ragpicker is also a figure for the poet who sifts through the detritus of his society and finds uses for what that society discards. At the same time, the ragpicker is a figure for Benjamin himself, for the critic and historian who assembles his critical montage from largely inconspicuous elements extracted with surgical precision from a body of evidence. Here and throughout Benjamin's studies of Baudelaire, we find a considered identification with the poet: with the social isolation, with the commercial failure, with the recourse to a "secret architecture" in writing, and in particular with the fathomless melancholy that suffuses every page.

Benjamin concludes this first section of the essay by contrasting Baudelaire with Pierre Dupont, an avowed social poet, whose work strives for a direct, indeed simple and tendentious, engagement with political events of the day. In contrasting Baudelaire with Dupont, Benjamin brings to light a "profound duplicity" at the heart of Baudelaire's poetry—which, he contends, is less an index of support for the cause of the oppressed than a rude unveiling of their illusions. As Benjamin wrote in one of his notes to the essay, "There is little point in trying to integrate the position of a Baudelaire into the network of the most advanced positions in the struggle for human liberation. From the outset, it seems more promising to investigate his machinations where he was undoubtedly at home: in the enemy camp. . . . Baudelaire was a secret agent—an agent of the secret discontent of his class with its own rule" (SW, 4:92n).

By late 1938 Benjamin was convinced that traditional historiography, with its reliance on the kind of storytelling that presupposes a homogeneous continuity and inevitable process in historical change, "is meant to cover up the revolutionary moments in the occurrence of history. . . . The places where tradition breaks off—hence its peaks and crags, which offer footing to one who would cross over them—it misses" (AP, N9a,5). Benjamin's essay on Baudelaire's Paris is accordingly composed of a series of historical images or motifs "torn" from their original context—which is often on the margins of historical evidence, enmeshed in anecdote and secret history—and carefully worked into a text based on principles of montage. This method of composition arises from the conviction that such images, often the expression of seemingly inconsequential details of large historical structures, have been ignored as the dominant class ascribes truth-value to its own, ideologically inspired version of history. In order to uncover beneath the parade of historiographic enshrinement what he names "authentic historical time, the time of truth," Benjamin proposes "to extract, to cite, what has remained inconspicuously buried—being, as it was, of so little help to the powerful" (N3,1; J77,1). But how are we to understand the *relations* between the images in this revolutionary materialist historiography? Benjamin places all his faith in the "expressive" capacity of his image constellations. "The economic conditions under which society exists are expressed in the superstructure—precisely as, with the sleeper, an overfull stomach finds not its reflection but its expression in the contents of dreams, which, from a causal point of view, it may be said to 'condition'" (K2,5). These passages from *The Arcades Project*—and "The Paris of the Second Empire in Baudelaire" draws deeply on the decade of work on the arcades—all concern a textual space in which the speculative, the intuitive, and the analytical converge, a space in which images and the relays between them can be read in such a way that the *present* meaning of "what has been comes together in a flash." That crystallization of history in the present is what Benjamin calls the dialectical image. And "The Paris of the Second Empire in Baudelaire" is perhaps the most vivid and fully realized example of a critical practice built around dialectical images—the crowning achievement of Benjamin's literary-critical work in the 1930s.

The central section of "The Paris of the Second Empire in Baudelaire," titled "The Flâneur," examines the reciprocal relations between certain artistic genres and certain societal forms. In the crowded streets of the metropolis, the individual is not merely absorbed into the masses; all traces of individual existence are effectively effaced. And popular literary and artistic forms such as physiologies (paperbound documentaries of urban types) and panoramas (displays of "typical" historical and geographical tableaux) arose, Benjamin argues, precisely in order to quell the deep-seated unease that characterized this situation. Through their "harmlessness" these entertainments purveyed a "perfect bonhomie" devoid of all resistance to the social order of the day, a condition favorable to the "phantasmagoria of Parisian life." As we have seen, the term "phantasmagoria" in Benjamin emphasizes the illusionary quality of the modern urban environment, a quality that has a debilitating effect on the human ability to come to rational decisions and in fact to understand our own world. Physiologies are in this respect complicit with phantasmagoria, in that they encourage complacence by crediting their readers with an expertise they do not necessarily have. As Benjamin says in "The Paris of the Second Empire," physiologies "assured people that everyone could—unencumbered by any factual knowledge—make out the profession, character, background, and lifestyle of passers-by."

The "soothing little remedies" offered by physiologies could only be a temporary check on the unsettling character of life under modern conditions. Benjamin points out that another genre developed at this point (in the 1840s), one "concerned with the disquieting and threatening aspects of urban life." This genre was the detective story. If, in the dreamlike space of the urban phantasmagoria, the denizens of the city were confronted with recurrent shocks and an attendant disorientation, the detective story, with its militant, if usually eccentric, ratiocination, provided an apparent restorative, one that "allows the

intellect to break through this emotion-laden atmosphere." Baudelaire himself, Benjamin believed, was incapable of producing detective stories. "The structure of his drives" prevented such directly
rationalistic intentions in the poet: "Baudelaire was too good a reader
of the Marquis de Sade to be able to compete with Poe."

If Baudelaire's poetry neither catered to social conditions (as did
the physiologies) nor envisioned procedures for dealing with them (as
did the detective story), what exactly is the relationship of that poetry
to Parisian modernity? Benjamin champions Baudelaire precisely because his work, in allowing itself to be marked by the ruptures and
aporias of modern metropolitan life, reveals the hollowness in modern experience. At the heart of Benjamin's interpretation is thus a
theory of shock, developed in connection with a now-famous reading
of the poem "A une passante" (To a Passer-By). The speaker of the poem,
moving through the crowd in the "deafening" street, suddenly spies a
woman dressed in mourning walking his way, majestic in her grief,
and "with imposing hand/Gathering up a scalloped hem." The
speaker is as if possessed; his body twitches, wholly overcome by the
momentary encounter. The sight of this fugitive beauty has shattered
him and given him new life. Yet, Benjamin argues, the spasms running through the poet's body are not caused by "the excitement of a
man in whom an image has taken possession of every fiber of his being"; their cause is instead the powerful, isolated shock "with which
an imperious desire suddenly overcomes a lonely man."

This notion of a shock-driven poetic capability was a significant
departure from the understanding of artistic creation prevalent in
Benjamin's day and still widespread today. In this alternative view,
the poet is not an Olympian genius who "rises above" his age and captures its essence for posterity. For Benjamin, the greatness of Baudelaire
lies in his absolute *susceptibility* to the worst excrescences of modern
life; this masterly writer was possessed of an extraordinarily "sensitive disposition" enabling him to register, through cold reflective empathy, the character of his age. In Benjamin's broadly informed judgment, the "character of the age" was determined by spreading
commodification. Baudelaire was not simply *aware of* the processes of
commodification that generate phantasmagoria; he *embodied* those
processes in an emphatic manner.

When he takes his work to market, however hesitantly, the poet surrenders himself *as a commodity* to a certain unsealing and unselving—in short, to "the intoxication of the commodity immersed in a surging stream of customers." The poet's role as producer and purveyor of spiritual commodities opens him further to an intimate and estranging "empathy with inorganic things." And this, in turn, "was one of his sources of inspiration." Baudelaire's poetry is thus riven by tensions within and without—by the presentiment of doom enveloping its chosen task of *modernité,* and by a kaleidoscopic vision of history as nothing less than "permanent catastrophe." This is the sense in which the hapless Baudelaire was a "secret agent" of his own class's inner self-divestiture.

Approaching the conclusion to "The Paris of the Second Empire in Baudelaire" in the section entitled "Modernity," Benjamin makes a case for Baudelaire as the characteristic writer of modern life—its hero, in fact. "The hero is the true subject of modernity. In other words, it takes a heroic constitution to live modernity." Baudelaire as modern hero is more than the supersensitive flâneur strolling the streets of Paris with anamnestic attentiveness, more than the mimic purveyor of aesthetic commodities.[17] He is the unregenerate modern individual who, bit by bit, has been stripped of the possessions and security of bourgeois life and forced to take refuge in the street. As the harried denizen of the byways leading out from the Grands Boulevards, Baudelaire is rendered uniquely vulnerable to the shocks of modern life.

His heroism thus consists in his readiness to let the spirit of the age mark and scar his being. "The resistance that modernity offers to the natural productive élan of an individual is out of all proportion to his strength. It is understandable if a person becomes exhausted and takes refuge in death." Heroism thus assumes the form of mourning an always imminent loss—mourning as a form of vigilance—a Baudelairean notion that Benjamin places at the center of his reading. The pathos that infuses this section of the essay arises from the intense identification with Baudelaire's situation. The most prominent features of Baudelaire's biography—the penniless poet condemned, through lack of recognition, to an inner exile, and then, at the end of his life, to self-imposed exile in Belgium—conform closely to the situation of

Benjamin himself, one of the greatest writers of his generation deprived of a place on earth where, as he once put it, he could both earn a minimum wage and subsist on it. The temptation of suicide's release—"Modernity must stand under the sign of suicide, an act which seals a heroic will" (SW, 4:45)—was never far from Benjamin's thoughts in the period of his exile, and his imputation of "exhaustion" to Baudelaire was as much projection as description.

Yet the infernal character of modern life is not portrayed as flatly irredeemable. Through the focus of Baudelaire's poetry and prose, "The Paris of the Second Empire in Baudelaire" projects a parabolic understanding of that apparently unchangeable history—that "one-way street"—as the "object of a conquest." Even though the modern hero and the age that spawned him are "destined for doom," there exists a retrospective and wholly subterranean hope that modernity might harbor the elements of its own redemption. Baudelaire's question remains, the question as to "whether [modernity] itself will ever be able to become antiquity." If Victor Hugo saw in modern Paris so many palpable remainders of the ancient world that he could speak of "Parisian antiquity," Baudelaire, says Benjamin, conceives of a modernity bound to the past through shared *decrepitude,* through "mourning for what was and lack of hope for what is to come." Those aspects of the modern city made to appear "truly new" under capitalism soon reveal themselves as outdated. "Modernity has changed most of all, and the antiquity it was supposed to contain really presents a picture of the obsolete." In his 1929 essay on Surrealism, Benjamin had suggested that meaningful social change might be fueled by the "revolutionary energies" latent in what is obsolete. For the mechanisms of the capitalist process reveal themselves fully only in their waste products—in that which no longer serves a purpose and thus escapes the ideological control pervasive elsewhere. It is the illumination of processes of obsolescence, and through them of the coercive machinations of capitalism, that show the way to political action as a corrective. Baudelaire's spleen—the finely modulated wrath and disgust that complement his tenderness and his sorrow—bespeaks such promise.

No doubt the most revelatory potential raised in "The Paris of the Second Empire in Baudelaire" concerns the poet's language itself. Baudelaire's "prosody is like the map of a big city in which one can move about inconspicuously, shielded by blocks of houses, gateways, courtyards. On this map, words are given clearly designated positions before the outbreak of a revolt." How might such tactically situated words actually promote revolution? Benjamin's answer to this question involves a reconception of the notion of allegory developed in his *Trauerspiel* book of 1928. There he argued that the Baroque "plays of mourning," long neglected because of their apparently grave aesthetic flaws, in fact bore within them a responsible historical index of their age. In the allegorical mode of representation, dominant in the *Trauerspiel* and newly operative, Benjamin argues, in Baudelaire, "any person, any object, any relationship can mean absolutely anything else. With this possibility a destructive but just verdict is passed on the profane world: it is characterized as a world in which the detail is of no great importance."[18] In its spectral disintegrating power, its power of hollowing out and rendering transparent, allegory is the aesthetic form most attuned to an understanding of history as permanent catastrophe—the aesthetic form, therefore, most morally responsible for the present. The comparison of Baudelaire's prosody to a map indicates that it is less the words themselves than their *placement* in the topography of a text that makes for their revolutionary potential. This relational character of poetic language, its deployment of such stratagems as spacing and displacement, its "calculated disharmony between image and object," marks Baudelaire as an allegorist. And within the poetic spaces opened and articulated in this manner, Benjamin saw that experience of the utter groundlessness of modern existence might come into play—that, in other words, the phantasmagoria might be broken down and exposed for what it is. As he put it in *Central Park*, the collection of short reflections on which he also worked at this time: "To interrupt the course of the world—that was Baudelaire's deepest intention" (SW, 4:170).

What was specifically new in the theory of allegory in 1938 was what he had described in the letter of mid-April to Horkheimer—using the language of cinema and photography—as the "form-element" of allegorical perception, that is, the "dissolve" or superimposition *(Überblendung)*, by virtue of which antiquity appears in modernity and vice versa. Baudelaire is a poet for whom—as it is said in "The Swan," a poem structured by historical dissolves—everything turns to allegory. He is like the engraver Meryon, whom he championed in the latter's lifetime, and whose sequence of engraved views of Paris reveals an antiquity springing suddenly from an intact modernity; the "ancient face of the city" is uncovered "without abandoning a single cobblestone" of the new metropolitan Paris. "For in Meryon, too," comments Benjamin in the Paris essay, "there is an interpenetration of classical antiquity and modernity, and in him, too, the form of this superimposition—allegory—appears unmistakably."[19] And with this, the theory of allegory joins hands with that of the dialectical image, in which a particular past and present look through one another.

As he prepared to leave Denmark, Benjamin arranged—not without misgivings—to have his books, numbering in the hundreds, shipped to Paris. He was convinced that war was unavoidable, that the Munich accords promised anything but "peace in our time," and that the fascist alliance would simply shift its greedy gaze to new acquisitions. He strongly suspected that Paris itself would become yet another of the "transfer points" for himself and his possessions. "How long the European air will remain breathable—in a physical way—I don't know. Spiritually, it is no longer breathable after the events of the past weeks. . . . This much has now become indisputably clear: Russia has permitted the amputation of its European extremity" (BA, 277). He was somewhat heartened by the fact that his twenty-year-old son, Stefan, had settled down in the relative safety of England and that his former wife, Dora, was selling her property in San Remo, Italy, in order to follow Stefan to London. The situation of other friends must have seemed, in comparison, rather surreal: even as Europe descended toward war, he received a cheery letter from the Adornos, who were vacationing on Mount Desert Island in Maine. They had been visited by Egon Wissing and Gretel's sister, driving their new Ford convertible!

Benjamin left Denmark around October 15. His stay with Brecht had been unusually free of strife—which was itself a cause for concern, since he read Brecht's newfound willingness to listen as a sign of his friend's increasing isolation. "I don't entirely wish to exclude the more obvious explanation of the situation—that this isolation has diminished the pleasure he often used to take in the more provocative tactics during our conversations; a more authentic explanation, however, lies

34. Benjamin in 1939. Photo by Gisèle Freund (1912–2000) (© *Gisèle Freund-RMN. © RMN-Grand Palais/Art Resource, NY)*

in recognizing this growing isolation as a consequence of that loyalty to what we have in common" (C, 278).

Back in Paris, Benjamin met with a set of changes that exceeded his worst fears. His thirty-seven-year-old sister, Dora, who had been in generally poor health, was suffering from arteriosclerosis and was often bedridden for days at a time (she would make it through internment a year and a half later and die in a Swiss clinic in 1946). His younger brother, Georg, arrested by the Nazis in 1933 for his Communist sympathies, had been transferred to the prison at Bad Wilsnack in

Brandenburg, where he was part of a crew doing roadwork. "The great-est nightmare for those in his situation, as I often hear from people in Germany, is not so much the dawning of each new day behind bars as the threat of being sent to a concentration camp after years of impris-onment" (BG, 247). Georg would in fact perish in the Sachsenhausen concentration camp in 1942.

Benjamin now also feared the definitive loss of his personal ar-chives in Berlin. He had asked a friend, perhaps Helen Hessel, to make one last attempt to retrieve the books and papers that remained in his apartment, but this met with no success. He wrote to Gretel Adorno lamenting the loss of the papers of the brothers Fritz and Wolf Heinle (Benjamin's late friends from the German youth movement), the man-uscript of his own unpublished essay on Friedrich Hölderlin, and an "irreplaceable" archive of materials from the left-liberal wing of the youth movement, to which he had belonged. More generally, he feared the consequences of any French-German rapprochement in the wake of the Munich accords, and especially the potential effects on rela-tions between French and German residents in Paris. Lacking any al-ternative, he continued to pursue his application for French citizen-ship "circumspectly, but without illusions. If the chances of success were doubtful before, the usefulness of this measure has now also become problematic. The collapse of the legal order in Europe gives the lie to every kind of legalization" (BG, 247).

He was soon back in contact with his network of French friends. He first checked in with Adrienne Monnier to get her view of the cur-rent situation. In November he attended a banquet for contributors to *Les Cahiers du Sud* at the brasserie L'Alsacienne, where he saw Paul Valéry, Léon-Paul Fargue, Jules Supervielle, Jean Wahl, Rolland de Renéville, and Roger Caillois. He also was enjoying more frequent contact with the young scholar Pierre Missac, whom he had met in 1937 through Bataille; they shared an interest in film and architec-ture, among other things. They met often, sometimes at Benjamin's apartment, sometimes at the Café de la Mairie on the Place Saint-Sulpice. Of all his French friends, it was Missac who would later do the most to keep Benjamin's memory alive in France, publishing translations and critical essays and finally a book.[20] But Benjamin's French relationships were fragile. He asked Horkheimer, for example, to publish his negative review of Caillois's *Aridité* under the pseudonym "Hans Fellner" rather than risk incurring the displeasure of Callois's friend Renéville, who was shepherding Benjamin's citizenship application through his ministry. The review in fact appeared under the pseudonym "J. E. Mabinn," an anagram of "Benjamin."

Even amid the unrelentingly disastrous news from Germany, a few more positive signals emerged. His books arrived from Denmark, and Benjamin responded to a request from Horkheimer and Pollock for some form of reciprocation by contributing one of his gems, a four-volume history of the German book trade, to the institute's Paris library. He hoped that the gift would serve its intended purpose: namely, to furnish the "most important instrument for any future materialist history of German literature" (GB, 6:178). More of his German friends were now in Paris. Franz Hessel was the latest to emigrate. He had "sat in Berlin like a mouse in the timberwork for five and a half years" but had now come to Paris "with impeccable credentials and under powerful patronage": Jean Giraudoux, then a high-ranking official in the French foreign ministry, had procured a visa for him (BG, 247). The events of November 9–10—the pogrom formally known as Kristallnacht (Night of Broken Glass)—snuffed out any final glimmer of hope for peace, and Benjamin was led to meditate anew on the disastrous consequences looming for those left behind, such as his brother and Adorno's parents.

In mid-November Benjamin received what was probably the most crushing rejection of his career—the news, conveyed in a lengthy critique by Adorno, that the Institute of Social Research would not publish "The Paris of the Second Empire in Baudelaire" (BA, 280–289). The essay had been greeted not exactly with the bemused impatience he half expected but with thoroughgoing methodological and political objections. In his letter of November 10 Adorno, speaking for Horkheimer as well, accused Benjamin of neglecting the mediation that properly relates elements within a dialectical structure or presentation. He recognized the intentional fragmentariness through which Benjamin sought to reveal the "secret affinities" between general manifestations of industrial capitalism in big-city life and specific details of Baudelaire's work, but he judged the essay's aggregate method of construction a failure. Benjamin's idiosyncratic "materialist" approach, "this particular kind of concreteness" with "its behaviorist overtones," was methodologically unfeasible because, in its ascetic renunciation of interpretation and theoretical elaboration, it sought to place "conspicuous individual features from the realm of the superstructure" in an "unmediated and even causal relationship with corresponding features of the base." For Adorno, "the materialist determination of cultural characteristics is possible only when mediated through the *total social process*. . . . The holding back of theory" lends the material "a deceptively epic character on the one hand and, on the other, deprives the phenomena of their real philosophical-historical weight, since they are experienced merely subjectively." The suppression of theoretical formulation here results in a "wide-eyed presentation of mere facticity," an impenetrable layering of material "consumed in its own aura." In other words, Benjamin's study must be seen as lacking in sobriety, as indeed hexed, being located "at the crossroads of magic and positivism." Adorno reminds Benjamin, as he did in the Hornberg letter of 1935, of something Benjamin said during the memorable conversations at Königstein in 1929—namely, that every idea in the arcades project had to be wrested from a realm of madness—for there is something almost demonic, he charges, in the way the isolated contents of Benjamin's new essay conspire against the possibility of their own interpretation.

Adorno's critique was undoubtedly fueled by his suspicions that Brecht had exerted a malign influence on the essay. In pointing to the apparently unmediated juxtaposition of elements of the economic base (ragpickers) and corresponding elements of the superstructure (Baudelaire's poems), Adorno implicitly portrayed the entire essay as an exercise in the kind of vulgar Marxism the institute thought characteristic of Brecht's production. But a good deal more was at stake. In general, Adorno's critique represents not so much an immanent criticism of the essay as an expression of his antipathy to the unique allegorical materialism informing it. Benjamin was intent on working out a method of historical encapsulation through typifying images in shifting constellations, and he was convinced that the knowledge to which this motivic method gave access, knowledge of present and past in light of each other, could not be recuperated through any amount of abstract theorizing. Writing from the secure vantage of New York

City, where he now belonged to the inner circle of the institute, Adorno felt justified in rejecting not just a specific essay but a consummate expression of Benjamin's mature literary criticism. The reversal in their positions was complete. Not long before, Adorno had been Benjamin's disciple, composing a series of essays, plus a book on Kierkegaard, that were deeply indebted to Benjamin's work; delivering his inaugural lecture in Frankfurt as an homage; and teaching his first seminar on the *Trauerspiel* book. Now, aware that Benjamin was wholly dependent on the institute for his livelihood, he felt he could dictate not just the choice of subject matter but the intellectual tenor of Benjamin's work. And so, protesting that "this study does not represent you," he calmly and firmly pressured Benjamin—"this is a request on my part and does not represent an editorial decision or rejection"—to produce writing that would in fact approximate his own, with its often tenuous relationship to the material at hand and its remarkable, and remarkably abstract, systematically dialectical constructions. Adorno's material and moral support for Benjamin in these years was ongoing, but their intellectual exchange never fully recovered from this disagreement over Baudelaire.

It is hardly surprising that it took Benjamin almost a month to answer. Adorno's letter plunged him into a deep, immobilizing depression—it seems he barely stirred from his apartment for weeks—and he didn't really recover his balance until the spring of 1939. As he would later explain to Scholem, his near-total isolation made him morbidly sensitive to the reception of his work, and its outright rejection by his ostensible friends and allies was more than he could bear. In a letter dated December 9, Benjamin answered, point by point, Adorno's criticisms, but his main goal was to save the *structure* of the Baudelaire book, as he currently envisioned it, from Adorno's pressure to return to an earlier conception of the arcades project.

> If . . . I refused, in the name of my own productive interests, to develop my ideas in an esoteric direction and, in pursuit of other matters, to bypass the interests of dialectical materialism and of the institute, that was not just out of solidarity with the institute or loyalty to dialectical materialism but also out of solidarity with the experiences we have all shared over the past fifteen years. My deepest productive interests are also at stake here; I will not deny that

they may occasionally do violence to my original interests. An antagonism between them does exist. Overcoming this antagonism constitutes the problem of this work, and it is a problem of construction. (BA, 291)

Far from the abrupt and crudely subjective presentation of mere facticity that Adorno saw in the Paris essay, Benjamin's highly compressed mode of construction aimed at constituting the historical object, in the eyes of the present, as a monad. From the perspective of the book's overall structure, the essay submitted for publication had to be seen as consisting "primarily of philological material," while the projected first and third parts would furnish the theory demanded by Adorno. "The base lines of this construction converge in our own historical experience. In this way the object constitutes itself as a monad. And in the monad everything that formerly lay mythically petrified within the given text comes alive."

Benjamin concluded with a plea that "this text, which is indeed the product of a creative effort that is incomparable with that involved in any of my earlier literary efforts," somehow be published, if only to open the discussion to a wider audience. If he had no confidence in the judgment of his colleagues in New York, he did have a stubborn faith that history would gauge his work aright, if only it could see the light of day. Sensing in advance that his arguments would have little effect, he offered a final, desperate concession. He suggested that he revise the middle section of "The Paris of the Second Empire in Baudelaire"—the section "The Flâneur"—as an independent essay. Out of this maneuver would eventually emerge the bold theoretical initiative "On Some Motifs in Baudelaire," which was published in the *Zeitschrift.* Adorno, in this case, knew how to get what he wanted.

On January 5 Benjamin learned that the few things of value he had left behind at his home in Berlin—a large secretary, a rug, and, most important of all, a manuscript case and shelves full of books—would have to be moved, since his tenant, Werner von Schoeller, was leaving the apartment. Benjamin's friend Käthe Krauß saw to the sale of the secretary and rug, which paid his debt to his landlord; she agreed also to take care of the books and manuscript case. Neither the books nor the manuscript case—to say nothing of the latter's possible contents—was ever heard of again. On February 14 this material loss was succeeded by a more harrowing dispossession. Following on their discovery of an article—Benjamin's first "Letter from Paris"—published in 1936 under his own name in the Moscow journal *Das Wort*, the Gestapo initiated a procedure leading to the revocation of Benjamin's German citizenship. The decision on his expatriation was communicated to the German embassy in Paris in a letter dated May 26. He was henceforth stateless.

Venues for his work continued to shrink. Scholem reported that the German government had finally shut down Schocken Verlag (he also passed along the unexpected news that copies of Benjamin's dissertation, "The Concept of Criticism in German Romanticism," were still available, if only from the janitor who oversaw the cellars of the university in Bern). Benjamin nonetheless held out hope that Scholem could interest Schocken in publishing a book-length study of Kafka; he thus wrote a rather impatient letter to Scholem in late February, asking why he had not yet shown Schocken the letter on Kafka—with its demolition of Max Brod's biography—from the previous summer. Scholem replied that he had been anything but indolent in this regard. It turned out that Schocken had never read Brod and had no intention of doing so—or of publishing Benjamin's book, thus putting to rest yet another publishing prospect. In late January Benjamin's loyal Weimar publisher Ernst Rowohlt came through Paris after a rather hurried exit from Germany. Rowohlt had seen forty-six of the books on his list banned and burned in 1933, yet he had kept Jewish employees on his payroll as long as he could. Franz Hessel, in fact, served as one of the two main editors until 1938. Following the publication of the book *Adalbert Stifter* by Urban Roedl (the nom de plume of Bruno Adler), the German government forbade Rowohlt to work as a publisher because of his pseudonymous publication of the works of Jewish authors. Rowohlt joined the Nazi Party in 1937, but even this step failed to provide the security he sought for his family, and he was traveling through Paris on his way to Brazil in order to settle his wife and children there. Because of his support for Jewish authors and his loyalty to Hessel, Benjamin claimed that Rowohlt "can do no wrong in my book" (BS, 242).

Rowohlt was not the only acquaintance to have fled Germany so late. The Austrian writer and journalist Alfred Polgar, whom Benjamin knew from his Berlin days, arrived in Paris in late 1938; he had returned to Vienna from Berlin in 1933, and, after the Anschluß, sought a new home in Paris. Benjamin's old friend Wilhelm Speyer was on the run as well; he, too, had immigrated to Austria in 1933, and then to Paris in 1938. And Karl Thieme had felt compelled to leave even the seemingly safe haven of Switzerland. As part of the vocal Catholic opposition in Germany, he had emigrated in 1933, but now feared that the buildup of German troops at the Swiss border pointed to an imminent invasion. In better days, these refugees would have constituted welcome additions to Benjamin's circle of acquaintances in Paris; now they were primarily an occasion for more tales of misery. It seems that Benjamin avoided even his closest friends in January and February 1939; there is no evidence of meetings with Helen Hessel, Hannah Arendt, Germaine Krull, Adrienne Monnier, or Kracauer. And if he was reading anything, even mystery novels, there is no record of it—either in letters or in the list "Works Read in Their Entirety."

Despite his persistent depression, Benjamin struggled to resume work on the revision of the Baudelaire materials, a project from which he now felt "alienated" (BS, 240). Yet he could hardly afford to reveal that alienation to his colleagues in New York. In the course of the spring he allowed himself only the very occasional, subtle jab. He began one letter to Adorno with the phrase "either one is a philologist or one is not," and he reported progress to Horkheimer on his ability to integrate into his essay the "mediation" required by the institute—with the term "mediation" in quotation marks. In February he put aside the set of notes, reflections, and excerpts constituting "Central Park," which he had begun composing in April of the previous year, concurrently with "The Paris of the Second Empire in Baudelaire," and turned in earnest to a thoroughgoing revision of the Baudelaire materials, one that would satisfy the New York censors. He read the liberal economist and Physiocrat Anne-Robert Turgot and the nineteenth-century Leibnizian philosopher Hermann Lotze (both cited at length in *The Arcades Project*), as he thought about the concept of progress in relation to epistemology. He decided this work would be a continuation of historiographical ideas expounded in the essay on Eduard Fuchs. "The destruction of the idea of a continuum of culture, a destruction postulated in the essay on Fuchs," he wrote to Hork-heimer, "must be shown to have epistemological consequences, among which one of the most important is the determination of the limits that are set to the use of the concept of progress in history" (GB, 6:198). As he considered the materialist bases of his undertaking, he turned to Georg Simmel's *Philosophie des Geldes* (Philosophy of Money). Adorno had sharply criticized a quotation from Benjamin's old teacher in "The Paris of the Second Empire in Baudelaire." Benja-min now rose to Simmel's defense, asking whether "it is not time he was recognized as one of the forefathers of cultural bolshevism" and suggesting that there was much of interest in his philosophy of money, "as long as one is prepared to ignore the basic idea behind it" (BA, 311).

On February 1 Adorno sent what can only be characterized as an astonishingly intrusive letter agreeing to the publication of a revised version of "The Flâneur," the middle section of "The Paris of the Sec-ond Empire in Baudelaire." "Perhaps it would be advisable," he wrote, "if I make a number of further remarks on details of your text that could show what sort of alterations I had in mind" (BA, 300). He then in effect dictated long lists of major and minor changes to the text; the letter makes clear, despite the familiar tone of philosophical friend-ship, that these were not suggestions but *preconditions* with which Benjamin must comply if he wanted to see his work published in the *Zeitschrift*. Benjamin's reply, dated February 23, expressed gratitude for the "suggestive" remarks but took issue with Adorno on several matters, including the presentation of Baudelaire within a series of analogous types, the issue of fetishism, and the concept of phantas-magoria. Adorno continued to accuse Benjamin of subjectifying what Adorno insisted was the objective character of phantasmagoria. Benja-min's response on this point is telling:

> The selfsame [*Gleichheit*] is a category of cognition; strictly speak-ing, it has no place in soberly straightforward perception. Perception that is straightforward in the strictest sense of the word, free of all pre-judgment, could only ever encounter the "similar," even in the most extreme case. However, the kind of pre-judgment that as a rule innocuously accompanies our perception can become provocative in exceptional cases. It can openly reveal the percipient as one who is *not* so sober after all. This is the case with Don Quixote, for exam-

ple, when the chivalric romances have gone to his head. However various the situations which he encounters, he invariably perceives the same thing in all of them—namely, the adventure that is simply waiting for the knight-errant to come along. (BA, 309)

Rather than accede to Adorno's objection, Benjamin shifts the ground from the issue of subjectivity to that of perception and experience. Once there, he can return to the safe ground of economic theory.

> Equality makes a quite different appearance in Poe, not to mention in Baudelaire. But while the possibility of a kind of comic exorcism still flashes up in "The Man of the Crowd," there is nothing of the sort in Baudelaire. He artificially came to the aid of the historical hallucination of equality which had insinuated itself along with a commodity economy. . . . The commodity economy arms that phantasmagoria of sameness which simultaneously reveals itself, as an attribute of intoxication, to be the central image of illusion. . . . The price makes the commodity equal and identical to all those other commodities which could be purchased for the same price. The commodity . . . insinuates itself, not only and not merely with the buyer, but above all with its own price. And it is precisely in this respect that the flâneur accommodates himself to the commodity; he imitates it utterly; and since there is no economic demand, and therefore no market price, for him, he makes himself thoroughly at home in the world of saleable objects. (BA, 310)

But this strategy was an exception. In general, Benjamin was forced to accede to Adorno's demands. Yet he passed in silence over the question of the essay's methodology and structure. Still believing that he was working on the central section of a book-length study, he asserted in a letter to Scholem that the "key positions" of the Baudelaire project, which do not figure in the central section, remained untouched by the interference from New York (BS, 241).

He also carried on with his work on other projects. Early in the year he delivered extensive reviews of three books (by Dolf Sternberger, Richard Hönigswald, and Louis Dimier) to the *Zeitschrift für Sozialforschung*. He also wrote and submitted a substantial review of two volumes of the *Encyclopedia française* that had been published recently; this review was never published. As always, he was reading and thinking about Kafka. He sent Scholem a brief but rich series of observations: for Benjamin in 1939, the essential thing in Kafka was humor, though Kafka was clearly no ordinary humorist. "He was, rather, a man destined everywhere to run into people who made humor their profession: clowns. *Amerika [Der Verschollene]* in particular is one big clown act. And as for the friendship with Brod, . . . Kafka as Laurel felt the onerous obligation to seek out his Hardy—and that was Brod." Thus, "the key to Kafka" would belong to whoever could *"extract from Jewish theology its comic side* [komischen Seiten]" (BS, 243). He also made progress with a series of texts concerning Brecht. These included the brief "Note on Brecht," which nonetheless constitutes a significant essay on the writer, and the lengthy "Commentary on Poems by Brecht," to which he attached great importance. He made a number of attempts to find a publisher for this essay, enlisting friends in several countries in the effort, but it would remain unpublished during his lifetime—and would be one of the texts he entrusted to Georges Bataille's safekeeping before fleeing Paris in June 1940. His allegiance to Brecht remained unshakable, even as his opposition to the Soviet Union and its leadership of the left became entrenched.

On January 24 he sent the second of his long reports on French letters to Horkheimer. Although they remained unpublished, these reports were eagerly awaited in New York, and not only by the institute's research staff: Horkheimer informed Benjamin that they were being circulated among the Columbia University faculty. This second report is unusually critical. Alluding to the legacy of Apollinaire and of Surrealism, he opens with the remark that "the contemporary process of decomposition in French literature has weakened even those seeds that seemed to contain the potential for long-term development" (GB, 6:201). His most extensive commentary is reserved for *La Conspiration* (The Conspiracy), by Paul Nizan, an editor of the socialist daily *L'humanité*. Looking back at the formation and development of the Popular Front, this well-received work—at once political novel and novel of education—expresses Nizan's disillusionment with socialism. Benjamin calls the book an *"éducation sentimentale* of the Class of 1909" (GB, 6:198). He recommends Raymond Queneau's *Enfants du limon* (Children of Clay) with moderate enthusiasm; he faults

Queneau, the former Surrealist, for a certain timidity in taking up the legacy of Apollinaire. In commenting on a special issue of the *Nouvelle Revue Française* that dealt with the Collège de Sociologie and contained articles by Bataille, Caillois, and Michel Leiris, he singles out Caillois's contribution, "Le vent d'hiver" (The Wind of Winter) for particular scorn. He is surprisingly ambivalent regarding an article on anti-Semitism published by his close friend Adrienne Monnier in the *Gazette des Amis du Livre*; he finds that she is too cautious and too willing to compromise, perhaps out of solicitude for her own wealthy clientele. "The enfeebled moral consciousness of humanity needs nourishment above all—not doctoring" (GB, 6:203). He concludes with an extended summary, including quotations and ironic commentary, on Paul Claudel's last publication, a Catholic allegory of precious stones, issued as an exquisitely produced brochure available only at fashionable jewelry shops. A "new Beatitude," Benjamin calls it, whose innermost tendency may be "to establish the truly mystical congruence of social and theological registers" (GB, 6:208).

Early March brought a severe blow to Benjamin's waning confidence and resolve. Horkheimer had written, apologetically, with bleak news on the financial state of the Institute of Social Research; he told Benjamin that the institute would, in all likelihood, be forced to cancel his stipend in the near future. Benjamin replied on March 13, saying he had read the letter "with horror." He of course wished all the best for the institute's staff, but hinted that Horkheimer might not understand the difference between a reduction in stipend for the New York colleagues and its cessation for him in Paris: "We are all isolated individuals. And for the isolated individual the perspective opened by your letter, with its terrifying earnestness, overshadows all other plans" (GB, 6:231). Although it might have appeared that Horkheimer was preparing the way for a severing of the institute's ties to Benjamin, he at the same time vowed to increase his efforts to find a sponsor for Benjamin's work on the Paris arcades. At Horkheimer's behest, Benjamin sent off a revised version of the 1935 exposé of the project, hoping to aid Horkheimer in his search; a possible backer had appeared in the person of a New York banker named Frank Altschul. Besides dropping much factual material, the 1939 exposé, written in French, thoroughly recasts the section on Baudelaire—reflecting the current stage of the ongoing rewrite of the Baudelaire essay—as well as the sections on Fourier and Louis-Philippe, and adds a theoretical intro- duction and conclusion. "On the whole, this draft differs from the one you already know in that the confrontation of semblance and reality has become the primary focus right down the line. The succession of phantasmagorias that are indicated in the individual sections leads at the end to the great phantasmagoria of the universe in Blanqui" (GB, 6:233). And he began to cast about—though conscious of the futility of the enterprise—for sources of support in France. He explained his situ- ation to Gretel Adorno a few days later: "I have been following things here for long enough to know that, since the start of the emigration, no one who is working in a similar fashion and under similar condi- tions to my own has succeeded in making a living in France" (BG, 251). Even the people to whom he had frequently turned for emergency help were disappearing: Lévy-Bruhl lay dying, Sigmund Morgenroth was in America, and his letters to Elsa Herzberger had gone unan- swered since her return to America.

A letter to Scholem betrays his frustration with the situation in New York—along with a certain distrust of Adorno and Horkheimer: "As their letter indicates, these people had not been living on interest, as one would assume in the case of a foundation, but on the capital. The major portion of this is said to be still in existence but frozen, and the rest is supposed to be about to dry up" (BS, 248). A few weeks later he drew up a more considered, though no less pessimistic, assessment of his relationship to the institute:

> The same conditions that threaten my European situation will in all likelihood make emigration to the U.S.A. impossible. Such a move is only possible on the basis of an invitation, and an invitation could only come about at the instigation of the Institute. . . . I don't think it very likely that the Institute, even if it had the power to do so, would want to arrange my invitation at this time. For there is no reason to assume that such an invitation would solve the problem of my livelihood, and the Institute, I suspect, would find the immedi- ate linkage of these problems especially irritating. (BS, 251)

Yet some sort of immigration to America, or at least a visit to survey possible long-term sources of support, now seemed his only real hope.

He admitted to Margarete Steffin that his thoughts were turning westward, yet "to date I've only advanced as far as a few small Mexican images that are displayed in a nice half-surrealist exhibition here" (GB, 6:244). His reading began to orient itself increasingly to the New World. He met several times with the great translator Pierre Leyris, whom he knew through Klossowski, to discuss American literature, and especially Melville; he mentioned that he was particularly interested in Melville's representation of the physiognomy of New York in his novel *Pierre, or the Ambiguities.* By mid-April, he was pressing Horkheimer more directly for assistance in a move to New York, and he made a concerted effort to enlist Sigmund Morgenroth as his ally in this endeavor. He provided Morgenroth with two documents, one a brief introduction to the history and aims of the institute itself, the other a frank appraisal of his own current relationship to its directors. "Until now I've displayed no inordinate enthusiasm for going to America; it would be good if the directors of the Institute know for certain that a sea change has occurred in this regard. The growing danger of war and the increasing anti-Semitism are the reasons for this change" (GB, 6:258–259). We do not know exactly what role Adorno played in the institute's deliberations on Benjamin's fate. While there can be no question of his continued backing for the provision of Benjamin's stipend, it is conceivable that he remained ambivalent toward efforts to bring his philosophical friend to America. Given various indications that he was jealously aware of his wife's affection for Benjamin (the delay in revealing the news of the Adornos' wedding to Benjamin is one such indication), it is not at all clear that Adorno would have been happy with a situation in which all three of them lived in the same city. There may have been operating here something like unconscious betrayal.

Even as he looked for a chance to move to America, Benjamin once again sounded out Scholem on the question of immigration to Palestine, but, as Scholem immediately told him, he had waited too long. His "catastrophe at the Institute" coincided with "another one here." The situation was too unstable, and too many Jews were already flowing in from Austria and Czechoslovakia; tourist visas had been cut off, and there was simply no visible source of support for one more writer and intellectual (BS, 250). He had told Scholem that he could live under halfway human conditions if he were to receive the equivalent of 2,400 francs per month. "To sink below this level again would be hard for me to bear *à la longue*. For this, the charms of the world around me are too weak, and the rewards of posterity too uncertain" (BS, 248–249). With truly Benjaminian timing, a letter arrived from Scholem as he was about to seal his own; it brought news of Schocken's final rejection of his book prospectus. Schocken had celebrated the publication of a new edition of Karl Kraus's drama *Die letzten Tage der Menschheit* (The Last Days of Mankind) with a public reading and talks by Scholem and by Benjamin's former friend Werner Kraft. Scholem had filled his allotted time by reading from Benjamin's essay "Karl Kraus," which moved everyone in the room—except Schocken, who was mystified.

Hannah Arendt also sought help for her friend; her efforts were driven by special appreciation for his latest ideas. In a letter to Scholem in late May she wrote: "I am very worried about Benji. I tried to procure something for him here and failed miserably. Yet I am more than ever convinced of the importance of securing him a living for his further work. To my mind, his production has changed, right down to the stylistic details. Everything comes out much more definitely, much less hesitantly. It often seems to me that he is only now getting to the things that are decisive for him. It would be horrible if he were impeded in this."[21] (It is worth noting that the regard was mutual: Benjamin sent the manuscript of Arendt's study of Rahel Varnhagen to Scholem with an emphatic recommendation, noting that it "swims with powerful strokes against the current of edifying and apologetic Judaic studies" [BS, 244]). Genuinely moved by the support of his friends, Benjamin wrote to Gretel Adorno that "Europe is a continent in whose tear-laden atmosphere the signal flares of comfort now ascend only rarely to announce good fortune." He noted drily that "even the poorest devils" were doing what they could to get to the New World (BG, 254). Or, if not there, to a safer ground. He learned that the Brechts had closed their house in Skovsbostrand during the first days of March and moved to Stockholm. The news brought "melancholy reveries," as one more apparently safe haven was taken from him: "the chess games in the garden are now a thing of the past" (GB, 6:267).

By late February Benjamin was making somewhat tentative sorties out from the Rue Dombasle. He attended a concert by the Kolisch Quartet; he knew Rudolf Kolisch slightly through Adorno. And he began to see his friends once again, meeting Germaine Krull on her return to France from England and holding regular discussion evenings with Arendt, her companion Heinrich Blücher, and their mutual friend Fritz Fränkel. Despite these contacts, Benjamin frequently lamented his intellectual isolation. "How much it would mean to me to speak about it with you," he wrote to Gretel Adorno in early April, "or even any reasonable creature at all. . . . My current isolation harmonizes all too well with the current trend, which goes against everything that is ours. It is not purely intellectual in nature" (BG, 254). Friends and acquaintances continued to visit him, but their visits were brief, their destinations elsewhere. Two of his friends from the Brecht circle, the filmmaker Slatan Dudow and the novelist Bernard von Brentano, were in Paris, Brentano to be feted by his French publisher, Grasset, on the occasion of the appearance of his novel *Theodor Chindler* in French translation. Benjamin had never felt drawn to Brentano, and had in fact been harshly critical of some of his work. Like many left intellectuals of the day—Willi Münzenberg had recently published an open letter announcing his resignation from the Communist Party—Brentano was deeply embittered by what he saw as the Soviet Union's betrayal of socialism. Together with Ignazio Silone, Brentano had formed a kind of post-Dada, anti-Soviet avant-garde in Zürich. "I find it difficult to imagine how a political grudge such as Brentano's could be the daily bread of an author who is, after all, as significant as Silone. The notion that it is 'ten times worse' in Russia than in Germany is, Brentano would have us believe, the leitmotif of that Zurich avant-garde" (BG, 255).

In the late spring Benjamin was plagued by a persistent flu that confined him to his bed for several weeks. The pattern of his illnesses suggests, already in early 1939, that the strains and privations of exile were finally taking a toll on his health. The Benjamin who was laid so low by the flu was no longer the man who only a year before had delighted in walks into the mountains around San Remo. When he was able, he worked to revise his Baudelaire essay, however distasteful that work had become. He confided to Scholem on April 8, "You can surely understand that I have difficulty applying myself to projects oriented toward the Institute at the moment. If you add to this the fact that making revisions is less attractive than new endeavors anyway, you will understand that reformulating the flâneur chapter is making rather sluggish headway" (BS, 252). Despite external and internal resistance, he began to rethink the problem of Baudelaire's relationship to the flâneur under a new rubric: idleness. The flâneur would now appear "in the context of an investigation of the specific features acquired by idleness in the bourgeois age, amid the prevailing work ethic"—idleness as distinguished, that is, from the concept of leisure in the feudal age (BG, 254). He declared to Horkheimer in April that Baudelaire "embodies the trinity representative of idleness . . . : the flâneur, the gambler, and the student" (GB, 6:264). At about this time, Benjamin began a new convolute of arcades materials, a folder labeled "Idleness." Other things, too, indicate that the arcades project, with its theme of the fate of art in the nineteenth century, was on Benjamin's mind as he revised the Baudelaire. He sent a copy of the second, German version of the artwork essay to Gretel Adorno in early April so that she could make a typescript for reproduction and dissemination; he told her that this version had been expanded on the basis of a number of recent reflections. Although a folder with reflections related to the artwork essay was discovered at the Bibliothèque Nationale in 1981—presumably part of the material that Georges Bataille hid there after Benjamin's flight from Paris in 1940—the version sent to Gretel Adorno in April 1939 has not survived.

In late April a bit of sunlight broke through Benjamin's personal clouds for the first time in months. He learned that he had been awarded a grant from the Caisse des Recherches Scientifiques to spend a few weeks at the Foyer International d'Etude et Repos, a library and study center housed in the restored Abbaye de Pontigny, near the town of Auxerre, southeast of Paris; the center was run by the writer Paul Desjardins and his wife. Benjamin hoped to take advantage of the magnificent library, which held some 15,000 volumes, to advance the Baudelaire. The possibility of forging new links to the French intellectual scene was an added benefit. And, finally, the financial succor afforded by the visit—room and board were included in the invitation—played no small role. Arriving at the abbey in early May, he was encouraged by the "charming site" and the "magnificent complex" of ancient monastic buildings (GB, 6:276). Yet appearances proved deceptive. "Even though he walks only with difficulty, Desjardins came to meet me at the train; he makes, from the very first, the impression of a wholly broken man." Desjardins had overseen the complex with the help of an elderly English lady friend for decades, while living apart from his wife. His wife had returned two years before Benjamin's arrival and, according to him, had so wholly altered the intellectual layout as to "leave no stone unturned" (GB, 6:280). Benjamin remarked uncharitably on what he perceived as the role played by the wife in the decline of the proprietor: "There are moments when the husband's situation in these cases irresistibly reminds me of my own in San Remo" (BG, 259–260). The apparently idyllic setting thus soon turned to torture. Benjamin was plagued by his acute sensitivity to noise: his hope that work and recovery would be "one and the same" was disappointed by a visiting group of boisterous young people from Scandinavia who partook of daily instruction in the library, rendering it unusable for study. Instead of an intellectual community, he found only further isolation. He listened to a guest lecture by Emilie Lefranc, an official in a socialist educational organization, and commented that he hadn't previously recognized the extent to which vulgar Marxism could serve purely counterrevolutionary ends. (He himself spoke about his work on Baudelaire, apparently before a small audience.) Even his hope of forging new bonds to French writers was frustrated; he couldn't broach the subject with Desjardins, since a conversation of more than a few moments proved impossible with the aging *spiritus rector.*

Against the general clamor of disappointment and disparagement, Benjamin did find a few things worth his time at Pontigny. Among his discoveries in the library were the *Pensées* of Joseph Joubert (1754–1824), "the last of the great French moralists." Excerpts from this text play a key role in several sections of *The Arcades Project,* and Benjamin proclaimed that in matters of style the frank and subtle Joubert would henceforth play a definitive role "in everything I write" (BG, 260).[22] Finding himself barred from the library for hours at a time, he indulged in leisure reading. One particular book occasioned an observation on "the significant fact that the nineteenth century is the classic period of ghost stories": Henry James's "remarkable" novella *The Turn of the Screw*, in French translation. Gisèle Freund visited Benjamin in Pontigny and took one of the best-known photographs of her friend: she captured him standing pensively by its pond.

In late May Benjamin returned to a Paris rife with rumors of war and the coming internment of foreign nationals. The mood in the country was such that the French government saw itself compelled on April 21 to issue a *décret-loi* barring anti-Semitic propaganda. Benjamin's mood can be read pretty clearly from a number of passages in his letters. He comments with obsessive fascination on the deaths of the authors Joseph Roth and Ernst Toller. Toller, who had lived in the United States since 1934, had hanged himself in his room in the Mayflower Hotel in New York. Roth, who had lived a life parallel to Benjamin's in Paris, had long struggled with alcoholism. He died of a lung infection undoubtedly exacerbated by the effects of an abrupt detoxification. Benjamin passes along a morbid anecdote to a number of his correspondents: "Karl Kraus died too soon after all. Listen to this: the Vienna gas board has stopped supplying gas to Jews. A consequence of the gas consumption of the Jewish population was that the gas company lost money, since it was precisely the biggest users who did not pay their bills. The Jews preferred to use the gas to commit suicide" (C, 609).

Benjamin's financial situation, even after his stay as a guest at Pontigny, had grown more desperate. He wrote to friends asking for small amounts of money (and for tobacco), and he took the painful step of asking Stefan Lackner to pursue the sale in America of his most cherished possession, Paul Klee's aquarelle "Angelus Novus." In this state of mind, he pushed harder than ever for a move to New York. In early June he learned that, with the right invitation, he could get a tourist visa for America. Horkheimer responded very positively to this news and began to talk about specifics: "several" weeks of food and lodging and part of the travel expenses, namely the difference between what money Benjamin himself could raise, including proceeds from the sale of the Klee, and the actual cost of the ticket. The summer saw repeated approaches to his friends and supporters—to both Lackner and his father, to Wissing, and to Bryher—in an effort to raise the cost of his passage.

35. Benjamin at the Abbey of Pontigny, 1938. Photo by Gisèle Freund (1912–2000)
(© Gisèle Freund-RMN. © RMN-Grand Palais/Art Resource, NY)

The breadth and depth of Benjamin's reading remained unaffected by the political turmoil around him. He reported to Scholem, with some amusement, that he was acquiring new reading material from the widow of the Russian writer Lev Shestov, who lived in his building surrounded by uncut copies of her husband's collected works; as she made room for herself by discarding volumes, Benjamin added to his library. He was also reading the French novelist Jean Giono and the German novelist Elisabeth Langgässer—both of whom came in for acerbic commentary. More central to his interests were works by two friends and colleagues. Karl Thieme had published a well-received book dealing with Christian eschatology. Benjamin was fascinated by the "urbanity" with which Thieme could treat the concept of last days while balancing his theological and political interests. He says that such urbanity "is perhaps only the other side of courage," and he calls Thieme's eschatological speculations "genuine theology, something one rarely encounters anymore nowadays" (C, 605–606). Even more profitable to him was his reading of Karl Korsch's *Karl Marx*. This "riveting" book was in many ways Benjamin's most extensive encounter with Marx's own ideas; Korsch is cited in *The Arcades Project* more frequently than Marx himself. Much of his reading simply kept him afloat on the alien sea of French letters: Léon-Paul Fargue's *Piéton de Paris*, Maurice Sachs's *Souvenirs du boeuf sur le toit*, Georges Simenon's *La Marie du port*, Sartre's *Le mur*, and Valéry's "Pièces sur l'art." In addition to books there were movies, although we know relatively little about Benjamin's visits to the cinema other than that they were frequent. He did comment on Frank Capra's Oscar-winning 1938 film *You Can't Take It with You*. It struck him as not only meretricious but implicitly reactionary, prompting him to revise Lenin: it is not religion that is the opiate of the masses but "a certain kind of harmlessness—a narcotic in which the 'education of the heart' and 'tomfoolery' are the most important ingredients" (GB, 6:304–305). He saw the movie as evidence of the film industry's complicity with fascism, "even over there" (that is, in the United States).

During the late spring and early summer, he found comfort in frequent visits with friends, and especially with his former companion in libertinage, Franz Hessel, and Hessel's wife, Helen, one of Benjamin's staunchest allies in his last years. She worked tirelessly to help him in various ways, securing a number of invitations for weekends and meals among her friends. He was also meeting regularly with Pierre Missac at another of the Montparnasse venues, the Café de Versailles. His encounters with German acquaintances, even those with whom he had had differences in the past, took on a new tone in these darkening days. The writer Alfred Döblin, whose rather misty left-liberal views were once the target of his wrath, had come to be regarded more sympathetically. On June 23, in an address at the Cercle des Nations, Döblin remarked on the "incomprehensible" assimilation of many bourgeois Jews to Hitler's side. Benjamin's only reservation concerned Döblin's attitude to America: "Based on a stay of a few minutes in Roosevelt's study, and moreover without any knowledge of English, [Döblin] painted the future of America, as the apotheosis of freedom, against a rosy background. Europe is now supposed to look up to its big brother with complete confidence" (GB, 6:305). And Ferdinand Lion from *Maß und Wert* was in town; Benjamin had several amicable meetings with him where they discussed, among other things, the possibility of a book on Brecht by Karl Thieme.

Despite the advent of better weather and somewhat improved spirits, the Baudelaire material yielded only grudgingly to Benjamin's efforts to shape it. He attempted to work at a table on his balcony, so as to escape the din of the elevator in his building, but found that a "good-for-nothing" painter on a balcony opposite—"and God knows the street is narrow enough"—whistled to himself the whole day long. He tried stopping his ears with "wagon-loads" of wax, paraffin, and even concrete, to no avail (C, 608). As he often did when a deadline pressed, he took up an apparently marginal project. As a tribute to the 150th anniversary of the French Revolution, he put together a montage of letters by "Germans of 1789," expressing their reactions to the events in France. Modeled on his 1936 compilation *Deutsche Menschen*, "Allemands de quatre-vingt-neuf" brought him considerable pleasure, along with the discovery that the second volume of odes by the great German poet Friedrich Klopstock contained numerous poems about the revolution, a fact that German literary history had "systematically veiled" (C, 608). During composition of the text, he began working with a new translator, Marcel Stora, for whom he was full of praise. The piece appeared on his forty-seventh birthday, July 15, 1939, in

Stora's translation, in a special number of the journal *Europe* dedicated to the 150th anniversary of the revolution.

It was not until June 24 that he could report some progress on the Baudelaire; he sent Horkheimer an abstract of the new essay, an elaboration of the notes used for his talk at Pontigny. Benjamin reported that for the Baudelaire talk he employed a highly concentrated, almost "shorthand" delivery, and had managed to "galvanize for an instant even the broken Desjardins" (GB, 6:303). The abstract provides our first view of the article that was finally to result. It is clear from a number of remarks at this period that he saw the new Baudelaire essay as a kind of reentry visa to the Institute of Social Research. He was quick to assure his colleagues and friends in New York that the revision grew out of previously published work, particularly the essays on the technologically reproducible work of art and on the storyteller, and much less out of "The Paris of the Second Empire in Baudelaire." Emphasizing just this continuity between the new version and his "acceptable" works, including the arcades project, he gamely tells Gretel Adorno that "never before have I been so certain of the point at which all my reflections, even from the most differing perspectives, converge (and it now seems to me that they have always done so)" (BG, 262). At this late stage of the game, he could not risk telling Gretel all that he really felt about the assignment.

In late June Benjamin locked himself away in the Rue Dombasle, forgoing not just meetings with friends but all correspondence. His resolve was bolstered by a telegram from Horkheimer on July 11 offering him up to fifty pages in the next issue of the *Zeitschrift* if he could deliver the essay by the end of the month. In a bit less than six weeks, Benjamin completed the second Baudelaire essay—newly titled "On Some Motifs in Baudelaire"—and mailed it to Horkheimer on August 1. For Teddie and Gretel Adorno he playfully and triumphantly sketched a little allegory to frame the essay a week after it was sent off: "I'm allowing my Christian Baudelaire to be carried into heaven by nothing but Jewish angels. But arrangements have already been made so that, in the last third of the ascension, shortly before the entrance into glory, they will let him fall—as if by accident" (C, 612).

"On Some Motifs in Baudelaire" takes up many of the problems— and solutions—evident in "The Paris of the Second Empire in Baudelaire," although within a different context.[23] Whereas the earlier piece was a general consideration of Baudelaire's place in his era, the later essay examines Baudelaire's work from the perspective of its reception in the twentieth century. "If conditions for a positive reception of lyric poetry have become less favorable, it is reasonable to assume that only in rare instances does lyric poetry accord with the experience of its readers. This may be due to a change in the structure of their experience." Benjamin goes on to speculate about the nature of this change; he discriminates—in a formulation now given wide currency—between long experience *(Erfahrung)* and isolated experience *(Erlebnis)*. Long experience is understood as an accumulated body of knowledge, a seasoned wisdom not only retainable in human memory but transmissible from generation to generation; this is a notion first prominently aired in "The Storyteller," with its rather nostalgic assumption of a living tradition informing a precapitalist artisanal community and the "counsel" it passes on through stories. Isolated experience, on the other hand, emerges in "On Some Motifs in Baudelaire" as a form of immediate experience bound to the shocks encountered by individuals among the urban masses; far from being retainable or transmissible, isolated experience is usually parried by consciousness in such a way as to leave a trace in the unconscious. Of particular interest to Benjamin, though, is the case in which this defensive mechanism fails or is suspended—that is, when the shock is *not* parried by consciousness, but instead penetrates and deforms it. Such undeflected shocks give rise, as Benjamin sees it, to the characteristic images of Baudelaire's poetry.

The middle sections of "On Some Motifs in Baudelaire" turn to the social form in which urban shock experience *(Chockerlebnis)* is most prevalent: the crowd. Benjamin here elaborates his earlier analysis of "A une passante" and adds to it a brilliant reading contrasting Baudelaire's elemental social realism with the "distorting imagination" of Poe's story "The Man of the Crowd" (which Baudelaire translated). Drawing on the theory of estrangement advanced in the "Work of Art" essay, he argues that the isolation of the individual—the bourgeois retreat from the urban masses into domestic privacy and comfort—"brings those enjoying it closer to mechanization." The looming chaos of the streets, with hurtling cars and jostling pedestrians, is controlled technologically by advances as simple as traffic signals. Technology constitutes not just a prosthetic extension of the human sensory capacity, enabling a complex series of adaptations, but a veritable training school for the human sensorium that enables it to function in a world of "traffic."[24]

Benjamin delineates in Baudelaire's poetry a paradoxical capacity. Its imagery is engendered, on the one hand, by Baudelaire's creative submission to the variable shock experience of modern life—an attitude on his part at once splenetic and heroic. As indicated by the title of the first section of *Les fleurs du mal* ("Spleen et Idéal"), the splenetic energies of the verse, in their ebb and flow, are in tension with its operative ideal, its intention to fix in language "days of recollection [*Eingedenken*] not marked by any immediate experience [*Erlebnis*]." This constitutional tension is the source of that sober festivity animating the entire cycle of poems. Baudelaire's unquenchable sensitivity—to "modern beauty" in its dissonance and dissymmetry, to the resonance of antiquity in what is new, to the allegorical transparency of all things—is exemplified, for Benjamin, in two sonnets, "Correspondances" and "La vie antérieure." This, too, is part of the poet's heroism: the attempt to render an experience that would "establish itself in crisis-proof form." Benjamin's evocation of a life of plenitude—citing Baudelaire's *"luxe, calme et volupté"*—is not, as some readers have argued, the residue of a quixotic nostalgia; rather, it is in large part a *repoussoir*, a perspective device allowing Baudelaire, and Benjamin with him, "to fathom the full meaning of the breakdown which he, as a modern man, was witnessing."

The bracketing of the nostalgic dimension of Benjamin's reading is essential if the reader is to receive the explosive force of Baudelaire's modernité. What is called for instead is a dialectical nearness *in* distance. In the final sections of "On Some Motifs in Baudelaire" Benjamin suggests that Baudelaire's status as the representative poet of high-capitalist modernity reflects this tendency of his work to take upon itself the breakdown of "auratic" art. The term "aura" (meaning, literally, wind or breath) first appears with special theoretic emphasis in Benjamin's 1929 essay "Little History of Photography," but the most explicit definition—there is no full conceptual development of the term anywhere in Benjamin—is to be found in his "Work of Art" essay.

In keeping with his schematization for the Baudelaire book, specifically the third part, "The Commodity as Poetic Object," Benjamin credits Baudelaire with radical insight into the distancing phenomenon of the aura, with its paradoxical gaze of familiarity *(regards familiers)*. Yet Baudelaire's lyric poetry is great not just because of this insight, but because it is "marked by the disintegration of the aura." If auratic art, in its classic plenitude, seems to return our gaze, art marked by the loss of aura is disjointed and reticent, its gaze scattered or imploded.[25] Such art arises in technologically conditioned social situations, where humans in public spaces no longer habitually return the gaze of others. "Before the development of buses, railroads, and trams in the nineteenth century, people had never been in situations where they had to look at one another for long minutes or even hours without speaking to one another." Such a passenger, and such a poet, are hardly given to "daydreaming surrender to distance and to faraway things." In its dynamic inscription of the "figure of shock" within the fast-moving urban life of modernity, Baudelaire's poetry breaks through the brutal and seductive "magic of distance" with which it is nevertheless thoroughly conversant; it is like a viewer who "steps too close to the depicted scene" and thus shatters the illusions—not least the illusions fostered by auratic phenomena and, through them, by traditional systems of power.

In late 1863 Baudelaire published his essay "The Painter of Modern Life" in three installments of the newspaper *Le Figaro*. The reader encountering the Benjaminian interpretation of the poet will see that Benjamin's reinvention of Baudelaire as quintessentially modern was less the creation of a new Baudelaire than the recovery of formerly neglected or misunderstood features of the poet's work. When Baudelaire writes, "By 'modernity' I mean the ephemeral, the fugitive, the contingent, the half of art whose other half is the eternal and the immutable," we discern the physiognomy of Benjamin's poet riven by the splenetic and the ideal. "The Painter of Modern Life" is in fact shot through with themes later highlighted in Benjamin's essays on the poet: the fundamental shift in worldview from permanence and solidity to transience and fragmentation; the growing influence of fashion in all areas of culture; the abjection of the modern artist, and the regress of "genius" to a state of "convalescence"; the ascendancy of seemingly marginal, "kaleidoscopic" figures such as the dandy and the flâneur; the potentially fruitful estrangement of the individual in the urban mass, where "the spectator is a prince who everywhere rejoices in his incognito"; and even the insidious proliferation of phantasmagoria. In fact, the central theme of "On Some Motifs in Baudelaire"—the genesis of the poetic image from the experience of shock—is clearly sounded in "The Painter of Modern Life": "I am prepared to . . . assert that inspiration has something in common with a *convulsion* [*la* congestion], and that every sublime thought is accompanied by a more or less violent nervous shock which has its repercussions in the very core of the brain."[26]

CHAPTER ELEVEN

The Angel of History

Paris, Nevers, Marseilles, and Port Bou, 1939–1940

AFTER completing "On Some Motifs in Baudelaire," Benjamin scarcely had a chance to catch his breath. The Hitler-Stalin pact was signed on August 23, 1939, and on September 1 the German army invaded Poland. Benjamin lost no time in leaving Paris: in early September he fled to Chauconin, near the town of Meaux, east of Paris, where he stayed with the wife of the translator Maurice Betz. Helen Hessel was also staying as a guest, and had obtained an invitation for her friend. His greatest fear was conscription, to which he was subject until the age of fifty-two. Given the gravity of the situation and the dire uncertainty of his immediate future, Benjamin wrote to Horkheimer from Chauconin, asking humbly for an additional $15–$20 for each of the next two months.

Conscription turned out to be the least of his worries. Despite the general sense that war was imminent, the French authorities had apparently given no thought to the thousands of German and Austrian refugees within the borders of their country; the invasion of Poland left them no time to ascertain the political allegiances of the exiles. On September 3, placards were posted throughout the region, directing German and Austrian citizens to report with a blanket to the Stade Olympique Yves-du-Manoir in Colombes, a northwestern suburb of Paris. On September 9, or a few days after, along with thousands of other Germans and Austrians of military age, Benjamin was interned. The poet and critic Hans Sahl, a fellow internee, has left a vivid and revealing, if necessarily partial, account of Benjamin's two-month confinement. In this retrospective account, Benjamin is portrayed as the very embodiment of mandarin impracticality. "As he tried to orient himself to reality using his intelligence and his historical-political understanding, he distanced himself ever further from it."

Sahl's reading is undoubtedly influenced by his anti-Communism—he had gradually moved away from the radical left beginning in the mid-1930s—but the image of a Benjamin thwarted by his own penetrating intellect in his attempts to deal with a difficult practical situation resonates with what we know of his life in exile.[1] Impracticality, though, is not the dominant note Sahl strikes. He repeatedly characterizes Benjamin as someone sunk so deeply into himself that he comes to be viewed by those around him as a kind of seer. This, too, accords with the general sense people had of a man whose personal depths were sealed off behind the uniform and impenetrable façade of his courtesy.

The Stade de Colombes, as the detainees called it, with its partially roofed stands, afforded shelter from the elements to only a fraction of the inmates. They were fed a steady diet of cheap liver pâté spread on bread, and they were forced to build their own makeshift latrines. Sahl reports that the conditions were difficult even for the young and healthy; for Benjamin, who at forty-seven was one of the oldest detainees and already in a state of declining health, they were life-threatening. His life was no doubt saved by a young man, Max Aron, who came to his aid. "I noticed an older man," Aron remembered later, "on the first evening there, sitting quietly, motionless, on one of the benches. Was he really not yet fifty? . . . It was only when I noticed him the next morning, still sitting (as it seemed to me) in the same place, that I began to be concerned. There was something dignified both in his silence and in his posture. He simply didn't fit into those surroundings."[2] It seemed to Sahl that, "in the younger man's care for this physically frail individual, helpless in all things practical, [there was] an almost biblical respect for the spiritual in a time of plagues and dangers."

After ten days of confinement, the detainees were divided into groups and sent to internment camps *(camps des travailleurs volontaires)* throughout France. Benjamin and his friends—including not only Aron and Sahl but the playwright Hermann Kesten—made a concerted effort to remain together; they were transported under armed guard, first by bus to the Gare d'Austerlitz and then by train to Nevers, about 150 miles south of Paris and on the western border of Burgundy. Arriving in the late afternoon, the prisoners were forced to march two hours to the abandoned Château de Vernuche. The march was a torture for Benjamin, whose heart was taxed to the limit. He later told Adrienne Monnier that, although Aron carried his paltry belongings for him, he had collapsed en route. The 300 detainees found the château absolutely empty and slept on the floor until straw was brought a few days later. The series of shocks took a heavy toll on Benjamin; he needed more time than most of his fellows to adjust to the hardships, which included hunger, cold, filth, and "constant din." His health continued to suffer, and there were days on which he remained prostrate, unable even to read. With Aron's help, he established himself in a sort of lean-to beneath a circular stairway; a burlap drape allowed him something like privacy.

The challenges posed by life in the camp were of course hardly limited to material privation. The detainees were given no information regarding the intentions of the authorities: they were staring into an utterly blank future. Rumors circulated wildly, hinting sometimes of their imminent liberation, sometimes of the final termination of all liberty. And, in a continent torn by war, the detainees were largely cut off from news of friends and loved ones. Benjamin at least knew that Dora and Stefan were safe in London. He had no word, on the other hand, from his sister, and only after several weeks was there news from his friends in Paris and Switzerland. One of the notable features of Benjamin's last months in Europe was the solidification of his friendship with the writer Bernard von Brentano, a close associate of Brecht's; Brentano was one of the few people to whom Benjamin wrote at this time, and he took pains to keep him informed as to his whereabouts and condition. He feared, in addition, that the coming of war might mean the lasting disruption of his stipend, even if the institute was able to pay it; he knew that the bank accounts of the detainees had been at least temporarily seized. It remained unclear as to how foreign nationals might finally draw funds from French banks. He thus wrote to Juliane Favez, the institute's administrator in Paris, asking for her assistance in seeing the funds safely transferred and the rent on his apartment paid. He also asked her to keep Horkheimer and Pollock informed about his condition: "I rarely have the tranquility necessary to write directly to New York" (GB, 6:339). As it turned out, his sister and Milly Levy-Ginsberg (the wife of his friend the art historian Arnold Levy-Ginsberg, nephew of Else Herzberger) were seeing to his affairs and keeping an eye on his apartment and his belongings.

As often enough in the past, the present disruption in his life led him to transcribe his dreams. One, revolving around the motif of "reading," was memorable enough to share with New York:

> Last night, lying in the straw, I had a dream so beautiful that I cannot resist the temptation to share it with you. . . . The doctor by the name of [Camille] Dausse, who accompanies me in this dream, is a friend who looked after me when I was suffering from malaria [in the fall of 1933]. Dausse and I were in the company of several people whom I do not remember. At a certain point, Dausse and I parted company with this group. After we had left the others, we found ourselves in a pit. I saw that there were some strange beds almost at the bottom of it. They had the shape and the length of coffins; they also seemed to be made of stone. Upon kneeling down halfway, however, I saw that one could sink gently into them as if getting into bed. They were covered with moss and ivy. I saw that these beds were set up in pairs. Just as I was about to stretch out on one of them, next to a bed which seemed to be meant for Dausse, I realized that the head of that one was already occupied by other people. So we resumed our course. The place resembled a forest; but there was something artificial about the distribution of trunks and branches that lent this part of the scenery a vague resemblance to a nautical construction. Walking along some beams and crossing various paths in the forest, we found ourselves on a sort of miniature landing stage, a little terrace made of wooden boards. It was there that we found the women with whom Dausse was living. There were three or four of them, and they seemed to be very beautiful. The first thing that astonished me was that Dausse did not introduce me. That did not disturb me as much as the discovery I made when I set down my hat on a grand piano. It was an old straw hat, a "Panama" that I had inherited from my father. (It ceased to exist long ago.) Taking it off, I was struck by a large crack in the top of the hat. Furthermore, the edges of this crack showed traces of red.—I was brought a chair. That did not prevent me from fetching a different one myself, which I placed slightly away from the table where everyone was sitting. I did not sit down. In the meantime, one of the ladies had occupied

herself with graphology. I saw that she had something in her hand which I had written, and which had been given to her by Dausse. I was slightly unsettled by this examination, fearing that it would disclose some intimate traits of mine. I moved closer. What I saw was a cloth that was covered in pictures; the only graphic elements I could distinguish were the upper parts of the letter D, whose pointed lines revealed an extreme striving toward spirituality. This part of the letter had also been covered with a small piece of fabric with a blue border, and the fabric swelled up on the picture as if it were in the breeze. That was the only thing there which I was able to "read"— the rest offered indistinct, vague motifs and clouds. For a moment, the conversation turned to this writing. I do not remember the opinions that were put forward; I do know very well, however, that at a certain point I spoke these exact words: "It is a matter of changing a poem into a scarf." I had barely spoken these words when something intriguing happened. I saw that among the women there was a very beautiful one who had lain down in a bed. While listening to my explanation, she made a movement as quick as a flash. She lifted a very small corner of the blanket that was covering her in her bed. She performed this action in less than a second. And it was not to show me her body, but rather the pattern on her blanket, which showed a similar image to that which I had had to "write" many years ago as a present for Dausse. I knew very well that the lady had made this movement. But it was a sort of second sight that had given me this knowledge. For as far as my physical eyes were concerned, they were looking somewhere else, and I could not distinguish any of that which had been revealed by the blanket so fleetingly drawn back for me. (BG, 272–273; original in French)

Benjamin's greatest concern, however, was for the fate of his Baude-laire essay. He feared that the institute, unable to contact him, would make changes to his essay and publish it without his consent. He was somewhat heartened when he heard from his sister in late September, who passed along the text of a cable from New York: "Your admirable study on Baudelaire reached us like a ray of light. Our thoughts are with you" (BG, 271n). Although he was unable to read the proofs, the essay appeared, unchanged, in the next issue of the *Zeitschrift*.

Despite these worries, Benjamin, like most of the detainees, was heartened by a game of chess or by the "agreeable spirit of camaraderie" that prevailed in the château (BG, 270). Sahl describes that spirit in some detail: "A community that began to function was soon fashioned from the void; from chaos and helplessness emerged a society."[3] The detainees were soon organizing every aspect of camp life, from sweeping and cleaning with straw brooms and rags to the establishing of a primitive economy with cigarettes, nails, and buttons as currency. The camp offered an unusual diversity of intellectual opportunities. Sahl gave readings of his poetry (for example, his "Elegy for the Year 1939"); once he had recovered sufficiently, Benjamin delivered lectures (one of them was on the concept of guilt) and offered, for a fee, philosophical seminars "for advanced students." The fees were paid in the crude currency of the camp.[4]

At some point during the incarceration, a group of "film people" among the detainees convinced the commandant to give them day passes (they were issued armbands) in order to conduct research for a pro-French documentary; they returned from Nevers and regaled their envious comrades in the camp with stories of French wine and food. Inspired by the hope for an armband, Benjamin set out for the third time in his life—following his failed attempts with *Angelus Novus* in the early 1920s and *Krisis und Kritik* in the early 1930s—to found a journal. As editor of the projected *Bulletin de Vernuche: Journal des Travailleurs du 54e Régiment,* he assembled a first-class team of writers and editors from the camp population. The drafts for the first issue, which are held in the Akademie der Künste in Berlin, included sociological studies of camp life, critiques of camp art (chorales, amateur theatricals, etc.), and a study of the inmates' reading habits. Sahl's own proposed contribution, an analysis of the creation of a "society ex nihilo," might have taken the form of a chronicle along the lines of Defoe's *Robinson Crusoe*. Like its two predecessors, but for more obvious reasons, the journal was never published.

Sahl's account of the camp is harshly critical of the French authorities. Benjamin, on the other hand, was full of admiration for any and all French resistance to "the murderous rage of Hitler." Writing to Adrienne Monnier on September 21, he professed himself willing to serve "our cause" to the best of his ability, although his physical strength was "worthless" (C, 613). By mid-October, after more than fifty days in captivity, Benjamin could report to Brentano that he had recovered "the moral strength" to read and write (GB, 6:347). Many friends, above all Monnier, Sylvia Beach, and Helen Hessel, sent him chocolate, cigarettes, journals, and books. His reading consisted mainly of what was sent to him: Rousseau's *Confessions* (which he read for the first time) and Cardinal Retz's *Mémoires*. As Benjamin's fixation on the armband shows, thoughts of freedom were never far from his mind. He had already collected testimonials from Paul Valéry and Jules Romains in support of his citizenship application; he now added testimonials from Jean Ballard and Paul Desjardins, in the hope that they would buttress the attempts to have him released. Adrienne Monnier worked devotedly to the same end, ultimately convincing PEN, the international organization of writers and editors, to intervene with the Ministry of the Interior on behalf of Benjamin and Hermann Kesten, who was being held in another camp. By early November the first detainees were released. Benjamin's own liberation was pronounced by an interministerial commission on November 16, following the intervention of the diplomat Henri Hoppenot, a friend of Monnier's.

By November 25 Benjamin was back in Paris. His friends, concerned for his health, had arranged for Gisèle Freund to pick him up in a car. He had lost weight and was so exhausted that he was frequently forced to "pause halfway down the street because I am unable to go on" (C, 618–619). But on his return he wrote to Scholem (to whom he had not written during the internment, being limited to two letters per week) that he felt relatively well. He often found himself back in the camp in his thoughts. As one of the first detainees to be released, and at the very moment when wintry weather was setting in, he was very sensible of his good fortune: he corresponded with a number of his recent acquaintances still in Nevers and sent packages to several of them. One positive outcome of his experience in the camp was a burgeoning friendship with Kesten. Discussions with his friends in Paris often came around to the camp and the reasons for the internment of so many opponents of Hitler. He learned from Gisèle Freund that the situation in England was very different. Only Nazi sympathizers had been interned. The remaining Germans and Austrians, perhaps as many as 50,000 strong, had been required to submit to an interrogation before a tribunal: those who could document that they were victims of the German regime retained their freedom (GB, 6:352n).

Back at his desk in his apartment on the Rue Dombasle, he turned his thoughts to new projects. He sent a proposal to the Institute of Social Research for an essay on Rousseau's *Confessions* and Gide's journals, "a sort of historical critique of 'sincerity.'" And he mailed copies of "The Storyteller" to the German writer Paul Landsberg, whom he occasionally saw at the lectures of the Collège de Sociologie. Benjamin hoped that Landsberg's remaining contacts in the "Lutetia Circle" might help him publish the essay in French translation. Dedicated to the fall of the Hitler regime, the Lutetia Circle had been organized by Willi Münzenberg in 1935 and had continued its activities until late 1937. The group included Communists, Social Democrats, and members of the bourgeois center parties; among the participants had been Heinrich and Klaus Mann, Lion Feuchtwanger, and Emil Ludwig.

Benjamin still felt a deep attachment to Paris, which had been not only his home for seven years but also the object of his life's work: first with the tracing of the primal history of the nineteenth century, as it appeared in the murky light of the Parisian arcades, and now with the study of Baudelaire that had grown from it. He knew that "nothing in the world can replace the Bibliothèque Nationale for me" (C, 621). Yet he was quite aware that his freedom was only an interlude and that he would need to leave the city soon if he was to leave at all. His French friends (with the notable exception of Adrienne Monnier) urged him to go, and he remembered that his reluctance to cut all ties to another homeland—Germany—in 1933 had been overcome only at the urging of Gretel Adorno. He thus undertook a number of new initiatives aimed at his eventual departure from France. One of these was an attempt to learn English. He told Gretel that he had no difficulty reading her letters in English, and he composed, possibly with a friend's help, a letter of thanks in English to Cecilia Razovsky, a social worker in the Paris office of the National Refugee Service. On November 17 Razovsky had submitted a visa application for Benjamin to the American consul in Paris; it included affidavits of support from Milton Starr of Nashville, Tennessee, a wealthy businessman and patron of the arts. The unexpected appearance of this support galvanized Benjamin. Partially out of gratitude for PEN's willingness to intervene on his behalf during his internment, but certainly in an effort to acquire new allies, Benjamin stood as a candidate for the organization's division for German exiles. The candidacy was supported by letters from Hermann Kesten and Alfred Döblin; he learned from the writer Rudolf Olden, the director of the division, in early January 1940 that he was admitted as a member. This entitled him to a membership card—at a time when every piece of identification was precious. He also wrote to Horkheimer, pressing him to help find an opportunity to make use of the visa that was now in prospect. Horkheimer must have had a very clear picture of the probable fate of the German exiles still in France, yet he temporized, suggesting to Benjamin that the institute's stipend would continue to go further in Paris than it ever could in New York. Despite these mixed signals, Benjamin submitted his formal application for a visa to the American consulate on February 12, 1940.

Around the turn of the year he twice saw his former wife, Dora, who was traveling back and forth between San Remo and London as she transferred her business affairs. She had married the South African businessman Harry Morser in 1938 and was in the process of opening a boardinghouse in London. Accounts differ as to when she first met Morser. There is some evidence that her family, the Kellners, had friendly relations with the family of Heinrich Mörzer in Vienna; Dora may well have first met him, however, when he was a guest at her pension in San Remo. Mörzer had become a South African citizen early in the century and changed his name to Harry Morser. Most accounts—including those by Stefan Benjamin's two daughters—have assumed that Dora entered into a marriage of convenience in order to make possible her final immigration to England. Morser accompanied her, though, on at least one of the trips through Paris, where he made a favorable impression on Benjamin. Ernst Schoen also reported from London that Dora, Stefan, and "Herr Morser" had rejected all of their former friends, going so far as to conceal their address, which might suggest that they were living together as a family. Interestingly, Dora introduced Morser to Benjamin as a "friend." And she urged him—in vain—to follow them to England. This would be Benjamin's final meeting with his former wife. Dora lived a long life, running a series

36. Benjamin's library card, Bibliothèque Nationale, Paris, 1940 *(Bibliothèque Nationale de France)*

of boardinghouses in Notting Hill, London, and dying in 1964, eight years before the death of her son at fifty-three.[5] Stefan Benjamin was interned in Australia during the war, but he returned to London and became a dealer in rare books. Despite the ambivalence he evidently felt toward his father, at least one thing bound them: they were collectors.

As the new year began, Benjamin was still preoccupied with the details of a life that he had to reconstruct after his internment—details such as reopening his bank account, renewing his privileges at the Bibliothèque Nationale, and attempting to keep alive his dwindling opportunities for publication. His living conditions (an underheated, noisy apartment, with no heat at all for two weeks at the end of January) and his stagnant health (a heart that would not allow him to take his customary long walks) continued to impede his work. He reported to Gretel Adorno that he spent most of his time lying down. Yet he was driven forward by foreboding. Like many other residents of Paris, he purchased a gas mask early in the year; unlike many other residents, he could see in its material presence in his little world an ironic allegory, one superimposing the medieval on the modern and the spiritual on the technological: "A disturbing double of those skulls with which studious monks decorated their cells" (BG, 279). On January 11 he wrote to Scholem: "Every line we succeed in publishing today—no matter how uncertain the future to which we entrust it—is a victory wrested from the powers of darkness" (BS, 262). The last such major victories would seemingly have been the publication of "On Some Motifs in Baudelaire" and the Jochmann essay with Benjamin's introduction in the *Zeitschrift für Sozialforschung*, in the first days of 1940.

Yet Benjamin had almost nothing to say about the publication of the Baudelaire revision; there was a brief mention to Scholem asking for an opinion, and fervent thanks to Horkheimer for the support his acceptance of the essay represented, but nothing comparable to the letter of August 6, 1939, to Adorno, in which he discusses the "more precise articulation of the theoretical framework" in the reworked piece he had just sent off. The real enthusiasm was expressed by Adorno himself, whose "bad conscience" had now given way to "a rather vain feeling of pride" at having catalyzed "the most perfect thing you've done since the book on *Trauerspiel* and the essay on Kraus" (BA, 319). Remarkably enough, this extended letter details the ways in which Benjamin's essay, as Adorno saw it, responded to his own work. In reply, Benjamin formulated a typically mild deflection of Adorno's claim that "your theory of forgetting and the theory of 'shock' touches very closely indeed upon my musical writings":

> There is no reason to conceal from you the fact that the roots of my "theory of experience" can be traced back to a childhood memory. My parents would go on walks with us, as a matter of course, wherever we spent the summer months. There would always be two or three of us children together. But it is my brother I am thinking of here. After we had visited one or other of the obligatory places of interest around Freudenstadt, Wengen or Schreiberhau, my brother used to say, "Now we can say we've been there." This remark imprinted itself unforgettably on my mind. (BA, 320, 326)

The exchange with Adorno has much to say about Benjamin's state of mind in early 1940. His silence regarding "On Some Motifs in Baudelaire" attests to his lingering anger over the rejection of "The Paris of the Second Empire in Baudelaire" and to his ambivalent attitude toward the latter essay, with its forced subservience to an abstract theorizing. More remarkable, though, is the instantiation of childhood memory as a source of the late theory of experience, and the replacement of Adorno, and by extension the institute, by Georg Benjamin. Benjamin's siblings had played no role whatsoever in his recasting of the *Berlin Childhood around 1900* in 1938; two years later, with the internment camp behind him and war before him, his actual family had essentially taken the place of the institute, the intellectual family that had adopted him in the mid-1930s.

Any lingering reservations he may have had regarding "On Some Motifs in Baudelaire" did not color his general attitude toward the Baudelaire book, whose continuation was "much closer to [his] heart than any other work" (BG, 279). After a long period of debilitation and depression, he returned in early April to the schematization that he had composed in the summer of 1938 in Denmark, the schematization that yielded "The Paris of the Second Empire in Baudelaire." He never fully gave up hope that this first essay might be published—either separately or as part of his Baudelaire book. He expressed the hope to Stefan Lackner that "my first work on [the subject of Baudelaire] will someday fall into your hands" (GB, 6:441). That spring, as he told Adorno, he had opted to put aside the proposed essay on Rousseau and Gide, despite the fact that it would have been more amenable to the institute and more publishable in the *Zeitschrift:* "[Baudelaire] is the subject which stubbornly continues to present itself to me as the most pressing; and my most urgent task is to do full justice to its demands" (BA, 327). But this new period of labor produced only a series of notes on the reorganization of his materials and on specific aspects of the book, and no sustained piece of writing.

In early 1940 the success of the German armies in the east made a more general war seem inevitable. Benjamin's thoughts, understandably, turned increasingly to the present political situation. While he missed the fiery political debates he had been waging with Scholem since 1924, he told his old friend in January that there was no longer any point to them, presumably because he had lost all sympathy with the politics of the Soviet Union after the conclusion of the Hitler-Stalin pact. His sense of a renewed accord with Scholem undoubtedly sprang in some measure from the new text he was working on in early 1940, comprising a "certain number of theses on the concept of history" that brought together political, historical, and theological motifs in an original way. These theses ultimately became the text "On the Concept of History," Benjamin's last major work. He told several correspondents that they were motivated by the experience of his generation in the years leading up to Hitler's war. Just as important, however, was his intensive discussion with Arendt and Blücher in winter 1939–1940 of Scholem's *Major Trends in Jewish Mysticism*, which Scholem had sent Benjamin in manuscript. Arendt recalled their focus on Scholem's analysis of the Sabbatian movement of the seventeenth century. Its combination of a messianic mystical tradition with an active political agenda certainly provoked Benjamin to certain formulations in his new work—and especially to the messianic motifs that had largely lain dormant since the early 1920s. The theses themselves derived in part from the beginning of the essay on Eduard Fuchs and in part from reflections associated with the "theoretical armature" of the Baudelaire book; both of these sources, of course, had their textual ground in the arcades folders (GB, 6:400).

"On the Concept of History" opens with one of the most memorable set pieces in all of Benjamin. He imagines a chess automaton—a puppet in Turkish dress at a table beneath which is hidden a chess master, a hunchbacked dwarf—that can beat any opponent. The philosophic counterpart to this apparatus would have the puppet—historical materialism—vanquish any opponent so long as it takes into its service what is small, shriveled, and hidden, namely, the hunchbacked dwarf "theology" (SW, 4:389). As the very next section in the sequence of eighteen short sections makes clear, Benjamin's understanding of theology in 1940 is focused on a very particular kind of redemption: every generation is granted a "*weak* messianic power, a power on which the past has a claim."[6] The theological import of these late theses cannot be defined in terms of any single religious tradition; like all of Benjamin's writing that makes explicit use of theological motifs, it is drawn freely from Jewish and Christian sources. The notion of redemption at issue here presupposes the patristic category of apocatastasis (invoked, as we have seen, in Convolute N of *The Arcades Project*). Now the simple version of this term has it designating

universal salvation: no soul is ever lost to redemption. The term occurs in only one biblical passage, Acts 3:21, a discussion of the end
times. The term "apocatastasis" there denotes the putative *restitutio
in integrum*, the restoration of all things *after* the end times. Yet in
other sources that Benjamin knew—primarily Origen of Alexandria's
De Principiis, but a series of Stoic and Neo-Platonic texts as well—
apocatastasis has a persistent *cosmological* dimension involving the
rigorous alternation of ages of cosmic culmination and cosmic restitution. In Stoicism, the term refers to the *contraction* of the cosmos back
into the mind of Zeus, from which it emanates outward as the Logos;
more specifically, it refers to the process by which, in an all-encompassing
conflagration, the cosmos is reduced to its primal element—fire. Only
then can the rebirth of all existing things come about.

In one of the more subtle maneuvers of his late work, Benjamin
shifts this mythic-theological notion of the oscillation of cosmological ages onto a political and historiographical plane: "Only a redeemed
mankind is granted the fullness of its past—which is to say, only for a
redeemed mankind has its past become citable in all its moments."
Citability is the condition necessary for a living tradition. Benjamin
defines the task of the materialist historian—who, like everyone else,
is denied a full grasp of the past—as the appropriation of a "memory
as it flashes up in a moment of danger"; that (involuntary) memory has
the character of an "image that flashes up at the moment of its recognizability, and is never seen again." For "the true image of the past
flits by" and can be retrieved—that is, cited—solely in the present
that recognizes itself as intended *(gemeint)* in that image. The book
on Baudelaire—and the project of constructing a history of nineteenth
century France that lay behind it—understood itself as an attempt to
crystallize precisely such images and to present history itself as "the
subject of a construction." Benjamin was convinced that the authentic writing of history is a risk-filled, edgy venture, in contrast to the
conventional Rankean historicism, which aims, through intellectual
empathy, to grasp the past "as it really was." This is at bottom an empathy with one thing only: with the victor. All such efforts at en-
shrining, and hence reifying, the events of the past presuppose just
that empty homogeneous continuum that is shattered in the monadi-

cally concentrated "now-time" *(Jetztzeit)* of the dialectical image and its "tiger's leap" into "the thickets of long ago." "For in every case these [cultural] treasures have a lineage which [the historical materialist] cannot contemplate without horror. They owe their existence not only to the efforts of the great geniuses who created them, but also to the anonymous toil of others who lived in the same period. There is no document of culture which is not at the same time a document of barbarism." One may find hope in the past, Benjamin suggests, only if tradition is wrested from the conformism working to overpower it, only if it is opened to the momentary standstill and sudden threshold of "messianic time"—something beyond the causal nexus and chronological framework of modern scientific historicism. In the messianic experience of "universal and integral actuality,"[7] the present moment of remembrance is the "gateway" of redemption, the revolutionary chance in the fight for the oppressed (or suppressed) past. It follows that the Day of Judgment would not be distinguishable from other days. "To grasp the eternity of historical events," we read in paralipomena to the theses, "is really to appreciate the eternity of their transience" (SW, 4:404–407). This appreciation of eternal transience prepares the way for "genuine historical existence," where festivity and lament would be one. But whoever wishes to know exactly what this "redeemed humanity" might look like, and when it might come about, "poses questions to which there are no answers."

At the heart of the essay, and near the end of his life, Benjamin evokes the image that had accompanied him for almost twenty years: Klee's "Angelus Novus." Klee's angel, eyes wide, mouth open, wings outspread, has become the angel of history.

> His face is turned toward the past. Where a chain of events appears before *us*, *he* sees one single catastrophe, which keeps piling wreckage upon wreckage and hurls it at his feet. The angel would like to stay, awaken the dead, and make whole what has been smashed. But a storm is blowing from Paradise and has got caught in his wings; it is so strong that the angel can no longer close them. This storm drives him irresistibly into the future, to which his back is turned, while the pile of debris before him grows toward the sky. What we call progress is *this* storm. (SW, 4:392)

By late April or early May "On the Concept of History" was tentatively finished, and he sent a typescript to Gretel Adorno in New York. He was quite aware that the free interplay of historical materialism (including comments on Social Democracy and class struggle) with speculative theology in these theses would prove explosive. Despite their importance to him, he evidently had no intention of publishing them, let alone in their present experimental form: they would open the door to "enthusiastic misunderstanding" (BG, 286–287). With their abundant pessimism regarding the present and their scorn for any idea of progress that would bypass the present, the theses are clearly marked by the capitulations of Russia and the West to Hitler's will to power. Their animus is directed against those who have betrayed humanity: fascism, the Soviet Union, and finally those historians and politicians who have failed to grasp the order of the day. "On the Concept of History" stands more generally as a summa of Benjamin's thinking on history—a thinking that reaches back, through the arcades project, into the days following World War I. As he emphasized to Gretel Adorno in the letter enclosing the set of "notes," "The war and the constellation that brought it about led me to take down a few thoughts which I can say that I have kept with me, indeed kept from myself, for nigh on twenty years. . . . Even today, I am handing them to you more as a bouquet of whispering grasses, gathered on reflective walks, than a collection of theses" (BG, 286–287). The image of the heap of debris at the angel's feet evokes nothing so much as Benjamin's revisioning of the Baroque stage, with its randomly strewn yet subjectively charged historical objects. For Walter Benjamin, history remained from first to last a *Trauerspiel.*

As the tonality of this thesis-essay suggests, there was little that could alleviate Benjamin's increasing isolation—and the feelings of foreboding that were now never far off. Gustav Glück, his close friend and the inspiration for his 1931 essay "The Destructive Character," had escaped with his family to Buenos Aires. Pierre Klossowski, his friend and translator, had left Paris for Bordeaux, where he had taken a post with the municipal administration. The German-Czech journalist Egon Erwin Kisch had passed through on his way to exile in Mexico. Some newer friends, such as the musician Hans Bruck, were still in the internment camps that dotted the French countryside.

Other friends and acquaintances, including Paul Desjardins, the *spiritus rector* of the center at Pontigny, were now dead. The young illustrator Augustus Hamburger, whom Benjamin had come to know in the camp at Nevers, had committed suicide along with his companion, Carola Muschler. Hamburger had joined the Foreign Legion in order to get out of the camp, which had become intolerable. He and Muschler had spent the five-day holiday granted him for enlisting in the Hotel Georges V; on the fifth day they took their own lives.[8] Benjamin had written to Scholem that "the isolation that is my natural condition has increased owing to the present circumstances. The Jews seem not even to be holding on to the little intelligence they have left, after all they have been through. The number of those who are able to find their bearings in this world is diminishing more and more" (BS, 263). At other moments his sense of irony was still capable of surfacing; those same circumstances led him to speculate that an "ingenious synthesis" was in the process of being forged by history—a combination of Nietzsche's "good European" and his "last man." This synthesis "would result in the last European—something we are all striving not to become" (GB, 6:442).[9]

As spring came, Benjamin's health continued to deteriorate. The heart condition that had manifested itself during his internment had not improved with the return to Paris; he reported to Horkheimer in early April that his "weakness had progressed in disquieting proportion," so he seldom left his apartment. When forced to do so, he frequently found himself "bathed in sweat and unable to go on." He finally consulted a specialist; Dr. Pierre Abrami diagnosed tachycardia, hypertension, and an enlarged heart—a diagnosis that was confirmed by Egon Wissing, to whom Benjamin sent his X-rays in the course of the spring. The doctor's recommendation that he spend some time in the country was apparently delivered in all seriousness. As the cost of this medical care strained Benjamin's already precarious finances, he once again cast about for help. The Institute of Social Research responded with a generous special payment of 1,000 francs. The only positive side of the whole situation was his being pronounced unfit for military service—an ironic echo of his repeated and ultimately successful attempts to simulate illness in order to avoid service in World War I.

Well before the German armies invaded France on May 10, the aim of finding a safe haven in the United States had come to dominate Benjamin's thoughts. In the early spring he started English lessons together with Hannah Arendt and Heinrich Blücher, who had been married on January 16. He reported proudly on his first attempt to read an English text, Bacon's *Examples of the Antitheta* (from his *Advancement of Learning*), and he supplemented this with a book more closely related to the American experience, William Faulkner's novel *Light in August* (in French translation). The lessons continued, sporadically, even after Blücher was sent to an internment camp, but as Benjamin admitted, his spoken English never became more than halting. He was quite aware that he had waited too long: the opportunities to immigrate—to Palestine, to England, to Scandinavia—that he had passed up were coming back to haunt him. Months later, already on the run, he told Gretel Adorno, "You can be sure . . . that I have maintained the only state of mind befitting someone exposed to risks that he should have foreseen, and which he brought upon himself in the knowledge of their causes (or almost)" (BG, 289).

In late March Benjamin received a nasty shock. On reading the Jochmann essay and Benjamin's introduction in the *Zeitschrift für Sozialforschung*, his erstwhile friend Werner Kraft had sent a lengthy letter directly to Horkheimer in New York, accusing Benjamin not so much of plagiarism as of staking a claim to be Jochmann's discoverer when, according to Kraft, he himself had introduced Benjamin to the nineteenth-century writer. Horkheimer, always sensitive to the situation of the institute and its publications in a foreign country still reflexively hostile to any sign of leftism, was disturbed; Gretel Adorno counseled Benjamin to reply immediately and in detail so as not to jeopardize Horkheimer's goodwill precisely at the moment when he needed it most. Benjamin's reply, as we have related in Chapter 9, offered a straightforward account of his own discovery of Jochmann in the Bibliothèque Nationale and of the conversations with Kraft that followed this. There can be no doubt that Kraft introduced Benjamin to some of Jochmann's work, though evidently not to the writer himself.

Confined to his apartment, and unable to work with full concentration on the Baudelaire, Benjamin took on a diverse and at times seemingly arbitrary course of reading. He was studying not only Rousseau and Gide for his still-projected essay but also, with real absorption, the ethnologist Michel Leiris's autobiographical *L'âge d'homme* (1939), a book that he recommended to several friends. Of his friends and acquaintances in the Collège de Sociologie, it was the work of Leiris to which he felt the greatest affinity. He offered Adorno—in a letter to Gretel—a series of comments on Adorno's manuscript "Fragmente über Wagner"; Adorno's theorization of reduction as a phenomenon of phantasmagoria reminded him of his own, early remarks on Goethe's tale "The New Melusine." He told Brentano that he had read his new novel, *Die ewigen Gefühle* (Eternal Feelings), in "forty-eight hours." And he recommended Henri-Irénée Marrou's *Saint Augustin et la fin de la culture antique* to Karl Thieme, noting especially its treatment of late Roman decadence and its affinity to the work of Riegl.

On March 23 Benjamin sent a new overview of contemporary French letters to Horkheimer in New York. The bulk of the letter concerns three texts: a portrait of his adopted city entitled *Paris: Notes d'un Vaudois*, by the Swiss author Charles-Ferdinand Ramuz; Michel Leiris's *L'âge d'homme;* and a series of comments on the proto-Surrealist writer Lautréamont by Gaston Bachelard, presumably from his *Psychanalyse du feu* (Psychoanalysis of Fire). Benjamin pays tribute to Ramuz's study of Paris, which differs sufficiently in approach from his own arcades project to permit a genuine sympathy. The letter to Horkheimer is notable for articulating the nature of Benjamin's interest in Leiris: in the same way that much of Benjamin's work in the twenties and thirties explores paths opened by Surrealism, Leiris and the Collège de Sociologie in the later 1930s follow unconventional anthropological lines of inquiry that parallel Benjamin's own—at a distance. The Bachelard, too, is examined from a perspective derived from Benjamin's innermost concerns: he lauds Bachelard's interpretations of the latent content of Symbolist poetry—a series of "picture puzzles" *(Vexierbilder)* that carry a potential energy and import. The letter also contains shorter critiques of Jean Guéhenno's *Journal d'un "révolution"* (Diary of a "Revolution"); *Le regard* (The Gaze), by Georges Salles, to which Benjamin devoted a review (a second version of this appearing as a letter in Adrienne Monnier's *Gazette des Amis des*

Livres); and Caillois's "Théorie de la fête" (Theory of Festival). Another essay by Caillois on Hitler prompted the ironic observation that Caillois would spend the war years in Argentina, where he had followed the Argentine celebrity author Victoria Ocampo.

In early May Benjamin sent a long letter to Adorno in response to the draft of an essay on the correspondence between Stefan George and Hugo von Hofmannsthal. This letter constitutes Benjamin's last formal statement on literature; it combines insights into Kafka, Proust, and Baudelaire with a consideration of the neo-Romanticism of George and Hofmannsthal. Although Benjamin praises Adorno's courage in the attempt to "redeem" George at a time when he was being castigated in liberal circles as a protofascist, he is openly critical of Adorno's treatment of Hofmannsthal, and in fact offers an alternative reading.

> There are essentially two texts which, if taken together, are capable of revealing what I want to say. You refer to one of them yourself, when you cite Hofmannsthal's *Lord Chandos Letter* [of 1902]. And here I am thinking of the following passage: "I cannot say how often this Crassus and his moray eel comes to mind as a mirror-image of myself, tossed up over the abyss of the centuries . . . Crassus . . . , shedding tears over his moray. And I feel compelled to contemplate this figure, whose absurdity and contemptibility in the midst of a Senate that rules the entire world and deliberates upon the most elevated of matters is strikingly obvious, and compelled to do so by something unnameable that seems utterly foolish to me the moment I attempt to express it in words." (The same motif recurs in *The Tower* [1925]: with the insides of a slaughtered pig which the Prince was forced to look upon when he was a child.) As for the rest, the second passage I spoke of is also to be found in *The Tower:* namely, the conversation between Julian and the physician. Julian, the man who lacks nothing but a tiny effort of will, nothing but a single moment of commitment, to enjoy the highest experience imaginable, is a self-portrait of Hofmannsthal. Julian betrays the Prince: Hofmannsthal turned his back upon the task which emerges in his *Lord Chandos Letter.* His "loss of speech" was a kind of punishment for this. Perhaps the language which escaped Hofmannsthal was the very language which was given to Kafka at around the same time. For Kafka took on the task which Hofmannsthal had failed morally,

and therefore also poetically, to fulfill. (The highly suspect and fee-bly supported theory of sacrifice to which you refer bears all the traces of this failure.)/I believe that, throughout his entire life, Hof-mannsthal looked upon his own talents the way that Christ would have looked upon his Kingdom if he had been forced to establish it with Satan's assistance. His unusual versatility goes hand in hand, so it seems to me, with the awareness of having betrayed what was best in himself. (BA, 328–329)

This portrait of the great Austrian writer is a moving tribute to the one major figure who recognized and supported Benjamin's talent without trying to bend it to his own purposes.

As the German armies attacked first Belgium and the Netherlands and then France in early May, the French government began a new round of internments. Benjamin—together with Kracauer, the jour-nalist Hanns-Erich Kaminski, and the writer Arthur Koestler—was spared through the renewed intervention of Monnier's friend Henri Hoppenot. But more than 2 million people were now in flight before the Nazi armies. Benjamin hurriedly emptied his apartment and saw to the safekeeping of the bulk of his papers.[10] The least important of these were simply left behind in his apartment, where they were con-fiscated by the Gestapo; some of these papers vanished during the war, and the remainder were later confiscated by the Red Army and trans-ported to the Soviet Union, winding up eventually in East Berlin. A second group was left with a small number of friends. We know little about the fate of these papers during the war, but in 1946 they were in Zurich with his sister, Dora, who later sent them to Adorno in New York. The papers most precious to Benjamin—in particular, the cen-tral arcades materials, the 1938 revision of *Berlin Childhood around 1900*, the third version of "The Work of Art in the Age of Its Techno-logical Reproducibility," the author's copy of "On the Concept of His-tory," his sonnets, typescripts of "The Storyteller" and "Commentary on Poems by Brecht," and several theoretically central letters from Adorno—he gave to Georges Bataille.[11] Bataille entrusted the greater part of this material to two librarians at the Bibliothèque Nationale in Paris, where it remained during the war; after the war, Pierre Missac tracked down part of this hidden material, mainly the arcades convo-lutes, retrieved it from Bataille, and arranged for its eventual transfer by personal emissary to Adorno. The remaining papers, which also included the most advanced drafts and notes for the partially completed *Charles Baudelaire: A Lyric Poet in the Age of High Capitalism*, seemed for many years to be lost. In 1981 Benjamin's Italian editor, the philosopher Giorgio Agamben, discovered a body of material in Benjamin's hand in the Bataille archive at the Bibliothèque Nationale and in papers given him by Bataille's widow; this proved to be the missing trove of the manuscripts entrusted to Bataille in 1940. It remains unclear whether Bataille after the war had mistakenly retrieved only part of the manuscript collection left with him by Benjamin or whether this material had been stored separately and forgotten.[12]

With the help of French friends, Benjamin and his sister, Dora, who had been released only days before from an internment camp at Gurs, were able to secure places on a train leaving Paris on or around June 14—one of the last trains to carry refugees out of the city toward the south. Benjamin had with him a few toilet articles, his gas mask, and one book—the memoirs of Cardinal Retz. They got off the train at Lourdes, in the Pyrenees, where they found inexpensive accommodations. Benjamin was full of compliments for the locals: although the town was crowded with refugees—many of them Belgian—a sense of order and calm reigned. He immediately urged other friends still in Paris, and especially Gisèle Freund, to join him in the "beautiful countryside." Freund had waited in Paris so long that she was forced to flee on a bicycle; she found shelter in Saint-Sozy in the Dordogne region, where she remained until she was able to escape to Argentina in 1941. Hannah Arendt and Heinrich Blücher had been separated; when Blücher was released from his internment, he fled into the unoccupied zone, while Arendt went into hiding near Montauban. Both of them eventually made their way to Marseille, where Kracauer and his wife had preceded them. Other friends, too old or too weak to flee, were left behind. Benjamin wrote a touching note about the "remarkable valor" of Fritz Fränkel's mother, who had lived near him in Paris: "Baudelaire was right—"the 'petites vieilles' are sometimes those who demonstrate the most authentic heroism" (GB, 6:471).

Three weeks after his arrival in Lourdes, he wrote to Hannah Arendt that La Rochefoucauld's description of Cardinal Retz furnished an apt portrait of Benjamin himself: "His idleness sustained him in glory for many years, in the obscurity of an errant and secluded life." Despite the support of the townspeople, life in those weeks soon reached a state of utmost precariousness. Dora, suffering from anky-losing spondylitis and advanced arteriosclerosis, was all but immo-bile. Benjamin himself found that his heart condition was exacerbated not just by his general situation and the strains of daily existence but by the elevation as well. Even day-to-day living, given the lack of funds and the lack of contact with those close to him, posed an in-creasingly daunting challenge. "In the past few months," he wrote to Adorno, "I have seen a number of lives not just sink from bourgeois existence but *plunge headlong* from it almost overnight" (BA, 339). His sole comfort during the weeks in Lourdes seems to have been de-rived from literature, in particular a rereading of Stendhal's novel *The Red and the Black*.

Benjamin sensed a "glacial quietude" descending around him. His last letter to Gretel Adorno, written in mid-July, speaks of the comfort her letter had given him: "I would indeed say: the joy, but I do not know if I shall be able to experience that feeling in the near future" (GB, 6:471; BG, 288). Amid all this, Benjamin strove to maintain the kind of bearing and composure *(Haltung)* that he had recently, while still in Paris, described to Adorno: "I do not think it too bold to claim that we encounter someone's 'bearing' when the essential solitude of an individual properly manifests itself to us. That solitude which, far from representing the site of all the individual's richness, could well represent instead the site of the individual's historically conditioned emptiness, of the persona as the individual's sorry fate" (BA, 331).

In Lourdes, Benjamin's most immediate worry was the threat of reinternment, which would have led directly to a transfer into Ger-man custody. "The complete uncertainty about what the next day, even the next hour, may bring," he wrote to Adorno, "has dominated my life for weeks now. I am condemned to read every newspaper (they now come out on a single sheet here) as if it were a summons served on me in particular, to hear the voice of fateful tidings in every radio broadcast" (BA, 339). He thus cast about with increasing desperation for a means of escape, and obtaining a visa came to have a "primor-dial" importance (C, 635). Many of his friends, including Kesten and

Arendt, were making their way to Marseilles, where great numbers of refugees were gathering, all with the hope of escaping across the Pyrenees into Spain. Word also trickled through of the ongoing internment of a number of friends, including Hannah Arendt's husband, Heinrich Blücher. Soon after Benjamin and Dora arrived in Lourdes, however, the French authorities forbade all foreign nationals to travel without a permit, which was only obtainable upon presentation of a valid visa. On July 10 negotiations between the French and German governments resulted in the dissolution of the Third Republic and the formation of the Vichy regime under the collaborationist Marshal Philippe Pétain. The preceding cease-fire agreement, signed on June 22, had already included an article that effectively abolished the right of asylum for foreigners in France.[13] Benjamin's letters from these weeks reveal a rising panic: "My fear is that the time at our disposal may be far more limited than we supposed. . . . I hope that up to now I have given you the impression that I've remained composed even in difficult moments. You shouldn't think that has changed. But I cannot conceal from myself the peril of this situation. I fear that only a few will be able to save themselves."[14] Despairing of the possibility of reaching America, he even explored immigration to Switzerland, although the landlocked nation was hardly the safest of havens for a German Jew. He wrote to Hofmannsthal's friend Carl Jacob Burckhardt, a Swiss diplomat and historian, asking him to intercede in a situation that "in a very short time would have to be called hopeless [ausweglos]" (GB, 6:473). After the war, Burckhardt told Benjamin's friend Max Rychner that he had done what he could through Spanish friends to ease Benjamin's passage through that country, but by the time preparations could be made, it was too late.

Because contact with the world beyond Lourdes was intermittent, Benjamin knew little of the efforts being made on his behalf. Letters and postcards from the Institute of Social Research had arrived in Paris after his departure; some were lost, some reached him only weeks later. Benjamin did not learn until July that Horkheimer, despairing of quickly obtaining an American visa, had attempted to make possible his residence and employment in the Caribbean, first in Santo Domingo and later, after that plan had run aground, as a professor at the university in Havana on loan from the institute.

It took more than two months before Benjamin could join his friends in Marseilles. Finally, in early August, Benjamin learned that the institute had secured a non-quota visa enabling him to enter the United States and that the consulate in Marseilles had been duly informed. With this precondition satisfied, he obtained a safe-conduct pass and departed for Marseilles in mid-August. His sister Dora remained in Lourdes; she was able to find a hiding place on a farm in the country, and made her way to Switzerland in 1941. Arriving in Marseilles, Benjamin found a city crowded with refugees and dominated by an atmosphere of unrest. At the consulate, he was issued not only an entry visa for the United States but also transit visas for Spain and Portugal. What he could not obtain was an exit visa for France. Lists of German Jews and opponents of the regime were now posted at harbors and border crossings; Vichy militiamen searched internment camps, freeing Nazi supporters and handing over "enemies of the state" to the Gestapo.[15] Almost a month after receiving the visa for which he had struggled so long, Benjamin remarked to Alfred Cohn that "up to the present this has not served me in any significant way. It would be superfluous to inventory for you all my failed or reconceived schemes" (GB, 6:481). One of those schemes may have been an attempt, with Fritz Fränkel, to bribe their way onto a freighter, disguised as French sailors—surely the oldest and least practiced sailors in the history of maritime trade.[16] He also had his name entered on the list of refugees maintained by the Centre Américain de Secours, the organization founded by Varian Fry in support of antifascist exiles. Despite these efforts, the "sojourn" in Marseilles had by mid-September become a "terrible test of nerves"; he was weighed down by a powerful depression (GB, 6:481–482). There are indications, however, that even this urgent state of affairs could not extinguish his intellectual fires—or his playfulness. The novelist Soma Morgenstern tells of a lunch date with Benjamin in Marseilles at this time, during which the two writers talked about Flaubert.

> Hardly had we studied the menu and ordered something to drink than Walter Benjamin several times glanced at me insistently through his eyeglasses, as though he expected from me some obligatory but now overdue remark. . . . Finally, rather keyed up, he asked me:

"Haven't you noticed anything?" "We haven't eaten yet," I said, "what am I supposed to notice?" He handed me the menu and waited. I surveyed the list of dishes once again, but nothing caught my eye. At that point he lost all patience. "Haven't you noticed the name of this restaurant?" I glanced at the menu and saw that the innkeeper was named Arnoux. I communicated this finding to him. "Well," he went on, "doesn't that name mean anything to you?" I felt I had flunked; I was not equal to this exam. "Don't you remember who Arnoux is? [Madame] Arnoux is the name of Frédéric's beloved in *L'Education sentimentale!*" It was not until after the soup that he recovered from the disappointment I had caused him, and the subject of our lunchtime conversation that day was naturally Flaubert.[17]

In late September, Benjamin—accompanied by two acquaintances from Marseilles, German-born Henny Gurland and her teenage son Joseph—took the train from Marseilles into the countryside near the Spanish border. The prospects for a legal exit from France seemed non-existent, and Benjamin chose to attempt an illegal crossing into Spain; from there, he hoped to make his way through Spain to an embarkation point in Portugal, and on to the United States. In Port Vendres they joined Lisa Fittko, a thirty-one-year-old political activist who had lived in Vienna, Berlin, and Prague, and whose husband, Hans, Benjamin knew from the internment camp at Vernuche. Fittko was hardly a professional guide, but she had explored the possibilities for escape with real thoroughness. She could find her way along a path across the spurs of the Pyrenees and into the border town of Port Bou, Spain, with the aid of a description she had obtained from the mayor of Banyuls-sur-Mer, close to Port Vendres. From nearby Cerbère there was a more direct route to Port Bou that had served many refugees as their highway out of France, but the Vichy *gardes mobiles* had learned of this path and were closely guarding it. Refugees were now forced westward, higher into the mountains, along the "Route Lister"—so called because the narrow defile had in 1939 provided the escape route for Enrique Lister, a senior military official of the Republic who was in flight from the Spanish fascists. Lion Feuchtwanger, Heinrich and Golo Mann, Franz Werfel, and Alma Mahler-Werfel had all escaped by means of this rugged trail. Fittko asked Benjamin whether, in view of his fragile heart, he wanted to risk the exertion. "The real risk would be not to go," he replied.[18]

At this point the story of Walter Benjamin's last days becomes murky. On the advice of Mayor Azéma of Banyuls, Fittko led the little group on a reconnaissance of the first part of the path over the mountains. Benjamin probably left Banyuls on September 25.[19] Fittko noted Benjamin's carefully calculated pace—ten minutes of walking, followed by one minute's rest—and his refusal to have anyone else carry his heavy black attaché case, which contained, he said, a "new manuscript" that was "more important than I am."[20] Speculation has run wild as to the identity of this manuscript. Some have thought that it might be a completed version of the arcades project or of the Baudelaire book; neither of these is at all likely, given the state of Benjamin's health and his only sporadic ability to work in the last year of his life. The manuscript may have been a final text of "On the Concept of History," but he would have attributed this much importance to the version he was carrying only if it differed significantly from the versions he had given into the keeping of Arendt, Gretel Adorno, and Bataille. This, though, is only the first of the mysteries of his final days.

Benjamin must have suffered terribly on the walk through the Pyrenees, though he did not complain to Lisa Fittko and was even capable of making jokes and, drawing on his many years' experience of hill walking, helping them decipher the little handwritten map that was their only reference.[21] When Fittko, the Gurlands, and Benjamin reached the small clearing that was their goal for the day, Benjamin announced that he would sleep alone in the clearing; he was at the end of his powers and unwilling to attempt any segment of the journey more than once. His companions, having acquainted themselves with the first third of the trail, returned to Banyuls to sleep in an inn and rejoined him the next morning for the final, most difficult portion of the climb and the descent into Port Bou. Fittko remembers the contradiction between Benjamin's "crystal clear mind," his "unbending inner strength," and his otherworldliness. Only on one of the steepest sections did he falter, and Fittko and Joseph Gurland essentially dragged him up through a vineyard. Even under conditions such as these, Benjamin's ornate courtesy did not abandon him. When they had paused to eat and drink, he asked Fittko to pass a tomato: "With your kind permission, may I . . ." On the afternoon of September 26, when they were within sight of Port Bou, Fittko left the little party—which had grown slightly larger as they encountered other refugees, including Carina Birman and three companions.[22] Birman's first sight of Benjamin suggested that, on this "extremely hot" September day, he was on the point of cardiac arrest—"we ran in all directions in search of some water to help the sick man." Impressed by his bearing and manifest intellectuality, she took him to be a professor.[23]

Port Bou had remained a quiet fishing village well into the 1920s, but its strategic position on the rail line between Spain and France led to heavy bombing during the Spanish Civil War. Benjamin and the Gurlands reported, together with Birman's party, to the small Spanish customs office in order to obtain the stamp on their papers necessary for transit into Spain. For reasons that will presumably never be discovered, the Spanish government had recently closed the border to illegal refugees from France; Benjamin and his companions were told they would be returned to French soil, where they would face almost certain internment and transfer to a concentration camp. The entire group was escorted to a small hotel, Fonda de Francia, where they were kept under loose guard. Birman remembers hearing a "loud rattling from one of the neighboring rooms"; on going to investigate, she found Benjamin in "a desolate state of mind and in a completely exhausted physical condition. He told me that by no means was he willing to return to the border, or to move out of this hotel. When I remarked that there was no alternative [other] than to leave, he declared that there was one for him. He hinted that he had some very effective poisonous pills with him. He was lying half naked in his bed and had his very beautiful big golden grandfather watch with open cover on a little board near him, observing the time constantly."[24] He was visited by one of the two local doctors, bled, and given injections in the course of the afternoon and evening. At some point during the night of September 26, he composed a note for his companion in flight Henny Gurland—and for Adorno—the text of which was reconstructed from memory by Henny Gurland, who had felt it necessary to destroy the original:

In a situation presenting no way out, I have no other choice but to make an end of it. It is in a small village in the Pyrenees, where no one knows me, that my life will come to a close [*va s'achever*].

I ask you to transmit my thoughts to my friend Adorno and to explain to him the situation in which I find myself. There is not enough time remaining for me to write all the letters I would like to write.[25]

Sometime later that night, he took a massive dose of morphine; Arthur Koestler later remembered him leaving Marseilles with enough morphine "to kill a horse."

At this point the record of Walter Benjamin's last hours, and the fate of his body, becomes virtually impervious to historical inquiry. Henny Gurland later recalled that she received an urgent message from Benjamin early on the morning of September 27.[26] She found him in his room, where he asked her to depict his condition as the result of illness and gave her the note; he then lost consciousness. Gurland summoned a doctor, who pronounced him beyond help. According to Gurland, Benjamin died sometime on September 27. Birman recounts that news of Benjamin's death caused an uproar in the small town; several charged calls were made, perhaps to the American consulate in Barcelona, since Benjamin was carrying an entry visa for the United States. As Birman's party sat down for a meal in the hotel on September 27, a priest led a group of about twenty monks carrying candles and chanting a mass through the dining room. "We were told that they had come from a neighboring monastery to say a requiem at the deathbed of Prof. Benjamin and to bury him."[27] The municipal death certificate confirms some aspects of Gurland's recollections but not others—and it is contradicted at key points by the church register.[28] Identifying the deceased as "Dr. Benjamin Walter," it attributes his death to a cerebral hemorrhage. The Spanish doctor who examined Benjamin may have acceded to his final wish, hoping to conceal the suicide—or he may have been bribed by the other refugees, who would have wanted to avoid the kind of ruckus that might lead to their return to France. But it gives the date of death as September 26.

The next day the border was reopened.

Before leaving Port Bou, Henny Gurland followed Benjamin's last wishes and destroyed a number of letters—and perhaps, inadvertently, the manuscript he had carried over the Pyrenees. She also left enough money to rent a crypt for him in the communal cemetery for five years. The municipal death certificate records the burial on September 27; the ecclesiastical record, however, places the burial on September 28. Perhaps because the death certificate transposed his names, Walter Benjamin was buried in the Catholic section of the cemetery and not in the area reserved for those of other faiths (to say nothing of suicides). The municipal and ecclesiastical records again yield contradictory information on the exact number of the rented crypt—although a small memorial has been affixed to one of the possible resting places. A list of Benjamin's belongings, though not the belongings themselves, was discovered many years later in the municipal records, likewise under the name "Benjamin Walter." It mentions a leather attaché case (but no manuscript), a man's watch, a pipe, six photographs, an X-ray, a pair of glasses, a few letters and newspapers along with other papers, and a bit of money.

At the conclusion of the five-year lease, a new body was placed in the crypt in the cemetery at Port Bou. Benjamin's remains were in all probability transferred to a mass grave. A memorial by the Israeli artist Dani Karavan now looks out from the cemetery toward the little harbor of Port Bou and beyond that to the Mediterranean.

Epilogue

WHEN Walter Benjamin took his own life on the Spanish border in 1940, his name had long since begun to fade from European memory—which is only to say that he shared in the general oblivion imposed by the Nazi regime on freethinking German intellect. During the war years his reputation was kept alive—if only as a guttering flame—by a small circle of friends and admirers. There were meaningful gestures such as the dedication to Benjamin in Adorno's and Horkheimer's *Philosophische Fragmente* in 1944 (the first version of the book that would appear three years later in Amsterdam as *Dialectic of Enlightenment*)—but these found only a tiny audience. In the postwar years artists and intellectuals on both sides of the new border between the two German states struggled to forge continuities between the vibrant culture of the 1920s, effectively extinguished during the Third Reich, and their own. Theodor W. Adorno's publication of a two-volume edition of Benjamin's writings in 1955 inaugurated the rediscovery of his friend's work and built one bridge back to Weimar culture. Although the appearance of these volumes occasioned no widespread public discussion, they were noted and taken up by a number of writers and critics. Uwe Johnson, for example—arguably the most important German novelist in the second half of the twentieth century—was able to smuggle Adorno's edition into the German Democratic Republic, where Benjamin was considered insufficiently orthodox.

It was only with the rise of the student movement in the Federal Republic of Germany in the mid-1960s that Benjamin's works—at least some idea of them—started fueling debate. In the July 1967 issue of the prominent journal *Merkur*, the writer Helmut Heissenbüttel published an attack on Adorno's stewardship of Benjamin's legacy, making accusations that were echoed in other quarters. From very different political vantage points, both the West Berlin journal *Alternative* and Hannah Arendt amplified Heissenbüttel's charge that Adorno's editorial practices essentially continued the censorship of Benjamin's writing undertaken by the Institute of Social Research in New York in the late 1930s. What began as a debate about philology became a fierce war of words concerning the use and abuse of Marxist politics in the West. After 1968, with the "return to order" in West Germany, it became evident that this unresolved and unresolvable debate, though scarcely affecting contemporary politics, had awakened a readership for Benjamin's works. In Germany, an appreciation of the Benjaminian "capricious mosaic" was made possible, beginning in 1974, by the seven-volume *Gesammelte Schriften* (Collected Writings) edited by Rolf Tiedemann, Adorno's student and designated editorial heir, and Hermann Schweppenhäuser. In the English-speaking world, a decade separated the first two anthologies of selected essays by Benjamin, *Illuminations* of 1969 (edited by Hannah Arendt) and *Reflections* of 1978 (edited by Peter Demetz). Between those bookends, New Left Books in London published translations of Benjamin's book on the Baroque *Trauerspiel* and of major portions of his *Charles Baudelaire: A Lyric Poet in the Era of High Capitalism*, along with a volume of his essays on Brecht. From this point on, various journals started providing English-language scholars with translations of other key essays. The four-volume *Selected Writings*, which began appearing from Harvard University Press in 1996, finally made available a comprehensive, though by no means complete, collection of Benjamin's work.

By the early 1980s, the steady stream of popular and scholarly discourse on Benjamin was turning into a flood. The story of his life became shrouded in myth, and a pathos-ridden image of Walter Benjamin as the ultimate societal outsider and loser gained currency. A multitude of Benjamins emerged, as interpreters seized on distinct facets of his thought. The fire-breathing Communist stood alongside the Frankfurt School neo-Hegelian, with his infinite deferral of political action; the messianic Jewish mystic confronted uneasily the cosmopolitan assimilated Jew, with his fascination for Christian theology; the literary deconstructionist *avant la lettre*, astray in the hall of mirrors we call language, coexisted with the social theorist who envisioned a wholesale renovation of the human sensorium through the reform of modern media. Walter Benjamin's life and works provide material for each of these constructions; what runs through them all is the power of that material to resist stasis and reification. "To great writers," Benjamin remarked in *One-Way Street*, "finished works weigh lighter than those fragments on which they work throughout their lives. For only the more feeble and distracted take an inimitable pleasure in closure, feeling that their lives have thereby been given back to them." Coming generations of readers will undoubtedly find their own Benjamins in the encounter with that "mobile and contradictory whole" that is his lifework.

Abbreviations

The following abbreviations are used for citations in the text and the notes. Details are in the Selected Bibliography.

AP   Benjamin, *The Arcades Project*

AW   Benjamin, *The Work of Art in the Age of Its Technological Reproducibility, and Other Writings on Media*

BA   Benjamin and Theodor W. Adorno, *The Complete Correspondence*

BC   Benjamin, *Berlin Childhood around 1900*

BG   Benjamin and Gretel Adorno, *Correspondence*

BS   Benjamin and Scholem, *Correspondence*

C   Benjamin, *Correspondence*

EW   Benjamin, *Early Writings*

GB   Benjamin, *Gesammelte Briefe*

GS   Benjamin, *Gesammelte Schriften*

LY   Scholem, *Lamentations of Youth*

MD   Benjamin, *Moscow Diary*

OGT Benjamin, *The Origin of German Tragic Drama*

OH   Benjamin, *On Hashish*

SF   Scholem, *Walter Benjamin: The Story of a Friendship*

SW   Benjamin, *Selected Writings*

Notes

Previously published translations of Walter Benjamin's writings cited in this book have been modified in places for greater accuracy.

1. A BERLIN CHILDHOOD

1. Benjamin's brother, Georg (1895–1942), became a doctor, joined the Communist Party in 1922, and died in a Nazi concentration camp. His sister, Dora (1901–1946), a social worker who became seriously ill in the thirties, escaped with him from Paris in 1940 and thereafter lived in Switzerland.
2. Hilde Benjamin, *Georg Benjamin,* 13–14.
3. Hannah Arendt observes that the literature of the time was filled with representations of father-son conflicts. See her introduction in Benjamin, *Illuminations,* 26.
4. Benjamin, *Georg Benjamin,* 18.
5. *Walter Benjamins Archive* (Walter Benjamin's Archives) was published in conjunction with the exhibition of various of Benjamin's manuscripts and personal collections in the fall of 2006 at the Berlin Akademie der Künste; it has been published in English as *Walter Benjamin's Archive.* Benjamin's "Verzeichnis der gelesenen Schriften" (List of Books Read) is printed in GS, 7:437–476; the record of writings read before late 1916 has been lost.
6. Hilde Benjamin (née Lange; 1902–1989) played a decisive role in the Stalinist reorganization of East Germany's legal system from 1949 to 1967. As a judge, she gained the nickname "Bloody Hilde" on account of her frequent death sentences. She was minister of justice in the German Democratic Republic from 1963 to 1967. Her biography of her late husband was first published in 1977.
7. See Benjamin, *Georg Benjamin,* 14–15. See also Brodersen, *Walter Benjamin,* 17–19.
8. SF, 4.
9. Benjamin, "Die Landschaft von Haubinda" (ca. 1913–1914), in GS, 6:195.
10. See the anonymous festschrift article "Deutsche Landerziehungsheime" (German Country Boarding Schools), cited in GS, 2:827–828. To its chauvinist tendency was soon afterward added, as Brodersen points out, a "scarcely concealed anti-Semitism" (*Walter Benjamin,* 25). For a brief description of the "chapel" evenings at Haubinda, see SW, 2:322.
11. See Benjamin's *Anfang* essay of 1911, "The Free School Community," in EW, 39–45.
12. See Wyneken, *Schule und Jugendkultur,* 5–12. Benjamin commented on the first edition of this book in a letter of May 23, 1914: "His theory continues to lag far behind his vision" (C, 68 [Translations from this volume have been frequently modified in this biography to bring them closer to the original German. The translations in C are based on the first edition of Benjamin's

letters, the *Briefe* (1966), which contains many mistakes and omissions, and has been superseded by the *Gesammelte Briefe*.]).

13. "Benjamin's schoolmates included . . . Ernst Schoen, Alfred Cohn, Herbert [Belmore], Franz Sachs, Fritz Strauss, Alfred Steinfeld, and Willy Wolfradt. . . . These students formed a circle that met regularly to read and discuss works of literature. Fritz Strauss told me that this group regarded Benjamin as its leader and that his intellectual superiority was evident to all" (SF, 4).

14. See also Voigts, *Oskar Goldberg*, 127–128. On Benjamin's relation to Hiller, going back to ca. 1910, see SF, 15–16.

15. Scholem records a dream Benjamin had three days before the suicide of his aunt: " 'I was lying in a bed; my aunt and another person also lay there, but we did not mingle. People walking by outside were looking in through a window.' He said he did not realize until later that this had been a symbolic announcement of his aunt's death" (SF, 61–62). This dream takes on an added dimension when considered in light of Benjamin's own suicide.

16. Benjamin's school-leaving certificate notes his "regular attendance" and "commendable behavior," along with his "unsatisfactory" handwriting (Brodersen, *Walter Benjamin*, 30, 32).

17. In a letter of September 6, 1913, to Siegfried Bernfeld, a comrade in the youth movement, Benjamin refers to this high-school *Bierzeitung*, in which he published his "Epilogue" on the occasion of his graduation, as "my generation's humor magazine, particularly noteworthy for the fact that it was shown to teachers. Two friends and I had put it together behind the backs of the class and at the farewell banquet surprised both pupils and teaching staff" (GB, 1:172). The two friends may have been Fritz Strauss and Franz Sachs, though Ernst Schoen seems also to have been involved.

2. METAPHYSICS OF YOUTH

1. See Chapter 3. Benjamin refers to Heidegger several times in *The Arcades Project*; see especially AP, Convolutes N3,1 and S1,6. See also C, 168, 359–360, 365, 571–572; GB, 4:332–333, 341; GB, 5:135, 156. Heidegger mentions Benjamin briefly in correspondence with Hannah Arendt, on the occasion of her lecture on Benjamin in Freiburg in 1967, which Heidegger attended. (The lecture forms the basis of her introduction to *Illuminations*.) See Arendt and Heidegger, *Briefe*, 155, 321–322. See also Fuld, *Walter Benjamin*, 290–292. The difference between the two men, which has everything to do with their different backgrounds, is already apparent in their student years: Heidegger took no interest in the youth movement that was so important to Benjamin.

2. Walter Laqueur's *Young Germany* is still the most comprehensive and balanced treatment of the youth movement in English.

3. R. H. S. Crossman, introduction to Laqueur, *Young Germany*, xxii.

4. Autorenkollektiv (Authors' Collective), "Geschichte der deutschen Arbeiterjugend-Bewegung, 1904–1945" (1973), quoted in Benjamin, *Georg Benjamin*,

22–23. The passage in quotation marks at the end was formulated at the Meissner youth congress of October 1913 (discussed in this chapter); see note 29 below.

5. The reference is to Luke 17:21 and to Plato's *Symposium*.

6. Benjamin quotes the relevant lines in a 1928 review (SW, 2:105). He discusses *Hamlet*, "the tragedy of modern man," in his 1911 essay "Sleeping Beauty" (EW, 26–32).

7. As Benjamin would write in 1924, "Truth is not an unveiling that nullifies the secret but a revelation that does justice to it" (OGT, 31). (Translations of passages from the *Trauerspiel* book in this biography differ significantly from the more freely translated text of *The Origin of German Tragic Drama*.) See also the fragment from 1923, "On the Topic of Individual Disciplines and Philosophy": "There is no truth about an object [*über eine Sache*]. Truth is only *in* it" (SW, 1:404).

8. Benjamin quotes a sentence evidently written by Herbert Belmore (his correspondent here) in a letter that has not been preserved: "'It would truly be the torment of the Danaids to want to redeem the unredeemable [*das Unerlösbare erlösen zu wollen*]'" (C, 34). It is not clear with whom the phrase actually originates.

9. Nietzsche, *On the Advantage and Disadvantage of History for Life*, 37–38. The essay forms the second part of Nietzsche's *Unzeitgemässe Betrachtungen* (Untimely Reflections).

10. Novalis, *Werke in Einem Band*, 351 (first two sentences quoted in Benjamin's 1919 dissertation; see SW, 1:182). Compare Schlegel, *Lucinde and the Fragments*, Athenaeum fragment no. 147, on realizing antiquity within oneself (quoted on page 95 of this book).

11. For an early expression of Benjamin's theory of awakening, compare his poem "On Seeing the Morning Light," appended to a letter of September 10, 1917, to Ernst Schoen: "Where waking is not divorced from sleep / A radiance begins . . . In old dream's light [man] awakes" (EW, 281–282). On Wyneken's idea of awakening youth, see page 25. Benjamin was also acquainted with Ludwig Klages's 1914 treatise, "Vom Traumbewusstsein" (Dream Consciousness), now in Klages, *Sämtliche Werke*, 3:155–238; see esp. 158–189.

12. On the proximity of Benjamin's concept of "dialectical image" to early Christian ideas of the *kairos* (critical moment), see Agamben, *The Time That Remains*, 138–145, and, in a context that includes "the messianic time of Judaism," *Infancy and History*, 105, 111–115. Benjamin's idea of early Christianity was influenced by both Tolstoy (see note 30 below) and Martin Buber. Buber's *Three Addresses on Judaism* (1911), which Benjamin mentions in letters of this period, contains numerous comments on "early Christianity" as a distinctive epoch of authentic Jewish religiosity. See Buber, *On Judaism*, 45–47 and passim.

13. On the waking world, see AP, Convolute K1,3, and on now time (*Jetztzeit*), see SW, 4:395–397.

14. For an indication of Philipp Keller's "strong early influence" on Benjamin, see MD, 47.

15. Goldstein, "Deutsch-Jüdischer Parnaß," 286ff. This article is excerpted in Puttnies and Smith, *Benjaminiana*, 41–44.

16. The concept of "cultural Zionism" derives from the Russian-born Hebrew essayist Ahad Ha'am (Asher Ginsberg; 1856–1927), a liberal leader and internal critic of the Zionist movement who called for a revival of Hebrew and Jewish culture as prelude to an envisioned "national awakening" (see Puttnies and Smith, *Benjaminiana*, 60–61). In a diary entry of August 23, 1916, Scholem notes a conversation with Benjamin on Ahad Ha'am, remarking (despite his friend's explicit critique of nationalism) "how near Benjamin stands to Ahad Ha'am," by which he refers in particular to a shared appreciation of "the role of 'justice' in Judaism." Scholem, *Tagebücher*, 386.

17. Emil Ludwig, "Erinnerungen an Simmel," in Gassen and Landmann, eds., *Buch des Dankes an Georg Simmel*, 152.

18. Joël, quoted in Puttnies and Smith, *Benjaminiana*, 27; Belmore, "Some Recollections about Walter Benjamin," 120.

19. Kurt Tuchler, letter to Gershom Scholem, February 26, 1963, quoted in Puttnies and Smith, *Benjaminiana*, 40–41.

20. "Moral Education" (EW, 107–115) is the first text Benjamin published under his own name. He argues here for "the possibility of a moral education as an integral whole, although without systematic closure in the particulars." For even if "moral education has no system," it can serve to "combat all that is peripheral and without conviction in our scholarship, the intellectual isolation of our schooling." It does so by introducing "a new education in history," one in which the historian's own present day would find its relevance."

21. See the letters from Franz Sachs and Kurt Tuchler excerpted in Puttnies and Smith, *Benjaminiana*, 135. The Paris experience may be reflected in Benjamin's short story of ca. 1913, "The Aviator" (EW, 126–127).

22. "Studies in Metaphysics in Conjunction with the Writings of Henri Bergson" was the title of Rickert's course. Rickert was ultimately critical of Bergson's ahistorical philosophy of life; this criticism is echoed in Benjamin's "On Some Motifs in Baudelaire" (SW, 4:314, 336). See also AP, Convolute H1a,5. Benjamin gave a talk on Bergson in a seminar at Bern in 1918.

23. That Benjamin was not without antifeminist tendencies of his own is indicated by a review of 1928, in which he refers to Eva Fiesel's book on the linguistic philosophy of German Romanticism as "typische Frauenarbeit" (GS, 3:96); see Chapter 6. See also C, 133 (July 31, 1918).

24. According to Scholem (SF, 59) the essay is unfinished. See also C, 71, where Benjamin says that his "series" or "cycle" (*Zyklus*— his term for this piece) needs to be completed (July 6–7, 1914). The lyrical third part, "The Ball," introduces motifs of the masquerade and the round dance, the windowless hall in which time is captured, but otherwise does not develop thematically to any great extent, and is not treated here.

25. In 1913–1914 Benjamin published two pieces ("Youth Was Silent" and "Erotic Education") in Franz Pfemfert's *Die Aktion*, the well-known journal

of a politically attuned Expressionism. Pfemfert's publishing house, Die Aktion, published the third series of *Der Anfang*. On Benjamin's relationship to literary Expressionism, see SF, 65–66.

26. Compare the opening sentence of the essay's second part, "The Diary": "We wish to pay heed to the sources of the unnameable despair that flows in every soul."

27. See Bergson, *Matter and Memory*, 45–46, and *Creative Evolution*, 262. Consciousness and matter are complementary movements in Bergson's process philosophy.

28. In his autobiography, *Spiegelung der Jugend*, Werner Kraft tells of Benjamin's "ecstatic" reading of a Heinle poem to him in 1915, and of the air of "cultic mystery" with which Benjamin surrounded everything to do with his dead friend. He also mentions the disappointment later experienced by Hugo von Hofmannsthal on first reading Heinle's poetry. See C, 30 for a translation of Heinle's short poem "Portrait," and GS, 2:859–865 for examples of Heinle's prose writing (the *Anfang* piece, "Meine Klasse," along with a text from November 1913, "Die Jugend" [Youth], reminiscent of Benjamin's final essay for *Der Anfang*, "Experience") and of a nonsense poem, "Urwaldgeister" (Ghosts of the Primeval Forest), written together with Benjamin. See further Werner Kraft's two essays on Heinle: "Über einen verschollenen Dichter" and "Friedrich C. Heinle." Kraft quotes a number of surviving verses by Heinle, finds many of them moving, and considers them remnants of "a perhaps great poet."

29. Quoted in Benjamin, *Georg Benjamin*, 23–24. The proceedings of the Meissner congress were described in the November issue of *Der Anfang*, in an article by the journal's editor, Georges Barbizon (Georg Gretor); the report is printed in full in GS, 2:909–913. Laqueur devotes a chapter to the event ("At the Hohe Meissner") in his *Young Germany*.

30. The Russian novelist Leo Tolstoy (1828–1910) in his later years evolved a Christian anarchism, which led him to reject the authority of the Church, to oppose organized government, and to condemn private property, while affirming the moral development of the individual as the basis of social progress. Tolstoyism became an organized sect and around 1884 began to gain proselytes. Tolstoy's radical creed is reflected in such works as *A Confession* (1882), *The Kingdom of God Is within You* (1894), and *The Law of Love and the Law of Violence* (1908).

31. Dora Sophie Pollak to Herbert Blumenthal (Belmore), March 14, 1914; Scholem archive, quoted in Puttnies and Smith, *Benjaminiana*, 136.

32. Wyneken had given a lecture titled "Fichte as Educator" in the Berlin Sprechsaal on January 29, 1914 (GB, 1:193n). Fichte will have an important role to play in Benjamin's 1919 dissertation on German Romanticism (see Chapter 3).

33. From an account of Benjamin's "stirring" Weimar talk by Siegfried Bernfeld in *Der Anfang* (excerpted in GS, 2:877).

34. "The Life of Students" appeared in two versions during Benjamin's lifetime: first in the monthly *Der Neue Merkur*, in September 1915, and then in an expanded version (containing the lines from Stefan George at the end) in

the anthology *Das Ziel* (The Goal), published in 1916 by Kurt Hiller (1885–1972), a writer and a publicist of literary Expressionism, who in 1914 coined the term "literary activism" to refer to literature in the service of political intervention. As early as July 1916, Benjamin was regretting his participation in this second publication, and later, in a 1932 review entitled "The Error of Activism" (GS, 3:350–352), which invokes Trotsky and Brecht, he distanced himself from Hiller's rationalist position.

35. "In July 1914 [Grete Radt] spent some time with [Benjamin] in the Bavarian Alps. Toward the end of that month his father sent him a telegram with the terse warning 'Sapenti sat' [A word to the wise], presumably to induce him to leave the country for some neutral territory such as Switzerland. But Benjamin misinterpreted the message and replied by formally announcing that he was engaged to Grete Radt" (SF, 12). Of course we cannot be sure that this was a misinterpretation on Benjamin's part. See GS, 2:873–874 for Grete Radt's report on the Berlin Sprechsaal, as published in the March 1914 number of the *Anfang*. She is critical of the complacent resort to slogans instead of "wrestling with language for new expressions," and she argues, much like Benjamin at this time (see EW, 170), that "the only thing Youth can express is struggle [*Kampf*]." Grete Radt later married another close friend of Benjamin's, Alfred Cohn, and remained in touch with Benjamin until the end of his life.

36. Franz Sachs to Gershom Scholem, March 10, 1963; Scholem archive, quoted in Puttnies and Smith, *Benjaminiana*, 135.

37. Belmore, "Some Recollections of Walter Benjamin," 122–123.

38. A third Seligson sister, Gertrud (Traute), would commit suicide, together with Wilhelm Caro, in November 1915 (see GB, 1:213n).

39. Scholem relates that in October 1915, Benjamin "spoke about Hölderlin and gave me a typewritten copy of his essay, 'Two Poems by Friedrich Hölderlin'" . . . Only later did I realize that this gift was a sign of his great trust in me . . . Benjamin [referred] to Norbert von Hellingrath's edition of Hölderlin as well as to Hellingrath's study of Hölderlin's Pindar translations; Hellingrath's study had made a great impression on him" (SF, 17). Hellingrath had published an edition of Hölderlin's translations of odes by Pindar, together with his dissertation on these translations, in 1910. In February 1917 Benjamin wrote to Ernst Schoen about Hellingrath, whom he may have met in Munich in 1915: "Have you read that Norbert von Hellingrath died in the war? I had wanted to give him my Hölderlin study to read when he returned. The way Hellingrath framed the subject in his work on the Pindar translations was the external motivation for my study" (C, 85)—the internal motivation being, presumably, to commemorate Heinle. Whether the essay additionally has roots in a "talk about Hölderlin" given by Benjamin when still in high school (C, 146) cannot be determined, since no record of the talk has survived.

40. The form-content distinction is renovated in a luminous brief fragment from 1919: "Content makes its way toward us. Form holds back [*verharrt*], permits us to approach[,] . . . causes perception to accumulate." Content manifests the "currently effective messianic elements of the work of art"

and form manifests the "retarding elements" (SW, 1:213). On the "retarding" element, compare SW, 1:172, citing Friedrich Schlegel and Novalis.

41. This is concurrent with his invocation of the intoxication *(Rausch)* that accompanies "the highest intellectual clarity, . . . the consuming intoxication of creation, [which] is the consciousness of creating within the canon, according to the truth we fulfill." See "The Rainbow" (EW, 216–217).

42. In "Trauerspiel and Tragedy" (1916), Benjamin speaks of "the great moments of passivity" in which the meaning of a tragic fate emerges (EW, 242–243). Compare Friedrich Schlegel's idea of "true passivity" in his novel *Lucinde,* in *Lucinde and the Fragments,* 65–66 ("An Idyll of Idleness"). Wordsworth's phrase "wise passiveness," from his poem "Expostulation and Reply," may also be mentioned. Benjamin's idea of "motionless existence" *(reglose Dasein),* in the Hölderlin essay, points toward the "standstill" of the dialectical image.

43. Theodor W. Adorno remarks of Benjamin that he "viewed the world from the perspective of the dead." See "Zu Benjamins Gedächtnis" (1940), in Adorno, *Über Walter Benjamin,* 72. "Death . . . was the constant companion of our generation" (Gumpert, *Hölle im Paradies* [1939], quoted in GS, 2:881).

3. THE CONCEPT OF CRITICISM

1. Benjamin's German editors point to the letter of September 15, 1913, to Carla Seligson, in which he says, "We must not commit ourselves to one specific idea" (C, 54), as already indicating a slight distancing from Wyneken (GS, 2:865).

2. Willem van Reijen and Herman van Doorn suggest that the enigmatic second sentence of this passage may refer to Wyneken's homosexuality. See their *Aufenthalte und Passagen,* 235n.

3. Scholem, *Tagebücher,* 133; LY, 62 (July 23, 1915). The episode is also recounted in the later memoir (SF, 7).

4. See SW, 2:603–604.

5. In a letter of January 13, 1924, to Hugo von Hofmannsthal, Benjamin mentions that "nine years passed between my first attempts at a translation of the *Flowers of Evil* and the book's publication [in October 1923]" (C, 229). In this biography, previously published translations of Benjamin's letters have been modified in places for greater accuracy.

6. See C, 75. For translations of Benjamin's early writings on the aesthetics of color, which bears on a theory of perception and meaning that dissolves the "logic of solids," see "A Child's View of Color" (1914–1915) and "The Rainbow: A Conversation about Imagination" (ca. 1915), both in EW.

7. On Scholem's early mathematical studies, particularly in relation to the philosophy of time, see Fenves, *The Messianic Reduction,* 106–117.

8. Werner Kraft, a friend of both Benjamin and Scholem, was also present at this discussion, held in the Meeting Hall of the Berlin Independent Students' Association. See his autobiography, *Spiegelung der Jugend,* 59–69.

9. Unpublished book lists in the Walter Benjamin Archive in Berlin attest to Benjamin's extensive interest in the phenomenological school (information courtesy of Peter Fenves and Julia Ng).

10. Scholem, "Walter Benjamin und Felix Noeggerath," 135–136.

11. This understanding of the messianic realm influenced Scholem's own thinking decisively, as seen in his youthful "Remarks on Judaism and Time," which throw an interesting light on Benjamin's position: "The messianic realm is history in the present [*die Gegenwart der Geschichte*]. The prophets could speak about this idea only hypothetically by using the image of the future. What does 'And in those days' mean? If one thinks it through to the end, 'those days' refers to these days. The kingdom of God is the *present*. . . . Time in religion is always a decision, i.e., the present. . . . The future is a *command*, . . . for instance:. . . the command to spread holiness into the present moment" (LY, 245–246 [June 17, 1918]).

12. Scholem, *Tagebücher*, 401–402; LY, 142.

13. Dora Pollak to Herbert Blumenthal and Carla Seligson, June 29, 1915, Scholem Archive, quoted in Puttnies and Smith, *Benjaminiana*, 139–140; Belmore, "Some Recollections of Walter Benjamin," 119, 122.

14. His formulation in the essay is more complex, glancing as it does at the persistence of mythic elements in the figure of Socrates: "Socrates: this is the figure in which Plato has annihilated the old myth and received it" (EW, 233, 236n1). The composition of "Socrates" was roughly contemporaneous with that of several other short pieces: "The Happiness of Ancient Man," "On the Middle Ages," "'Trauerspiel and Tragedy," and "The Role of Language in *Trauerspiel* and Tragedy." The sequence was evidently capped by the composition of the essay "On Language as Such and on the Language of Man" in November. See C, 84.

15. Scholem remembers that "Buber made an angry remark about [Benjamin's letter (which he preserved)] when we met once in the winter of 1916. Later Buber supported Benjamin whenever he could . . . but the two men were simply of different temperaments" (SF, 27). See Chapter 6 on Buber's support for Benjamin in 1926–1927.

16. "Nacht," correcting the earlier reading of "Macht" (power) in the *Briefe* (GB, 1:327). Compare the maxim enunciated in "Socrates": "The radiant is true only where it is refracted in the nocturnal" (EW, 234).

17. When he gave Scholem a copy of the essay in December, he spoke of adding two more parts. See SW, 1:87–91 for an indication of his ideas for continuation.

18. On the priority of word to concept, see SW, 2:444. On "the magical side of language" and "the magical realm of words," see SW, 1:424 and 2:212, as well as the letter to Buber cited above.

19. Years later, on the subject of dream houses, Benjamin writes: "Arcades are houses or passages having no outside— like the dream" (AP, 406 [L1a,1]).

20. In the *Moscow Diary*, Benjamin formulates the problem of communication somewhat differently. He speaks of "the polarity that exists in every linguistic entity: to be at once expression and communication [*Mitteilung*]. . . . The development of the communicative aspect of language to the exclusion of all else . . . inevitably leads to the destruction of language. On the other hand, the way leads to mystical silence if its expressive character is raised

to the absolute. . . . In one form or another, a compromise is always necessary" (MD, 47 [1926]).

21. Benjamin's distinction between the *intensive Totalität* and *extensive Totalität* of language (GS, 2:145) recalls Rickert's distinction between intensive and extensive infinities.

22. Compare Benjamin's comments on the relation of the word to art, truth, and justice (C, 83 [ca. end of 1916]; also 108 [February 28, 1917]).

23. At the end of the essay, after having argued that "language never gives *mere* signs" (EW, 260), although "man makes language a means . . . and therefore also, in one part at any rate, a *mere* sign" (264), Benjamin observes that "the relation between language and sign . . . is original and fundamental" (266).

24. With its invocation of "the night that bears the light," night as "the bleeding body of the spirit," this letter to Belmore bears a close relation to the letter of July 17, 1916, to Buber, discussed previously in the text.

25. The note is preserved together with one from Carla Seligson to Benjamin: "Lieber Walter, ich möchte Dich bitten zu mir zu kommen. Carla" (Dear Walter, I would ask you to come see me. Carla), evidently representing an attempt to salvage the friendship after their last meeting on July 9 (GB, 1:368).

26. Belmore, "Some Recollections of Walter Benjamin," 123.

27. There was an emotional exchange of letters in late 1917 between Scholem and Benjamin concerning this essay; Scholem read the interpretation of Prince Myshkin as secretly having reference to Benjamin's dead friend, Fritz Heinle. See SF, 49, and C, 102.

28. We have corrected two errors in the translation of this passage in C that derive from misreadings, on the part of the editors of the *Briefe* (1966), of Benjamin's manuscript: "eleusinisch" (Eleusinian) was construed as "unsinnig" (insanely), and "unentweiht" (inviolate) as "unentwegt" (without deviation). See GB, 1:363, which prints material omitted in the *Briefe* and in C.

29. Schlegel, *Lucinde and the Fragments*, 180 (Athenaeum fragment 147).

30. In a short, Hölderlin-inspired piece from the end of 1917, "The Centaur," discussing the "spirit of water" in Greek myth, Benjamin refers to the liquid element as the animating medium, *Medium der Belebung*, which, "because it was a medium, . . . was the unity of [*über*] opposites" (EW, 283). Compare *Medium der Reflexion* in the dissertation, begun some three months later.

31. Compare what Benjamin says about *Theorie* as the "welling fruitfulness of our production," in a letter of December 4, 1915, to Fritz Radt (GB, 1:298–299).

32. First published in 1963.

33. Benjamin's term is *systematische Spezifikation der Erkenntnis*. In a note of March–June 1888, Nietzsche writes, in connection with his concept of *Kraftzentrum* (center of force), that "Perspectivism is only a complex form of specificity [*Spezifität*]. . . . Every specific body strives to become master over all space and to extend its force" (*The Will to Power*, 340 [no. 636]).

34. Kant is later invoked at a key point in *The Arcades Project*, when Benjamin, alluding to the author's preface to the second edition of *The Critique of Pure Reason*, speaks of a "Copernican revolution in historical perception" (Convolute K1,2). See Chapter 6, note 43.

35. The letter to Schoen, written from Locarno, is dated February 28, 1918 (GB, 1:435); it is misdated in *The Correspondence of Walter Benjamin*. It was during this period, in early 1918, that Benjamin first manifested his tendency toward microscopic handwriting. See SF, 45; also the editors' comments in GS, 7:573–574.

36. The surviving pages of Benjamin's *Büchlein* devoted to the "thoughts and opinions" of his son, which he intended to have typed for Scholem's archive, are translated in *Walter Benjamin's Archive*, 109–149.

37. Early examples of this interest are the fragment "A Child's View of Color" (1914–1915) and the discussion of children's picture books and games involving color in "The Rainbow: A Conversation about Imagination" (ca. 1915), both in EW.

38. Scholem had been drafted into the German army in the spring of 1917, but after telling army doctors of his "visions," he was diagnosed with a form of schizophrenia and confined to a mental ward, where he spent his time writing letters on themes of Torah, History, and Messiah. By August 1917 he was back in Berlin, having been released from the military (LY, 162–163).

39. In his diary, Scholem mentions a conversation on May 5, 1918, a day after his arrival in Switzerland, in which he and Benjamin talked about "an academy where we are for ourselves" (LY, 235).

40. See SF, 58; C, 134, 222; GS, 4:441–448 ("Acta Muriensa" [1918–1923]); and GB, 3:304n.

41. See GB, 2:107 (1920), on *Religion of Reason*. Benjamin generally cites Cohen respectfully in published essays. See, for example, SW, 1:206, 249, 304, 348, and 2:797. In a letter of December 22, 1924, Benjamin writes Scholem of their ongoing "critique of Cohen's system" (GB, 2:512). During this same period, in the prologue to the *Trauerspiel* book, he criticizes the origin-logic developed in Cohen's *Logic of Pure Knowledge* as insufficiently historical, a defect he will remedy in his own conception of particular origin (*The Origin of German Tragic Drama*, 46). There are related criticisms of Cohen in SW, 4:140 and GB, 2:215n. Benjamin's creative appropriation of Cohen's philosophy of religion is discussed in Chapter 4.

42. Benjamin includes one of the theologian Overbeck's letters to Nietzsche in *German Men and Women* (1936); see SW, 3:217–219. Bernoulli's *Franz Overbeck und Friedrich Nietzsche* was published in 1918. Benjamin later refers to it as "scholarly colportage" (C, 288). See also Benjamin's "Review of Bernoulli's *Bachofen*" (SW, 1:426–427).

43. By the beginning of June 1918, Scholem was confiding his doubts about Walter and Dora to his diary: "There are moments—may God and the two of them forgive me for this—when I consider them to be perfectly ignoble, especially in their behavior." Two weeks later, he complains that "they tell lies out of aesthetic pleasure. . . . Only gradually am I realizing how deceitful their lives are—also in their relationship to me. His honesty is in his poetry and

philosophy." On June 23, he asks: "And Walter? . . . I think that only from afar can a person have an absolute relation with him. . . . With him I have to keep silent about almost everything that gives me fulfillment. . . . I can only say that I don't know where Walter is, he's just not where I am (this much I see); it only seems that he is." The pattern continued into the fall. He writes on October 7: "Worst of all, there is the lurking danger that I'll completely lose my faith in Walter's purity in everyday life. He frequently seems to lack what one calls honesty. . . . Above all, Dora stands between us. . . . She says I don't love her. But here I must say that I have loved her unendingly, boundlessly. But now the sun has set. Why? Because I didn't expect daily life with them to be like this. . . . They don't know, but I do, that over the past three years, I've always done the opposite of what they've advised me." A month later: "I'm again beginning to have an inexpressible love for Dora. . . . We are now like *one* family: I am beyond all doubts" (LY, 240, 245, 252, 268, 273–274).

44. "The Bolshevik Revolution and the collapse of Germany and Austria, as well as the ensuing pseudorevolution, brought current political events into our conversation again for the first time since we had agreed on our attitude toward the war. . . . I was not deeply involved, however" (SF, 78). Scholem goes on to say that their sympathies were largely with the Social Revolutionary Party in Russia, which was later liquidated by the Bolsheviks.

45. On the debates between Benjamin, Ball, and Ernst Bloch, see Kambas, "Ball, Bloch und Benjamin."

46. Ball, *Die Flucht aus der Zeit*, 201–202.

47. From a 1974 interview, cited in Brodersen, *Walter Benjamin*, 100.

48. In letters to Scholem and Ernst Schoen written in September 1919, Benjamin mentions his idea of reviewing *Geist der Utopie* and says that Bloch himself has "already transcended" and "is ten times better than" his book, which "exhibits enormous deficiencies . . . [but] is nevertheless the only book on which, as a truly contemporaneous and contemporary utterance, I can take my own measure" (C, 146–148).

49. In paragraph 10 of *Sein und Zeit* (1927), Heidegger also distinguishes literary history *(Literaturgeschichte)* from the history of problems *(Problemge-schichte)*, suggesting that the former is turning into the latter. See *Being and Time*, 30.

50. Compare the formulation in a fragment, "The Theory of Criticism," from 1919–1920: "Works of art are ways in which the ideal of the philosophical problem makes itself manifest. . . . [E]very great work [of art] has its sibling . . . in the realm of philosophy" (SW, 1:218–219). And further: "The only philosophical ideas that can enter into the structure of art are those which concern the meaning of existence" (SW, 1:377 [1923]).

51. In a fragment of 1923, "On the Topic of Individual Disciplines and Philosophy," Benjamin puts it this way: "Our gaze must strike the object in such a way that it awakens something within it that springs up to meet the intention. . . . The intensive observer finds that something leaps out at him from the object, enters into him, takes possession of him. . . . This language

of the intentionless truth (that is to say, of the object itself) possesses authority. . . . It leaps into existence as the result of an immersion of the object
in itself provoked by the external gaze" (SW, 1:404–405).

52. Compare the definition of experience as "systematic specification of knowledge" in "Program of the Coming Philosophy" (discussed earlier in the
text). Benjamin points out that Schlegel himself did not make use of the
term "medium." Benjamin uses the term in two of his own pieces from this
period: in the language essay of 1916, where it designates the peculiar
"infinity" of language, which is limited by nothing external to itself but
communicates itself *in* itself, and in "The Centaur" of 1917, where it is associated with a functional unity of opposites (see note 30 above).

53. See Weber, *Benjamin's -abilities.*

54. On what Benjamin calls the "afterlife" or "survival" or "continuing life" of
the work of art, see SW, 1:164. See, further, SW, 1:177–178, 254–256; 2:408,
410, 415, 464; OGT, 47; and AP, 460 (N2,3). Benjamin discusses the afterlife
(Fortleben) of letters in a letter of September 19, 1919, to Ernst Schoen (C,
149).

55. Now in GS, 2:615–617.

56. Compare GB, 2:101, 127, for indicators that he did not read the Sorel book
until early 1921.

57. Her father, Leon Kellner, had been a close associate of the founder of Zionism, Theodor Herzl, and her brother Viktor would help found a village in
Palestine.

4. ELECTIVE AFFINITIES

1. See the fragment "According to the Theory of Duns Scotus," SW, 1:228.

2. This and all further currency conversions are based upon a database maintained by Harold Marcuse of the University of California, Santa Barbara,
and published at http://www.history.ucsb.edu/faculty/marcuse/projects/cur
rency.htm.

3. Scholem, *From Berlin to Jerusalem*, 80.

4. Excerpts from the book are available in English in Gutkind, *The Body of
God.* Gutkind had anglicized his first name after immigrating to America
in 1933.

5. Scholem, *From Berlin to Jerusalem*, 81.

6. For a reliable account of the Forte circle and its publications, see Faber and
Holste, eds., *Potsdamer Forte-Kreis.*

7. Kraft, *Spiegelung der Jugend*, 63.

8. SF, 91.

9. Benjamin, *Georg Benjamin*, 45–46.

10. Erwin Levy, letter to Gary Smith, cited in Puttnies and Smith, *Benjaminiana*, 23.

11. SF, 84.

12. GB, 2:108–109. The word "third" in this letter is controversial. Scholem
read it as "first" and related it to a bipartite schema for the politics; the editors of Benjamin's collected letters have argued convincingly for a tripartite
schema (111n).

13. See SW, 3:305–306, 306n1 for an indication of the uncertainty of the dating of the piece. Recent opinion favors a date of 1920 or 1921. Benjamin adduces Bloch's *Geist der Utopie* (The Spirit of Utopia; 1918) in support of his rejection of the political justification of theocracy.

14. On "eternal transience" *(ewige Vergängnis)*, see SW, 1:281 (1920–1921); AP, 348, 917 (1935); and SW, 4:407 (1940).

15. Benjamin found Müller's *Zwölf Reden über die Beredsamkeit und ihren Verfall in Deutschland* (Twelve Speeches on Eloquence and Its Decline in Germany; 1816) sloppy in its systematics, but full of insight; he remarked that he hoped to use it for the composition of his essay on "the true politician" (GB, 2:141). The book is mentioned in the 1921 essay fragment "Capitalism as Religion" (SW, 1:288–291).

16. See GB2, 107 (letter of December 1, 1920), to Scholem, documenting Benjamin's brief but favorable first impression of the recently published text of *Religion of Reason*.

17. One of the manifestations of this divine violence *(göttliche Gewalt)* is an "educative power [*erzieherische Gewalt*], which in its perfected form stands outside the law. . . . These [manifestations] are defined . . . by the expiating moment in them that strikes without bloodshed, and . . . by the absence of all lawmaking." For there is "something rotten in the law" (SW, 1:250, 242). Sorel speaks of the "educational value" of the general strike at the end of section 2 of chapter 4, "The Proletarian Strike," in *Reflections on Violence*.

18. Kohlenbach, "Religion, Experience, Politics," 65.

19. Ibid., 78.

20. SF, 96–97.

21. Ibid., 91.

22. *Walter Benjamin's Archive*, 124.

23. See Kraft, *Spiegelung der Jugend*, 65, and Wolff, *Hindsight*, 67–68.

24. Wolff, *Hindsight*, 68. Wolff describes the placement of the Klee aquarelle in Benjamin's Grunewald study: "Walter and I used to sit opposite each other at a long oak table, covered with his manuscripts. The walls of his room were made invisible through rows of books which reached from floor to ceiling. There was, however, one large space left on the back wall to house a picture Walter loved—the 'Angelus Novus' by Paul Klee. He had a personal relationship with this picture, as if it were part of his mind. . . . In time I understood that it expressed a lucidity in composition and 'touch' " (67).

25. Quoted in GB, 2:175n.

26. Wolff, *Hindsight*, 64–65.

27. Dora Benjamin to Gershom Scholem, quoted in GB, 2:154n.

28. SF, 95. Scholem asks at this point: "Was the reason for this [apparent incorporeality] some lack of vitality, as it seemed to many, or was it a convolution of his vitality (which often enough burst forth in those years) with his altogether metaphysical orientation that gained him the reputation of being a withdrawn person?" Compare to this the letter of September 6, 1936, from Theodor W. Adorno to Benjamin, in which Adorno locates "the heart of our debate" in his difference with Benjamin's "undialectical ontology of the

body": "It is as if for you the human body were the measure of all concreteness [*Maß der Konkretion*]" (BA, 146).

29. Wolff, *Hindsight*, 69.

30. Compare SW, 2:271.

31. Ibid., 70. From this perspective, Walter Benjamin resembles another eminently Nietzschean character, Baron Clappique in André Malraux's *Man's Fate*. Clappique's own failed erotic conquests may be compared to Benjamin's: "He was drunk with his lie, with this heat, with the fictive world he was creating. When he said he would kill himself he did not believe what he was saying; but, since she believed it, he was entering a world where truth no longer existed. It was neither true nor false, but real. And since neither his past which he had just invented, nor the elementary gesture, presumably so close, upon which his relationship to this woman was based—since neither of these existed, nothing existed. The world ceased to weigh upon him" (Malraux, *Man's Fate*, 246–247). Like Clappique in Shanghai, Walter Benjamin may have been the only man in Berlin who absolutely did not exist.

32. Schiller-Lerg, "Ernst Schoen," 983.

33. Adorno, "Benjamin the Letter Writer" (C, xxi).

34. Schiller-Lerg, "Ernst Schoen."

35. Dora Benjamin to Gershom Scholem, quoted in GB, 2:153–154n.

36. Benjamin, "Zwei Gatten sind Elemente . . . ," and "Über die Ehe," GS, 6:68.

37. GS, 7:64. The sonnet was inscribed in the notebook reserved for Stefan's "opinions and pensées."

38. SF, 53–54.

39. On George and his circle, see Norton, *Secret Germany*.

40. Regler, *The Owl of Minerva*, 103–104.

41. Benjamin, "Über Stefan George," GS, 2:622–623.

42. "Capitalism as Religion," SW, 1:288–291. *Verschulden* means both "to make financially indebted" and "to make morally guilty."

43. Gutkind to van Eeden, May 10 and 30, 1920, in van Eeden Archive, Amsterdam; quoted in Jäger, *Messianische Kritik*, 76.

44. Wolff, *Hindsight*, 68–69.

45. SF, 106–107.

46. Ibid.

47. The Buber comment is in an unpublished note quoted in Jäger, *Messianische Kritik*, 1.

48. GB, 3:16. The best analysis of the collaboration between Rang and Benjamin remains Steiner, *Die Geburt der Kritik*. See also Jäger, *Messianische Kritik*.

49. Jäger reads the incident more straightforwardly, pointing to Benjamin's interest in esoteric theories of language and in the cultural production of the mentally ill (*Messianische Kritik*, 95). The ironic view of Lyck taken by the monarchist Hans Blüher, who was at this time a friend of Rang's, recalls Benjamin's tone: "When Lyck fell into that ecstatic state that the Greeks called Mania, he would speak of the bird Roch and of Greif and of the transformative force that emanated from them; and then he would allow one to see, without explicitly articulating it, that he himself was this kind of

legendary bird-king whenever he returned to the place from which he had come." Hans Blüher, *Werke und Tage* (1953), 23, quoted in Jäger, *Messianische Kritik*, 95.

50. Benjamin defines the matter of myth by way of hints: "'Eternal return' is the *fundamental* form of . . . mythic consciousness. (Mythic because it does not reflect.) . . . The essence of the mythical event is return" (AP, D10,3). In the Goethe essay of 1921–1922, he writes similarly: "All mythic meaning strives for secrecy [*Geheimnis*]" (SW, 1:314).

51. Cohen, *Religion of Reason*, 46–48, 6.

52. In the 1912 "Dialogue on the Religiosity of the Present," the lead speaker says: "We've had Romanticism and we are indebted to its powerful insight into the night side of the natural. At bottom, the natural is not good; it's strange. dreadful, frightening, repugnant—crude. But we live as though Romanticism had never occurred" (EW, 68). See also the letter of July 30, 1913, to Herbert Belmore: "I was of the opinion that a dread of nature is the test of a genuine feeling for nature. A person who can feel no dread in the face of nature will have no idea of how to begin to treat nature" (C, 48).

53. It should be noted in this context that *One-Way Street* concludes with reference to an emergent *physis*—"the new body" (SW, 1:487).

54. Compare Cohen's critique of "the pantheistic sickness" in *Religion of Reason*, 33, 45, and passim. Benjamin debates the merits of pantheism in connection with Goethe in "Dialogue on the Religiosity of the Present" (EW, 66–69). For an indication of the differences between Benjamin's and Cohen's concepts of myth, see Menninghaus, "Walter Benjamin's Theory of Myth," 299–300.

55. Kraft, *Spiegelung der Jugend*, 64.

56. Letter from Gert Caden to Alfred Hirschbroek, undated, in Sächsische Landesbibliothek, Dresden, Handschriftensammlung, Nachlaß Caden; quoted in Finkeldey, "Hans Richter and the Constructivist International," 105.

57. For a facsimile translation of the journal *G* and a number of essays that situate it in its period, see Mertins and Jennings, eds., *G: An Avant-Garde Journal of Art, Architecture, Design, and Film*.

58. In all of this, Moholy-Nagy must be counted the central figure. Although documentation of the friendship between Benjamin and Moholy-Nagy is sparse, it is significant that in a graphic representation of Benjamin's human relationships—"resembling a series of family trees"—produced in conjunction with his *Berlin Chronicle*, one entire branch on the chart ends with Moholy-Nagy's name. See SW, 2:614, and GS, 6:804.

59. Craig, *Germany*, 450.

5. ACADEMIC NOMAD

1. Kracauer, *Ginster*, in *Werke*, 7:22.

2. Rosenzweig, *The Star of Redemption*, 4. On "language as the organon of revelation," see 110, 295, and passim.

3. On Rosenzweig, see SW, 2:573 ("Privileged Thinking"; 1932) and SW, 2:687 (note of 1931–1932).

4. See GB, 2:386n.

5. See Adorno, *Notes to Literature*, 2:322 ("Benjamin's *Einbahnstraße*"; 1955).

6. Benjamin's position here is adumbrated in the first paragraph of his 1915 essay "The Life of Students" (discussed in Chapter 2).

7. See especially the undated draft of a letter to Schultz from ca. fall 1923, in which Benjamin says that Schultz "particularly suggested" the topic (GB, 2:354).

8. Benjamin composed the short essays "*Trauerspiel* and Tragedy" and "The Role of Language in *Trauerspiel* and Tragedy" in 1916.

9. On the Frankfurt circle, see Jäger, *Messianische Kritik*, 183.

10. Kracauer, "Deutscher Geist und deutsche Wirklichkeit [German Spirit and German Reality]," in Kracauer, *Schriften*, 5:151; first published in *Die Rheinlande* 32, no. 1 (1922).

11. The scene with Dora is mentioned without explanation in a letter Scholem wrote from Frankfurt on July 9, 1923, to his fiancée, Elsa Burchhardt, a letter describing a violent flare-up with Benjamin himself over a telephone call in which Benjamin refused to allow Scholem to bring his cousin Heinz Pflaum (later a professor of Romanticism in Jerusalem) with him for a visit (GB, 2:337–340n).

12. See Müller-Doohm, *Adorno*, 108.

13. Fuld, *Walter Benjamin*, 129–130; SF, 14.

14. Benjamin claimed never actually to have read Barth's epoch-making commentary on Romans (C, 606), but Barth's ideas were very much in the air in the 1920s, and the similarities between his way of thinking and Benjamin's have been noticed. See especially Taubes, *The Political Theology of Paul*, 75–76, 130. Benjamin's understanding of the theological situation in the era of the confessional wars was also greatly aided by discussions with Rang.

15. Volkmann, *Historisch-Kritische Nachrichten aus Italien*.

16. Goethe, *Italian Journey*, 128–129.

17. Benjamin, "Mai-Juni 1931," GS, 6:424.

18. Hessel published Benjamin's translation of Baudelaire's introductory poem "Au lecteur," and of "Le mort joyeux," "L'horloge," and "À une madone" from the "Spleen et idéal" section of *Les fleurs du mal*.

19. Tiedemann, Gödde, and Lönitz, "Walter Benjamin," 161.

20. Lacis, *Revolutionär im Beruf*, 45–46.

21. Ibid., 48.

22. Ibid., 47.

23. Benjamin, review of Jakob Job, *Neapel: Reisebilder und Skizzen* (1928), GS, 3:132. The Camorra is a Neapolitan criminal organization.

24. Adorno asserted that the text was Benjamin's alone— "There can be little doubt that this work was completely Benjamin's product"—a judgment in keeping with a general tendency on the part of Benjamin's friends and readers to denigrate Lacis and her role in his life. A corrective to this position is supplied by Ingram, "The Writings of Asja Lacis."

25. See, for example, the radio play *Lichtenberg* (1932–1933) in GS, 4:696–720.

26. Bloch, "Italien und die Porosität," in *Werkausgabe*, 9:508–515.

27. Benjamin, review of Job, *Neapel* (GS, 3:133).

28. See, for example, "A Child's View of Color" (1914–1915) and "The Rainbow: A Conversation about Imagination" (ca. 1915), in EW, 211–223.
29. See GB, 2:515n and 3:19n.
30. Lacis, *Revolutionär im Beruf*, 53.
31. See Wizisla, *Walter Benjamin and Bertolt Brecht*, 25–31.
32. Lindner, "Habilitationsakte Benjamin," 150.
33. It was Werner Fuld who, in *Walter Benjamin: Zwischen den Stühlen*, 161, initially made the claim that Schultz participated in the book burning. Burkhardt Lindner, in "Habilitationsakte Benjamin," 152, adds that Fuld, in a private conversation, said that he based his claim on the testimony of Werner Fritzemeyer, who had been a student at the university at the time.
34. OGT, 55. We have referred throughout this biography to Benjamin's book on the Baroque play of mourning as *Origin of the German Trauerspiel*. Osborne's translation of the title as *The Origin of German Tragic Drama* represents a serious misunderstanding of the text, which attempts to discriminate the play of mourning precisely from the "tragic drama." We have amended Osborne's translations elsewhere in our quotations from the *Trauerspiel* book.
35. Witte, *Walter Benjamin*, 128.
36. Cornelius, "Habilitations-Akte Benjamin," quoted in Lindner, "Habilitationsakte Benjamin," 155–156.
37. Burkhardt Lindner's 1984 study of the record of Benjamin's candidacy revealed an ironic footnote to the whole sad story. Cornelius not only asked Benjamin for a summary but also asked two of his assistant professors for their evaluations of the dissertation. One of these assistants was Max Horkheimer, who soon would be given a chair at Frankfurt and control of the Institute of Social Research, and who would be primarily responsible for lending Benjamin financial support and affording him opportunities for publishing his work during the years of exile. This same Horkheimer reported, according to Cornelius's recommendation, that he "was incapable of understanding" Benjamin's study.
38. Goethe-Universität, "Habilitationsakte Benjamin," cited in Lindner, "Habilitationsakte," 157.

6. WEIMAR INTELLECTUAL

1. See "Büchereinlauf" (1925), in GS, 4:1017–1018.
2. Haas, "Hinweis auf Walter Benjamin," *Die Welt*, October 9, 1955, quoted in Brodersen, *Walter Benjamin*, 175.
3. The authorship of "The Weapons of Tomorrow" is uncertain. It was signed with Dora's initials, DSB, but appears in the index of published articles Benjamin maintained. Its language would seem to point to Walter Benjamin as the author.
4. The translation of "Anabase" into German has a curious history. A second translation was undertaken by Bernhard Groethuysen in 1929, but that, too, remained unpublished. When the first published translation, by Herbert Steiner, appeared in 1950 in the journal *Das Lot*, an editorial note stated that it was based on a previous version by Benjamin and Groethuysen—

who, to the best of anyone's knowledge, never collaborated on this or any other translation. Benjamin's translation was preserved among Rilke's papers and first published in GS, Supplement 1 (1999), 56–81.

5. SW, 1:424–425.
6. Mann, "Die Entstehung des *Doktor Faustus*," 708. Thomas Mann is mentioned in Benjamin's 1912 "Dialogue on the Religiosity of the Present" in such a way as to suggest that Benjamin did not always "hate" him (EW, 72–73).
7. Benjamin, *Georg Benjamin*, 176.
8. Lacis, *Revolutionär im Beruf*, 52–53. Lacis confuses the years, remembering Benjamin's departure from Hamburg as fall 1924 rather than August 1925.
9. Ibid., 56.
10. SW, 1:474.
11. Lacis, *Revolutionär im Beruf*, 57.
12. *Walter Benjamin's Archive*, 123.
13. Jay and Smith, "A Talk with Mona Jean Benjamin, Kim Yvon Benjamin and Michael Benjamin," 114.
14. Schöck-Quinteros, "Dora Benjamin," 75.
15. Ibid., 79.
16. Reventlow, *Tagebuch*, quoted in Wichner and Wiesner, *Franz Hessel*, 17.
17. Hessel, *Tanz mit dem Jahrhundert*, 14, quoted in Nieradka, *Der Meister der leisen Töne*, 75.
18. Hessel, "Die schwierige Kunst spazieren zu gehen," 434.
19. Kracauer, "Travel and Dance," 65, 66.
20. Ernst Penzoldt, "Lob der kleinen Form," quoted in Köhn, *Straßenrausch*, 9.
21. Tergit, *Käsebier erobert den Kurfürstendamm*, 35, quoted in Köhn, *Straßenrausch*, 7.
22. Benjamin's position here is similar to that of his "Theological-Political Fragment" (SW 3:305–306).
23. Bloch, *Tagträume*, 47, quoted in Münster, *Ernst Bloch*, 137.
24. Bloch, "Recollections of Walter Benjamin" (1966), in Smith, ed., *On Walter Benjamin*, 339.
25. Kracauer, "Lad and Bull," 307.
26. This uncertainty is reflected in their inability to decide between the formal *Sie* and the familiar *Du* as a form of address.
27. MD, 9.
28. See Dewey, "Walter Benjamins Interview," containing a German translation of the short interview with Benjamin, which was conducted on December 18, 1926, in the hall of the All-Russian Association of Proletarian Writers, and was published on January 14, 1927. See also MD, 86. In the interview, after noting the dead end of Italian Futurism, Benjamin refers to the "stagnation" of German art since the decline of Expressionism and mentions Paul Scheerbart as the most noteworthy, if not widely read, representative of contemporary German literature, one whose works are pervaded by "the pathos of technology, . . . the pathos of machinery," a theme new to literature. The production of machines, in Scheerbart, is "important not on economic grounds but as a demonstration of certain ideal truths" (this proposition

evidently raised the ire of Reich and Lacis). Benjamin goes on to claim that Soviet Russia is the only country at present where art is advancing and where it is assuming an "organic character."

29. For Benjamin, film unfolds "all the forms of perception, the tempos and rhythms, which lie preformed in today's machines, such that all problems of contemporary art find their definitive formulation only in the context of film" (AP, Convolute K3,3). On film aesthetic, see also K3a,1–2; Q1a,8; Y1,4; H°,16; M°,4; O°,10.

30. Benjamin later conveyed to Buber (who helped finance the trip to Moscow) his hope that some readers would realize "that these 'visual' [optischen] descriptions have been introduced into a grid of ideas" (C, 316), while to another correspondent at this time he wrote that, from his position outside the Party and outside the language, he had grasped in his essay what was there to be grasped—admittedly, not all that much (GB 3:275; compare 252).

31. See GB, 3:249–250, and Brodersen, *Walter Benjamin*, 169, for excerpts from these two reviews.

32. See BA, 106, and AP, Convolute O, "Prostitution, Gambling."

33. See SF, 132. Benjamin's projected three-part essay on politics is discussed in Chapter 4.

34. On the principle of shrinkage in criticism, see SW, 2:408, 415–416, and chapter 7, note 33.

35. See GB, 3:263 (letter of June 5, 1927, to Kracauer) for what may be the first recorded mention of the arcades work. The first explicit mention is in a letter of October 16 (292–293).

36. "Arcades" is now in AP, 871–872 ("Early Drafts"); see also 919–925 ("Materials for 'Arcades'"). Van Reijen and van Doorn cite evidence for a date of composition in mid-July 1927 (*Aufenthalte und Passagen*, 95, 237n86).

37. See "Program for Literary Criticism," SW, 2:290. For Adorno's claim that Benjamin intended the arcades project to be pure "schockhafte Montage des Materials," made up of citations alone, a claim disputed by Rolf Tiedemann, editor of the *Passagen-Werk*, see GS, 5:1072–1073. See also Tiedemann's introduction to the *Passagen-Werk*, "Dialectics at a Standstill," trans. Gary Smith and André Lefevere, rpt. in AP, 930–931, 1013n6.

38. For details on the transmission of the text, see GS, 5:1067–1073. The manuscripts of first sketches and early drafts were sent to Adorno in the United States in 1941 by Dora Benjamin, the writer's sister. The two exposés were written for the Institute of Social Research, to which they were sent by Benjamin. Additional papers relating to organizational schemas for the *Arcades* materials were discovered in 1981 by the Italian philosopher and Benjamin editor Giorgio Agamben among manuscripts donated to the Bibliothèque Nationale by Bataille's widow.

39. Tiedemann chose the title on the basis of Benjamin's customary usage in the letters, where the project is referred to under different rubrics, such as "Passagenarbeit," "Passagenwerk," "Passagenpapieren," and "Passagen-Studien."

40. The distinction between *Forschung* and *Darstellung* is invoked in AP, Convolute N4a,5 (citation of Marx); see also BS, 100.

41. On *Urgeschichte* as "primal history," see SW, 2:335 ("Julien Green" [1930]). Compare AP, Convolute D10,3 and following, and Convolute N2a,2.

42. *Jetzt der Erkennbarkeit*—a formula dating back to 1920–1921 (see SW, 1:276–277). The concept of dialectical image as memory image also draws significantly on Proust, as discussed later in this chapter.

43. With the concept of a "Copernican revolution in historical perception" (Convolute K1,2), Benjamin alludes to Kant's preface to the second edition of *The Critique of Pure Reason* (B xvi–xvii). Just as for Kant an object of experience is constituted in conformity with the faculties of an experiencing subject, so for Benjamin the historical object is constituted in conformity with the concerns of a living present.

44. Benjamin might also have cited the preface to *Beyond Good and Evil* (1886), in which Nietzsche, like Marx and Michelet, historicizes the old messianic theme of awakening, referring to all those like himself—all "good Europeans"—who have woken from the nightmare of philosophic dogmatizing, and "whose task is [now] wakefulness [*Wachsein*] itself" (2). The idea is echoed in the "Nestor" chapter of Joyce's *Ulysses*, where Stephen Dedalus remarks to Mr Deasy that "history . . . is a nightmare from which I am trying to awake" (34).

45. For Benjamin, citation is not just a critical method but an iterative or mimetic process in the occurrence of history itself: the French Revolution cites ancient Rome ("On the Concept of History," in SW, 4:395). See also "Karl Kraus," SW, 2:442, on citation as mimetic *(mimisch)* unmasking.

46. See SW, 2:244. Benjamin speaks here of "the universe of intertwining." What is at issue, therefore, is a *spatiotemporal* conception. Compare K1,4, in which the spacetime *(Zeitraum)* of the nineteenth century is understood as a dreamtime *(Zeit-traum)*.

47. For example, N10,3; N11,4; J38a,7. See also OGT, 47–48.

48. Kracauer's essay was published in the *Frankfurter Zeitung*, October 28, 1927. See Kracauer, "Photography." Benjamin mentions Kracauer's "great essay" in his letter to the Cohns.

49. See SW, 2:494–500, 794–818; SW, 3:322–329; SW, 4:407.

50. See OGT, 138–158.

51. The text was reprinted, slightly emended and expanded, in GS, vol. 6 (1985), and was translated in OH.

52. The Nietzschean idea of creative intoxication is echoed in Benjamin's 1915 dialogue on aesthetics and color, "The Rainbow: A Conversation about Imagination" (EW, 215–216). In addition to Baudelaire's *Artificial Paradises*, Benjamin mentions, as important to his thinking about hashish, Hermann Hesse's novel *Der Steppenwolf* (1927).

53. Compare MD, 25: "One knows a spot only when one has experienced it in as many dimensions as possible." Compare also the "prismatic" power of film to reveal "unexpected stations" in familiar milieux (SW 2:17).

54. See AP, Convolute M2,4. This passage goes on to describe the once-popular "mechanical picture," with its composite imagery, as an example of "colportage illustration." According to Benjamin, the exact connection between colportage—a system of distributing books, linens, notions, and other wares

by traveling peddlers in eighteenth- and nineteenth-century France—and the "colportage phenomenon of space" remains to be explained (AP, M1a,3).

55. On aura, see OH, 58, 163n2. See also SW, 2:515–519 ("Little History of Photography" [1931]), discussed in Chapter 7.

56. Puttnies and Smith, *Benjaminiana*, 113–114. The reviews by Kracauer, Bloch, Hessel, Brion, Stoessl, and Milch are printed at the back of vol. 8 of *Werke und Nachlaß*. See also SF, 154. The label of "outsiderism," applied by Milch to Benjamin, is echoed in a letter from the Königsberg professor Hans Schaeder to Hofmannsthal, quoted in SF, 147–149. Schaeder speaks of an "altogether personal scholasticism . . . which can lead only to intellectual solipsism."

57. See Newman, *Benjamin's Library*, 195–197. The *Trauerspiel* book was reviewed in the spring 1930 issue of *Modern Language Review*. The review is signed with the initials "R.P." Brief but generally positive, it is the first appearance of Benjamin's name and the only contemporaneous review of his work in an American journal (Fenves, "Benjamin's Early Reception in the United States").

58. Now in GS, 4:497–502, 502–509; translated in SW, 2:80–84, 91–97. See also the account in French by Pierre Bertaux, who was present at the interview (and about whom Benjamin was silent), printed in GS, 7:617–624.

59. Compare Benjamin's remarks, in regard to graphology and physiognomics, on "an unceasingly renewed dialectical adjustment [*Ausgleich*]," which can never be found in "the golden middle way" (SW 2:133).

60. The emphasis is somewhat different, if no less dialectical, in the article "André Gide and Germany," printed (at Gide's request) in the more conservative *Deutsche allgemeine Zeitung*: "The community of nations is something that can be created only where national characters achieve their highest, most precise forms, but also only where they achieve their most stringent spiritual purification. No one knows this better than the man who wrote many years ago: 'The only works we recognize as valuable are those that at their most profound are revelations of the soil and race from which they sprang'" (SW 2:83).

61. Adorno's reference to their "philosophischen Freundschaft" echoes Benjamin's phrase "philosophische Kameradschaft" (BA, 108, 10).

62. The three pieces on toys are translated in SW, 2:98–102, 113–116, 117–121. See also Benjamin's letter of December 21, 1927, to Kracauer, in GB, 3:315–316.

63. Compare section XVI of "On the Concept of History" (SW 4:396).

64. See Häntzschel, "Die Philologin Eva Fiesel." The decision to omit a bibliography in the book reviewed by Benjamin was evidently made by the publisher. Fiesel's book was reprinted in 1973.

65. Compare the letter of July 31, 1918, to Ernst Schoen, in which, apropos of a book by Luise Zurlinden, *Gedanken Platons in der deutschen Romantik* (1910), Benjamin remarks: "The horror that grips you when women want to play a crucial role in discussing such matters is indescribable. This contribution is truly base" (C, 133). The term "shamelessness" is likewise applied

here. These sentiments do not exactly accord with statements made five years earlier on the task of transcending the categories "man" and "woman" (see Chapter 2).

66. Compare the final section of *One-Way Street*, "To the Planetarium," on "the new body" and the new *physis*, with its unprecedented velocities and rhythms, being organized in modern technology, and the new political constellations emerging as a result (SW 1:486–487).

67. "Metaphysics of Youth" (1913–1914) begins: "Each day, like sleepers, we use unmeasured energies. What we do and think is filled with the being of our fathers and ancestors." "The Life of Students" (1915) similarly proclaims at the outset: "The elements of the ultimate condition . . . are deeply embedded in every present in the form of the most endangered, excoriated, and ridiculed creations and ideas" (EW, 144, 197).

68. "The messianic world is the world of universal and integral actuality. Only in the messianic realm does a universal history exist. Not as written history, but as festively enacted history. This festival is purified of all celebration. . . . Its language is liberated prose" (SW, 4:404).

69. In 1932 Benjamin will refer to the Surrealists' "reactionary career" (SW, 2:599).

70. Hansen, "Room for Play," 7.

71. Benjamin, "The Work of Art in the Age of Its Technological Reproducibility" (first version), 19.

7. THE DESTRUCTIVE CHARACTER

1. Dora kept the house and lived off the proceeds from its sale after she left Germany in 1934. See Jay and Smith, "A Talk with Mona Jean Benjamin, Kim Yvon Benjamin, and Michael Benjamin," 114.

2. Puttnies and Smith, *Benjaminiana*, 144–147.

3. See GB, 4:47, and Puttnies and Smith, *Benjaminiana*, 166 (letter from Dora to Scholem, August 15, 1931). According to Mona Jean Benjamin (the author's granddaughter), Stefan Benjamin believed that his mother never stopped loving his father. After the separation, Stefan made weekly visits to see his father (Jay and Smith, "A Talk with Mona Jean Benjamin, Kim Yvon Benjamin, and Michael Benjamin," 114).

4. See GS, 2:1495, which quotes at length from Lacis's *Revolutionär im Beruf*. Lacis says she found Benjamin's representation of her theses too complicated for her own use and asked for a rewrite.

5. Compare "Curriculum Vitae (III)," from early 1928, in which Benjamin speaks of his "programmatic attempt to bring about a process of integration in scholarship—one that will increasingly dismantle the rigid partitions between the disciplines that typified the concept of the sciences in the nineteenth century—and to promote this through an analysis of the work of art" (SW, 2:78). The idea of an integration of academic disciplines is central to Benjamin's early writings on education, particularly "The Life of Students" (see Chapter 2). He will return to the theme of childhood in various autobiographical writings, beginning in 1932.

6. Compare the distinction between the first and second technology in the second version of "The Work of Art in the Age of Its Technological Reproducibility" (SW, 3:107).

7. See Lacis, *Revolutionär im Beruf*, 49. See also SF, 155.

8. Asja Lacis reports that she first introduced Benjamin to Brecht in November 1924 in Berlin, that Brecht was not very forthcoming, and that nothing further developed at the time (*Revolutionär im Beruf*, 53). Her report is confirmed by Erdmut Wizisla, who documents other encounters of the two men between 1924 and 1929. See his *Walter Benjamin and Bertolt Brecht*, 25–31.

9. Puttnies and Smith, *Benjaminiana*, 150–151 (letter of July 24, 1929). See also 148, which cites Franz Hessel's journal entry of June 21, 1929, describing Benjamin dancing "wooden-legged" with one of the "ladies." See further "A Berlin Chronicle" (SW, 2:599) and note 63 below, concerning the "Green Meadow."

10. Hannah Arendt, introduction to Benjamin, *Illuminations*, 14–15.

11. See Lacis, *Revolutionär im Beruf*, 64.

12. Brecht invited Bernhard Reich and Asja Lacis to go with him to see *The Circus*, which opened in Berlin at the beginning of 1929. See Reich, *Im Wettlauf mit der Zeit*, 305 (cited in Fuld, *Zwischen den Stühlen*, 215).

13. Benjamin was, however, critical of Korsch's *Marxismus und Philosophie*. See GB, 3:552.

14. See Brecht, *Arbeitsjournal*, 1:15, entry for July 25, 1938 (cited in Brodersen, *Walter Benjamin*, 313n88). See also SF, 176.

15. Benjamin apparently owned a copy of Joyce's *Ulysses* in German translation. See BG, 16 (undated list of books in Benjamin's possession, possibly compiled by Gretel Karplus in 1933). *Ulysses* was first translated into German in 1927.

16. See Chapter 2 on the derivation of this interpretive principle from Nietzsche and the early Romantics. The principle is formulated concisely in "Excavation and Memory" from 1932 (SW, 2:576; see also 611).

17. On the educational uses of entertainment, compare AP, Convolute K3a,1; and "Theory of Distraction," in SW, 3:141–142. See also "Zweierlei Volkstümlichkeit" (1932), in GS, 4:671–673, and the conclusion of the 1932 essay "Theater and Radio," in SW, 2:585.

18. See GS, 7:68–294 ("Rundfunkgeschichten für Kinder" and "Literarische Rundfunkvorträge"), and GS, 4:629–720 ("Hörmodelle," which includes two *Hörspiele*). On Benjamin's radio work, see Schiller-Lerg, *Walter Benjamin und der Rundfunk*. On the work with Schoen in particular, see Schiller-Lerg, "Ernst Schoen." There are no known recordings of Benjamin's voice.

19. Quoted in a letter of April 10, 1930, from Ernst Schoen to Benjamin (GS, 2:1504).

20. See *Revolutionär im Beruf*, 68, where Lacis mentions her surprise at Benjamin's decision, at this time, not to accompany her on the train to Frankfurt.

21. There is a photograph of the little Swiss-style house in which they met—presumably a restaurant or inn—in van Reijen and van Doorn, *Aufenthalte und Passagen*, 116.

22. Puttnies and Smith, *Benjaminiana*, 166.
23. Ibid., 166, 164. Hergesheimer is quoted on 166.
24. On the meeting between Proust and Joyce, see Ellman, *James Joyce*, 523–524.
25. It is more likely that M. Albert was the model for Jupien. See Benjamin's "Abend mit Monsieur Albert," evidently not written for publication, in GS, 4:587–591.
26. SF, 162–164.
27. On Activism, see Chapter 2, note 34, concerning Kurt Hiller. On Expressionism and Neue Sachlichkeit, see also SW, 2:293–294, 405–407, 417–418, 454.
28. See the short political allegory entitled "Möwen" (Gulls), a section in the cycle "Nordische See" (Nordic Sea), published in the *Frankfurter Zeitung* in September 1930 (GS, 4:385–386).
29. On the picture puzzle or rebus *(Vexierbild)*, compare "Dream Kitsch" (SW, 2:4) and AP, Convolute G1,2; I1,3; J60,4.
30. Concerning the last two named, see "The Storyteller" (SW, 3:143–166) and AP, Convolute S. The proposed volume of essays in literary criticism was never completed.
31. In a diary entry from August 1931, Benjamin suggests that, with the "literarization of living conditions," by which work gains a voice, the newspaper could become the site for the regeneration of the printed word it had formerly helped debase (SW, 2:504–505; compare 527, 741–742). See Wizisla, *Walter Benjamin and Bertolt Brecht*, 206, for Brecht's idea of a "fully literarisized life"; see also the discussion of Benjamin's 1931 essay "Karl Kraus" later in this chapter.
32. In a curriculum vitae from early 1928, Benjamin likewise speaks of the work of art as an "integral expression of the religious, metaphysical, political, and economic tendencies of its age" (SW, 2:78). On Benjamin's film theory, see Chapter 6.
33. Benjamin refers to Adorno's 1930 essay "New Tempi." See Adorno, *Night Music*, 104–117, esp. 106–107: "Works shrink and contract over time [*schrumpfen in der Zeit ein*]; their various elements draw closer together." See also "Arnold Schoenberg, 1874–1951," in Adorno, *Prisms*, 171, on Schoenberg's "shriveled diction" *(geschrumpften Diktion)*. Benjamin had already used the term in his 1927 essay on Gottfried Keller (discussed in Chapter 6) and in a hashish protocol of 1928 (OH, 53). It appears later in "The Little Hunchback" (BC, 121). Compare also *Walter Benjamin's Archive*, 49: "Memory . . . makes things grow smaller, compresses them" (from a previously unpublished manuscript); and "A Berlin Chronicle" (SW, 2:597).
34. *Abmontieren* is not to be confused with the Husserlian and Heideggerian term *Abbau*, which is also translated as "deconstruction." On Benjamin's *Abbau der Gewalt* (deconstruction of violence), see GS, 2:943 (1919–1920), and C, 169. See also GS, 1:1240 (1940), on Benjamin's *Abbau der Universalgeschichte* (deconstruction of universal history).
35. Compare the collector's object as "magic encyclopedia" and the arcade as "a world in miniature," in AP, 207, 3. Such phenomena of historical encapsulation

in this text and elsewhere in Benjamin belong under the general heading of "monadology." See also EW, 197 (1915), on the "focal point," and SW, 1:225 (1919–1920), on the "smallest totality."

36. See C, 365; also 359–360, where Heidegger is mentioned in connection with the "theory of historical knowledge." The reading circle seems to have dissolved before it could get to Heidegger. Benjamin's radio talk on Brecht is in SW, 2:365–371; his first Brecht commentary, 374–377.

37. On the abortive journal project of 1930–1931, see chapter 3, "Krise und Kritik," in Wizisla, *Walter Benjamin and Bertolt Brecht*, 66–97. The more popular form "Krise" (rather than "Krisis"), the form evidently preferred by the publisher Rowohlt, is used here. Concerning the protocols of the editorial discussions, five of which are documented, see 190–203 and 69n.

38. Benjamin's memorandum is printed in GS, 6:619–621; see also 827, concerning the list of contributors. The names of Döblin, Hindemith, Musil, and the film director Dudow were later crossed out, and a question mark was placed after Kracauer's name. Kracauer attended a meeting of the journal's editorial board in November and, as he later wrote to Adorno, found the discussion "dilettantish" (quoted in Wizisla, *Walter Benjamin and Bertolt Brecht*, 90).

39. Benjamin puts it rather differently in his letter of February 1931, to Brecht: "The journal was meant to contribute to the propaganda of dialectical materialism *by applying it to questions that the bourgeois intelligentsia is forced to acknowledge as its own most characteristic questions*" (C, 370). See Chapter 6 (regarding the trip to Moscow) on Benjamin's ambivalence toward the Communist Party.

40. See Wizisla, *Walter Benjamin and Bertolt Brecht*, 206. In this same discussion, Brecht posits the goal—realizable only through revolution—of a "fully literarisized life" (206).

41. During this cruise he may have worked on Jouhandeau's story "La Bergère 'Nanou'" (The Shepherdess Nanou), from *Prudence Hautechaume* (1927), which appeared in Benjamin's translation in *Die literarische Welt* in April 1932. "Nordische See" was published in the *Frankfurter Zeitung* in September 1930 (GS, 4:383–387).

42. See Schmitt, *Hamlet or Hecuba*, 59–65 (appendix 2). Schmitt argues, against Benjamin, that Shakespeare's *Hamlet* is not Christian in any specific sense.

43. Scholem describes Gustav Glück as "a man of extraordinarily noble character and profound culture, but (and this was somewhat uncommon in those circles) he had no literary ambitions and was completely free of vanity" (SF, 180).

44. See SW, 1:469 (from *One-Way Street*); SW, 2:110 ("Karl Kraus Reads Offenbach," 1928); SW, 2:194–195 ("Karl Kraus [Fragment]," 1928); and GS, 4:552–554 (review of Kraus's drama *The Unconquerable*, 1929). The essay "Karl Kraus" of 1931 is in SW, 2:433–458.

45. See Chapter 6 on citation in *The Arcades Project*.

46. Benjamin mentions this conversation in a letter to Brecht in February 1931 (C, 370), but a letter of February 5 to Scholem suggests that he remained

open to the possibility of coediting the journal for at least a month after the conversation with Brecht (see GB, 4:11).

47. Compare Benjamin's statement in "Kavaliersmoral" (November 1929), his first published piece dealing with Kafka: "Kafka's work, which is concerned with the darkest areas of human life, . . . harbors this theological mystery deep within itself, while outwardly appearing plain, unpretentious, and modest. So modest was Kafka's entire existence" (GS, 4:467).

48. Quoted from an undated postcard in the collection of Martin Harries, signed only "E" and referring to the early departure of "Lotte." The author is certainly Wissing; Lotte is Liselotte Karplus, Gretel Karplus Adorno's sister and Wissing's second wife.

49. But see the moving letter of July 15, 1941, written in English by Benjamin's ex-wife, Dora, to Scholem, where it is suggested that Benjamin experienced suicidal feelings as early as 1917. The letter is cited in part in Chapter 11, note 5, and in full in Garber, "Zum Briefwechsel," 1843. The expression of such feelings in June and July 1932 is discussed later in this chapter.

50. Passages on the "other nature" and the "optical unconscious" (SW, 2:510, 512) and on the aura as a "strange weave of space and time" (518–519) are taken up practically verbatim in the "Work of Art" essay.

51. Quoted from "Little History of Photography" in Benjamin, The Work of Art in the Age of Its Technological Reproducibility, 276–77. This version differs from that published in SW.

52. See AP, 22, where "modern beauty" is said to be the linchpin of Baudelaire's entire theory of art, and 671–692 (Convolute Y, "Photography"), which contains material on Nadar and nineteenth-century photography.

53. Puttnies and Smith, Benjaminiana, 33.

54. See Valero, Der Erzähler, 36–58. This is a translation of Experiencia y pobreza: Walter Benjamin en Ibiza, 1932–1933 (2001).

55. Selz, "Benjamin in Ibiza," 355.

56. Ibid., 355–356.

57. See Valero, Der Erzähler, 119, 155.

58. Ibid., 83–94.

59. SF, 188–189. Parem later told Scholem that Benjamin took her refusal "so badly that he never again asked about her when he saw her eventual husband, Philipp Schey; Schey was in the Brecht circle and associated with Benjamin in Paris for a long time later." See also Valero, Der Erzähler, 98–99.

60. Valero, Der Erzähler, 130.

61. Benjamin's friendship with Wilhelm Speyer would founder a year and a half later after Speyer's failure to pay Benjamin what he was owed for this collaboration. See BG, 74–76, 80.

62. The four letters are in GB, 4:115–120.

63. Benjamin no doubt puns here on the address of the Hôtel du Petit Parc, with its "view of the park": 6 Impasse Villermont. Impasse in French means both "cul-de-sac" and "impasse." The "Green Meadow," referred to in the letter that follows, was a bed. It is memorialized, as the site of sexual adventures, in Benjamin's "Berlin Chronicle": "the 'Green Meadow'—a bed that still

stands high above the couches spreading all around, on which we composed a small, complaisant, orientally pallid epilogue to those great sleeping feasts with which, a few years earlier in Paris, the Surrealists had unwittingly inaugurated their reactionary career. . . . On this meadow we spread out such women as still amused us at home, but they were few" (SW, 2:599).

64. Benjamin's will, "Mein Testament," is printed in full in GB, 4:121–122n, and partially translated in SF, 187–188.

65. Benjamin also incorporated, with various adaptations, the section "Enlargements" from *One-Way Street* (see SW, 1:463–466) into *Berlin Childhood around 1900*.

66. Compare the formulation in a letter of September 21 to Jean Selz: *"une série de notes"* (GB, 4:132). The letter continues: "It is a sort of reminiscence of childhood, but exempt from all markedly individual or familial accent. A sort of tête-à-tête of a child with the city of Berlin around 1900."

67. *Berliner Kindheit um Neunzehnhundert* first appeared in book form in 1950, with the sequence of texts determined by Adorno. This was the basis of the 1972 Adorno-Rexroth edition in GS, 4:235–304. Only with the discovery in 1981, in Paris, of the manuscript of the 1938 revision, the so-called final version ("Fassung letzter Hand"), edited and published in 1989 in GS, 7:385–433, did we have Benjamin's own arrangement of the pieces, though this cannot be considered a definitive version in view of his drastic reduction of the 1932–1934 text. For more on the publication history of the work, the different extant versions, and Benjamin's revisions, see GS, 7:691–705, 715–716, 721–723; and the translator's foreword to BC. The unfinished draft "Berliner Chronik" was first published in 1970 and reprinted, with editorial amendments, in 1985 in GS, 6:465–519 (trans. in SW, 2:595–637).

68. On the palimpsest structure of memory, see the section entitled "The Palimpsest" toward the end of Baudelaire's *Artificial Paradises* (147–149), which Benjamin first read in 1919 (the material in question deriving from De Quincey). In 1921, Benjamin wrote: "Since the Middle Ages, we have lost our insight into the complex layers that compose the world" (SW, 1:284). Compare also Adorno's comment: "[Benjamin] immersed himself in reality as in a palimpsest" ("Introduction to Benjamin's *Schriften*" [1955], in Smith, *On Walter Benjamin*, 8). The superimposition *(Überblendung)* of past and present plays an important role in *The Arcades Project*, as indicated in Chapter 6, and in Benjamin's conception of allegory in his writings on Baudelaire (see, for example, SW, 4:54, and GB, 6:65).

69. See SW, 2:479. The subject of dwelling *(Wohnen)* was also of fundamental importance to Heidegger after World War II. See in particular his essay "Building Dwelling Thinking" from the early 1950s, in Heidegger, *Poetry, Language, Thought*, 141–159.

70. In his 1938 foreword to the text, Benjamin says he "sought . . . insight into the irretrievability—not the contingent biographical but the necessary social irretrievability—of the past" (BC, 37).

71. "Nachwort zur *Berliner Kindheit um Neunzehnhundert*" (1950), in Adorno, ed., *Über Walter Benjamin*, 74–77.

72. See Brodersen, *Walter Benjamin*, 198–200, for names of several students in the class who went on to become Germanists, sociologists, art historians, and journalists, and for excerpts from the surviving protocols of the summer semester, 1932, documents which have been published in the *Adorno Blätter* IV (Munich, 1995), 52–57. No records of the following winter semester of the course have been preserved.

73. See the letters to Carl Linfert from this period in GB, vol. 4. The first version of the review is translated in SW, 2:666–672.

74. "Lichtenberg: Ein Querschnitt" (Lichtenberg: A Profile) was completed at the end of February or beginning of March 1933, shortly before Benjamin's flight from Germany, and published posthumously in GS, 4:696–720. Preliminary notes for the radio play, which incorporates clements derived from Paul Scheerbart's *Lesabéndio*, appear in GS, 7:837–845. See C, 391, 383, and 84 (1916); also GB, 4:87n, 59–60n. A letter of Lichtenberg's is included in "German Men and Women" (SW, 3:168–170).

75. "The Mummerehlen" was published in May 1933 in the *Vossische Zeitung*. See BC, 131.

76. The two texts are translated in SW, 2:694–698, 720–722. See also the fragmentary material from ca. 1933–1935 on the mimetic faculty, in GS, 2:955–958. Benjamin's thoughts on similarity in language were stimulated by Rudolf Leonhard's "onomatopoetic theory of the word," as set forth in his book *Das Wort* (1931), from which Benjamin quotes in his two new texts; see his letter of October 25, 1932 (BS, 22).

77. On the use of the term "medium," see, for example, the 1916 "On Language as Such and on the Language of Man" (EW, 253–255, 267), discussed in Chapter 3.

8. EXILE

1. "Curriculum Vitae (VI): Dr. Walter Benjamin" (SW, 4:382).

2. See Selz, "Benjamin in Ibiza," 360, citing a letter of March 1933 to Selz from Felix Noeggerath, to whom Benjamin had written before leaving Berlin, in order to make arrangements for his stay on Ibiza.

3. Palmier, *Weimar in Exile*, 2.

4. Estimates of the exact number vary by 10,000; see ibid., 685n153.

5. He later remarked to Scholem about the Musil novel: "I have lost my taste for it and have taken leave of the author, having come to the conclusion that he is far too clever for his own good" (BS, 52).

6. "Only what burned bright was extinguished/when you descended to the Hotel Istria;/everything was different on the Rue Campagne, No. 1,/in 1929, toward the noon hour."

7. See the birthday letter of July 15, 1934, from Dora, cited in part in GB, 4:476–477n.

8. See Selz's brief account of their evenings in Barcelona's bohemian red-light district, Barrio Chino, in "Benjamin in Ibiza," 361. See also GB, 4:244, and SF, 189.

9. Selz, "Benjamin in Ibiza," 362.

10. The name belonged to a character in Wilhelm Speyer's play, *Ein Mantel, ein Hut, ein Handschuh* (A Coat, a Hat, a Glove), on which Benjamin had

collaborated the year before. See Walter Benjamin and Gretel Adorno, BG, 6n5.

11. Selz, "Benjamin in Ibiza," 361. They eventually translated into French five sections of the text (printed in GS, 4:979–986), before their friendship cooled later in the summer. See GB, 4:374–375, 393–394.

12. "An Experiment by Walter Benjamin" (1959), trans. Maria Louise Ascher, in OH, 147–155.

13. "Crock Notes," in OH, 85. On Benjamin's hashish use, see Chapter 6.

14. See the account by Georg's wife, Hilde Benjamin, who states that he was murdered at Mauthausen, in *Georg Benjamin*, 207–291. The relevant material is summarized in Brodersen, *Walter Benjamin*, 208–209. Benjamin's sister, Dora, was likewise still in Germany at this time, but she spent the years 1934 and 1935 in Paris (where she and Walter renewed contact) before escaping to Switzerland, where she died in 1946.

15. Brecht, *Poems 1913–1956*, 319.

16. Valero, *Der Erzähler*, 119–120.

17. He mentions the *Europäische Revue*, in which Adorno published music criticism that spring and summer. Adorno's recommendation of Benjamin to the journal's editor, Joachim Moras, proved fruitless. See GB, 4:196n, 211n.

18. BS, 41.

19. Benjamin puts it poignantly to Scholem: "If ever God has smitten a prophet by fulfilling his prophecies, then this is the case with George" (BS, 59). Despite his authoritarian conservatism, George was strongly opposed to the rise of Nazism; he refused money and honors offered him by the Nazi government and went into exile in 1933, at the end of his life. It was one of his followers, Count von Stauffenberg, who attempted to assassinate Hitler in July 1944.

20. See Selz, "Benjamin in Ibiza," 359–360. "Am Kamin," originally published under the pseudonym Detlef Holz, is reprinted in GS, 3:388–392. See also section XV of "The Storyteller": "The reader of a novel . . . swallows up the material as a fire devours logs in the fireplace. The suspense which permeates the novel is very much like the draft of air which fans the flame in the fireplace and enlivens its play" (SW, 3:156). Benjamin tells Scholem that "Am Kamin" contains "a theory of the novel that bears no resemblance to Lukács's theory" (BS, 48).

21. Compare the formulation in "Experience and Poverty" (1933), discussed later in this chapter (p. 413).

22. Scholem likewise discouraged the idea of sending Benjamin's son, Stefan, with his strong leftist leanings, to Palestine. See BS, 49.

23. Compare AP, 388: "Proust could emerge as an unprecedented phenomenon only in a generation that had lost all bodily and natural aids to remembrance and that, poorer than before, was left to itself to take possession of the worlds of childhood in merely an isolated, scattered, and pathological way" (Convolute K1,1).

24. On the theme of "the new," compare AP, 11 (Exposé of 1935, section V), which quotes the last line of Baudelaire's "Le voyage": "Au fond de l'Inconnu pour trouver du *nouveau!*" (Deep in the Unknown to find the *new*). An echo

of this line may be heard at the end of "Experience and Poverty," in the phrase *das von Grund auf Neue* (literally, "what is new from the ground up"). This is where Benjamin refers to "the cause of the fundamentally new."

25. For a short biography of Anna Maria Blaupot ten Cate, see van Gerwen, "Angela Nova," 107–111.

26. See van Gerwen, "Walter Benjamin auf Ibiza," 2:981 (cited in GB, 4:504n). Van Gerwen, who interviewed Toet Blaupot ten Cate and Jean Selz, suggests that a copy of Benjamin's "Agesilaus Santander" (discussed in this chapter) was presented as a gift for Blaupot ten Cate's thirty-first birthday on August 13, 1933 (the date of composition of the second version of the text). He quotes from her letter of June 1934 to Benjamin, in which she says: "You [*Sie*] are much more than a good friend to me. . . . You understand me unconditionally, that's what it is," but then asks, in regard to their relationship: "Why do you want something that doesn't exist and cannot be, and why do you not see how wonderfully good that is which already exists?" (van Gerwen, "Walter Benjamin auf Ibiza," 971–972). Benjamin's two poems to Blaupot ten Cate, written in the summer of 1933, are printed in GS, 6:810–811.

27. Cited in *Global Benjamin*, 972 (Valero, *Der Erzähler*, 182–183).

28. The three "Geschichten aus der Einsamkeit" are printed in GS, 4:755–757.

29. See Scholem, "Walter Benjamin and His Angel." The two versions of "Agesilaus Santander" first appeared in this essay. See also van Reijen and van Doorn, *Aufenthalte und Passagen*, 139.

30. On the motif of waiting for a woman, compare BC, 72–73, and AP, 855 (M°,15). Waiting is a central theme of the latter text, where, transposed from its ancient theological context, it is associated with such topics as boredom, flânerie, dream, hashish, and the "parasitic elements" of the city. Even the commodity waits to be sold (O°,45). At one point Benjamin speaks of the need for "a metaphysics of waiting" (O°,26). Compare EW, 7–8 (1913). See also Kracauer, "Those Who Wait" (1922).

31. Benjamin arranged to have their translation published in the *Cahiers du Sud* in 1935, despite serious misgivings about its quality (see GB, 4:414–415).

32. See AP, 331, 342 (Convolute J56a,8 [*Kalvarienberg*]; J57,1 [*Opfergang*]; J64,1 [*Passionsweg*]), and SW, 4:167 ("Central Park," Section 10).

33. Selz, "Benjamin in Ibiza," 364.

34. In March 1934, the more important of Benjamin's books reached Skovsbostrand (Brecht's residence in Denmark) in five or six packing cases, but today only a small remnant of Benjamin's library is preserved in Moscow. His collection of manuscripts of the Heinle brothers, which formed part of his Berlin archives, was likewise lost. See BS, 72, 82–83, 102, and GB, 4:298n. See also *Walter Benjamin's Archive*, 4.

35. Palmier, *Weimar in Exile*, 228.

36. For comprehensive histories of the Institute of Social Research, see Jay, *The Dialectical Imagination*, and Wiggershaus, *The Frankfurt School*.

37. The best study of Austro-Marxism remains Rabinbach's *The Crisis of Austrian Socialism*.

38. Kluke, "Das Institut für Sozialforschung," 422–423.

39. See especially Ogden, "Benjamin, Wittgenstein, and Philosophical Anthropology," and Gess, " 'Schöpferische Innervation der Hand.' "

40. His commentary, "Brecht's Threepenny Novel" (SW, 3:3–10), written ca. January–February 1935, remained unpublished during his lifetime.

41. See Wizisla, *Walter Benjamin and Bertolt Brecht*, 49–51, for an indication of the projected novel's plot and leading motifs. It was to concern blackmail and, though undertaken as a kind of literary *jeu*, was to serve the authors' concern with laying bare the mechanisms of bourgeois society.

42. Sperber, quoted in Palmier, *Weimar in Exile*, 184.

43. Lottmann, *Rive Gauche* (Paris, 1981), cited in Palmier, *Weimar in Exile*, 190.

44. Scholem refers to the section entitled "Sexual Awakening" (BC, 123–124). See BS, 25, on their exchange about this in early 1933.

45. On overcoming specialization, compare EW, 204 ("The Life of Students"), and SW, 2:78 ("Curriculum Vitae [III]").

46. Here, as so often, Benjamin imbricates elements of his reading of other books: a key moment in Malraux's *Man's Fate*, which Benjamin read in January 1934, shows the self-alienation of Kyo, the protagonist, through his failure to recognize his own voice on a gramophone record.

47. Compare Hermann Cohen: "Redemption . . . clings to every moment of suffering, and constitutes in each moment of suffering a moment of redemption" (*Religion of Reason*, 235). Compare also the "redemption of the unredeemable" (C, 34 [1913]).

48. Letter from Gustav Glück to Benjamin, December 22, 1933, cited in GB, 4:298n.

49. Ruth Berlau, *Brechts Lai-tu* (Darmstadt, 1985), cited in Brodersen, *Spinne im eigenen Netz*, 233.

50. The term "Jewish fascism" had been current in Germany since the late twenties, often in association with attacks on Zionism. See Wizisla, *Walter Benjamin and Bertolt Brecht*, 166n.

51. Karl Kraus, "Warum die Fackel nicht erscheint" in *Die Fackel*, Heft Nr. 890–905 (July 1934), 224, cited in GB, 4:469.

52. GB, 4:477n.

53. Horkheimer, *Briefwechsel 1913–1936*, 246.

54. Smollett, *Travels through France and Italy*, 188–189.

55. He refers to the 1933 review "Am Kamin." See note 20 above.

56. BS, 153n1.

57. Benjamin's notes for his Kafka revision are printed in GS, 2:1248–1264.

58. "Auf die Minute" is in GS, 4:761–763, and "Conversation above the Corso: Recollections of Carnival Time in Nice" is in SW, 3:25–31.

59. The first edition of Bloch's *Erbschaft dieser Zeit* (Zurich, 1935) appeared in late 1934. An expanded edition appeared in 1962; this appears in English as *Heritage of Our Times*. We quote from 8, 221, 207–208, 339, 346. On Ador-

no's criticisms of Bloch's book (in a letter of 1935 now lost), see BG, 129–130, 134.

60. Witness the fragment of ca. August 1934, "Hitler's Diminished Masculinity" (SW, 2:792–793), which, some six years before Chaplin's film *The Great Dictator*, compares the persona of Hitler to "the feminine cast of the little tramp."

9. THE PARISIAN ARCADES

1. Dora Benjamin to Walter Benjamin, March 28, 1935 (Walter Benjamin Archiv 015: Dora Benjamin 1935–1937, 1935/3), and Dora Sophie Benjamin to Walter Benjamin, May 29, 1935 (Walter Benjamin Archiv 017: Dora Sophie Benjamin 1933–1936, 1935/5).

2. See Täubert, *"Unbekannt verzogen . . ."*

3. *Adrienne Monnier et La Maison des amis des livres 1915–1951*, ed. Maurice Imbert and Raphaël Sorin (Paris, 1991), 43, cited in BG, 170.

4. See GS, 5:1262.

5. The full documentation of the congress was published only in 2005. See Teroni and Klein, *Pour la défense de la culture*. For a magisterial evaluation of the congress, see Rabinbach, "When Stalinism Was a Humanism: Writers Respond to Nazism, 1934–1936," in *Staging Anti-Fascism*.

6. Rabinbach, "When Stalinism Was a Humanism."

7. Wolfgang Klein and Akademie der Wissenschaften der DDR, Zentralinstitut für Literaturgeschichte, *Paris 1935: Erster Internationaler Schriftstellerkongress zur Verteidigung der Kultur: Reden und Dokumente mit Materialien der Londoner Schriftstellerkonferenz 1936* (Berlin: Akademie-Verlag, 1982), 60, cited in Rabinbach, "When Stalinism Was a Humanism."

8. Klein, *Paris 1935*, 56, cited in Rabinbach, "When Stalinism Was a Humanism."

9. Klein, *Paris 1935*, 61; cited in Rabinbach, "When Stalinism Was a Humanism."

10. Rabinbach, "When Stalinism Was a Humanism."

11. Dora Benjamin to Walter Benjamin, March 28, 1935, Walter Benjamin Archiv 015: Dora Benjamin 1935–1937, 1935/3.

12. The Sagrada Familia, or Church of the Holy Family, is Antonio Gaudí's still unfinished basilica in Barcelona; the Tibidabo is a mountain in the Serra de Coliserola range that overlooks Barcelona.

13. On Ursel Bud, see GB, 5:166–167n.

14. See Hansen, *Cinema and Experience*.

15. Elsewhere Benjamin conceives of aura (from Greek *aura*, "breath," "air in motion") as something appearing in all things, and he refers to the paintings of Van Gogh: "Perhaps nothing gives such a clear idea of aura as Van Gogh's late paintings, in which . . . the aura appears to have been painted together with the various objects" (OH, 58, 163n2).

16. On the legend of the Chinese painter, compare *Berlin Childhood around 1900* (SW, 3:393).

17. Surya, *Georges Bataille*, 146.

18. Ibid., 221-222.

19. Adorno and Horkheimer, *Briefwechsel*, 165.

20. Horkheimer to Benjamin, March 18, 1936 (quoted in GS, 1:997).

21. Bernhard Reich to Benjamin, February 19, 1936, Walter Benjamin Archive 1502-1503.

22. For Benjamin's French translation, "Le Narrateur," which he completed in the summer of 1937, and which was first published in 1952 in *Mercure de France*, see GS, 2:1290-1309.

23. Benjamin reviewed the following books for a 1937 number of the *Zeitschrift für Sozialforschung:* Helmut Anton, *Gesellschaftsideal und Gesellschaftsmoral im ausgehenden 17.Jahrhundert* (Breslau, 1935); Hansjörg Garte, *Kunstform Schauerroman* (Leipzig, 1935); Oskar Walzel, *Romantisches. I. Frühe Kunstschau Friedrich Schlegels. II. Adam Müllers Ästhetik* (Bonn, 1934); Alain, *Stendhal* (Paris, 1935); Hugo von Hofmannsthal, *Briefe 1890-1901* (Berlin, 1935); Hermann Blacker, *Der Aufbau der Kunstwirklichkeit bei Marcel Proust* (Berlin, 1935); Hermann Broch, *James Joyce und die Gegenwart: Rede zu Joyces 50. Geburtstag* (Vienna, 1936). The review is reprinted in GS, 3:511-517.

24. Quoted in Wizisla, *Walter Benjamin and Bertolt Brecht*, 59.

25. Ibid.

26. SF, 202.

27. See GS, 3:482-495.

28. Dora Sophie Benjamin to Walter Benjamin, April 19, 1936, Walter Benjamin Archive 015, Dora Sophie Benjamin 1935-1937, 1936/4.

29. Dora Sophie Benjamin to Walter Benjamin, July 10, August 16, and October 16, 1936, Walter Benjamin Archive 015, Dora Sophie Benjamin 1935-1937, 1936/8 and 1936/10.

30. Dora Sophie Benjamin to Walter Benjamin, January 26, 1937, Walter Benjamin Archive 015, Dora Sophie Benjamin 1935-1937.

31. Wilhelm Hoffer to Dora Sophie Benjamin, May 24, 1937, Walter Benjamin Archive 018, Dora Sophie Benjamin 1937-1939, 1937/5.

32. AP, 470 (N7,6); AP, 918 (Materials for the Exposé of 1935).

33. That Benjamin's attitude toward the question of contemplation is characteristically ambivalent is indicated by a passage from the "First Sketches" section of *The Arcades Project*: "In *The Arcades Project*, contemplation [*Kontemplation*] must be put on trial. But it should defend itself brilliantly and justify itself" (AP, 866 [Q°,6]). See also H2,7, on the " 'disinterested' contemplation" of the collector.

34. For the text of Horkheimer's and Löwenthal's letters to Benjamin (of March 16, 1937, and May 8, 1937, respectively), see GS, 2:1331-1337, 1344-1345.

35. There is a letter of May 17, 1937, written in English by Benjamin to Leyda, offering him—in apparent disregard of Horkheimer's request in his letter of December 30, 1936—a German original of the artwork essay for translation. See GB, 5:530, 458-459n.

36. From Kraft's letter of April 30, 1940, to Horkheimer, cited in GS, 2:1402. See 1397-1403 for other documents relating to the Benjamin-Kraft dispute over the rediscovery of Jochmann.

37. Sohn-Rethel, *Warenform und Denkform*, 87ff.
38. Krenek in the *Wiener Zeitung*, May 18, 1937, cited in Müller-Doohm, *Adorno*, 342.
39. Adorno and Horkheimer, *Briefwechsel*, 240.
40. See esp. Falasca-Zamponi, *Rethinking the Political*.

10. BAUDELAIRE AND THE STREETS OF PARIS

1. Lackner, " 'Von einer langen, schwierigen Irrfahrt,' " 54–56.
2. Young-Bruehl, *Hannah Arendt*, 122.
3. SF, 205–214.
4. Paulhan, "Henry Church and the Literary Magazine 'Mesures.' "
5. Denis Holier, quoted in Surya, *Georges Bataille*, 261.
6. See Bataille et al., *The College of Sociology, 1937–1939*.
7. Adorno and Horkheimer, *Briefwechsel*, 340.
8. Benjamin, *Georg Benjamin*, 255–256. The passage from *German Men and Women* is in SW, 3:173.
9. Benjamin, *Georg Benjamin*, 256.
10. This sentence appears, in revised form, as Convolute J51a,6, in *The Arcades Project*. The published translation of this letter to Horkheimer has been extensively modified here to bring it closer to the original German.
11. The manuscript of this revision, the so-called Final Version ("Fassung letzter Hand"), comprising thirty sections and two addenda, and featuring a textual arrangement by the author, was discovered in 1981 in Paris by Giorgio Agamben and published in GS, vol. 7, in 1989. The so-called Adorno-Rexroth version, containing forty-one pieces from the years 1932–1934 in an arrangement by the editors, was published in 1972 in GS, vol. 4. The first book publication of *Berliner Kindheit um Neunzehnhundert* was arranged by Adorno in 1950.
12. The French phrase, meaning "stubborn contemplation of tomorrow's work," comes from section 6 of Baudelaire's article "Conseils aux jeunes littérateurs" (Advice to Young Men of Letters; 1846). The passage is cited in Convolute J4,2 in *The Arcades Project*.
13. Brecht wrote to Benjamin in 1936: "The chess board lies orphaned; every half hour a tremor of remembrance runs through it; that was when you made your moves." Cited in Wizisla, *Walter Benjamin and Bertolt Brecht*, 59. "The little community of exiles took with a passion to board and card games. Chess was played most often, but also Monopoly, which was patented in 1936, table billiards, poker, and 66 (a card game)" (58).
14. See "Diary Entries, 1938," in SW, 3:335–343.
15. The entry continues: "Our bourgeoisie thinks it is mankind. When the heads of the aristocracy fell, at least their pricks remained erect. The bourgeoisie has contrived to ruin even sexuality." Cited in Wizisla, *Walter Benjamin and Bertolt Brecht*, 36. Benjamin refers to this conversation in Convolute O11a,3 in *The Arcades Project*. See also GS, 7:737.
16. "The Paris of the Second Empire in Baudelaire" appears in SW, 4:3–92.
17. On Baudelaire as "the mime who has taken off his makeup," see AP, Convolute J52,2 and following, particularly J56,5 and J62,6.

18. OGT, 175.
19. SW, 4:53–54. Compare AP, Convolute M1a,1, Convolute S2,1, and Convolute M°,4 *(Superposition, Überdeckung)*; and SW, 2:94 *(surimpression)*. Compare also Adorno's 1955 characterization of Benjamin: "He immersed himself in reality as in a palimpsest" ("Introduction to Benjamin's *Schriften*," 8).
20. Missac, *Walter Benjamin's Passages*.
21. Hannah Arendt in a letter to Scholem, May 29, 1939, quoted in SF, 220. See also GB, 6:255.
22. Benjamin cites Joubert on stylistics in AP, Convolute N15a,3: "On the style one should strive for: 'It is through everyday words that style bites into and penetrates the reader. It is through them that great thoughts circulate and are accepted as genuine . . . for nothing is so clear, when it comes to words, than those we call familiar; and clarity is something so characteristic of the truth that it is often confused with it.'"
23. "On Some Motifs in Baudelaire" appears in SW, 4:313–355.
24. "We live in an age of socialism, of the women's movement, of traffic, of individualism" (EW, 26 [1911]).
25. See section XI of "On Some Motifs in Baudelaire," where, in connection with this idea, Benjamin cites statements by Novalis ("Perceptibility is an attentiveness"), by Valéry ("The things I look at [in dreams] see me just as much as I see them"), and (in a note) by Karl Kraus ("The closer one looks at a word, the greater the distance from which it looks back"). SW, 4:338–339, 354n77. On the possible influence of Léon Daudet's 1928 book *La melancholia* on Benjamin's concept of "aura" (Daudet refers to Baudelaire as a "poet of the aura" and to photography and cinema as "transmitters of aura"), see Agamben, *Stanzas*, 44–45.
26. Baudelaire, *The Painter of Modern Life*, 8.

11. THE ANGEL OF HISTORY

1. Sahl, "Walter Benjamin in the Internment Camp," 348.
2. Memoirs of Max Aron, 1939, Jewish National and University Library, Jerusalem; cited in Scheurmann and Scheurmann, eds., *Für Walter Benjamin*, 115.
3. Sahl, "Walter Benjamin in the Internment Camp," 349.
4. Ibid., 349–350.
5. Dora was devastated by the news of Walter Benjamin's death. She wrote to Scholem in English on July 15, 1941: "Dear, dear Gerhard, I cried when I saw your handwriting and at last got a letter from you after seven years. . . . Dear Gerhard, Walter's death has left a vacuum which is slowly but surely sucking in all my hopes and wishes for the future. I know that I shall not survive him long. You will be surprised at this, because I no longer formed part of his life, but he formed part of mine. . . . I thought and felt, that if the world was able to keep alive a creature of his worth and sensitiveness, it could not, after all, be such a bad world. It seems that I was wrong. / This is his birthday. I need not tell you more. . . . He would not have died if I had been with him. He did not die in 1917. . . . When I saw him last, in January 1940, and before that in the summer of 1939, I implored him to come to Lon-

don, where his room was ready for him." Cited in Garber, "Zum Briefwechsel zwischen Dora Benjamin und Gershom Scholem nach Benjamins Tod," 1843. See also Jay and Smith, "A Talk with Mona Jean Benjamin, Kim Yvon Benjamin, and Michael Benjamin."

6. An early, untitled draft of the theses contains two additional sections, dropped in later manuscript versions. See SW, 4:397. See also *Über den Begriff der Geschichte*, 30–43, for the text of Benjamin's "Handexemplar" (author's copy), which contains nineteen sections, including the one labeled XVIIa in the paralipomena and which begins: "In the idea of classless society, Marx secularized the idea of messianic time. And that was a good thing" (SW, 4:401–402).

7. This phrase in the "Paralipomena to 'On the Concept of History'" comes from Benjamin's 1929 essay "Surrealism," where it is associated with the concept of "image space" (SW, 2:217). In regard to "messianic time," compare "*Trauerspiel* and Tragedy" from 1916 (EW, 242).

8. Sahl, *Memoiren eines Moralisten*, 82–85.

9. On the good European, see Nietzsche's *Human, All Too Human*, aphorism 475. On the last man, see the fifth section of the prologue to Nietzsche, *Thus Spoke Zarathustra*.

10. Concerning the preservation of Benjamin's *Nachlaß* (posthumous papers), see Tiedemann, *Dialektik im Stillstand*, 151–155.

11. Benjamin's sonnets are printed in GS, 7:27–67. They were composed ca. 1913–1922, though the dating is uncertain.

12. Missac himself thinks that Bataille in 1945 simply forgot about part of the papers, which included an unpublished essay on film history by the young Missac that Benjamin had preserved among his own working documents. Missac, *Walter Benjamin's Passages*, 121–122.

13. Ingrid Scheurmann, "Als Deutscher in Frankreich: Walter Benjamins Exil, 1933–1940," in Scheurmann and Scheurmann, eds., *Für Walter Benjamin*, 96.

14. GB, 6:475–476 (letter of August 2, 1940, to Adorno). The last four sentences of the passage quoted are omitted in BA, 339–340.

15. Fabian and Coulmas, *Die deutsche Emigration in Frankreich nach 1933*, 85ff.; cited in Scheurmann, "Als Deutscher in Frankreich," 97.

16. See Fittko, "The Story of Old Benjamin," 947. This essay is reprinted in Lisa Fittko, *Escape through the Pyrenees*, trans. David Koblick (Evanston, IL: Northwestern University Press, 1991). Fittko's recollections of Benjamin's crossing of the Pyrenees in September 1940 constitute much of what we know about Benjamin's last days. A more recent addition to the scant store of facts is the memoir of her own flight across the Pyrenees by Carina Birman, *The Narrow Foothold* (London: Hearing Eye, 2006).

17. Soma Morgenstern to Gershom Scholem, December 21, 1972. Cited in Puttnies and Smith, *Benjaminiana*, 203–205.

18. Fittko, "The Story of Old Benjamin," 947.

19. The exact dates of Benjamin's walk across the Pyrenees, arrival in Port Bou, and death are not certain. The evidence we have for these dates— memoirs by Lisa Fittko, Henny Gurland, and Carina Birman, municipal

and ecclesiastical records, and Benjamin's own last letter—is itself contradictory. Fittko gives the date of the group's departure as September 26.

20. Fittko, "The Story of Old Benjamin," 950, 948.

21. According to a telephone communication from Lisa Fittko to the authors before her death in Chicago in 2005.

22. Fittko later served as guide for other fleeing groups before she herself escaped in 1941. She spent eight years in Havana before finally settling in Chicago, where she supported herself and her husband through work as a translator, secretary, and office manager. For a brief biography by Lisa Fittko's niece, Catherine Stodolsky, see http://catherine.stodolsky.userweb.mwn.de.

23. Birman, *The Narrow Foothold*, 3.

24. Ibid., 5.

25. GB, 6:483. Translated in AP, 946.

26. Many of the details that follow are found in a letter from Henny Gurland written in October 1940; see GS, 5:1195–1196. The letter is translated by Harry Zohn in SF, 224–226.

27. Birman, *The Narrow Foothold*, 9.

28. For facsimiles of this and other relevant documents, see Scheurmann and Scheurmann, eds., *Für Walter Benjamin*, 101ff.

Selected Bibliography

WORKS BY WALTER BENJAMIN

Das Adressbuch des Exils, 1933–1940, ed. Christine Fischer-Defoy (Leipzig: Koehler & Amelang, 2006).

The Arcades Project, trans. Howard Eiland and Kevin McLaughlin (Cambridge, MA: Harvard University Press, 1999).

Berlin Childhood around 1900, trans. Howard Eiland (Cambridge, MA: Harvard University Press, 2006).

Walter Benjamin and Theodor W. Adorno, *The Complete Correspondence, 1928–1940*, trans. Nicholas Walker (Cambridge, MA: Harvard University Press, 1999).

Walter Benjamin and Gretel Adorno, *Correspondence 1930–1940*, trans. Wieland Hoban (Cambridge: Polity Press, 2008).

The Correspondence of Walter Benjamin, trans. M. R. and E. M. Jacobson (Chicago: University of Chicago Press, 1994).

Walter Benjamin and Gershom Scholem, *The Correspondence of Walter Benjamin and Gershom Scholem, 1932–1940*, trans. Gary Smith and Andre Lefevere (New York: Schocken Books, 1989).

Early Writings, 1910–1917, ed. Howard Eiland (Cambridge, MA: Harvard University Press, 2011).

Gesammelte Briefe, 6 vols., ed. Christoph Gödde and Henri Lonitz (Frankfurt: Suhrkamp Verlag, 1995–2000).

Gesammelte Schriften, 7 vols., ed. Rolf Tiedemann and Hermann Schweppenhäuser (Frankfurt am Main: Suhrkamp Verlag, 1974–1989).

Moscow Diary, ed. Gary Smith (Cambridge, MA: Harvard University Press, 1986).

On Hashish, ed. Howard Eiland (Cambridge, MA: Harvard University Press, 2006).

The Origin of German Tragic Drama, trans. John Osborne (London: New Left Books, 1977).

Selected Writings, 4 vols., Michael W. Jennings, general ed. (Cambridge, MA: Harvard University Press, 1996–2003).
Volume 1: *1913–1926*, ed. Michael W. Jennings and Marcus Bullock.
Volume 2: *1927–1934*, ed. Michael W. Jennings, Howard Eiland, and Gary Smith.
Volume 3: *1935–1938*, ed. Michael W. Jennings and Howard Eiland.
Volume 4: *1938–1940*, ed. Michael W. Jennings and Howard Eiland.

Werke und Nachlaß: Kritische Gesamtausgabe, Christoph Gödde and Henri Lonitz, general eds. (Berlin: Suhrkamp Verlag, 2008–).
Volume 3: *Der Begriff der Kunstkritik in der deutschen Romantik*, ed. Uwe Steiner.
Volume 8: *Einbahnstraße*, ed. Detlev Schöttker.
Volume 10: *Deutsche Menschen*, ed. Momme Brodersen.

Volume 13: *Kritiken und Rezensionen*, ed. Heinrich Kaulen.

Volume 16: *Das Kunstwerk im Zeitalter seiner Technischen Reproduzierbarkeit*, ed. Burkhardt Lindner.

Volume 19: *Über den Begriff der Geschichte*, ed. Gérard Raulet.

"The Work of Art in the Age of Its Technological Reproducibility" (first version), trans. Michael W. Jennings, *Grey Room* 39 (Spring 2010).

The Work of Art in the Age of Its Technological Reproducibility, and Other Writings on Media, ed. Michael W. Jennings, Brigid Doherty, and Thomas Y. Levin (Cambridge, MA: Harvard University Press, 2008).

The Writer of Modern Life: Essays on Charles Baudelaire, ed. Michael W. Jennings (Cambridge, MA: Harvard University Press, 2006).

PRIMARY SOURCES

Theodor W. Adorno, *Aesthetic Theory*, trans. Robert Hullot-Kentor (Minneapolis: University of Minnesota Press, 1997).

———, *In Search of Wagner*, trans. Rodney Livingstone (London: Verso, 1981).

———, *Kierkegaard: Construction of the Aesthetic*, trans. Robert Hullot-Kentor (Minneapolis: University of Minnesota Press, 1989).

———, *Minima Moralia*, trans. Edmund Jephcott (London: Verso, 1978).

———, *Night Music: Essays on Music 1928–1962*, trans. Wieland Hoban (London: Seagull, 2009).

———, *Notes to Literature*, 2 vols., trans. Shierry Weber Nicholsen (New York: Columbia University Press, 1991–1992).

———, *Prisms*, trans. Samuel and Shierry Weber (Cambridge, MA: MIT Press, 1981).

———, *Über Walter Benjamin*, rev. ed. (Frankfurt: Suhrkamp Verlag, 1990).

Theodor W. Adorno and Max Horkheimer, *Briefwechsel*, vol. 1, *1927–1937* (Frankfurt: Suhrkamp Verlag, 2003).

Guillaume Apollinaire, *Selected Writings*, trans. Roger Shattuck (New York: New Directions, 1972).

Louis Aragon, *Nightwalker (Le paysan de Paris)*, trans. Frederick Brown (Englewood Cliffs, NJ: Prentice-Hall, 1970).

———, *Une vague de rêves* (Paris: Seghers, 1990).

Hannah Arendt, *Men in Dark Times* (New York: Harcourt, 1968).

Hannah Arendt and Martin Heidegger, *Briefe, 1925–1975* (Frankfurt: Klostermann, 1998).

Hugo Ball, *Die Flucht aus der Zeit* (Lucerne: Josef Stocker Verlag, 1946).

Georges Bataille et al., *The College of Sociology, 1937–1939*, ed. Denis Hollier, trans. Betsy Wing (Minneapolis: University of Minnesota Press, 1988).

Charles Baudelaire, *Artificial Paradises*, trans. Stacy Diamond (New York: Citadel, 1996).

———, *Intimate Journals*, trans. Christopher Isherwood, with an introduction by T. S. Eliot (1930; rpt. Westport, CT: Hyperion, 1978).

———, *Les fleurs du mal*, trans. Richard Howard (Boston: David Godine, 1983).

———, *Oeuvres complètes*, ed. Marcel A. Ruff (Paris: Seuil, 1968).

———, *The Painter of Modern Life and Other Essays*, trans. Jonathan Mayne (1964; rpt. New York: Da Capo, 1986).

————, *Selected Writings on Art and Literature,* trans. P. E. Charvet (London: Penguin, 1972).

Henri Bergson, *Creative Evolution,* trans. Arthur Mitchell (Mineola, NY: Dover, 1998).

————, *Matter and Memory,* trans. N. M. Paul and W. S. Palmer (New York: Zone, 1991).

Carina Birman, *The Narrow Foothold* (London: Hearing Eye, 2006).

Ernst Bloch, *Heritage of Our Times,* trans. Neville Plaice and Stephen Plaice (Berkeley: University of California Press, 1990).

————, "Italien und die Porosität," in *Werkausgabe,* vol. 9, *Literarische Aufsätze* (Frankfurt: Suhrkamp Verlag, 1965).

————, *The Spirit of Utopia,* trans. Anthony Nassar (Stanford, CA: Stanford University Press, 2000).

Bertolt Brecht, *Arbeitsjournal* (Frankfurt: Suhrkamp Verlag, 1973).

————, *Brecht on Theatre,* ed. and trans. John Willett (New York: Hill and Wang, 1964).

————, *Poems 1913–1956,* ed. John Willett and Ralph Manheim (New York: Methuen, 1979).

André Breton, "Manifesto of Surrealism," in *Manifestoes of Surrealism,* trans. Richard Seaver and Helen R. Lane (Ann Arbor: University of Michigan Press, 1969).

————, *Nadja,* trans. Richard Howard (New York: Grove, 1960).

Max Brod, *Franz Kafka: A Biography,* trans. G. Humphreys Roberts and Richard Winston (New York: Schocken Books, 1963).

Martin Buber, *On Judaism,* ed. Nahum Glatzer (New York: Schocken Books, 1967).

Hermann Cohen, *Kants Theorie der Erfahrung* (Berlin: Bruno Cassirer, 1918).

————, *Religion of Reason: Out of the Sources of Judaism,* trans. S. Kaplan (New York: Frederick Ungar, 1995).

Johann Gottlieb Fichte, *The Science of Knowledge,* trans. Peter Heath and John Lachs (1970; rpt. Cambridge: Cambridge University Press, 1982).

Lisa Fittko, "The Story of Old Benjamin," in Walter Benjamin, *The Arcades Project,* trans. Howard Eiland and Kevin McLaughlin (Cambridge, MA: Harvard University Press, 1999).

Stefan George, *Gesamt-Ausgabe der Werke,* 15 vols. (Berlin: Georg Bondi, 1927–1934).

André Gide, *Pretexts: Reflections on Literature and Morality,* trans. Justin O'Brien (New York: Meridian, 1959).

Johann Wolfgang von Goethe, *Conversations with Eckermann, 1823–1832,* trans. John Oxenford (San Francisco: North Point Press, 1984).

————, *Elective Affinities,* trans. R. J. Hollingdale (London: Penguin Classics, 1978).

————, *Italian Journey,* trans. W. H. Auden and Elizabeth Mayer (1962; rpt. London: Penguin, 1970).

Moritz Goldstein, "Deutsch-Jüdischer Parnaß," in *Der Kunstwart* 25, vol. 11 (March 1912).

Friedrich Gundolf, *Goethe* (Berlin: Georg Bondi, 1916).

Eric Gutkind, *The Body of God: First Steps toward an Anti-Theology*, ed. Lucie B. Gutkind and Henry Le Roy Finch (New York: Horizon Press, 1969).

Willy Haas, *Gestalten der Zeit* (Berlin: Kiepenhauer, 1930).

Adolf von Harnack, *Lehrbuch der Dogmengeschichte*, 3 vols. (Freiburg: J. C. B. Mohr, 1888–1890).

Martin Heidegger, *Being and Time*, trans. John Macquarrie and Edward Robinson (New York: Harper and Row, 1962).

———, *Poetry, Language, Thought*, trans. Albert Hofstadter (New York: Harper, 1971).

Franz Hessel, "Die schwierige Kunst spazieren zu gehen," in *Ermunterung zu Genuß, Sämtliche Werke*, vol. 2 (Hamburg: Igel Verlag, 1999).

Friedrich Hölderlin, *Essays and Letters on Theory*, trans. Thomas Pfau (Albany: State University of New York Press, 1988).

———, *Selected Poems*, trans. Christopher Middleton (Chicago: University of Chicago Press, 1972).

Max Horkheimer, *Briefwechsel, 1927–1969* (Frankfurt: Suhrkamp Verlag, 2005).

———, *Critical Theory: Selected Essays*, trans. Matthew J. O'Connell et al. (New York: Continuum, 1995).

Alexander von Humboldt, *Schriften zur Sprache*, Michael Böhler, "Nachwort" (Stuttgart: Reclam, 1973).

Franz Kafka, *The Blue Octavo Notebooks*, trans. Ernst Kaiser and Eithne Wilkins (1954; rpt. Cambridge: Exact Change, 1991).

———, *The Castle*, trans. Mark Harman (New York: Schocken Books, 1998).

———, *Complete Stories*, various translators (New York: Schocken Books, 1995).

Immanuel Kant, *Critique of Pure Reason*, trans. Norman Kemp Smith (1929; rpt. New York: St. Martin's Press, 1965).

Ludwig Klages, *Sämtliche Werke*, vol. 3 (Bonn: Bouvier, 1974).

Karl Korsch, *Marxism and Philosophy* (New York: Monthly Review Press, 1970).

Siegfried Kracauer, *Schriften*, 9 vols., ed. Inka Mülder-Bach et al. (Berlin: Suhrkamp Verlag, 2011).

———, "Travel and Dance," "Lad and Bull," "Photography," "Those Who Wait," and "On the Writings of Walter Benjamin," in *The Mass Ornament*, trans. Thomas Y. Levin (Cambridge, MA: Harvard University Press, 1995).

———, *Werke in neun Bänden*, vol. 7, *Romane und Erzählungen*, ed. Inka Mülder-Bach (Frankfurt: Suhrkamp, 2004).

Werner Kraft, *Spiegelung der Jugend* (Frankfurt: Fischer, 1996).

Asja Lacis, *Revolutionär im Beruf: Berichte über proletarisches Theater, über Meyerhold, Brecht, Benjamin und Piscator* (Munich: Rogner & Bernhard, 1971).

Georg Lukács, *History and Class Consciousness: Studies in Marxist Dialectics*, trans. Rodney Livingstone (Cambridge, MA: MIT Press, 1971).

———, "On Walter Benjamin," *New Left Review* 110 (July–August 1978).

———, *The Theory of the Novel*, trans. Anna Bostock (Cambridge, MA: MIT Press, 1974).

André Malraux, *Man's Fate*, trans. Haakon M. Chevalier (New York: Random House, 1969).

Thomas Mann, "Die Entstehung des *Doktor Faustus*" (1949), in *Doktor Faustus* (Frankfurt: S. Fischer, 1967).

Detlef Mertins and Michael W. Jennings, eds., *G: An Avant-Garde Journal of Art, Architecture, Design, and Film, 1923–1926* (Los Angeles: Getty Research Institute, 2010).

László Moholy-Nagy, *Painting—Photography—Film* (Cambridge, MA: MIT Press, 1969).

———, "Production/Reproduction," in *Photography in the Modern Era: European Documents and Critical Writings*, ed. Christopher Phillips (New York: Metropolitan Museum of Art, 1989).

Friedrich Nietzsche, *Beyond Good and Evil: Prelude to a Philosophy of the Future*, trans. Walter Kaufmann (New York: Vintage, 1966).

———, *On the Advantage and Disadvantage of History for Life*, trans. Peter Preuss (Indianapolis, IN: Hackett, 1980).

———, *Thus Spoke Zarathustra*, trans. R. J. Hollingdale (Baltimore: Penguin, 1961).

———, *The Will to Power*, trans. Walter Kaufmann and R. J. Hollingdale (New York: Vintage, 1968).

Novalis (Friedrich von Hardenberg), *Werke in Einem Band* (Berlin: Aufbau, 1983).

Marcel Proust, *Swann's Way*, trans. C. K. Scott Moncrieff and Terence Kilmartin, rev. D. J. Enright (New York: Modern Library, 2003).

———, *On Art and Literature*, trans. Sylvia Townsend Warner (1957; rpt. New York: Carroll and Graf, 1984).

Florens Christian Rang, *Deutsche Bauhütte: Ein Wort an uns Deutsche über mögliche Gerechtigkeit gegen Belgien und Frankreich und zur Philosophie der Politik* (Leipzig: E. Arnold, 1924).

———, *Historische Psychologie des Karnevals* [1927–1928] (Berlin: Brinkmann und Bose, 1983).

Gustav Regler, *The Owl of Minerva*, trans. Norman Denny (New York: Farrar, Straus and Cudahy, 1959).

Bernhard Reich, *Im Wettlauf mit der Zeit* (Berlin: Henschel Verlag, 1970).

Alois Riegl, *Late Roman Art Industry*, trans. Rolf Winkes (Rome: Giorgio Bretschneider, 1985).

Franz Rosenzweig, *The Star of Redemption*, trans. W. Hallo (New York: Holt, Rinehart and Winston, 1971).

Max Rychner, "Erinnerungen," in *Über Walter Benjamin*, ed. T. W. Adorno et al. (Frankfurt: Suhrkamp Verlag, 1968).

Hans Sahl, *Memoiren eines Moralisten: Das Exil im Exil* (Munich: Luchterhand, 2008).

———, "Walter Benjamin in the Internment Camp" (1966), trans. Deborah Johnson, in *On Walter Benjamin: Critical Essays and Recollections*, ed. Gary Smith (Cambridge, MA: MIT Press, 1988).

Paul Scheerbart, *Glass Architecture*, and Bruno Taut, *Alpine Architecture*, trans. James Palmes and Shirley Palmer (New York: Praeger, 1972).

———, *Lesabéndio: Ein asteroïden-Roman* (Munich: Müller, 1913).

Friedrich Schlegel, *Friedrich Schlegel: Kritische Ausgabe seiner Werke*, 35 vols., ed. Ernst Behler, Jean-Jacques Anstett, and Hans Eichner (Paderborn: Schöningh, 1958–2002).

———, *Lucinde and the Fragments*, trans. Peter Firchow (Minneapolis: University of Minnesota Press, 1971).

Carl Schmitt, *Hamlet or Hecuba*, trans. David Pan and Jennifer R. Rust (New York: Telos Press, 2009).

———, *Political Theology: Four Chapters on the Concept of Sovereignty*, trans. George Schwab (Chicago: University of Chicago Press, 2006).

Gershom Scholem, *From Berlin to Jerusalem: Memories of My Youth*, trans. Harry Zohn (New York: Schocken Books, 1980).

———, *Lamentations of Youth: The Diaries of Gershom Scholem, 1913–1919*, trans. Anthony David Skinner (Cambridge, MA: Harvard University Press, 2007).

———, *Major Trends in Jewish Mysticism* (New York: Schocken Books, 1941).

———, *Tagebücher 1913–1917* (Frankfurt: Jüdischer Verlag, 1995).

———, *Walter Benjamin: The Story of a Friendship*, trans. Harry Zohn (New York: Schocken Books, 1981).

———, "Walter Benjamin and His Angel" (1972), in *On Walter Benjamin: Critical Essays and Recollections*, ed. Gary Smith (Cambridge, MA: MIT Press, 1988).

———, "Walter Benjamin und Felix Noeggerath," *Merkur*, February 1981.

Detlev Schöttker and Erdmut Wizisla, *Arendt und Benjamin: Texte, Briefe, Dokumente* (Frankfurt: Suhrkamp Verlag, 2006).

Jean Selz, "Benjamin in Ibiza," in *On Walter Benjamin: Critical Essays and Recollections*, ed. Gary Smith (Cambridge, MA: MIT Press, 1988).

Tobias Smollett, *Travels through France and Italy* (London: John Lehmann, 1949).

Alfred Sohn-Rethel, *Warenform und Denkform* (Frankfurt: Suhrkamp Verlag, 1978).

Georges Sorel, *Reflections on Violence*, trans. T. E. Hulme (London: Collier-Macmillan, 1950).

Gabrielle Tergit, *Käsebier erobert den Kurfürstendamm* (Frankfurt: Krüger, 1977).

Sandra Teroni and Wolfgang Klein, *Pour la défense de la culture: Les textes du Congrès international des écrivains, Paris, Juin 1935* (Dijon: Editions Universitaires de Dijon, 2005).

Erich Unger, *Vom Expressionismus zum Mythos des Hebräertums: Schriften 1909 bis 1931*, ed. Manfred Voigts (Würzburg: Königshausen & Neumann, 1992).

Paul Valéry, *The Art of Poetry*, trans. Denise Folliot (Princeton, NJ: Princeton University Press, 1958).

———, *Leonardo, Poe, Mallarmé*, trans. Malcolm Cowley and James R. Lawler (Princeton, NJ: Princeton University Press, 1972).

Johann Jakob Volkmann, *Historisch-Kritische Nachrichten aus Italien, 1770–71*, cited in Gunter Grimm, "Bäume, Himmel, Wasser—ist das nicht alles wie gemalt? Italien, das Land deutscher Sehnsucht," *Stuttgarter Zeitung*, July 4, 1987.

Ernest Wichner and Herbert Wiesner, *Franz Hessel: Nur was uns anschaut, sehen wir* (Berlin: Literaturhaus Berlin, 1998).

Charlotte Wolff, *Hindsight* (London: Quartet Books, 1980).

Karl Wolfskehl, *Gesammelte Werke*, vol. 2 (Hamburg: Claassen, 1960).

Gustav Wyneken, *Schule und Jugendkultur*, 3rd ed. (Jena: Eugen Diederich, 1919).

SECONDARY SOURCES

Theodor W. Adorno et al., ed., *Über Walter Benjamin* (Frankfurt: Suhrkamp Verlag, 1968).

Giorgio Agamben, *Homo Sacer: Sovereignty and Bare Life* (Stanford, CA: Stanford University Press, 1998).

———, *Infancy and History*, trans. Liz Heron (London: Verso, 1993).

———, *Potentialities*, ed. and trans. Daniel Heller-Roazen (Stanford, CA: Stanford University Press, 1999).

———, *The Signature of All Things: On Method*, trans. Luca D'Isanto with Kevin Attell (New York: Zone, 2009).

———, *Stanzas*, trans. Ronald L. Martinez (Minneapolis: University of Minnesota Press, 1993).

———, *The Time that Remains: A Commentary on the Letter to the Romans*, trans. Patricia Dailey (Stanford, CA: Stanford University Press, 2005).

Robert Alter, *Necessary Angels* (Cambridge, MA: Harvard University Press, 1991).

H. W. Belmore, "Some Recollections of Walter Benjamin," *German Life and Letters* 28, no. 2 (January 1975).

Andrew Benjamin, *Style and Time* (Evanston, IL: Northwestern University Press, 2006).

———, ed., *The Problems of Modernity: Adorno and Benjamin* (London: Routledge, 1989).

——— and Peter Osborne, eds., *Walter Benjamin's Philosophy: Destruction and Experience* (Manchester: Clinamen, 2000).

Hilde Benjamin, *Georg Benjamin*, 2nd ed. (Leipzig: S. Hirzel Verlag, 1982).

Russell A. Berman, *Modern Culture and Critical Theory* (Madison: University of Wisconsin Press, 1989).

Ernst Bloch, "Recollections of Walter Benjamin" (1966), trans. Michael W. Jennings, in *On Walter Benjamin: Critical Essays and Recollections*, ed. Gary Smith (Cambridge, MA: MIT Press, 1988).

Norbert Bolz and Bernd Witte, *Passagen: Walter Benjamins Urgeschichte des XIX Jahrhunderts* (Munich: Wilhelm Fink, 1994).

Momme Brodersen, *Walter Benjamin: A Biography*, trans. Malcolm R. Green and Ingrida Ligers (London: Verso, 1996).

Susan Buck-Morss, *The Dialectics of Seeing: Walter Benjamin and the Arcades Project* (Cambridge, MA: MIT Press, 1989).

———, *The Origin of Negative Dialectics: Theodor W. Adorno, Walter Benjamin, and the Frankfurt Institute* (New York: Free Press, 1977).

Eduardo Cadava, *Words of Light: Theses on the Photography of History* (Princeton, NJ: Princeton University Press, 1997).

Roberto Calasso, *The Ruin of Kasch*, trans. William Weaver and Stephen Sartarelli (Cambridge, MA: Harvard University Press, 1994).

Stanley Cavell, "Benjamin and Wittgenstein: Signals and Affinities," *Critical Inquiry* 25, no. 2 (Winter 1999).

Howard Caygill, "Benjamin, Heidegger and the Destruction of Tradition," in *Walter Benjamin's Philosophy: Destruction and Experience*, ed. Andrew Benjamin and Peter Osborne (Manchester: Clinamen, 2000).

———, *Walter Benjamin: The Colour of Experience* (New York: Routledge, 1998).

T. J. Clark, "Should Benjamin Have Read Marx?" *boundary 2* (Spring 2003).

Gordon Craig, *Germany, 1866–1945* (New York: Oxford University Press, 1980).

Paul DeMan, "Conclusions: Walter Benjamin's 'The Task of the Translator,'" in Paul DeMan, *Resistance to Theory*, 73–105 (Minneapolis: University of Minnesota Press, 1986).

Jacques Derrida, *Acts of Religion*, various translators (New York: Routledge, 2002).

———, "Des tours de Babel," in *Difference in Translation*, ed. and trans. Joseph F. Graham (Ithaca, NY: Cornell University Press, 1985).

Michel Despagne and Michael Werner, "Vom Passagen-Projekt zum Charles Baudelaire: Neue Handschriften zum Spätwerk Walter Benjamins," *Deutsche Vierteljahresschrift für Literaturwissenschaft und Geistesgeschichte* 58 (1984).

M. Dewey, "Walter Benjamins Interview mit der Zeitung *Vecherniaia Moskva*," *Zeitschrift für Slawistik* 30, no. 5 (1985).

Terry Eagleton, *Walter Benjamin, or Towards a Revolutionary Criticism* (London: New Left Books [Verso], 1981).

Howard Eiland, "Reception in Distraction," in *Walter Benjamin and Art*, ed. Andrew Benjamin (London: Continuum, 2005).

———, "Superimposition in Walter Benjamin's *Arcades Project*," *Telos* 138 (Spring 2007).

———, "Walter Benjamin's Jewishness," in *Walter Benjamin and Theology*, ed. Stéphane Symons and Colby Dickinson (forthcoming).

Richard Ellman, *James Joyce* (New York: Oxford University Press, 1959).

Richard Faber and Christine Holste, eds., *Der Potsdamer Forte-Kreis: Eine utopische Intellektuellenassoziation zur europäischen Friedenssicherung* (Würzburg: Königshausen & Neumann, 2001).

Ruth Fabian and Corinna Coulmas, *Die deutsche Emigration in Frankreich nach 1933* (Munich: K. G. Saur, 1978).

Simonetta Falasca-Zamponi, *Rethinking the Political: The Sacred, Aesthetic Politics, and the Collège de Sociologie* (Montreal: McGill–Queen's University Press, 2012).

Peter Fenves, *Arresting Language: From Leibniz to Benjamin* (Stanford, CA: Stanford University Press, 2002).

———, "Benjamin's Early Reception in the United States: A Report," *Benjamin-Studien* (forthcoming).

———, *The Messianic Reduction: Walter Benjamin and the Shape of Time* (Stanford, CA: Stanford University Press, 2011).

David S. Ferris, ed., *The Cambridge Companion to Walter Benjamin* (Cambridge: Cambridge University Press, 2004).

———, ed., *Walter Benjamin: Theoretical Questions* (Stanford, CA: Stanford University Press, 1996).

Bernd Finkeldey, "Hans Richter and the Constructivist International," in *Hans Richter: Activism, Modernism, and the Avant-Garde*, ed. Stephen C. Foster (Cambridge, MA: MIT Press, 1998).

Eli Friedlander, *Walter Benjamin: A Philosophical Portrait* (Cambridge, MA: Harvard University Press, 2012).

Paul Fry, *The Reach of Criticism* (New Haven, CT: Yale University Press, 1983).

Werner Fuld, *Walter Benjamin: Zwischen den Stühlen* (Frankfurt: Fischer, 1981).

Klaus Garber, "Zum Briefwechsel zwischen Dora Benjamin and Gershom Scholem nach Benjamins Tod," in *Global Benjamin: Internationaler Walter-Benjamin-Kongreß 1992*, ed. Klaus Garber and Ludger Rehm (Munich: Fink, 1999).

Kurt Gassen and Michael Landmann, eds., *Buch des Dankes an Georg Simmel: Briefe, Erinnerungen, Bibliographie* (Berlin, Dunckner und Humbolt, 1958).

J. F. Geist, *Arcades: The History of a Building Type*, trans. Jane Newman and John Smith (Cambridge, MA: MIT Press, 1983).

Wil van Gerwen, "Angela Nova: Biografische achtergronden bij Agesilaus Santander," *Benjamin Journal* 5 (Fall 1997).

———, "Walter Benjamin auf Ibiza: Biographische Hintergründe zu 'Agesilaus Santander,'" in *Global Benjamin: Internationaler Walter-Benjamin-Kongreß 1992*, ed. Klaus Garber and Ludger Rehm (Munich: Fink, 1999).

Nicola Gess, "'Schöpferische Innervation der Hand': Zur Gestensprache in Benjamins 'Probleme der Sprachsoziologie,'" in *Benjamin und die Anthropologie*, ed. Carolin Duttlinger, Ben Morgan, and Anthony Phelan (Freiburg: Rombach, 2011).

Davide Giuriato, *Mikrographien: Zu einer Poetologie des Schreibens in Walter Benjamins Kindheitserinnerungen, 1932–1939* (Munich: Wilhelm Fink, 2006).

Jürgen Habermas, "Walter Benjamin: Consciousness-Raising or Rescuing Critique (1972)," in Habermas, *Philosophical-Political Profiles*, trans. Frederick G. Lawrence (Cambridge, MA: MIT Press, 1983).

Werner Hamacher, "Afformative, Strike," trans. Dana Hollander, in *Walter Benjamin's Philosophy: Destruction and Experience*, ed. Andrew Benjamin and Peter Osborne (London: Routledge, 1994).

———, *Premises: Essays on Philosophy and Literature from Kant to Celan*, trans. Peter Fenves (Cambridge, MA: Harvard University Press, 1996).

Miriam Bratu Hansen, *Cinema and Experience* (Berkeley: University of California Press, 2012).

———, "Room for Play," *Canadian Journal of Film Studies* 13, no. 1 (Spring 2004).

Beatrice Hanssen, *Walter Benjamin's Other History: Of Stones, Animals, Human Beings, and Angels* (Berkeley: University of California Press, 1998).

Hiltrud Häntzschel, "Die Philologin Eva Fiesel, 1891–1937," in *Jahrbuch der Deutschen Schillergesellschaft*, 38. Jahrgang (Stuttgart: Kröner, 1994).

Geoffrey H. Hartman, *Criticism in the Wilderness* (New Haven, CT: Yale University Press, 1980).

Stéphane Hessel, *Tanz mit dem Jahrhundert: Eine Autobiographie* (Zurich: Arche Verlag, 1998).

Susan Ingram, "The Writings of Asja Lacis," *New German Critique*, no. 86 (Spring–Summer 2002).

Lorenz Jäger, *Messianische Kritik: Studien zu Leben und Werk von Florens Christian Rang* (Cologne: Böhlau Verlag, 1998).

Martin Jay, *The Dialectical Imagination: A History of the Frankfurt School and the Institute of Social Research, 1923–1950* (Boston: Little, Brown, 1973).

———, "Politics of Translation: Siegfried Kracauer and Walter Benjamin on the Buber-Rosenzweig Bible," *Publications of the Leo Baeck Institute*, Year Book 21, 1976 (London: Secker and Warburg).

Martin Jay and Gary Smith, "A Talk with Mona Jean Benjamin, Kim Yvon Benjamin and Michael Benjamin," in *Benjamin Studies/Studien 1* (Amsterdam: Rodopi, 2002).

Michael W. Jennings, *Dialectical Images: Walter Benjamin's Theory of Literary Criticism* (Ithaca, NY: Cornell University Press, 1987).

———, "Absolute Fragmentation: Walter Benjamin and Romantic Art Criticism," *Journal of Literary Criticism* 6, no. 1 (1993): 1–18.

———, "Benjamin as a Reader of Hölderlin: The Origin of Benjamin's Theory of Literary Criticism," *German Quarterly* 56, no. 4 (1983): 544–562.

———, "Eine gewaltige Erschütterung des Tradierten: Walter Benjamin's Political Recuperation of Franz Kafka," in *Fictions of Culture: Essays in Honor of Walter Sokel*, ed. Stephen Taubeneck (Las Vegas, NV: Peter Lang, 1991), 199–214.

———, "Towards Eschatology: The Development of Benjamin's Theological Politics in the Early 1920's," in *Walter Benjamins Anthropologisches Denken*, ed. Carolin Duttinger, Ben Morgan, and Anthony Phelan (Freiburg: Rombach Verlag, 2012), 41–58.

———, "Walter Benjamin and the European Avant-Garde," in *The Cambridge Companion to Walter Benjamin*, ed. David S. Ferris 18–34 (Cambridge: Cambridge University Press, 2004).

———, "Walter Benjamin and the Theory of Art History," in *Walter Benjamin, 1892–1940: Zum 100. Gerburtstag*, ed. Uwe Steiner, 77–102 (Bern: Peter Lang, 1992).

James Joyce, *Ulysses* (1922; rpt. New York: Modern Library, 1992).

Chryssoula Kambas, "Ball, Bloch und Benjamin," in *Dionysus DADA Areopagita: Hugo Ball und die Kritik der Moderne*, ed. Bernd Wacker (Paderborn: Ferdinand Schöningh, 1996).

———, *Walter Benjamin im Exil: Zum Verhältnis von Literaturpolitik und Ästhetik* (Tübingen: Niemeyer, 1983).

Robert Kaufman, "Aura, Still," *October* 99 (Winter 2002); rpt. in *Walter Benjamin and Art*, ed. Andrew Benjamin (London: Continuum, 2005).

Heinrich Kaulen, "Walter Benjamin und Asja Lacis: Eine biographische Konstellation und ihre Folgen," in *Deutsche Vierteljahrsschrift für Literaturwissenschaft und Geistesgeschichte*, 69. Jahrgang, 1995 (Heft 1 / März).

Frank Kermode, "Every Kind of Intelligence," *New York Times Book Review*, July 30, 1978.

———, "The Incomparable Benjamin," *New York Review of Books*, December 18, 1969.

Wolfgang Klein and Akademie der Wissenschaften der DDR, Zentralinstitut für Literaturgeschichte, *Paris 1935. Erster Internationaler Schriftstellerkongress zur Verteidigung der Kultur: Reden und Dokumente mit Materialien der Londoner Schriftstellerkonferenz 1936* (Berlin: Akademie-Verlag, 1982).

Paul Kluke, "Das Institut für Sozialforschung," in *Geschichte der Soziologie*, vol. 2, ed. Wolf Lepenies (Frankfurt: Suhrkamp Verlag, 1981).

Margarete Kohlenbach, "Religion, Experience, Politics: On Erich Unger and Walter Benjamin," in *The Early Frankfurt School and Religion*, ed. Raymond Geuss and Kohlenbach (Houndmills: Palgrave Macmillan, 2005).

Eckhardt Köhn, *Strassenrausch: Flânerie und kleine Form—Versuch zur Literaturgeschichte des Flâneurs bis 1933* (Berlin: Das Arsenal, 1989).

Werner Kraft, "Friedrich C. Heinle," *Akzente* 31 (1984).

———, "Über einen verschollenen Dichter," *Neue Rundschau* 78 (1967).

Stephan Lackner, " 'Von einer langen, schwierigen Irrfahrt': Aus unveröffentlichten Briefen Walter Benjamins," *Neue Deutsche Hefte* 26, no. 1 (1979).

Walter Laqueur, *Young Germany: A History of the German Youth Movement*, introduction by R. H. S. Crossman (1962; rpt. New Brunswick, NJ: Transaction Books, 1984).

Esther Leslie, *Walter Benjamin: Overpowering Conformism* (London: Pluto Press, 2000).

———, ed., *Walter Benjamin's Archive* (London: Verso, 2007).

Burkhardt Lindner, ed., *Benjamin Handbuch: Leben-Werk-Wirkung* (Stuttgart: Metzler Verlag, 2006).

———, "Habilitationsakte Benjamin: Über ein 'akademisches Trauerspiel' und über ein Vorkapitel der 'Frankfurter Schule' (Horkheimer, Adorno)," *Zeitschrift für Literaturwissenscahft und Linguistik* 53/54 (1984).

———, ed., *Links hatte noch alles sich zu enträtseln . . .": Walter Benjamin im Kontext* (Frankfurt: Syndikat, 1978).

Geret Luhr, ed., *Was noch begraben lag: Zu Walter Benjamins Exil—Briefe und Dokumente* (Berlin: Bostelmann und Siebenhaar, 2000).

John McCole, *Walter Benjamin and the Antinomies of Tradition* (Ithaca, NY: Cornell University Press, 1993).

Kevin McLaughlin, "Benjamin Now: Afterthoughts on *The Arcades Project*," *boundary 2* (Spring 2003).

Jeffrey Mehlman, *Walter Benjamin for Children: An Essay on His Radio Years* (Chicago: University of Chicago Press, 1993).

Winfried Menninghaus, *Walter Benjamins Theorie der Sprachmagie* (Frankfurt: Suhrkamp Verlag, 1980).

———, *Schwellenkunde: Walter Benjamins Passage des Mythos* (Frankfurt, Suhrkamp Verlag, 1986).

———, "Walter Benjamin's Theory of Myth," in *On Walter Benjamin: Critical Essays and Recollections*, ed. Gary Smith (Cambridge, MA: MIT Press, 1988).

Pierre Missac, *Walter Benjamin's Passages*, trans. Shierry Weber Nicholsen (Cambridge, MA: MIT Press, 1995).

Stefan Müller-Doohm, *Adorno* (Frankfurt: Suhrkamp Verlag, 2003).

Arno Münster, *Ernst Bloch: Eine politische Biografie* (Berlin: Philo & Philo Fine Arts, 2004).

Rainer Nägele, *Theater, Theory, Speculation: Walter Benjamin and the Scenes of Modernity* (Baltimore: Johns Hopkins University Press, 1991).

———, ed., *Benjamin's Ground* (Detroit: Wayne State University Press, 1988).

Magali Laure Nieradka, *Der Meister der leisen Töne: Biographie des Dichters Franz Hessel* (Oldenburg: Igel, 2003).

Jane O. Newman, *Benjamin's Library: Modernity, Nation, and the Baroque* (Ithaca, NY: Cornell University Press, 2011).

Robert E. Norton, *Secret Germany* (Ithaca, NY: Cornell University Press, 2002).

Blair Ogden, "Benjamin, Wittgenstein, and Philosophical Anthropology: A Reevaluation of the Mimetic Faculty," in Michael Jennings and Tobias Wilke, eds., *Grey Room* 39 (Spring 2010).

Michael Opitz and Erdmut Wizisla, eds., *Aber Ein Sturm Weht vom Paradies Her: Texte zu Walter Benjamin* (Leipzig: Reclam, 1992).

———, *Benjamins Begriffe*, 2 vols. (Frankfurt: Suhrkamp Verlag, 2000).

Peter Osborne, *Philosophy in Cultural Theory* (New York: Routledge, 2000).

———, *The Politics of Time: Modernity and Avant-Garde* (London: Verso, 1995).

Jean-Michel Palmier, *Walter Benjamin: Lumpensammler, Engel und bucklicht Männlein—Ästhetik und Politik bei Walter Benjamin*, trans. Horst Brühmann (Berlin: Suhrkamp Verlag, 2009).

———, *Weimar in Exile: The Antifascist Emigration in Europe and America*, trans. David Fernbach (New York: Verso, 2006).

Claire Paulhan, "Henry Church and the Literary Magazine *Mesures:* 'The American Resource,'" in *Artists, Intellectuals, and World War II: The Pontigny Encounters at Mount Holyoke College*, ed. Christopher Benfy and Karen Remmler (Amherst: University of Massachusetts Press, 2006).

Hans Puttnies and Gary Smith, *Benjaminiana* (Giessen: Anabas, 1991).

Anson Rabinbach, *The Crisis of Austrian Socialism: From Red Vienna to Civil War, 1927–1934* (Chicago: University of Chicago Press, 1983).

———, *In the Shadow of Catastrophe: German Intellectuals between Apocalypse and Enlightenment* (Berkeley: University of California Press, 2001).

———, *Staging Anti-Fascism in the Era of Hitler and Stalin*, forthcoming.

Willem van Reijen and Herman van Doorn, *Aufenthalte und Passagen: Leben und Werk Walter Benjamins* (Frankfurt: Suhrkamp Verlag, 2001).

Gerhard Richter, *Thought-Images: Frankfurt School Writers' Reflections from Damaged Life* (Stanford, CA: Stanford University Press, 2007).

——, *Walter Benjamin and the Corpus of Autobiography* (Detroit: Wayne State University Press, 2000).

Avital Ronell, "Street Talk," in Rainer Nägele, ed., *Benjamin's Ground* (Detroit: Wayne State University Press, 1988).

Charles Rosen, "The Ruins of Walter Benjamin," *New York Review of Books*, October 27, 1977.

Monad Rrenban, *Wild, Unforgettable Philosophy in Early Works of Walter Benjamin* (Lanham, MA: Lexington Books, 2005).

Ingrid Scheurmann, ed., *Neue Dokumente zum Tode Walter Benjamins* (Bonn: Arbeitskreis selbständiger Kultur-Institute und Gemeinde Port-Bou, 1992).

Ingrid Scheurmann and Konrad Scheurmann, eds., *Für Walter Benjamin* (Frankfurt: Suhrkamp Verlag, 1992).

Sabine Schiller-Lerg, "Ernst Schoen (1894–1960): Ein Freund überlebt—Erste biographische Einblicke in seinen Nachlaß," in *Global Benjamin: Internationaler Walter-Benjamin-Kongreß 1992*, ed. Klaus Garber and Ludger Rehm, 2:982–1013 (Munich: Fink, 1999).

——, *Walter Benjamin und der Rundfunk* (Munich: Saur Verlag, 1984).

Eva Schöck-Quinteros, "Dora Benjamin: '. . . denn ich hoffe nach dem Krieg in Amerika arbeiten zu können'—Stationen einer vertriebenen Wissenschaftslerin, 1901–1946," in *Barrieren und Karrieren: Die Anfänge des Frauenstudiums in Deutschland* (Berlin: Trafo, 2000).

Christian Schulte, *Ursprung ist das Ziel: Walter Benjamin über Karl Kraus* (Würzburg: Königshausen & Neumann, 2003).

Gary Smith, "Das jüdische versteht sich von selbst: Walter Benjamins frühe Auseinandersetzung mid dem Judentum," *Deutsche Vierteljahresschrift für Literaturwissenschaft und Geistesgeschichte* 65 (1981): 318–334.

——, ed., *On Walter Benjamin: Critical Essays and Recollections* (Cambridge, MA: MIT Press, 1988).

Susan Sontag, "Under the Sign of Saturn," in *Under the Sign of Saturn* (New York: Farrar, Straus and Giroux, 1980).

Uwe Steiner, *Die Geburt der Kritik aus dem Geiste der Kunst* (Würzburg: Königshausen und Neumann, 1989).

——, *Walter Benjamin: An Introduction to His Work and Thought*, trans. Michael Winkler (Chicago: University of Chicago Press, 2010).

——, "The True Politician: Walter Benjamin's Concept of the Political," *New German Critique* 83 (Spring-Summer 2000).

——, ed., *Walter Benjamin, 1892–1940: Zum 100. Geburtstag* (Bern: Peter Lang, 1992).

Michael Surya, *Georges Bataille: An Intellectual Biography*, trans. Krzysztof Fijalkowski and Michael Richardson (New York: Verso, 2002).

Peter Szondi, "Hoffnung im Vergangenen: Walter Benjamin und die Suche nach der verlorenen Zeit," in *Zeugnisse: Theodor W. Adorno zum sechzigsten Geburtstag*, ed. Max Horkheimer (Frankfurt: Europäische Verlagsanstalt, 1963); translated by Harvey Mendelsohn as "Hope in the Past: On Walter Benjamin," in Walter Benjamin, *Berlin Childhood around 1900* (Cambridge, MA: Harvard University Press, 2006).

Bruno Tackels, *Walter Benjamin: Une vie dans les textes* (Arles: Actes Sud, 2009).

Klaus Täubert, *"Unbekannt verzogen...": Der Lebensweg des Suchtmediziners, Psychologen und KPD-Gründungsmitgliedes Fritz Fränkel* (Berlin: Trafo, 2005).

Jacob Taubes, *The Political Theology of Paul* (1987), trans. Dana Hollander (Stanford, CA: Stanford University Press, 2004).

Rolf Tiedemann, *Dialektik im Stillstand* (Frankfurt: Suhrkamp Verlag, 1983).

Rolf Tiedemann, Christoph Gödde, and Henri Lonitz, "Walter Benjamin, 1892–1940: Eine Ausstellung des Theodor W. Adorno Archivs, Frankfurt am Main in Verbindung mit dem Deutschen Literaturarchiv Marbach am Neckar," *Marbacher Magazin* 55 (1990).

Siegfried Unseld, ed., *Zur Aktualität Walter Benjamins: Aus Anlaß des 80. Geburtstages von Walter Benjamin* (Frankfurt: Suhrkamp Verlag, 1972).

Vicente Valero, *Der Erzähler: Walter Benjamin auf Ibiza 1932 und 1933*, trans. Lisa Ackermann and Uwe Dehler (Berlin: Parthas, 2008).

Manfred Voigts, *Oskar Goldberg: Der mythische Experimentalwissenschaftler* (Berlin: Agora Verlag, 1992).

Samuel Weber, *Benjamin's -abilities* (Cambridge, MA: Harvard University Press, 2008).

———, "Genealogy of Modernity: History, Myth and Allegory in Benjamin's *Origin of the German Mourning Play*," *MLN* (April 1991).

———, "Taking Exception to Decision: Walter Benjamin and Carl Schmitt," *diacritics* (Fall–Winter 1992).

Daniel Weidner, *Gershom Scholem: Politisches, esoterisches und historiographisches Schreiben* (Munich: Wilhelm Fink, 2003).

Sigrid Weigel, *Entstellte Ähnlichkeiten: Walter Benjamins theoretische Schreibweise* (Frankfurt: Fischer Verlag, 1997).

———, *Body- and Image-Space: Re-reading Walter Benjamin*, trans. Georgina Paul, Rachel McNicholl, and Jeremy Gaines (New York: Routledge, 1996).

Rolf Wiggershaus, *The Frankfurt School: Its History, Theories, and Political Significance*, trans. Michael Robertson (Cambridge, MA: MIT Press, 1994).

Bernd Witte, *Walter Benjamin: An Intellectual Biography*, trans. J. Rolleston (Detroit: Wayne State University Press, 1991).

———, *Walter Benjamin: Der Intellektuelle als Kritiker—Untersuchungen zu seinem Frühwerk* (Stuttgart: Metzler, 1976).

Erdmut Wizisla, *Walter Benjamin and Bertolt Brecht: The Story of a Friendship*, trans. Christine Shuttleworth (New Haven, CT: Yale University Press, 2009).

Irving Wohlfarth, "Et cetera? Der Historiker als Lumpensammler," in *Passagen: Walter Benjamins Urgeschichte des XIX Jahrhunderts*, ed. Norbert Bolz and Bernd Witte, 70–95 (Munich: Wilhelm Fink, 1994).

———, "On the Messianic Structure of Walter Benjamin's Last Reflections," *Glyph* 3 (1978).

———, "The Politics of Youth: Walter Benjamin's Reading of *The Idiot*," *diacritics* (Fall–Winter 1992).

————, "Re-fusing Theology: Benjamin's Arcades Project," *New German Critique* 39 (Fall 1986).

Elisabeth Young-Bruehl, *Hannah Arendt: For the Love of the World,* 2nd ed. (New Haven, CT: Yale University Press, 2004).

Acknowledgments

We owe a special debt of gratitude to Lindsay Waters, the godfather of this book and progenitor of the well-established faith in the work of Walter Benjamin prevailing at Harvard University Press. More than thirty years ago, Erich Heller and Walter Sokel provided the initial impetus for a lifetime's involvement with Benjamin. Erdmut Wizisla and the staff at the Benjamin Archive at the Akademie der Künste in Berlin were helpful at many stages of the project. Final preparation of the manuscript was greatly aided by Shanshan Wang at Harvard University Press and by the expert production team at Westchester Publishing Services. Many friends, scholars, and colleagues have, over the years, contributed generously to this book as we discussed issues large and small, pestered them for details, and tested theses on them. We are enormously grateful to Michael Arner, Alexander Bove, Eduardo Cadava, Matthew Charles, Bo-Mi Choi, Ingrid Christian, Norma Cole, Stanley Corngold, Brigid Doherty, Kurt Fendt, Peter Fenves, Devin Fore, Hal Foster, Michael Hamburger, Martin Harries, Robert Kaufman, Alexander Kluge, Tom Levin, Vivian Liska, James MacFarland, Daniel Magilow, Kevin McLaughlin, Winfried Menninghaus, Ben Morgan, Jane Newman, Tony Phelan, Andy Rabinbach, Gerhard Richter, Eric Santner, Gary Smith, Uwe Steiner, Jeffrey Stuker, Jiro Tanaka, Stephen Tapscott, David Thorburn, Joseph Vogl, Arnd Wedemeyer, Daniel Weidner, Sigrid Weigel, and Tobias Wilke. The students in our classes and seminars—and the many young scholars at the biennial conferences of the International Walter Benjamin Society—have over the years challenged us to refine our understanding of Benjamin's work. And Julia Prewitt Brown and Susan Constant Jennings have provided the kind of unstinting inspiration and support—to say nothing of patience—of which most authors can only dream.

Index

Note: Pages numbers in *italics* indicate photographs. Page numbers followed by n or nn indicate notes. WB is Walter Benjamin and DPB is Dora Pollak Benjamin.

Abbaye de Pontigny, 332, 534, 636, *639*
Abrami, Dr. Pierre, 663
Adorno, Gretel. *See* Karplus, Margarete "Gretel"
Adorno, Theodor Wiesengrund, 33, 144, 189, *192*, 325, 427, 472, 586; on WB, 4, 8, 688n43; *Dialectic of Enlightenment*, 165, 604, 677; WB's *The Arcades Project* and, 280, 287, 290, 476–478, 493–494, 541, 552, 553, 700n37; WB's "philosophical friendship" with, 301; Königstein conversations and, 332–333; indebtedness to WB, 359–360; *Kierkegaard: Construction of the Aesthetic*, 359, 386, 525; WB's *Berlin Childhood around 1900* and, 381, 385; WB's *Origin of the German Trauerspiel* and, 385–386; Karplus and, 414, 472–473, 570–571, 633; *Singspiel*, "The Treasure of Indian Joe" and WB's opinion, 447–448; WB's "Franz Kafka" critiqued, 475; WB's "Paris, the Capital of the Nineteenth Century" critiqued, 493–495; essay on Berg, 527, 569; WB's *Charles Baudelaire* and, 532–533, 578; WB's *Deutsche Menschen* and, 538; Jochmann's "Die Rückschritte der Poesie" and, 561; Sohn-Rethel's "Sociological Theory of Knowledge" and, 562–563; literary work with WB, 562–566, 569; Kracauer's *Orpheus in Paris* and, 563–564; *Minima Moralia*, 564; in New York, 575, 586–587; *Versuch über Wagner* (In Search of Wagner), 576, 603; WB mediates between Brecht and, 607–608; WB's "The Paris of the Second Empire in Baudelaire" critiqued, 623–625, 628–629, 657–658; WB's "On Some Motifs in Baudelaire" critiqued, 657;

WB's last statement on literature and, 666–667; WB's work published posthumously by, 677–678
Afterlife of cultural antiquity, 295
Afterlife of works, 59, 109, 112, 158, 289, 343
Agamben, Giorgio, 668, 684n12, 700n38, 715n11, 716n25
Agnon, Shmuel Yosef, 123; "The Great Synagogue," 442
Ahad Ha'am (Asher Ginsberg), 83, 685n16
Die Aktion, 61, 63, 685–686n25
Albert Ludwig University, 32–45, 51–53, 55–61
Allegory, 9, 18–19, 91, 198, 217, 289, 475, 492, 596, 602, 708n68; "allegorical perception," 18; in *Origin of the German Trauerspiel*, 228–230; WB on Baudelaire and, 617–619
Alternative (journal), 677
Altschul, Frank, 631
Der Anfang (journal), 28–29, 53, 60, 152; WB's pseudonymous articles in, as student, 49–50, 61–62
Angelus Novus (WB's proposed journal), 150–157, 173, 182–183; WB's plans for first and second issues of, 157, 160–161, 169, 442
Antifascist aesthetic, of International Congress of Writers, 504
Apokatastasis, 548, 604, 659–660
Aragon, Louis, 236, 279, 281, 335, 394; *Paysan de Paris* (Paris Peasant), 285, 310, 490
The Arcades Project (Benjamin), 1–2, 160, 165–166, 254, 286, 304, *319*, 325, 429, 515; WB and significance of prostitution, 56; Hessel and, 256; "The Gambler," 280–281; Adorno and, 280, 287, 290, 476–478, 493–494, 541, 552, 553, 700n37; ideas and plans for, 285–287, 337, 700n37; "Paris

The Arcades Project (continued)
  Arcades I," 286; "Paris Arcades II,"
  286–287; literary montage and
  dialectic method in, 287–293,
  701nn43–46; manuscripts hidden in
  Bibliothèque Nationale, 287, 700n38;
  "Notes and Materials," 287; structure
  of, 291, 293, 306, 337, 363, 388, 390,
  429, 450, 484, 548, 566, 569, 573, 595,
  659; "Photography," 293; intoxication
  and, 296, 297, 298; work on, 305–306,
  317, 501–502; gambling and, 333,
  389–390, 484–485, 485; suicide and,
  362; cross-fertilization with other
  works, 386, 573; "crock" and manifold
  interpretability in, 400; "Central
  Park," 418, 618, 627; Korsch and, 465,
  640; sociological and historical
  direction adopted, 478; reviews of,
  480; "Paris, the Capital of the
  Nineteenth Century" exposé,
  483–484, 489–495, 631–632; visual arts
  focus develops, 502–503; collective
  unconscious and, 532; construction
  and destruction and, 548; Jungian
  psychology and, 566; Baudelaire and,
  567; Joubert and, 637, 716n22
Arendt, Hannah, 322, 580–581, 634–635,
  659, 664, 678
Die Argonauten (journal), 127, 137, 150
Aron, Max, 648–649
Aron, Raymond, 520, 584
Arp, Hans, 106, 171
Atget, Eugène, 363, 365
Auerbach, Erich, 196; *Mimesis,* 196
Aura, WB's concept of, 59, 146, 295, 298,
  364–365, 514–515, 517, 623, 644–645,
  713n15, 716n25; merger of theory of
  language and Marxism, 581–582; in
  process of decay, 602
Awakening, dialectics of, 289–291, 298,
  493–494
Awakening youth motif, 24–25, 28, 39,
  44, 684n11

Baader, Franz von, 81–82, 449, 460, 530
Bachelard, Gaston, *Psychanalyse du feu*
  (Psychoanalysis of Fire), 665
Bachofen, Johann Jakob, 81, 436, 473–474
Bakunin, Mikhail, 106, 127
Ball, Hugo, 105–106, 171

Ballard, Jean, 265, 467
Barbizon, Georges (Georg Gretor), 28, 61
Barbusse, Henri, 503
Barrès, Maurice, 404
Barth, Friedy, 544
Barth, Karl, *Epistle to the Romans,*
  129–130, 198, 697n14
Barthes, Roland, *Mythologies,* 258
Basseches, Nikolaus, 268
Bassiano, Princess di, 261
Bataille, Georges, 518–519, 609; WB's
  papers entrusted to, 287, 591, 630,
  636, 667–668, 717n12; countering of
  Surrealism and, 519–520; Collège de
  Sociologie and, 574–575, 589
Baudelaire, Charles, 577; WB character-
  izes as secret agent, 6, 613, 616; WB's
  translation of, 76, 124, 137, 186–188,
  193–194, 209, 688n5; *Artificial
  Paradises,* 114, 296; spleen and, 170,
  596, 617, 644; conception of "modern
  beauty," 226; hatred of journalism,
  352; George's translation of, 407, 611;
  portrayed as flâneur, 492; "Le peintre
  de la vie moderne" (The Painter of
  Modern Life), 545, 645–646; influence on T. S. Eliot, 610–611. *See also*
  Charles Baudelaire: A Lyric Poet in
  the Age of High Capitalism
  (Benjamin)
Baumgardt, David, 29
Beach, Sylvia, 336, 435, 653
Becher, Johannes R., 503; *Levisite oder
  der einzig gerechte Krieg* (Levisite,
  or the Solely Just War), 267
Belmore, Herbert, 27, 30, 34, 35, 39, 51,
  55–56, 59, 84–85; on DPB, 68, 93; WB
  breaks with, 71, 92–93
Benda, Julien, 404, 503, 504; *Un régulier
  dans le siècle* (A Soldier in This
  Century), 588
Benjamin, Dora (sister), 19–20, 485, 505;
  relationship with WB, 126, 334,
  446–447, 505; educational and
  professional life of, 245–246, 682n1;
  WB's gambling and, 484; Fränkel and,
  495–496; health of, 505, 620; WB's
  internment and, 649, 651; WB's papers
  and, 667; flight from France at start of
  war, 668, 669, 670, 682n1, 710n14; *The
  Arcades Project* and, 700n38

Benjamin, Dora Sophie Kellner Pollak
(wife), 64, 67–68, 69, 99–101,
113–116, 121, 180, 191, 216, 243, 279,
280, 303, 401, 434, 447; marriage to
Pollak, 67, 84–85; Scholem and, 83,
84, 691–692n43; marries Benjamin,
91–92; WB's health and, 91–92; birth
of son, 100; as book and art collector, 100, 124, 135, 218; work life of,
100, 121–122, 191, 235, 301, 360, 395;
marriage to WB, 103–105, 141–147,
155–156, 691n43, 694n28; health of,
114, 153–154, 155, 174, 180; theatrical
ambitions, 135; Schoen and, 143–147,
315; WB's friendships and, 155, 157;
divorce from WB, 252, 314–317, 333,
334, 337, 350, 357–358, 703n1, 703n3;
WB's love for, 357; improved
relationship with WB, 360, 467–468;
WB's suicide plans in 1932 and, 379;
pension in San Remo, 395, 466,
565–566, 574, 619; WB's work and,
428; WB's gambling and, 484;
concern about Stefan's psychological
condition, 542–545, 568; German
warrant for arrest of, 543; in London
at start of war, 649, 655–656; marries
Morser, 655; death of, 656; on WB's
death, 716n5
Benjamin, Emil (father), 14, 15, 16–17,
29, 46, 60, 113–114, 115, 173–174, 263,
350, 687n35
Benjamin, Georg (bother), 15, 19–20, 20,
126, 221, 245, 247, 250, 658, 682n1;
political activity, arrests, and death,
240, 246, 295, 400–401, 434, 447, 495,
506, 541–542, 594, 620–621, 682n1,
710n14; education and professional
life of, 246, 682n1; marriage, 246,
250, 526
Benjamin, Hilde Lange (sister-in-law),
36–37, 594; professional life and
politics of, 20, 246–247, 682n6;
marries Georg Benjamin, 246, 250,
526
Benjamin, Michael (nephew), 594
Benjamin, Mona Jean (granddaughter),
703n3
Benjamin, Pauline Schoenflies (mother),
14, 15, 17–18, 46, 113–114, 115, 308,
335, 349–350

Benjamin, Stefan Rafael (son), 279, 542;
WB's use of childhood sayings of,
100–101, 135, 145–146, 218, 243–245;
birth, 100; as child, 114, 115, 174,
180, 191, 216, 218, 220, 221–222, 279;
remarks on Brecht, 349; parents'
divorce and, 360, 703n3; Nazi rule
and question of being sent to
Palestine, 395, 710n22; in San Remo,
395, 468, 472, 575; safety concerns as
war looms, 401, 434, 447; concern
about psychological condition of,
542–545, 568; in London at start of
war, 619, 649; death, 656
Benjamin, Walter, radio broadcasts of,
325, 331–332; "Bert Brecht, 323;
"Franz Kafka: Beim Bau der
Chinesischen Mauer," 358–359; "On
the Trail of Old Letters," 362;
"Recent Literature in Russia," 278;
"Young Russian Writers," 278, 346
Benjamin, Walter, works of: "Against a
Masterpiece," 329; "Agesilaus
Santander," 416–418, 422, 711n26;
"Am Kamin," 408, 710n20; "Analogy
and Relationship," 114; "André Gide
and Germany," 702n60; "The Author
as Producer," 405, 439–442, 449, 505;
"Berlin Chronicle," 13, 320, 368–369,
380, 382; "Brecht's Threepenny
Novel," 474; "The Cactus," 373–374;
"Capitalism as Religion," 149, 182;
"The Centaur," 690n30; "Central
Park," 418, 618, 627–629, 711n32;
"Collection of Frankfurt Children's
Rhymes," 236; "Commentary on
Poems by Brecht," 630, 667; "The
Concept of Criticism in German
Romanticism" (1919 dissertation),
81, 94, 95, 99, 105, 107–113, 118, 139,
158, 194, 343, 547, 626, 686n32,
690n30; "Conversation above the
Corso," 475–476; "Conversation with
André Gide," 300; "Conversation
with Ernst Schoen," 330–331;
"Critique of Violence," 128, 131–134,
152, 175, 193; "Crock Notes," 400;
"Death of the Father," 60; "The
Destructive Character," 130, 307,
351, 362, 662; Deutsche Menschen
(German Men and Women), 362, 367,

Benjamin, Walter, works of *(continued)* 430, 536–539, 593–594, 641; "Dialogue on the Religiosity of the Present," 40, 107, 150, 696n52, 696n54; "Doctrine of the Similar," 87, 388; "Dostoevsky's *The Idiot*," 109, 127; "Eduard Fuchs, Collector and Historian," 344, 388, 406, 478, 488, 510, 529, 546–551, 627–628; "Ein deutsches Institut freier Forschung" (A German Institute for Independent Research), 573; "Epilogue," 30–31, 683n17; "Epistemo-Critical Prologue," 87; "Evening with Monsieur Albert," 336; "The Eve of Departure," 370; "'Experience,'" 49–50; "Experience and Poverty," 186, 412–414, 422, 425, 443; "Fantasy on a Passage in *The Spirit of Utopia*," 130; "Fate and Character," 114, 127, 132, 152; "Food," 363; "Franz Kafka: *Beim Bau der Chinesischen Mauer*," 439, 442–446, 454–457, 474–475; "From World Citizen to Haut-Bourgeois," 537–538; "Garlanded Entrance," 495–496; "German in Norway," 425; "Germans of 1789," 641–642; "Goethe's Elective Affinities," 117, 119, 132, 148, 152, 160, 161–169, 187, 191, 193, 229, 239, 279, 343, 344, 361, 444, 511, 567, 609; "Gottfried Keller," 282; "The Handkerchief," 370; "Hashish in Marseilles," 297, 418, 481; "Ibizan Sequence," 384; "Idea of a Mystery," 294; "In the Sun," 371–372; "J. P. Hebel's *Treasure Chest of the Rhenish Family Friend*," 425; "Julien Green," 325; "Karl Kraus," 350–354, 390, 634; "Karl Wolfskehl: On His Sixtieth Birthday," 81; "Left-Wing Melancholy," 340; "Letter from Paris" on Gide, 474, 555, 626; "Letter from Paris" on painting and photography, 555; "Life and Violence," 130; "The Life of Students," 39, 43, 51, 56, 64, 65–67, 72, 128, 158, 365, 491, 686n34, 703n5; "The Light," 416; "Literary History and the Study of Literature," 344, 547–548; "Little History of Photography," 293, 325, 363–368, 390, 441, 445, 511, 644; "May–June 1934," 357; "Metaphysics of Youth," 43–44, 55, 56–59, 72, 88, 337, 685n24; "Moral Education," 53, 685n20; "Moscow," 271–272, 277, 700n30; *Moscow Diary*, 268–275, 487, 689n20; "Myslovice-Braunschweig-Marseilles," 297; "Naples," 210–212, 697n24; "Nordic Sea," 348; "Note on Brecht," 630; "Notes from Svendborg," 464; "Old Forgotten Children's Books," 218–220; "On January 6, 1922," 145–146; "On Language as Such and on the Language of Man," 57, 87–90, 158–159, 388, 689n14, 709n77; "On Some Motifs in Baudelaire," 625, 642–646, 647, 657, 685n22, 716n2; "On the Concept of History," 133, 169, 312, 416, 549, 659–662, 667; "On the Critical Liquidation of Apriorism: A Materialist Analysis," 562–563; "On the Image of Proust," 249, 326–328, 382, 390; "On the Mimetic Faculty," 87, 388, 422; "On the Present Situation of Russian Film," 275; "On the Program of the Coming Philosophy," 95–98, 102, 103, 108, 150, 693n52; "Paris Diary," 308–309, 311, 335; "The Paris of the Second Empire in Baudelaire," 567, 606, 609–619, 622–625, 628–629; "Paris, the Capital of the Nineteenth Century," 483–484, 489–495, 631–632; "Paul Scheerbart: *Lesabéndio*," 91–92; "Paul Valéry: On His Sixtieth Birthday," 363; "Peintures chinoises à la Bibliothèque Nationale," 557; "The Poet," 28; "The Political Groupings of Russian Writers," 271; "Politics," 127–129, 130; "The Present Social Situation of the French Writer," 387, 403–406, 448, 449; "Privileged Thinking," 367, 368; "Problems in the Sociology of Language," 428, 439; "Program for a Proletarian Children's Theater," 320; "Rastelli's Story," 510; "Reply to Oscar A. H. Schmitz," 275; "Response," 184–185; "The Return of the Flâneur," 330; "The Rigorous Study of Art," 386, 393–394; "The Ring of

Saturn," 309–310; "The Role of Language in *Trauerspiel* and Tragedy," 90; "Russian Toys," 278–279; "Sad Poem," 401–402; "San Gimignano," 328–329; "School Reform, a Cultural Movement," 38–39; "Short Shadows," 320, 367; "Socrates," 58, 85, 689n14; "Some Remarks on Iron Construction," 287; "Spain, 1932," 369; "Stefan George in Retrospect," 407–408; "Story of a Love in Three Stations," 416; "The Storyteller," 370, 408, 412, 530–532, 572, 643, 654, 667, 710n20; "Surrealism," 264, 295, 296, 298–299, 310–312, 326, 365, 390, 406, 491, 587, 617, 703nn66–68, 717n7; "The Task of the Critic," 342; "The Task of the Translator," 87, 130, 152, 157–160, 194, 576; "Theological-Political Fragment," 129–130; "Theories of German Fascism," 339–340; "Theory of the Novel," 468; "Thought Figures," 426; "To the Minute," 475; translation of "Anabase," 238, 698n4; translation of Baudelaire, 76–77, 137, 186–188, 193–194, 209, 573, 697n18; "*Trauerspiel* and Tragedy," 58, 90, 688n42, 689n14, 717n7; "The True Politician," 194; "Two Poems by Friedrich Hölderlin," 30, 56, 66, 70–74, 76, 85, 109, 111, 112, 337, 387n39, 387n40, 688n41, 688n42, 688n43; *Über Haschisch*, 297; "Unpacking My Library," 362–363; "Various Things of Human Interest about the Great Kant," 363, 367, 387; "The Weapons of Tomorrow," 237, 698n3; "What Is Epic Theater? A Study of Brecht," 367; "Youth Was Silent," 63. See also *The Arcades Project; Berlin Childhood around 1900; Charles Baudelaire: A Lyric Poet in the Age of High Capitalism; One-Way Street; Origin of German Trauerspiel;* "The Work of Art in the Age of Its Technological Reproducibility"

Benjamin, Walter Benedix Schoenflies, *34, 262, 278, 345, 590, 639;* character of, 5–6, 18–19, 84–85, 118, 136–137, 220, 307, 315–316, 322, 431, 648, 673–674; gambling and, 5, 6, 280–281, 389–390, 484–485; intellectual concerns of, 6–9; political convictions and sympathies of, 9–10, 127–134, 184–186, 240–241, 259–260, 273–274, 320–322, 448–449; reading habits, 9, 22, 24, 27, 52–53, 60, 77, 81–82, 93–94, 98, 114, 116, 123–124, 133, 137, 181, 183–184, 197–198, 225–226, 236, 239, 247–248, 266, 317, 348, 350, 374, 409, 449–450, 471, 506, 526–527, 558–559, 587–589, 609, 633, 637–638, 665, 699n6; posthumous publishing, 10–11, 677–679; childhood, 12–20, *15, 20;* early education, 16, 21–30, *23,* 683n13, 683n16; pseudonyms of, 38, 161, 386, 407, 420, 439, 536, 622, 710n20; solitude in community and, 41–42, 51, 67, 221; visits Paris for first time, 53–55; sexual initiation, 54–55; attempts to enlist in World War I military, 69–70; described, 77–78, 153, 367, 373, 376; marries Dora Pollak, 91–92; as book and art collector, 98, 124–125, 213, 218, 315, 316, 332, 463–464, 506, 640; birth of son, 100–101; tensions in marriage to DPB, 103–105, 141–147, 155–156, 691n43, 694n28; habilitation work in Heidelberg, 115–120, 123–124, 139–141, 147–150, 175–176; financial dependence on parents, 120–121, 126–127, 173–174, 191, 197, 216, 220, 235, 314; intellectual circles of, 122–123, 134, 152, 171–172, 180, 184–185, 205, 295–296, 306, 321–325, 654; studies Hebrew, 124–125, 126, 284–285, 307–308, 328; emigration to Palestine considered, 135, 410–411, 428, 429, 633–635; engagement with contemporary visual art, 137–139, 140, 171, 694n24; attempts to start journal *Angelus Novus,* 150–157, 160–161, 169, 173, 182–183, 442; habilitation work in Frankfort, 177–178, 183–184, 188–191; depression and, 180–181, 214, 222–223, 424, 435, 446, 462, 507–508, 624, 627, 671; German culture and reasons not to flee Germany, 195–196; in Capri, 198–216; life outside academy

Benjamin, Walter Benedix Schoenflies
(continued)
    imagined and shift to interest in
    modern culture, 205–208, 217–218;
    Soviet Union and, 205, 607; political
    shift to left, 206–208, 218; health of,
    214, 421–422, 423–424, 465, 495, 533,
    596, 635, 648–649, 656, 663, 669;
    income from publishing opportuni-
    ties pursued, 235–239; disposition of
    papers, 287, 591, 621, 630, 636,
    667–668, 675–676, 717n12; divorce of
    DPB and effects of, 252, 287, 314–317,
    333, 334, 337, 350, 357–358, 591, 630,
    636, 703n1, 703n3; reorientation
    toward popular culture, 256–257; in
    Marseilles, 264–266; in Moscow,
    267–277, 273, 274, 278, 699n28,
    700n29; on typewriter, 281–282;
    experiments with hallucinogens,
    296–299, 309, 349, 399–400, 451,
    495–496, 701n52, 701n53; growing
    reputation as man of letters, 299–313;
    cultural/literary/political writing, in
    late 1920s, 317–333; on meaning of
    theater, pedagogy, and childhood,
    320–321, 703n5; cultural/literary/
    political writing, in early 1930s,
    338–345, 355–357; attempts to start
    journal *Krisis und Kritik*, 346–348,
    354–355, 394, 609, 706n38, 706n39; on
    Ibiza, 369–375, 369–376, 391–422;
    library of, 421–422, 578–579, 619, 622,
    625–626, 711n34; in Denmark in
    1934, 451–466; Nazi power observed
    by, 460–461, 482; official expatriation
    ordered by Gestapo, 474; in Monaco,
    484–488; International Congress of
    Writers for the Defense of Culture,
    504; path to radical thought, 519–521;
    concern about Stefan's psychological
    condition, 542–545, 568; on difficul-
    ties of publishing in exile, 554;
    appearance of, 581; French literary
    politics and, 582–589; Collège de
    Sociologie and, 590–591; requests for
    French naturalization and growing
    concern over legal status, 592–593,
    621, 622, 653; revocation of German
    citizenship, 626; emigration to
    America considered, 632–633, 638,

654–655, 664; interned in France,
    647–653; transcription of dream while
    interned, 650–651; attempts to start
    journal while interned, 652; studies
    English, 654, 664; overview of
    contemporary French letters, 665–667;
    attempts to flee France at start of war,
    668–674; death of, 674–676
Benn, Gottfried, 436
Bennett, Arnold, 418; *The Old Wives'
    Tale*, 408–409; *Clayhanger*, 408
Benoist-Méchin, Jacques, 435
Berg, Alban, 527, 569
Bergmann, Hugo, 525
Bergson, Henri, 33–34, 55, 58–59, 73, 88,
    310, 327, 382, 580, 685n22
Berl, Emmanuel, 336
Berlau, Ruth, 452
Berlin Childhood around 1900
    (Benjamin), 2, 13, 18–19, 239, 299,
    320, 368–369, 380–385, 667; "Two
    Enigmas," 21; "Beggars and
    Whores," 55; suicide and, 70,
    361–362; "Loggias," 214, 403; Adorno
    and, 381, 385; "A Christmas Angel,"
    381; "The Otter," 381; structure of,
    381–382, 475, 708n67; "Excavation
    and Memory," 382; "The Mum-
    merehlen," 384, 388, 390; "Winter
    Morning," 384–385; French transla-
    tion of, with Selz, 399, 421, 447;
    "The Little Hunchback," 403, 458;
    "The Moon," 403, 422; attempts to
    publish, 437–438, 533, 598–600;
    "Sexual Awakening," 712n44
Bernanos, Georges, *Les grands ci-
    metières sous la lune (A Diary of My
    Times)*, 587
Bernfeld, Siegfried, 61, 544, 683n17
Bernoulli, C. A., 102, 248, 691n42
Bern, University of: WB's dissertation,
    98–100, 107–113; WB's doctorate
    awarded, 113–114
Bertaux, Félix, 499
Betz, Maurice, 647
Bibliothèque Nationale: WB's papers
    and, 10, 287, 636, 667–668; WB's
    research and, 283, 429, 450, 466, 489,
    501–502, 512, 525, 558, 561, 567–569,
    571, 574, 578, 654, 656, 656; Bataille
    and, 518–519, 636

Bihalji-Merin, Oto, 439
Birman, Carina, 674
Blanqui, Louis-Auguste, 574; *L'éternité par les astres* (Eternity via the Stars), 578
Blass, Ernst, 127, 137
Blaupot ten Cate, Anna Maria, 414–418, 462–463, 711n26
Blei, Franz, 412
Bloch, Ernst, 106–107, 127, 135, 156–157, 201, 206, 237, 323, 434, *459*, 498, 499–500, 555, 692n48; Simmel and, 49; *The Spirit of Utopia*, 107, 116, 128–129, 692n48; review of Lukács, 206; "Italy and Porosity," 212; WB on, 213; WB in France and, 261–262, 264; drugs and, 297; reviews of WB's work, 299, 479; copying of WB's work and, 328; WB's suicide plans in 1932 and, 379; flees Germany, 391; WB's view of success of, 458, 499; *Heritage of Our Times*, 478–480
Bloch, Linda, 500
Blossfeldt, Karl, 303–304
Bloy, Léon, 279
Blücher, Heinrich, 580, 635, 659, 664, 668, 670
Blum, Léon, 526, 571
"Body space" *(Leibraum)*, 10, 310, 312
Bohème, WB's essay on Baudelaire and, 611–612
Bourgeois sexuality, crisis of, 607
Boy, Eva, 348, 366
Brecht, Bertolt, 1, *324*, 357, 391; WB's friendship with, 153, 309, 322–323; Monnier, 201; WB meets, 221, 321, 704n8; *Threepenny Opera*, 314, 453, 474, 535, 572; influence on WB, 340, 430–431; *Krisis und Kritik* and, 346, 354, 355; WB's "Franz Kafka" and, 358, 445; "To Those Born Later," 402; Karplus's concern for influence on WB, 430–431; *Threepenny Novel*, 430, 474; WB's "Author as Producer" and, 441–442; "refunctioning" and, 441; with WB in Denmark, 451–466, 534–535, 604–607, 619–620; attitude toward Kafka, 454–455; *Round Heads and Pointed Heads*, 466; *Saint Joan of the Stockyards*, 466; WB's *The Arcades Project* and, 490; International Congress of Writers for the Defense of Culture, 504; "To Walter Benjamin, Who Killed Himself Fleeing from Hitler," 534; WB's "The Work of Art in the Age of Its Technological Reproducibility," 535–536; *Gewehre der Frau Carrar* (Señora Carrar's Rifles), 572; WB mediates between Adorno, Horkheimer and, 607–608; on Soviet Union, 607
Brecht, Marianne, 201
Bredel, Willi, 532, 536, 539, 553–555
Bremer Presse, 238, 537
Brentano, Bernard von, 346, 354, 357, 391, 432, 649; "Kapitalismus und schöne Literatur," 355; *Prozeß ohne Richter* (Trial without a Judge), 559; Soviet Union and betrayal of socialism, 635; *Theodor Chindler*, 635
Brentano, Margot von, 357
Breton, André, 236, 386, 504, 519–521
Breysig, Kurt, 49
Brill, Hans Klaus, 520–521
Brion, Marcel, 280, 285, 299, 466, 473, 481, 572, 588
Brod, Max, 444, 458, 600, 602–603, 630
Bruck, Hans, 662
Brüning, Heinrich von, 391, 482
Bryher. *See* Ellerman, Annie Winifred (Bryher)
Buber, Martin, 46, 63, 86, 88, 122–123, 155, 184, 185, 194, 272, 309, 689n15
Buchholtz, Erich, 171
Buchholz, Inge, 415, 418, 463
Bud, Ursel, 507, 545, 570, 593
Budzislawski, Hermann, 555
Bulletin de Vernuche: Journal des Travailleurs du 54e Régiment (WB's attempted journal), 652
Burchhardt, Elsa, 147
Burckhardt, Carl Jacob, 670
Burschell, Friedrich, 412
Busoni, Ferruccio, 101, 145

Caden, Gert, 171
Cahiers du Sud, 265, 280, 467, 481, 567, 584, 588, 609, 621
Caillois, Roger, 574–575, 590–591, 621; Collège de Sociologie and, 589; Aridité, 622; "Le vent d'hiver" (The

Caillois, Roger *(continued)*
Wind of Winter), 631; "Théorie de la
fête" (Theory of Festival), 666
Capitalism, WB on, 149, 291–292, 513
Capital (Marx), 149
Capra, Frank, *You Can't Take It with
You,* 640
Car, Wilhelm, 687n38
Cassirer, Ernst, 49, 304
Cassirer, Paul, 187
Cassou, Jean, 503, 504, 532
Cavelli-Adorno, Agathe, 446
Céline, Louis-Ferdinand, 553, 566;
Voyage au bout de la nuit, 404;
Bagatelles pour un massacre, 582, 583
Centre Américain de Secours, 671
Chagall, Marc, *Sabbath,* 138
Chaplin, Charlie, 277, 713n60; *The
Circus,* 322–323
Charlantanism, in *The Arcades Project,*
573
*Charles Baudelaire: A Lyric Poet in the
Age of High Capitalism* (Benjamin):
research and preparatory work,
169–170, 572–573, 574, 576–578,
604–606, 609–610; suicide and, 362;
Adorno and, 532–533, 578, 628–629;
Horkheimer and, 552–553; schematization and metaphorical formulation
of, 595–596, 605–606, 658; WB on
parallels with Kafka, 600–603;
sociophysiognomic approach,
611–615; language and allegory and,
617–619; Institute of Social Research
declines to publish, 622–625; as
monad, 625; revision of and attempt
to publish, 627–629, 635–636,
641–642, 651; flâneur and idleness,
636; "On Some Motifs in Baudelaire," 642–646, 657–658; historiography and, 660; fate of manuscript,
668; posthumous translation and
publishing of, 678
Church, Henry, 584
Citation, theory and practice of: in *The
Arcades Project,* 286–288, 290,
352–353; in "Karl Kraus," 352–353,
701n45
"Classless society," *The Arcades Project*
and Adorno's critique of, 491, 494
Claudel, Paul, 631

Cocteau, Jean, 261; *Les enfants
terribles,* 448; *Chevaliers de la table
ronde,* 572, 573–574
Coeducation, Wyneken and, 55, 75
Cohen, Hermann, 33, 102, 132, 444,
691n41; *Religion of Reason out of
the Sources of Judaism,* 102, 163
Cohn, Alfred, 22, 71, 85, 142, 143, 221,
307, 395, 434, 592; WB's suicide plans
in 1932 and, 379; in Barcelona, 434,
473, 485–486, 509; and "The Work of
Art in the Age of Its Technological
Reproducibility," 523; Spanish Civil
War and, 535
Cohn, Grete Radt, 67, 79, 85, 142, 395,
687n35
Cohn, Jula. *See* Radt-Cohn, Jula
Cohn-Bendit, Erich, 580
Collector and collecting, 218–219, 292,
363, 389–390, 705n35, 714n33
Collège de Sociologie, 574–575, 584,
589–591, 609
"Colportage phenomenon of space,"
298, 317, 701n54
Comité d'aide et d'accueil aux victimes
de l'antisémitisme en Allemagne,
422–423
Commentary, as divergent from
critique, 167–168
Commodification, 291, 339–340, 563,
615–616
Communication, problem of, 88–89,
689n20
Communism, 366; radical communism,
206; WB and, 406, 431, 448–449;
International Congress of Writers for
the Defense of Culture and, 503–505;
Gide and, 555–556. *See also* Marxism
Communitarianism, 64
Conference of the International Congress
for Unified Knowledge, 567–568
Constructivist International, 172
Contre-Attaque (journal), 519–520
Cornelius, Hans, 178, 189–190, 223,
231–232, 427, 698n37
Criticism: theory of, 8, 71–72, 118–119,
157–158, 161–165, 192–194, 230,
342–345, 692n50; Form-content
distinction, theory of, 72, 687n40;
Romantic concept of, 94; WB's
dissertation on German Romantic

criticism, 107–113; problem-historical context versus literary-historical context, 109, 692n49
Croce, Benedetto, 71, 73, 201
Cultural historiography, WB's concern with, 547, 551
Cultural Zionism, 47, 685n16
Curie, Marie, 209
Curtius, Ernst Robert, 248, 300, 326
Cysarz, Herbert, 361

Dalsace, Jean, 435–436
Danske Komité til Støtte for landsfl ygtige Aandsarbejdere (Danish Committee for the Support of Refugee Intellectual Workers), WB's appeal to, 459–460
Däubler, Theodor, 122
Décades de Pontigny, 332, 534
Demetz, Peter, 678
Denkbild (figure of thought), 3, 182, 211–212, 214, 258, 320, 380, 426
Desjardins, Paul, 332, 534, 636–637, 663
Desnos, Robert, 335
Detective novels: WB's reading of, 123, 248, 397, 409, 449, 471, 481; doctrine of humors and, 248; WB and possible writing of, 430, 561; urban phantasmagoria and, 614–615
Detective plays, Speyer and, 328, 378, 433, 437
Deutsche Vierteljahresschrift für Literaturwissenschaft und Geistesgeschichte (journal), 187
Dialectical image, 44, 90, 289, 333, 389–390, 477, 491–494, 541, 614, 619, 661, 684n12; Adorno and psychologization of, 493–494; Fuchs essay and, 547–548; used in Charles Baudelaire, 613–614
Diebold, Bernhard, 363
Dimier, Louis, 629
Dimitrov, Georgi, 504
Döblin, Alfred, 267, 430, 441, 641, 655
Dollfuß, Engelbert, 461
Doolittle, Hilda (H.D.), 524
Dreams: dream image and dialectic and, 491; WB's transcription of dream while interned, 650–651
Du Bos, Charles, 436, 475
Dubosc, Pierre, 557

Dudow, Slatan, 347, 635, 706n38
Duns Scotus, John, 118
Dupont, Pierre, 612
Dürer, Albrecht, Melancholia, 60, 295
Dwelling, as WB's "favorite topic," 358, 383, 708n69

Eddington, Arthur, The Nature of the Physical World, 600–601
Ehrenburg, Ilya, 503, 504
Ehrenreich, Elizabeth "Lili," 264
Eisler, Hanns, 466
Elias, Norbert, Über den Prozess der Zivilisation (The Civilizing Process), 588
Eliot, T. S., 534, 610–611
Ellerman, Annie Winifred (Bryher), 524
Encyclopedia française, WB's review of, 629–630
Engländer, Sigmund, 450
Etiemble, René, 540
Experience, Theory of, 7–8, 10, 49, 88, 96–97, 102, 103, 108, 133–134, 280–281, 289–290, 298–299, 311–312, 382–383, 388–389, 399–400, 412–414, 492, 513–514, 530–531, 600–602, 642–646, 657 658, 693n52
Expressionism, 28–29, 45, 46, 52, 56–57, 61, 68, 105–106, 122, 134
"Expressionism debate," 607

Falke, Konrad, 555
Fargue, Léon-Paul, 335–336, 621
Favez, Juliane, 649
Febvre, Lucien, Un destin: Martin Luther, 409
Fessard, Gaston, 584
Feuchtwanger, Lion, 430, 532, 654, 672
Feuilleton pages, in newspapers, 202, 235–236, 257–259
Fichte, Johann Gottlieb, 65, 108, 109–110; Addresses to the German Nation, 65
Fiesel, Eva, 685n23; Die Sprachphilosophie der deutschen Romantik (The Philosophy of Language in German Romanticism), 304–305, 702nn64–65
Film: WB's thoughts about, developed in Moscow, 274–277, 311–312, 700n29; treated in "The Work of Art," 513–518; WB on Capra, 640

First Student Pedagogic Conference, 62
Fischer, S. (publishing house), 124, 438
Fittko, Lisa, 672–674, 717n16, 717n19, 718n22
Flâneur: F. Hessel as, 256; Hessel's *Spazieren in Berlin*, 285–286; *The Arcades Project* and, 288, 292, 296, 297, 298, 329; WB's literary criticism and philosophy of, 329–330; *Charles Baudelaire* and idleness, 636
Flattau, Dov, 198–199
Flaubert, Gustave, 93, 374, 529, 671–672; *Sentimental Education*, 293–294
Forster, E. M., 503, 504
Forster, Georg, 594
Forte circle, 122–123, 184
Fourier, Charles, 9, 292, 321, 450, 491, 572–573, 632
Francesco, Grete de, 573
Franco, Francisco, 400
Fränkel, Fritz, 296, 391–392, 451, 505, 580, 635, 671; Wissing's drug use and, 495–496
Frankfurt Circle, 184–185
Frankfurter Zeitung, 235–236, 377–378; WB published in, 81, 212–213, 236, 237, 278–279, 302, 304, 328, 350–351, 362, 367–370, 381, 386–387, 407, 408, 422, 426, 439, 458, 475, 502, 536–537, 599; Kracauer and, 189, 256, 264, 410, 433; WB reviewed in, 194, 209, 279, 299; Helen Hessel and, 254–255; Roth and, 261; Wolfskehl and, 295; Cohn and, 307; Lehning and, 307; Brecht and, 346; Sternberger and, 511
Frankfurt School, 333, 427
Frankfurt University, 177–178; WB's attempts to earn habilitation at, 183–184, 188–191, 222–223
Free German Youth, 36, 62–65
Free School Community, at Wickersdorf, 24, 27, 29, 36, 62–63
Freie deutsche Forschung (journal), 597
Freies Jüdisches Lehrhaus (Free Jewish House of Learning), 178, 188
Freund, Gisèle, 260, 573, 638, 653, 668
Friedrich Wilhelm University, in Berlin, 48–51, 61–67, 77–78
Fromm, Erich, 427
Fry, Vivian, 671

Fuchs, Eduard, 406, 428, 510, 546–547, 549–550, 561
Fuld, Werner, 194, 698n33

G (journal), 151, 172, 293
Galerie des Beaux-Arts exhibition, 579
Gallimard publishers, 248–249, 525, 540
Gauguin, Paul, 398
Geheeb, Paul, 24
Geiger, Moritz, 79
Genesis, book of, 89–90
George, Stefan, 3, 71, 80, 102–103, 147–148, 194, 309; *Denkbild* and, 182; WB's review of, 407–408; translation of Baudelaire, 611; WB's last statement on literature and, 666–667; opposition to National Socialism, 710n19
German Communist Party, 120, 271, 354, 465, 495, 534; Georg Benjamin and, 240, 246, 295, 400; WB and, 260, 273–274, 582
German Romanticism, WB and, 93–96, 98–100, 107–113
G Group, 171–172, 205, 263, 324
Giacometti, Augusto, 410
Gide, André, 299–300, 521, 577, 702n59, 702n60; *Strait Is the Gate*, 114; WB on, 404, 405–406, 474; *Lafcadio's Adventures (Les caves du Vatican)*, 405–406; International Congress of Writers for the Defense of Culture and, 503; *Return to the USSR*, 555
Giedion, Sigfried, 347; *Bauen in Frankreich* (Architecture in France), 317
Gilbert, Stuart, 521–522
Giraudoux, Jean, 622
Glück, Franz, 533
Glück, Gustav, 307, 350, 351, 379, 662, 706n43
Goethe, Johann Wolfgang von, 102–103, 547; "ideal of content" and, 112–113; "The New Melusine," 137, 665; *Italian Journey*, 199; WB and Marxist perspective on, 249–250; WB's *Great Soviet Encyclopedia* essay on, 249–250, 304; maxim of, 272; centennial of, 369; *Maxims and Reflections*, 435
Goldberg, Oskar, 133, 134, 156, 294, 324, 469

Goldschmidt-Rothschild, Baroness, 423
Goldstein, Moritz, 46–47
Gonzague de Reynold, Frédéric, 98
Grab, Hermann, 360–361
Graeff, Werner, 171, 172
Gramsci, Antonio, 106
Great Soviet Encyclopedia, WB's essay
  on Goethe for, 249–250, 304
Green, Julien, 303, 325, 334, 335, 342,
  374, 404–405, 471
Groethuysen, Bernhard, 540
Grossman, Maria, 357
Großman, Rudolf, 279
Großman, Stefan, 302
Grosz, George, 464
Grünberg, Carl, 426
Gryphius, Andreas, 183, 224
Guéhenno, Jean, 504; Journal d'un
  "révolution" (Diary of a "Revolu-
  tion"), 665
Gumpert, Martin, 156; Hölle im
  Paradies: Selbstdarstellung eines
  Arztes, 50, 688n43
Gundolf, Friedrich, 147–148, 201, 347, 497
Gurland, Henny, 672–676
Gurland, Joseph, 672–674
Gutkind, Erich, 81, 121–123, 124, 152,
  173, 174, 178, 183, 196, 198–199,
  323–324; Siderische Geburt:
  Seraphische Wanderung vom Tode
  der Welt zur Taufe der Tat, 122
Gutkind, Lucie, 81, 178, 183, 198–199
Guttmann, Simon, 61, 431
Guys, Constantin, 545

Haas, Willy, 236–237, 299, 323, 368, 387,
  425, 437, 537
Häberlin, Paul, 98
Haecker, Theodor, 367
Hallmann, Johann Christian, 224
Halm, August, 67
Hamann, J. G., 87
Hamburger, Augustus, 663
Hansen, Miriam Bratu, 8, 312, 512
Harnack, Adolf von, 198
Hasenclever, Walter, 46
Hauptmann, Elisabeth, 357, 379, 430, 432
Hauptmann, Gerhart, 27, 62, 205
Hausmann, Raoul, 171, 172, 399
Haussmann, Baron, 429, 492–493
Heartfield, John, 500–501

Hebrew University, 284, 338, 449, 460
Hegner Verlag, 302–303
Heidegger, Martin, 32, 33–34, 57, 346,
  580, 683n1, 692n49; "The Problem of
  Historical Time," 91; The Doctrine
  of Categories and of Meaning in
  Duns Scotus, 118; Sein and Zeit,
  346, 692n49
Heidelberg University, 115–120,
  123–124, 139–141, 147–150, 175–176
Heidenrich, Karl, 580
Heine, Heinrich, 527
Heinle, Christoph Friedrich (Fritz), 54,
  215, 621; WB's friendship with, 53,
  59–61, 431, 686n28; Anfang and, 61;
  suicide of, 70–71, 74, 361, 687n38,
  707n49; WB's introduction to
  collected poems of, 160, 169
Heinle, Wolf, 60, 105, 157, 175, 181, 621
Heissenbüttel, Helmut, 677–678
Hellingrath, Norbert von, 71, 687n39
Hennings, Emmy, 105–106
Hepburn, Katharine, 605
Herbertz, Richard, 99, 100, 115, 117
Hergesheimer, Joseph, 335, 360
Herzberger, Alfons, 460
Herzberger, Else (Elfriede), 446, 460, 571,
  574, 632
Herzfelde, Wieland, 68, 464, 500, 532
Herzl, Theodor, 693n57
Hesse, Hermann, 299, 437–438
Hesse-Burri, Emil, 357
Hessel, Alfred, 254
Hessel, Franz, 251–253, 253, 255–256, 283,
  323, 332, 337, 622, 626, 640; back-
  ground, 201–202, 253–257; translation
  of Proust with WB, 248–249, 251, 254,
  279, 309, 349; marriage of, 252, 254; as
  flâneur, 255–256; On Foot in Berlin,
  WB's review of, 285–286, 330;
  Heimliches Berlin (Unknown Berlin),
  293; reviews of WB's work, 299; WB's
  suicide plans in 1932 and, 378, 707n63
Hessel, Helen Grund, 255, 283, 323, 647;
  marriage of, 252, 254; WB and,
  254–255, 498, 640–641; Vom Wesen
  der Mode (On the Nature of Fashion),
  498; WB's internment and, 653
Hessel, Johanna, 254
Hessel, Stéphane, 254
Hey, Heidi, 599–600

Heym, Georg, 29, 54, 340
Hilberseimer, Ludwig, 171
Hiller, Kurt, 29, 77, 128
Hindenburg, Paul von, 391
Hirschfeld, Gustav, 20
History, theory of, 43, 129–130, 225–229, 288–292, 325, 344–345, 477–478, 491–492, 547–549, 603–604, 613–614, 617–618, 659–662, 703n68
Hobrecker, Karl, 218
Höch, Hannah, 171
Hoffer, Wilhelm, 545
Hoffmanswaldau, Christoph Hoffmann von, 224
Hofmannsthal, Hugo von, 45, 187–188, 196–197, 237, 238, 295–296, 300–301, 686n28; *Buch der Freunde* (Book of Friends), 181; *The Tower*, 250, 301; death of, 329; WB's last statement on literature and, 666–667
Hölderlin, Friedrich, 27, 57, 76, 159, 159–160, 621
Hönigswald, Richard, 629
Hoppenot, Henri, 653, 667
Horkheimer, Maidon, 570
Horkheimer, Max, 387; *Dialectic of Enlightenment*, 165, 604, 677; Königstein conversations and, 333; WB's Fuchs essay and, 388, 549–550; background, 426–427; Institute of Social Research and, 426, 427, 446, 454, 466–467; habilitation thesis of, 427; WB's "The Work of Art in the Age of Its Technological Reproducibility" and, 518; WB and Klossowski's translation, 521; WB's essay on Baudelaire, 532, 552–553; WB's essay on Jochmann and, 559–561; WB mediates between Brecht and, 607–608; attempts to help WB flee France, 670–671; WB's thesis and, 698n37
Huelsenbeck, Richard, 106
Humboldt, Wilhelm von, 73, 177, 238–239, 284, 537
Husserl, Edmund, 32, 33, 79; *Ideas: On a Pure Phenomenology*, 79
Huxley, Aldous, 504

Ibsen, Henrik, 27, 529
Ideal, Baudelaire and, 170

"Ideal of content," of Goethe, 112–113
Ideas, theory of, 230–231
Ihering, Herbert, 346
"Image space" *(Bildraum)*, 10, 310, 312
Independent Students' Association, 36, 45, 51, 52, 61, 63–64, 67
Innervation, 310–312
Insel Verlag, 238, 361
Institute for the Study of Fascism, 439
Institute of Social Research, 147, 387–388, 426–427, 575, 678; WB's stipend from, 446, 454, 470, 483, 484, 487, 506, 524, 571–572, 583, 631–632, 647, 649, 663; WB's library and, 449, 622; move to America, 466–467; WB and French literary politics, 582–589; declines to publish *Charles Baudelaire*, 622–625; WB's possible move to New York and, 633; attempts to help WB flee France, 670–671
International Congress of Philosophy, 567–568
International Congress of Writers for the Defense of Culture, 503–505
Internationale Revue i10, 237–238, 278, 307, 324–325
Intertwined time *(verschränkte Zeit)*, 291, 327, 327–328, 383

James, Henry, *The Turn of the Screw*, 638
Janko, Marcel, 106
Jaspers, Karl, 148, 574
Jazz music, WB and Adorno and, 528
Jentzsch, Robert, 29, 68
"Jewish fascism," 455, 715n50
Jewish identity and Zionism, 45–48, 134; Scholem and, 83–86; WB and, 83–86, 337–338; DPB's family and, 115–116, 693n57; WB's study of Hebrew, 124–125, 126, 284–285, 307–308, 328; converts and, 179–180; growing anti-Semitism, 195; *Berlin Childhood* and Scholem, 438–439; Ahad Ha'am and, 685n16
Joachim, Hans Arno, 532
Jochmann, Carl Gustav, 136, 664; *Über die Sprache* (On Language), 559–561
Joël, Ernst, 51, 76, 175, 296, 496
Johnson, Uwe, 677
Jokisch (stranger on Ibiza), 373

Joseephi, Friederike (aunt), suicide of, 29, 683n15
Joubert, Joseph, *Pensées*, 637, 716n22
Jouhandeau, Marcel, 279, 336, 348
Journalism, WB on impact on criticism, 342, 352, 705n31
Jouve, Pierre Jean, 522
Die Jugend (journal), 407
Jugendstil, 73, 289, 291, 317, 342, 407–408, 479, 529
Jules and Jim (film), 252, 254
Jung, Carl Gustav, 81, 541, 552, 553, 566
Jünger, Ernst, 339

Kafka, Franz, 236, 240, 294; "The Penal Colony," 91; *The Trial*, 294, 443, 455, 470; WB's ideas about, 358–359, 707n47; WB's "Franz Kafka: *Beim Bau der Chinesischen Mauer*," 439, 442–446, 454–457, 474–475; *The Castle*, 443, 444; "The Judgment," 443; "The Cares of a Family Man," 444, 601; "interpretive monopoly" and, 458; WB on parallels with Baudelaire, 600–603; "A Common Confusion," 601; "The Trees," 601; *Amerika* [*Der Verschollene*], 630
Kaiser Friedrich School, 16, 21–22, 27–29, 683n13
Kállai, Ernø, 172
Kaminski, Hanns-Erich, 667
Kampfbund für deutsche Kultur, 347
Kandinsky, Wassily, 80, 122, 123; *Concerning the Spiritual in Art*, 123
Kant, Immanuel, 7, 33, 41, 60, 79, 85, 87, 88, 94, 102, 134, 231, 367, 562; *Foundations of the Metaphysics of Morals*, 53; *The Critique of Judgment*, 55; knowledge and, 96–98, 691n34; experience and, 108–109, 693n52; *The Critique of Pure Reason*, 701n43
Kantorowicz, Ernst, 497–498; *The King's Two Bodies*, 497
Kapp, Wolfgang, 130
Karavan, Dani, 676
Karplus, Liselotte, 598
Karplus, Margarete "Gretel," 302, 307, 434, 481–482, 576; WB's relationship with, 301, 348, 414–415, 418, 496–497, 541; Königstein conversa-

tions and, 333; WB's suicide plans in 1932 and, 379; WB's work and, 381, 430–431, 597, 664; WB in Ibiza and, 395, 397, 399–400, 402, 422; WB's finances and, 424–425, 460, 486–487; Wissing and WB's archives, 447; Adorno and, 472–473, 570–571, 633; in New York, 586–587
Kästner, Erich, 340–341
Kelbort, Chanan, 580
Keller, Gottfried, 282
Keller, Philipp, 45, 46, 52
Kellner, Leon, 100, 173, 693n57
Kellner, Viktor, 395, 693n57
Kemény, Alfréd, 172
Kessler, Harry Graf, 464
Kesten, Hermann, 430, 648, 653, 655, 669
Key, Ellen, 24
Kierkegaard, Søren, 53, 359, 386; *Either / Or*, 53
Kirchner, Ernst Ludwig, 54
Kisch, Egon Erwin, 267, 662
Kitsch, 310, 317
Kläber, Kurt, 432
Klages, Ludwig, 62, 63, 80, 81, 169, 253; *The Mind as Adversary of the Soul*, 348; *On Cosmogenic Eros*, 552
Klee, Paul, 579; "Die Vorführung des Wunders," 124, *125*; *Angelus Novus*, 138–139, *140*, 349, 416, 579, 638, 661, 694n24
Klemperer, Otto, 325
Klopstock, Friedrich, 641
Klossowski, Pierre, 260, 518–519, 520, 584, 662
Kluckhohn, Paul, 187
Knoche, Herr (tutor), 21
Koestler, Arthur, 439, 667, 675; *Spanish Testament*, 587–588
Kohlenbach, Margarete, 133
Kojève, Alexandre, 574–575
Kolisch, Rudolf, 565, 635
Kolmar, Gertrud, 20
Kolzow, Michail, 432
Kommerell, Max, 439; *The Poet as Leader in German Classicism*, 329, 339
Korff, Hermann August, 190–191; *Spirit of the Age of Goethe*, 190
Korsch, Karl, 106, 323, 464–465; *Marxism and Philosophy*, 465; *Karl Marx*, 640

Kracauer, Siegfried, 1, 185–186, 190, 205–206, 209, 210, 242, 275, 304, 323, 430, 433, 572, 580, 667; *Ginster*, 177; WB meets, 181, 189; "*Travel and Dance*," 256–257; on *Thomas Münzer as the Theologian of Revolution*, 264; WB in France and, 264, 265–266; "Two Planes," 266; "Photography," 293; reviews of WB's work, 299; *White-Collar Workers*, 340–341; flees Germany, 391; *Georg*, 499; *Orpheus in Paris: Offenbach and the Paris of His Time*, 563–564, 576

Kraft, Werner, 105, 123, 124, 136, 169, 442, 458, 474, 475, 524, 634, 664, 686n28, 688n8; WB breaks with, 135–136, 560–561

Kraus, Karl, 103, 137, 180, 303, 306, 342, 461, 524; WB's "Karl Kraus," 350–354, 390, 634; *Die letzten Tage der Menschheit* (The Last Days of Mankind), 634

Krauß, Käthe, 625

Die Kreatur (journal), 272

Krenek, Ernst, 564, 592

Krisis und Kritik (journal), 346, 354–355, 394, 609; WB's plans for, 347–348, 354–355, 706n38, 706n39

Krull, Germaine, 363, 572, 582, 592, 635

Kubin, Alfred, 80

Kurella, Alfred, 62, 175, 354, 394, 403, 429, 609

Lacis, Asja, 4, 203, 216, 220–221, 240, 487, 522; meets WB in Capri, 203–204; WB introduced to Soviet culture, 204–206; "Naples" and, 210–212, 697n24; introduces WB to Brecht, 221, 321, 704n38; WB visits in Latvia, 242–243; WB visits in sanatorium, 267–269, 273; breakdowns of, 267, 332; WB's divorce and, 314–317; WB's leftist politics and, 320–322; internment of, 321; Königstein conversations and, 333; WB's love for, 357, 418; WB's suicide plans in 1932 and, 379; in Moscow, 508

Lackner, Stephan (Ernest Gustave Morgenroth), 557, 579, 581, 638; *Jan Heimatlos*, 583

Landauer, Gustav, 122

Landerziehungsheim Haubinda, 22–24, 27

Landry, Harald, 532

Landsberg, Paul, 654

Lange, Hilde. *See* Benjamin, Hilde Lange (sister-in-law)

Langen, Albert, 438

Language: masculine and feminine modes of, 57–58; language of silence and language of words, 57; WB's theory of, 85–91, 219–220, 581–582, 689n20, 690n21, 690n23; *Sprachgeist*, WB's theory of language and, 87–90; WB's use of Stefan's childhood sayings, 100–101, 135, 145–146, 218, 243–245; *Origin of the German Trauerspiel* and, 231; similarity and mimesis and, 388–390; "physiognomics" of, 428; polytechnic education and training and, 440–442; Jochmann on politics and, 559–561; "Onomatopoetic theory of the word," 709n76

Lasker-Schüler, Else, 68, 464

Laurencin, Marie, 252

League for Free School Communities, 51

Lechter, Melchior, 80, 201

Lederer, Emil, 133, 175

Lefranc, Emilie, 637

Lehmann, Siegfried, 53

Lehmann, Walter, 80

Lehning, Arthur, 237, 307, 324–325

Leichter, Otto, 595

Leiris, Michel, 575, 589, 631; *L'age de l'homme*, 591, 665

Lenya, Lotte, 357, 430

Leonhard, Rudolf, 709n76

Leskov, Nikolai, 529–532

Lévi, Israel, 422

Levy, Erwin, 127

Lévy, Sylvain, 446

Levy-Ginsberg, Arnold

Levy-Ginsberg, Milly, 507, 649

Lewy, Ernst, 73, 123, 154

Leyda, Jay, 554, 714n35

Leyris, Pierre, 633

Lichtenberg, Georg Christoph, 212, 366, 388, 709n74

Lichtenstein, Alfred, 340

Lieb, Fritz, 529, 530, 572, 582

Liebert, Arthur, 568

Lietz, Hermann, 24

Lindner, Burkhardt, 223, 232, 698n33, 698n37
Linfert, Carl, 393–394, 403
Lion, Ferdinand, 555, 573, 593, 599
Lissitzky, El, 171, 172, 205
Lister, Enrique, 672
Die literarische Welt: WB published in, 52, 236–237, 252, 271, 275, 277, 279, 282, 293, 295, 300, 302, 308–310, 326, 328–330, 335, 341, 344, 362–363, 367–368; DPB published in, 100, 301; WB reviewed in, 299; Cohn published in, 307
Litthauer Verlag, 220, 235
"Little form," in newspapers. *See* Feuilleton pages, in newspapers
Lohenstein, Daniel Casper von, 183, 224
Loos, Adolf, 350
Lotze, Hermann, 627–628
Löwenthal, Leo, 147, 427, 528–529, 550
Ludwig, Emil, 654
Ludwig Maximilian University, Munich, 78–91
Lukács, Georg, 10, 49, 106, 127, 607, 608; *History and Class Consciousness,* 157, 206–207; *Theory of the Novel,* 206–207; *Soul and Form,* 206
Luserke, Martin, 62
Lutetia Circle, 654
Lüttwitz, Walther von, 130
Luxemburg, Rosa, 127
Lyck, Hugo, 156, 695n49

Macke, August, 138
Macpherson, Kenneth, 524
Magnes, Judah L., 284–285, 307–308, 338
Mahler-Werfel, Alma, 672
La Maison des Amis des Livres (bookshop), 336, 499
Malik Verlag, 464
Malraux, André, 449, 503, 521, 522; *Man's Fate (La condition humaine),* 406; *L'espoir (Man's Hope),* 587
Mann, Golo, 672
Mann, Heinrich, 79, 429, 436, 441, 654, 672
Mann, Klaus, 430, 437, 458, 474, 654
Mann, Thomas, 80, 381, 555; *Doctor Faustus,* 134; *The Magic Mountain,* 239–240, 348

Mannheim, Karl, 176, 561–562
Marc, Franz, 80
Marcuse, Herbert, 427; "Philosophie und kritische Theorie," 588–589
Marcuse, Ludwig, 49
Marinetti, Filippo Tommaso, 213, 339–340
Marx, Karl, 9–10, 90, 106–107, 149, 272, 289–291, 337, 353, 465, 524, 562, 640, 701n44, 717n6; *Capital,* 502
Marxism: Bloch and, 106; WB and, 127, 168, 182, 204–205, 320–322, 323; literary theory and, 225; Institute of Social Research and, 426; Brecht and, 431; Korsch and, 465; Rubel and, 524; theory of art and, 550–551. *See also* Communism; Materialism
Marx-Steinschneider, Kitty, 393, 409, 410, 423, 424, 509, 523
Maß und Wert (journal), 555, 573, 593, 599
Materialism: theory of reading and, 386; historical materialism in WB's late work, 659–662
Mayer, Dr. Max, 285
Mayer, Hans, 589
Maync, Harry, 98
Meinecke, Friedrich, 33
Meins, Hans, 439
Melville, Herman, *Pierre, or the Ambiguities,* 633
Memory, 327–328, 382–383, 444, 643–644, 660–661; Palimpset nature of, 288, 382–383, 492, 708n68
Mendelsohn, Anja, 544
Merkur (journal), 677
Meryon, Charles, 525, 619
Messianism and Messianic realm, 9, 82, 102, 108, 129–130, 168, 659–662, 689n11, 703n68
Mesures (journal), 583–584
Meyerhold, Vsevolod, 269, 274
Michel, Ernst, 185
Michelet, Jules, 290
Mies van der Rohe, Ludwig, 171, 172
Milch, Werner, 299, 702n56
Mimesis and mimetic mode of perception, 18, 101, 103, 312, 374, 384, 388–390, 428, 709n76
Missac, Pierre, 4, 621, 641, 667–668, 717n12

Moholy-Nagy, László, 1, 171–172, 205, 238, 363, 696n58; "Production-Reproduction," 171; Lehning's journal and, 324–325

"Monad," 73, 291, 660–661; *Charles Baudelaire* as, 625

Monadology, 291, 382, 705–706n35

Monnier, Adrienne, 279, 336, 474, 499, 500, 522, 572, 582, 631, 653; *Fableaux*, 375; *Gazette des Amis des Livres*, 665–666

Montage: mechanisms of, 276; dialectical method and, 287–293, 701nn43–46; used in *One-Way Street*, 288; WB on Bloch's use of, 479; used in *Charles Baudelaire*, 613–614

Morgenroth, Sigmund, 632, 633

Morgenstern, Soma, 671–672

Morser, Harry, 655

Müller, Adam, 130, 694n15

Müller, Anton, 60

Mulnier, Thierry, *Mythes socialistes*, 539

Münchhausen, Thankmar von, 238, 252–253, 261, 394, 395

Münter, Gabriele, 80, 122

Münzenberg, Willi, 635, 654

Münzer, Thomas, 156

Muschler, Carola, 663

Musil, Robert, 503, 504; *The Man Without Qualities*, 393, 709n5

Myth: treated in WB's work, 73–74, 152, 162–167, 443–444, 492–494, 601–602, 689n14, 696n50; mythic violence, 132–133; criticism and differentiation of truth from, 166–167

Natorp, Paul, 62

Naturalist movement, WB on Löwenthal and, 528–529

Neher, Carola, 357, 453

Neher, Caspar, 201

Neo-Kantianism, 33, 49, 96, 102

Neopathetisches Cabaret, 28, 134

Neoromanticism, 532

Nettlau, Max, 131

Neue Club, 28–29, 134

Neue Deutsche Beiträge (journal), 197

Neue Sachlichkeit, 267, 313, 705n27

Die Neue Weltbühne (journal), 555

Niebuhr, Reinhold, 525

Nietzsche, Friedrich, 8, 43, 65, 102, 143, 212, 289, 695n31; "On the Advantage and Disadvantage of History for Life," 25–26, 548; *politeia* and, 41–42; WB's criticism of "intellectualized philistinism" of, 47–48; *On the Future of Our Educational Institutions*, 65; creative intoxication and, 297, 701n52;

Nihilism, 9, 130, 132, 207, 227, 311, 326, 340, 404, 444; revolutionary messianism and, 168; clinical nihilism, 553, 566, 583

Nizan, Paul, *La Conspiration* (The Conspiracy), 630

Noeggerath, Felix, 80–81, 369–375, 394, 419, 420

Noeggerath, Hans Jakob (Jean Jacques), 371, 374, 472, 711n26

Noeggerath, Marietta, 371

Nouvelle Revue Française, 436, 466, 473, 583–584, 591, 631

Novalis, 43, 108, 109, 110, 111

"Now of recognizability," 44, 225, 289, 327, 511

Ocampo, Victoria, 665–666

One-Way Street (Benjamin), 2, 172, 181–182, 205, 239, 606, 679; suicide and, 70, 361; dread of nature and, 163–164, 696n53; "Gloves," 163–164; "Chinese Curios," 204; "Imperial Panorama," 208; "Flag," 215–216; "Half-Mast," 215–216; Rang and, 215–216; "To the Planetarium," 227; "Not for Sale," 241–242; mechanical cabinet described in, 241; "Ordnance," 242; "Stereoscope," 243; feuilleton form and, 257–259; as "user's guide" to WB's new critical methods, 257–259; "Filling Station," 259; montage cover of, 263; "Manorially Furnished Ten-Room Apartment," 270; publication and reviews of, 279, 294, 299, 702n56, 702n57; montage and, 288, 293; composition and tonality of, 333; contemporary culture and politics and, 338; language and, 440; Bloch's review of, 479

Opie, Redvers, 570

Oprecht, Emil, 573

Origin of German Trauerspiel (Benjamin), 117, 119, 168, 239, 698n34; work on, 183–184, 191–192, 197–198, 201, 207, 209, 213–214; format determined, 217, 222; as fulcrum of WB's career, 224–231; rejected as habilitation thesis, 231–234, 698n37; preface to, 233; publication and reviews of, 239, 266–267, 279, 294, 299, 606, 702n56, 702n57; inscribed to Hofmannsthal, 300; Adorno and, 359–360; academic use of, 385; connection with *The Arcades Project*, 386; posthumous publication of, 678

Ossietzky, Carl von, 542, 555
Osten, Maria (Maria Greßhöhner), 532
Overbeck, Franz, 98, 102, 691n42

Palmier, Jean-Michel, 392, 425
Panofksy, Erwin, 295–296
Papen, Franz von, 377, 460
Paquet, Alfons, 185
Parem, Olga, 375–376, 378, 395, 707n59
Pariser Passagen (Paris Arcades) manuscript page, *318*
Patmos circle, 180, 184
Paul, Eliot, 373
Paulhan, Jean, 261, 436, 473, 584
Péguy, Charles, 114, 124, 283, 404
PEN, 653, 655
Penzoldt, Ernst, 258
Perse, Saint-John (Alexis Leger), 238
Persitz, Shoshana, 428
Pfemfert, Franz, 61, 63
Phantasmagoria, 296, 341, "second nature" and, 10; *Origin of the German Trauerspiel* and, 225–226; flâneur and, 492; as eighteenth-century illusionistic device, 516; used in *Charles Baudelaire*, 614–615, 628–629, 632
"The Philosophical Group," 324
Photography, WB on, 293, 363–368
Picabia, Francis and Gabrielle, 260
Piper Verlag, 249, 309, 349
Plato, 25, 29, 40–42, 85, 96, 231, 327, 689n14
Plekhanov, Georgy, 354
Polgar, Alfred, 325, 626–627

Pollak, Dora Sophie Kellner. *See* Benjamin, Dora Sophie Kellner Pollak (wife)
Pollak, Max, 67, 84, 85
Pollock, Friedrich, 426, 449, 489, 522, 524, 565, 571–572, 606
Positivism, 33, 623
Prampolini, Enrico, 213
Primal history, theme of *(Urgeschichte)*, 288, 325, 477, 478, 491, 600–601, 654, 701n41
Prostitution, Belmore and cultural significance of, 55–56
Proust, Marcel: WB's translation of, 238, 248–249, 251, 254, 265, 266, 279, 309, 349; WB and philosophical way of seeing, 326–328; WB and "Monsieur Albert" in, 336; WB on, 404–405
Pufahl, Helene, 21
Pulver, Max, 81
Puni, Ivan, 171

Queneau, Raymond, *Enfants du limon* (Children of Clay), 630–631
Quint, Léon-Pierre, 335, 424, 466

Rabinbach, Anson, 503
Radio: WB's complaints about politization and commercialization of, 330–331; "listening models" of WB, 594–595. *See also* Benjamin, Walter, radio broadcasts of
Radt, Fritz, 142, 221, 242, 263, 266, 309, 348, 472, 535
Radt, Grete. *See* Cohn, Grete Radt
Radt-Cohn, Jula, 79, 137, *144*, 148, 266, 309, 348, 458, 472; WB and, 67, 141–143, 145, 147, 148, 153, 242–243, 269, 315, 357, 418, 687n35; in Paris, 251, 252, 253, 262–263; WB's suicide plans in 1932 and, 378; Spanish Civil War and, 535
Raiffeisen Society, 155
Ramuz, Charles-Ferdinand, *Paris: Notes d'un Vaudois*, 665
Rang, Emma, 198, 208, 215
Rang, Florens Christian, 127, 154–155, *154*, 175, 196, 198–199, 208; Forte Circle and, 122–123, 152; German politics and, 180; Frankfurt Circle and, 184–185; WB's work and,

Rang, Florens Christian (*continued*)
184–185, 188, 192–193, 196–198; death
of, 214–216; "theological thinking"
of, 471–472
Rathenau, Walter, 123
Razovsky, Cecilia, 654
Redemption, 9, 42, 108, 160, 168, 170,
290–291, 446, 603–604, 659–661
Reflection, WB on criticism and,
109–112, 692n51
Regler, Gustav, 147–148, 534
Rehbein, Grete, 243, 244
Reich, Berhard, 201, 203, 216, 220, 249,
268–269, 273, 278, 314, 321, 522
Reich, Daga, 203–204, 210, 220
Reiss, Erich, 438
Renéville, Rolland de, 621, 622
Renger-Patzsch, Albert, 441
Reproducibility of art, treated in "The
Work of Art," 513–515
Reventlow, Fanny zu, 80, 253,
254
Richter, Hans, 134, 171, 172
Richter-Gabo, Elisabeth, 134, 171
Rickert, Heinrich, 33, 40, 55, 106, 148,
685n22
Riegl, Alois, 226, 267, 386
Rilke, Rainer Maria, 79–80, 123, 143,
238, 394, 518
Roché, Henri-Pierre, 254, 255
Roedl, Urban (Bruno Adler), *Adalbert
Stifter*, 626
Roessler, Rudolf, 536, 593–594
Röhm, Ernst, 460
Rolland, Romain, 123
Romantic anticapitalism, 127–128, 149,
206
Rosenberg, Alfred, 347
Rosenstock-Huessy, Eugen, 179–180
Rosenzweig, Franz, 178–180, 336–337,
581; *The Star of Redemption*, 179
Rothacker, Erich, 187
Roth, Joseph, 261, 430, 638
Rothschild, Baron Edmond de, 422
Rowohlt, Ernst, 346, 606, 626
Rowohlt Verlag, 202, 236, 239, 254, 266,
279, 293, 294, 299, 302–303, 307;
collapse and bankruptcy of, 342, 355,
363
Rubel, Maximilien, 523–524
Rychner, Max, 326, 355–356, 367, 403, 670

Sachs, Franz, 45, 67–68
Sahl, Hans, 523, 647–648, 652
Salles, Georges, *Le regard* (The Gaze),
665
Salomon-Delatour, Gottfried, 178, 189,
202, 222, 224, 232–233, 263
Sander, August, 363, 365
Saxl, Fritz, 295–296
Scheerbart, Paul, 91–92, 205, 413–414,
582, 699n28; *Lesabèndio*, 128,
709n74
Schey, Philipp, 707n59
Schickele, René, 133
Schiller-Lerg, Sabine, 143–144
Schlegel, August Wilhelm, 588
Schlegel, Friedrich, 95, 108, 119, 588;
allegory and, 18; reflection and,
110–111; criticism and, 112; *Alarcos*,
137
Schleicher, Kurt von, 391
Schleiermacher, Friedrich, 177
Schmidt, Johannes, 597
Die Schmiede, 248–249
Schmitt, Carl, 184; *Political Theology*,
198, 350; *Hamlet or Hecuba*, 350,
706n42
Schocken, Salomon, 600, 602–603, 626,
634
Schocken Verlag, 437, 458, 474–475, 626
Schoen, Ernst, 22, 63–64, 70–71, 99, 107,
114, 119, 123, 144, 220, 221, 244, 263,
325, 433, 472, 655; DPB's affair with,
143–147, 315; G group and, 172; WB
and radio and, 220, 330–332; WB's
suicide plans in 1932 and, 379; arrest
and eventual escape from Nazis, 391
Schoenflies, Arthur Moritz (great-
uncle), 20, 178, 308
Scholem, Erich, 306
Scholem, Escha, 525
Scholem, Gershom, 45, 68, 78, 94–95,
101, 121, 188, 280, 283–284, 581,
691n38; on Kaiser Friedrich School,
22; WB and DPB's marriage and, 68,
103–105, 188, 691n43; WB meets,
77–78; on WB, 79–80, 82–83;
disappointment with WB's character,
83–84; theory of language and, 86–87;
on Gutkind, 122; WB's study of
Hebrew and, 124–145, 126; "Greeting
from the Angelus" poem, 138–139; on

Rang, 175; emigration to Palestine, 182, 195; Frankfurt Circle and, 188; *Amtliches Lehrgedicht der Philosophischen Fakultät der Haupt-und Staats-Universität Muri* (Official Didactic Poem of the Philosophical Faculty of the University of Muri), 306; on WB and Marxism, 320; WB's Judaism and, 338; WB's letter to Rychner and, 355, 356; *WB's Berlin Childhood* publication and, 438–439; WB's politics and, 448–449; WB's Kafka project and, 455–457; suggests WB visit Palestine, 469–470; as WB's archivist, 482; WB's relationship with, 509–510, 539–540, 608–609; Peel Commission and questions of Jewish state, 568–569; report on visit to New York, 584–587; on Horkheimer and WB, 586; *Major Trends in Jewish Mysticism*, 659

Scholem, Reinhold, 123

Scholem, Werner, 401

School Reform Units, at universities, 35–37; at Freiburg, 37–38, 45, 52; in Berlin, 51

Schottlaender, Rudolf, 248

Schuler, Alfred, 80, 81

Schultz, Franz, 178, 183, 187, 189, 191, 222–224, 232, 698n33

Schuschnigg, Kurt, 591

Schutzverband deutscher Schriftsteller im Ausland (Defense League of German Authors Abroad), 556

"Schwabinger Bohème," 80

Schweppenhäuser, Hermann, 678

Schwitters, Kurt, 171, 172

"Second nature," 10

Seghers, Anna (Netty Reiling), 556–557, 565, 572; *Revolt of the Fishermen of Santa Barbara*, 556

Seligson, Carla, 39–40, 52, 53, 64, 84, 92

Seligson, Gertrud (Traute), 687n38

Seligson, Rika, 70

Sellier, Louis, 418, 463

Selz, Dorothée, 376

Selz, Guy, 399

Selz, Guyet, 376, 399, 419, 420

Selz, Jean, 373, 376, 394, 419–421, 447; "Une expérience de Walter Benjamin," 399

Seume, Johann Gottfried, 536

Seyss-Inquart, Arthur, 591

Shapiro, Meyer, 595

Shestov, Lev, 640

Shock, WB's theory of, 277, 512, 615, 643–646, 657

"Shrinkage" *(Schrumpfung)*, 282, 344, 705n33

Silone, Ignazio, 635

Similarity, 374, 388–390, 709n76

Simmel, Georg, 49, 106, 178, 206; *Philosophie des Geldes* (Philosophy of Money), 628

Sinclair, Upton, 123

Smollet, Tobias, 467

Socialist Realism, 441–442

Sohn-Rethel, Alfred, 202, 212–213, 242; "Sociological Theory of Knowledge," 562–563

Sorel, Georges, 114; *Réflexions sur la violence*, 131–132, 693n56, 694n17

Soupault, Philippe, 323

Sovereign violence, 132–133, 694n17

Sperber, Manès, 433, 439

Speyer, Wilhelm, 316, 323, 328–329, 357, 387, 423, 433; WB's collaboration with, 376, 379–380, 437, 707n61; WB's suicide plans in 1932 and, 379; emigration of, 391, 627

Spitteler, Carl, 53

Spitzer, Moritz, 437, 458

Spleen, Baudelaire and, 170, 596, 617, 644

Stalinism, characterized as humanism, 503–504

Stalin, Josef, 441–442

Starr, Milton, 654

Steffin, Margarete, 430–432, 462, 522; *Threepenny Novel*, 430, 474

Steiner, Rudolf, 81

Steinschneider, Karl, 393

Stern, Günther, 580

Stern, Hilde, 20

Stern, William, 20

Sternberger, Dolf, 511, 629; *Panorama: Ansichten des 19. Jahrhunderts* (Panoramas of the Nineteenth Century), 597–598

Stoessl, Otto, 299

Stone, Sasha, 263, 293, 363

Stora, Marcel, 641–642

Straßer, Georg, 347

Strauss, Leo, 325
Strauß, Ludwig, 40–41, 46–48, 123, 125
Stritzky, Else von, 106, 135
Suicide: WB's thoughts of, 5, 357–358,
    361–362; WB's family and, 29, 127,
    683n15; of Heinle, 70–71, 74, 361,
    687n38, 707n49; WB's plans for and
    will written in 1932, 377–379,
    707n63; WB on modernism and, 617;
    of Hamburger and Muschler, 663; of
    WB, 674–676
Supervielle, Jules, 621
Surrealism, 76, 172, 236, 290, 450, 478,
    591, 630, 665; Bataille's countering
    of, 519–520. See also under Benja-
    min, Walter, works of
Surya, Michel, 519–520
Symbolisme, 279

Täuber, Sophie, 106
Taut, Bruno, 121
Teachings, concept of (Lehre), 94–96.
    See also Knowledge
Tergit, Gabriele, Käsebier Conquers the
    Kurfürstendamm, 259
Thieme, Karl, 502, 525, 536, 592, 627,
    640; Das alte Wahre: Eine Bil-
    dungsgeschichte des Abendlandes
    (Old Verities: A History of Personal
    Formation in the West), 471–472
Tiedemann, Rolf, 287, 288, 678, 700n37,
    700n39
Tillich, Hannah, 585
Tillich, Paul, 525, 585
Time: language and problem of, 42–44,
    90–91; immortal and developmental,
    58–59; messianic, 661, 684n12,
    717n6, 717n7. See also Intertwined
    time (verschränkte Zeit); "Now of
    recognizability"
Toller, Ernst, 638
Tolstoy, Leo, 30, 48, 64, 128, 684n12,
    686n30
Tonnelat, Ernest, 436
Trakl, Georg, 57
Tretyakov, Sergei, 522, 607
Truth and Truth Content, 40, 58, 72–73,
    112–113, 119, 150–151, 158–160,
    164–168, 230–231, 343–344, 684n7
Tschesno-Hell, Mischa, 432
Tuchler, Kurt, 45, 52, 53–54

Tucholsky, Kurt, 555
Tumarkin, Anna, 98
Turgot, Anne-Robert, 627–628
Tzara, Tristan, 106, 171

Unger, Erich, 156, 221, 294, 324; Politik
    und Metaphysik, 133–134, 260

Valero, Vicente, 371, 402, 416, 419
Valéry, Paul, 261, 279, 284, 363, 404–405,
    621
Van Doesburg, Theo, 171, 172
Van Eeden, Frederick, 122
Van Hoddis, Jakob (Hans Davidsohn),
    29, 122
Varèse, Edgard, 145
Varō, Tomás, 375
Vasari, Ruggero, 213
Verspohl, Maximilian, 419–420
Vitalism, 33
Vita Nova press, 536, 593–594
Von Schoeller, Werner, 394–395, 449,
    625
Vossische Zeitung, 237, 299, 381, 386,
    387, 532, 698n3

Wackenroder, Wilhelm Heinrich,
    588
Wagner, Richard, 576, 583, 603
Wahl, Jean, 522, 557, 579–580, 621
Walden, Herwarth, 508
Wandervögel ("walking birds"), 36, 37
Warburg, Aby, 267, 284, 295–296
Weber, Alfred, 149, 176
Weber, Marianne, 149, 175
Weber, Max, 106, 133, 149
Wedekind, Frank, 27, 80
Weidlé, Wladimir, Les abeilles d'Aristé:
    Essai sur le destin actuel des lettres
    et des arts, 559
Weigel, Helene, 451–452, 462, 463,
    572
Weil, Felix, 426
Weil, Hermann, 426
Weill, Kurt, 357, 430
Weissbach, Richard, 127, 137, 150, 161,
    169, 170, 173, 194, 201
Die Weltbühne (journal), 212, 555
Werfel, Franz, 236, 672
Wiegand, Willy, 238
Wieland, Christoph Martin, 408

Wigand, Karl von, 191
"Will to art" (Kunstwollen), 226
Winckelmann, Johann Joachim, History of the Art of Antiquity, 199
Wish image, 491–492
Wissing, Egon, 349, 357, 359, 447, 472, 486, 663; WB's suicide plans in 1932 and, 378–379; death of wife, 424, 433; drug use, 433–434, 495–496, 509; WB's relationship with, 496–497; in Moscow, 508, 509; marriage of, 598
Wissing, Gert, 349, 357, 598; WB's suicide plans in 1932 and, 378–379; death of, 424, 433
Witte, Bernd, 231
Wizisla, Erdmut, 534, 704n8
Wolff, Charlotte, 137, 138, 141–142, 143, 153, 201, 694n24
Wolff, Kurt, 124
Wölfflin, Heinrich, 79, 304; Classical Art, 79
Wolfskehl, Karl, 80–81, 253, 294–295, 391
Work of art, theory of, 71–73, 108–113, 119, 164–165, 192–193, 513–515, 547–548, 693n54
"The Work of Art in the Age of Its Technological Reproducibility" (Benjamin), 2, 172, 325, 339, 483, 503, 511–523, 667; film and photography and, 275–277, 363, 365–366; Brecht and, 535–536; publication issues, 553–554; Baudelaire project and, 643, 644–645
World events and politics: World War I, 69–70, 75–76, 91–92; collapse of Austria-Hungary, 105, 692n44; Germany's collapse, 105, 692n44; Russian revolution, 105, 692n44; Kapp Putsch, 120, 130, 131; Ruhr uprising, 120, 131; Weimar Republic's political and economic crises, 120, 130–131, 141, 174, 180–182, 191, 194–195; Palestine, emigration to, 135, 428, 429, 633–634; Hitler's advance to power, 195, 377, 391, 460–461; Weimar Republic's ban on travel out of, 200; fascism in Italy, 208; National Socialists' seizure of power and exclusion of Jews from German life, 333, 391–395; National

Socialists' growing power, 347, 366, 375, 377–378; German Reichsschriftumskammer "chamber" for writers established, 432; Night of the Long Knives, 460–462; July Putsch, 461; Popular Front in Spain, 474, 526, 567, 571, 630; Palestine conflicts, 525–526, 556, 568–569; Moscow show trials, 535, 540–541, 567, 582, 607; Spanish Civil War, 535, 556, 584, 587–588; Anschuluß and arrest of opponents to National Socialism, 591–592; growing threat to Jews in 1930s, 591–593; Munich Pact and invasion of Sudetenland, 609–610; Kristallnacht, 622; Hitler-Stalin Pact, 647, 658; Belgium, Netherlands, and France fall, 667–668
Das Wort (journal), 474, 532, 533, 536, 539, 554, 607, 626
Wyneken, Gustav, 38, 51, 52, 62–63; educational program of, 24–28, 27–28; influence on WB, 25–26, 29, 39, 44, 45, 48; Schule und Jugendkultur (School and Youth Culture), 25, 682n12; School Reform units proposed, 35–39; views on coeducation, 55, 75; WB's break with, 75–76, 688n1, 688n2

Youth movement, cultural transformation, and critique of academia, 32–74; activities in Freiburg, 32–45, 51–53, 55–61; school reform movement, 32–45; politics and, 40–41, 48–51; Jewish identity and Zionism and, 45–48, 685n16; activities in Berlin, 48–51, 55–67; WB's metaphysical understanding of, 56–59; WB's call for transformation of academic life, 65–68; WB's forming as metropolitan intellectual, 68–74

Zeitschrift für Sozialforschung, 406, 427, 428, 429, 437, 439, 483, 489, 546, 564, 573, 606, 629, 657, 664
Zhdanov, Andrei, 504–505
Zionism. See Jewish identity and Zionism
Zurich Dadists, 105–106, 171
Zweig, Stefan, 209–210